**Teacher Prep**

TEACHER PREP

MERRILL
PRENTICE HALL

www

Your Class. Their Careers. Our Future. Will your students be prepared?

We invite you to explore our new, innovative and engaging website and all that it has to offer you, your course, and tomorrow's educators! Preview this site today at www.prenhall.com/teacherprep/demo. Just click on "go" on the login page to begin your exploration.

Organized around the major courses pre-service teachers take, the Teacher Preparation site provides media, student/teacher artifacts, strategies, research articles, and other resources to equip your students with the quality tools needed to excel in their courses and prepare them for their first classroom.

This ultimate online education resource will provide you and your students access to:

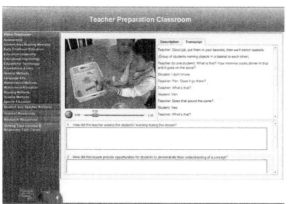

Online Video Library. More than 250 video clips—each tied to a course topic and framed by learning goals and Praxis-type questions—capture real teachers and students working in real classrooms.

Student and Teacher Artifacts. More than 200 student and teacher classroom artifacts—each tied to a course topic and framed by learning goals and application questions—provide a wealth of materials and experiences to help your students observe children's developmental learning.

Lesson Plan Builder. Step-by-step guidelines and lesson plan examples support students as they learn to build high-quality lesson plans.

Articles and Readings. Over 500 articles from ASCD's renowned journal *Educational Leadership* are available. The site also includes Research Navigator, a searchable database of additional educational journals.

Strategies and Lessons. Over 500 research-supported instructional strategies appropriate for a wide range of grade levels and content areas.

Licensure and Career Tools. Resources devoted to helping your students pass their licensure exam; learn standards, law, and public policies; plan a teaching portfolio; and succeed in their first year of teaching.

How to ORDER *Teacher Prep* for you and your students:

For students to receive a *Teacher Prep* Access Code with this text, instructors **must** provide a special value pack ISBN number on their textbook order form. To receive this special ISBN, please email **Merrill.marketing@pearsoned.com** and provide the following information:
- Name and Affiliation
- Author/Title/Edition of Merrill text

Upon ordering *Teacher Prep* for their students, instructors will be given a lifetime *Teacher Prep* Access Code.

COLLABORATION AND SYSTEM COORDINATION FOR STUDENTS WITH SPECIAL NEEDS

From Early Childhood to the Postsecondary Years

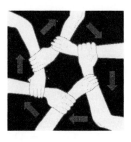

CAROL A. KOCHHAR-BRYANT
The George Washington University

PEARSON

Merrill · Prentice Hall

Upper Saddle River, New Jersey
Columbus, Ohio

Vice President and Executive Publisher: Jeffery W. Johnston
Executive Editor: Ann Castel Davis
Editorial Assistant: Penny S. Burleson
Senior Production Editor: Linda Hillis Bayma
Production Coordination: Rebecca K. Giusti, GGS Book Services
Design Coordinator: Diane C. Lorenzo
Photo Coordinator: Lori Whitley
Cover Designer: Bryan Huber
Cover Image: SuperStock
Production Manager: Laura Messerly
Director of Marketing: David Gesell
Marketing Manager: Autumn Purdy
Marketing Coordinator: Brian Mounts

This book was set in Garamond by GGS Book Services. It was printed and bound by R.R. Donnelley & Sons Company. The cover was printed by R.R. Donnelley & Sons Company.

Photo Credits for Chapter Openers: Michelle D. Bridwell/PhotoEdit Inc.: p. 290; Corbis RF: pp. 4, 60; Scott Cunningham/Merrill: pp. 260, 370; Krista Greco/Merrill: p. 28; Anthony Magnacca/Merrill: pp. 174, 342, 396; Robin Nelson/PhotoEdit Inc.: p. 202; Michael Newman/PhotoEdit Inc.: pp. 118, 228; Mark Richards/PhotoEdit Inc.: p. 146; © Tom Stewart/Corbis, All Rights Reserved: p. 314; U.S. Congress, Office of Technology Assessment: p. 90.

Pearson Education Ltd.
Pearson Education Singapore Pte. Ltd.
Pearson Education Canada, Ltd.
Pearson Education—Japan

Pearson Education Australia Pty. Limited
Pearson Education North Asia Ltd.
Pearson Educación de Mexico, S.A. de C.V.
Pearson Education Malaysia Pte. Ltd.

10 9 8 7 6 5 4 3 2 1
ISBN-10:   0-13-114519-3
ISBN-13: 978-0-13-114519-1

This book is dedicated to my husband, John, as it would not have been possible without his extraordinary patience, humor, and unwavering encouragement. This work is also dedicated to my students over the years who have graduated with master's and doctoral degrees and who are exercising their leadership every day in their collaborative work to improve educational and human service systems at local, state, and national levels. Their capacity and commitment to make a difference in the field for youth with special needs and their families are the true measure of our work.

PREFACE

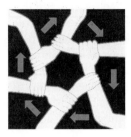

As students navigate the developmental journey through schooling and into adulthood, they encounter a spectrum of professionals along the way in their school and community. These professionals must work in partnership to help their students achieve realistic goals, and build upon their strengths, abilities, and talents to shape personal visions for their futures.

Collaboration and system coordination have become essential to improving the lives of students with special needs and their families. The skills and abilities of professionals to form partnerships have become so important that just about every set of new standards for the professional qualifications of teachers, administrators, and related school personnel now addresses collaboration and system coordination. This book, therefore, is concerned with connecting systems—within schools and between schools and communities, from early childhood programs through high school—and the extraordinary collaboration and coordination it takes to accomplish it.

This book also emphasizes the important transitions in the process of development from early childhood programs through to high school graduation. The transition from one level to another (e.g., kindergarten to first grade, elementary to middle, middle to high school, and high school to higher education or employment) can be an exciting time or it can be daunting for a child with disabilities and his or her parents. Recent research has indicated that over half of children with special needs demonstrate moderate to serious difficulties with such transitions. However, the complexities of negotiating special educational and supportive services can be reduced if the services are known to parents and well coordinated by professionals. Open and continuous communication and collaboration among professionals and families are essential throughout the school years.

Many components of the educational system have historically evolved together to provide education and support services to students with special needs, but have never fully connected. For example, special education has not fully connected with general education, nor general education with related and support services, nor preschool with elementary schools, nor middle schools with high schools, nor high schools with postsecondary institutions, nor schools with community service agencies. Although many exemplary efforts to create a seamless educational system exist across the United States, we have a great distance to go. This book examines how these separate systems can be better connected, creating communities that work more effectively for children and youth and their future.

Finally, this book centers on the role of collaboration and coordination as central to problem solving and change in classrooms, schools, and school–community systems. Collaboration and coordination are essential to change in relationships among people, which lead to change in practices, which ultimately lead to change and progress in students. The chapters address how collaboration and coordination work, who takes responsibility for the process, and how broken links in the chain can be reconnected. The primary goal is to explore the possibilities and potential of professional collaboration and system coordination for improving educational services and, ultimately, student outcomes.

Today, general education teachers, in collaboration with special educators and related service specialists, are expected to develop educational programs that are designed for a very diverse population, including students with disabilities, those at risk academically in the general education setting, gifted students, former school dropouts, students with limited English proficiency, teen parents, and many others. Each of these student groups may be considered a special population that possesses unique needs requiring specialized educational strategies and supports. Today these special populations represent a majority of students in many school systems across the United States. Teachers are expected to improve the achievement and development of every student in a culture of shared responsibility for inclusion and full participation—*they are all our kids.*

THE STUDENT AND FAMILY IN THE CENTER

This exploration of school collaboration and system coordination is anchored in many ideas, philosophies, and principles that have guided the movement toward a shared responsibility for the development and achievement of children and youth. Framing the exploration is the contemporary service philosophy of "self-determination." This book places student and family self-determination goals and tasks of the individual at the center of the discussion of school collaboration and system coordination. The roles of many individuals and professionals—parents, teachers, support services personnel, guidance counselors, administrators, community service, postsecondary personnel, business leaders, and many others—are examined with consideration of their impact on the individual student's ability to determine his or her own future (self-determination). Threaded through the discussions of school collaboration and system coordination is the principle that the individual and his or her family remain at the center of developmental planning and should exercise as much personal decision making as is possible throughout schooling and at key transition points. Self-determination of the student and family becomes an organizing force for structuring professional collaboration and for connecting the system.

WHAT IS THE AUTHOR'S RELEVANT EXPERIENCE?

This book is based on over 30 years' experience developing, managing, and studying school and community agency coordination for individuals with special needs at local, state, and national levels. The material in the book reflects my work in initiating and helping schools develop collaborative interagency agreements and helping states define interagency arrangements that improve collaboration and coordination among agencies to improve services to students. My work in evaluation has also contributed to the development of this book, including evaluation of service coordination programs and defining measures of effectiveness; evaluation of special education resource centers, job development programs, and their coordination; correctional education programs, community residential programs, and university-based programs.

I have contributed to federal legislation that addresses interagency coordination and collaboration; written resource manuals, chapters, and articles on service coordination and collaborative leadership; and designed university graduate courses in interagency coordination, professional collaboration, and system change for teachers, administrators, and interagency personnel. This book has also been shaped by years of research and countless interviews with teachers, school administrators, local and state coordinators, parents, students, and others involved in making collaboration and coordination work.

Finally, my perspective has been deeply enriched by my experience as a parent of a youth with disabilities who has needed specialized and supportive services from a variety of agencies and professionals for many years. He is now navigating the tumultuous passage through late adolescence and transition to adulthood, gradually gaining ground in his daily struggle to overcome multiple challenges from within. Together over the years, he and I have negotiated services from five different agencies to provide the combination of supports he has needed. Together we have deeply learned just how important the parent is in the collaboration and coordination process, and just how unpredictable the journey.

WHAT ARE THE AUTHOR'S UNDERLYING BELIEFS AND ASSUMPTIONS?

In any research endeavor, facts are collected, hypotheses formed, preconceptions challenged, and new theories constructed and tested. Because the study of educational collaboration and system coordination is relatively new, facts are scarce and conclusions are often more speculative than those in more established fields of study. My goals are to (a) present what we do know about the effectiveness of collaboration and coordination in the field of education, (b) introduce ideas from a variety of disciplines that have relevance for improving collaboration and coordination in education, (c) explore faulty assumptions still held by the public about the developmental needs of children, and (d) examine misunderstandings about collaboration among professionals that create roadblocks along the educational continuum.

My aim is to provide the reader with an understanding of the possibilities and potential of collaboration and system coordination to contribute to positive outcomes, as well as to promote improvements in educational services for children and their families. It is hoped that new or veteran professionals entering the field of special or general education or related fields, and who aspire to leadership, will be inspired to help advance developments in collaboration and system coordination. Professional collaboration and system coordination, implemented as a systematic set of interventions, can make the difference in a student's journey toward successful school completion and long-term adjustment to adult life. A great deal more research and development is needed by creative professionals to continue to advance our knowledge and practice of collaboration and system coordination.

For Whom Was This Book Written?

This text is designed for teacher preparation courses and for the professional development of human services personnel who want to improve school collaboration and the coordination of services for children and youth with special needs and their families. Whereas the book is particularly valuable for professionals working with students with special needs, it is useful for any professional concerned with any child who receives services that require professional collaboration within the school or among schools and community agencies. The book will be of interest to anyone concerned with coordination of services for students who need supportive or related services while in school, and youth who are preparing to make the transition from schooling to employment, postsecondary education, and adult services. The material is appropriate for those preparing for professional roles in a variety of education and human services fields, including special and general educators, administrators, early intervention specialists, parents and parent advocates, guidance counselors, school counselors and mental health workers, professional development coordinators, school-to-careers and transition coordinators, college student services personnel, social workers, youth workers, juvenile services personnel, and business and industry collaborators.

How Is This Book Different From Others?

Numerous books have been written on the topic of school collaboration, so what would motivate anyone to write another textbook on this subject? The goal of this work is to fill a gap in the literature for a text that broadly addresses school collaboration and system coordination within education for children and adolescents, and to connect it with contemporary service philosophies and practices. This book addresses in-school collaboration among professionals as well as broader system linkages required of schools today—the coordination among schools and human service agencies in the community. It differs from books on case management which have a specialized focus on individual service coordination in medical, nursing, rehabilitation, school psychology, or social work fields. This book provides a broader treatment of the subject of professional collaboration and system coordination in education with emphasis on serving students with special learning needs. It focuses on how collaboration and coordination processes work to ensure that they are executed, monitored, and evaluated. At the heart of these complex processes are some important questions: Who takes responsibility for its implementation? What happens when a link in the collaborative chain breaks and a student is not receiving needed services?

This book explores why school collaboration and system coordination have been so difficult to accomplish within the field of education and provides useful models and strategies for building local capacity. It urges change in how professionals think about the way education and human services agencies should respond to individuals with multiple service needs. It also discusses new directions in the use of interagency agreements for school improvement in the wake of new school improvement and accountability initiatives under the No Child Left Behind Act of 2001 and IDEA of 2004.

Collaboration and system coordination represent a range of relationships among disciplines within schools and among schools and community service agencies that serve children, youth, and families. This text explores and analyzes the role and structure of collaboration and coordination in education and human services.

It examines the ideas, philosophies, and principles that have stimulated and guided a movement toward collaborative professional communities, interagency partnerships, and shared responsibility for the development and well-being of all students.

WHAT ARE THE UNIQUE FEATURES OF THIS BOOK?

1. ***Developmental Framework.*** Drawing on perspectives and data from multiple disciplines, a comprehensive examination of school collaboration and system coordination is presented in a developmental framework, from early childhood through adolescent transition from high school. The concept and practice of self-determination is a theme throughout the continuum from early childhood to adolescence and beyond. Attention is given to models of effective school collaboration and system coordination from early intervention through transition from high school to careers and postsecondary education.

2. ***Case Illustrations.*** Each chapter contains case illustrations that provide concrete examples of collaboration and coordination and serve as a window on real-world applications. They serve primarily to make the unfamiliar familiar and to give readers a common language about collaboration and coordination. Case illustrations provide narratives that serve as a basis for class discussion, and challenge students to apply the concepts they have learned in the chapters and in real-life situations. Cases illustrations differ from information delivered through lecture, problems, or exercises because they present real-life scenarios that offer complex questions for readers and require that they analyze the situations. Case illustrations are also designed to engage students and to assess whether they have mastered material in the chapters well enough to apply it.

3. ***Reflections and Perspectives.*** "Reflections and perspectives" on school collaboration and system coordination by parents, students, and professionals are included throughout the book. Threaded throughout are "essential questions" that are designed to provoke and inspire reflection, and to help readers think beyond conventional wisdom and their own biases.

4. ***Research on Effectiveness of Coordination and Collaboration.*** The book provides a review of current research on the effectiveness of school collaboration and system coordination for improving educational and social outcomes for children and youth. Additionally, readers are introduced to innovative state practices with interagency agreements and coordination to aid school improvement and accountability efforts for low-performing schools under the No Child Left Behind Act.

5. ***Structured for Teaching and Professional Development.*** Readers are provided with practical tools to (a) explore their own knowledge about school and community-based services and coordination; (b) reflect on their beliefs and assumptions about collaboration and system coordination; and (c) assess how they make different choices and decisions about students based on their assumptions and beliefs. Guiding questions provide a framework for the chapter content and for the end-of-chapter exercises, and key terms and phrases draw students' attention to new terms and concepts. Framing questions are revisited in the end-of-chapter key content questions, questions for reflection and thinking, and skill-building activities.

Concrete case illustrations are interwoven to apply new concepts and principles to real-world situations and settings. Such examples may address lessons learned, recommendations and strategies for students and families, recommendations and strategies for practice, implications for school policy development, and strategies and tools for critical review and assessment of current practices (e.g., for students and school personnel to use to examine their own school collaboration initiatives and interagency cooperative agreements).

ACKNOWLEDGMENTS

I wish to thank many colleagues who have contributed to the material in the book, reviewed drafts of chapters, and helped to improve its accuracy, clarity and coherence. I want to acknowledge the following contributors to specific chapters:

Laura Peters, Principal, Pathways School nonpublic special education facility for students with emotional disabilities, Maryland. Contributor, case illustration, Chapter 1.

Patti Ralabate, Senior Special Education Advisor, National Education Association, Washington, DC. Contributor, case illustrations, Chapter 4.

Kendra Hill, Special Educator, Contributor, case illustrations, Chapters 5 and 8.

Diane Oglesby, Senior Project Associate, IDEA Partnership, National Association of State Directors of Special Education, Virginia. Contributor, Chapter 6.

Deanna Ortiz, Special Educator. Contributor, case illustration, Chapter 7.

Kerri Larkin, Special Educator. Contributor, case illustration, Chapter 7.

Ashby Rushing, Special Educator. Contributor, Chapter 7.

Tracy Price, Ed.D. Special Education Coordinator. Coauthor, Chapter 9.

Robert M. Baer, Ph.D., Kent State University, Center for Innovation in Transition and Employment. Coauthor, Chapter 13.

Renee Lacey, Ed.D. Director, Alternative Education, Prince William County Public Schools, Virginia. Coauthor, Chapter 14.

Anjali Kochhar, Early childhood educator, Montessori School, Virginia, for her tireless assistance with the permissions work for the manuscript.

I am indebted to the following colleagues whose detailed and thoughtful critique of various parts of the book has added immeasurably to its balance, fairness, and accuracy: James F. Austin, University of Akron; Dennis Campbell, Arkansas State University; Gary Clark, University of Kansas; Lee Cross, University of Central Florida; Gloria Dye, Washburn University; Joy Fuqua, Fort Hays State University; Chris Givner, California State University–Los Angeles; Peg Hughes, San Jose State University; Colleen Klein, University of Central Florida; Martha Larkin, State University of West Georgia; Kathleen McCoy, Arizona State University; Verna Nassif, Southwest Minnesota State University; Jane Newacek, Appalachian State University; Marie Patterson, Wichita State University; Sharyn Rhodes, Loyola College in Maryland; Tamar F. Riley, Florida Memorial University; Kathy Dickinson Rockwood, Manhattanville College; Denise Skarbek, Indiana University–South Bend; Lorraine Tullis, California State University–Bakersfield; Donna Wandry, West Chester University; and Daryl Wilcox, Wayne State College.

DISCOVER THE MERRILL RESOURCES FOR SPECIAL EDUCATION WEBSITE

Technology is a constantly growing and changing aspect of our field that is creating a need for new content and resources. To address this emerging need, Merrill Education has developed an online learning environment for students, teachers, and professors alike to complement our products—the *Merrill Resources for Special Education* Website. This content-rich Website provides additional resources specific to this book's topic and will help you—professors, classroom teachers, and students—augment your teaching, learning, and professional development.

Our goal is to build on and enhance what our products already offer. For this reason, the content for our user-friendly Website is organized by topic and provides teachers, professors, and students with a variety of meaningful resources all in one location. With this Website, we bring together the best of what Merrill has to offer: text resources, video clips, Web links, tutorials, and a wide variety of information on topics of interest to general and special educators alike. Rich content, applications, and competencies further enhance the learning process.

The *Merrill Resources for Special Education* Website includes:

- video clips specific to each topic, with questions to help you evaluate the content and make crucial theory-to-practice connections;
- thought-provoking critical analysis questions that students can answer and turn in for evaluation or that can serve as basis for class discussions and lectures;
- access to a wide variety of resources related to classroom strategies and methods, including lesson planning and classroom management;
- information on all the most current topics related to special and general education, including CEC and Praxis™ standards, IEPs, portfolios, and professional development;
- extensive Web resources and overviews on each topic addressed on the Website; and
- a search feature to help access specific information quickly.

To take advantage of these and other resources, please visit the *Merrill Resources for Special Education* Website at

http://www.prenhall.com/kochhar

CONTENTS

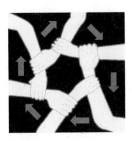

PART ONE

FOUNDATIONS FOR COLLABORATION AND SYSTEM COORDINATION

PART TWO

PEOPLE MAKE THE DIFFERENCE IN COLLABORATION AND SYSTEM COORDINATION

PART THREE
COLLABORATION AND COORDINATION FROM EARLY CHILDHOOD THROUGH POSTSECONDARY TRANSITION

NOTE: Every effort has been made to provide accurate and current Internet information in this book. However, the Internet and information on it are constantly changing, so it is inevitable that some of the Internet addresses listed in this textbook will change.

PART ONE

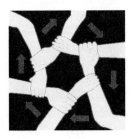

FOUNDATIONS FOR COLLABORATION AND SYSTEM COORDINATION

Part 1, *Chapters 1 through 5,* provides the foundations for understanding the concepts of collaboration and system coordination. These chapters define collaboration and system coordination work among professionals, families, schools, and communities, and how both are now considered to be essential for improving the lives of students with special needs and their families, as well as for the work of professionals. Four core functions for collaboration and coordination are presented, which serve as a framework for remaining chapters. A variety of foundational theories of collaboration and system coordination are presented, with applications in school practice.

Chapters 4 and 5 introduce the reader to federal laws and policy initiatives that promote school collaboration, system coordination, and a stronger role for parents in their children's education. They also explore important research evidence that collaboration and system coordination actually result in positive outcomes for student achievement, improved teaching and support practices, and school improvement. New efforts in policy and research have led to some creative and enduring new relationships between schools and community agencies and have led to a better understanding of how these relationships can improve outcomes for children and families.

The development of collaborative relationships among professionals does not develop in a tidy, step-by-step, linear fashion. Instead it is messy, complex, and unpredictable. However, in the past two decades, research has demonstrated that the challenges and opportunities presented by special learners have led to close collaboration and unity among personnel who have not previously worked together. Such collaboration has also resulted in new organizational relationships, practices, and policies that were unprecedented for schools and that have benefited all students. New patterns of relationships have emerged that are very different from the traditional isolation and independent work that had been characteristic of the teachers, school support staff, and parents in the past. The extent to which our educational systems support children through the developmental process ultimately expresses our will to invest in the future of the nation. From the perspective of costs—both school resources and human costs—it is a national imperative that we view successful transitions through school as a primary objective for which schools are held accountable.

Professionals at each stage of the developmental continuum can best support the student as a team, through multiple lenses, alert to needs and signs of progress. Schools are becoming centers for learning, not only for students but also for families and professionals. The value of collaboration and system coordination has emerged as a central theme in the reform and renewal of our educational institutions as we struggle to embrace all children.

CHAPTER ONE

WHY ARE COLLABORATION AND SYSTEM COORDINATION IMPORTANT?

This is not a tidy tale; collaboration is an untidy business, full of uncharted territories, ambiguities, and institutional complexities. —MARILYN JOHNSTON, 1997

Never underestimate that a small group of thoughtful, committed people can change the world, indeed it's the only thing that ever has. —MARGARET MEAD

PERSPECTIVES

Teacher

I read about collaboration theories and strategies in my teacher preparation program, but it is only through experience in the schools that I really "got it." I learned quickly how vital teamwork is in the school's efforts to improve education for all our children. I learned that I cannot watch from the sidelines, but had to participate continually and be a part of the process. It had to become a way of thinking.

— (Conversation with a Middle School Teacher, 2005)

High School Student

They say I've got to be prepared to graduate from high school, so I've got to be involved in my own planning. I can make decisions for my future. I can be part of it. I don't just want my parents and teachers making all the decisions for me. Yes, I might need help, but they have to listen to me, too. I mean, who else is going to walk into my future but me. I have to be the main player on the court!

— (Conversation with a High School Student, 2005)

INTRODUCTION

Collaboration and system coordination—what images do these words conjure up in the education stetting? Do they suggest people talking together and solving problems in their classrooms in a constructive way? Do they project the image of people sharing resources on effective strategies for working with diverse students? Do you see images of people coming together in new combinations—perhaps people who have never worked together before—to stimulate new thinking and new ideas?

This chapter explains collaboration and system coordination among professionals, families, schools, and communities, and how both have become essential for improving the lives of students with special needs and their families. It discusses the importance of collaboration in educational reform and improvement and in ensuring appropriate education for every student. The reader is introduced to a variety of theories of collaboration and system coordination. Four core functions for collaboration and coordination are defined and serve as a framework for the remaining chapters. Finally, this chapter emphasizes the important "transitions" in a child's development from early childhood programs to high school graduation. These passages can be daunting for any child, particularly one with a disability. Close communication and collaboration among professionals and families are essential throughout the years.

WHAT IS COLLABORATION?

The overarching goal of education is to promote the highest possible levels of academic, social, and career–vocational functioning for each child, with and without disabilities. Achieving these goals necessarily involves change in students as they grow and develop, but it also requires change in professionals, in families, and in schools and systems. Change that promotes student progress depends on the individuals involved and how they collaborate with one another to bridge the different and separate worlds of family and school, of academic disciplines, of professional roles, and of school and community.

The concepts of collaboration and coordination are not simply pleasing abstractions—they must lead to effective practices. For what purpose are we collaborating or coordinating? Too often collaborative initiatives are launched among professionals in schools, or between schools and community service agencies, without a clear objective, goal, or end in mind. Yet, clarity of purpose is often the key ingredient in the success or failure of a collaborative effort. Without a map, you won't know where you're going or when you'll get there.

Several components of the educational system (early intervention services, general education, special education, related services, guidance and counseling, career education, transition services, community-based services) have developed side by side, to provide various education and support services to children and youth with special learning needs. However, many of these components of the system have never fully connected with each other in a manner that promotes the child's fullest potential within the educational continuum. For example, special and general educators have traditionally taught classes in separate rooms or buildings. Guidance counselors have traditionally not had students with disabilities on their caseloads. There are several reasons for these disconnections. First, historically, the various components of the educational system have evolved separately. Second, there are natural barriers that occur between people who work within those sectors. Factors that separate them and prevent them from effective collaboration are rooted in differences in their roles, professional "languages" or terminology, expectations for students, policies that guide them, practices, and backgrounds and training of individuals.

The ability of professionals and parents to collaborate to solve problems and to improve education has become so important that just about every set of new standards for the preparation of teachers, administrators, and related school personnel now addresses collaboration and coordination. Expectations for collaborative practices are embedded in the Individuals With Disabilities Education Improvement Act of 2004, which will be referred to in this book as IDEA 2004, and in the No Child

Left Behind Act of 2001 (NCLB), as well as in a variety of additional laws aimed at protecting educational opportunities and the civil rights of individuals with disabilities. IDEA and NCLB define the specific educational services and supports that must be provided to eligible students. Collaboration and coordination refer to relationships and strategies designed to ensure that quality services are provided to meet each student's educational needs.

Defining Collaboration

A definition of **collaboration** can be drawn from the Latin root *col-laboratus,* meaning to work (*laboratus*) together (*col*) (Random House, 2001). Therefore, collaboration, most simply, can be defined as work done jointly with others. Collaboration is a term that is used widely today in education and human service fields. We commonly refer to collaboration among different groups of people within and outside the schools—among teachers, between teachers and parents, among teachers in different schools, among teachers and related services personnel (e.g., speech therapist, audiologist, counselor, psychologist, reading specialist), and among teachers and community agency personnel. *Collaboration is generally defined as a process of participation through which people, groups, and organizations form relationships and work together to achieve a set of agreed-upon results.* At the heart of effective and long-lasting school collaboration are effective relationships among professionals. Collaboration represents a range of relationships among people in different roles and disciplines within schools and among schools and human service agencies in the community that provide services to children and families. The terms *collaboration* and *coordination* represent:

- *ideas* about how people can work together to improve teaching and learning, student development and achievement, and the engagement of community service agencies;
- *philosophies* about how creative change blends or synthesizes a variety of perspectives and values among people to make things possible for students, families, professionals, schools, and systems;
- *practical strategies and processes* through which people can effect change, solve problems, or improve practices; and
- *commitment* to working together constructively and embracing new ideas.

Collaboration can be thought of as the "people part" and **system coordination** as the "organizational," or broader system part. However, collaboration and system coordination are inextricably linked: Collaborative relationships are essential in order for system coordination to occur. Results of collaboration may affect an individual student (e.g., collaboration on an Individual Education Program team or child study team), a group of professionals (coteaching team), or a whole organization (school improvement team). Recently, collaboration has also been defined as:

1. the process of shared creation between two or more individuals with complementary skills interacting to create a shared understanding that none had previously possessed or could have come to on their own. Collaboration creates a shared meaning about a process, a product, or an event (Montiel-Overall, 2005).

2. the sharing of resources among school community stakeholders to accomplish goals and objectives or solve problems (Glover, 2003).

3. team-building activities that develop mutual trust and promote collaborative decision making that meets the diverse needs of the school community (Lambert, 2003).

4. communities of practice; that is, groups of people who share a concern or a passion for something they do and who interact regularly to learn how to do it better (Wenger, McDermott, & Snyder, 2002).

5. relationships that provide opportunities for mutual benefit and results beyond what any single organization or sector could realize alone (Drucker, 2002).

6. a style of interaction that professionals use in order to accomplish a goal they share, often stressed in inclusive schools. Collaboration emphasizes common goals, relationships, and mutual interdependence and is a way to build community as well as being a way of life within a community (Friend & Cook, 2000).

7. planning, deciding, and acting jointly, but also *thinking together*. There is a commitment to shared resources, power, and talent (John-Steiner, Weber & Minnis, 1998, p. 776).

From these seven definitions arise six common themes, indicating that collaboration:

1. involves new *relationships* among people,
2. involves *sharing of resources* (human or other),
3. involves *trust* among people working together in peer (nonhierarchical) relationships,
4. involves *joint responsibility* for outcomes, and is aimed at achieving specific *results* or change,
5. involves *joint decision making* and actions, and
6. involves thinking together to create new solutions.

Expectations for collaborative practices are a centerpiece of the Individuals With Disabilities Education Improvement Act of 2004 (referred to as IDEA 2004), the No Child Left Behind Act of 2001 (NCLB), and a variety of related education and disability laws that will be discussed in Chapter 4. The IDEA of 2004 requires several kinds of collaborative teams along the **developmental continuum** for children from early childhood to high school.

Collaboration, Consultation, and System Coordination

Collaboration can be distinguished from the terms *consultation* and *system coordination*. Consultation, a form of collaboration, typically refers to one-time or short-term services that teachers and other professionals offer or receive from one another or offer to parents. It involves a request for a service or an advisory opinion. Consultation can also involve problem-solving relationships in which a group of peer professionals share their skills and experiences and provide joint recommendations to improve a situation for a child or group of children, or solve an organizational problem (Chrispeels, Strait, & Brown, 1999; Dettmer, Dyck, & Thurston, 2005).

Collaboration can also be distinguished from *system coordination*. As mentioned previously, collaboration refers to the relationships among people working together (e.g., special education teachers and general education teachers), and system coordination refers to the organizational or institutional relationships among agencies that are linked in their efforts to educate and support students and their families (e.g., the school counseling unit and the community mental health service agency). As stated earlier, we can think about collaboration as the "people part" and system coordination as the "organizational," or broader system part. However, collaboration and system coordination are *inextricably linked: Collaborative relationships are essential in order for system coordination to occur.*

WHO IS INVOLVED IN SCHOOL COLLABORATION?

Although it may sound trite, it does indeed *take a whole school* to work toward successful collaboration and build a collaborative culture. At the heart of effective and long-lasting school collaboration are effective relationships among professionals. Collaboration in education represents a range of relationships among people in different roles and disciplines within schools and among schools and human service agencies that serve children and families in the community. To make it work, the football coach and the music teacher must be just as committed to collaboration on behalf of all students as is the general education teacher and the administrator. Table 1.1 presents the spectrum of individuals who may be involved in planning for students' educational and developmental needs.

TABLE 1.1   It Takes a Whole School

Educational Needs	Support Services Needs	Social, Physical, and Extracurricular Needs
• The student	• Social worker	• Classmates
• General education teacher	• Rehabilitation counselor	• Physical education teachers
• Special education teacher	• Case manager	• Coaches
• Career-vocational education teacher	• School or guidance counselor	• Personal assistant
• Principal or administrator	• Psychologist	• School club leaders
• Parent or guardian	• Occupational therapist	• Music and theater arts teachers
	• Physical therapist	
	• Reading specialist	
	• Speech/language therapist	
	• Job coach or placement specialist	

These participants may work together in a variety of teams for a variety of purposes. Examples of collaboration that occur in schools include collaborative teaching, individualized education planning, collaboration for student assessment, collaboration between career vocational and special educators, collaborative work groups and learning communities, and collaboration for school reform, improvement, or evaluation.

Outside of the school setting, there are many human service agencies that are essential for comprehensive planning for students with disabilities and special learning needs. Examples of the community-based agencies include private tutoring and academic support services, as community mental health, social service agencies, family services, public health services, juvenile court services, substance abuse services, postsecondary institutions, or vocational rehabilitation agencies.

WHO ARE SPECIAL NEEDS LEARNERS?

Today, general education teachers, in collaboration with special educators and related service specialists, are expected to develop educational programs that include diverse students, including those with disabilities, those who are gifted students, students at-risk for failure in the general education setting, former school dropouts, students with limited English proficiency, teen parents, and many others. Each of these groups may be considered a special population of students that possesses unique needs requiring specialized educational strategies and supports.

Special learners is a broad term that include students with disabilities who are receiving special education, those who are at risk of being identified as needing special education, and those who are at risk of failure in the educational system for reasons other than disability. A *student with a disability* refers to a child with any of the disorders identified under IDEA, including mental retardation, hearing impairments (including deafness), speech or language impairments, visual impairments (including blindness), emotional disturbance, orthopedic impairments, autism, traumatic brain injury, other health impairments, or specific learning disabilities, who needs special education and related services.

IDEA 2004 has broadened its definition of individuals with special learning needs to include students who are at risk of failure in the educational system. This category includes students in K–12 who are suspected of having a disability, who need additional academic and behavioral support to succeed in a general education environment, and who are being provided with **early intervening services** to prevent referral to special education. This group also includes those who are limited in English proficiency, economically disadvantaged, migrant, and homeless (Sec. 613(a) (2) (C)). These populations are discussed in greater detail in Chapter 4. Teachers are expected to work together in a climate of shared responsibility: They are *all our kids.*

WHY IS THERE A GROWING INTEREST IN SCHOOL COLLABORATION AND SYSTEM COORDINATION?

Collaboration and coordination among teachers, administrators, parents, and community agency personnel are arguably the most important factors in the success or failure of educational programs for students with special learning needs, and indeed for all children. Since the education system has a mandate to educate each child as a *whole child*, collaboration and coordination are the pivot upon which that mission turns. Yet these are among the most challenging goals for individuals to achieve.

Every aspect of educational development to improve teaching, support, and student learning involves the ability of people to work together effectively for positive change. Many educational reforms, innovations, and good ideas have failed primarily because of the human challenges with implementing them or sustaining them. Conversely, many initiatives owe their success to human creativity, perseverance in problem solving, and the power of the basic human drive for continuous learning. An essential paradox for collaboration is that human nature and human interaction harbor both the promise of, and the threat to, creative problem solving. With skilled leadership that harnesses the creativity and basic motivation of people to apply new knowledge in solving problems, collaboration can result in powerful and positive long-term change.

Why are collaboration and coordination watch words in education today? Why have researchers and policymakers over the past few decades pointed to the need to improve collaboration among professionals, among schools and community agencies, and among professionals and parents? Over the past 20 years, major transformations have occurred in educational, social, political, and economic arenas that continue to impact the education and development of children and youth with special learning needs and the institutions that support them. Children with disabilities are now typically educated in inclusive settings along with their peers without disabilities. Antidiscrimination laws have improved access to early childhood education programs, community schools, and postsecondary education and employment for youth and young adults with disabilities. A greater national commitment is being made to assist all individuals to gain access to education and support services and to increase social and economic independence. Teachers are now prepared to deliver **differentiated instruction** in the classroom, modifying materials and methods to accommodate a wide range of diverse learners, including students with disabilities. Successful transitions into the educational system for very young children, and out of secondary school for young adults, are becoming recognized as a chief indicator of the effectiveness of our educational system for preparing children for adult independence.

Transition from family to preschool, through schooling, and into responsible adulthood involves changes in the self-concept, motivation, and development of the individual and is a fragile passage for each child or adolescent seeking to make difficult life choices (German, Martin, Marshall, & Sale, 2000; Michaels, 1994). This passage is even more delicate for children who need additional support and preparation to make the journey. For professionals seeking to help students on their journey, the process requires seamless linkages among educators, parents, and human service personnel.

Growing Complexity of the Service System

Collaboration and system coordination are vital characteristics of an effective education and human service system. The education and human service system has become increasingly complex and more difficult for the individual family to navigate when their child needs specialized services. Such children and youth often need a variety of support services from different agencies to help the family cope as a unit, help the student participate and progress in education and social settings and function as independently as possible. There are, however, often "cracks" or "gaps" in the service system when students need special education and related services within the school or from external community agencies. These gaps present several perplexing challenges for education and human service personnel including:

- the frustrations and anxieties that arise when a single individual in need must acquire special education services and supports from several separate and uncoordinated sources;
- the risk that the youth or family will be unable to find help because of the gap in services (e.g., absence of speech and hearing services near the school elimination of a school-based psychologist or mental health counselor position due to budget cuts or inadequate transportation to service agencies in a rural or remote area);
- the differences among families in their capacity to access and effectively use services within the system.

The system "gap," may mean incomplete links between schools and community service agencies. It may mean that there is no single access or entry point to help students and families identify the services they need and how to become eligibile for them.

New Philosophies in Education and Human Services

Collaboration with families has become increasingly important as a result of new philosophical views on disability, education, and the role of schools and human service agencies in the **empowerment** of students and families to make decisions about

Anthony Magnacca/Merrill

School professionals provide resources to empower students and families to participate in decisions and choices about services and educational goals.

services and to assume more control over educational planning **(self-determination)**. Empowering also means equipping parents and extended families with the tools— knowledge and skills—to help their children to learn and to collaborate effectively with professionals. Student self-determination and individual planning to achieve educational goals have become central to collaboration and coordination initiatives for students. Teachers, administrators, and parents are expected to collaborate and coordinate services in ways that support student self-determination.

Collaboration Improves Conditions for Learning

Collaboration has gained increasing attention because people accomplish more and make better decisions when they work effectively together. Collaborative groups or teams may work on decision making, curricular reform, development of new programs, or restructuring. Students of collaboration have observed that the traditional structure of schools promotes isolation and impedes collaboration (Friend & Cook, 2000). Teachers work in isolation, administrators try to accomplish tasks with little input from personnel, and the responsibility of implementing new ideas falls to individuals. Collaborative teams have many advantages over individuals working in isolation. Teams tend to be better at solving problems, have a higher level of commitment, and include more people who can help implement an idea or plan. Moreover, teams are able to generate energy and interest in new strategies or ideas. Both research and practice demonstrate the advantages that teams bring to accomplishing school improvement goals. But effective teams do not develop by accident. Teams take time, skills, and knowledge to be successful (North Central Regional Educational Laboratory, 2001).

Current Legislation Strengthens Collaboration Between General and Special Education

Over the past several decades, considerable interest and professional controversy has been centered on the practice of labeling and providing separate special education services to students with disabilities. In 1986, Madeleine Will, then Assistant Secretary of the U.S. Office of Special Education and Rehabilitation Services, argued that many students who could benefit from regular education were being excluded, and many schools withheld special services or supports until the student failed, rather than providing services to prevent failure (Will, 1986, p. 411). Will's call for reform and a "shared responsibility" for educating all children, is referred to as the *Regular Education Initiative* (REI) (Semmel, Abernathy, Butera, & Lesar, 1991; Will, 1986). Since the inception of the REI debate, there has been a growing recognition in the United States that the education of all children in least restrictive settings relies upon close collaboration among professionals within and outside the school.

Professional collaboration has become even more important because of its relevance in achieving new school reform requirements that promote full participation of children with disabilities in education. These requirements include early childhood transition to preschool, youth transition to employment and postsecondary education, access to general education and standardized assessment, special education monitoring requirements, parent collaboration, and teacher performance. These trends and higher expectations for schools demand that educators develop a wider range of collaborative skills and that schools develop an infrastructure to support more collaborative efforts (Sharpe & Hawes, 2003).

Schools are also required under IDEA to coordinate needed **related services** that are written into a **student's individualized education** plan. Related services include educational, supportive, and other services that children need in order to participate and to make progress in their education programs. Examples include transportation; developmental, corrective, and other supportive services; speech–language pathology and audiology services; psychological services; physical and occupational therapy; recreation, including therapeutic recreation; social work services; counseling services, including rehabilitation counseling; orientation and mobility services; and medical services for diagnostic and evaluation purposes.

Both the IDEA and NCLB have strengthened provisions for system coordination, including school–community coordination, formal interagency agreements, and coordination of educational services with services provided by health, rehabilitation, and social service agencies (IDEA, 2004).

Effectiveness of a Shared Responsibility

Schools and school-linked agencies are finding that as they improve their ability to coordinate services, outcomes for students improve as well. A **shared responsibility** and shared approaches to addressing student educational and developmental needs—helping the "whole child"—bring to bear the combined thinking, planning, and resources of many professionals in the schools and in a variety of agencies upon the needs and problems of a child and family (Conzemius & O'Neill, 2001). There is a growing recognition of the economic value of sharing resources across agencies to close persistent gaps in services for children and families who need them. Unfortunately, schools are experiencing widespread difficulties in establishing cooperative agreements and sustaining interagency relationships that support student education and transition (Fowler, Donegan, Lueke, Hadden, & Phillips, 2000; Kochhar-Bryant, 2003a; Kohler, 2003). However, there are new initiatives in federal education policy and at the state and local levels to improve formal agreements.

Expanding Early Childhood Services

Recent research and practice have confirmed the value of early intervention services in preparing children to make the often precarious transition from family to preschool and elementary school settings. In response to this new knowledge, IDEA 1997 and 2004 mandated an expanded role for educators and related services personnel in collaborating with families to prepare students for such transitions.

The Expanding Role of Business Partnerships

Business and industry have emerged over the past few decades as important collaborative partners with education and youth development efforts. Through active commitment and involvement, the private sector is coordinating with education and community services to help them address the health, academic, career-vocational, and independent living needs of all youths, particularly those with disabilities.

Expanded private sector involvement is based on the assumption that more effective school and community programs produce a better workforce.

Giving People a Voice

Schools and communities are effectively using collaboration to give a stronger voice to people who previously have had little influence in community decision making and are enabling a broad array of community members to work together constructively to address issues they care about. This is referred to as building "stakeholder involvement" (Otterbourg, 2003).

Let's See It in Action, below, illustrates how collaboration for change in a single school may begin as an untidy process but leads to long-lasting and positive schoolwide changes. An interdependence emerged among people working together for a common purpose—a system. The culture and organization of the school was permanently changed. This experience with systemic change also established new patterns of relationships very different from the traditional isolation and independent work that had been characteristic of teachers, school support staff, and parents in the past.

 LET'S SEE IT IN ACTION! CASE ILLUSTRATION: ALL OUR KIDS INITIATIVE

From Rocky Beginning to Positive Change

The Sunrise Valley Middle School eighth-grade teachers all shared a common challenge. They were about to receive a group of 12 students with emotional and learning disabilities who had been transferred from a separate special education center into the community school. The special education center was being closed as part of a countywide budget reduction, and the 12 students were to be part of a new **inclusion** initiative. The students were to be integrated into general education classes with the support of collaborating special education teachers. Due to circumstances beyond the control of the middle school, the program was implemented on very short notice, the special education lead teachers/coordinators were brand new, and none of the teachers had planning time to prepare for their new charges.

In August, before the fall semester began, a few of the teachers met briefly with Principal John Harris to discuss their roles, how they would collaborate to develop IEPs, and how they would deliver an integrated curriculum with curriculum accommodations. This year, for the first time, they were combining English and history into a blocked class, and math and science into another block for all students. Although the teachers were excited and very supportive of the inclusion initiative, they did not feel ready to receive the 12 new students and had to spend a great deal of extra time before the semester reviewing the students' backgrounds to become familiar with their instructional, social, and behavioral needs.

Several problems arose during the fall semester. Some of the *general education teachers* had not been involved in the August meetings and, therefore, were not aware of the students' disabilities and needs. Other school staff, such as the physical education staff, cafeteria staff, the new nurse, the new guidance counselor, and the music teachers, were unaware that these students were to be transferred in under the new inclusion initiative. Several of the students requested extra help with the long-term classroom projects, help with organizational skills, and extensions of time for taking quizzes and tests and turning in assignments. There were numerous adjustment difficulties and behavioral incidents with a few of the students, which resulted in a variety of consequences such as in-school suspensions. In three cases, the use of in-school suspensions resulted in midyear course failures. When in in-school suspension, students were not permitted to complete their work and turn in homework and, as a result, lost all points for projects and homework. Teachers did not know how to put behavioral strategies to work in their classrooms to prevent escalation of these incidents. In addition, two of the students had probation officers who were not known to the teachers, but who were required to visit the students in their school. None of the 12 students were adjusting well to their new school. Several parents joined forces to complain to the principal about what was wrong with the "inclusion experiment."

In mid-December, the teachers met again to review the outcome of the *inclusion initiative*. They determined that many things were seriously wrong with the initiative and that a major intervention was needed—quickly! Mary Masters, the head special education coordinator, had done some homework and had checked on the special education center from which the students had been transferred. She learned that they had been taught in classes with ratios of one teacher to six to eight students. The students also had regular group counseling and the support of a mental health therapist who frequently intervened before small problems became big ones.

Mary also believed that a great deal needed to be done to improve the collaboration among the teachers. First, in collaboration with Principal Harris, she arranged for a series of meetings and discussions with all of the teachers involved with the students, including key support staff, to discuss the students and their needs. An *external specialist/consultant* experienced with educating youth with emotional and learning disabilities was brought in to consult on strategies for positive behavioral supports, classroom management, instructional modifications (changes in the instruction or curriculum materials), and classroom accommodations (changes in the physical classroom or seating).

Second, a series of *follow-up training* sessions were arranged with Mary and the consultant to help general education teachers increase their skills in working with students with special needs. In addition, ongoing technical assistance and staff coaching by the consultant was arranged, with in-school observations over the balance of the year and with follow-up in the subsequent year. This training series included "critical analysis" sessions in which teachers learned to model, observe, and analyze their own instructional techniques and to coach each other. Consultation and training was built into a 2-year *personnel development plan* for the school.

Third, the special educators and general education teachers also established a process for *communicating with parents* on a regular basis in order to intercede early when student problems emerged. Parents typically were the first to anticipate student problems or crises, and open communication between parents and teachers could help defuse problems early. Parents were invited to communicate openly with the special or general education teachers or school counselor. They were encouraged to alert staff in instances that could affect student behavior in school, for example if the student: (a) was having trouble adjusting to a new medication, (b) needed extra help to organize assignments, (c) was anxious about a large project coming due, or (d) had just been placed on house arrest by their probation officer for violating a curfew. Teachers could then be ready to provide extra support.

Fourth, an *emergency response policy* was defined and implemented for students whose behavior was challenging and disruptive in class. This policy included a process of teacher staffing for students who were having difficulty adjusting and who needed team consultation for problem solving. One school counselor's caseload was reduced so that he could establish an ongoing support group for students throughout the year. Mary, the special education coordinator, located an online "academy" program for the resource library that teachers could use to research useful and tested strategies to accommodate students with learning, emotional, and behavioral disabilities or any student with challenging behaviors.

Fifth, a process was created by which *information on students with special needs*, who had been identified for transfer into the school, would be forwarded and made available to teachers well in advance. In addition, when possible, transition visits to the school were arranged for the students and their families to promote the students' adjustment. A teacher-mentor was assigned to each incoming student to provide continuity of support.

Finally, the special education coordinator, a general education lead teacher, and Principal Harris held a series of meetings with the general school staff to *orient them to the goals of an inclusive community*, the needs of the new students, and the channels of communication if students should need additional support or intervention. As an alternative to the traditional label of "inclusion program," the staff adopted the term "All Our Kids Initiative" to emphasize the goal of building a community that emphasizes quality educational experiences, universal design for learning, and responds to the diverse needs of *all* children and youth. The Sunrise Valley High School staff established a learning community to advance their own ongoing professional development and improve their work with students with special needs. They established a system for evaluating the initiative and for making adjustments along the way. They also arranged learning seminars with other middle schools to share their challenges and successes with the initiative.

Questions for Discussion

Reflect on the case illustration as you consider the following questions:

- What were the central challenges or problems, and what solutions were created to address them?
- How did the staff collaborate in search for solutions?
- What factors or conditions led to teacher frustration and initial resistance to the initiative?
- What strategies or actions on the part of the special educator and principal were aimed at improving morale among teachers? Which were aimed at increasing their skills?
- What strategies were designed to create long-term, whole-school change to ensure the success of the initiative?

This case example illustration shows that collaboration for change typically does not develop in a tidy, step-by-step linear fashion. Instead it is messy, complex, and unpredictable. However, the initial challenges and instability provided ample motivation for the principal and teachers to find solutions to some serious problems.

This challenge led to creative thinking, close collaboration and unity among personnel who had not worked together previously, and new leadership among staff. It also resulted in new relationships, practices, and policies that were unprecedented for the school.

HOW DOES COLLABORATION LEAD TO SYSTEM CHANGE?

Collaboration in Systems: An Untidy Process

Collaboration is about change—in people, in practices, or in organizations. More broadly, it is about **systemic change**, or changing a *system* (Chrispeels, Strait & Brown, 1999; Dettmer, Dyck & Thurston, 2005; Pounder, 1999). The term **systemic change** has emerged over the past 60 years from the biological and physical sciences. Over two decades ago, Kaufman (1980), borrowing from Von Bertalanffy's (1968) seminal work on *general* **system theory**, defined a system as a collection of parts that interact to function purposefully as a whole. For example, a pile of airplane parts is not a system, but a functioning jet is. *A system, therefore, is an interdependent group of things that work together to achieve a common purpose.*

Human systems involve interdependent groups of people who work together for a common goal. Relationships among people and the contexts in which they live and work become interrelated aspects of change. We all live in systems and with systems: A nation, a family, a school, a community, or a person can each be viewed as a whole system. Acting within a *whole system* or *ecological perspective* means that if we want to create a change in a system, we have to examine all the parts of that system—personnel, relationships, roles, resources, leadership, organization, and others—and how they are related to each other in context (Bronfenbrenner, 1979). Nothing is irrelevant.

Systems are "open" when they are free to interact with their larger environment. They are not isolated or cut off from that environment or any component of the setting. Because of their constant state of interaction with their environment, such systems grow, develop, and change but not in a linear fashion. In the first case example (see p. 15), the teacher collaboration did not develop in a linear fashion or in a tidy, step-by-step manner. Instead it was messy, complex, and at times unstable.

Understanding systemic change and our individual relationship to it as a professional, requires a change in our worldview—a paradigm shift. Such a shift requires a change in the way we think about our professional role and practices, our relationships, and the environments in which we work. As the previous case example showed, the teachers changed their traditional assumptions about how to work together in order to help the new students with disabilities that they shared in their classes.

Group or organizational change processes mirror the process of individual change. As mentioned earlier, the paradoxical nature of humans can both facilitate and threaten collaborative relationships. When individuals are challenged to change their thinking or behavior, they often react with resistance or fear (Cooperider, Sorensen, Whitney & Yaeger, 1999; Costa & Kallick, 2000). Often they require a powerful psychological stimulus, either internal or external, to motivate the change. The initial stimulus for change is frequently situational, such as a life crisis. Internal motivation may include guilt, dissatisfaction with one's life, or a desire for self-improvement. Examples of external motivation include spouses' or parents' demands

FIGURE 1.1

Systemic Change
Process for a
Collaborative
Community

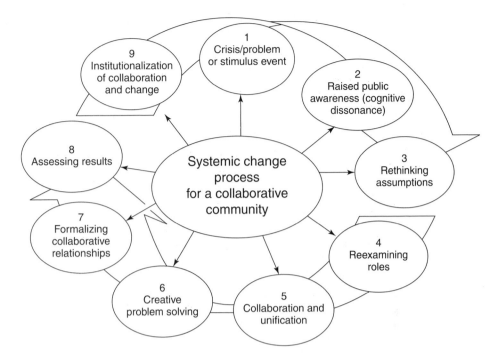

for change, fear of the judgments of colleagues, fear of losing a job or a counselor's encouragement to change, or a court order to cease a behavior. In the Sunrise Valley case example, the teachers' crash course in systemic change followed a path similar to that shown in Figure 1.1.

The teachers were highly motivated by the strong stimulus (crisis or problem) provided by the hastily introduced inclusion initiative, which was in turn triggered by the county budget crisis. These conditions, which challenged their base of knowledge and created great discomfort (cognitive dissonance), also led to a reexamination of their assumptions and beliefs about collaboration, teaching, and learning. As they searched for new structures for collaboration to solve the problems of including students with disabilities in the general education classroom and school system as a whole, they also had to reexamine their professional roles. First, they created informal analysis and problem-solving teams. Then they formalized the collaboration by establishing long-term learning and support teams and by assessing results through evaluation teams. The creation of long-term teams institutionalized the collaboration, or helped increase the likelihood that the collaboration would be sustained over time. The school was forever changed, as were the teachers.

One might argue, in hindsight, that the early "errors," "failures," "barriers," or "challenges" for the staff could have been prevented. However, in the framework of *system theory*, they could not have been averted. When introduced to a new and complex set of stimuli or changes in the environment (i.e., the sudden mandate to implement the inclusion initiative), the system was not yet ready for the required change. The problem-solving process and actions could *not* have been forecast or anticipated. Instead they had to be *constructed together* by a group of creative people sharing a common experience. Therefore, the initial stimulus presented by the

FIGURE 1.2
Creating a Stimulus
for Change

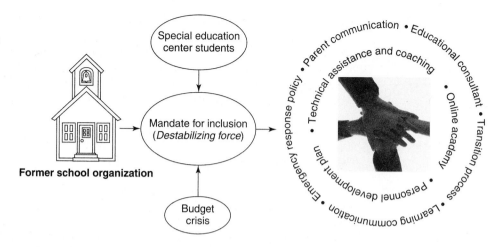

inclusion challenge can be viewed as a powerful condition for the development of deep and sustainable change, as illustrated in Figure 1.2.

Several factors in the system can affect the change process and ultimate success of the school's response: (a) the clarity and strength of the mandate, (b) the leadership to guide the inclusion initiative, (c) the needs of special education center students being transferred, and (d) the budget resources to support the initiative. If these change forces are aligned well to support the process, a stronger collaborative unit in the school will be created. However, if one of the interacting forces or conditions is weak (e.g., the inclusion plan is well conceived and the students are ready, but there are inadequate resources or leadership) then the initiative may be seriously undermined.

While crisis is not a necessary condition for effective collaboration and sustainable change, untidy and unpredictable processes are typical. For these reasons, systemic change can at once be thrilling, fascinating, and extremely challenging. Leading such change is not for the lighthearted. Collaboration for change does not develop in a step-by-step linear fashion. As Hall and Hord (2001) observed, change is a process, not an event. It is rare that human systems transform both rapidly and effectively; they need time for adjustment, reflection, problem solving, and evaluation. Without these, new processes or reforms are likely to erode and decay over time.

The Challenge of Studying Systems

The unpredictable nature of the change process in human systems makes it a difficult process to study and to evaluate. It is, therefore, also a challenge to predict the outcomes of human collaboration. According to system theorists, whole systems are dynamic and are continually changing, moving, and developing. We cannot simply "freeze frame" and examine a system at a single point in time, or examine one isolated part of a system in order to understand the whole. Oceanographers would not net off a section of the ocean to study the "whole" sea. Nor would educational researchers close off a small wing of a school for observation in order to study the whole school. Human groups, as live systems, are subject to growth, change, and development, and are continually interacting with their larger environments.

A change in any single part of a complex interdependent system causes change in other parts. To understand open, living systems, it is important to recognize their complexities and interdependencies (Capra, 1996; Dettmer, 1997; Gaynor, 1998; Hall & Hord, 2001; Kuhn, 1970; Sutherland, 1973; Thagard, 1992; Von Bertalanffy, 1968; Weinberg, 2001). The next section explores four functions of collaboration that incorporate its complexities and possibilities within human systems.

HOW DOES COLLABORATION SERVE AS AN INSTRUMENT OF CHANGE?

Four Reciprocal Functions

The term *reciprocal* is defined as *mutual,* or *expressing a mutual relation* (Random House, 2001). Systemic change in education and human service systems relies upon cooperation and effective relationships among people who are working together. Like all living systems that are characterized by complexity and nonlinearity, collaborative relationships seldom develop in a linear fashion. Although we may try to plan for and implement collaborative initiatives in a step-by-step process, it is typically untidy, unstable, and unpredictable. Collaboration places complex demands on a system and can be thought of as having four overlapping functions. These functions reflect the complex dimensions of collaboration and their instrumentality in contributing to problem solving and change. *Instrumentality* means using collaboration as an instrument, tool, medium, or lever for creating change in knowledge or understanding, relationships among people, practices, or problem-solving approaches. The four **reciprocal functions of collaboration** and their applications are:

1. *Collaboration as discovery* refers to the use of collaborative relationships and processes to *construct new knowledge* through action research or team investigation, or to transfer new knowledge between and among groups of professionals. Examples include the use of classroom- or school-based action research teams, study groups, committees and task forces, teaching internships, and teacher exchanges. In the Sunrise Valley Middle School case example, the teachers developed an inquiry team to explore strategies that other schools use successfully to include students with learning and emotional disabilities in the middle school curriculum.

2. *Collaboration as synthesis of ideas* refers to the use of collaboration to *connect the thinking and knowledge of people* in different disciplines or groups within a school or organization in order to guide decisions and actions, redefine or solve problems, or develop new policies and processes. Examples of collaboration as synthesis include teams involved in the development of Individual Family Service Plans (IFSP) or Individualized Education Plans (IEP), interdisciplinary problem-solving groups, and parent advisory groups. In the Sunrise Valley case, teachers established a response team that combined the thinking of special and general education teachers, counselors, and related services personnel to solve immediate student problems and to create new policies.

3. *Collaboration as the development of practice* refers to the *application of collaborative practices to analyze, develop or make more effective educational and support practices and role relationships.* Examples of these include collaborative or team teaching, teacher networks, personnel development programs, partnerships with Institutions of Higher Education (IHEs), interschool planning teams, mentoring or coaching relationships, parent and family resource centers, and local school improvement teams.

In the Sunrise Valley Middle School, the special education teacher and an external consultant established a professional development program for all personnel. The program was embedded within a long-term technical assistance initiative to support teacher practices for the balance of the school year and the following year.

4. *Collaboration as building professional community* refers to the *creative use of collaboration to connect school personnel with the larger external professional community* to create broad, sustainable change within the school. It means bringing the professional community into the school to facilitate change. This function may also involve the creative use of collaboration for the purpose of linking the first three functions, which involve research or new knowledge creation, development of practice, and collaborative decision making. Examples of this form of collaboration include linking with professional associations, connecting teachers with national or regional resource centers, connecting with web-based professional communities, and creating partnerships with universities to enhance the school's capacity to improve learning for all children.

A collaborative initiative typically involves a blend of two or more of these functions. Choosing the best form of collaboration to address a particular system challenge depends a great deal on the purpose, goals, and the results that are defined.

Strategic Collaboration for Results

Research on organizational change has demonstrated that attempts to change systems to improve teaching, learning, and support for students involve new collaboration among people and their roles, and involve ongoing inquiry and reflection (Cooperider et al., 1999; Cushman, 1998; Ettling, 2002; Fullan, 1999; Hall & Hord, 2001; Hargreaves, 2000; Hinde, 2003; Osguthorpe & Patterson, 1998). This means that making change requires people to (1) learn new information and reflect on what they have learned in the past (discovery); (2) think and work together differently and in new combinations (synthesis); (3) clarify expected results, or define what needs to be changed or improved; (4) create new practices and processes (development of practices); (5) decide who takes responsibility for the process and how to resolve problems when the collaboration is "broken"; and (6) participate in continuous self-development and learning in connection with the wider professional community (building professional community).

Strategic collaboration involves a purposeful effort to change how people work together, how they perform their roles, and how the environment supports their goals. For example, never has the issue of cooperation and community building been more important than in the integration of general education and special education to support students who are special learners in the general curriculum. The effectiveness of collaboration depends on how well the desired results are envisioned and defined, how carefully the goals are developed, and how precisely the collaborative activities are aimed at the actual problem or need being addressed. This reflects a "backward design" process that begins with the end in mind (Covey, 2004; Wiggins & McTighe, 2001).

For example, suppose a physician is presented with a complex set of symptoms in a few new patients. Suspecting that this may be a new or previously unidentified illness, she decides to collaborate with physicians from two other specialty areas to diagnose the problem and develop appropriate treatment plans. The effectiveness of that collaboration (defined by results) depends upon the clear goals defined for the collaboration. Evaluators could have examined only the *processes* of collaboration, for example, the roles of the other physicians, how they worked together, how often they meet, how they established the treatment plan, or how decisions were made. Or, they could have evaluated the *results* of the collaboration, for example, accurate diagnosis of the problem, effectiveness of the treatment plan, new combination of medications prescribed, and ultimately, improvements in the patients' conditions within a reasonable period of time. The patients improve, the doctors have an identified illness, and the collaboration is deemed essential to the overall effort.

Obviously in the example above, the target results of the collaboration are quite clear—heal the patient. With collaboration in education and human services, the target results or outcomes are seldom so defined. In fact, they are usually highly complex and affect several groups and levels within the organization. But the old adage still applies—if you don't know where you're going, you'll probably end up somewhere else.

WHAT ARE THE DEVELOPMENTAL ASPECTS OF COLLABORATION?

The questions posed earlier about achieving change through effective collaboration become a little more complex when considered across the **developmental continuum** of the child. Questions about the effectiveness of collaboration then become: *For what purposes? For what children? At what stage in their development?* Figure 1.3

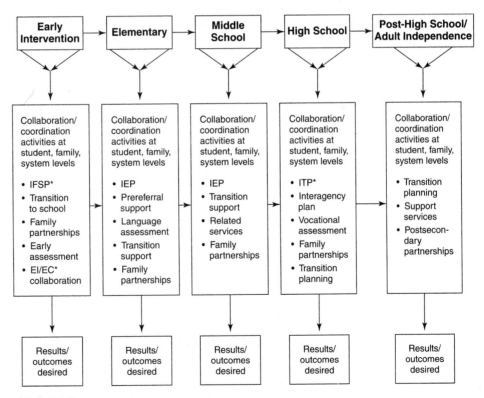

FIGURE 1.3

Collaborative Results Continuum: Focus on Purpose and Results

*IFSP: Individual Family Services Plan; EI/EC: Early Intervention/Early Childhood; IEP: Individual Education Plan; ITP: Individual Transition Plan.

presents the kinds of collaboration and coordination activities that occur at student, family, and system levels at each stage of the student's pathway through school. Specific results for students, families, and staff can be identified for each stage along the way.

Considering school collaboration and system coordination within the student's developmental framework is important because collaborative activities necessarily change in response to the changing needs of the student. Chapters 10 to 15 closely examine collaboration and coordination needs and strategies in each of these developmental stages from early childhood through to postsecondary education.

Educators and related service personnel are typically focused on one particular stage in students' continuum of development. Teacher preparation is structured so that teachers are prepared for early childhood, elementary, middle school, or high school teaching. Although specialization is necessary in the preparation of personnel, it is also important to promote understanding and planning for future needs of students and families along the continuum. For example, it is often a challenge for early childhood specialists and elementary teachers to think ahead to the expectations of middle and high school years and to planning for transition to adult life. Similarly, it is often difficult for middle and high school teachers to reflect on the experiences of students and early influences of family, health, or education on the student with a disability. It is crucial for children and families for professionals to help them become familiar with the options and array of services in the school and community at each transition point from early childhood through high school. Professionals are more effective when they possess a broader understanding of the full continuum of passages for students.

CAN COLLABORATION BE EVALUATED?

Shared Responsibility for Outcomes

Systemic change is not likely to occur if the principal or administrator alone has a clear understanding of what needs to be accomplished. To create a shared commitment to collaboration, everyone involved in producing results needs:

- a clear rationale for why a change in practice or relationships is needed, including expected results;
- an explanation of how the new collaborative relationships will help achieve the results;
- an understanding of each participant's role in the process, including how they can expect their role and work to change; and
- incentives or rewards associated with participation in the collaborative initiative (tangible and intangible).

It is important that collaborative leaders remain clear about their purposes or goals for a collaborative initiative. Most purposes for collaboration fall into the four major functions for collaboration—*discovery, synthesis, development of practice,* and *professional community*. These purposes for collaboration, which can serve as a basis for evaluation, may include relationships established, indicators of improved teaching, student learning, services coordinated, resources shared, personnel development provided, agreements developed, information shared or disseminated, consensus reached on issues or policies, problems identified, and expanded stakeholder participation.

It is important to determine the purpose for the collaboration, the outcomes or results desired, the environment, the tasks, the responsibilities, and the manner of evaluating the success of a collaborative initiative. The following mnemonic—POETRE—might help readers to remember essential questions for evaluating a collaborative initiative:

1. (P) What is the *purpose* for the collaboration (what problems need to be addressed, or what questions need to be asked)?
2. (O) What *outcomes* (results) are collaborators expecting?
3. (E) What is the appropriate *environment* to accomplish the outcome (people, location, setting, materials)?
4. (T) What is the sequence of *tasks* to be accomplished?
5. (R) Who should be assigned *responsibility* for the tasks?
6. (E) How do we *evaluate* so we know that we have achieved the results we want?

Focusing on these questions helps collaborative leaders to make decisions that can guide the collaborative activity and keep it focused. Let's See It in Action, below, applies the POETRE questions.

LET'S SEE IT IN ACTION! Case Illustration: Know What You Want from Your Meeting

Middle school principal Amy Jeffords and a few of her teachers decided to bring people together to talk about ways the school could improve students' preparation for transition to the high school. The meeting was planned hastily, and invitations were sent out broadly to individuals within and outside the school. When the meeting came together, there were elementary and middle school teachers, a high school counselor, a speech and language therapist, a social worker, as well as district staff and a school improvement specialist. The meeting was unproductive because it degenerated into a tense complaint session in which school personnel were put on the defensive about what resources were available to make changes, who was responsible, why there were no high school teachers there, and why this had not been brought up during the last school improvement team meeting. It felt to some participants like a monitoring meeting.

After the meeting, Principal Jeffords and school staff stayed to debrief. They had not thought through what they wanted from the meeting. The debriefing yielded the following information about purpose, results desired, environment, tasks, responsibility, and evaluation (POETRE).

1. P: *What was the purpose (question being asked)?* How can our school improve transition services and supports for students moving from middle school to high school?
2. O: *What outcome/results did they expect?* Although Principal Jeffords expected to produce a set of brainstormed ideas about strategies that could be pursued further with the high school staff, she did not clearly communicate to participants that this was an expected result.

3. E: *What is the appropriate environment to accomplish the outcome (people, location, setting, materials)?* Principal Jeffords realized that perhaps first she should have held a smaller brainstorming session with staff to organize their thinking, examine needs within the middle school, and become better prepared to present needs and set goals for a larger meeting. Also, realizing that place and setting is important and symbolic, staff suggested a more neutral setting, or to have the next meeting at the high school.

4. T: *What are the next tasks to be accomplished?* Another meeting was set for school personnel to hold an open discussion about transition and to prepare for a larger meeting in which concrete plans could be developed.

5. R: *Who should be assigned responsibility for the tasks?* Principal Jeffords took responsibility to invite participants from the middle school and assigned the assistant principal to conduct a schoolwide survey of ideas that could be brought to the next meeting.

6. E: *How do we evaluate so we know that we have achieved the results we want?* Principal Jeffords decided to evaluate the activities by providing staff with a summary of the needs survey, a summary of the group discussion outlining the suggested ideas and strategies to improve transition, and a summary of proposed next steps. All staff were invited to provide feedback, individually, in writing, or in a general staff meeting.

Summary of Key Points

- Collaboration is a process of participation through which people, groups, and organizations form relationships and work together to achieve a set of agreed-upon results.
- System coordination refers to the organizational relationships among schools and agencies that are linked in their efforts to provided services.
- Collaboration and system coordination must respond to students' changing developmental needs.
- Collaboration is complex and unpredictable and does not develop in a tidy, step-by-step linear fashion.
- Effective collaboration depends on how well desired results can be defined and how well the collaborative activities are aimed at the expected results.
- Collaboration and coordination reflect the belief that people and their relationships are fundamental to solving problems and making progress in any field or discipline.

Key Terms and Phrases

- Collaboration (p. 7)
- System coordination (p. 7)
- Developmental continuum (p. 8)

- Early intervening services (p. 10)
- Special learners (p. 10)
- Differentiated instruction (p. 11)
- Empowerment (p. 12)
- Self-determination (p. 13)
- Individualized education plan (p. 14)
- Related services (p. 14)
- Shared responsibility (p. 14)
- Inclusion (p. 15)
- System theory (p. 18)
- Systemic change (p. 18)
- Reciprocal functions of collaboration (p. 21)
- Strategic collaboration (p. 22)
- Developmental continuum (p. 23)

Questions for Reflection, Thinking, and Skill Building

1. Why are human systems referred to as "messy, complex, unstable, and unpre-dictable"? What are the implications of this assumption for developing collaborative relationships?
2. Why are collaboration and system coordination important for assisting children and youth to make transitions along the developmental continuum? Identify a few barriers or impediments to collaboration and system coordination?
3. Find out in your school or local school district how collaboration and system coordination support the work of the schools. How many kinds of collaborative activities or initiatives can you identify operating (e.g., team teaching, study teams, task forces, school improvement teams, teacher–parent partnerships)? What kinds of system coordination activities can you find (e.g., school–community partnerships, interagency agreements, cross-agency study teams or advisory groups)?
4. Organize the various collaboration and system coordination activities you identified above by the four reciprocal functions of collaboration and coordination.

CHAPTER TWO

HOW DOES SCHOOL
COLLABORATION WORK?

Be the change you want to see in the world. —GANDHI

- What is collaboration and collaborative culture?
- What factors influence collaboration?
- How are school collaboration and system coordination linked?
- How are reciprocal functions applied in collaborative practices?
- What are foundation theories for collaboration and applications in practice?
- What are ten principles for successful collaboration and coordination?

PERSPECTIVES

Administrator

One of the most noticeable benefits of collaboration is teacher reflection—having the opportunity to interact with others, learn about others' beliefs, knowledge, and attitudes, and consequently, to "develop shared language for expressing ideas and critiquing practice" (Brownwell et al., 1997, p. 346). Teachers become more reflective practitioners. They construct new frameworks for teaching and extend these frameworks through conversation with their colleagues and practice in their classrooms. They reflect on past and present teaching practices.

—THERESA STARR, DISTRICT ADMINISTRATOR

Counselor

I read about collaboration theories and strategies in my counseling preparation program, but it was only through my experience in the schools that I really "got it." I learned quickly how vital teamwork is in the school's efforts to improve the overall environment for students. I learned that I cannot expect others to create the change, but I had to be a part of the process.

—HIGH SCHOOL COUNSELOR

INTRODUCTION

Collaborative practices in education are rooted in theories that have emerged within a variety of fields, including organizational development, sociology, physical sciences, health professions, and psychology. Concerned with the quality of education to meet higher standards for a more diverse student population, educators are seeking to learn from the theories and models of related disciplines. For example, when Peter Senge, world-renowned organizational development expert and author of

The Fifth Discipline (1994) was asked if schools are considered to be *learning organizations*, his response was this:

> Definitely not. A learning organization is an organization in which people at all levels are, collectively, continually enhancing their capacity to create things they want to create. Most of the educators I talk with don't feel as though they're doing this. Most teachers feel oppressed trying to conform to all kinds of rules, goals, and objectives, many of which they don't believe in. Teachers don't work together; there's very little sense of collective learning going on in most schools. (O'Neil, 1995, p. 20)

Since that interview, educators have begun to identify barriers that schools face in becoming learning organizations that can promote progress for all its children. These include (a) the overly large size of schools, particularly middle and high schools; (b) a shortage of well-prepared teachers and administrators; (c) the increasing challenge to help special learners participate in the general education curriculum; (d) little time for collaboration and pressure to perform too many activities; (e) diminishing resources to support the needs of special learners; (f) few resources to support teacher research to improve teaching practices; and (g) inadequate staffing and resources to support collaboration among schools, community-based agencies, and business and industry. In the search for solutions, educational leaders are exploring ideas from other fields, including the following:

1. Creating smaller communities among people for professional practice development, inquiry, problem solving, and decision making (communities of practice, learning communities, inquiry teams, and technical-assistance communities).
2. Connecting disciplines within schools and connecting schools with human service agencies.

The educational profession is challenged with the weight of its mandate and complexity of its structure. It is searching for answers to how to connect professionals with one another, with students, families, and the larger community. Many educators view the educational experience through the eyes of their students and ask: Are schools structured in a way that best supports their learning and their social development? Are schools structured in a way that best supports teachers' abilities to share responsibility for children, to blend their expertise to deliver the highest quality instruction and create effective and safe learning environments? Are schools able to connect with supportive services and human service agencies in the community in order to link children and families with the extra services they may need to benefit from their educational experience? And the most difficult questions of all are: Do children and youth feel good about being in school, about staying in school, and about their futures? How do educators and school organization promote a positive view of school by students, or contribute to a negative view? These are among the most challenging questions being debated by educators across the United States and around the world.

Human collaboration and coordination lie at the heart of each of these questions, and the solutions we seek will determine the very future of education and its ability to embrace all children. The purpose of this chapter is to explore the concept of collaboration and its underlying theories, its many forms found in schools today, and the professional roles involved.

WHAT IS COLLABORATION AND COLLABORATIVE CULTURE?

School-based collaboration refers to collaborative relationships among professionals of different disciplines and units within a school setting in order to provide educational and related services within a school (Bos, Nahamias, & Urban, 1999; Dettmer, Dyck, & Thurston, 2005; Friend & Cook, 2003; Glover, 2003; Walther-Thomas, Korinek, McLaughlin, & Williams, 2000). *System coordination* (discussed in Chapter 3) refers to relationships between schools and school-linked human service agencies that work to address the needs of students who require a more coordinated approach (Abrams & Gibbs, 2000; Kohler, 2003; Mogharreban & Branscum, 2000; Rosman, McCarthy, & Woolverton, 2001; Simmons, 2002; U.S. Department of Health and Human Services, 2001).

Within this broad definition, collaboration can also be defined as a complex process that involves *networking, coordination, cooperation,* and *collaboration* (Himmelman, 1992; 1996). The degree of collaboration among professionals will depend on a variety of factors, including the strategic goals of the partners, the administrative and organizational support and culture, the kinds of stresses or threats to the process, and the kind of learning that is desired or required to accomplish the task.

The degrees of intensity of collaboration range from the less complex *communication* and *networking,* to the most complex and uncommon state of total *integration* of roles, groups, units, or organizations. *The difference in degree reflects the complexity of the kind of interaction required and the kind of learning that needs to occur.* At one end of the continuum, teachers may simply request and provide information. But at the highest level of learning, thinking and interaction within the group is characterized by the exchange of ideas, transformation, and integration of perspectives, attitudes, and opinions (Cohen, 2004; Friend & Cook, 2003). Figure 2.1 depicts the five degrees of collaboration and their relationship to the complexity of learning. The concept of degrees of collaboration is interpreted below in the context of professional collaboration between general and special educators.

FIGURE 2.1
Degrees of
Collaboration

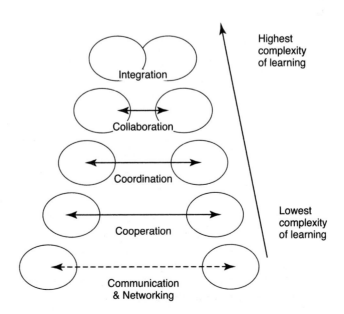

Communication and Networking means the discussion or sharing of information between teachers or other professionals for the purposes of maintaining relationships, understanding roles, and sharing information about a student or a teaching strategy. This may occur on an ad hoc, intermittent, or as-needed basis. The teachers do not undertake any joint activities or projects, and interaction involves requesting and providing information.

Cooperation refers to ongoing communication between general and special educators that occurs on a regular basis. The teachers or other professionals have structured their communication or information-sharing events into their schedules, expect and anticipate them, and prepare for them. They have similar interests, plan together, negotiate mutual roles, and share resources to achieve joint goals, but they maintain separate role identities (Taylor-Powell, Rossing, & Geran, 1998). As partners, they need only to come to an agreement on how to work together to achieve a general goal (Himmelman, 1996; Taylor-Powell et al., 1998). Cooperative activities do not in any way limit the status of the individual and his or her role, or the team or unit, but they retain separate identities. Interaction remains at the information-sharing level.

Coordination means specific shared, ongoing activities beyond discussion or information sharing that occur between general and special educators or among several professionals. Examples include creation of procedures for referring students for special education, creation of coordinated staff development activities, or development of policies that promote coordinated activities between special educators and counselors.

Collaboration refers to formalized and substantial involvement among professionals in which teachers work closely together within a common classroom or common community of practice. Collaboration typically includes a process in which two or more people with complementary skills work together to create a shared understanding that none had previously possessed or could have come to on their own. This can involve a process through which parties who see different aspects of a problem can explore their differences constructively, and search for and implement solutions that go beyond their own limited vision of what is possible (Taylor-Powell, Rossing, & Geran, 1998). For example, two teachers may create an adapted lesson that accommodates students at different reading levels.

Collaborative activities may include coteaching, classroom consultation, inquiry teams, professional-development teams, decision-making teams, and other activities in which people develop common standards, language, and procedures to facilitate working together. The kinds of thinking and interaction within the group is of a highly complex cognitive level, characterized by the exchange of ideas, information, perspectives, attitudes, and opinions. Teachers may also deliberately discuss conflicting views or attitudes that place them into cognitive conflicts. As they explain and defend their views, those conflicts can be reconciled. Thus, through discussion, they arrive at *negotiated meaning* (understanding that is constructed through social interaction). In doing so, individuals reformulate their own thinking and alter their knowledge structures; that is, they learn (King, 2002).

Integration means the unification of two or more previously separate groups, units, or agencies under common control, or the combining of activities and roles of two or more professionals that were previously carried out separately and independently.

Examples include (a) teachers who are credentialed in both general and special education and have integrated roles; (b) the merging of two professional subject matter teams into one; and (c) the merging of two administrative units within a school so that it shares authority and makes decisions together. Integration can occur as a response to extreme pressures—for example, financial instability. Or it can result from longer-term strategies that are based on the need to combine complementary knowledge and skills. The nature of and success of collaboration within a group or school depends upon the culture of that school, the leadership to guide and support it, and the preparation of all professionals within that school who work together to improve education of children.

What Is Collaborative Culture?

Over two decades ago, John Goodlad (1984) observed that American teachers feel that their work is more satisfying when they are involved in problem solving, influencing teaching and schoolwide decision making. The school reform movements of the 1980s brought interest in collegiality to general education, and eventually the term that characterized reform work became known as collaboration (Friend & Cook, 2000). As Marzano (2003) observed, coordinated teacher schedules can allow teachers to capitalize on individual strengths in meeting students' needs. Schoolwide committees can encourage teachers to take an interest in the school beyond their classrooms and to expand their leadership. However, none of these can transform a school (Marzano, 2003). Creating *schoolwide collaboration* requires the development of a **collaborative culture**. School leaders and educators agree that a collaborative culture benefits a diverse population of students and professionals.

Anne Vega/Merrill

Schools with a culture of collaboration promote interchange between professionals whenever and wherever it is needed.

Peterson and Brietzke (1994) defined collaborative schools as places where the underlying norms, values, and beliefs support, encourage, and reinforce teamwork, collegiality, and interactions about problems of practice. According to Jackson and Davis (2000), building a collaborative culture means:

- creating a democratic school community,
- fostering skills and practices of strong leadership,
- establishing regular and common planning time among instructional and support personnel, and
- embedding professional development into the daily life of the school.

Jackson and Davis (2000) further explain that a collaborative culture in the school means creating structures that promote a culture of high-quality teaching and learning and related services, establishing small learning communities within the school, lowering student–teacher ratios where possible, and building parent and community partnerships. In a collaborative culture, members of the school community work together effectively and are guided by a common purpose. All members of the community—teachers, administrators, students, and their families—share a common vision of what the school should be like. Together they set goals that lead them toward this vision. In doing so, they create a culture of discourse in which the most important educational matters facing the school are openly and honestly discussed. Members respect each other, value their differences, and are open to each other's ideas. Even when there is disagreement, people listen to each other because they believe deeply that resolving differences in viewpoints is vital in moving their school forward. The many different voices within the school community add to its strength and vitality.

Let's See It in Action, below, is based on a true story, providing a glimpse of the struggles and rewards of collaboration.

LET'S SEE IT IN ACTION! Case Illustration: A Principal Fights for Collaboration

For the past two years, I have been the principal of Whiteman Academy, a private special education school located on the grounds of a public school. The purpose of the program is to integrate students with disabilities into the general education population and curriculum. In my first year, the site was in its fourth year of operation. My predecessor had achieved some measure of collaboration between general and special education teachers, enough to permit two students to be served in inclusive classes.

I began my first year as principal assuming that there was a high degree of collaboration within the system, but quickly discovered that the public school administration was not as welcoming as I had hoped. The goal of inclusion was an extremely fragile one, and Mr. Paul Lynden, the public school principal, required extensive documentation "proving" a student's readiness to attend a class within his building. He also wanted one of my staff to accompany our students and remain with them during class. I assured Mr. Lynden, the teachers, and the staff that our students could be successful in general education, and I provided them the necessary support and technical assistance. Persistence finally paid off, and we were able to successfully include three students into a total of eight classes by the end of the first year. During the process, I identified several challenges within the system that I had inherited.

First, our school program was located in two temporary classrooms outside of the public school building in a courtyard, and from the beginning the public school students viewed our students as different. Next, the school day was arranged so that our students arrived later than the rest of the student body to avoid "problems with the buses" and to allow staff to avoid the early start time of the public school at 7:15. This meant that our students missed morning announcements and homeroom and were unable to attend first period classes. Every Wednesday our school closed early to allow for extra planning and staff development, but this arrangement prohibited students from attending after-school activities and dances, afternoon assemblies, and afternoon inclusive classes. Finally, our staff had very little interaction with the public school staff because of the different hours, the physical location, and the limited involvement of our students. All of these factors limited opportunities for our students to interact with their peers without disabilities.

The most significant barrier to true collaboration was the preconceived belief that we had nothing unique to offer the public school. For the first two years, I struggled with my feelings of being a perpetual guest. For every student opportunity I sought, I had to ask permission, request favors, offer thanks, or even offer some type of compensation. The amount of effort needed to keep a foot in the door was extraordinary. I was frustrated and exhausted and knew I needed a new lens on the problem to make a different kind of change.

Collaboration is the key ingredient in the success of a program like this, but in our case the arrangement had been completely one-sided. The only way to open the door to real collaboration was to recognize that we had something to offer the public school. What we had to offer was our knowledge and skills that could benefit all teachers and their diverse learners. The public school system had already been offering coteaching classes in some schools (classes taught by both a general education content area teacher and a special educator), and such an arrangement offered greater support to all students. I proposed that our staff could work in teams with general educators to create a reciprocal (two-way) relationship with our host school. From the moment that I suggested to Principal Lynden that we do this, our relationship changed. The new program was a greater success than I could have anticipated. The components of the new program included many improvements:

1. My two special education teachers cotaught two classes with general education teachers within the public schools.
2. Our students attended these classes and received academic support and socializing opportunities.
3. The school counselor worked closely with special education teachers and students to provide additional support.
4. Our students were permitted to enter additional inclusive classes if they maintained appropriate behavior, and many attended these classes without direct staff supervision.
5. Special educators joined one of the four academic teams—groups of 8 to 12 content area teachers who share the same concerns about integrated students.
6. Students attended special field trips and assemblies.

Our students now feel like students of the public school, and our staff members experience the benefit of belonging to a team. They attend team meetings and are part of the planning and reflection process within that group. We have also made changes to our school day schedule and now follow the same schedule as the public school. We use the same buses, and our students are spared the social discomfort of riding special education buses. The benefits for students were clear, but the change in the perception of school personnel has made all the difference. Probably the greatest measure of the success of this new program is the gratitude I hear from Principal Lynden—our greatest obstacle in the beginning. He now praises my staff and my students and finally views me as an equal. (Laura Peters, Principal, 2005)

Questions for Discussion

- What was Principal Peters' first step in the process of collaboration? What proactive steps did she make to begin changing relationships?
- What did she realize about the nature of collaboration that made it effective?
- What evidence is there that the collaborative relationship is effective in achieving results?

In the preceding case illustration, Principal Peters first reflected on the original structure of the program and how that would influence the professional collaboration and ultimately the inclusion effort (e.g., separating students and teachers physically and by school arrival time and schedule). Second, she realized that collaboration was not only an organizational structure but also a philosophy. It had to be a *reciprocal relationship* in which the participants were equals—no one was a "guest" in the school. Everyone had something to offer each other in the public school.

Third, Principal Peters realized that only through a *strategic change process* (focused on actions) could she achieve her goals. She realized that her teachers had expertise in designing and delivering special education services, and that the coteaching model was the solution for inclusion, student support, and teacher collaboration. Fourth, Principal Peters engaged the public school principal and forged a new relationship. Together they constructed the coteaching arrangements and also restructured the relationships among special and general education professionals to ensure that **collaborative teams** became a part of the everyday culture of the school.

WHAT FACTORS INFLUENCE COLLABORATION?

There is no one model for successful collaboration in schools. The challenges and turbulence of the educational environment today means that practices must be carefully tailored to the particular circumstances of the schools and communities. Success depends on a range of factors, including history, preparation of personnel, attitudes and commitment of collaborating partners, and school culture (Aiello & Bullock, 1999; Rosman, McCarthy, & Woolverton, 2001).

Factors That Influence Collaborative Behavior

Collaboration involves human beings who often behave very differently in groups than they do alone. Based on studies of cooperation and competition among groups, there are a variety of factors that have been shown to positively or negatively affect the development of cooperative and collaborative behavior among people and groups:

- *Size and composition of the group:* size of the group and composition in terms of gender balance, ethnic diversity, age, and other demographic factors that can impact the development of alliances, trust, and communication.
- *Alliances and the presence of norm violators:* the kinds of friendships and alliances formed during the collaborative activity, as well as the presence of group members who are known to, or demonstrate a willingness to break "the rules" or the group norms in order to achieve consensus (e.g., ganging up against members who are opposed to a certain position).
- *Availability of information and obligation to cooperate:* the adequacy of information group members have to help them make sound decisions, and the pressure of a superior on group members to achieve cooperation and reach a consensus on an issue or decision. Collaboration will be affected by the degree of comfort group members feel about their decision-making power and the high stakes of the outcomes.
- *Theory:* the availability of or group construction of a theory about the problem being addressed can aid decision making and can promote cooperation and reduce conflict. A theory can serve as an anchor, focus, or guiding set of principles for the deliberations.
- *Communication skills of the group:* the ability of the group (and its leader) to communicate constructively, reduce conflict, and achieve a consensus.
- *Uncertainty or mistrust:* uncertainty or skepticism about the outcome of the cooperative action or decisions or how they may be used by superiors.
- *Noise and environmental conditions:* the amount of environmental noise in the room or building, which can greatly affect the communication among group members, and therefore impact their ability to achieve consensus. Other environmental factors can include air quality, availability of food and drink, temperature, and other factors that can distract the group's work.
- *Payoffs:* the existence of rewards or incentives for the group to achieve a positive outcome or consensus. Celebrating collaborative activities that occur in the school can also help reinforce collaborative culture.
- *Past choices and decisions:* the record or institutional history of previous decisions related to the problem the group is addressing, written in the organization's policies, regulations, or informal documents.
- *The presence of an external threat:* the existence of a threat to the group, such as an external group who is interested in influencing the outcome (Axelrod, 1997; Bendor, 1993; Hammerstein, 2003; Herasymowych & Herasymowych, 2000; Ridley, 1998; Singer, 2000; Stump & Hagie, 2005).

Although many factors affect collaborative decision making, several factors related to the unpredictability of groups can strengthen a collaboration. These can be classified into four groups: (1) unexpected *synergy*, harmony, or team spirit among the collaborators; (2) unexpected *synthesis* and *creativity*; (3) unanticipated *complementary expertise* and experience within the team; and (4) unexpected *leadership* that emerges from within a group. The strategy of choice for establishing a positive climate for collaboration is helping professionals appreciate how collaboration increases the likelihood of achieving their desired professional goals and how collaboration can enhance each others' competence (Himmelman, 1996; Hutt et al., 2000; Reason, 1999). Furthermore, administrators who support collaborative innovation provide necessary resources and time for team members to work together and provide opportunities for continued professional development in areas of interest and need (Stump & Hagie, 2005).

Structure of Collaborative Teams

Friend and Cook (2000) described collaboration as existing in two different dimensions, characterized by *structure* and *purpose*. In relation to the first dimension, teams can be structured as *multidisciplinary, interdisciplinary*, or *transdisciplinary* teams:

- *Multidisciplinary* teams are formed to implement evaluation and placement procedures for students with disabilities and are comprised of combinations of professionals, including special educators, general educators, related service specialists, administrators, parents, and students.
- *Interdisciplinary* teams involve two or more professionals representing different disciplines who meet frequently to share information on student progress or to make decisions about a student.
- The *transdisciplinary* team includes special and regular educators and related service specialists who collaborate closely and may blend or share roles to deliver an intervention to a student.

Teams are also formed for various purposes, which can often impact the way in which the team is structured (Schwartz, Shanley, Mewer, & O'Cummings, 2003). These purposes may include monitoring, problem solving, or instruction. *Monitoring teams* ensure that services are being provided in accordance with special education law. Or they may serve as a child-study team, school assessment team, prereferral team, placement team, planning team, or multidisciplinary team (Friend & Cook, 2000). *Problem-solving teams* solve problems related to student needs. Examples include *teacher assistance teams* (TATs offer support to teachers working to accommodate students in the classroom), *intervention assistance teams* (IATs identify and coordinate resources in a school), and *prereferral intervention teams* (PITs offer recommendations and interventions for teachers with concerns regarding student performance and behavior to prevent referral for special education services) (Schwartz et al., 2003).

Instructional teams provide instruction to children with special needs. The teams work together on all types of classroom practices involving planning, executing, and assessing lessons. They may be organized as coteaching, teaching, or grade-level teams.

How Are School Collaboration and System Coordination Linked?

School collaboration and system coordination have important differences, but they are also closely linked. As mentioned earlier, school collaboration refers to the work conducted among people within schools (the people part). System coordination refers to institutional and human relationships among people who work between schools and community agencies (the interagency and organizational part). These community services may even be located within the school. It is useful to define the variety of forms that collaborative relationships can take within a school and between schools and community service agencies. Figure 2.2 depicts the variety of collaborative and coordinating relationships. As this figure shows, although the range of possible relationships are infinite, they can be grouped into

FIGURE 2.2

Spectrum of Collaborative Relationships Among Professionals

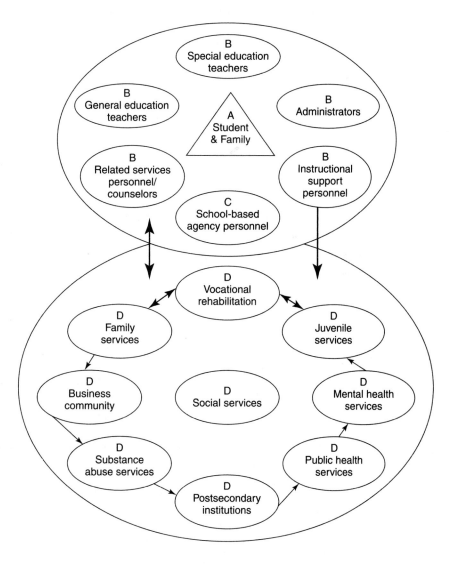

two broad categories—*collaboration* among people, and *system coordination* among institutions or agencies. The possible configurations are explained below.

School Collaboration

- **A→B:** collaboration between student or family and school professionals (special and general education teachers, related services personnel, administrators)
- **A→C:** collaboration among students, families, school-based agency personnel, and community agency professional who may be colocated at the school
- **Within B:** collaboration among professionals within a single professional grouping or discipline within a school (e.g., among science teachers, among special educators, among related services personnel)
- **B→B:** collaboration between two professional groups in a school (e.g., general educators and special educators)
- **B→B→B→C:** collaboration among several groups of professionals within a school (e.g., among special educators, related services personnel, administrators, and vocational rehabilitation personnel)

System Coordination (between schools and community agencies)

- **B→D or B→B→D:** coordination among professionals in the school and in one school-linked community agency (e.g., special educators and vocational rehabilitation personnel)
- **B→D→D or B→B→D→D:** coordination among professionals in the school and professionals in two or more community agencies
- **B→B or B→C:** formal and informal agreements to link and establish ongoing activities, relationships among units, and coordination of services within the school (e.g., agreement between the counseling and guidance unit and special education unit)
- **B→D and B→B→D→D:** formal and informal agreements to link and establish ongoing activities, relationships among school and community-based groups, and coordination of services (e.g., agreement among the school, vocational rehabilitation division, community mental health agency, and adult services)

HOW ARE RECIPROCAL FUNCTIONS APPLIED IN COLLABORATIVE PRACTICE?

As introduced in Chapter 1, reciprocal functions reflect the complex dimensions of collaboration and their contributions to problem solving and change. The four functions include collaboration *as discovery, as synthesis of ideas, as development of practice,* and *as building professional community.* In the following sections, collaboration activities are described in relation to these functions. In actual systems, of course, there is overlap among these categories and functions.

Applying Collaboration for Discovery and Learning

Collaboration within the school serves as a tool to conduct inquiry or research within a school setting, such as the use of classroom or school-based action research teams. For example, four ninth-grade middle school coteaching teams of special and general educators established an inquiry team to collect data on whether students with disabilities performed better in their mathematics achievement when they introduced a new hands-on method of teaching in which students used foam shapes as manipulatives to learn basic algebra. They agreed to share student performance data and discuss their own delivery of the new method. Other examples of applied action research include:

- teachers' joint examination of how a new classroom assessment impacts students' learning,
- study of how the inclusion of two students with severe learning disabilities is positively impacting the general education classroom environment, and
- study of how a new collaborative learning strategy is helping students improve discussion skills.

Collaboration for discovery also includes study groups, committees, task forces, and professional internships. For example, a school needed to help teachers learn new strategies for working with students with disabilities integrated into general education classes and strategies for classroom management. A schoolwide system was established to work with and receive support and assistance from a state special education technical assistance center. The school established an "advance team," or support team composed of special educators, general educators, related services specialists, and counselors who were identified to become school team leaders. These team leaders would then teach others in a staged process of professional development that would ultimately reach everyone in the school. The support team also included a consultant from the local university who was knowledgeable in scientifically based research and practice on teaching and learning and familiar with the development of learning communities. The consultant led teacher teams through the process of collaborative research on new practices, through planning for their implementation, and finally through joint evaluation of the effectiveness of the practices for student learning and their own teaching.

Applying Collaboration to Synthesize Ideas for Decision Making

In applying collaboration for a synthesis of ideas, collaborators are seeking to develop consensus among teachers and administrators on key decisions of broad importance to the school. Examples of such decisions include how to restructure staffing, how to create effective discipline policies, who should have authority to refer English language learners to special education, or how to work together in the development of individual family service plans (IFSPs), IEPs, or individual transition plans (ITPs).

School improvement processes are anchored in collaboration (Slater, 2004). Many schools have achieved their success by ensuring that teachers—and often parents and students—have a voice in governance. There is evidence that teacher participation in school decision making can lead to improved academic achievement for students (California School Redesign Network, 2005a; Kilgore & Webb, 1997; Martin, Marshall, & De Pry, 2002; Smylie et al., 1996). Sergiovanni (1994) proposed that the sources of authority for leadership are embedded in shared ideas, not simply in the power of position. This assumption echoes a core concept of democracy: Power is derived from the consent of the governed. Democratic decision making at the school level models the collaborative work that effective teachers expect from their students (and indeed the democratic process of the larger society).

School personnel also collaborate at the student level to make decisions about individualized education planning and services.

Collaboration for Student Placement and Individualized Education Planning.
Professionals are required to collaborate closely to determine the least restrictive environment (LRE) for children and most appropriate education plan. IDEA requires that, to the maximum extent appropriate, children with disabilities are expected to be educated with children who do not have disabilities.

Teachers and professionals also collaborate in decision making with parents to develop and implement comprehensive IEPs. Close collaboration is needed to make joint decisions about the child's present level of educational performance, annual goals, special education and related services, supplementary aids and services, program modifications or supports that will be provided for the child, extent to which the child is expected to participate with nondisabled children in the regular class, needed accommodations to participate in state or district standardized assessments of student achievement, and the manner in which parents will be regularly informed of their child's progress. The IEP process reflects the best of collaboration, combining the expertise of professionals from multiple disciplines, the expertise of parents about their child, and the self-knowledge of the student.

Collaboration With Paraprofessionals.
The paraprofessional or instructional aide collaborates closely with teachers to make decisions about supports to students in the classroom (Bowe, 2005; Demchak & Morgan, 1998). They typically serve in the following roles: administrative support (copying and distributing papers, supplies, tests, and setup for classroom activities); assistance with classroom management (monitoring student behavior, reinforcing behaviors, and recording results); student assistance (note taking for students, turning pages for a student with a physical disability); elaboration and review (amplifying and illustrating what teachers say during a lesson); and instruction (leading a parallel group) (Bowe, 2005).

Collaboration for Related and Supplemental Services.
As the IEP team—special and general education teachers, administrator, parents, student, and related service personnel—works closely together to consider a student's comprehensive evaluation and to make a team decision about needed educational, related, or supportive services. Close collaboration is needed to determine appropriate modifications in learning environments and to incorporate and implement instructional and assistive technology into the educational program. In the event that a child is at risk for referral to special education, they collaborate to develop prevention and early intervening strategies (designed to intervene to prevent referral for special education), and help design instructional methods to strengthen and compensate for learning deficits (e.g., such as in perception, comprehension, memory, and retrieval). They also determine whether and how instruction might be provided in community-based settings.

Collaboration for Student Assessment.
Teachers and specialists collaborate closely to help students and parents make decisions about participation on standardized tests. They discuss and decide how the student will participate in the assessments, design

testing accommodations when they are needed, and, through the IEP team process, they identify students who may need to take alternative assessments. Professionals work together to design formal and informal approaches for identifying students' interests and preferences related to educational experiences and postschool goals. They work together to ensure that assessment instruments and procedures are used in a manner that does not discriminate against persons with disabilities, or on the basis of race, religion sex, national origin, age, political practices, family or social background, or sexual orientation (Council for Exceptional Children, 2001a).

Collaboration for Secondary Transition.   At the secondary level, students and parents collaborate closely with members of the IEP team to plan a course of studies and needed services to support transition to postsecondary settings. Together they help the student to develop postschool goals and objectives, basing them on the interests and preferences of the student. Transition specialists, in collaboration with teachers and guidance personnel, provide information to families about transition education, services, support networks, and postschool options. They also coordinate the development of exit IEPs and *summaries of performance* (now required under IDEA 2004 amendments) that help the student communicate information about services and accommodations that have been successful in the K–12 setting and that should continue into the postsecondary setting. Transition specialists provide professional development for colleagues on transition requirements in federal law. Finally, they collaborate with adult service personnel to participate in transition planning and anticipate service needs after the student graduates.

Applying Collaboration to Develop Practice

In applying collaboration for the development of practice, special and general educators are joined to accommodate all students in general education. General education teachers are joined in new ways across their content area disciplines in order to plan together for instruction or student assessment. Within the school, collaborative teams for developing practice include coteaching teams, problem-solving groups, critical friends groups, coaching or mentoring, and teacher networks to support new practices. Collaborative relationships are instrumental today for the development and continual improvement of (a) developmentally appropriate practice, (b) collaborative teaching, (c) integrating academic and vocational curriculum, and (d) aligning standards-based education and transition.

Collaboration for Developmentally Appropriate Practice.   Teachers and related service personnel collaborate to create and continually improve developmentally appropriate practices (DAP) for young children, elementary children, and middle-school youth. They collaborate to ensure that classroom practices emphasize child-initiated activities and that learning activities and materials are concrete and relevant to children's lives and stage of development (Adams & Edgerton, 1997). (Chapter 10 provides a detailed discussion.)

Development of Collaborative Teaching.   Collaboration is essential between general and special education teachers when students are included in the general education classroom. In the collaborative model, the general education and special education teachers each bring their skills, training, and perspectives to the team to strengthen teaching and learning opportunities, methods, and effectiveness. It is in this nexus of classroom level collaboration that the individualized instructional process for students with disabilities and the standards-based process for all students are brought into alignment.

Collaboration to Integrate Academic and Career-Vocational Curriculum. Collaboration is an important instrument in assisting secondary students with disabilities to participate in career-vocational education courses with appropriate specialized services and supports. Under the Carl D. Perkins Career and Technical Education Improvement Act of 2006, schools are required to promote the development of services and activities that integrate academic, vocational–technical instruction, and community-based experiences, and that link secondary and postsecondary education. The alignment of academic and career-vocational curricula requires the close collaboration among vocational educators, general educators, and special educators.

Collaboration to Align Standards-Based Education and Transition Services. Professional collaboration is essential to the development of an alignment between the general curriculum that requires students to meet state learning standards (standards-based education) and transition planning and services. The 2004 IDEA emphasizes two important goals for students with disabilities: (1) to be involved in and make progress in the general education curriculum and (2) to access needed individualized transition services and supports. The challenge for educators is to align standards-based education policies with those under IDEA that are based on individual rights and an individualized educational process. Transition, therefore, must be viewed as a comprehensive framework (a) to ensure effective alignment between secondary education and transition services, and (b) to guide planning and decision making among students, families, and professionals (Kochhar-Bryant & Bassett, 2002b). Together the IEP team conducts a careful backward design and planning process with a clear eye to the final outcome—the postsecondary goal. The course of study requirement of IDEA connects transition planning with curriculum standards and assessment for all students. The field is currently experimenting with collaborative initiatives to develop effective practices to align these systems (Chapter 4 provides a detailed discussion).

Applying Collaboration to Build Professional Communities

School collaboration serves as a tool for connecting school personnel with the external professional community to create broad, lasting change within the school. Building professional community may also involve the linking of new knowledge, development of practice, and collaborative decision making. Examples of this form of collaboration include linking with professional associations, connecting teachers with national or regional resources centers or web-based professional communities, providing professional development, and creating partnerships with universities to enhance the school's capacity to improve learning for all children.

Collaboration for Professional Development and Teacher Renewal. Effective teachers and related school professionals are not only well-prepared for their roles, they are also continually learning. Expertise in teaching—as in many other fields—comes from a process of sharing, attempting new ideas, reflecting on practice, and developing new approaches (California School Redesign Network, 2005b). Traditionally conceived as one-shot training events, personnel development has come to involve much more creative kinds of activities that embed collaborative practices. Examples of these include focused content training, study groups, teacher networks, mentoring or coaching relationships, university–school district collaboration for preservice (initial preparation) and inservice (continuing preparation), committees and task forces, internships, technical assistance embedded in training, and communities of practice. Personnel development initiatives are now more likely to be designed to be cyclical (offered on a recurring basis) and some to be progressive (i.e., a staged process in which advanced training builds on previous training). In many initiatives, the training involves *cohort participation*, in which groups of personnel from the same school or district participate in the same training. Training is aligned with the actual work and goals of personnel and promotes active learning and analysis of their practices.

What Are Foundation Theories and Applications in Practice?

Collaboration as a phenomenon and a subject of study has fascinated researchers for decades in a variety of fields, including psychology, organizational studies, business, human resources development, human services fields, and education. Theories of collaboration are constantly being tested, modified, and refuted as new ideas and evidence about human behavior emerge.

The English word *theory* comes from the Greek root word *theo-rós*, meaning spectator. This derives from the same root as the word *theater*. A theory is a logical explanation, general group of principles, or a model that is based on extensive observation, analysis of facts, testing of hypotheses, and reasoning that attempts to explain the phenomena of collaboration (Montiel-Overall, 2005). Theories help explain complex phenomena, such as collaboration. Christman (2001) referred to *theories of action* as an important ingredient for change.

Theories Underlying Collaboration

Social Learning Theory and Modeling.   **Social learning theory** focuses on learning that occurs within a social context—people learning from one another. In relation to the four functions of collaboration, social learning theory is particularly relevant for collaboration as *discovery* or creation of new knowledge and as application in the *development of practice*. Social learning theory is a general theory of human behavior developed by Bandura (1977), who advanced the premise that individuals learn through vicarious experience by observing others. Children and adults acquire attitudes, emotional responses, and new styles of conduct through the *modeling* of behavior by those around them, which can have as much impact as direct experience. For example, the principal's and teachers' modeling of pride in their students is contagious and influences the behavior of newly hired teachers.

Research on peer learning—for both students and professionals—has shown that the interaction between and among the learners in a group influences the cognitive activity that is occurring, and it is this cognitive activity that accounts for the learning that takes place (King, 2002; O'Donnell & King, 1999; Webb & Palincsar, 1996). Different types of interaction facilitate different kinds of learning. For highly complex learning to take place (e.g., learning how to change attitudes), the thinking and interaction in the group must be carefully structured and guided. It must be of a high cognitive level, involving exchange of ideas, information, perspectives, attitudes, and opinions, as well as resolving disagreements or cognitive conflicts (Cohen, 2004; King 2000).

Modeling teaches new behaviors, influences the frequency of previously learned behaviors, encourages previously forbidden behaviors, and increases the frequency of similar behaviors. Furthermore, when people are shown how to perform a behavior, they are more likely to engage in the behavior and to believe they are capable of executing it successfully. In other words, they will experience increased *self-efficacy*, or self-confidence in their ability to learn and perform. Self-efficacy creates joy and satisfaction in carrying out activities, promotes effort and persistence in activities, and deepens learning and achievement. For collaborative leaders, the challenge is to (a) create opportunities for social learning in which behaviors, attitudes, and performances are modeled for those who need to learn them and (b) to increase self-efficacy among the collaborating learners.

Social Constructionism. Constructionism is a sociological theory of learning and a theory of knowing related to social learning theory. First articulated by Peter Berger and Thomas Luckmann (1966), the focus of **social constructionism** is to examine how individuals and groups participate in and create their perceived reality (make meaning of their world) and how that meaning becomes part of the school culture and tradition. For example, student assessments, grades, and teacher career ladders are social constructions created to judge and reward student and teacher performance. Positive behavioral support programs are emerging social constructions aimed at creating healthy social environments for learning. In relation to the four functions of collaboration, social constructionism is particularly relevant for collaboration as a synthesis of ideas—a use of collaboration to connect the thinking and knowledge of people in different disciplines, units, or groups within a school or district in order to guide decisions and actions, redefine or solve problems, or develop new policies.

In relation to collaborative learning, the theory is based on the assumption that cognition (knowledge) is formed and reformed based on experiences, beliefs, values, sociocultural histories, and prior perceptions. Individuals construct meaning from their own personal values, beliefs, and experiences. The social nature of learning is emphasized, and shared inquiry is a central activity (Bruner, 1966; Dewey, 1938; Feurstein, 1990; Fosnot, 1992; Gardner, 1983; Lambert et al., 1995; Piaget & Inhelder, 1971). Thus, knowledge is always "under construction" and evolving as individuals interpret, understand, and achieve new learning in groups.

A major theme in the theoretical framework of Bruner (1966) is that learning is an active process in which learners construct new ideas or concepts based upon their current and past knowledge. The learner selects and transforms information, constructs hypotheses, and makes decisions, relying on *cognitive structure* to do so. Cognitive structure (i.e., schema, mental models) provides meaning and organization to experiences and allows the individual to move beyond the information given to be able to apply it in new situations (e.g., applying positive behavioral support strategies in different classrooms). Collaborative problem solving and decision making requires individuals to construct new ideas and concepts through a group consensus-building process. The group process, as distinct from the individual process (creating personal meaning), is referred to as social constructionism.

Reciprocal Knowledge Construction.

The effects of social interaction on learning have been the concern of developmental psychologists for decades (Piaget & Inhelder, 1971, 1964; Vygotsky, 1978). The term *reciprocal* is defined as mutual, or expressing a mutual relation (Random House, 2001). **Reciprocal knowledge construction** refers to the principle that governs how people share or exchange knowledge in the process of learning and collaboration. This principle is relevant for the function of collaboration as discovery or creation of new knowledge.

Emerging research on teaching and learning is increasingly focused on the role of communicative practices in learning for both students and teachers (Boudah & Knight, 1999; Brownwell, Yeager, Reinells, & Riley, 1997; Cheney, 1998; da Costa, Marshall, & Riordan, 1998; Heron & Reason, 2001; Jarzabkowski, 2001; Murawski & Swanson, 2001). The classroom, the conference room, the counselor's office, and the media room are viewed as places in which students and teachers construct knowledge and negotiate meanings together. In other words, the teaching–learning process for both students and for professionals learning to collaborate is a complex social situation (Jarvela, Lehtinen, & Hamalainen, 1997). For example, a group of teachers might meet regularly to share resources on teaching students with learning disabilities and share successful strategies that they have used. Every act of communication requires the participants' mutual commitment—a temporarily shared social world. Collaborative leaders create opportunities for collaborators to enter into shared social worlds for the purposes of creating shared meanings.

Transformative Learning.

Since first introduced by Jack Mezirow in 1978, the concept of **transformative learning** has been a topic of research and theory building in the field of adult education (Taylor, 1998). Transformative learning involves experiencing a deep, structural shift in one's basic premises of thought, feelings, actions, and consciousness that dramatically and permanently alters one's view of oneself, others, and the world (O'Sullivan, 2003). This principle is directly relevant for the functions of collaboration as discovery or creation of new knowledge, and as building professional community, the creative use of collaboration to connect school personnel with the larger external professional community.

Transformative learning promotes understanding of the world in a different way, changing the way we experience it and the way we behave in our daily lives. For example, a group of high school graduates with severe disabilities (now college students) were invited for a conversation with high school teachers. Their sharing of what helped and hindered their progress profoundly influenced the teachers' assumptions about, and expectations for, students with disabilities. For learners to change their *meaning schemes* (beliefs, attitudes, and emotional reactions), "they must engage in critical reflection on their experiences, which in turn leads to a perspective transformation" (Mezirow 1991, p. 167). Perspective transformation is the process of becoming critically aware of how and why our assumptions have come to constrain the way we perceive, understand, and feel about our world and then making choices and acting on these new understandings. For collaborative leaders, the challenge is to create transformative learning experiences that can change attitudes and perceptions of collaborators to help them understand the world in a different way and to make changes in relationships and practices.

General Systems Theory.   **General system theory** and philosophy (Bertalanffy, 1969; Hall & Hord, 2001; Sutherland, 1973) provide basic principles that are useful in their application to collaborative processes in schools. System theory is particularly relevant to the functions of collaboration, synthesis of ideas, and building professional communities. In education, professionals work together to address the needs of the individual student as a whole person, facilitating system responses that are integrated rather than fragmented. The following principles, selected from the work of Bertalanffy (1969) and Sutherland (1973), apply basic general system principles to collaborative work and system coordination:

1. *The Individual Is Viewed as a Whole Person (Holistically).* In general system theory, people are viewed as whole individuals who are greater than the sum of their parts. This means that to understand human growth, development, or behavior, individuals must be viewed as a dynamic, whole system in continuous interchange with their environments—the individuals with whom they interact, their physical surroundings, and their culture. System thinkers seek to understand individuals and their needs in the context of their relationships with their environment or surroundings. For example, when students have multiple needs that require services from several sources, they need professionals to address each need in collaboration—not in isolation—with others, nor can different service agencies attend to the needs of a shared client in isolation of one another. For example, a school counselor is not concerned with academic performance alone but also with factors that affect performance, such as student motivation, family circumstances, health, and physical status.

2. *Interdisciplinary Communication Is Essential.* Specialists from diverse fields can better communicate if they develop a common dialog and vocabulary and a common set of philosophical principles and practices to respond to students with special learning needs.

In summary, a system approach to collaboration means addressing the holistic needs of the student and helping the service system develop responses that are integrated rather than fragmented.

Ecological Theory.   Bronfenbrenner's (1979) **ecological theory**, derived from general system theory, views a child's development within the context of the system of relationships that forms his or her environment. Ecological theory, applied to adult collaboration, is most closely aligned with the synthesis of ideas function of collaboration. Bronfenbrenner's theory defines complex layers of environment, each having an effect on a child's (or adult's) development. He defined a whole-system, or ecological perspective, and theorized that in order to create a change in a system, we have to examine all the parts of that system—personnel, relationships, roles, resources, leadership, organization, and others—and how they are related to each other in context (Bronfenbrenner, 1979). Brofenbrenner (1986) later refers to a social context system that involves interaction among people who influence the student at multiple levels of a student's social organization—family, peers, school, and wider community. An application of this model is the concept of interdisciplinary teaming (Hart, Zafft & Zimbrich, 2001). The collaborative team model is compatible with social systems context theory, since the focus is on the individual, at the center of the system. (Chapter 7 provides a detailed discussion.)

Applying Theory to Collaborative Practice

Learning Communities. Collaborative practices help professionals apply theories in order to better understand how they work and how they affect children. Wenger (2004) recently observed that the world is rapidly growing smaller, interdependent, and unpredictable. He echoes the view of several theorists that systems are very untidy.

> We are facing daunting challenges that require accelerated learning at various levels of scale at once, from individuals, to communities, to organizations, to regions, to worldwide learning systems. Understanding how to enhance our learning capabilities in this multidimensional nexus is taking increasing urgency. (Wenger, 2005, p. 1).

A few of the questions that have been of particular interest to students of collaboration include the following:

- How does human collaboration lead to change in the individual and change in group behavior?
- Does collaboration lead to effective decision-making processes?
- Does collaboration make professionals more effective in their roles in a way that positively impacts children?
- Does collaboration improve the motivation of professionals to improve their own performance and effectiveness?
- What is effective leadership to facilitate collaboration?

In the *learning community*, a concept grounded in system theory, change is easier to achieve when those affected by the change are directly involved. School professionals operate in a constantly changing environment, learning new teaching, counseling, or related services strategies, using information and data on students in new ways, and learning how best to accommodate all students' learning needs in the classroom. Learning communities can be described as a family of strategies that pursue action (or change) and research (new knowledge or understanding) at the same time (Dick, 1999). Often this occurs in a cyclical or spiral process which alternates between action and critical reflection on new understanding, continuously refining methods, data, and interpretation in the light of the understanding developed in the earlier cycles. Research has demonstrated that collaboration advances the process of continuous learning that is one of the defining characteristics of professional practice.

Schon (1987) introduced the term *knowing in action*, which refers to the kind of knowing that we reveal in our intelligent action, in our publicly observable performance in the classroom, or in another setting. Knowing in action is dynamic, whereas facts, procedures, rules, and theories are static. When our actions as a teacher or related service professional result in unexpected outcomes, the reflective practitioner stops to think, to question assumptions, to reframe the problems, or to restructure the strategies. Reflection shapes our future action and is referred to by Schon as the "artistry" of professional practice that good teachers often display in their everyday work. **Learning communities** provide support for learning, risk-taking, and innovation, and the collaborative structure helps overcome fear and resistance to the unfamiliar.

Appreciative Inquiry.

Appreciative inquiry, also grounded in system theory, is a highly affirmative approach to collaborative or organizational change that departs from traditional problem-based management. Appreciative inquiry is a philosophy of knowing or learning about organizational needs, and it is a methodology for leading and managing collaborative change (Cooperider & Dutton, 1998; Cooperider & Whitney, 1998). "Appreciative" refers to recognizing the best in people or the world around us; affirming past and present strengths, successes, and potentials; and perceiving those things that give vitality to living systems. "Inquiry" refers to exploration and discovery, asking questions, and remaining open to seeing new potential and possibilities (Random House, 2001).

Within schools, appreciative inquiry refers to the process of exploring and discovering ways for schools and human service organizations to change that involve recognizing strengths and potentials rather than focusing on problems and weaknesses. The orientation to helping teams of professionals or schools change and improve centers on the question: What is going well and how can we build on it? For example, teachers in a school might ask, what is it about our current team structure that is working. Strengths-based principles involve a deliberate focus on strengths, assets, existing capacities, and competencies; explore existing natural supports; develop plans that build on the full range of people's assets and strengths; and match strengths to workplace or role functions (Cooperider & Whitney, 1998).

The process of implementing appreciative inquiry involves four steps: (1) *discover* (discerning needs and identifying what is working well); (2) *dream* (visualizing what can be, what we *really* want to accomplish); (3) *design* (preserving what works and moving toward the vision); and (4) *deliver* (acting). As Cooperider & Whitley (1998) observe, the single most prolific thing a group can do, if it aims to consciously construct a better future, is to make the positive change core (what's working) the common and explicit property of all.

Self-Determination and Self-Advocacy.

When professionals collaborate in the IEP process, the student is viewed as a central participant. Two terms that are in wide use to reflect such participation are **self-determination and self-advocacy**, terms that are both rooted in ecological theory and social learning theory. Many youth and young adults with disabilities have difficulty assuming control of their lives and participating in the educational decisions that are made each year about their educational program. In 1993, the U.S. Office of Special Education developed and adopted the following working definition of self-determination: "choosing and enacting choices to control one's own life to the maximum extent possible, based on knowing oneself, and in pursuit of one's own needs, interests and values" (Campeau & Wolman, 1993, p. 2). Definitions of self-determination have been modified and expanded over the past decade to include some common themes. These common themes are reflected in a summary of definitions offered by Field, Martin, Miller, Ward, and Wehymer (1998b), as part of a position statement for the Division on Career Development and Transition, Council for Exceptional Children:

> Self-determination is a combination of skills, knowledge, and beliefs that enable a person to engage in goal-directed, self-regulated, autonomous behavior. An understanding of one's strengths and limitations together with a belief in oneself as capable and effective are essential to self-determination. When acting on the basis of these skills and attitudes, individuals have greater ability to take control of their lives and assume the role of successful adults. (p. 2)

Self-determination theory (Deci & Ryan, 1985, 2000; Ryan & Deci, 2000; University of Illinois at Chicago National Research & Training Center, 2002) is based on the assumption that people have inborn tendencies to grow and develop psychologically, to strive to master challenges in their environment, and to integrate experience into their self-concepts. This theory holds that these human tendencies are fully expressed only within a supportive social context. That is, self-determination is not achieved simply because an individual has certain requisite knowledge and skills; it is also important that key people and institutions in the person's life provide a context conducive to self-determination. Table 2.1 relates the concept of self-determination to collaboration.

The process of building self-determination depends upon the collaboration and shared decision making between the individual, the family, and the professionals in decisions that affect the future of the individual. Along with building individual capacity to make informed choices and decisions also comes a greater responsibility and accountability for the outcomes of those decisions.

Shared Governance.   *Shared governance* is an application of social constructionism and means a process of democratic and collaborative decision-making in which there are shared norms and values (Katz, Miller, & Peters, 2002) that guide the work of teachers, parents, and students. Collaborating professionals develop a "synthesis of values" or a strong consensus about what matters to members of the school community and develop priority goals for student learning, teaching, and support. These reference points are used to guide decisions, for example, about creating student policies, establishing peer evaluations, developing collaborative teams, making curriculum decisions, setting standards for assessing student and teacher work, and creating professional development programs. Within the framework established by these shared norms and with ongoing collaboration in school-level decisions, effective schools place day-to-day decision-making authority with those who are instructionally closest to the students and who best know their needs: teachers and related services professionals. This localized decision-making structure allows teachers to respond quickly and flexibly to changes in students' needs (Wallach, Lambert, Copland, & Lowry, 2005).

Collaborative Work as Developmental.   The process of collaborative change is developmental, whether the goal is individual, group, or institutional change, and occurs in stages (Stump & Hagie, 2005). These stages mirror the five degrees of collaboration introduced earlier in this chapter—*communication and networking, cooperation, coordination, collaboration,* and *integration.* Each stage represents an

| TABLE 2.1 | Aligning Self-Determination and Collaboration |

Forms of Collaboration and Coordination	Self-Determination Opportunities for Students
Information and referral for services	• Proactively request information about available education, support, and transition services and supports (both in-school and out-of-school youth). • Talk to other students in the school or program.
Identification and preparation for entry to transition services	• Ask peers about educational services, supports, and opportunities. • Talk with the family about goals and interests. • Get involved in early planning.
Assessment and evaluation	• Understand one's own learning needs, interests, and postschool goals. • Understand one's own career–vocational interests and levels of functioning. • Seek to understand the assessments and evaluation information.
IEP/transition planning and development	• Learn self-determination skills. • Learn how to choose short- and long-range goals and understand what the time lines mean. • Learn how to direct an IEP meeting.
Service coordination and linking	• Learn about community agencies and the services they provide. • Keep in regular contact with the coordinator or case manager. • Help the case manager stay in touch with the family.
Classroom monitoring and follow-along	• Help teachers and service coordinators know what has been accomplished at school and at home (they may miss things). • Utilize the expertise of both the general and special educator. • Advocate for your instructional needs. • Know what supports and accommodations work best for you.
Individual and interagency advocacy	• Join support groups and self-advocacy groups in the high school or postsecondary institution. • Join youth advisory groups and disability rights groups. • Join youth policy advisory groups.
Service evaluation and follow-up	• Let teachers and service coordinators know what services and supports were most helpful through high school. • Let professionals know what happens after high school. • Let them know what adult or community services you enroll in, and which ones benefit you the most. • Return to high school as a guest to help others plan for transition. • Get back in touch if you do not complete high school.

increasingly closer collaborative relationship among professionals and includes sharing information, discussing adaptations and modifications, providing supports in the classroom, sharing instruction, and participating in coinstruction.

Let's see how the stages of change can be applied to a teacher team working together to accommodate a student in the general education class. The stages include: (a) *sharing information* about the needs of the student identified as having disabilities and found eligible for special education services (e.g., how the disability will affect learning); (b) *discussing adaptations and modifications* (e.g., the types of interventions most appropriate for supporting student participation and learning in the classroom); (c) *providing supports* in the classroom (e.g., monitoring student work and behavior; preteaching or reteaching skills), (d) *sharing instruction* in the classroom (e.g., alternating roles of lead and support teacher), and (e) *coinstruction* (e.g., team teaching). Understanding the developmental nature of collaboration can aid teams in setting reasonable goals for their work together and lead to sustainable collaborative programs (Stump & Hagie, 2003).

Professional Communities of Practice.

In education communities, knowledge involves shared learning that is the basis for change and growth. An important concept in the discussion of shared learning is **communities of practice** (CoP). Theories of professional communities underlie collaborative or collegial learning on the basis of a shared curiosity and a desire to expand skills and knowledge individually and collectively (Pugach & Johnson, 1999; Wald & Castleberry, 2000; Wenger, 1998; Wenger, McDermott, & Snyder, 2002). Communities of practice are aligned with the collaborative function, *building professional community*, or using collaboration to connect school personnel with the larger external professional community.

Etienne Wenger's pivotal work, *Communities of Practice: Learning as a Social System* (1998) builds on previous work of developmental psychologists and social learning theorists. *Communities of practice* are groups of people who share a concern or a passion for something they do and who interact regularly to learn how to do it better (Wenger, 1998; Wenger, McDermott, & Snyder, 2002). Communities of practice are formed by people who engage in a process of collective learning in shared activity, such as a group of teachers and counselors working on together to improve student motivation for learning, a gathering of first-time district administrators helping each other cope with new legal requirements on school discipline, or a small group of students with disabilities in community college who support each other as they seek to negotiate needed accommodations in their classes.

A CoP is not just a club, a group of friends, a chat room, or a group of people who share similar interests. Rather, according to Wenger (1998), a CoP has an identity that is defined by a shared domain or area of interest. Membership implies a commitment to the domain and therefore a shared competence that distinguishes members from other people. In pursuing their interest in their domain, members engage in joint activities and discussions, help each other, and share information. They build relationships that enable them to learn from each other. A group of teachers having the same job title is not a CoP unless they interact and learn together to achieve a common purpose:

> Members of a community of practice are practitioners. They develop a shared repertoire of resources: experiences, stories, tools, ways of addressing recurring

problems—in short a shared practice. This takes time and sustained interaction . . . In the course of all these conversations, they have developed a set of stories and cases that have become a shared repertoire for their practice. (Wenger, 1998)

Communities develop their practice through a variety of activities. A few examples are provided in Table 2.2.

Wenger describes the life cycle of a community of practice over time, as depicted in Figure 2.3 (Wenger, McDermott, & Snyder, 2002, p. 69).

For Wenger, indicators for the formation of a community of practice include the following: (1) sustained mutual relationships, whether harmonious or filled with conflict; (2) shared ways of engaging in doing things together; (3) a rapid flow of information and propagation of innovation; (4) quick setup of a problem to be discussed (substantial overlap in participants' descriptions of who belongs); (5) knowing what others know and can do and how they can contribute to an enterprise; (6) ability to assess the appropriateness of actions and products; (7) shared stories, inside jokes, jargon, and shortcuts to communication; (8) shared symbols of membership and shared discourse reflecting a certain perspective on the world.

Communities of practice are becoming vital instruments for knowledge acquisition and the exploration of new ideas. So important has this idea become in education, that

TABLE 2.2	Activities and Examples Based on Communities of Practice
Problem solving	"Can we work on designing this accommodation for my student and brainstorm some ideas? I'm stuck."
Requests for information	"Where can I find the text of the law related to student discipline?"
Seeking experience	"Has anyone dealt with a student in this situation before?"
Reusing assets	"I have a proposal for an action research project that I wrote for the district supervisor last year. I can send it to you, and you can easily tweak it for this new initiative."
Coordination and synergy	"Can we pool some of our budget funds to purchase and share the assessment instruments we need?
Discussing developments	"What do you think of the new online professional development academy? Is it helping you with new strategies for working with students?"
Documentation projects	"We have talked about this problem five times now. Let's write down our process for solving it."
Visits	"Can we come and see your new student court program? We would like to establish one in our school."
Mapping knowledge and identifying gaps	"Who has expertise with behavioral assessment? What are we missing? What other groups should we connect with to learn more?"

Source: From Learning for a Small Planet: A Research Agenda, by E. Wenger, 2004. Accessed January 11, 2005, http://www.ewenger.com/theory. Adapted with permission.

FIGURE 2.3

Life Cycle of a Community of Practice

Source: From *Cultivating Communities of Practice* (p. 69), by E. Wenger, R. McDermott, and W. M. Snyder, 2002, Cambridge, Cambridge University Press. Copyright 2002 by Combridge University Press. Reprinted with permission.

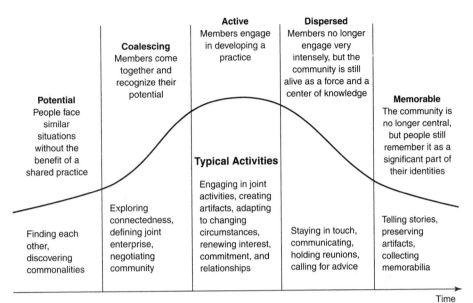

Stages of Development

Potential
People face similar situations without the benefit of a shared practice

Coalescing
Members come together and recognize their potential

Active
Members engage in developing a practice

Dispersed
Members no longer engage very intensely, but the community is still alive as a force and a center of knowledge

Memorable
The community is no longer central, but people still remember it as a significant part of their identities

Typical Activities

Finding each other, discovering commonalities

Exploring connectedness, defining joint enterprise, negotiating community

Engaging in joint activities, creating artifacts, adapting to changing circumstances, renewing interest, commitment, and relationships

Staying in touch, communicating, holding reunions, calling for advice

Telling stories, preserving artifacts, collecting memorabilia

Time

the U.S. Office of Special Education Programs (2003b) has recently established a National Communities of Practice Technical Assistance Network to help state educational agencies establish communities of practice to develop new insights into problems and solutions.

WHAT ARE TEN PRINCIPLES FOR SUCCESSFUL COLLABORATION AND COORDINATION?

Successful collaboration begins with the adoption of a common set of principles that can serve as an anchor and guide for building a collaborative culture. Based on evidence from theory and research, the following ten principles have been defined. They can be applied in the development and evaluation of both collaboration and system coordination practices and policies and represent recurring themes for the remaining chapters.

Principle 1. Collaboration and system coordination are long-term developmental processes that impact students' abilities to achieve their maximum level of potential. Some students with special learning needs require short-term support in education and community settings and during periods of transition from one setting to another. Others require extended support services or intermittent intensive support services. Effective collaboration for educational planning and support is flexible and designed to assist the student to achieve as much independence as is possible in as many areas of functioning in which there are assessed needs. School and school-linked agency personnel work together to strengthen the service system. For example, efforts to improve K–12 education for students depend on engaging related services within the school, such as speech and audiology, counseling, psychological services, social work services, and medical diagnostic services. The system as a whole benefits by coordinating efforts to improve outcomes. Research shows that individuals make greater developmental, physical, and educational progress when services are received in integrated settings with persons without disabilities (Chapter 5 provides a discussion of research on collaboration).

Principle 2. Collaboration and system coordination initiatives are interventions to achieve change in relationships, processes or services, institutions, or systems. Expected results must be clearly defined, and outcomes evaluated and communicated to all professionals and consumers involved. Federal and state education laws now require collaboration within schools, as well as interagency agreements between schools and community service agencies to provide needed services for students as required by their IEPs. In most communities, however, collaboration and interagency linkages are still largely informal and voluntary collaborations. As Beaumont and Hagebak (1992) counseled over 15 years ago, although collaborative initiatives may be mandated, their results cannot be, because collaboration and coordination depend upon local processes and the will and abilities of people to work cooperatively. The intended student outcomes must be clearly specified and interagency resources focused to achieve those outcomes.

Principle 3. Planning for collaboration and system coordination initiatives is vital to the strength and sustainability of the initiatives. While many collaborative initiatives spring up in response to crises or sudden changes (as illustrated in the Sunrise Valley Middle School case see p. 15), an organized planning process should be established as soon as possible to provide a "rudder" for navigating the change process.

Planning also involves assessing the readiness of people or groups for collaboration or coordination by asking several guiding questions. What is the goal or mission of the collaborative initiative? What are the expected results and how will they be measured? What do the participants (or participating school units or agencies) bring to the relationship in terms of resources, missions, and philosophies? What is the extent of their knowledge, skills and attitudes about collaboration and about the population of students being served? What combination of people could help to address the goals of the collaboration and coordination? Planning that is focused by such guiding questions join people strategically and can lead to sustainable change.

Principle 4. Collaboration must engage all the people (stakeholders) who will be affected by the change process. The success of any collaboration or coordination effort will depend on the ability of the planning team to create a supportive community environment and engage all of the key participants who are likely to be affected by the change initiative.

Principle 5. Collaboration initiatives can start small and emerging from any part of a system. As was discussed earlier, human systems involve complex relationships and interdependent groups of people who work together for common aims. Change in human systems does not develop in a tidy, linear, step-by-step fashion and is often messy, unstable, and unpredictable. A collaboration for change that emerges in one part of the system can trigger a larger change process within the whole system.

Principle 6.   Child- and family-centered collaboration and coordination promote the self-determination and engagement of the student and family. Effective collaboration promotes the student's and family's ability to make decisions (self-determination) in planning for education and support services. Collaboration and system coordination activities strengthen or reinforce self-help and informal support networks that include the individual's parents, siblings, and extended family.

Principle 7.   The effectiveness and sustainability of collaboration and system coordination are based on the level of commitment people have to the process. This principle may seem like a platitude, but if a school or organization attempts systemic change without clear commitment from the people being affected, the change is not likely to last. Collaboration among people of different professional roles, disciplines, beliefs, and attitudes is a complex undertaking, even under the best of circumstances. Systemic change is not likely to occur if the leader, the principal, or the administrator alone is committed. Nor can it be successful if only some of the people have a clear picture of what needs to be accomplished.

Principle 8.   The effectiveness and sustainability of collaboration and system coordination depend on how professionally prepared people are to participate. Along with commitment, professional preparation is vital to the effectiveness of collaboration. Ability to collaborate effectively with others is not innate; it involves a complex repertoire of skills that must be modeled and learned. That repertoire includes knowledge of the underlying foundational ideas and principles of collaboration, skills to participate effectively and to facilitate collaboration, and dispositions (beliefs, attitudes, and ethics) that are essential to effective practice in collaboration and coordination.

Principle 9.   The environment for collaboration influences its potential. There are many aspects of the local environment that can either support or undermine the development and effectiveness of collaboration or system coordination. A supportive environment for collaboration and system coordination is one in which there is dedicated leadership for the initiative and a focus on *outcomes* and *benefits* of the collaboration for students and families. In addition, there are adequate resources, technical assistance and support to the collaborators, formal agreements where needed, and a quality review and evaluation process.

Principle 10.   Early defeat in an attempt to collaborate does not necessarily mean long-term failure; such initiatives often lie dormant and rise again when conditions change. In any system, a collaborative initiative based on a sound idea, once begun,

---

BOX 2.1   A Window Opens Somewhere

Representatives of three agencies met with excitement to talk about cooperation among the Fairley Public School District, the community services agency (CSA) (the adult mental health, mental retardation, and substance abuse services system), and the vocational rehabilitation agency (VR). The representative of the community service agency initiated and hosted the meeting. The goal was to draft the first cooperative agreement among the three agencies to improve access to and coordination of services for youth with disabilities exiting the school system who needed adult services and VR services. The initiative would be led by the CSA with the school district and rehabilitation agency as equal partners. After several meetings, a cooperative agreement was crafted and the "pioneer" team was feeling pleased with its work. The agreement was presented to the director of the CSA, who praised the initiative, but did not approve the agreement. It was dead on arrival.

The team was extremely discouraged and asked for an explanation for the decision. The CSA director explained that it was not considered within the scope of the CSA to be the lead agency in initiating and managing such an agreement with the school system, and it would require additional resources that the CSA did not have. The team believed the decision was short-sighted and was forced to disband. However, after one year, the team member from the Fairley school district dusted off the agreement and carried it forward, creating a public school-initiated agreement with the VR and CSA. The CSA signed on this time, since the school system would take the lead and manage it.

This story began over 30 years ago, and the interagency agreement has been sustained and strengthened and is now a nationally known interagency collaborative that expanded statewide and has served as a model for other states. Although the original initiators of the interagency agreement at the CSA may feel wistful that they will never be recognized for their initial leadership, they learned that when a door closes on an initiative in one part of the system, often a window opens up somewhere else.

---

is hard to suppress. Once it is brought to life and a small core of "champions" or leaders has emerged who are invested in it, somehow it will find a way to take root. Box 2.1 illustrates Principle 10 and is based on a true story.

Summary of Key Points

- Human collaboration lies at the heart of most important problems and solutions in educating students today.
- School-based collaboration refers to collaborative relationships among professionals of different disciplines and units within a school. System coordination means relationships between schools and school-linked human service agencies in the community to address the needs of students who require a coordinated approach.
- Creating schoolwide collaboration requires the development of a collaborative culture in which norms, values, and beliefs support and encourage teamwork and interaction about problems of practice.
- Collaboration can be viewed as having four functions: discovery and learning, synthesis of ideas for decision making, development of practice, and building professional communities.
- Building a collaborative culture means creating a transformation in the way we think about structuring educational roles and environments for all the children in all of the activities and opportunities a school has to offer.

Key Terms and Phrases

- Collaborative culture (p. 33)
- Collaborative teams (p. 36)
- Social learning theory (p. 45)
- Social constructionism (p. 46)
- Reciprocal knowledge construction (p. 47)
- Transformative learning (p. 47)
- Ecological theory (p. 48)
- General systems theory (p. 48)
- Appreciative inquiry (p. 50)
- Learning communities (p. 50)
- Self-determination and self-advocacy (p. 50)
- Communities of practice (p. 53)

Questions for Reflection, Thinking, and Skill Building

1. Provide at least three examples of school collaboration in relation to each of the four functions of collaboration.

2. Write up your own personal collaboration development profile. Trace your own professional development path in terms of (a) the information you received as a child or youth about collaboration with your peers, (b) your early career awareness or exposure to collaborative groups and practices, (c) your reactions to your early career experiences with collaboration, (d) the collaborative skills and training that you have gained, (e) contacts with collaborative role models, and (f) help and feedback you have received while developing your collaborative skills.

3. Discuss your beliefs about how ready your professional peers are to participate effectively in collaborative initiatives in your school or agency. What skills do you think they need to become more effective? What skills and attitudes (dispositions) do they need to strengthen?

4. Analyze your state teacher preparation documents (e.g., teacher licensing regulations, policy guidelines, curriculum guidelines, training agenda) for evidence of a philosophical basis or commitment to collaboration. What philosophical ideas related to collaboration appear to be reflected either implicitly or explicitly in the documents? To what extent do they reflect the expectation that school districts create a culture of collaboration?

CHAPTER THREE

How Does System Coordination Work?

Collaboration is like dancing with an octopus. The work of building
and sustaining school/community collaborations is a dance with multifaceted
partners. —LEVINE, 1998, P. 1

Great discoveries and improvements invariably involve the cooperation
of many minds. I may be given credit for having blazed the trail, but when I look
at the subsequent developments, I feel the credit is due to others rather than
to myself. —ALEXANDER GRAHAM BELL

- What is system coordination?
- How has system coordination evolved?
- What does a service coordinator do?
- What are the functions of system coordination?
- What are the various models of system coordination?

- What principles and practices contribute to effective system coordination?
- What system coordination practices improve the education and well-being of students and families?
- Can system coordination be evaluated?

PERSPECTIVES

Administrator

In my 28 years in education, this was the hardest thing I've ever done, moving from a communitywide "silo" mentality to a blended funding model that wraps services around children and families with multiple needs—reducing costs and litigation in the process. School districts cannot underestimate the value of putting parents, educators, and others in a position to help children on the same team—with a wide array of options to choose from in building a supportive system.

—Executive Director, Education Service District

Service Coordinator

Dreams can sometimes be difficult to put into a written plan, but it is necessary to have a direction, especially for young children who have a lifetime of promise ahead of them. Our consumers are children from birth to five years of age, and we see children with all types of disabilities. Families are referred to us by social workers, teachers, doctors, and other professionals. We often are the first to link them to services. Listening to the aspirations parents have for their children and then trying to create a plan to provide a child with the services necessary to reach those goals are important first steps for a service coordinator working in the early intervention program.

—Service Coordinator, Early Childhood Center

INTRODUCTION

It has long been recognized that schools alone cannot provide all the services that children and youth with disabilities and their families need. As discussed in Chapter 1, shared responsibility for a community's children has recently become a watchword for educators and human services personnel. As the perspectives introduced above illustrate, the notion of shared responsibility also implies working across school and community agency boundaries to create a well-coordinated service system to meet the holistic needs of students. Coordination is about connecting people within systems and the extraordinary commitment that is required to accomplish it.

Over the past few decades, the benefits of case management and interagency coordination in systems such as health care, mental health, rehabilitation, and adult disability services, have caught the attention of educators and policymakers. Since more than 90% of children with disabilities are being served in their base public schools, there is a growing interest in linking the educational system with human service agencies to provide a comprehensive system of services and supports for children and their families (Dunst & Bruder, 2002; Kendziora, Bruns, Osher, Pacchiona, & Mejia, 2001; National Center on Outcomes Research, 2001; Research and Training Center on Service Coordination, 2001; Whelley, Hart, & Zafft, 2002; U.S. Department of Education, 2003c; U.S. General Accountability Office, 2004c). Such an approach requires that schools reach out beyond their boundaries and seek a shared responsibility from the many agencies that provide services for students.

This chapter defines *system coordination*, examines the ideas and theories that underlie these definitions, and reviews the kinds of school–community or interagency relationships that are emerging. The chapter also discusses practical issues associated with building a local coordinated system, including interagency agreements and preparation of service coordinators.

WHAT IS SYSTEM COORDINATION?

Recently, educators have come to recognize that effective education and support for students with disabilities requires much more than collaboration among professionals within the school environment. Rather, it involves a wider collaboration among schools, among local and state human service agencies, and among a wide range of community public and private agencies that share a common concern about children and youth. The term **system coordination** builds upon earlier concepts that emerged in the fields of health, mental health, mental retardation, and rehabilitation in the 1960s—case management and interagency cooperation. More than two decades ago, Bachrach (1986) defined case management within the mental health discipline as,

> . . . the integration of services on the patient level . . . someone in the system is taking charge and seeing to it that all the little bits and pieces of the fragmented service system begin to come together in some coherent way for the chronically mentally ill individual. It embodies the concepts of continuity and comprehensiveness in a personalized manner. (p. 174)

Figure 3.1 depicts this shared system today.

In education and human services, a systematic approach means developing goals, activities, and approaches in an organized and coordinated manner to address the multiple needs of children and youth with disabilities. The individual is viewed as having complex and interconnected needs that require coordinated responses from multiple service agencies (e.g., the school, mental health agency, family services, public health services, social services, juvenile court services, or legal services). The underlying principle of system coordination is that the student remains at the center, is assisted to link with the services needed to be successful in

FIGURE 3.1

Laws and the Shared Responsibility for the Service System

Source: Adapted from Successful Inclusion: Practical Strategies for a Shared Responsibility. by C. Kochhar, L. West, & J. Taymans, 2000, Upper Saddle River, NJ: Merrill/Prentice Hall, p. 112. Reprinted by permission.

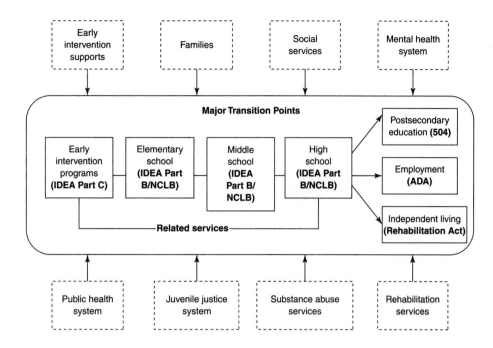

the academic program, and is encouraged to exercise as much personal decision making in planning for graduation and adult life as is possible.

This means that each part of the system is dedicated to ensuring that each child, from early intervention through transition from high school, is connected with the services they need along the way. Each professional or agency in a system is dedicated to contributing to the well-being and development of children with disabilities and their families as they respond to their changing needs and the changing educational environment.

A Framework for Defining System Coordination

Coordinated services refer to the delivery of services across systems to address the holistic (whole person) needs of students. Students in need of special education services, whether integrated into general education or not, are often in need of related services that are not available in the school but in the community. When families seek services from two or more agencies that have different rules for eligibility, a mechanism for assisting them to connect with these agencies is extremely helpful. Without such assistance, many students fail to access services they need. School–community coordinators can facilitate access to services by serving as liaisons between families and service providing agencies (Bonner-Thompkins, 2000).

Interagency partnerships and agreements are relationships that involve the school and at least one agency that coordinate for a common purpose. The definition of system coordination reflects four assumptions:

1. Interagency relationships are formalized in *written cooperative agreements* in which the role of the agencies and professionals are made clear.

2. Interagency relationships are *dynamic* and *responsive to changes* in the needs of children and families and in the service environment.

3. Interagency relationships are *continuous*, if needed, throughout the course of the child's educational journey from early childhood to high school graduation.

4. The system relationships should result in *goals and strategies* that systematically anticipate and address the problems and priority needs of persons being served by the system.

A *coordinated interagency service system*, therefore, can be defined as follows:

> A coordinated interagency service system means a systematic, comprehensive, and coordinated system of education and support services for individuals with disabilities, which is provided in their communities in the most integrated settings possible, and in a manner that promotes individual choice and decision-making. (Kochhar-Bryant, 2003a)

A synthesis of the literature on planning for educational services for students with disabilities (Kochhar Bryant, 2003a) shows that there are several important elements of a coordinated system.

1. *A formal long-range interagency plan for a system of education and support services* for students in integrated settings, from early intervention through postsecondary transition.

2. *Special supports for the critical "passages"* or transitions between educational settings, such as from early intervention to preschool, elementary to middle school, and high school to postsecondary education.

3. *A statewide system of personnel development* to prepare teachers and support personnel to work within a coordinated interagency system of services, which includes preservice preparation as well as continuing (inservice) preparation of all school personnel and the training of parents.

4. *Innovative cooperative partnerships* among public schools, related service agencies, area colleges and universities, private service providers, related services agencies, and parents to achieve common goals for the inclusion of students with disabilities into general education and extracurricular activities.

5. *Ongoing evaluation* of system coordination efforts and student outcomes (Benz, Lindstom, & Yovanoff, 2000; Dunst & Bruder, 2002; Hurth, 1998; Kim-Rupnow, Dowrick, & Burke, 2001; National Center on Outcomes Research, 2001; Rosman, McCarthy, & Woolverton, 2001; Stodden, 2001; U.S. General Accounting Office, 2003d).

System coordination is a cornerstone in the educational success of individuals with disabilities and their families.

A coordinated interagency service system is both an ideal and a strategy. It is a service structure for responding to individuals with special needs within their communities, in the most integrated setting possible, and in a manner that promotes individual decision making. The general goal of service coordination is to ensure that students receive education and support services in a manner that is timely, appropriate, accessible, comprehensive, and flexible (Bogdan, 1999; Braddock, Hemp, Parish, & Rizzolo, 2000).

Levels of Service Coordination

System coordination can be viewed as a process that occurs on different levels of the service delivery system—the individual or student, family, and peer group and the *system* level or the school, community, and state educational system (Figure 3.2). At the individual student and family level, coordination activities are aimed at assisting the individual or family to access the services and supports they need to achieve educational and developmental goals. The expected outcome is individual change. The goal of system coordination at the local and state levels becomes one of broader system change and improvement, rather than one of change in the individual child. The expected outcome at the local and state system level is to expand the entire service network that affects all school districts, or make it more responsive and flexible.

Individual Student/Family Level: Strengthening Self-Determination.   For children who receive school-linked services, service coordination is focused on the needs of each individual student. System coordination activities at the individual level are designed to directly affect the individual in a program or classroom. **Individual level coordination** may involve determining the match between individual needs and appropriate services. It may involve direct linking of the student or family with the agency to help them access services, ensure continuity of services, or advocate for services when there are service gaps. **System level coordination** helps students achieve the greatest possible level of social, economic, and physical integration or inclusion of students into the range of learning environments in the school system (Dunst & Bruder, 2002; Hurth, 1998; National Center on Outcomes Research, 2001; Neubert, 2000; Neubert & Moon, 1999). System coordination based on principles of **self-determination** also means helping the

FIGURE 3.2
Levels of System Coordination

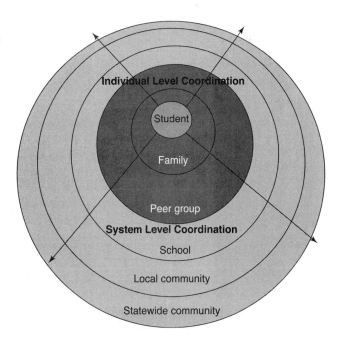

student to participate to the extent possible in decisions that are made about services that will be obtained from nonschool or community agencies. At the individual level, coordination *functions and activities* are intended to accomplish several objectives and result in a variety of individual outcomes, as Table 3.1 shows.

Interagency System Level.   At the school–community system level, coordinators are concerned with establishing appropriate cooperation between the school and multiple service providers in order to establish a local system of service options and pathways to access them. The IDEA 2004 requires local educational agencies to provide related and supportive services to all youth with disabilities in coordination with community-based agencies. IDEA 2004 also requires interagency service agreements between schools and community agencies, either through formal interagency agreements or memoranda of understanding (MOUs), informal guidelines for coordinating with potential service providers, or assignment of service coordinators to work with participating agencies.

At the system level, schools and community agencies work to (a) make services more available to students and families, (b) make services easier to coordinate

TABLE 3.1 Individual Level Functions and Outcomes for Student Self-Determination	
Individual Level Functions	**Individual Outcomes**
• Promote self-determination or increased participation of students and families in decision making. • Assure equitable access to a range of needed services. • Ensure that changing needs of the student and family are recognized and appropriately met through ongoing relationships. • Assist the individual in achieving the maximum level of potential. • Improve the quality of life and learning environment of the individual. • Promote community integration. • Assist the individual to improve health and physical well-being • Reinforce informal support networks. • Promote integration into community-based service systems. • Use evaluation methods that focus on individual outcomes and service improvements.	• Improvements in individual access to a needed service • Progress on developmental milestones of a child as a result of services • Increased participation in decision making about agency services in relation to IEP goals • Access to assessment and diagnostic services for the individual • Improved individual performance and motivation of a student • Improved health of an individual or family • Improved academic or vocational achievement • Improved work skills and employment for a young adult • Improved attendance of youth in high school • Improved family relationships • Higher rates of program or grade completion

among schools and agencies, (c) improve linkages among services at key transition points for students, (d) improve projections of service needs among students and close gaps in services, (e) improve interagency training of professionals, and (f) evaluate service outcomes. Service coordination functions are focused on expanding or sustaining the availability of school-linked services to a whole population of students within a school, school cluster, local school district, or state.

Dimensions of System Coordination

System coordination involves several dimensions that must be aligned or in agreement in order for the interagency relationship to work effectively. Figure 3.3 depicts these levels, functions, and **dimensions of system coordination**.

The dimensions in Figure 3.3 include (1) service philosophy and principles, (2) policies and legal requirements, (3) procedures for interagency agreements, and (4) service coordination outcomes. If these dimensions are not in agreement with each other, then the effectiveness of system coordination will be diminished. In other words, if a local interagency agreement has an inclusive service philosophy but its policies and procedures do not match that philosophy, then the intended results will not be achieved.

System coordination represents a range of relationships among disciplines and service agencies because no single solution for improving coordination can be applied to all individuals or all communities. Educational needs are best addressed, not from the perspective of a single institution but from multiple perspectives and a

FIGURE 3.3

Dimensions of
System Coordination

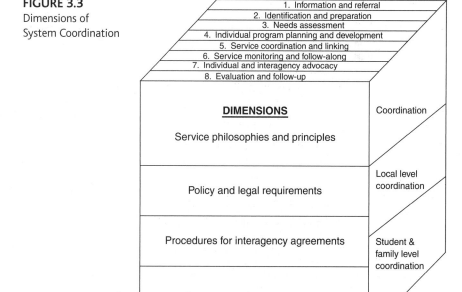

FIGURE 3.4
Continuum of
Transition Passages

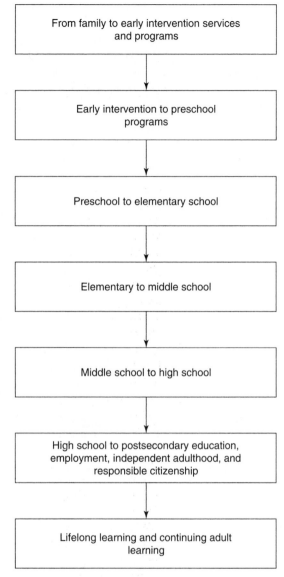

From family to early intervention services and programs

Early intervention to preschool programs

Preschool to elementary school

Elementary to middle school

Middle school to high school

High school to postsecondary education, employment, independent adulthood, and responsible citizenship

Lifelong learning and continuing adult learning

broadly shared understanding. Many community sectors must bring their collective knowledge and skills together to address the complex developmental and educational needs of individuals with disabilities as they make difficult transitions throughout their lives (Figure 3.4).

As a result of their training, educators and human services personnel generally remain narrowly focused on their own segment along the developmental continuum from early intervention to high school. Professionals who collaborate to provide coordinated holistic services are more effective when they understand the full continuum of passages in a student's life.

Let's See It in Action, below, illustrates a system's response to the very complex needs of an individual youth and his family.

LET'S SEE IT IN ACTION! Case Illustration: A Family's Desperate Struggle

The following actual case tells the story of a 16-year-old boy and his family's struggle to find the right services at the right time to save his future.

The worried family of Eric, a very bright 16-year-old, recently attended an interagency team meeting that included representatives from the county public schools, mental health services, alcohol and drug services, and juvenile services/probation. Eric was failing 9th grade a second time, was on a Child in Need of Supervision (CHINS) petition through juvenile services, was participating in alcohol and drug services by court order, and had been in weekly private mental health therapy. He was participating in outpatient alcohol and drug treatment services but was failing urine tests regularly. His parents and former therapists all believed he needed intensive behavioral therapy in a residential treatment program. Although Eric had been privately diagnosed with ADHD, emotional disabilities, and substance abuse, the school special-education evaluation team would not refer him for special education because they believed his primary problems were conduct disorder and substance abuse and "IDEA did not provide services for students with these problems." The private mental health counselor said he could not continue to work with Eric because he needed to "get clean first," and the family was wasting its money. He recommended residential treatment. The alcohol and drug services staff said they could not refer Eric for residential treatment as long as he was willing to participate in outpatient treatment, and the parents would need to make a formal drug charge against him before a court could order him into residential treatment.

At the interdisciplinary team (IDT) meeting among agencies, after all the reports were reviewed, the IDT leader explained that because Eric was over age 14, under state law, this team could not forcibly place Eric into residential treatment unless he had a charge filed against him, but they could only recommend a "level of service." They recommended a dual diagnosis program and specifically referred him to an intensive adolescent day treatment program in the local community. Eric's mother asked for copies of all reports from the agencies being represented at the IDT. They said they could not release them since Eric was 16 and permission was needed.

Eric's mother, a paragon of patience and a master of record keeping after years of being Eric's "case manager," proceeded to contact each of the agencies separately to obtain the reports. She immediately made an appointment to visit the day treatment program. She learned that the program was a dual diagnosis program for youth with mental health and substance abuse problems, and it seemed to be what Eric needed. The program accepted 22 students during the year and had a classroom ratio of 1 to 5. It was combined with an alternative school that was part of the public school system and aligned with the state curriculum. It had a structured behavioral component, a mental health counseling component, and family counseling services. Eric and the family would have a case manager and would also continue to receive outreach services from his probation officer during the evening and weekends. The family believed that this program represented hope for Eric's future.

Questions for Discussion

- What experiences did Eric and his mother have that indicated that there was fragmentation, or lack of coordination, in the system of services?
- What agencies were involved in Eric's case?
- Why did the mother refer to herself as Eric's "case manager"?

The kind of struggle to obtain services from multiple agencies (seen in the case illustration above) is common across the nation for adolescents who pass the age by which parents can place them into treatment programs without the involvement of law enforcement agencies. Although this kind of case is among the most challenging and complex, obtaining services from multiple agencies in less complex cases continues to be difficult even for the most savvy families. For example, a student with attention deficit disorder and learning disabilities who is experiencing a family divorce may require speech-language services, academic tutoring, and short-term counseling. The student and family will need assistance to obtain the needed services in a timely fashion.

How Has System Coordination Evolved?

System Coordination Has a Long History

There is a long history in the United States of providing noneducational services to children within a school setting—a shared responsibility between schools and communities. Initially, as part of social reform efforts early in the 1900s, health services in schools were provided primarily by public health doctors and dentists who volunteered their services. As health and social services became embedded in the schools, the services became more school-centered and less family-oriented, focusing on improving school attendance and academic performance. Over the past 50 years, the number of noneducational staff and the ratio of these staff to students has increased dramatically. The goal for providing school-linked health and social services shifted toward (1) improving academic performance, (2) improving international competitiveness, or (3) meeting the health and social needs of underserved children (children at risk) (Tyak, 1992).

From the 1950s through the early 1980s, schools and community agencies reported little formal interagency collaboration and minimal use of formal interagency agreements, even though there was a strong consensus on the need to develop such agreements (Neubert, 2000; Storms, O'Leary, & Williams, 2000b). During the 1990s, however, several factors stimulated the development of interagency coordination to support the development of children and youth in the schools. These included (a) better definitions of interagency coordination goals and functions, (b) laws that encouraged interagency coordination in order to carry out transition planning requirements for students with disabilities, (c) greater willingness of agencies to reduce barriers that have hindered collaboration, (d) development of state and local resources to develop interagency cooperative activities, and (e) lessons learned about the effectiveness of interagency coordination in other disciplines (e.g., social work, mental health, public health, and rehabilitation). Recent outcome data now confirm the effectiveness of interagency services coordination activities in improving access, quality of services, and outcomes for students and families. (Chapter 5 provides a discussion.)

National Policies Promote Coordination.   Over the past two decades the corner-stone of the Regular Education (Inclusion) Initiative has been collaboration among teachers, specialists, and parents (Stainback & Stainback, 1996; Welch & Brownell, 2002). More recently, collaboration and system coordination strategies together have become central policy tools or instruments embedded in major education and disability-related laws. The IDEA of 1997, IDEA Amendments of 2004, No Child Left Behind Act of 2001, and Rehabilitation Act Amendments expanded cooperative arrangements at the federal, state, and local levels. It is important to understand how collaboration and system coordination are central to implementing free and appropriate public education for students with disabilities and for improving educational outcomes.

State and Local Communities Recognize the Value of School-Linked Services.
Recent arguments for implementing coordinated school-linked services rest on six basic premises. First, educators and policymakers have come to recognize that all facets of a child's well-being impact his or her potential for academic success. Second, demographic trends indicate that an increasing number of American school-age children can be considered at risk for school failure and other social problems such as substance abuse and incarceration (Centre for Educational Research and Innovation, 1998; Cuban & Usdan, 2002; Hodgkinson, 2003). Third, prevention is more cost-effective for society than correction or remediation. For example, Hodgkinson (2003) reports that there is an established relationship between dropping out of school and the probability of committing a crime, and that dropout prevention costs less in the long run than incarceration. Fourth, at-risk children come to school with multiple problems that cut across conventional health, social, and education systems boundaries, problems that schools are ill-equipped to handle alone (Cuban & Usdan, 2002; Kirst, 1994). Fifth, the current system of child-related service delivery is fragmented, often characterized by duplication, waste, and lack of coordination. Consequently, many children fall through the cracks and don't get the services they need (Abrams & Gibbs, 2000; Kirst, 1994). Finally, because schools have sustained, long-term contact with children, they are the logical gateway for providing multiple services to children (Adelman & Taylor, 1997; Kirst, 1994; Wagner, Golan, & Valdes, 2003).

WHAT DOES A SERVICE COORDINATOR DO?

System coordinators, or **service coordinators**, provide the link between the needs of students and families and appropriate services in the school and community as required by students' Individualized Education Programs (IEPs) or Individualized Family Services Plans (IFSPs), if they are in early intervention services, and by IDEA and NCLB requirements for school–community collaboration. System coordinators facilitate the efficient and effective use of resources. They provide a single contact, or single point of entry, into the broader service system within and outside the

Krista Greco/Merrill

The service coordinator provides the link between the student and family and appropriate services in the school and community as required by student's by student's IEP.

school for students with disabilities and their families. A service coordinator (often referred to as a case manager) facilitates the individualized education plan (or IFSP for the child in early intervention services) by linking the student and his or her family with the needed services within and outside the school. The coordinator identifies the role of each provider and coordinates all needed services. The student and family can expect the following services to be provided by their coordinator:

- Meet with the student and family on a regular basis and include the student and family in all aspects of planning services to meet needs.
- Ensure that service providers identified in the IFSP or IEP are of quality and are the best match for the student and family.
- Work with service providers to ensure that the student and family can access the services and help resolve problems with service providers.
- Assist in obtaining and maintaining all services that the student is entitled to under the law and that are written into their IEP.

Service coordinators also assess needs of the child and family, broker the needed services, and act as liaisons between district staff, classroom teachers, other school staff, and parents. They facilitate school-based teams, IEP teams and other collaborative meetings, maintain records, and facilitate smooth transitions at the elementary, middle, and high school levels. They determine eligibility for services, provide monitoring and tracking of services, advocate for families, and advocate for greater service availability.

The coordinator's role is *dynamic*—that of advocate, mentor, and coordinator of a set of services. For example, a coordinator at the elementary level may recommend tutoring for a child with learning disabilities in the general education classroom, but in the middle school, the student may be referred for counseling and family support.

Effective service coordinators are well trained and know the community, individuals, and families whom they serve. They should be competent, sensitive, and committed to representing the interests and preferences of the individual and his or her family. They must provide reliable information, help explore options, coach individuals and families, and guide them to make informed decisions about services and supports. Finally, they assist in the coordination of service providers in a manner that strengthens the informal resources (family, friends, neighbors, church) and ensures the participation of students in defining personal goals for the future (Jackson, 2003; The ARC, 2003). In some schools teachers or special education consulting teachers may also serve as service coordinators.

WHAT ARE THE FUNCTIONS OF SERVICE COORDINATION?

This section defines the essential elements or functions of service system coordination in the educational continuum. A synthesis of over three decades of literature (1970–2005) by this author resulted in a set of eight categories by which system coordination activities can be categorized. These categories represent eight basic **service coordination functions** that are performed by schools and school-linked agencies to provide services to students and families (Kochhar, 1995; Kochhar-Bryant, 2003a). They include:

1. Information and referral
2. Identification and preparation
3. Needs assessment and evaluation
4. Individual program planning and development
5. Service coordination and linking
6. Service monitoring and follow-along
7. Individual and interagency advocacy
8. Evaluation and follow-up

These functions operate at the individual and system levels and are discussed separately in the following sections.

Function 1: Information and Referral.   Information and referral activities vary widely among interagency systems, which define the function either (a) narrowly, as information-giving to the public and the referral of youth and families to agency services for which they are eligible; or (b) broadly, with extensive outreach activities, aggressive parent and community education, and interagency case-finding activities to identify different groups of individuals needing services. Information and referral activities include outreach to eligible in-school students or those in alternative educational placements who are not currently benefiting from related and supportive services; distribution of information to students and families about community resources and how to access them; development of a single point of entry or contact for services; and decreasing the amount of time between initial contact and entry into services or programs. Improved outreach and identification of eligible target groups increases the likelihood that needed services reach the students who need them.

Function 2: Identification and Preparation. Identification and preparation involve procedures for matching individual service requests with appropriate supportive agencies. Identification and preparation activities may include creating a reliable system database on students identified and served; developing criteria for early evaluation and diagnosis of the disability or learning need; making services accessible in terms of physical access, hours of operation, transportation, and costs; obtaining and documenting informed consent; and involving families in early planning.

Function 3: Needs Assessment and Evaluation. Needs assessment and evaluation is a process by which diagnostic evaluation and general information is collected, analyzed, and interpreted among the service coordinator, student, family, teachers, and other relevant personnel. An evaluation should focus on both the individual's current level of functioning as well as his or her highest level of functioning before seeking services. A needs assessment should also address the whole person, including academic, social, vocational, and independent living domains (Halpern, Herr, Doren, & Wolf, 2000; Sitlington, Neubert, Begon, Lombard, & Leconte, 1966; Sitlington, Neubert, & Leconte, 1997; Tindle, Leconte, Buchanan, & Taymans, 2004). Based on an assessment of individual needs, the service coordinator can establish priorities for services to the student and incorporate needed services into the IEP.

Comprehensive evaluation addresses strengths and developmental needs in relevant functional domains, including academic, physical development, independent functioning, social, family and natural support, behavioral, academic and vocational, employment, health, and psychological. It also involves periodic renewal of evaluations, communicating and interpreting evaluation information, adapting evaluation tools for individuals with disabilities, and making recommendations for interventions on individual education and transition plans. Needs assessment and evaluation is an ongoing process that extends throughout the course of the student's school program. System level needs assessment involves activities such as data analysis and surveys of systemwide needs of populations for services.

Function 4: IFSP/IEP and Transition Planning. The development of a comprehensive service plan as part of the IEP (individual education plan) or IFSP (individual family service plan) is an essential function of service coordination from early intervention through high school transition. Individualized plans represent the service agreements or contracts among the student, the family, the school, and the service providers. The plans document the responsibilities and commitments of the student, teachers, family members, and other agency service providers. They are based on information obtained from the individual evaluations and assessments described in Function 3. Planning activities engage the interdisciplinary team and families in education planning; address all of the functional domains, including family supports; address the continuity of needed supplemental and support services as the student moves from one educational level to the next; involve regular review of the plan; and ensure active participation and decision making of students and their families in the process. Program planning also occurs at the system level and typically results in the development of an interagency cooperative agreement.

Function 5: Service Coordination and Linking. At the individual level, service linking means identifying appropriate service agencies and individuals to deliver the services identified in an IFSP or IEP. For example, for families of children and youth with disabilities, it may mean providing a central point of contact to link the student and family with a variety of services such as speech and hearing, school counseling, or assistive devices or equipment. For individuals with chronic health needs, it may mean providing information and linking with public health services, nursing services, and providers of in-home health-related and adaptive equipment. For secondary youth preparing for postsecondary placement, it may mean linking the student with vocational rehabilitation services, post-secondary institutions, and employment preparation. At the individual level, linking activities may include establishing a service coordinator or point of contact for each individual or family; identifying and contacting needed services within the agency's catchment (service) area (or outside, if needed); and linking students and families with needed services during key transitions from early childhood through exit from high school.

At the system level, linking means coordinating and sharing resources among agencies on behalf of children and youth with special needs. Shared resources include financial, human and intellectual, and material resources that belong to cooperating agencies, which could be dedicated to system coordination activities defined in a cooperative agreement. Interagency linking activities can help prevent duplication of services among many agencies and make the service system more efficient.

Function 6: Service Monitoring and Follow-Along.   At the individual level, the purpose of service monitoring is to (a) ensure that students receive services that are described in the IEP and (b) evaluate the student's progress in achieving the goals and objectives included in the plan. Monitoring also involves documenting services actually received, documenting gaps in services for students and efforts to locate services outside the community, documenting barriers in services for the student, and maintaining continuity in service coordination through key transition points. Monitoring requires that the service coordinator and IFSP or IEP team maintain ongoing contact with students receiving services and the agency(ies) providing them.

Service monitoring at the *system level* means observing the delivery of services of cooperating agencies and contract service providers to ensure that services are delivered according to the intended schedule; reach the students they were intended to serve; are delivered in a manner that complies with established local, state, and national laws; and are delivered with an acceptable level of quality. Monitoring activities at the system level include documenting progress and performance of cooperating agencies and contract service providers, collecting data on referrals to agencies and services needed by individuals or families, and collecting information from students and families about how they perceive the quality, appropriateness, and accessibility of services. The monitoring function can offer valuable information about the quality and effectiveness of service coordination in the service delivery system.

Follow-along activities are an important part of the monitoring function. Follow-along includes activities by the service coordinator that provide mentoring, provide emotional support, foster relationships of trust with the student, and maintain close contact and communication with the family. Follow-along activities may include home visits to families, visits to youth in their school or work-based programs, informal and supportive counseling with students or families, addressing family support needs, or providing behavioral or crisis intervention. The follow-along function includes the personal support component of service coordination. It can be instrumental in preventing student dropout from needed services or programs and even preventing dropout from school.

Function 7: Individual and Interagency Advocacy.   *Advocacy* is a very broad term that has different meanings to different groups of people, but it is a particularly important function of service coordination. At the individual level, advocacy means actively seeking services on behalf of a student or assisting the student to advocate on his or her own behalf (self-advocacy). Advocacy activities at the individual level include recommending to IFSP or IEP teams specific services for the student, sharing information with a family about services to solicit their consent to approve a student's participation, and educating general educators about how supportive and assistive services can help a student with special needs progress in general education.

System level advocacy means advocating in similar ways to those described above but doing so on behalf of a population of students. Examples of advocacy activities include (a) developing a shared interagency understanding of the needs of groups of students with disabilities or special learning needs, (b) addressing multicultural and language minority issues with service agencies to negotiate the development of special supports or accommodations, (c) communicating service barriers and service gaps to decision makers, (d) communicating and protecting human rights and due process procedures for groups of students, (e) promoting an emphasis on self-determination and informed decision making for students and their families, (f) helping local agencies meet new legal requirements, and (g) increasing support services for groups of students as they transition between grades or programs. As local agencies respond to new requirements for system coordination, advocacy can help build a shared capacity to meet the multiple needs of students and their families.

Function 8: Evaluation and Follow-Up.   Evaluation and follow-up are essential to effective service coordination. Although evaluation may be a final step in assessing the value and quality of services for children, it is the first step in their improvement. Evaluation is a process by which information about educational programs and services is collected in order to measure results or effects of the services and programs on students and families; determine if the interagency partnership is achieving the goals that it set for itself; and make decisions about the future of the interagency agreement. Because evaluation is closely linked to the decision-making process, it is most powerful if the information it generates becomes part of the decision-making process (Rossi, Freeman, & Lipsey, 1999).

Follow-up activities are used to track the path or disposition of students once they have exited the program or service agency (e.g., from preschool to elementary, or from high school to college or employment). Follow-up activities are designed to answer questions such as the following: What happens to students once they have left the school and the services in which they have been participating? Do the students return to community agencies for additional services and are they more likely to access services again in the future? Do students experience long-term benefits or impacts as a result of receiving services (e.g., continued postsecondary education; independent living; improved physical health, mobility, or social, financial, and family relations; employment; and general functioning)?

Follow-up methods at the *individual level* include student or family surveys or interviews to determine perceptions about quality, accessibility, and appropriateness of services; outreach to students who did not complete high school to determine what additional services are needed; and evaluation of transition plans for students and their families. Follow-up information informs us about whether or not the benefits or progress made by students who receive school-based or or school-linked services endure over time. While they may be known by different labels in different educational agencies across the nation, the eight functions discussed above represent the basic tasks performed by system coordinators in schools and school-linked agencies.

What Are the Various Models of System Coordination?

Models of System Coordination

There are several models for system coordination in use across the United States to facilitate services for students and families. These models differ in the types of roles that service coordinators play, the functions that are performed, the scope of the authority for coordination (federal, state, or local level), and the kinds of interagency agreements developed. The following models have been defined and classified based on a series of studies of service coordination models in the United States (Kochhar, 2003, 1995, 1987).

Generalist Model.   A single school-based service coordinator or transition coordinator is responsible for all eight service coordination functions at the individual student level. This model most closely resembles the traditional social casework model but is applicable in a variety of disciplines. This type of model (Figure 3.5) is particularly effective in long-term support systems for students with severe or multiple disabilities (cognitive, physical, or emotional/behavioral) who need long-term assistance through schooling and into adulthood. Under this model, each student is provided a single coordinator who is their primary point of contact and with whom they can communicate regularly. Service coordinators use a variety of skills and perform the full range of functions described earlier in this chapter. Service coordinators have considerable autonomy in their daily activities, maintain complete records on a student, and maintain a high level of accountability.

Specialist Model.   The service coordination process is divided up into specialties in which one coordinator, for example, conducts individual planning, another conducts assessments, and another conducts monitoring and follow-up. Typically, coordination may involve two or more functions. This model is most often used with individuals who have significant or multiple disabilities and who need comprehensive support services. Teaming among coordinators provides support and enhances shared problem solving and creativity.

Embedded Coordination Model.   In the embedded model, the coordination function is attached to a primary role of teacher, counselor, or therapist. Individuals who need ongoing support require a professional who knows them well and can

FIGURE 3.5
Generalist Model

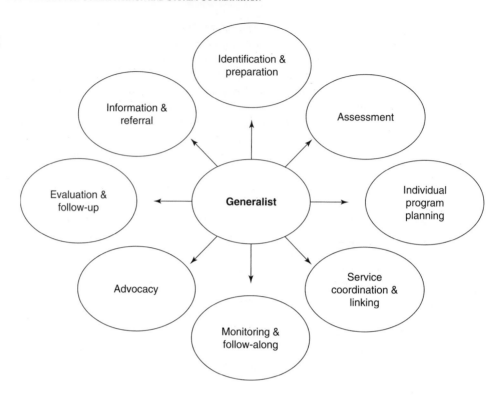

also assist in linking with other related and support services in the community. This model is most effective when the professional is trained in coordination functions and carries a reasonable caseload (number of students to whom they provide services).

Family Model. The family model has traditionally meant that the service coordination rests with the individual's family. Parents or guardians act as coordinators for their child. This is common among families of young children with disabilities, adolescents in high school, and youth entering employment or postsecondary education. Some educational systems are recognizing the important role families play in negotiating services among agencies and are providing families with information, training, and support to enable them to become more informed advocates. The family model is very much evolving.

Natural Support Model. The natural support model is built around the natural support structures in the community. Members of the community are selected as coordinators or ombudsmen who are matched with a single child. They may be other parents, volunteers, retired persons, or outreach workers. These coordinators provide information to students, maintain ongoing mentor relationship, provide supportive counseling, or conduct outreach and follow-up. In some districts, they are provided with regular training and supervision through the school system. Volunteers can greatly extend the capacity of an agency or group of agencies to perform service coordination functions. This model has been particularly effective in rural and remote geographical regions.

Local System Coordination Model.   Drawing from three decades of planning in the mental health and public health disciplines, many local service systems are adapting a *core services* model for linking the individual with related and supportive services in the community. Under the core services model, the interagency system defines the core interagency service coordination functions that are considered to be absolutely essential for linking the student with needed services that support their IFSP or IEP (Alamprese, 1994; New York 2001–2005 Statewide Comprehensive Plan for Mental Health Services, 2001). The key agencies that provide these services are then identified and an interagency agreement is developed.

State and Federal Level System Coordination Model.   State interagency initiatives typically result from federal initiatives or policies, but sometimes they emerge independently. They involve efforts to form partnerships between one or more state agencies to conduct activities such as statewide assessment of student support and transition needs, identifying funds to support local interagency service coordination, providing advocacy for target populations, assuring continuity of services and access, developing professional training and technical assistance programs, and developing policies that support system coordination. State governments and agencies play a pivotal role in stimulating and shaping local service coordination (Adelsheim, Carrillo, & Coletta, 2001; Braddock, Hemp, Parish, & Rizzolo, 2000).

The federal level model links several national health, education, and human service agencies in order to create interagency policies and to provide leadership to stimulate similar efforts at the state and local levels. An example of federal-level interagency coordination is the linkages forged over the past decade between the U.S. Department of Education and Department of Labor to assist youth with disabilities to prepare for and enter employment and with Health and Human Services to improve mental health services for students. National level coordination includes activities such as joint priority setting, policy development, resource sharing, research and demonstration projects, and joint training projects. Federal interagency activities can provide powerful leadership to encourage state and local efforts (U.S. Office of Special Education Programs, 2003b).

These models for system coordination represent those in use across the United States to facilitate services for students and families. In most states several of these models are integrated to respond to unique local needs.

WHAT PRINCIPLES AND PRACTICES CONTRIBUTE TO EFFECTIVE SYSTEM COORDINATION?

Principles for System Coordination

Research has confirmed that system coordination and a shared responsibility for the student are vital for preserving the hard-earned gains made in the past few decades to integrate individuals with disabilities into general education, postsecondary programs, employment, and the community. Several consumer-centered philosophical principles facilitate effective coordination to assist students with disabilities to reach their greatest potential. Eight **consumer-centered principles** are presented below that reflect recurring themes in most of today's discussions of reform and improvement in the quality and effectiveness of education and human service systems.

1. *Principle 1.* Service coordination assists the student to achieve the maximum level of potential and promotes self-determination.
2. *Principle 2.* Service coordination activities result in improvements in the quality of life and learning environment of the individual.
3. *Principle 3.* Service coordination promotes community integration.
4. *Principle 4.* Service coordination assists the individual to improve health and physical well-being.
5. *Principle 5.* Service coordination assures equitable access to a range of needed services.
6. *Principle 6.* Service coordination reinforces the informal support network.
7. *Principle 7.* Service coordination promotes integration into community service delivery systems.
8. *Principle 8.* Service coordination employs evaluation methods that focus on individual outcomes and service improvements.

These also represent guiding principles that have helped shape existing models for interagency service coordination.

The Circle of Commitment

To the consumer-centered principles introduced above, is added the **circle of commitment,** which is closely related to concepts of strategic planning. When applied to system coordination, the term *circle of commitment* helps to define the range of resources, both human and material, that must be invested in an interagency effort to improve educational outcomes for special learners and their families (Figure 3.6). Key stakeholders responsible for education and development of children and youth, along with supporting material and financial resources, form the partnership's circle of commitment, which includes the following six elements:

1. *The Human Commitment:* the key partners—school and community personnel, students, and families.
2. *The Resource Commitment:* the financial and material resources that cooperating agencies commit to the partnership for improving services and outcomes.
3. *The Values Commitment:* a shared set of values and a belief in the shared responsibility for children and youth with disabilities and their families.
4. *The Action Commitment:* a shared mission, written cooperative agreement, and common goals for the interagency partnership.
5. *The Outcome Commitment:* a shared set of expectations for development and education outcomes for those who will be served or impacted by the interagency partnership (infants, toddlers, children, youth, and families).
6. *The Renewal Commitment:* a shared long-term plan (a) to continue to review the course of the interagency partnership, (b) to recognize and celebrate the unique contributions that each agency and its staff make to the relationship, and (c) to continue those commitments.

This commitment represents the range of resources and tools that system coordinators need to improve education and support services for students and their families.

FIGURE 3.6

Circle of
Commitment

Source: Adapted from
Successful Inclusion:
Strategies for a Shared
Responsibility by
C. Kochhar, L. West, &
J. Taymans, 2000, Upper
Saddle River, NJ:
Merrill/Prentice Hall.
Reprinted by permission.

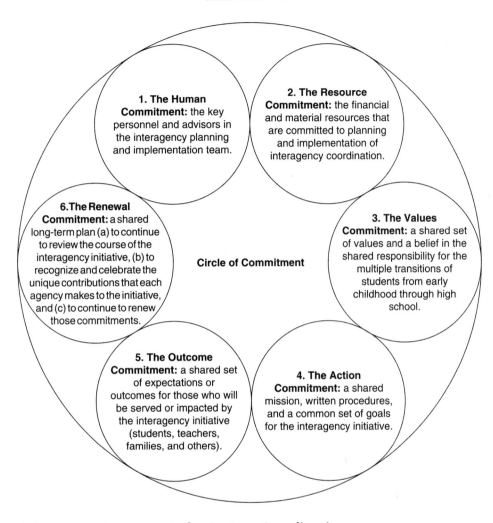

Interagency Agreements for System Coordination

Schools and partner agencies make many decisions about how they will define and manage their relationships and how they will cooperate to provide services. For example, they must plan together to define their target population(s) and assess service needs, to determine what agencies will participate and who will take the leadership responsibility (lead agency), to decide how decisions will be made, to establish a client information database to track services, to conduct ongoing evaluation of services, and to determine how it will include families in the planning and evaluation of the effort.

In order to define such complex relationships, coordinating schools and community agencies establish formal **interagency cooperative agreements** that define the roles of each agency in the planning and service provision, communication and coordination, and training of key personnel. Echoing the characteristics of systems in Chapter 1, planning for system coordination is a dynamic process. Planning must support flexibility in the service system so that it can respond to changes in direction, environments, student and system needs (Future Educational Funding Council, 2002; Martinelli, 2002).

The First Step: Establish a Joint Vision and Shared Mission.   Once system coordination needs have been assessed and potential resources identified, the action phase of the process can begin—that of establishing the shared mission. In this step, collaborating agencies meet to discuss a joint vision for a partnership and hammer out broad goals and strategies for achieving that shared vision. The goal of this step is to develop a written mission statement for the cooperative relationship and a signed formal interagency agreement or memorandum of understanding (MOA) that embodies the principles of shared responsibility. It is important to view an agreement as more than a linkage, but as a shared strategy for improving outcomes for children and youth in the community.

Components of the Interagency Mission Statement.   A mission statement is a broad description of the vision of the partnership. It serves as a preamble to a cooperative agreement that further defines specific goals, objectives, and actions for the partnership. Each community defines its interagency mission differently, so no two mission statements will look alike. However, a few fundamental elements should be included in every mission statement:

1. *A statement of context or history:* a brief introductory paragraph that broadly describes the interagency partnership, how it was initiated, how it addresses current student and family needs, how it improves upon current educational practices, and how the partnership improves services.

2. *A statement of the authority for the interagency agreement:* an introductory section that refers to the legal basis for the agreement and may list the local, state, and federal laws, regulations, or policies that give authority to the agreement.

3. *General statement of purpose of the agreement and expected outcomes:* a broad statement of what the partnership expects to accomplish and the results it hopes to obtain for children and families.

4. *The broad goal and outline of roles and responsibilities:* a description of roles and responsibilities of each cooperating partner.

The Next Step: Developing the Cooperative Agreement.   The next step involves negotiating among cooperating agencies the specific agreements for action to achieve the mission. The cooperative agreement incorporates the mission statement and then elaborates on the commitments of the agencies involved. The cooperative agreement answers the questions: How does the team develop such a cooperative agreement to meet specific annual goals? How can goal statements be crafted so that the team can measure the results of the coordination activities? What should be the timetable for action?

The cooperative agreement defines the structure, processes, and local authority for action among the collaborating agencies. It also defines what can be expected from each agency—their activities, responsibilities, and contributions to the service delivery system. Cooperative agreements accomplish four things:

1. *Identify resources to support interagency relationships:* The agreement broadly outlines each cooperating agency's contribution and the time it will commit, including funds, staff, equipment, consultation time, vehicles, space, and other resources.

2. *Identify goals, objectives, and activities:* The agreement describes the goals, objectives, and activities to be performed by the cooperating agencies, as well as the role and authority of the interagency coordinator and planning team.

3. *Identify expected results (outcomes):* The agreement defines the expected results for students and families and for the cooperating agencies. It should also describe the interagency planning team's authority for evaluating and monitoring the coordination activities and the roles of cooperating agencies, students, and families in the process.

4. *Establish a timetable:* The agreement establishes the date the agreement takes effect, the schedule for accomplishing objectives, and the dates for reviewing and modifying the agreement.

Objectives for the agreement should be specific, measurable, and time-limited. If the interagency team defines its goals and objectives early in the development of the relationship, it is much easier to evaluate what is accomplished and whether or not students and families are benefiting from the services provided.

WHAT SYSTEM COORDINATION PRACTICES IMPROVE THE EDUCATION AND WELL-BEING OF STUDENTS AND FAMILIES?

Several new service coordination model practices have emerged in the past decade designed to bring together the resources of the community, family, and school to meet the needs of children and their families. These models include systems of care, integrated services, community schools, school-linked services, full service schools, and wraparound services. The following sections describe these programs.

Systems of Care

A system of care, based on ecological theory, is a consortium of agencies organized to work together to provide related and supportive services to individuals. A model that emerged out of the mental health profession, it is designed to help children or adolescents with emotional and behavioral disorders to obtain the services they need in or near their homes and community. Effective systems of care help reduce costly alternative school placements or out-of-home placements, improve children functional behavior, improve school performance, and reduce delinquency of students (Kendziora, Bruns, Osher, Pacchiona, & Mejia, 2001; Rosenblatt & Woodbridge, 2003; Woodruff, et al., 1999).

In systems of care, local public and private organizations work in teams to plan and implement a tailored set of services for each child's physical, emotional, social, educational, and family needs. Services that may be included in a system of care include service coordination, counseling, crisis residential care, crisis outreach teams, day treatment, education/special education services, family support, health services, independent living supports, in-home family-based counseling, protection and advocacy, respite care, self-help or support groups, tutoring, and vocational counseling. System of care teams include family advocates and may be comprised of representatives from mental health, health, education, child welfare, juvenile justice, vocational rehabilitation, recreation, substance abuse, or other organizations.

Teams identify and build upon the strengths of a child and his or her family, rather than focusing solely on their problems.

Integrated Services Model

Similar to the system of care is the integrated services model. Integrated services (IS) is a coordinated, holistic approach to addressing the needs of children or youth, particularly the complex, interrelated problems of at-risk children, by providing a comprehensive range of educational and human services (Abdal-Haqq, 1993; Hanson, Deere, Lee, Lewin, & Seval, 2001). School-linked integrated services programs focus on prevention, promoting wellness for children and their families, and providing services that overcome barriers to school readiness and academic success (Blackorby, Newman, & Finnegan, 1998; Briar-Lawson & Lawson, 1997a; Hanson, Deere, Lee, Lewin, & Seval, 2001). These services include tutoring and remedial education, mentoring, dropout prevention, after-school care, drug abuse counseling, health care, job training and counseling, parent education, programs to reduce student conflict, gang-diversion programs, and programs for homeless youth.

Integration is characterized by features such as common intake and "seamless" service delivery, where the student/client may receive a range of services from different programs without repeated registration procedures, waiting periods, or other administrative barriers. Such a model contrasts with traditional communities in which clients may have to visit different agency locations and re-register for each program to obtain services (Martinson, 1999). Integrated services schools are the hub of a coordinated network of service providers who link services with children and their families.

There is no one model for implementing school-linked integrated services programs. Programs are designed to offer a comprehensive continuum of services, avoid duplication and gaps in services through communication and collaboration among service providers, and ensure that each child and family has a personal relationship with a coordinator (Blackorby, Newman, & Finnegan, 1998; Hanson, Deere, Lee, Lewin, & Seval, 2001).

Community Schools Models

In many communities across the United States, the school is the center of the community, offering more than academic instruction during traditional school hours. Dryfoos (2002) traced the concept of community schools to the early 20th century when "John Dewey brought the school into the community and Jane Addams brought the community into the school" (p. 2). A community school is defined as:

> a school, operating in a public school building, that is open to students, families, and the community before, during, and after school, seven days a week, all year long . . . It is jointly operated and financed through a partnership between the school system and one or more community agencies . . . Families, students, principals, teachers, youth workers, neighborhood residents, college faculty members, college students, and business people all work together to design and implement a plan for transforming the school into a child-centered institution." (Dryfoos, p. 2)

The purpose of the community school is to reengage community members in the planning of new facilities and daily life of the schools; foster new partnerships that serve both student needs and community needs; use information about student learning outcomes for local planning; and establish a K–12 education system that is as seamless as possible. Additional community resources and services are located in local school facilities during afternoons, evenings, and weekend hours, including health and mental health services, social services, recreation activities, and parenting and adult education classes.

School-Linked Services

School-linked services are defined as a system of interrelated resources that link schools, families, and public and private service agencies (Adelman & Taylor, 1997; Briar-Lawson & Lawson 1997a; Wagner & Gomby, 2000). These programs may engage health services, social services, housing, law enforcement agencies, transportation services, local businesses, institutions of higher education, libraries, museums, and religious institutions. They are designed to increase access and delivery of school and community resources to students and families, improve student learning and social and physical development, enhance the professional's ability to link families with community resources, and promote resilience among children and families (Wang, Haertel, & Walberg, 2002).

Full-Service Schools and Wraparound Services

Educators and human service agency personnel are not in agreement about the extent to which services should be provided directly within the school. The most comprehensive approach to school-linked services combines school restructuring with service delivery in what some educators term *full-service schools*. The full-service school model puts the best of school reform together with all other services that children, youth, and families need, most of which can be located in a school building. The challenge to community agencies is to bring into the school services such as health, mental health, employment services, child care, parent education, case management, recreation, cultural events, welfare, and community policing. The result is a new kind of seamless institution, a community-oriented school that ensures flexibility, accessibility, and continuity of services for those most in need (Briar-Lawson & Lawson, 1997a; Dryfoos, 1994, p. 12; North Central Regional Education Laboratory, 2001; Wagner, Golan, & Valdes, 2003; Wagner & Gomby, 2000).

Wraparound is a process of service delivery typically found in full-service schools that is intended to improve the lives of children and families who have complex needs. The wraparound process includes several important principles. First, it includes a comprehensive service plan based on the unique strengths, values, and preferences of the child and family. Services and supports are community-based, and the services cut across traditional agency boundaries through multi-agency involvement and funding. A service coordinator helps link the student and family to needed services and provides follow-along. And finally, outcome measures are identified and the plan is evaluated periodically (Miles & Frantz, 2001).

Services and supports are tailored to the unique values and cultural needs of the child and family.

CAN SYSTEM COORDINATION BE EVALUATED?

Outcomes and Benefits of System Coordination

Policymakers, researchers, and practitioners recognize the benefits—positive outcomes—of service coordination to support children and their families as they enter, progress in, and exit the school system. Achieving system coordination, however, is a highly complex human endeavor. Although system coordination has been required by legislation for decades, the development of interagency agreements among districts across the United States remains a continuing challenge (Adelman & Taylor, 1997; Sussman, 2000; U.S. Department of Health and Human Services, 2003, 2001c; U.S. Government Accountability Office, 2003a; Wagner & Gomby, 2000). Evaluation of benefits and outcomes, therefore, also remains a challenge.

Benefits and outcomes refer to what interagency planners hope to see change as a result of the services or service coordination effort. Outcome evaluation of system coordination measures the extent to which interagency services cause desired change in the student/consumer population and in partner agencies.

Factors That Facilitate Effective System Coordination

Although there are many organizational, attitudinal, and knowledge factors that serve as barriers to complex system collaboration, there are many that can facilitate the development of effective coordination. *Organizational facilitators* include formal interagency agreements, time lines for action, investment of agency resources, reward systems for staff to reinforce group-centered approaches and collaboration, reasonable caseloads, a focus on outcomes and accountability for results, a broad range of services offered by organizations, geographic proximity among organizations, clear lines of communication and clear roles, an active state role in developing and improving services, and shared evaluation of the effectiveness of the interagency agreement.

Knowledge facilitators include research on effective models for coordinating services, adapting models to fit local conditions, staff assigned to agency boundary-crossing roles, service coordinators with an adequate base of knowledge and values to carry out their duties, leadership styles that facilitate collaboration, state standards that communicate the responsibilities of local education agencies for system coordination, and shared definitions and service philosophies among agencies.

Attitudinal facilitators include perceived need for collaboration; prevailing organizational and environmental norms that value collaboration; a history of effective relationships between organizations; relationships among participants that are based on trust, respect, and mutual understanding; flexibility and adaptability; a process for recognizing and celebrating collective achievements and individual contributions; shared common commitment to the interagency goals; and a process for sharing information between families and professionals that facilitates service access yet ensures confidentiality (adapted from Ingram, Bloomberg, & Seppanen, 1996; Kirst, 1994).

Seven Action Steps for Evaluating Interagency Agreements

The following action steps are useful for designing an evaluation of interagency agreements for system coordination:

1. *Who will participate?* Decide who will participate in design of the evaluation and defining outcomes to be measured. Ensure that all agencies, units, or organizations that will be impacted by the interagency agreement are represented in the evaluation. Engage a consultant if needed.

2. *What will you evaluate?* Select the elements of the interagency agreement that need to be evaluated (informing the community, assessing needs, developing shared resources, shared mission, cooperative agreement, outcomes, or all of these). Decide whether to evaluate individual level outcomes or system level outcomes. Outcomes can be measured at the individual and system (interagency) levels. Individual level outcomes include measures of achievement or progress of children and families in education or transition from one educational level to the next (e.g., successful transition from early intervention to preschool), improved academic performance, improved access to related services, increased involvement of families in the IEP process, reduced dropout, and successful transition from high school to postsecondary settings. *System level outcomes* include measures of improvements in the service system as a whole, in the way agencies coordinate their services to serve students, and how well the system is improving access to services for all students with IEPs (e.g., creation of a formal interagency agreement or memorandum of understanding, joint needs assessments, joint cross-agency training activities, coordinated database and information sharing, and coordinated evaluation of service delivery.

3. *What questions will you ask?* Outcome evaluation addresses several questions: How do we know that the programs and services are helping students and families achieve education goals? How can we improve the interagency partnership to increase access to services included in student's IEPs? How do students and families judge the quality and accessibility of the education and support services? How well are the interagency partners accomplishing the goals in their cooperative agreements? To what extent are students and families benefiting from the services?

4. *What will be your evaluation design and methods?* Evaluation supports decision making and should be built into the cooperative agreement early in the planning stage. Evaluation measures should be closely aligned with objectives in the cooperative agreement. Interagency coordinators play central roles in the planning and implementing of evaluation and in defining measures of success. It is important that interagency evaluation is supported at the highest leadership levels within coordinating agencies and that the partners communicate evaluation results and use them for future planning. Interagency evaluation planning teams include representatives from all collaborating agencies and families.

5. *How will you collect and analyze your data?* Data collection and analysis should yield useful information about results and benefits for participants. Identify the sources of information needed to answer evaluation questions (e.g., interviews, surveys, site visits and observations, records reviews). Select data analysis procedures such as quantitative information on numbers of participants, trends in participation, or measures of student progress or qualitative information such as analysis of interviews and open-ended questionnaires that solicit students' and families' judgments of the quality of the services.

6. *Develop your report of evaluation results.* Distribute the final report to partners and key stakeholders.

7. *How will you use the evaluation information for change and improvement?* Ensure that evaluation results are acted upon. Evaluation reinforces and supports program management, accountability, and continuous improvement. Have the evaluation design and methods evaluated by an external consultant. Equally important as collecting evaluation data from multiple sources is acting upon evaluation data to improve the service system. Evaluation information should be (1) analyzed and communicated in a manner that is understandable and usable by different stakeholder groups (e.g., service coordinators, teachers, counselors, families, administrators) and (2) applied in decisions about service system change and improvement. Evaluations reveal valuable information about the general quality, weaknesses, barriers, and gaps in services, and they inform future decisions about how the interagency agreement needs to change to improve services for students.

Summary of Key Points

- A coordinated interagency service system means a systematic, comprehensive, and coordinated system of education and support services for individuals with disabilities that is provided in their communities in the most integrated settings possible and in a manner that promotes individual choice and decision making.
- School and community leaders apply the concept of community to creating new partnerships and structures for the benefit of children, youth, and families.
- There is no one model for successful system coordination; best practices need to be carefully tailored to the particular circumstances of the schools and communities and of the students and families they serve.
- Educators and related services professionals are challenged to look beyond traditional service boundaries and to consider relationships across their disciplines, across the educational continuum, and across agency boundaries.

Key Terms and Phrases

- System coordination (p. 62)
- Individual level coordination (p. 65)
- Self-determination (p. 65)
- System level coordination (p. 65)
- Dimensions of system coordination (p. 67)
- Service coordinator (p. 71)
- Service coordination functions (p. 73)
- Consumer-centered principles (p. 79)
- Circle of commitment (p. 80)
- Interagency cooperative agreements (p. 81)

Questions for Reflection, Thinking, and Skill Building

1. Why is system coordination important in helping children and youth at the critical transition points?

2. How does service coordination at the individual and system levels differ? What is a student-centered approach?

3. Discuss your beliefs about how ready your professional peers are to participate effectively in system coordination activities in your school or agency. What skills and attitudes do you think they need to become more effective? What skills or attitudes do you need to strengthen?

4. Review the case of Eric at the beginning of the chapter. What agencies are coordinating to provide services for Eric? What was the mother's role in the process and what barriers did she experience in obtaining services for Eric? Do you believe Eric ended up in the program he needed? Why or why not? What do you think the lessons learned by the family tell us about interagency coordination in the county system highlighted in the illustration? What recommendations would you make to improve the processes for coordination?

5. Interview one to five case managers or service coordinators who work with youth with disabilities. What is their caseload size? What are their duties? Do they serve more than one role? How do they judge the effectiveness of their position? What barriers do they face? How do they overcome them? What training do they receive? What are their qualifications? What recommendations do *they* have for improving their services?

6. Find out what is being done in your school or district to promote coordination and team building among families, professionals, and agencies.

CHAPTER FOUR

WHAT EDUCATION LAWS PROMOTE SCHOOL COLLABORATION AND SYSTEM COORDINATION?

World history is the progress in the consciousness of liberty. —FREDERICK HEGEL

- Who are children with disabilities?

- What philosophical ideas are reflected in our education laws?

- Why do federal policies promote school collaboration and system coordination?

- How does IDEA promote collaboration and system coordination: Early childhood to postsecondary?

- What provisions of the No Child Left Behind Act of 2001 promote collaboration and coordination?

- How do NCLB and IDEA differ in principles and policies?

- What provisions of the Americans with Disabilities Act promote collaboration and system coordination?

- What provisions of the Job Training Improvement Act/Rehabilitation Act Amendments promote collaboration and system coordination?

- What provisions of the Carl D. Perkins Career and Technical Education Improvement Act promote collaboration and system coordination?

PERSPECTIVES

Middle School Teacher

I never quite understood the tensions surrounding the No Child Left Behind Act and the Individuals with Disabilities Education Improvement Act, but I knew that they were important. I never really understood just whom it directly affected. As a general educator, my lens was undoubtedly blurred, as I failed to understand how I was factored into the equation of the new laws.

Middle School Counselor

In my counseling masters program at the University, I never had to take courses in special education and knew little about laws affecting students with disabilities. I came to realize what a barrier that was for me. I cannot provide guidance and counseling to all my students if I am unfamiliar with the needs and expectations of students with disabilities.

INTRODUCTION

In the past few decades, state and federal laws have promoted school collaboration, system coordination, and a stronger role for parents in their children's education. Collaboration and system coordination are the cornerstones for several educational movements affecting students with disabilities: inclusion and universal design, school accountability, community schools, and transitions from early childhood programs through postsecondary education. As a result, collaboration and system coordination strategies have become central policy tools or instruments for improving education that are embedded in a variety of education and disability related laws. This chapter introduces federal laws and initiatives that promote school collaboration, system coordination, and a stronger role for parents in their children's education. It will discuss new expectations for students' participation in their own education and transition planning.

Borrowing from decades of experience in the social services and mental health fields, collaboration and system coordination in education began as a way to improve the delivery of education and related services, improve efficiency, and lower costs for services. These efforts have led to some creative and enduring new relationships among schools and community agencies and to a better understanding of how these relationships can improve outcomes for children and families. Both the **Individuals with Disabilities Education Improvement Act of 2004** (IDEA 2004) and the No Child Left Behind Act of 2001 include new language that requires collaboration and coordination. They require (1) coordination of early intervention and education for children with special needs with health, rehabilitation, and social service agencies; (2) strategies to overcome systemic barriers to the delivery of early intervention, educational, and transition services to children with disabilities; and (3) coordination of related services written into the student's individualized education program (IEP) (IDEA, 2004, P.L. 108–446). This chapter explains how collaboration and system coordination among people and agencies are essential in order to achieve the intent of the laws.

WHO ARE CHILDREN WITH DISABILITIES?

Special learners refers to a broad group of students, including those with disabilities, who are receiving special education, those at risk of being identified as needing special education, and those who are at risk of failure in the educational system for reasons other than disability. Under IDEA 2004, states must identify, locate, and evaluate all children with disabilities (and those suspected of having disabilities) residing within the state, including children who are homeless, wards of the state, attending private schools, and who are in need of special education and related services (IDEA 2004 Regulations, Child Find, 300.111).

Defining "Individuals With Disabilities"

IDEA identified specific categories of disabilities under which children may be eligible for special education and related services. **Students with disabilities** are children with any of the following disorders defined below who needs special education and related services (IDEA, 2004, Sec. 1401).

Learning Disability: a disorder of one or more of the basic psychological processes involved in understanding or in using language, spoken or written. Such a disability may manifest itself in the imperfect ability to listen, think, speak, read, write, spell, or do mathematical calculations. Under IDEA 2004, a local educational agency (LEA) is no longer required to take into consideration whether a child has a severe discrepancy between achievement and intellectual ability in oral expression, listening comprehension, written expression, basic reading skill, reading comprehension, mathematical calculation, or mathematical reasoning (20 U.S.C. 1414, 2004). A local educational agency may use a *response to intervention* or RTI evaluation process—usually implemented by a collaborative team—to determine if a child responds to research-based interventions. RTI will be discussed in greater depth later.

Mental Retardation: substantial limitations in levels of functioning that adversely affect a child's educational performance. It is characterized by significantly impaired intellectual functioning, existing concurrently with deficits in adaptive behavior (the ability to cope with the demands of the environment, self-help, communication, and social skills), and manifested during the early developmental period.

Autism: a developmental disability that significantly affects verbal and nonverbal communication and social interaction, is generally evident before age three, and adversely affects educational performance. Other characteristics include repetitive activities and stereotyped movements, resistance to change in the environment or in daily routines, and unusual responses to sensory experiences. Autism is also referred to as Autism Spectrum Disorder and includes Pervasive Developmental Disorder Not Otherwise Specified (PDD-NOS) and Asperger's Syndrome.

Hearing Impairment (including deafness): means an impairment in hearing, permanent or fluctuating, which adversely affects a child's educational performance.

Speech or Language Impairment: refers to problems in communication and related areas such as oral motor function, stuttering, impaired articulation, language impairments, or a voice impairment that adversely affects a child's educational performance (Hamaguchi, 2001).

Visual Impairment (including blindness): an impairment in vision, including both partial sight and blindness, that even with correction, adversely affects a child's educational performance.

Emotional Disturbance: involves one or more of the following characteristics, displayed over a long period of time and to a marked degree, that adversely affects a child's educational performance including: (1) an inability to learn that cannot be explained by intellectual, sensory, or health factors; (2) an inability to build or maintain satisfactory interpersonal relationships with peers or teachers; (3) inappropriate behavior and feelings under normal circumstances; (4) a general pervasive mood of unhappiness or depression; and (5) a tendency to develop physical symptoms or fears associated with personal or school problems. The term does not apply to children who are "socially maladjusted" or have a "conduct disorder," unless they also have an emotional disability.

Orthopedic Impairments: a severe orthopedic impairment that adversely affects a child's educational performance. The term includes impairments caused by congenital anomaly (i.e., clubfoot, absence of an extremity), impairments caused by disease (i.e., poliomyelitis, bone tuberculosis), and impairments from other causes (i.e., cerebral palsy, amputations, and fractures or burns that cause muscle contractures).

Traumatic Brain Injury: an acquired injury to the brain caused by an external physical force, resulting in total or partial functional disability or psychosocial impairment, or both, that adversely affects a child's educational performance. The term applies to open or closed head injuries resulting in impairments in one or more areas, such as cognition; language; memory; attention; reasoning; abstract thinking; judgment; problem solving; sensory, perceptual, and motor abilities; psychosocial behavior; physical functions; information processing; and speech.

Other Health Impairments: having limited strength, vitality, or alertness, including a heightened alertness to environmental stimuli, which results in limited alertness with respect to the educational environment and which affects educational performance. Such impairments may be due to chronic or acute health problems such as asthma, attention deficit disorder or attention deficit hyperactivity disorder (ADD/HD), diabetes, epilepsy, a heart condition, hemophilia, lead poisoning, leukemia, nephritis, rheumatic fever, and sickle cell anemia.

Defining Students "At Risk"

IDEA 2004 has added new definitions of individuals with special learning needs who are at risk of failing in the educational system. **Students' "at risk"** include students in K–12 public schools who are suspected of having a disability, who need additional academic and behavioral support to succeed in a general education environment, and who are being provided with early intervening services to prevent referral to special education. These individuals also include those who are **limited English proficient**, economically disadvantaged, or migrant (IDEA Amendments, Sec. 601, 613(f)).

Limited English proficient students (also referred to as English Language Learners or ELL) include those aged 3–21 whose difficulties in speaking, reading, writing, or understanding the English language may impact their ability to attain levels of proficiency on state assessments, to achieve in the classroom, or to fully participate in society (NCLB, Sec. 9101). They may either (a) be born outside the United States and have a native language other than English; (b) be Native American or Alaskan native; or (c) be migratory.

Economically disadvantaged students live in families with low incomes according to income data from the U.S. Department of Commerce. Such learners often have life circumstances that predispose them to learning difficulties. The households where youth grow up, the resources available in them, and the characteristics of the families who head them can have implications for students' economic security and emotional support (Wagner, Cameto, & Guzmán, 2003). National data show high rates of dropout and wide gaps in academic achievement between students from low and high socioeconomic communities.

Today these "special" populations represent a majority of students in many school systems across the United States. The percentage of the total school population with disabilities who are receiving special education services ranges from 8.9% nationally (U.S. Department of Education, 2003b, 25th Report to Congress, 2003) to over 20% as reported by some individual states. The percentage of total school population of all of these special learner groups can range from 25–80% in some urban areas (Blechman, Fishman, & Fishman, 2004). Teachers are now expected to work to improve the achievement and development of each of these groups of students.

WHAT PHILOSOPHICAL IDEAS ARE REFLECTED IN OUR EDUCATION LAWS?

Education and disability laws are rooted in several fundamental philosophical ideas. Knowing how these principles and values are embedded in the laws deepens our understanding of the requirements and strengthens skills for implementation. These ideas include equal access, a shared responsibility, inclusion, and full participation.

The movement for full participation and inclusion is an expression of a broad human rights movement that has been in progress for centuries around the world. The term **inclusion** has a relatively long history in the United States. It is an extension of the civil rights movement that arose out of the struggle of African Americans and Native Americans for their freedom in America in the 1800s and early 1900s. Before 1975, more that half of all children with disabilities in the United States were either institutionalized or did not receive educational and support services appropriate to their needs or potential abilities (IDEA, 2004). The U.S. Congress, parents, and advocates recognized that throughout the United States, education, health, and employment outcomes for children and youth with disabilities remained far below those of their typically developing (nondisabled) peers. In response, several federal laws were passed to ensure that state and local educational agencies provided equal access for all children to educational programs and services that were appropriate to their needs. In coordination with community services agencies, schools were required to provide free, appropriate education and supportive services in the least restrictive environment (LRE). Students with disabilities were expected to be educated with their peers without disabilities.

Recent demands to increase educational quality and equity for all children are now being systematically addressed in education and human service policies throughout the states. *Quality improvement* refers to the general effort to define and improve standards in the services provided. *Equity* refers to efforts to decrease *social inequality* by providing *equal access* to and *equal opportunity* for all to benefit from education programs and services available to all (National Center for Education Statistics, 2000; Nieto, 2000; Shapiro, 1990). *Social equality* refers to protecting the rights of the individual, and to a commitment to making cultural experiences and development of human potential (through education) generally available to all (Harvard Civil Rights Project, 2004; Shapiro, 1990). The way schools are organized, the way teachers collaborate to teach, the way curriculum is structured, and the manner in which children with particular disadvantages are supported and included in basic education, can either decrease or perpetuate *social inequality*. Education serves both an ideological and economic role in improving equity in all societies (Hart, Zafft, & Zimbrich, 2001; Shapiro, 1980).

Inclusion, although not a term used in IDEA, generally refers to social and legal mandates designed to ensure that children have access to educational programs and services without regard to race, gender, ethnic origin, age, level of education, or disability. **Full participation** is a broader term used more recently in the United States that refers to educational policies that also emphasize social integration, participation in nonacademic activities and student progress in an educational program, in addition to access. The IDEA 2004 Regulations, released in August 2006, introduced the term *full educational opportunity goal* (FEOG), referring to the requirement that states establish a goal of providing full educational opportunity to all children with disabilities, aged birth through 21 years. Furthermore, the state must ensure that children with disabilities have available to them the variety of educational programs and services available to nondisabled children, including art, music, industrial arts, and vocational education (20 USC 1412(a)(2), 1413(a)(1)). FEOG and inclusion also refer to the provision of the range of necessary support services and guidance needed by a student in order to make necessary progress and to complete an educational program. The concept of full educational opportunity has emerged because of the concerns of educators, policymakers, and families that access to educational programs and support services alone has resulted in minimal improvements in educational, economic, and social outcomes for children and youth. Once children gain access to educational programs and services, professionals within the system are also accountable for their progress and successful completion. Implementation of programs that promote full participation also requires support services to help students make successful transitions from elementary through high school and into employment or postsecondary education.

The philosophy and practice of ensuring full participation also mean that no one lives in isolation, but rather, each student is interconnected or interdependent with other people and with their communities. There is a close interrelationship between the economic participation (employment) and independence of individuals and the economic development of the community and the nation (Arat, 1991; Lynch, 1994; Kochhar & Gopal, 1997; Zuckerman, 2003). In short, learning, earning, and the economy are interconnected.

An effective education system must be inclusive of all children and youth for whom productive employment and community participation are long-term goals. Educators and policymakers recognize the connections among education, personal decision making, and the ability to participate in the work of a community. In order to shift resources from supporting people in states of dependency (welfare and social services) to the arena of independence and self-sufficiency, a community invests in education and training for all children and youth (Center for Workforce Development, 2003; Lynch, 1994). Therefore, *concepts of liberty, democracy, and individual rights are integrated into educational planning at local, state and national levels.*

Educational reform initiatives over the past several decades have emerged to help students with disabilities and learners at risk to succeed in inclusive settings. These principles and strategies associated with the *special education paradigm* include (1) individualized education programming to accommodate diverse needs, (2) interdisciplinary teacher collaboration and service coordination, (3) modified and alternative educational performance standards (4) strategies for family and community involvement, (5) peer and mentor support models, (6) supports for the multiple transitions throughout school years, and (7) work preparation and community-based learning options (Bailey, 2001; Center for Workforce Development, 2003; Greene & Kochhar-Bryant, 2003).

Several changes in philosophy about integrating people with differences into general society have accelerated the inclusion movement for children and youth with disabilities. Over the past few decades, service models have focused less on "fixing" problems within the individual and more on seeking ways to change educational environments in order to build capacity to improve the development and learning of all children. Some in the disability community advocate for a shift from disability-centered terms and the label "inclusion program," and toward broader terms that emphasize a change in the culture of schooling. Such a culture embraces the responsibility to celebrate diversity in the full sense of the term, emphasizing standards of quality and equity for educating all children.

WHY DO FEDERAL POLICIES PROMOTE SCHOOL COLLABORATION AND SYSTEM COORDINATION?

Fulfilling the Intent of the Laws

Collaboration and system coordination strategies represent promising interventions that engage both schools and the community in a **shared responsibility** to improve the achievement of all students. It is important to understand how current laws emphasize the role of collaboration and system coordination for implementing core provisions. Figure 4.1 depicts the continuum of shared responsibility among professionals and agencies.

The Individuals with Disabilities Education Improvement Act of 2004 (P.L. 108–446) holds schools responsible for ensuring that students with disabilities receive appropriate educational and related services and transition assistance. Lawmakers recognize that planning for education and support services cannot be done in isolation, but must reach beyond the school boundaries into the community. As a result, the IDEA required schools to establish linkages with community-based and postsecondary agencies and to share the responsibility for education and transition supports. States are required to establish statewide, coordinated service systems for students with disabilities, ages 3 to 21, who need services from the school and other community-based human service agencies (unless the 3 to 5 age group or 19 to 21 age group is inconsistent with state law).

FIGURE 4.1

A Shared Responsibility for the Service System

Source: Adapted from *Successful Inclusion: Practical Strategies for a Shared Responsibility* (p. 112), by C. Kochhar, L. West, and J. Taymans, 2000, Upper Saddle River, NJ: Merrill/Prentice Hall. Reprinted by permission.

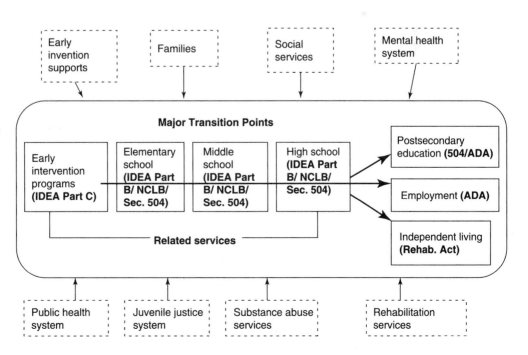

The No Child Left Behind Act of 2001 (NCLB), first authorized as the Elementary and Secondary Education Act of 1965, also requires strategic cross-agency planning as well as collaboration for students' transition plans. In addition, two civil rights laws—the Americans With Disabilities Act of 1990 (ADA) and **Section 504 of the Rehabilitation Act of 1973** (and 1998 amendments) protect individuals against discrimination on the basis of disability in education and employment settings. These laws are discussed later in this chapter.

New Emphasis on Accountability

Over the past few decades, educators, policymakers, and the general public have been concerned about the effectiveness of public education programs and how well they provide equitable opportunities for all students. During the 1950s, 1960s, and 1970s, with the passage of Brown *v* Board of Education of Topeka, Kansas, and the Education for All Handicapped Children Act of 1975 (P.L. 94–142), educational reforms centered on achieving equity and increasing general access to public schools for all students without regard to race or disability. The single largest source of federal support for K–12 education was the Elementary and Secondary Education Act (ESEA of 1965), the centerpiece of President Lyndon Johnson's War on Poverty. After 1965, providing equal educational opportunity was insufficient, and the goal of achieving equal, or near-equal, outcomes for all students, regardless of race, class, religion, ethnicity, or sex, became the new benchmark. Access alone was insufficient; public schools had to educate all children (Lagemann, 2000).

Since the 1980s, educational improvement legislation, including IDEA 2004 and the No Child Left Behind Act of 2001 (NCLB, 107–110), has sought to improve public school programs for *all students* (National Center for Secondary Education and Transition, 2002). These laws promote comprehensive planning to enable all students to achieve high academic standards, while holding educators responsible for the progress of students. The ESEA of 1994 encouraged the states to adopt two types of voluntary standards: (1) *content standards* which identify what students are to learn in one subject (P.L. 103–227, sec. 3 (4)) and (2) *performance standards* that define the quality of the performance considered satisfactory (sec. 3 (9)). When ESEA was reauthorized in 2001 as the No Child Left Behind Act, it strengthened the focus on curriculum standards, requiring states and districts to develop challenging academic content standards and state assessments (Kochhar Bryant & Bassett, 2002a).

Students with disabilities are expected to be included, to the extent possible, in the general education curriculum and in standardized assessments. To support these goals, educational laws reflect stronger mandates for collaboration between general and special education teachers; between teachers and related services professionals; among teachers, families, and students; between preschool and elementary schools; between elementary and middle schools; between middle and high schools; between high schools and postsecondary institutions (colleges and universities); and between school and community agencies. NCLB and IDEA 2004 emphasize that children with disabilities must be considered to be general education students first. States are responsible for implementing a single accountability system for all students based on strong academic standards for what every child should know and be able to do, including children with disabilities. The following sections describe federal education laws that promote collaboration and system coordination as central strategies for achieving the goals of educational excellence and equity for all children.

HOW DOES IDEA PROMOTE COLLABORATION AND SYSTEM COORDINATION? EARLY CHILDHOOD TO POSTSECONDARY

Why a Special Law for Individuals With Disabilities?

In 1975, Congress passed the **Education for All Handicapped Children Act of 1975** (Public Law 94–142). At the time, most children with disabilities were not receiving an education appropriate to their needs, or were served in institutions or segregated schools, or remained at home. More than one-half of the children with disabilities in the United States were not receiving appropriate educational services. Over one million children were entirely excluded from the public school system and did not complete the educational process with their peers. Many children with disabilities were participating in regular school programs, but their disabilities were undetected and prevented them from having a successful educational experience. Because of the lack of adequate services within the public school system, families were often forced to find services outside the public school system, often at great distance and at their own expense. Congress recognized that these conditions for children demanded federal intervention and a civil rights law (Education for All Handicapped Children Act, 1975, Findings).

Since 1975, more than 30 years of research has demonstrated that outcomes for children with disabilities improve with (a) higher expectations; (b) increased access to the general curriculum; (c) stronger parent participation; (d) coordination of educational services with other community agencies; (e) inclusion of students with disabilities in school improvement efforts; and (f) high-quality, intensive professional development for all personnel who work with children with disabilities in order to address their learning needs (IDEA, 2004; U.S. Senate Report 108–185, 2003).

What Is the Purpose of IDEA?

The driving purpose of IDEA (as it was first authorized in 1975 as P.L. 94–143) was to ensure that all children with disabilities, ages 3–21 (varies in some states), have available to them a **free appropriate public education** that emphasizes special education and related services. Such services are to be provided in the *least restrictive environment*, designed to meet students' unique needs, and prepare them for college, employment, and independent living. The least restrictive environment means an educational setting in which a child with a disability can receive a free, appropriate public education while being educated to the extent possible with her or her nondisabled peers.

The aim of the law then and now is to equalize the opportunity for children with disabilities to become all that they can be academically and socially. The act is designed to ensure that the rights of children with disabilities and their parents are protected. Furthermore, the act is designed to assist states, local school districts, and school-linked agencies to support the education of all children with disabilities.

In the 1980s, Congress expanded the target group to include children ages 0–5 and charged states with implementing statewide, comprehensive, coordinated, multidisciplinary, interagency systems of **early intervention services** for infants and toddlers with disabilities and their families. Recognizing that schools would need extra resources to create systemic change and improve results, the act provided funding for coordinated research and preparation of personnel; coordinated technical assistance, information dissemination, and support; and technology development and media services. Finally, the act was to monitor the progress of students in education. The words *coordination* and *collaboration* appear throughout the act, reflecting lawmakers' understanding that personnel in schools and community agencies needed to work together to improve results for children.

Resources and Flexibility to Build a Coordinated Service System

Under IDEA 2004, Congress sent a clear signal about its commitment to coordinated services, particularly in the early years, and included many new provisions specifically designed to expand cooperative arrangements at the federal, state, and local levels. These provisions include (1) state and local interagency agreements; (2) flexibility to allow local educational agencies discretionary use of 15% of the total federal allotment to develop and implement coordinated early intervening services for students, grades K–12 (focusing on K–1), who need extra academic and behavioral support to succeed in the general education environment; (3) requirements for coordination between Part C (early intervention services) and Part B (K–12 special education services) to ensure a smooth transition of services; (4) resources to promote systematic school interventions, behavioral supports, and services in interim alternative education settings; and (5) resources to support stronger links between schools and school-based community mental health services, and to improve interim alternative education settings by promoting interagency coordination of service delivery (Sec. 300.154; 300.74). Although local flexibility is permitted in choosing how to design a coordinated service system, all initiatives are expected to be designed *to improve results for children and families*, including children with disabilities and their families (20 U.S.C. 1413[f]).

Collaboration and "Civil Rights" Under IDEA (Procedural Safeguards)

IDEA ensures that any state or local educational agency that receives funding through IDEA establishes and maintains **procedural safeguards** that protect the rights of children with disabilities to receive a free appropriate public education. Procedures that protect children's rights include (a) the provision of a free appropriate public education; (b) the opportunity for the parents of a child with a disability to examine all records relating to their child; (c) the opportunity to participate in meetings related to the identification, evaluation, and educational placement of the child; (d) the right to obtain an independent educational evaluation; (e) written prior notice to parents in the native language when there is a proposed change in the identification, evaluation, or educational placement of the child; and (f) an opportunity to present complaints with respect to any matter relating to the identification, evaluation, educational placement, or provision of a free appropriate public education (IDEA, Sec. 1415).

Collaboration, Dispute Resolution, and Mediation. Procedural safeguards not only protect rights, but also protect and strengthen the collaborative process between parents and professionals by providing a constructive way to resolve disagreements.

Disagreements can arise between parents and professionals over issues such as identification of students' needs for special education, developing and implementing IEPs, and determining the appropriate education setting. Collaboration among professionals and families is essential to resolve disagreements.

School districts and families have at least three formal processes for resolving disagreements or disputes: state complaint procedures, due process hearings, and mediation. A *state complaint procedure* is a review by the state education agency (SEA) to determine whether a state or a local school district has violated IDEA. A *due process hearing* is an administrative process in which an impartial hearing officer receives evidence, provides for the examination and cross-examination of witnesses by each party, and then provides a report of the findings of facts and decisions. In order to provide an alternative, less costly, and less adversarial process for resolving conflicts, the 1997 and 2004 IDEA amendments required that states offer opportunities for voluntary mediation when a request for a due process hearing is filed (20 USC 1415, 2004).

Mediation is a negotiation process that employs an impartial mediator to help people in conflict resolve their disputes through the development of a mutually accepted written agreement. IDEA strongly encouraged states to promote the use of mediation to resolve disagreements (U.S. Government Accountability Office, 2003e). The effectiveness of these procedures in protecting families and children, and ensuring that schools comply with the law, depend on close coordination and communication among school personnel, mediation specialists, attorneys, and families when complaints arise. Mediation can provide an opportunity for professionals to strengthen or repair relationships between parents and professionals, resolve disputes at a much lower costs, and share information with parents about services and how they can best utilize the system.

Collaboration and the Least Restrictive Environment

IDEA mandates that, to the maximum extent appropriate, children with disabilities, including children in public or private institutions or other care facilities, are expected to be educated in the **least restrictive environment** (LRE) with children who are not disabled. The use of special or separate classes, separate schooling, or other removal of children with disabilities from the regular educational environment should occur only when the nature or severity of the disability of a child is so problematic that educating the child in the general education class with the use of supplementary aids and services cannot be achieved satisfactorily (20 USC 1412, 2004). Close collaboration and communication among special and general education teachers and related service personnel, through the IEP process, is essential for decisions related to LRE. Such decisions include determining the extent to which children will be included in general education classes, their removal from such classes, and the supports provided within those classes or in alternative education settings.

Collaboration and the Individualized Education Plan

The process of developing and implementing an **individualized education plan** (IEP) for a child with a disability depends on considerable collaboration among people and agencies. The IEP is essentially a legally required service contract between the student/family and the educational service system. The effectiveness of that contract depends on how well the partners collaborate to assess students' needs, determine appropriate educational and related services to meet the needs, and deliver those services as planned. Specifically, the contract, or written statement for each child with a disability (in preschool or elementary through high school), includes information on:

a. the child's present levels of academic achievement and functional performance, including how the disability affects the child's involvement and progress in the general education curriculum, or participation in appropriate activities in the case of preschool children;

b. measurable annual goals, including academic and functional goals designed to meet the child's needs and enable the child to participate in and make progress in the general education curriculum;

c. how the child's progress towards meeting annual goals will be measured and when periodic reports on the child's progress will be provided (e.g., use of quartly reports along with report cards);

d. a statement of special education, related services, supplementary aids, and services needed by the child;

e. program modifications or supports for school personnel that will be provided to enable the child attain their annual IEP goals, to make progress in the general education curriculum, and to participate in extracurricular and other nonacademic activities with nondisabled peers;

f. extent, if any, to which the child will not participate with nondisabled children in the regular class and nonacademic activities;

g. individual appropriate modifications that are necessary to measure the academic achievement and functional performance of a child on state and districtwide assessments of student achievements (if the IEP team determines that the child will not participate in such an assessment or will participate in an alternate assessment, a rationale statement is included with an explanation of how the child will be assessed);

h. the projected date for the beginning of the services and modifications and the anticipated frequency, location, and duration of those services and modifications;

i. beginning not later than the first IEP to be in effect when the child turns 16 (or younger, if determined appropriate by the IEP team), and updated annually, a statement of the appropriate, measurable postsecondary goals based on age-appropriate transition assessments related to training, education, employment, and independent living skills and the transition services, including courses of study, needed to assist the child to reach their goals; and

j. beginning not later than one year before the child reaches the age of majority under state law (typically 18 or 21), a statement that the child has been informed of the rights under Part B that will transfer to him or her upon reaching the age of majority (20 USC 1414, 2004).

The IEP is the *service contract* for the student that brings together the IEP team.

The IEP Team: A Collaborative System. IEP planning is designed to be a coordinated process among professionals and programs within the school and often between schools and community service agencies as children progress through the years and prepare for advancement from one grade level to the next. The IEP team means a collaborative group that includes (1) the student and his or her parents; (2) at least one regular education teacher of such child (if the child is, or may be, participating in the regular education environment); (3) at least one special education teacher; (4) a representative of the local educational agency that is providing services to the child; (5) an individual who can interpret the instructional implications of evaluation results; and (6) individuals invited by the parents who have knowledge or special expertise regarding the child, including related services personnel.

The child's general education teacher is also a member of the IEP team and should participate in the development of the IEP of the child, including the determination of appropriate positive behavioral interventions and strategies and the determination of supplementary aids and services, program modifications, and support for school personnel. Finally, and most importantly, the child with a disability should be included on the IEP team and be prepared to participate in the meeting to extent possible, including directing the meeting if the student is capable.

Differences Between the IEP and Section 504 Plans

There has been confusion about the relationship between IEPs and individual plans under Section 504 of the Rehabilitation Act (504 Plans). Successful collaboration depends on understanding their differences. The federal government provides school districts with a portion of the per-pupil expenditure (through Part B of IDEA) to cover special education costs, in combination with state and local funds. Section 504 is governed by the Office of Civil Rights, and schools are obligated to provide services or accommodations to students with disabilities at their own expense. *It is important to understand that Section 504 falls under the management responsibility of the general education program.*

Section 504 was enacted to "level the playing field"—to eliminate impediments to full participation—by persons with disabilities who are not eligible for services or identified under IDEA. In legal terms, the statute was intended to prevent intentional or unintentional discrimination against persons with disabilities, persons who are believed to have disabilities, or family members of persons with disabilities (Rosenfeld, 2005). If a child is found ineligible for special services and accommodations under IDEA, he or she may still qualify for services under Section 504. Any person who (1) has a physical or mental impairment that substantially limits one or more major life activity, (2) has a record of such an impairment, or (3) is regarded as having such an impairment is eligible for a Section 504 plan (Rehabilitation Act, Sec. 504). Major life activities include walking, seeing, hearing, speaking, breathing, learning, working, caring for oneself, and performing manual tasks. Section 504 requires the development of a plan, but it is not required to be written. Section 504 requires students to be educated with nondisabled peers to the maximum extent appropriate. Though enacted almost 25 years ago, until recently Section 504 has been virtually ignored by schools (Rosenfeld, 2005).

The objective of Section 504 is to remove barriers that could stop a capable student from accessing or progressing in general education. For example, the physical layout of a school might prevent a child in a wheelchair from entering the computer lab, or a faulty air conditioning system might prevent a student with asthma from attending chemistry class. A student with attention deficit disorder may not need special education services and may be able to perform adequately within the general education class with some help with organizing subjects and project work. Often 504 plans include fairly minor accommodations for students with disabilities. In the first two examples, the student's disability does not affect his or her learning, only access—it is the environment that needs "special attention." In the third example, the student can perform in the general education curriculum with only minor accommodations.

The IEP, on the other hand, addresses the needs of students whose disabilities significantly interfere with their learning so that they need *specialized instruction and supports* to progress in general education or special education classes. Eligibility requirements for special education are much more specific than those of Section 504, as discussed earlier.

Like IDEA, parents of students with 504 Plans must be notified regarding identification, evaluation, changes in the plan, or a significant change in placement. Written notice is recommended. Furthermore, similar to IDEA, evaluation and placement procedures under Section 504 require that information be obtained from a variety of sources in the area of concern; that all data are documented and considered; and that decisions are made by a group of persons knowledgeable about the student, evaluation data, and placement options. Section 504 requires periodic reevaluations, but does not specify any timelines for such evaluations. To be in compliance with Section 504, schools must (1) provide written assurance of nondiscrimination; (2) designate a 504 coordinator to manage the program; (3) provide grievance procedures to resolve complaints; (4) provide notice of nondiscrimination in admission or access to its programs or activities (in a student/parent handbook); (5) provide parents or guardians with procedural safeguards; (6) annually identify and locate all qualified children with disabilities who are not receiving a public education; (7) annually notify persons with disabilities and their parents or guardians of the district's responsibilities under Section 504; and (8) conduct a self-evaluation of school district policies, programs, and practices to make sure discrimination is not occurring. Figure 4.2 presents a flowchart for decisions about IEPs and 504 plans.

Box 4.1 and 4.2 provide case examples and questions for discussion.

Related and support services are crucial for helping students progress in the educational setting and achieve IEP goals. Connecting the students with these services requires close collaboration among professionals within the school and with community agencies. The term **related services** means services that are required to assist a student with a disability to benefit from special education, including transportation; developmental, corrective, and other supportive services including speech–language pathology and audiology services; psychological services; physical and occupational therapy; recreation; social work and counseling services; orientation and mobility services; medical services for diagnostic purposes; and early identification and assessment. The term **supplementary aids and services** means, aids, services, and other supports provided in the general or special education class to enable children with disabilities to be educated with nondisabled children to the maximum extent appropriate. Examples include modifications to the curriculum or classroom, extended time to complete tasks, assistive technology, or an aide or notetaker.

Early Intervention and Preschool Under IDEA

Services to children with disabilities, ages 5–21, began with the Education for All Handicapped Children Act, Public Law 94–142, in 1975. In 1986 and 1990, the law extended free and appropriate public education to preschoolers with disabilities

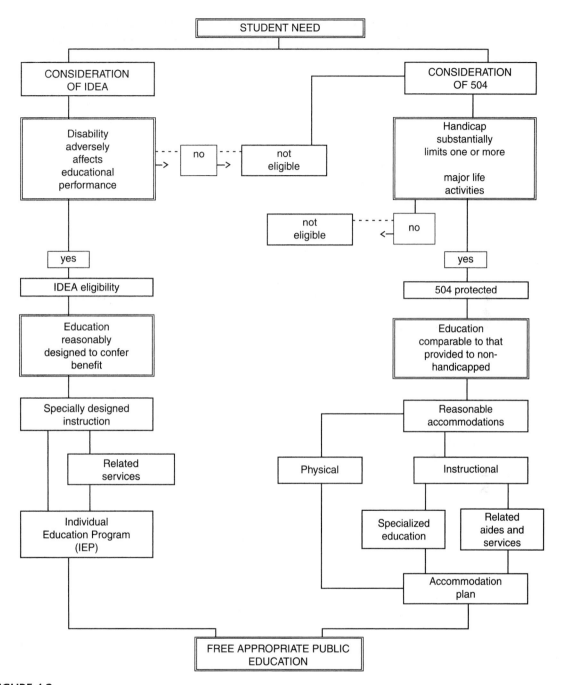

FIGURE 4.2

IDEA/504 Flow Chart

Source: From *Section 504 and the ADA Promoting Student Access: A Resource Guide for Educators,* by Council of Administrators of Special Education, Inc. Albuquerque, NM: Author. Reprinted with permission.

BOX 4.1   IEP and 504 Plan: Case Analysis 1

Joel is a 15-year-old with a moderate to severe permanent hearing loss. Without his hearing aid, he cannot hear normal conversation, but can hear loud noises. When he wears his hearing aid, he can hear within the normal range although there is distortion if there is loud background noise. He does not need a sign language interpreter and has no other disabilities. Joel has been identified under IDEA as a student with a disability since he was 3 years of age when his hearing impairment was first diagnosed. Each year his IEP has included special education services and speech and language therapy.

At his IEP meeting, the team decides that he no longer qualifies for special education services or speech and language therapy because he is now at grade level. He works hard as a student and gets mostly Bs. Some team members are concerned that he still be provided with accommodations, such as extra time for testing or testing in a quiet setting. Consider the following:

1. Is he eligible for accommodations under Section 504? If so, what accommodations do you think he needs?
2. Who do you think should be involved in his 504 team?
3. If not eligible, how would you assure that he continues to receive the support he needs?

BOX 4.2   IEP and 504 Plan: Case Analysis 2

Theresa is 8 years old and in third grade. Although she has received individual reading support from her classroom teachers and is now receiving remedial reading, she remains at 6 months below grade level in reading. She has just been diagnosed by her physician as having attention deficit disorder without hyperactivity. Her ADD symptoms include difficulty paying attention to and remembering verbal information and high distractibility. Her doctor reports that he believes that her ADD behaviors could substantially impair her ability to learn in a general education classroom without accommodations. Theresa's classroom teacher has a different opinion. She describes Teresa as unmotivated. She says Teresa gets into conflicts with her peers because she is "nosey" and talks too much in class. Consider these questions:

1. Is Teresa eligible for accommodations under Section 504?
2. What accommodations do you think she needs? Should she be involved in her 504 team?
3. If not eligible, how would you ensure that she receives the support she needs?

---

and established a new discretionary program for infants, toddlers, and their families (Part H, now called Part C). The purpose of the Part C program was to (1) enhance the development of infants and toddlers with disabilities and to minimize their potential for developmental delay; and (2) enhance the capacity of families to meet the special needs of their infants and toddlers with disabilities.

Early Intervention Law Includes Infants, Toddlers, and Young Children.   IDEA 2004 includes two programs for young children and their families: (1) the *Early Intervention Programs for Infants and Toddlers with Disabilities, Part C*, which is designed to enhance the development of infants & toddlers from birth through age 2; and (2) the *Preschool Program of Part B*, which provides services to children from ages 3–5. The purpose of the Part C program is to (a) enhance the development of infants and toddlers with disabilities and to minimize their potential for developmental delay; (b) enhance the capacity of families to meet the special needs of their infants and toddlers with disabilities; (c) provide financial assistance to increase the capacity of state and local agencies to create statewide, comprehensive, coordinated, multidisciplinary, interagency systems of services for children birth to age 3 with disabilities or developmental delays.

Together these programs represent an important effort to expand the scope of services available to the nation's youngest children with disabilities and their families. Public schools are required to provide special education and related services to young children before they enter first grade. Data from the 2005 school year show that 2.3% of the nation's infants and toddlers, ages 0 to 3, and 5% of all U.S. preschool-age children were served under IDEA (U.S. Department of Education, 2003; Westat, 2006).

Defining Children Who Need Early Intervention.

An *infant or toddler with a disability* means a child under 3 years of age who needs early intervention services because she or he is (1) experiencing substantial developmental delays, as measured by appropriate diagnostic instruments and procedures in one or more of the areas of cognitive development, physical development, communication development, social or emotional development, and adaptive development; or (2) has a diagnosed physical or mental condition which has a high probability of resulting in developmental delay and may be an at risk infant or toddler (20 USC 1432, 2004). In order to determine eligibility, a timely, comprehensive, multidisciplinary evaluation of the functioning of each infant or toddler must be conducted along with an assessment of family needs to assist their infant or toddler. Furthermore, each infant or toddler with a disability in the state must have an **individualized family services plan** (IFSP) that includes provisions for service coordination (20 USC 1401, 2004).

What Services Must Be Provided?

Early intervention services for children age 3 years and younger means services are designed to meet the developmental needs of infants or toddlers with disabilities, in areas such as physical and cognitive development, communication, social and emotional development, and speech and hearing. Examples of early intervention services include family training, counseling, service coordination services, home visits, special instruction, speech-language and audiology services, occupational therapy, early identification and screening, health services, social work services, vision services, assistive technology devices, and transportation.

These services, to the extent possible, are most effective when provided in natural and inclusive environments such as the child's home and in community settings in which children without disabilities participate (IDEA, 1997, 2004). A multidisciplinary assessment and an IFSP developed by a multidisciplinary team and the parents is an essential part of early intervention services (20 USC 1435, 2004). Service coordination or case management services are expected to be available for every eligible child and his or her parents. The IFSP must identify the service coordinator who will be responsible for the implementation of the plan and coordination with other agencies and persons, including transition services (20 USC 436, 2004).

Quality early intervention services are provided by qualified personnel, including special educators, speech–language pathologists and audiologists, occupational therapists, physical therapists, psychologists, social workers, nurses, nutritionists, family therapists, orientation and mobility specialists, and pediatricians and other physicians (20 USC 1432, 2004). Training of personnel should prepare them to coordinate transition services for infants and toddlers with disabilities from an early intervention program to preschool or other appropriate services.

Ages 3 to 5. When a child with disabilities nears the age of 3, he or she must be considered for services beyond early intervention services. These services include, but are not limited to, special education preschool programs (under Part B of the IDEA), Head Start programs, and public or private preschool programs. Planning for transition services occurs at this time to ensure that children continue to receive services and support as they move within and between service delivery systems, such as from early intervention to preschool.

Special education preschool programs are available to children with disabilities who are 3 to 5 years old. If a child is eligible for preschool special education services, he or she must have an Individualized Education Program (IEP) in place by age 3, unless the child is continuing to receive early intervention services under Part C (20 USC 1419, 2004). The person responsible for ensuring the completion of the transition and service plan is the service coordinator. The service coordinator is required to inform a child's local school district that the child is nearing the age of 3 and must, with the permission of the family, schedule a meeting with the family, other team members, and the local school district representative. The purpose of this meeting, which must be held at least 120 days before the child's 3rd birthday, is to discuss what is needed to determine whether the child is eligible for special education preschool services. A representative of the child's local school district must attend this transition planning conference. Team members review existing evaluations, assessments, and progress reports. If the team determines that it is likely that the child will be eligible for special education preschool services, a multifactored evaluation is completed to determine the areas of documented disability or deficit, and an IEP is then developed.

Coordination for Transition to Preschool. The 2004 reauthorizations of IDEA included an emphasis on "transition from Part C to Preschool Programs." Researchers and practitioners had brought to the attention of lawmakers the fact that too many children participating in Part C early intervention were not experiencing a smooth and effective transition to preschool programs (Government Accountability Office, 2005a). The parents and the local education agency are required to participate in transition planning conferences (Individualized Family Service Plan, IFSP) arranged by the designated lead agency. At the system level, each state is required to develop a statewide system to support such transition planning for children and their families. The state must establish an interagency coordinating council and a plan for interagency agreements between early intervention, preschool, and other early intervention programs (e.g., Head Start) (20 USC 1412, 2004).

Collaboration and Coordination in Middle School, Secondary Education, and Transition From High School

In an effective educational system, youth with disabilities participate in transition planning as far in advance as possible before graduation. As with all students, career interests and postsecondary options are considered in the middle school so that the course of study can be determined as the student moves into high school. In high school, postsecondary goals become more crystallized as a student's interests, preferences, and abilities are assessed. Through a process of backward planning from the postsecondary goal, a program of study and support is designed to advance the student toward graduation goals. Postsecondary goals may include college, employment, or military. **Transition services** means a coordinated set of activities for a child that:

1. is designed to be within a results-oriented process that is focused on improving academic and functional achievement and that promotes movement from school to postschool activities, including postsecondary education, vocational education, integrated employment (including supported employment), continuing and adult education, adult services, independent living, or community participation;
2. is based upon the individual's needs, taking into account the student's preferences and interests; and
3. includes instruction, related services, community experiences, the development of employment and other postschool adult living objectives, and, if appropriate, acquisition of daily living skills and functional vocational evaluation (20 USC 1401, 2004).

The IEP, beginning no later than the first IEP in effect when the child turns 16 (or younger if determined appropriate by the IEP team) and updated annually, must include a statement of appropriate measurable postsecondary goals based on age-appropriate transition assessments related to training, education, employment and independent living skills. The student's success will depend on his or her active participation in establishing postsecondary goals and a secondary course of study, and the collaboration among parents and professionals.

System Coordination for Transition.   Transition services depend on the formal ability of schools and community agencies, including postsecondary institutions, to coordinate to provide the transition services described in the student's IEP. For example, if the IEP indicates that the student needs an assessment for vocational rehabilitation services by the VR agency, for example, but that agency cannot provide such an assessment, then the local education agency is required to reconvene the IEP team to identify alternative ways to meet the transition objectives.

The 1997 IDEA required that the IEP contain a "statement of needed transition services for the child, including, when appropriate, a statement of the interagency responsibilities or any needed linkages." The 2004 IDEA deleted this specific language, but preserves language under the definition of the IEP and its components that the IEP include the projected date for the beginning of services and modifications, the anticipated frequency, location and duration of those services (20 USC 1414, 2004).

Furthermore, if a participating agency fails to provide the transition services described in the IEP, the local educational agency shall reconvene the IEP team to identify alternative strategies to meet the transition objectives for the child set out in the IEP (20 USC 1414, 2004). Interagency responsibility to provide needed services to support students' programs of study and postsecondary goals continues to be an expectation. This requirement for interagency collaboration and shared responsibility means that (a) schools must develop a seamless system of supports to assist the student to make a successful transition to postsecondary life; (b) the student and family must be engaged in transition planning well before graduation; and (c) there must be formal interagency agreements between schools and cooperating agencies.

Education Laws Align General and Special Education and Promote Collaboration

Educators are grappling with many complex questions as they attempt to comply with the mandate to improve access to the general education curriculum for students with disabilities (Center on Education Policy, 2003). How can the standards-based curriculum be reconciled or aligned with the individualized education process? How should students with disabilities be included in standardized assessments? The standards-based education model is grounded in the assumption that all students should meet *common standards* for what should be taught and learned. However, the individualized education process is grounded in the principle of "appropriate" education that meets *individual education needs* of each student. As a result, professional collaboration to align these two systems has taken center stage in IDEA 2004 and NCLB.

WHAT PROVISIONS OF THE NO CHILD LEFT BEHIND ACT OF 2001 PROMOTE COLLABORATION AND SYSTEM COORDINATION?

The **No Child Left Behind Act of 2001** (NCLB) is the most sweeping reform of the Elementary and Secondary Education Act (ESEA) since it was enacted in 1965. It redefines the federal role in K–12 education and aims to help close the achievement gap between disadvantaged and minority students and their peers. The ESEA is the principal federal law that affects education from kindergarten through high school. The four "pillars" of the act are (1) accountability for results, (2) emphasis on doing what works based on scientific research, (3) expanded parental options, and (4) expanded local control and flexibility. The new law requires states to test children annually in reading and math from third to eighth grades, and to analyze and report the results publicly by race, English proficiency, income, and disability. Schools have until 2014 for all students to reach the levels of proficiency on standardized tests that are established by the states.

The goals are ambitious, but there is broad recognition that schools cannot work alone to achieve the expected results. NCLB incorporates service coordination and school–community collaboration as a primary policy instrument for creating change. There are many provisions within the act that require new levels of formal coordination between schools and community agencies in order to share responsibility for improving education to help students achieve new academic standards. These are discussed in the following sections.

Local Educational Agency Coordination of Services

Each local educational agency (LEA) must have a plan for implementing NCLB (NCLB, Title I, Part A). These local plans must describe how the LEA will coordinate with other agency services to children, youth, and families and integrate services with other educational initiatives or programs at the local educational agency or individual school level (e.g., Head Start, Reading First, preschool programs, transition from preschool to elementary, programs for English language learners, adult education, vocational and technical education, children with disabilities, migratory and homeless children, immigrant children, neglected or delinquent youth, Native American children) (20 USC 6312, 2002). It is expected that such coordination will increase the effectiveness of the programs, eliminate duplication of services, and reduce fragmentation of the instructional program (U.S. Department of Education, 2004b).

Schoolwide Reform Strategies for Adequate Yearly Progress

Like IDEA, the NCLB promotes schoolwide reforms to improve results for all children in the school, but particularly the needs of low-achieving children and those at risk of not meeting the state academic achievement standards. Such reforms may include counseling, college and career awareness, career guidance, personal finance education, applied learning and team-teaching strategies, integration of vocational and technical education programs, violence prevention programs, nutrition programs, Head Start, and reading readiness programs (20 USC 6311, 2002).

NCLB funds may also be used for targeted assistance to schools for comprehensive services. *Targeted assistance* means providing resources to help specific groups of students who are at risk for not meeting the state academic achievement standards, for dropping out, or who are identified as having the greatest need for special assistance (NCLB, Title I, Part A., Sec. 1115). Targeted assistance may include health, nutrition, social services, provision of basic medical equipment (e.g., eyeglasses and hearing aids), service coordination, and professional development of teachers, parents, and related services personnel. To implement a targeted assistance plan, the school is required to conduct a comprehensive needs assessment and to establish a formal collaborative partnership with local service providers.

Under NCLB, schools are expected to make **adequate yearly progress** (AYP) toward meeting state student academic achievement goals. In passing NCLB, Congress recognized that some schools experience chronic underachievement, and the performance of students on standardized tests in those schools was unacceptable. The AYP status of a school is determined using student assessment data, but the data must be broken out by subgroups of students (general education, students in special education, English language learners, low-income students, and specific ethnic groups) (20 USC 6311, 2002). One hundred percent of students in general education, and in each subgroup (with a 1% exception for students with disabilities) must reach the state-defined *proficient* levels in reading and math assessments by 2013–14 (U.S. Department of Education, 2004). A lack of progress (10% improvement is required each year) by any of these subgroups could cause an entire school to be designated as *needing improvement* under the federal definition.

Reassessments of these accountability requirements will be conducted by the U.S. Department of Education in the coming years.

Districts and schools that fail to make AYP toward that goal face a series of escalating consequences. If a school fails to achieve AYP, then a system of corrective actions come into play to help the school improve. These include the following:

1. Level 1, School Improvement Status (Missed AYP for 2 years): Revise the school improvement plan for a 2-year period, seek technical assistance, and provide students with an option to transfer to another school.

2. Level 2, School Improvement Status (Missed AYP for 3 years): Make supplemental educational services (e.g., tutoring) available to students through approved providers and continue to make transfer options available.

3. Level 3, Corrective Action Status (Missed AYP for 4 years): Implement a corrective plan identified by the district and continue requirement in Level 2.

4. Levels 4 and 5, Restructuring Status (Missed AYP for 5 or 6 years): Prepare a plan for major restructuring of the school and its governance (20 USC 6311, 2001).

NCLB requires that each local education agency receiving funds have a plan for implementing the law, including processes for coordination and integration of services for all children. For example, in many schools seeking to improve the performance of all students, especially those with disabilities and from high-risk groups, specialists are being trained as in-school service coordinators with case-loads of students for whom they are responsible. These coordinators become the main contacts for the students, help arrange support services when needed, obtain assessments, and maintain records of service needs and progress of each student. Examples of service coordination activities, which support broad change efforts and school restructuring, include those that (a) restructure preschool programs to incorporate health and social services to improve general readiness for elementary school; (b) restructure schools, classrooms, teaching, and curriculum to improve basic academic and vocational outcomes for students in K–12 and incorporate social service and family supports; and (c) restructure secondary schools to better link with two- and four-year colleges and provide outreach to adults in need of retraining and continuing education (Volpe, Batra, Bomio, & Costin, 1999). Administrators report that coordinating with other organizations to meet the needs of special learners improves student outcomes, expands schools' access to resources, increases efficiency and effectiveness by engaging students and families, and builds stronger schools and communities (American Association of School Administrators, 2001).

How Do NCLB and IDEA Differ in Principles and Policies?

In considering the twin goals of excellence and equity in education, it is important to distinguish between the principles of NCLB and IDEA. For more than three decades, the primary policy tool for improving outcomes for students with disabilities has been the special education law, now known as the Individuals with Disabilities Education Improvement Act and its provisions for free and appropriate education and protection of individual rights and individualized education programming. Standards-based education under NCLB has introduced a fundamentally different set of policies and practices that are based on uniform learning standards within a *standards-based curriculum*. The students' mastery of the curriculum content is measured by standardized tests or assessments. Standards-based education (SBE) is based on the assumption that *common standards for all students* are a catalyst for improved educational results and serve as a basis for what should be taught and for measuring what students should be expected to know (Kochhar-Bryant & Bassett, 2003; McDonnel, McLaughlin, & Morison, 1997). SBE is also based on the assumptions that content and performance standards can be clearly and precisely defined, student performance can be measured validly and reliably, and accountability can be strengthened through public reporting of aggregate data on student performance.

In contrast to the assumption of common performance standards, special education services are guided by the special education framework which defines the rights of students with disabilities to a free and appropriate education and specifies the responsibilities of school systems to accommodate their individual needs (McDonnel, McLaughlin, & Morison, 1997). Individualized education relies on a *private process*—the IEP is centered on the *needs of the individual student*, and *students' individual rights* are enforced through a set of procedural safeguards. Also, in contrast to the focus on academic outcomes that are the hallmark of standards-based education, the special education framework for students with disabilities encompasses a broader range of educational outcomes for students with disabilities. Observers of standards-based education for all students claim that states have crafted standards that are too narrow and do not allow for educators to include nonacademic learning objectives such as those that are focused on social and behavioral skills, career and vocational development, physical and health development, and functional skills (Center on Education Policy, 2005; Kochhar-Bryant & Bassett, 2003; Vreeberg-Izzo et al., 2001).

IDEA 1997 and 2004 emphasized the importance of an equitable accountability system and required states to include students with disabilities in general state and districtwide assessments and school improvement efforts. States are now required to revise their state improvement plans to establish goals for the performance of children with disabilities, and to assess their progress toward achieving those goals. They must establish indicators such as student participation in assessments, dropout rates, graduation rates, and guidelines for alternate assessment of children with disabilities. However, *IDEA also protects the child's right to "appropriate" and "individualized" methods for achieving common standards and goals, including nonacademic goals*. The challenge for educators is to align standards-based education policies with those under IDEA that are based on individual rights and individualized educational processes. Such an alignment requires the close collaboration among special and general educators, parents, related, and support personnel.

WHAT PROVISIONS OF THE AMERICANS WITH DISABILITIES ACT PROMOTE COLLABORATION AND SYSTEM COORDINATION?

The ADA of 1990 guarantees equal access for all individuals with disabilities in employment, public accommodations, state and local government services, transportation, and telecommunications. As a civil rights act, the ADA requires employers and other private entities to make reasonable accommodations for qualified individuals with disabilities to perform essential job functions (Horne & Morrison, 1998). Under the ADA, reasonable accommodations in the workplace include making facilities physically accessible and usable by individuals with disabilities. Other examples of reasonable accommodations include job restructuring, modified schedules, the acquisition of equipment and devices, modifications to examinations or training materials, and the provision of qualified readers or interpreters (42 USC 12101, 1990).

The ADA promotes nondiscrimination in any private entity (including colleges and universities, postsecondary vocational–technical schools, employer-based training programs, and other private training programs) on the basis of disability. The law promotes collaboration among general, special, vocational, and postsecondary personnel to assist youth to exercise their rights to access postsecondary programs or employment. The promise of equal opportunity and full participation for *all youth* cannot be realized unless students with disabilities have access to the range of opportunities in the secondary and postsecondary systems. New provisions for documentation of disability under IDEA also promote coordination between secondary and postsecondary systems to assist youth to enroll in and access needed services. Under ADA, local plans for postsecondary institutions must describe how they will provide eligible students with comprehensive academic and career guidance, vocational counseling, educational and physical accommodations, and assistance with application to postsecondary education.

WHAT PROVISIONS OF THE JOB TRAINING IMPROVEMENT ACT OF 2005 AND THE REHABILITATION ACT AMENDMENTS OF 1998 PROMOTE COLLABORATION AND SYSTEM COORDINATION?

Educators who teach adolescents must necessarily work in cross-agency relationships to assist youth to prepare for and make successful transitions to postsecondary education and employment. The Workforce Investment Act of 1998 (WIA) (P.L. 105–220), now being reauthorized as the job Training Improvement Act of 2005, creates a comprehensive job training system with local one-stop centers that provide youth with employment and training services at central locations, outreach and intake, initial assessment of skill levels, job search and placement assistance, career counseling, assessment of skills necessary for jobs, service coordination, and short-term prevocational services (job readiness) (NCSET, 2002; Sussman, 2000 U.S. Congress HR27). Because the focus is on inclusion, JTIA promotes a philosophy of service delivery that is consistent with the ADA. JTIA requires that services be provided in the most integrated setting possible for persons with disabilities and that they be universally accessible to all. For youth with disabilities, JTIA includes individualized services and access to integrated education opportunities similar to those found in IDEA. Both acts include specific provisions for preparing for the transition from school to employment (National Center for Secondary Education and Transition, 2002).

At the system level, JTIA creates linkages with state vocational rehabilitation programs and youth programs in order to provide youth with disabilities comprehensive supportive services to improve their education and job skills, support transition to postsecondary education, and provide effective connections to employers. The requirement to provide preparation for postsecondary education and unsubsidized employment and create linkages between academic and occupational learning, indicates the strong intersection between JTIA's and IDEA's transition goals. Both JTIA and IDEA serve youth ages 14–21; however, under IDEA, students with disabilities become ineligible for services upon graduation with a regular high school diploma, or by exceeding the age eligibility for FAPE (free appropriate public education) under state law.

Rehabilitation Act Amendments of 1998

The Rehabilitation Act Amendments of 1998 is a major nondiscrimination law that comprises the major portion of the Job Training Improvement Act of 2005. The Rehabilitation Amendments of 1998 extended the federal vocational rehabilitation (VR) program for 5 years. Primary principles at the core of the Rehabilitation Act are nondiscrimination, improving access to rehabilitative services through coordination, and focus on improving the quality of life for the whole person. Several provisions apply to secondary and postsecondary schools. Section 504 of the Rehabilitation Act of 1973 requires that, "No otherwise qualified individual with a disability in the United States . . . shall, solely by reason of her or his disability, be excluded from the participation in, be denied the benefits of, or be subjected to discrimination under any program or activity receiving Federal financial assistance" (Section 504, 29 USC Sec. 794). As discussed earlier in this chapter, most school districts have policies and procedures, and often the coordinator of special education serves as the district 504 coordinator.

Coordination With Rehabilitation Services for Transition From High School.
Several provisions of the Rehabilitation Act address coordination with high schools in order to improve transition services for students who will be eligible for vocational rehabilitation (VR) services after leaving school. Recognizing that some youth with disabilities leaving school will require assistance, state VR agencies are encouraged to participate in the cost of transition services for any student determined eligible to receive VR services (Horne, 2001). The State Educational Agency (SEA) must create a plan that transfers responsibility for transitioning students from the school to the vocational rehabilitation agency. This provision links the IEP and the Individual Plan for Employment (IPE) under the Rehabilitation Act to accomplish rehabilitation goals before high school graduation.

WHAT PROVISIONS OF THE CARL D. PERKINS CAREER AND TECHNICAL EDUCATION IMPROVEMENT ACT PROMOTE COLLABORATION AND SYSTEM COORDINATION?

The Carl D. Perkins **Career and Technical Education Improvement Act of 2005** (formerly the Vocational and Technical Education Act of 1998, Public Law 105–332), is referred to as the *Perkins Act*. The purpose of the law is to develop more fully the academic, career, and technical skills of secondary and postsecondary students who elect to enroll in career and technical education (CTE) programs. The 1990 and 1998 Amendments required states to ensure equal access to career and vocational–technical education for youths with disabilities, including access to recruitment, enrollment, and placement activities in the full range of vocational education programs in the public schools (Perkins Act, Sec. 113 [c]). Perkins requires local vocational education programs to coordinate with special education and related services to support students in vocational programs, provide information about career preparation courses, and recruit students into vocational programs and transition services (Association for Career and Technical Education, 2005). Youth with disabilities must be provided the support services to ensure that they have the same opportunity as all other youth to enter career–vocational education. Examples of such supports include curricular accommodations, adaptive equipment, classroom modifications, supportive personnel, and instructional aids.

Career-vocational education includes several programs that require coordination between schools and outside agencies. One such program is *cooperative education*, which means a method of combined classroom-based and community-based instruction (including required academic courses and related vocational and technical education instruction) in a job context, delivered under cooperative arrangements between a school and employers (Perkins Act, Sec. 124, (c) (4)). A *tech-prep program* refers to a program of study that combines 2 years of secondary education with a minimum of 2 years of postsecondary education. A sequential course of study integrates academic and vocational–technical instruction in a career field using work-based or worksite learning (Perkins Act, Sec. 2).

Summary of Key Points

- Consistent with IDEA, under NCLB children with disabilities must be considered to be general education students first. States are responsible for implementing a single accountability system for all students based on strong academic standards for what every child should know and learn, including children with disabilities.
- The IEP is essentially a legally required service contract between the student/family and the educational service system. The effectiveness of that contract depends on how well the partners in that contract collaborate and deliver on the educational and related services required to meet the student's needs.
- IDEA 2004 defines an effective educational system as one that promotes service integration and the coordination of state and local education, social, health, mental health, and other services to address the full range of student needs to maximize their participation and learning in school and the community.

Key Terms and Phrases

- Special learners (p. 92)
- Students with disabilities (p. 92)
- Individuals with Disabilities Education Improvement Act of 2004 (p. 92)
- Students "at-risk" (p. 94)
- Limited English proficient (p. 94)

- Inclusion (p. 95)
- Full participation (p. 95)
- Shared responsibility (p. 97)
- Section 504 of the Rehabilitation Act of 1973 (p. 98)
- Free appropriate public education (p. 99)
- Education for All Handicapped Children Act of 1975 (P.L. 94–142) (p. 99)
- Procedural safeguards (p. 100)
- Early intervention services (p. 100)
- Least restrictive environment (p. 101)
- Individual education plan (p. 101)
- Supplementary aids and services (p. 104)
- Related services (p. 104)
- Individualized family services plan (p. 107)
- Transition services (p. 109)
- No Child Left Behind Act of 2001 (p. 110)
- Adequate yearly progress (p. 111)
- Americans with Disabilities Act of 1990 (p. 113)
- Career and Technical Education Improvement Act of 2005 (p. 115)

Questions for Reflection, Thinking, and Skill Building

1. What does it mean to say that "Congress has recognized and employed collaboration and coordination as a major policy instrument for improving excellence and equity in educating all children?" Discuss this in a small group.
2. Provide a rationale for why nonschool agencies should share responsibility with schools to educate children with disabilities. Identify some of the nonschool agencies that IDEA 2004 refers to.
3. In what ways do NCLB and IDEA differ in their principles, and how do they complement each other in ensuring equal educational opportunities for all children? In improving the quality of education for all children?
4. Interview a teacher and an administrator in a school in your district (preferably those who have been in their positions for at least 5 years). Ask if their roles have changed over the years in terms of new expectations for collaboration and system coordination. What broader changes in the school have they observed?
5. Conduct a mock "hearing" before "Congress" in which members of the class divide into two groups: (1) a group of members of Congress inquiring about the status of the inclusion of students with disabilities into general education and service coordination and (2) a group of administrators, teachers, parents, students, and others who will provide testimony on the status of educational services from state/local perspectives.

CHAPTER FIVE

WHAT RESEARCH EVIDENCE LINKS COLLABORATION AND SYSTEM COORDINATION WITH RESULTS FOR STUDENTS?

There comes a time when the mind takes a higher plane of knowledge but can never prove how it got there. All great discoveries have involved such a leap. The important thing is not to stop questioning. —ALBERT EINSTEIN

- Why conduct research on collaboration and system coordination?

- Collaboration and community: Is there a basis in biology and brain research?

- Does collaboration improve results for students from early childhood to the postsecondary years?

- Do collaboration and system coordination promote student and family self-determination?

- What have we learned from national studies of system coordination?

PERSPECTIVES

School people and their relationships to one another will make or break reform. How do teachers relate to each other? How do school professionals interact with parents and community? What are principal–teacher relations like? The answers to such questions are central to determining whether schools can improve.

—DAVID T. GORDON, HARVARD'S KENNEDY SCHOOL OF GOVERNMENT CONFERENCE ON SCHOOL ACCOUNTABILITY

We believe that there is always one answer to a problem, regardless of its complexity. Despite our repeated experiences in life, we persist in looking for one answer, the quick fix, or the ultimate solution that will solve all our problems. . . . [educational leaders and supervisors] should encourage their people to ask impertinent questions regarding quick fixes, a questioning typical of critical thinkers.

—STEPHEN BROOKFIELD, CRITICAL THINKERS, 1995

INTRODUCTION

As discussed in Chapter 1, collaboration and coordination are essential to change processes aimed at improving student achievement. The essential question in this chapter is: What evidence is there that collaboration and system coordination actually result in the kinds of change or outcomes we expect in student achievement, improved teaching and support practices, and organizational change? This question about evidence becomes a little more complex when we begin to think about the effects of collaboration across the *developmental continuum* of students with special needs. The chapter discusses research that provides evidence of a link between collaboration and coordination and positive results for students, families, and for a variety of professionals who work together on their behalf. This discussion is organized to address findings at the student, family, and system levels, and along the developmental continuum, from early childhood through transition from high school.

Collaboration occurs in the context of clearly defined results, or desired effects on personnel, students, and families. The driving question is: Does collaboration work?

What do we mean by "effective" collaboration? What results should be expected from collaboration? This chapter explores research evidence that collaboration promotes student achievement, quality of instruction, parent engagement in education, and more effective linkages between schools and human service agencies.

WHY CONDUCT RESEARCH ON COLLABORATION AND SYSTEM COORDINATION?

The development of theories on collaboration has a history that began with the early Greek philosophers. For example, in the fourth century B.C., Aristotle, in *Politics*, wrote extensively about the behavior of a citizen as a member of a community (McKeon, 1947). Concerns about social intercourse among people advanced with the philosophical treatises in 1600s and 1700s on the nature of human interaction and communication (Hume, 1748; Locke, 1690; Rousseau, 1762). More contemporary studies explored the social nature of teaching and learning, communities of practitioners, and organizational behavior of schools (Bruner, 1990; Habermas, 1987; Thagard, 1997; Vygotsky, 1978). Most recently, the practices and effects of collaboration and system coordination have moved to the forefront of the national agenda for educational reform and accountability, and have become integral elements in new education and human services legislation. Reform requires creativity and change. Bennis and Biederman (1997) observed that the single most important characteristic of creativity and productivity during the 20th century was collaboration. In their study of the most significant inventions in the 20th century, they concluded that the world has become so complex that no single individual can expect to accomplish on his or her own what could be achieved by working with others.

In the field of education, new educational reform laws have reflected recent research that provides scientific evidence of the benefits of collaboration and system coordination (**evidence-based research**). Educational practices have been shaped by research designed to gain a better understanding of the methods of implementing collaborative processes. Research means the systematic investigation (i.e., the gathering and analysis of information) of a subject in order to contribute to our general knowledge (Code of Federal Regulations, Title 45 CFR Part 46, 2001). Table 5.1 provides examples of four categories of research.

Research in collaboration and system coordination reflect all of these categories of research. Some research studies on collaboration and system coordination are conducted to gain a better understanding of the processes, or the social phenomena (*descriptive* and *exploratory research*). Other research studies explore cause and effect relationships between two or more variables related to collaboration. For example, a study might seek to explore the relationship between administrator support and the effectiveness of team teaching in schools (*explanatory research*). In other cases, research is conducted to understand whether particular policy choices, programs, and collaborative partnerships are actually helping to solve problems or achieve intended goals for students and families (*evaluation research*).

Descriptive and *exploratory* research studies have examined the processes of professional collaboration or coordination and recommend more attention to the creation of **collaborative cultures** in schools (da Costa, Marshall, & Riordan, 1998; Dettmer, Dyck, & Thurston, 2005; Gallego & Cole, 2001; Kampwith, 1998;

TABLE 5.1	Four Categories of Research
Type	**Example Question**
Descriptive	• How many schools have interagency agreements with their local mental health agencies? How frequently do parents attend IEP team meeting?
Exploratory	• What are the attitudes of teachers toward collaborative partnerships with parents? How do administrators define "collaborative cultures"?
Explanatory (causal)	• Do supportive transition plans that require coordination between elementary and middle school teachers improve students' adjustment in the 7th grade (shows a causal relationship between the coordination activities and measures of students' adjustment)?
Evaluation	• Should new school policies that require collaborative curriculum planning between special and general education teachers be continued? Are they resulting in improved accommodations for students with disabilities (adapted from Bickman & Rog, 1997; Maxwell, 2004)?

Lieberman, 1999b). Such studies explore strategies for promoting social relationships and collaborative environments among teachers, among related service professionals, or between teachers and parents. Other studies have examined issues of trust among professionals and concluded that schools with a high degree of *relational trust* are far more likely to sustain change that raises student achievement. Improvements in areas such as classroom instruction, curriculum development, teacher preparation, and professional development have little chance of succeeding without improvements in a school's social climate (Bryk & Schneider, 2002). Conclusions from most studies on the collaborative climate of schools remain speculative since they are mainly descriptive, exploring the conditions for improving student outcomes through collaboration.

There are few systematic studies that meet the standard of being *explanatory*, or *evidence-based*. This term means that there is research evidence that shows a significant causal relationship between a particular collaborative technique or process and specific results (outcomes) for students, families, or professionals. Such studies provide evidence of *exemplary* or *model practices* in the field because they are based on scientific studies with experimental or quasi-experimental designs. Most research on collaboration offers findings that are less scientific (speculative) pointing instead to promising practices that hold promise for yielding positive results. According to Dettmer, Dyck, and Thurston (2005), the education field could benefit from a deeper understanding of collaboration, efficacy, and effectiveness, and how they can be measured.

Barriers to Reliable Conclusions

Several barriers impede sound research to measure the effects of professional collaboration and coordination on students and families. First, the use of non-rigorous methods (qualitative or quantitative) and the inadequate preparation of educators to conduct research leads to studies that lack credibility. Second, the lack of control or comparison groups in studies prevents the comparisons between students or professionals who participate in a program or intervention (treatment) and those who do not. Third, when studying impacts of interventions on children, investigators often fail to devote attention to age-related or developmental changes in their subjects over time, as well as to the complex and dynamic interactions among student, family, teacher, peers, and the environment. Such changes in students or their environment during a study create intervening factors that undermine the validity of the research (Hipp & Huffman, 2002). Other barriers to sound research include failure to clearly define measures of collaboration, and lack of objective behavioral data about collaboration.

COLLABORATION AND COMMUNITY: IS THERE A BASIS IN BIOLOGY AND BRAIN RESEARCH?

How does our biology affect our desire and ability as adults to work together collaboratively, or our resistance to it? Is behavior among adults stable, patterned, and predictable, or is it flexible and malleable? Does the behavior of teachers and administrators become increasingly rigid or institutionalized when they work in highly structured bureaucratic organizations? Like the organization, does it become resistant to change, and what does this mean for collaboration and professional relationships? Can we apply biological principles when we explore the phenomenon of collaboration, and is there a **biological basis** for such behavior in our brains? Researchers investigating education and human behavior say that, yes, we can apply biological principles to the study of collaboration.

Three areas of inquiry that focus on human societies, brains, and cells are now converging to help explain the biology of behavior:

1. **Evolutionary psychology** and *psychobiology* explores why we develop cooperative communities, create nurturing family environments, and support activities such as the arts and religion (Sylwester, 2003, p. 17).

2. *Imaging technology* is the study of body–brain properties and brain activity during cognitive tasks.

3. *Genetics* is the study of processing systems that regulate cell activity and division.

Psychobiologists—those who study the biology of our psychological processes and development—are interested in how human psychology has changed during our evolution as a species. For example, Barkow, Cosmides, and Tooby (1992), in *The Adapted Mind*, present three premises about human behavior. First, there is a universal human nature which exists at the level of evolved psychological mechanisms. The mechanisms are innate, or rooted in our biology, rather than in culturally learned behavior. The second premise is that these evolved psychological mechanisms are

adaptations which were created through **natural selection** (survival of the fittest or those with beneficial traits) over evolutionary time. The third assumption is that the evolved human mind is adapted to the way of life of early hunter–gatherers and has not yet caught up with the accelerated change in our modern world. So, from an *evolutionary perspective*, we are still thinking and behaving as hunter–gatherers, but are now living in a world quite different from the one from which we evolved. We may be experiencing the fastest technological progress ever known to humankind, but we are doing this with brains that evolved under very different conditions— conditions that did not include living in large cities, working in large organizations, and using advanced technology (Baron-Cohen, 1995; Cosmides & Tooby, 1997; Gazzaniga, 2000; Herasymowych & Herasymowych, 2000; Pinker, 2002).

Understanding evolutionary psychology is useful because it provides a new and provocative way to think about human nature and to identify aspects of behavior that are inborn and universal. It also offers a framework for understanding why people tend to act as they do in groups and organizational settings (Nicholson, 1998).

From Competition to Cooperation

Over the past few decades, many other researchers have attempted to link evolu- tionary biology to psychology and then to culture and **cooperative communities** (Axelrod, 1997; Axelrod & Dion, 1988; Badcock, 1991; Bendor, 1993; Bendor & Mookherjee, 1990; Bicchieri, 1990; Glance & Huberman, 1994; Hammerstein, 2003; Harcourt, 1992; Herasymowych & Herasymowych, 2000; Hinde & Groebel, 1991; Ridley, 1998; Singer, 2000). Current research in evolutionary biology (the study of human evolution) which has previously been focused on competition, is now focused on defining and expanding *models of cooperation*. Evolutionary psycholo- gists and biologists have analyzed the conditions under which cooperative behavior has evolved. Based on Charles Darwin's (1895) premise that human behavior is shaped by natural selection, these analyses show that cognitive mechanisms for engaging in cooperation can be selected for only if they solve certain complex information-processing problems (Axelrod & Cohen, 1999; Barkow, Cosmides, & Tooby, 1992). Understanding the mechanisms of cooperation has relevance for a variety of fields other than biology, and particularly for education.

Over the past 2 decades, research studies have examined the functioning of the brain during cooperative activities. Investigators have studied cooperation among people using a variety of creative structured games. For example, McCabe, Houser, Ryan, Smith, and Tourard (2001), building on previous research (McCabe & Smith, 2000; Nowak & Sigmund, 1998), conducted a brain imaging study (functional imag- ing) of cooperation in two-person reciprocal exchanges. Competing for cash awards, participant subjects played two-person "trust and reciprocity" games, both with human and with computer partners. The researchers hypothesized that coop- eration between two people requires the ability to infer each other's mental states in order to form shared expectations about how the cooperation would result in mutual gains or advantages, and about how they might achieve these gains. The researchers also hypothesized that the front of the brain, known as the *prefrontal cortex*, was involved in the processing of such cooperative actions. Through brain imaging, they found that the prefrontal regions of the brain were more active when subjects were playing the game with a human than when they were playing against a computer, and more active with highly cooperative subjects than with noncooperative subjects.

Applying evolutionary concepts at the classroom level, Sylwester (2003) argues that collaboration is a form of social adaptation (a structure, process, or behavioral trait that evolves over time). It is innate within our democratic society, and we spend a great deal of cognitive energy trying to solve problems. Humans are biased toward challenge and much of our cognitive energy is focused on solving problems. When things are running smoothly, we tend to go searching for trouble—at both the personal and greater community levels. As Sylwester (2003) observes, democracy is an unfinished process, replete with dangers and opportunities, and our social nature prefers a continuing collaborative search for the solutions. Our nation began with a determination to succeed as a democracy, and then worked collaboratively through the legislative process to temporarily solve each successive challenge it confronted.

The Genetic Link

According to Herasymowych and Herasymowych (2000), resistance to change, which is really resistance to loss, is innate. Humans are hardwired to resist losing control over their environments. This shows up as increased complaints, dissatisfaction, stress-related illnesses (e.g., depression), anxiety, and a lack of motivation. You may ask: If humans are hardwired to resist loss, then why do some people seem to thrive in ambiguous and changing conditions? Why are some people "thrill-seekers" who get bored with sameness and predictability in their lives? Some researchers believe such characteristics are genetically based—in other words, some have a thrill-seeking gene—although in many cases such behavior is learned. We know that DNA makes brains unique, and each brain develops in a unique environment to form an individual personality (Goldsmith, Lemery, Aksan, & Buss, 2000; Hamer & Copeland, 1998; Kagan, 2003). Scientists who search for answers like these study the field of **behavior genetics**. These scientists have discovered a genetic link between the genes that we carry in our DNA and our behavior. These behaviors dictate who we are and how we behave in certain situations.

All behavior lies on a continuum, and people display these behaviors in varying degrees. People also display these behaviors differently in different contexts or situations. For example, they may display considerable risk-taking behavior in their home life but the opposite in their work life. On the other hand, they may avoid expressing anger in their professional life but have anger management problems in their personal life. Individual dispositions to these genetic behaviors have significant implications for an organization's ability to learn and negotiate the changes it must undergo.

Practical Implications for Collaboration in Schools

What do evolutionary biology and psychology, universal patterns of behavior, and human nature have to do with educational collaboration and schools? The classical evolutionary biologists, beginning with Konrad Lorenz (1974) and Niko Tinbergen

(1970), who are considered to be the founders of *ethology* and who shared a Nobel prize in 1973, have told us that human behavior in many ways mirrors that of animal behavior (Allen & Beckoff, 1995; Beckoff & Allen, 1997; Cummins & Allen, 1998; Griffin, 1982; Lorentz, 1974). The evolutionary psychologists have also told us that we are not designed to live in large cities and work in large organizations. Instead, we are designed to live and work in small, connected communities in which we know everybody by name and reputation. This creates a level of stability, and humans are hardwired to work best in this kind of environment. This is precisely the type of environment that most people want to achieve in schools, in community agencies, or in large organizations. There are several practical implications for collaboration and system coordination emerging from research by evolutionary psychologists:

1. *Small Communities for Learning.* There is an emerging interest in creating smaller **communities for learning** among people for professional conversations, inquiry, problem solving, and decision making. There is an explosion of interest by business, education agencies, and human services in applying the concept of community to create *communities of practice, learning communities, communities of inquiry,* and *technical assistance communities* (discussed in greater detail in Chapter 3). As Parker Palmer poetically put it:

> Today our images of biological reality have been transformed. Ecological studies offer a picture of nature less focused on the terrors of combat than on the dance of communal collaboration, a picture of the great web of being . . . . This transformation of images of reality—from fragmentation and competition to community and collaboration—has gone on in virtually every academic discipline over the past fifty years. (Palmer, 1998, p. 96)

2. *Learning Styles and Collaboration.* The term *learning styles* refers to the preferred (generically based) ways by which people learn. Common learning styles include visual, auditory, and tactile (hands-on). These variations in preferred ways of learning affect the learning processes that must occur as adults and students enter into new collaborative relationships. Many organizations concerned with adult learning (e.g., universities, technical colleges, businesses, professional training organizations) have used a variety of tools to assess learning preferences and learning styles and to facilitate learning. These include the Myers–Briggs assessment of personality type, learning styles inventories, cognitive styles inventories, perceptual modality and sensory preference instruments, social interaction assessments, and study strategies (Miller, 1998).

3. *Multiple Intelligences, Learning, and Collaboration.* Howard Gardner (1983), professor of education at Harvard University, suggested that the traditional notion of intelligence, based on IQ testing, is far too limited. He originally proposed seven kinds of intelligence spanning three domains (physical, cognitive, and affective) to account for a broader range of human potential in children and adults. Multiple intelligences include logical–mathematical, verbal–linguistic, visual–spatial, bodily–kinesthetic, musical–rhythmic, interpersonal, and intrapersonal. An eighth intelligence, naturalistic, was added later, and others, including existential and olfactory–gustatory (smell and taste) are under study (personal communication, Harvard Seminar, 2005). Because our understanding of the brain and human behavior is continually expanding, so likely will the concept of intelligence. This variation in types of intelligences among people (and differences in how they learn best) represent assets to collaboration and group problem solving because it can bring together complementary strengths and interests.

4. *Resistance to Change.* Different behavioral dispositions and styles of learning can lead to resistance to change or collaboration if the change leader is inflexible and his or her leadership style does not allow for sensitivity to the different learning styles of the team members.

Teachers, related service personnel, and administrators face major challenges adapting to environments that are in constant change. Although most people in organizations recognize that change is a constant, possessing this knowledge doesn't necessarily mean they will cope with it well. School leaders often encounter resistance to change, despite the recognition among people that change is needed. Unless personnel and supervisors gain a deeper understanding of why people resist change, they may be inclined to believe that these resistors are acting in an irrational or malicious manner. Let's See It in Action, below, presents a principal's effort to respond to teachers' resistance to change.

When professionals work together, the continually make choices. Those choices are affected by biological and psychological motives of which they are often unaware. As people improve their ability to understand what motivates them and others (self-

LET'S SEE IT IN ACTION! CASE ILLUSTRATION: ARE PEOPLE NATURALLY RESISTANT TO CHANGE?

Principal Jackson of Harford Middle School wants to increase the collaborative nature of her team and believes that it will promote cross-disciplinary instruction as well as collaboration between special and general education teachers. Currently, the teachers work in individual classrooms with closed doors. To facilitate collaboration, Principal Jackson wants to remove physical barriers, such as walls and doors, and replace them with flexible, sliding walls that will allow for merged classes when needed. When Principal Jackson announces this to the team, she encounters a revolt from most of the team members. They proceed to raise a variety of reasons why the plan would be a bad idea. Is this resistance to change? According to evolutionary psychology, the short answer is yes . . . and no. The longer answer is that humans resist losing the familiarity of what they know and are reluctant to buy into a future that they are uncertain about. If Principal Jackson knows this, she will understand the reason for the behavior and will be likely to negotiate it in an effective way. She can work with the team, help them to understand their initial reactions and how collaboration will actually benefit the team in its work, and invite the team's suggestions for building collaboration. These solutions may not involve removing physical barriers such as doors and walls. The key is to ensure that the team participates in and has some control in creating the solution. When the team feels they have some control over the process and outcome, the team might be more willing to change.

On the other hand, if Principal Jackson fails to explore the reasons why the team is behaving in a resistant manner, she may punish the team, and even force the team to comply with her plan. Such authoritative actions can send the revolt underground, connecting to other hard-wired behaviors: gossip and rumor, all built on the fear and anger that is being suppressed by the principal's actions (adapted from Herasymowych & Herasymowych, 2000).

knowledge), they can better evaluate their professional behavior in the midst of changing circumstances or during the challenge of a new collaborative relationship. A basic understanding of the principles of evolutionary psychology can be very helpful.

DOES COLLABORATION IMPROVE RESULTS FOR STUDENTS FROM EARLY CHILDHOOD THROUGH POSTSECONDARY?

Professional collaboration has become even more important in recent years because of its relevance in achieving new accountability requirements for schools to improve academic achievement for *all students*. Accumulating research is providing evidence of links between student achievement and collaboration: professional-to-professional, teacher-to-student, special educator-to-general educator, teacher-to-parent, IEP team collaboration, and school-to-community professional coordination. Effective collaboration and system coordination have been linked to a variety of student, family, and professional outcomes. These include gains in student achievement; improved collaboration among teachers and related services personnel; systematic assistance and support to beginning teachers; an expanded pool of ideas, methods, and materials that benefit all teachers; greater engagement of parents in their children's education; and improved coordination among schools and school-linked agencies to support student services and school improvement planning (Abrams & Gibbs, 2000; Chrispeels, Strait, & Brown, 1999; Dettmer, Dyke, & Thurston, 2005; DuFour, 2003; Friend & Cook, 2003; Glover, 2003; Kendziora, Bruns, Osher, Pacchiona, & Mejia, 2001; Knight & Boudah, 2003; Little & Lauver, 2005; Osher & Osher, 2002; Sharpe & Hawes, 2003). Creating a professional collaborative culture may be the single most important factor in successful school improvement initiatives to improve student outcomes (Newman & Wehlage, 1995).

A body of knowledge is emerging on the effectiveness of collaboration and school consultation. *Emerging* means that investigators are at the stage of describing and identifying key variables in the collaboration and consultation processes and outcomes (Dettmer, Dyke, & Thurston, 2005) and searching for correlations with student results (e.g., successful integration in the general education class and academic test scores). The following sections provide a summary of selected research on collaboration and system coordination in relation to developmental stages from early childhood to postsecondary transition.

Collaboration and Student Outcomes in Early Childhood and Elementary Years

A study by the Research and Training Center on Service Coordination (2001) examined results for children and families one year after beginning early intervention. Children in all age groups were advancing developmentally, with significantly higher percentages of children in each group showing mastery of selected milestones one year after entering early intervention. Notably, after one year, significantly more families felt confident about their ability to help their children learn and develop. They reported that their children's communication and motor skills improved, and over two-thirds of families reported that early intervention had had a considerable impact on the child's development (U.S. Department of Education,

Annual Report to Congress, 2002d). High-quality services were identified as those that produced the following outcomes: (a) Children and families receive appropriate supports and services that meet their individual needs; (b) children reach their full potential; (c) children are healthy; (d) children's development is enhanced; (e) children experience successful transitions; (f) families are involved in decision making; (g) families are informed about resources and services; (h) families and professionals work together as a team (Dunst & Bruder, 2002; Lourie, Stroul, & Friedman, 1998; National Center on Outcomes Research, 2001).

Facilitating Transition From Early Childhood Programs to Elementary.

The entrance into kindergarten marks children's first interaction with formal schooling, and research shows that success during this first year may predict later school success (National Center for Early Development and Learning, 2002; Pianta, 1999; Pianta, Cox, Taylor, & Early, 1999). Recent studies of the effectiveness of early childhood programs have centered on factors that include collaboration between prekindergarten, kindergarten, and elementary programs.

A survey by the National Center for Early Development and Learning of 3,600 kindergarten teachers about transition to kindergarten and elementary school (Pianta, Cox, Taylor, & Early, 1999) reported that while 52% of all children have a successful entry into kindergarten, 48% experience moderate to serious problems. The survey revealed that communication between teachers and parents is a primary factor in successful transition, and high poverty school districts experience the greatest challenges. These findings suggest the importance of transition support through collaboration among professionals and families in preschool, kindergarten, and first grade (National Center for Early Development and Learning, 1999; Pianta, Cox, Taylor, & Early, 1999).

Some school districts are demonstrating significant student achievement gains from new collaborative initiatives that link early childhood and elementary programs. For example, Maryland's *Early Success Performance Plan* demonstrates gains in student achievement. Plans that began 3 years ago in kindergarten, now reap significant benefits among second-grade students, and those who are African-American, Hispanic, from low socioeconomic communities, in special education, and English language learners (Weast, 2003). Maryland's program serves as the basis for the coordination of prekindergarten and early elementary programs and services. Together with an alignment of instructional programs through grade 12, the plan is focused on improving student achievement in reading, writing, mathematics, and language. The Early Success Performance Plan is built around five major components: (1) challenging curriculum for reading, writing, and mathematics; (2) ongoing assessment of progress; (3) expanded instructional time; (4) intensive, targeted, and sustained professional development for teachers in collaborative teaching based on the Skillful Teaching Course (Brookfield, 1995, 2001); and (5) meaningful family involvement and community collaboration, including descriptive report cards with detailed information about child development and progress (Weast, 2003).

Special Education Elementary Longitudinal Study.

Initiated in 2000, the U.S. Department of Education conducted a 5-year series of studies to examine the programs and services for children with disabilities in elementary school, including their experiences with transition in and out. This study, the *Special Education Elementary Longitudinal Study* (SEELS, 2002), is the largest of its kind and involved 11,000 students ages 6–12 in elementary school receiving special education from first grade or higher. The following provides highlights from this study.

Age at identification and first service. Some disabilities, such as genetic disorders, and some conditions that result from premature birth, affect children from birth and throughout their lives. Other disabilities emerge when children reach the age of typical developmental milestones and exhibit delays in acquiring skills such as walking or talking (Blackorby & Wagner, 2002, p. 12). Still others have disabilities that remain unidentified until the child makes the transition into elementary school (or even later in middle or high school) and is required to perform more sophisticated cognitive tasks such as reading, mathematics, complex homework projects, and standardized tests. Finally, accidents can occur at any age and result in a disability such as a traumatic brain injury or spinal cord injury that require specialized educational services and supports. Age at identification is an important indicator of the extent of the disability and families' experiences with the disability and the service system

One of the SEELS studies reported several findings from the sample of 8,483 students. About one in four elementary students (24%) had disabilities that first were recognized when they were infants or toddlers. Another 22% had disabilities or delays first identified in their preschool years, and more than half (54%) were first identified when they were elementary school age (5 or older). Even larger proportions of children did not begin receiving professional services until they entered school (74%). More than one-third of children (34%) were first served at age 6 or 7, and more than one fourth (26%) were served at age 8 or older. These data show that, for many children, disabilities that may not have been noticed earlier, emerge in the years of formal schooling and begin to impact the child in the new context of learning and performance. Processes that improve collaboration and communication among general and special educators and related services professionals is essential for early identification.

Collaboration Between General and Special Educators Leads to a Reexamination of the "Pull-Out" Model.   In most studies that explore ways to increase elementary student achievement through school reform, *teacher collaboration* typically appears along with variables such as lower student–teacher ratios, increased per-pupil expenditures, and increased resources for teachers (Grissmer, Flanagan, Kawata & Williamson, 2000; Haimson 2000; Pritchard, 2000). Collaboration between special and general educators is now viewed as among the most important factors in the success of a school that is inclusive of all children. While rigorous research studies need to be developed, several educational researchers have demonstrated tentative links between general and special educator collaboration and student achievement.

Some elementary level special educators discussed discomfort with their current "pull-out" services and have begun redefining their roles and relationships with general educators (Thompson, Thurlow, Parson, & Barrow, 2000; Zigmond, 2003). In fact, there is a strong case for the instructional and social benefits of providing for the needs of all students in inclusive classrooms with differentiated instruction

(England, 1996; Swartz, 2004). A model practice referred to as *push-in* delivery of services (as opposed to *pull-out*), in which special and general education teachers collaborate to provide services, is yielding benefits for students. Special education teachers become more involved with the instruction that is delivered in general classrooms and, therefore, are perceived as integral members of the instructional team. Students benefit from the reduced stigma of being identified as having "special needs"; they also benefit from better alignment of teaching strategies and cooperation among the various teachers they work with (Swartz, 2004). Not only does inclusive education for children with disabilities improve academic functioning, it also expands opportunities for socialization with typical peers (without disabilities) in general education settings (Pavri & Monda-Amaya, 2000).

Social Relationships Among Professionals Affect School Improvement and Student Achievement.

Several studies have reported *improved social skills* for both special and general education students where coteaching was practiced. Some investigators have measured relationships among key school stakeholders—the principal, teachers, and parents—and link them to student achievement. For example, Bryk and Schneider (2002) conducted research during the early 1990s on 12 Chicago elementary schools in the process of restructuring. They theorized that effective relationships among school stakeholders facilitate school environments that promote school improvement and ultimately student outcomes.

According to Bryk and Schneider, *relational trust*—their term that means effective social relationships—acts as both a foundation for and an agent of school improvement. Relational trust is the level of trust that individuals or groups have for each other based on their perceptions of how well or how poorly the other meets their expectations. For example, parents expect that teachers will use the accommodations written into their children's IEP in the general education classroom. Teachers expect parents to provide extra support at home for their children so that they will be prepared for class each day. If either party fails to meet expectations, levels of relational trust between teachers and parents will be negatively affected. The investigators found that in three Chicago elementary schools, schools with high relational trust between parents and teachers were more likely to partner in ways and experiment with practices that helped students learn. Students in schools with strong relational trust among stakeholders showed *gains in test scores*, whereas students in schools with weak relational trust showed stagnant and sometimes falling test scores.

There is research evidence that in cotaught classrooms, nondisabled students also show appreciation for the uniqueness of their peers. Staff provide more individualized attention to students and develop academic adaptations for students. As a result, social performance appears to be enhanced because students have a better understanding and greater tolerance for differences (Baker & Zigmond, 1995; Hines, 2001; Hunt, 2000; Salend, 2001; Salend & Duhaney, 1999; Walther-Thomas, 1997a).

Whole School Collaboration Yields Student Achievement Gains.

Recent research has shown that the general performance of students improves when schools use whole school improvement approaches, based on comprehensive professional collaboration and coordination. For example, the *Onward to Excellence* I and II (OTE) national model demonstration, developed by the Northwest Regional Educational Laboratory (2001) under contract with the U.S. Department of

Education, was designed to help schools and communities work together. Onward to Excellence has been operating for 20 years, and more than 1,000 schools have participated in the process. The model is characterized by several key elements: *collaborative decision making and professional learning communities, shared leadership and continuous learning for improvement.* Although it is difficult to fully measure the impact of complex whole-school reform processes, OTE schools have produced several measurable outcomes or gains. They have raised student achievement; established a common focus for all staff across grade levels, departments, and disciplines; helped teachers learn how to work together, support, and trust each other through professional development; aligned teaching with state standards and standardized assessments; and involved parents and the community in the improvement work (Dorfman & Fisher, 2002; Northwest Regional Education Laboratory, 2001). Furthermore, two studies showed that OTE schools led to more teacher collaboration and research-based teacher practices, and that the model was most effective in high poverty districts (NWREL, 2001).

Collaboration and Student Outcomes in Middle School Years

Improved Supports in Middle School Improve Students' Performance.
Collaborative practices and supports for youth with disabilities in middle school can have profound effects on their future success in high school and beyond. The advancement from elementary school to middle school represents a major transition in the life of the adolescent that requires additional attention and support. Research has confirmed what teachers and parents have known for decades—that a significant number of children show changes in academic performance, perceptions about school, and self-perceptions as they make the transition and adjustment to middle school. Students who participate in supportive transition activities and are placed in *interdisciplinary teams* make more successful transitions to middle school. Closer collaboration among professionals in sending and receiving schools can impact student outcomes in several areas:

1. *Academic Performance.* Youth exhibit decreased academic performance and are at greatest risk for failure in the time of their transition to and adjustment in eighth to ninth grade (Bilig, 2001; George, 1999; Henderson & Raimondo, 2002; Hines, 2001; Kilgore, Griffin, Sindelar, & Webb, 2001; Mullins & Irvin, 2000; Ritter, Michel, & Irby, 1999; Sanders & Epstein, 2000; Wilson & Horch, 2004).

2. *Grade Point Average.* Students show a general decline in grade point average (GPA) in grades six through ten, with the most dramatic drop in GPA at the transition point between grades six and seven (Blyth, Simmons & Carlton-Ford, 1983; Crockett, Petersen, Graber, Schulenberg, & Ebata 1989; Fenzel, 1992; Gronna, 1998; Mullins & Irvin, 2000). Achievement scores have also been shown to be affected by the nature of supports in the transition year in middle school; students grouped into interdisciplinary teams during their transition year perform significantly better on standardized achievement tests than students who are in departmentalized schools (Alspaugh & Harting, 1997; Mullins & Irvin, 2000).

3. *Perceptions of School.* Students' perceptions of their educational experiences generally influence their motivation to perform in school. When students have a history of struggle in school, it is particularly difficult for them to stay motivated. When they

believe that their poor performance is caused by factors out of their control, such as a disability, they are unlikely to see any reason to hope for an improvement (Anderman, Maehr, & Midgley, 1999; Collins, 1996; Eccles, Lord, & Midgley, 1991; Mullins, 1997; Phelan, Davidson, & Yu, 1998; Roeser, Eccles, & Sameroff, 2000; Sadowski, 2003; Sanders & Epstein, 2000; Wigfield, Eccles, MacIver, Reuman, & Midgley, 1991).

4. *Student Self-Perceptions.* Exploring the possible effects of the transition from elementary to middle school on the self-esteem of young adolescents, several studies have documented the lowest self-esteem ratings and highest self-consciousness ratings from students between the ages of 12 and 14 (Mullins, 1997; Simmons, Rosenberg, & Rosenberg, 1973). Furthermore, girls who made no school transition during early adolescence, remaining in a K–8 setting maintained higher self-esteem ratings than girls who had made a school transition. More recent studies have concurred that the decline in self-esteem for boys and girls is magnified if there is a disability or other significant life changes such as onset of puberty, initiation of dating relationships, change of residence, or parental divorce (Collins, 1996; Eccles, Lord, & Midgley, 1991; Eccles, Wigfield, Reuman, & MacIver, 1987; Mahdi, Christopher, & Meade, 1996; Mullins, 1997; Phelan, Davidson, & Yu, 1998; Roeser, Eccles, & Sameroff, 2000; Sadowski, 2003).

In supportive interdisciplinary teams, students maintain their sense of academic competence as well as their sense of perceived social acceptance as they make the transition to middle school (Arowosafe & Irvin, 1992; Billig, 2001; George, 1999; Mizell, 1999; Mullins, 1997).

Mismatch Between Adolescents' Developmental Needs and the School Environment.
Professional collaboration, interdisciplinary teaming, and peer support are becoming central features in the structure of most middle school programs. Middle school educators claim that professional teaming helps students to maximize their learning (Hines, 2001; Roeser, Eccles, & Sameroff, 2000; Walther-Thomas, 1997a). Such collaboration can have significant impact on the middle school student since there is such wide diversity among them developmentally. Diversity is a hallmark of middle level learners. Middle school children range from childlike to adultlike, from socially awkward to socially adept, from emotionally insecure to highly confident, and from concrete to abstract in thinking—sometimes seemingly all in the same student on the same day (Tomlinson, Moon, & Callahan, 1998).

Until the late 1980s, most research examining life transitions, adjustments, and performance as students moved from elementary to middle school and from middle school through high school was shaped by the theory that problems with coping were caused by rapid cognitive, physical, and social-emotional changes. More recently, however, researchers are asking: Are there factors that aren't centered in the adolescent, but rather are associated with the middle school environment that may create some of the stress? They began looking at the structure of classes, student decision making (or lack thereof), increased school size, greater departmentalization, ability grouping, increased use of competition as a motivator, and increased rigor in grading and testing. Studies have suggested that as students mature, they want more autonomy and opportunity for self-management and personal decision making (Bremer, Kachgal, & Schoeller, 2003; Deci & Ryan, 2000; Doll, Sands, Wehmeyer, & Palmer, 1996; Eisenman & Chamberlin, 2001; Field, Hoffman, & Spezia,

1998; Martin, Marshall, & DePry, 2002; Wehmeyer, Abery, Mithaug, Powers, & Stancliffe, 2003).

These desires are expressions of adolescents' developmental needs as they search for their own identity, yet the school environment in the middle years typically limits these opportunities to exercise decision making. Many schools respond to students with highly controlling management and discipline policies, which can actually increase misbehavior and decrease motivation (Stuhlman, Hamre, Pianta, 2002). Educators' perceptions of students' capacity for decision making and autonomy tended to mirror those at the elementary level and clearly do not match student's self-perceptions. Students believe that they should be allowed to make decisions in middle school and learn to make them even before the transition to high school (Alspaugh, 1998; Eccles, Lord, & Midgley, 1991; Mullins, 1997; Mullins & Irvin, 2000; Phelan, Yu, & Davidson, 1994).

Several studies have concluded that factors associated with the middle school setting may have a deleterious effect on students' successful transition, and adjustment, and performance for both those with and without disabilities (Mizelle & Mullins, 1997). Young adolescents mature at vastly different rates and at different stages between grades 4 and 10. Transitioning students from classrooms designed for children to those designed for young adolescents cannot be done effectively by treating all students as though they develop physically, emotionally, socially, and cognitively at the same rates (Hough, 2003).

Much more research is needed in order to understand more clearly the phenomena of students' experiences as they move from elementary into middle schools and how programs might be better structured to respond to the developmental needs and capacities of young adolescents. Recent reforms in middle schools are showing great promise for addressing barriers to successful transition and performance in middle school and lessening the often overwhelming challenges for youth, particularly those with special needs, at this vulnerable stage in development.

Professional Teaming in Middle School Improves Students' Performance.

Developmental diversity presents a special challenge for teacher collaboration, as well as for the interaction among students with and without disabilities. The sense of belonging is especially crucial during early adolescence and is increased when students are given the opportunity to interact with others and learn to appreciate abilities, interests, and differences (Burt, Resnick, & Novick, 1998; Carnegie Council on Adolescent Development, 2000; Forest & Pearpoint, 1997). Most comprehensive school reform models involving increased collaboration among teachers and other professionals have been implemented at the elementary school level, leaving many with unanswered questions about how this approach to increased student achievement might work at the middle school level for students with disabilities (Hines, 2001). The U.S. Office of Educational Research and Improvement (OERI) and Johns Hopkins University's Center for Social Organization of Schools (2000) have developed a comprehensive school reform model oriented toward middle and secondary schools. A key component is the collaboration among teachers, students, and families. Box 5.1 provides a research-based example of school reorganization to promote collaboration among teachers.

Teacher collaboration also affects teacher expectations of students' abilities and students' expectations of themselves. Teachers who provide the majority of

---

BOX 5.1   School Reform for Collaboration in the Middle School

Teachers, students, and families are encouraged to develop strong bonds and close relationships facilitated by innovative approaches to the school's organization. For example, some faculty remain with the same students for 2 or more years (called *looping*), and teacher teams share students and common planning time, during which they are provided training (called *semidepartmentalization*). Semidepartmentalization helps cut down class size, improves student–teacher bonds, and enables the teacher to better connect subject matter across disciplines. There is evidence that the model can realize substantial gains in student performance while improving both student and staff morale. For example, in reading, students from one model school outgained comparison students by 5 scale score points, while students from the other model school outscored comparison students by 12 points. Both model schools continue to display outstanding and broad-based achievement gains in all years for which data are available (Johns Hopkins University, Center for Social Organization of Schools, 2000).

---

their services through team teaching or consultation with general educators in standards-based environments, expect a greater number of their students to meet high standards, work with more students on using accommodations, and discuss standards with more IEP teams than teachers at other grade levels who provided most or all of their services in separate special education classrooms and resource rooms (Thompson, Thurlow, Parson, & Barrow, 2000). Middle school students, their parents, and teachers share the belief that middle level students with mild to moderate disabilities included in the general classroom experience (1) increased self-confidence, (2) camaraderie, (3) support of the teachers, (4) higher expectations, and (5) avoid low self-esteem that can result from placement in a special education setting (Hines, 2001; Hines & Johnson, 1996; Ritter, Michel, & Irby, 1999).

Collaboration and Student Outcomes in Secondary and Postsecondary School Years

Research has demonstrated that effective high schools and effective departments within high schools are characterized by strong *professional collaboration* (McLaughlin & Talbert, 2001). Deschler, Schumacher, and Woodruff (2004), who have studied effectiveness of secondary inclusion strategies for over 2 decades, have indicated that while progress has been made, there is a distance to go. They have concluded that *collaboration is among the most important elements in building school capacity to improve education for all children.* Schools build capacity to help students with disabilities progress in general education by using a variety of group and team strategies, including teacher planning teams, critical friends groups, and advisory groups. For example, many schools use *critical friends groups*, which are small groups of teachers and administrators who work together over a period of time to solve problems, critique work, and obtain support and feedback to improve their practices. Deschler, Schumacher, and Woodruff (2004) and others have concluded that it is the strength of the coteaching relationships among teachers and the personal relationships with students that make the inclusion model work (Eick, Ware, & Jones, 2004; Rice & Zigmond, 2000).

When schools and agencies coordinate their services, students benefit in many ways, including increased participation in career assessment and employment programs, and increased referrals of students with disabilities to a variety of adult service agencies following high school (Hasazi, Furney, & DeStefano, 1999). Hasazi also found that written agreements among agencies were essential for interagency coordination, concluding that "the presence of sustained interagency collaboration emerged as a defining characteristic" among model secondary and transition sites (Hasazi, Furney, & DeStefano, 1999, p. 563).

DO COLLABORATION AND SYSTEM COORDINATION PROMOTE STUDENT AND FAMILY SELF-DETERMINATION?

Recently, educational researchers have sought clearer correlations among professional collaboration, student self-determination, and student outcomes. Although the special education literature contains many recommended strategies to promote self-determination, more research is needed to demonstrate that these strategies actually improve educational outcomes for children and youth with disabilities (Wehmeyer, Field, Doren, Jones, & Mason, 2004). Currently only 55% of schools offer self-advocacy or self-determination curriculum to students with disabilities (25th Annual Report to Congress). Wehmeyer et al., (2004) conducted a comprehensive review of the literature on self-determination and found that while most studies lack a scientific research base, several empirically based studies have demonstrated a link between self-determination and improved educational outcomes for youth with disabilities. Their review yielded several important findings. Children who help choose school activities show enhanced motivation to perform those tasks and are more likely to achieve their goals. Students with higher self-determination scores in their final year of high school are more likely to have expressed a preference to live independently, have a savings or checking account, and be employed for pay. Instruction in self-determination increases participation and independence of students with mild and moderate to severe disabilities. Self-determination skills are enhanced when students and families become active participants in the educational team and collaborative conferences (Algozinne, Brauder, Test, & Wood, 2001; Field, Martin, Miller, Ward, & Wehmeyer, 1998b; Martin & Marshall, 1995; Wehmeyer, 2003; Wehmeyer, Agran, & Hughes, 1998; Wehmeyer, Agran, Palmer, & Blanchard, 1998).

Most studies of self-determination are focused on adolescents and adults; additional research is needed to examine the effects of self-determination on children ages 5–13 (Algozzine et al., 2001). Algozzine and colleagues (2001) identified 22 studies that were scientifically rigorous and determined the impacts of interventions on students. Most of these studies reported modest changes in **self-determination outcomes** as a result of instructional interventions. These findings are relevant for professionals who seek to collaborate with parents and other school professionals to ensure that self-determination is an integral part of student IEP and postsecondary planning.

WHAT HAVE WE LEARNED FROM NATIONAL STUDIES OF SYSTEM COORDINATION?

Coordination initiatives for students with disabilities, encouraged under IDEA, are grounded in research demonstrating that fragmented approaches to service provision do not work in meeting the complex needs of children with disabilities and their families. While there is a dearth of systematic studies of the effects of school-linked services and students' outcomes, a few studies show promising linkages.

National Study of School-Linked Services

Wang, Haertel, and Walberg (1998, 2002) conducted a study with two components: (1) a program analysis of six coordinated **school-linked service programs**, and (2) a quantitative synthesis of 44 studies of the effects of school-linked programs on children's cognition, affect, and behavior. The purpose of the quantitative synthesis of research and practitioner journals in education, psychology, public health, public policy, and social services, and 44 organizations was to identify key characteristics of coordinated school-linked services and their effects on student outcomes.

The 44 programs analyzed in the synthesis served preschool through high school students and reported specific student outcome data. Most of the coordinated school-linked programs from the 44 quantitative studies were targeted for urban, low-achieving, and economically disadvantaged children, youth, and their families. About 80% of programs indicated that school-linked services programs produced positive results. The five most commonly measured student outcomes in studies and evaluations of school-linked programs were: attendance, academic performance (i.e., achievement test scores, grade point average, and academic grades), reduced behavior problems, self-esteem, and dropout rates (Wang, Haertel, & Walberg, 1998). Additional outcomes examined include student cognition, affect, behavior, number of services delivered, new knowledge and skills acquired by family members, reduced drug usage, and reduced teenage pregnancy rates. Direct access to services was emphasized in the programs.

The most frequent collaborators were schools, families, and social and health care workers. Practices of coordinated school-linked service programs included case management and interdisciplinary teams that link students to services; emphasized prevention, not just crisis management; provided outreach services to families of students; shared management of collaborative operations; provided technical assistance to collaborating agencies and service providers; received frequent referrals from teachers to the collaborative staff; included all key stakeholders in planning meetings; used written interagency agreements; and identified common outcomes that reflect common goals among all collaborating agencies. Effective coordination of services relies on several kinds of collaborative processes including planning for inclusive procedures, sharing expertise, managing operations, interacting frequently about the program, and identifying common outcomes.

Table 5.2 shows that the influence of school-linked services on specific student outcomes was very positive in the 44 programs examined. The number of positive results reported ranged from reduced behavior problems (76% of the 44 programs studied) to reduced dropout rates (89% of programs). These results suggest that school-linked service programs are correlated with increased student engagement in

TABLE 5.2 Effect on Student Cognition, Affect, and Behavior		
Type of Student Outcome	Total Number of Programs Reporting Student Outcomes (N = 44)	Number of Programs Reporting Positive Student (N = 44)
Attendance	18	15 (83%)
Academic Performance	36	29 (81%)
Reduced Behavior Problems	17	13 (76%)
Self-Esteem	12	10 (83%)
Dropouts	9	8 (89%)

Source: From *The Effectiveness of Collaborative School-Linked Services,* by M. Wang, G. Haertal, and H. Walberg, 1998, Philadelphia: Mid-Atlantic Laboratory for Student Success. Reprinted with permission.

the life of the school, improve academic performance, reduce behavior problems, and increase self-esteem.

The positive results from the programs that reported outcomes suggest that coordinated services hold promise as a means of enhancing the well-being of children and youth, especially those in adverse circumstances (Wang, Haertel, & Walberg, 1998, 2002).

U.S. Department of Education Study of IDEA Implementation: A Distance to Go

Initiated under IDEA 1997, the U.S. Department of Education's Office of Special Education Programs (OSEP) conducted a national study from 2000–2005 to examine how the changes in the legislation are affecting infants and toddlers, children and youth with disabilities, and their families in the states, districts, and schools. The *Study of State and Local Implementation and Impact of the Individuals with Disabilities Education Act* (SLIIDEA, 2003) was designed to address the following issues of interest to Congress and the public: improving performance for students with disabilities; supporting students with disabilities in the least restrictive environment; facilitating the use of positive behavioral supports; increasing positive parent involvement; improving service coordination; promoting successful transitions for young children to school and young adults to postschool life.

Data collected from 50 states over a 5-year period on children with disabilities (2000–2005) yielded several findings related to system coordination and interagency agreements. Coordination was found to be most frequent between schools and mental health agencies. Resources available for service coordination were fairly limited. There is no clear designation of responsibility for service coordination (e.g., school social work or guidance counselor). No resources such as professional development or training were available to learn about service coordination or resources that might be available in the community. Finally, in many communities, there are few agencies and community resources with which to coordinate.

Even though service coordination has been embedded in special education legislation for decades, these findings indicate that much more needs to be done. Greater federal incentives and guidance are needed to promote school-linked service coordination, but such guidance must be based on sound research into the effectiveness of coordination and its impacts on students and families.

Research on the Full Service and Community Schools and Students with Disabilities

Full-service schools have been described as one-stop centers in which the educational, physical, psychological, and social requirements of students and their families are addressed in a coordinated, collaborative manner using school and community services and supports (Dryfoos, 1994, 2002; Fox, Leone, Rubin, Oppenheim, Miller, & Friedman, 1999; Hocutt, Montague, & McKinney, 2002). In the **full-service school model**, schools house a variety of health care, mental health, and related services for children and their families. Offering services on school grounds alleviates many of the problems that interfere with families obtaining services for their children (e.g., the lack of transportation, lack of understanding of public health and social service systems, inability to take time away from work, and lack of health insurance).

Full-service schools address several areas of need: (1) *prevention* to provide services to children early, when learning or behavior problems are first detected; (2) *support* for students with disabilities who come disproportionally from families who are living in poverty, living with physical or mental health needs, or with educational needs (e.g., literacy); and (3) *integrated services* that also provide non-curricular services to support the total well-being of the student. The full-service school program particularly benefits students with disabilities because it provides easy access to services. Further, providing school-based services may reduce concerns of general education personnel regarding complex medical or behavioral problems by providing access to specialists.

Preventive services include adult education, immunizations, family planning, recreation, after-school care, social services to access basic living resources, economic services/job placement, quality early childhood education, mental/physical health screening, consultation, drug and alcohol prevention, dropout prevention, school meal programs, and child care. *Early intervening services* (to prevent placement in more restrictive settings) include guidance and counseling, tutoring, public health care, conflict resolution, child abuse education, juvenile alternative services, latch-key services, and mental health counseling. *Intensive treatments for chronic disabling conditions* include special education services, related services, emergency crisis treatment, and case management (Dryfoos, 2002). Traditionally, full-service school programs have been designed for at-risk children, but the potential of full-service school programs for students with disabilities is only beginning to become apparent.

Dryfoos (2002) examined 49 community school initiatives that have been evaluated across the United States and which cover a broad continuum, from highly developed community schools in operation for over a decade to schools that are new. Results showed that 15 of the 20 initiatives in this study reported improvement in student academic achievement, as measured by improved grades in school courses and scores in proficiency testing. Thirty-six of the 49 programs reported academic gains. More than half of the evaluations looked for and found evidence of positive development as measured by a variety of indicators, including reductions in behavior or discipline problems, rates of substance abuse, teen pregnancy, suspensions; improved attendance; greater compliance with school assignments and rules; increased access to physical and mental health services; improvements in reading and mathematics scores; greater contact with supportive adults; improvements in personal and family situations and increased parent involvement; increased access to support services; higher teacher attendance rates; improved access to health care and lower hospitalization rates; higher immunization rates; after-school programs available; and improved access to child care.

The accumulating evidence of the value of system coordination for students with disabilities underscores the need to continue to advance research and validate the connections between coordination and student outcomes. Let's See It in Action, below, presents an investigation into the effects of full-service school models for prevention and early intervening services for children with emotional and behavioral disabilities.

The concept of full-service schools is closely aligned with recommended practices in special education that form interagency and family collaborations and integrate comprehensive services into the student's educational program. Full-service schools hold promise for preventing problems from becoming so serious that the student is referred to more intensive support programs. They provide early intervening services, supporting students with multiple risk factors in accessible locations and providing comprehensive intervention support in school settings. More research is needed to explore specific features of how students with disabilities may be served in full-service school models.

LET'S SEE IT IN ACTION! CASE ILLUSTRATION: IMPACT OF THE COMMUNITY SCHOOL MODEL ON STUDENT OUTCOMES

One of the schools that turned itself around was East Hartford High School located in East Hartford, Connecticut. East Hartford High School in 2001–2002 had student demographics very similar to many large urban school districts in the country. They had 2,400 students who spoke 40 different languages and originated from 70 different countries, and 72% of the student population consisted of students of color. The school provided services to a large number of transients and students on free and reduced lunch (Edwards, 2002).

In 1992, East Hartford High School had high gang activity, violence was commonplace, drugs and weapons were present in the schools, tension among the ethnic groups was prevalent, there were excessive suspensions, and the dropout rate was at 28% (Edwards, 2002). Principal Steve Edwards was charged with improving the school. He immediately began to increase extracurricular activities and student clubs so that the students would have more opportunities to participate in school. He started personal responsibility and diversity awareness seminars, and recruited a team of student leaders who helped the school and worked on issues of conflict and difference (Fix, 2000). He solicited ideas from students and started focusing on their health issues. Principal Edwards, with the assistance of Ken Gwozdz, created the student center for conflict resolution, career counseling, and other forms of personal assistance. This center was named the Student Assistance Center (the Center) and consisted of many services, a few examples of which are listed below:

1. The Peer Mediation Program offers student-directed, neutral mediation to decrease conflict and violence and promote communication and resolution.
2. Students who are referred for additional educational and emotional support are paired with one of the 25 faculty members of the Student Assistance Team.
3. The Drug and Alcohol Counseling and Conflict Resolution programs tackle acute problems with individual and group counseling.
4. Juniors and seniors participate in Career Beginnings, a partnership program that offers mentoring and counseling on educational and career opportunities.

The Center's staff included interns from counseling, education, and social work programs around Connecticut. East Hartford High School community partners include: The State Department of Children and Families (DCF), United Way, Connecticut Education Association, Alcohol and Substance Elimination, and Connecticut Regional Educational Council (CREG). These organizations provide guidance and support to the Center, as well as funding for SAC to train students and pay for transportation fees.

From 1993 until 2002, there were no expulsions in 8 years, there was a 60% reduction in fighting, a 50% reduction in suspensions, a reduced dropout rate to 1.8%, raised standardized test scores, increased graduation rates by 12%, and a 20% increase of students going on to college. This application of the **community school model** yielded unexpected positive results for youth (Edwards, 2002, by permission).

Summary of Key Points

- In education, particular attention has been devoted to the benefits and impacts of collaboration and system coordination, although few studies are systemic and rigorous enough to prove causation between collaborative strategies and particular results for children.
- Extensive research has confirmed the benefits of collaborative relationships among school professionals, professionals and parents, and school and community personnel.
- Professionals become less isolated, increase their effectiveness, and become more innovative when they collaborate.
- When school and community personnel coordinate, students and families are more likely to receive the related and support services they need to progress in general education. They are more likely to experience improved transition services at key transition points from early intervention to high school transition.

- The evidence of effectiveness of collaboration and system coordination is accumulating and has led to the incorporation of such practices in major education legislation and in state and national professional standards for teachers and administrators.

Key Terms and Phrases

- Collaborative cultures (p. 120)
- Evidence-based research (p. 120)
- Biological basis (p. 122)
- Evolutionary psychology (p. 122)
- Adaptations (p. 123)
- Cooperative communities (p. 123)
- Natural selection (p. 123)
- Behaviour genetics (p. 124)
- Communities for learning (p. 125)
- Developmental diversity (p. 133)
- Self-determination outcomes (p. 135)
- School-linked service programs (p. 136)
- Full-service school model (p. 138)
- Community school model (p. 139)

Questions for Reflection, Thinking, and Skill Building

1. What does brain research tell us about the relationship between human biology and collaboration and community? Can you provide an example from your experience that illustrates this relationship?

2. Identify at least five ways that collaboration and system coordination improve results for students and families, from early childhood through postsecondary.

3. What are full-service schools? What are the assumptions about the effectiveness of the community schools model?

4. Examine in your own organization or school how collaboration and system coordination support the work of the organization. How many kinds of collaborative activities or initiatives do you see operating? Summarize how these collaborative activities or initiatives are benefiting students and/or professionals, and others.

5. Initiate a *community of inquiry* in your organization or school to address a problem or need. Maintain a journal of the activities in which you describe the impact of the collaborative activity on the participants, the problem being addressed, and on yourself.

PART TWO

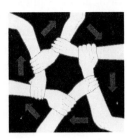

PEOPLE MAKE THE DIFFERENCE IN COLLABORATION AND SYSTEM COORDINATION

The national priority to promote access to general education for students with disabilities has inspired new models for collaboration between special and general education teachers, with related services professionals, and with families. Effective collaboration and coordination implies change in the way people work together and in their beliefs about their own effectiveness as collaborative professionals.

Part 2, *Chapters 6 through 9,* explores the relationships and essential skills for effective communication, collaboration, and coordination. Chapter 6 describes the characteristics of effective collaborative teams and how to create them. The challenges and barriers faced by professionals are explored along with strategies for overcoming them. Chapter 7 explores why the collaboration between special and general education teachers is important for students and teaching. This chapter examines how special and general education teachers collaborate, the barriers to their work, and how they can improve collaborative work. Special attention is given to planning for collaboration and coteaching and how to best prepare teachers for the challenges.

Chapter 8 examines (a) the crucial role of parents and families in the collaborative process and their potential to participate as decision makers in the process and (b) principles and strategies for facilitating family involvement. Chapter 9 introduces a factor in human interaction that makes collaboration and coordination even more complex yet deepens our understanding of the concept and its importance—cultural and linguistic diversity. The chapter is designed to improve educators' ability to establish meaningful collaborative relationships with culturally and linguistically diverse students, parents, and communities. A theoretical framework for understanding diversity and culture is provided, along with principles for working with culturally and linguistically diverse students and parents.

Diversity among people and among perspectives is also an essential dimension of creative collaborative work. People do not learn to step outside their traditional ways of thinking unless they bump up against other, often opposing, ideas. Throughout these chapters, particular emphasis is given to viewing the issues and challenges through the lens of parents and family members.

CHAPTER SIX

WHAT ARE THE ESSENTIAL SKILLS FOR EFFECTIVE COMMUNICATION, COLLABORATION, AND COORDINATION?

Collaborative leadership does not mean working alone or at the top. It does not mean working at the fringes. Rather, it means working in the thick of things, with people, in communities. It is a state of mind that must be shaped during the professional preparation process. Collaboration and communication are vital to change processes. People do not learn to step outside their traditional ways of thinking unless they bump up against others, often against opposing ideas.
— PARKER PALMER, 2000

- What is the connection between adult learning and collaboration?

- What strategies can help collaborative teams improve communication?

- What are the barriers to collaboration and how can they be overcome?

- What attitudes and beliefs (dispositions) about collaboration and coordination help people work together more effectively?

- What professional development content and standards promote collaboration and coordination skills?

PERSPECTIVES

Secondary Teacher:

I read about collaboration theories and strategies in my teacher preparation program, but it is only through experience in the schools that I really "got it." I learned quickly how vital teamwork is as schools try to improve education. I learned that I cannot watch from the sidelines, but have to participate continually and be a part of the process.

College Professor:

It is our responsibility in the academic institution as teacher educators to address collaboration throughout the curriculum. We must make certain that we send into the schools qualified teachers who are prepared for collaboration, team leadership, and partnerships with other professionals and parents. They will never be prepared, and will always be vulnerable to the pressures of isolation and territorialism if we don't address their "dispositions," or attitudes, about collaboration, its importance, and their role in making it work.

INTRODUCTION

The overarching goal of education is to promote the highest possible levels of academic and social functioning for each child, with and without disabilities. Achieving these goals for each student requires collaboration among professionals from multiple disciplines and agencies. Improved interpersonal competence goes to the heart of effective school collaboration. While collaboration involves two or more people, it is important to understand that *each individual is an essential element in any change process*. Each individual affects the quality of relationships and ultimately the success of a collaborative initiative. Organizations do not change until the individuals within them change (Hall & Hord, 2001).

Often both the successes and difficulties with the collaborative process can be traced to problems in professional and personal relationships. Likewise, the cornerstones of coordinated interagency relationships are the personal relationships of the individuals involved. The quality of these relationships depends on the *team skills* and *beliefs and attitudes* of the people involved. Effective collaboration and coordination imply change in the way people work together and in their beliefs about their own effectiveness as collaborative professionals. Diversity and conflict are also essential dimensions of creative collaborative work. People's traditional ways of thinking are not challenged until they encounter others who are different and have opposing ideas.

It has been observed that the cornerstone of the inclusive education movement is collaboration on the part of teachers, specialists, administrators, and parents (Stainback & Stainback, 1996; Welch & Brownell, 2002). IDEA 2004 and NCLB require that educators work to reduce the barriers to professional collaboration since they share the responsibility for the success of students. Such collaboration is, by its very nature, team-driven and multidisciplinary. Multidisciplinary teams are organized to combine the expert contributions of teachers, parents, related professionals, paraprofessionals, and students, who can work in concert to ensure that students with disabilities receive appropriate individualized education and support services. This challenge raises several questions. How do professionals from different disciplines work together and blend their skills and talents to achieve these goals? How do professionals work across the institutional boundaries of schools and community agencies to meet children's multiple needs? What attitudes and beliefs about collaboration are needed to work together toward change effectively? Who takes responsibility for the collaborative process, and who intervenes when the process breaks down?

This chapter describes the characteristics of effective collaborative teams and how to create them. The challenges and barriers faced by professionals are explored along with strategies for overcoming them.

WHAT IS THE CONNECTION BETWEEN ADULT LEARNING AND COLLABORATION?

Knowledge of how adult learners learn best and what motivates them is vital to understanding how collaborative professional relationships can be developed and sustained. Also essential is an understanding of the important connections among learning, relationships, community building, and change.

There are important connections between the characteristics of adult learners and the development of collaborative practice. Attention to *adult learning theory* is important since collaborative team building is a learning opportunity for all involved. Certain conditions facilitate adult learning and learners' capacity to incorporate new knowledge into their professional practice.

Classic *adult learning theory* postulates that learning is facilitated when people are responsible for their learning, subject matter is relevant and meaningful, new material is applied to real-world examples, and self-evaluation is used to assess progress (Knowles, 1984; Rogers, 1969). The **adult learner**, of course, differs from the child or youth physically, emotionally, cognitively, and experientially. Box 6.1 presents characteristics of the adult learner which are synthesized from the works of Dewey, Piaget, Vygotsky, Knowles, Hord, Gardner, Greene, and others.

Learning must be meaningful for the adult learner and relevant to his or her current role and life circumstances. Self-directed, participatory, and transformative

---

BOX 6.1   Key Points About Adult Learners

- Adults (individually and in collaborative groups) learn by doing.
- Adults come with a wealth of life experiences, values and world views, and learning styles which are tapped by effective teachers and team leaders.
- Adults are task-focused in their approach to learning.
- Adults need to "play" with their learning. In other words, they need to apply it to real world situations.

Adults learn best when:

- they have input into the selection of the content and even development of the learning experiences (or goals of a collaborative group);

- the learning is connected to the vast background of knowledge and experience that the adult brings to the table;
- the learning is both received and processed in more than one way;
- the learning is collegial and directed at solving specific job-related problems;
- the learner has ample opportunity to reflect on how to use new competencies; and
- following initial training, they are provided with ongoing support that can take the form of peer coaching or study groups. (Tate, 2004, pp. 24–25)

---

learning are terms frequently used to describe adult learning. **Self-directed learning** refers to an adult learner who initiates learning, explores problems, seeks solutions, and evaluates learned information. For example, the self-directed adult (a) voluntarily chooses to participate in a professional development seminar, (b) applies new information to seek solutions to problems in his or her school environment, and (c) reflects on the value or quality of the information for his or her profession. **Participatory learning** refers to the collaboration between the learner and the teacher/facilitator in decisions about the content of the material to be learned (the curriculum) as well as the instructional process employed. **Transformative learning** occurs when the adult learner reflects on and critiques prior thinking and assumptions as he or she learns new content. Individuals are transformed as they consciously make and implement plans that bring about new ways of defining their world (Imel, 1999). The aim of transformational learning is to change both the adult learner's awareness and understanding. The role of learner changes from receiver of information to one of learner-initiator, information seeker, problem solver, and evaluator (Mezirow, 1997, 2000a; Payne, 2004). Transformative learning is critical to successful collaboration as individuals learn to think, reflect on, and dialogue about, their shared work.

For example, a group of teachers from several subject areas are about to participate in planning for the integration of students with disabilities into the general education classroom. They will have students diagnosed with mild to moderate learning disabilities in some of their classes, supported by a consulting special education teacher. They are asked to discuss their beliefs about the value of inclusion in the general education class for students who have previously been in segregated classrooms or schools. They learn that the attitudes of the group range from openness to all possibilities to outright resistance and firm belief that such students will make it more difficult for them to teach. They view a film from a national research organization demonstrating that students with learning disabilities not only can make remarkable academic progress in the general education classroom, but also can benefit socially and emotionally from working with their general education peers. Furthermore, they learn that research has demonstrated that students without disabilities benefit from understanding the unique learning challenges these students have. The teachers are then asked to discuss their reactions to the film. *Transformative learning* opportunities can be very powerful in the development of collaborative initiatives, as individuals and teams learn to reflect on new information, create new conversations around their shared work, and modify old thinking in order to permit new ways of looking at their world.

Personality and Collaboration

Why are some people viewed as natural collaborators who find it easy to work with others? They are usually highly optimistic people and often highly resilient—they can suffer personal or professional defeat and quickly rekindle their innate optimism. Rarely do they allow their personal struggles to interfere with relationships. Is this characteristic a result of past experiences or is it rooted in individual personality? Some students of human behavior believe it is both but that individual predispositions toward relationships are rooted in our genes.

According to behavioral geneticists and brain researchers, DNA makes each of our brains unique. However, each brain develops in a unique environment to form an individual personality that dictates how we will behave in certain situations. For example, research has demonstrated that three behaviors that are genetically linked include *thrill seeking or risk taking, harm avoidance*, and *anger* (Cohn, Macfarlane, Yanez, & Imai, 1995; Deery, 1999; Donohew, Zimmerman, Cupp, Novak, Colon, & Abell, 2000; Hamer & Copeland, 1998). According to behavior geneticists Hamer and Copeland (1998), all behavior lies on a continuum, and adults display these behaviors in varying degrees in different contexts or situations. Dispositions to these genetic behaviors have significant implications for an individual's ability to learn, collaborate with peers, and adapt to change his or her environment. Gaining an awareness that behavior has a genetic as well as environmental basis helps individuals understand why they may behave as they do in groups, and how they can modify their own behavior to become more effective collaborators.

Thrill seeking is a genetic predisposition to taking risks, and it can take different forms—physical (predisposition to mountain climbing or skydiving) or experiential (predisposition to look for new ways to stimulate one's life or look for new perspectives). People who have a high disposition to risk taking seek and create change, challenge, and complexity in their lives. Those with a low predisposition to risk taking may resist change by seeking stability and repetitiveness. Change agents, charged with leading change through collaboration, are more effective when they recognize that some individuals will welcome their efforts and others will resist them.

Harm avoidance is a genetic predisposition to worry about what may happen, and this worry can take different forms. Harm avoidance is a cluster trait that includes anxiety, fear, inhibition, shyness, depression, tiredness, and hostility (Hamer & Copeland, 1998). People with a predisposition to harm avoidance tend to be emotionally sensitive to both punishment and criticism. They tend to see the darker side of life, focusing more on what can go wrong rather than what can go right. They are often viewed as pessimists. Of all of the genetic traits, harm avoidance shows up in humans very early in their lives, persists throughout life, and can be a difficult trait to overcome. *Collaboration generates fear* in those who seek to avoid harm through relative isolation and avoidance of others. Palmer (1998) expresses this concept in an interesting way as he discusses the "culture of fear":

> We collaborate with the structures of separation because they promise to protect us against one of the deepest fears at the heart of the human being—the fear of having a live encounter with alien "otherness," whether the other is a student, a colleague, a subject, or a self-dissenting voice within. We want these encounters on our own terms so we can control their outcomes and they will not threaten our view of the world and self. (p. 168)

What does this mean for collaboration in times of change? Some collaborators will be optimistic about what will happen to them (low predisposition to harm avoidance), and others will be pessimistic (high predisposition to harm avoidance). Some may be impatient for change and may challenge anything they can—the status quo, the pace of change, the leader of change, or the decision process (predisposition to risk taking). Some will fall somewhere in between.

Anger is a genetic predisposition to intense emotions and aggression, which, of all of the traits, has the greatest effect on thinking patterns. It can cause individuals to behave in ways that are inappropriate for a given situation. During a change process, uncertainty can trigger emotions and anger, which, if not addressed, can undermine relationships and social systems that are crucial for successful collaboration.

Change efforts can bring out both the best and worst in people, but the facilitation strategies chosen can make a great difference. For change agents and participants, the knowledge that behavior has its roots in our genes (personality) as well as our background and experiences, can bring perspective to the process of collaboration and prepare them for the challenges. It can help both the change leader and the participants (a) identify sources of resistance and manage them; (b) marshal the forces of the "risk takers" to help propel and shape the process; (c) be more sensitive to the pace of change and shore up patience in team members who resist change efforts; and (d) appreciate that apparent "resisters" (harm avoiders or naysayers) are valuable because they raise important questions or concerns that may go unexamined in a change process.

It is important that collaborative team leaders and participants understand that the complexity of the task itself, coupled with the challenge of teamwork among very different personalities, can form a "perfect storm" for interpersonal stress. Intervention skills are essential along with an appreciation for one of the great paradoxes of human behavior—desire for control while desiring group acceptance.

What Strategies Can Help Collaborative Teams Improve Communication?

Effective teams are important catalysts for development and change in schools. Team participants represent a range of values, experiences, technical skills, and cultural traditions. In today's environment of school accountability and performance, teams charged with creating new policies and practices or providing technical assistance are often pressured to produce results quickly. Under these conditions, teams need to model values of empowerment, participation, and flexibility. In such settings, traditional team building is not enough. Instead, teams need an in-depth understanding of how effective collaboration is essential for student progress, school improvement, and ensuring access to appropriate education for all children.

As discussed previously, some people are naturally collaborative, like to work in teams, enjoy discussions, and readily open up and share information with one another. This is an easy group to work with or lead. But as mentioned earlier, collaboration often requires the combined thinking of people who view the world and their roles differently, do not enjoy working together, and prefer to work alone. How then do we think about building effective collaboration? What strategies can help create cohesion among groups of diverse individuals? It is not enough to say: We just have to learn to trust each other. Change is difficult from the human side, but it is also difficult from the practical, structural, organizational, and logistical side (Beyerlein, McGee, Klein, Nemiro, & Broedling, 2003). Change through team collaboration is highly complex, but essential in the work of today's schools and school-linked agencies. Experts who advocate the use of collaborative teams make the following assumptions:

- Effective collaborative teams develop creative solutions to difficult problems and tend to be successful in implementing complex plans.
- Teams make good use of diverse talents, knowledge, and experience as they improve decision making and the quality of projects and programs.
- Teams can increase flexibility in rapidly changing environments and can produce rapid responses.
- Teams permit professionals to feel a sense of ownership and empowerment in their jobs to make meaningful contributions to the effectiveness of their organizations and to student progress.
- Teams build commitment and support for new ideas among staff and community members as they become part of the learning process of professionals (Hayden, Frederick, & Smith, 2003; Maeroff, 1993; Sartorius, 2005).

It is important to appreciate the challenge that comes with developing into effective, well-functioning teams.

Adult Learners and the Stages of Team Growth

Collaborative teams and work groups are formed for a variety of reasons. Some form for brief periods of time to complete short-term projects (e.g., a short-term recruitment team to hire a new teacher). Such teams tend to pass rapidly through the stages of team growth (*forming, storming, norming, performing,* and *adjourning*), first defined by Tuckman and Jensen (1977) and depicted in Figure 6.1.

However, if a collaborative team is expected to remain in place for a long period of time, or to become an enduring part of the structure of the school or organization, the "human element" takes on profound importance as the group seeks to reach and sustain the "norming" and "performing" stages. Attention to *adult learning theory* is important for sustained or long-term team building since it represents a continuous learning process for all involved. As mentioned earlier, classic *adult learning theory* indicates that learning is facilitated when people are responsible for their learning, the subject matter is relevant and meaningful, new material is applied to real-world examples, and self-evaluation is a part of assessing performance and

FIGURE 6.1

Phases in Team Formation

Source: From "States in Small Group Development," by B. W. Tuckman and M. A. C. Jensen, 1977, *Group and Organizational Studies, 2,* p. 419. Reprinted with permission.

Phase 1: Forming. Individuals begin to see themselves as a group with a common task. Central issues are revolvement and adhesion.

Phase 2: Storming. Group members vie for leadership and control. Issues are direction and conflict management.

Phase 3: Norming. Group develops expectations about "correct" behaviours and an identity that sets it apart from other groups. Issues are agreeing on expectations and dealing with failure of some to meet expectations.

Phase 4: Performing. Group members are actively involved in doing a task, accomplishing objectives. Issues include individual performance and coordination.

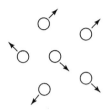
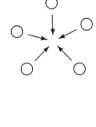
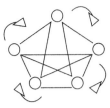

progress. Adults (and adults in collaborative teams) learn by doing; come with a wealth of life experiences, values, and worldviews; are task-focused in their approach to learning, and need to apply new knowledge to real world situations. Learning must be meaningful for the adult learner (or group member) and relevant to their current roles and life circumstances (Kasl & Yorks, 2004; Knowles, 1998; Payne, 2004; Rogers, 1969; Schwandt & Marquardt, 2000). Development of effective collaborative teamwork involves *self-directed, participatory and transformative learning processes* in which adults critically reflect on their assumptions and beliefs. Transformative learning is essential in achieving the "performing" stage of collaborative work.

Ten Blocks to Effective Communication and Strategies to Overcome Them

Communication and effective interpersonal relationships are the building blocks for collaborative work. Communication among personnel can be improved when they become aware of the habits or behaviors that can either facilitate or undermine communication and relationships and divert a team from their task. The following presents habits and behaviors that can block communication, adapted from the work of Gerlach (2003):

   1. *Unequal Status.* Someone in the team sends a verbal or nonverbal message (unconscious message sent through voice tone or body language) that is received as "*I don't view you or respect you as an equal on this team.*" Team leaders should be aware that communication is effective only when each participant believes that they have equal status with others and feel respected.

   2. *Mismatch in Communication.* Two or more team members' communication needs conflict—for example, Bill needs to "vent" or express frustration, and Jane needs to persuade Bill to adopt an idea or position. The communication needs are mismatched and can create conflicts, which could be avoided if team members were aware of each other's needs. Help the team members identify their individual communication needs and understand that different needs can conflict at times.

3. *Mixed Message.* A team member may communicate a double or mixed message (their words say one thing and their voice or manner imply another (e.g., the person shouts—"*I am NOT angry with you!*" with arms folded tightly across the chest). The response to such communication is often confusion and distrust of the person speaking. Such double messages occur when the speaker has two conflicting thoughts at the same time and is not honest in his or her communication. The team can help the speaker to become aware of the double message being sent.

4. *Distraction.* One or more team members are distracted in the team meeting and can't focus or attend well to the work of the group. They may be distracted by (a) physical discomfort (e.g., pain, thirst, sleepiness, full bladders, headaches); (b) worry, anxiety, or other strong emotion; or (c) environmental factors such as noise, sirens, flashing lights, or room temperature; and yet they try to communicate in the group. The team leader should be aware of the potential for environmental and personal distractions.

5. *Interruptions.* When a team member frequently interrupts the group or their partner, they are communicating an implicit message that "*I'm superior and my needs and ideas are more important than yours.*" This behavior also suggests that the interrupting team member is preparing his or her response without really listening to the other, or is rushing the speaker. The other person may feel discounted or insulted and may react with defensiveness or resentment. The most constructive response in a team situation is to respectfully make the interrupter aware of the behavior and calmly say, "*I really need you to stop interrupting me.*"

6. *Withholding Emotions.* Sometimes people withhold emotions either purposefully or unconsciously as they communicate. Others in the group are left feeling unsafe or confused about the person's meaning or may misinterpret them ("*You don't trust me because you're hiding something*"). Chronic anxiety and distrust in the group can result. However, some people (particularly the "harm avoiders") have difficulty expressing emotions and need encouragement to understand how this communication block hinders effective problem solving and creativity.

7. *Focus on the Past.* Occasionally a team member may have the habit of focusing continually on the past or the future ("*We tried that in the past and it didn't work*"; "*I know what's going to happen in the future, so I don't want to be part of this*"). Such behavior can be deliberate or unconscious, but usually serves to avoid confronting problems in the present. The team member needs an awareness of how this behavior affects communication effectiveness and relationships. The team member is also seeking reassurance that patterns of the past will not be repeated.

8. *Focus on Self.* Some individuals are habitually self-centered, causing others to feel ignored or resentful. They may repeatedly or suddenly change the subject to divert the conversation, or they may exhibit nonstop talking which undermines communication and keeps people at an emotional distance. Awareness and respectful assertion on the part of other team members can intervene constructively ("*I notice that you change the subject when we talk about getting technical assistance*").

9. *Preaching or Moralizing.* A team member may have the habit of preaching to others or advising them, which can undermine team relationships, implying—*I know how to fix your problem and you don't.*" If someone needs to express their feelings or to vent, they want to be respectfully heard and don't necessarily need to have someone insist on "fixing" the problem.

10. *Withdrawal and Lack of Eye Contact.* Physical or emotional withdrawal can communicate to others: "*You scare or overwhelm me,*" or "*I am not interested in what you have to say right now.*" Habitual lack of eye contact can also communicate to others a feeling of inferiority or intimidation which, over time, may result in loss of respect by team members and ineffective communication. Either message undermines communication and leaves others frustrated and mistrustful ("*Greg, every time I suggest that we try a different approach in the classroom, you just say 'fine!' and then become silent. Is there something that's troubling you?*"). Constructive intervention involves honest feedback to the individual to respectfully explore what is triggering the withdrawal.

To overcome barriers such as these, it is important to make time for team members to discuss how communication habits can undermine relationships. *Metatalk* is a useful term that means talking about how one communicates with others (Gerlach, 2003). When conflicts arise and do not seem to be resolved over time, team members must ask, "Are we actually problem solving, or are we doing something else?" Excessive and prolonged interpersonal problems at work lead to negative affective reactions such as increased stress, lower job satisfaction, and reduced organizational and professional commitment (Billingsly, 2003). For these reasons, teams need clear signals from team leaders and superiors that (a) they have permission to explore their communication habits freely; and (b) all team members are responsible for their communication blocks, for improving their team communication, and for resolving disputes.

Traditional organizations are set up to reinforce individual work and can actually contribute to competition and conflict (Beyerlein & Harris, 2003; Brownell et al., 2005). However, humans are social beings and naturally create relationships, networks, and communities. The successful **change agent** looks for opportunities to harness this natural tendency to create communities and to use it to address the important work of improving education for all children. He or she strives to create places, spaces, times, and opportunities for both formal and informal networking and community building.

Six Strategies to Improve Communication and Collaboration

The following set of six strategies for improving communication and collaborative work are defined and explained in the context of a case illustration (Boxes 6.2–6.7) in which a change agent, the principal, led a group of staff through a very challenging change process to establish a new collaborative structure within the school. Adult learning principles are reflected in the process and expected outcomes for each strategy are identified:

Strategy 1. Affirm the importance of the common goal of the collaboration. Clearly communicate the goal of the change process or initiative and affirm the purpose and value of each individual team member (see Box 6.2).

Each collaborating team member must be clear about the purpose and goal of the change initiative to which he or she will be devoting time and energy. The

---

BOX 6.2   Hope Middle School Tackles a Difficult Challenge: Strategy 1

Anna Hayworth, principal of Hope Middle School, wanted to establish a working team to design and establish a *prereferral process* (early intervening services) for students for whom English was their second language (ESOL). Her charge to the group was to come up with a process that would help differentiate among students who were falling behind due to language acquisition challenges, those who had learning disabilities that required special education, and those who had both. The goal was to make the most appropriate placement and intervention decisions for these students. She began by calling together general education and special education teachers, the school counselor, the psychologist, the language resource teacher, and others who could provide input. She also provided a strong rationale for why the school needed to embark on this initiative, using demographic information and new legal requirements, and confirming this as a school improvement priority for the coming year. She explained why she had chosen each member of the team, what she thought they could bring to the change effort, and how they would be compensated for their time (*continued* in Box 6.3).

BOX 6.3   Hope Middle School: Strategy 2

Principal Hayworth invited a consultant, Dr. Niancopolous ("Dr. Nick," for short), from the local university to lead the change team through a series of exercises beginning with the selection of a project name (this consulting role could also be filled by someone within the school system with strong collaborative leadership skills). The team then presented, discussed, and reflected upon a variety of cases of students who had both English language challenges and learning disabilities. They learned about the difficulties in distinguishing between second language difficulties and learning disabilities unrelated to second language acquisition. They examined models for prereferral (early intervening services) that were being used in states in which there were high concentrations of students from immigrant families. The goal was to help the team understand the complexity of the problem, appreciate its importance, recognize the need within their own school, and become familiar with successful approaches in other districts and schools (*continued* in Box 6.4).

---

expected outcome of this strategy is the appreciation of team members for each other's roles and contributions, the sense of being individually valued as members of the team, the sense of participating in an important change event, and intellectual "buy-in" or commitment to the process.

Strategy 2. Build a personal commitment to the collaborative goal. Facilitate the personal engagement, investment, or "connection" of each person to the change goal or initiative (see Box 6.3).

In order to be as effective as possible and to overcome natural dispositions discussed earlier (harm avoidance, anger, etc.), each collaborator had to feel committed to the goal of the initiative. Such commitment may not occur immediately, but is more likely to develop if team members believe in the need and see the merits of the mission.

The expected outcome of this strategy is the emotional and attitudinal commitment of each team member, the development of a group bond or team identity, understanding of the complex nature of the problem, and appreciation of its importance to students, families, and the school. In addition, the goal is to help staff develop a sense of possibility by examining actual program models and progress that other schools were achieving.

Strategy 3. Build a common commitment to the power of the team. Create an appreciation for and commitment of each team member to the potential of the collective group to create change that can impact students (see Box 6.4).

Team members are more engaged when they connect their individual and collective power of collaboration to the goal and outcome of the project. This means that they must understand how collaborative relationships are fundamental to building and sustaining a development initiative. To build a "team lens," they must also understand how their individual professional roles and expertise relate to the new structures being created. Therefore, the expected outcome of this strategy is the appreciation of collaborators that the power of the team lies in the collective expertise and commitment of professionals working to create a common solution that affects students.

Strategy 4. Clearly communicate the collaborative principles or rules of engagement. Establish a climate and set of rules for constructive collaboration so that the work of planning, problem solving, and implementing actions can proceed in a manner that supports the group process (see Box 6.5).

All collaborators must feel safe in the group process and feel that their expertise and experience is valued and respected. While this may be affirmed in the beginning of a collaborative venture, it may become undermined at any time during the process. Consultant Dr. Nick framed the "rules" in the form of *essential principles,* reflecting sensitivity to the adult learner and his or her need for an explicit and reasoned process.

The expected outcomes of this strategy include a team process that is characterized by (a) constructive dialog; (b) respect for diverse opinions; (c) a reflective approach to conflict, moving beyond impulsive or defensive reactions, and toward deeper interpretation of conflicts and concerns in terms of the overall goal; and

---

BOX 6.4   Hope Middle School: Strategy 3

Dr. Nick, the university consultant, designed each planning session so that it had a collaborative team-building component. The purpose of this was to ensure that collaborative behavior could be observed, reinforced (nurtured), or intervened in if breakdown occurred. The second purpose was to teach the team about collaborative group processes and their role in it. Therefore, at the first planning session, Dr. Nick discussed collaboration, what facilitates it and what undermines it, and how it is connected to the overall purpose and objectives of the change initiative. They explored and discussed examples of change initiatives that had failed because of group factors such as conflicting personalities and behaviors, communication failures, lack of information, disciplinary territorialism, weak team leadership, inability to keep the group on task, lack of commitment to the goals, and shifting priorities of the school leader. They examined the reasons that each team member was selected to be on the permanent "Early Response Team" and why each kind of expertise was functionally essential to the prereferral review and decision-making process being created. This helped each team member connect their roles with the new procedures being created. Finally, they developed a way of evaluating their work as a team, including effective *group performance* rather than individual performance (*continued* in Box 6.5).

BOX 6.5   Hope Middle School: Strategy 4

During a planning session, consultant Dr. Nick presented "rules of engagement" for the collaborative work. He explained that these rules were essential principles for teams that were associated with effective group performance and could help strengthen the team, reduce conflicts, and improve the quality of their work. These principles included the following:

- We are committed to the goal and purpose of this collaboration, and all have something to learn in the process.

- We understand that each individual's role and domain of expertise is needed in combination to address the solution.

- We respect diversity of perspective and opinion and believe that it enhances the quality of the solution.

- While we appreciate the collective history of the team members within the organization, we will free ourselves to search outside our traditional ways of doing things in order to consider new ideas.

- We understand that conflicts may arise, and within these conflicts we will look for issues, concerns, and questions that are worthy of examination by the group.

- We understand that we all have unique personality characteristics that will interact with the group process, and we will commit to harnessing and applying them to pursue the goal.

- We are committed to sustaining this collaboration.

After that Dr. Nick encouraged team members to discuss experiences they have had with effective and productive teams and ineffective teams and what made them that way. Finally, he asked the team to commit to addressing problems or threats to the process by reviewing the essential principles and recommitting to the overall goal (*continued* in Box 6.6).

BOX 6.6   Hope Middle School: Strategy 5

During several development meetings of the Early Response Team, Principal Hayworth encouraged team members to bring in, send to her in advance, or attach by email, any articles or information that they could find related to the prereferral process. She particularly encouraged articles that were critical of the process, represented different perspectives on the process, or that highlighted potential pitfalls. These were discussed at team meetings, and team members were encouraged to discuss the prereferral processes, including critical issues from their professional perspectives. During these sessions, Principal Hayworth always remembered to share a funny story about collaborating groups to start off with a laugh (*continued* in Box 6.7).

(d) a set of governing principles that shape team behavior, help troubleshoot threats to collaboration along the way, and serve as the basis for self-assessment or evaluation of team performance.

Strategy 5. Facilitate the sharing of knowledge, new information, and prior experience. It is important to nurture collaborators' ability to share new information about the work at hand as well as their prior experiences (see Box 6.6).

Each team member needs to know that his or her concerns and questions about the change process are being considered seriously and that problems encountered will not be insurmountable. Remember that the "harm avoiders" are often pessimists who worry about what can go wrong and can anticipate problems. You need them! As Parker Palmer advises, a healthy respect is needed for truth sought through conflict. Conflict is a result of complex communication, testing ideas that serve to redefine the meaning and context of knowledge . . . the dynamic conversation of a community that keeps testing old conclusions, and coming into new ones is where truth exists (1998). Conflict is essential, but it must also be harnessed and managed. The techniques of raising understanding about sources of conflict and researching and sharing new ideas that represent different perspectives can address concerns about change.

The anticipated outcome for this strategy is the understanding by the team that a critical and reflective approach to conflict (examining pitfalls and opposing viewpoints) actually strengthens the work of the team and is not to be feared.

Strategy 6. Address problematic behavior swiftly and constructively. Take decisive action to preserve the team, its work, and its progress when serious threats are brought about by the undermining behavior of single members (see Box 6.7).

The collaborative team leader—who may be the principal, a lead teacher, or a consultant—must remain aware that sometimes individual behaviors can undermine and threaten the work of and survival of the team. Collaborative systems are not always predictable, and stress may cause unpredictable reactions. Team leaders are not aware of all of the daily stresses of the individuals working together, what they bring into the workplace with them, or their physical or emotional states. Team leaders must be ready to act and intervene constructively if the stress mounts and the team is threatened by behaviors such as personal hostility among team members, threats to leave the team, criticisms of the team leader, domination of the team by one or two members which excludes participation of others, refusal of a member to interact or participate, or criticism of the team process or team members in a destructive way outside the meetings. In these cases, it is up to the team leader to meet with the "troubled" individual to discuss the underlying problems, reconfirm

---

BOX 6.7   Hope Middle School: Strategy 6

During one development team meeting, the discussion about appropriate placement of students became heated. The language arts teacher, Mr. McNulty, raised issues of behavior in the classroom as a result of "different cultural standards," as he put it. The language resource teacher, Maria Jimenez, accused the general education teacher of "wanting all special education kids and all non-English-speaking kids out of his general education classroom!" Behavioral issues for students with disabilities and English language learners had not come up before, and this was a trigger for some anger and hostility. Mr. McNulty became enraged, red in the face, and threatened to resign from the team altogether.

Principal Hayworth, who had been carefully observing the strategies of Dr. Nick, intervened and asked Mr. McNulty to share experiences he had had with English language learners and students with disabilities as it related to behavior concerns. This helped defuse Mr. McNulty's emotions and shifted the attention of the group from the personal conflict to defining the particulars of his concern about behavior. Mr. McNulty described circumstances in which some of his students were falling behind and which he believed led to some acting-out behavior. He felt unprepared to accommodate or help the students with learning disabilities and the English language learners. The discussion was triggering his feelings about his sense of competence because he was an award-winning teacher with a 20-year successful history with the school. Mrs. Jimenez then pointed out that in her view the prereferral process that they were designing would actually help provide support to both students and teachers who have students with disabilities and English language learners in their classrooms. At the next meeting, Mr. McNulty brought in an article and asked that the team discuss a professional development program that could help everyone.

that person's importance on the team, and regain his or her commitment to the mission. Communication effectiveness is key to getting results from collaborative work and is a shared responsibility of all participants.

What Are the Barriers to Collaboration and How Can They Be Overcome?

Earlier in the chapter, communication barriers were discussed. The following sections examine barriers to collaboration and to collaborative practice which can fall into two broad categories: (1) attitudinal and knowledge barriers that prevent an individual from interacting effectively with one or more colleagues; and (2) systemic and structural barriers that make collaboration difficult, if not impossible, to achieve within the organization or setting without the intervention of an administrator or other leader. Educators and human service professionals take pride in their professional status and independence. Such independence, however, can sometimes lead to isolation and can create barriers to professional collaboration and system coordination.

Organizational, Attitudinal, and Knowledge Barriers

It is also useful to view barriers to collaborative practice as falling into three clusters: **organizational, attitudinal, and knowledge barriers:**

1. *Organizational barriers*: barriers related to the differences in the way collaborative or interagency relationships are structured and managed, how they are led, how resources are provided, and how the overall environment supports them.
2. *Attitudinal barriers*: barriers related to the beliefs, motivations, attitudes, and fears (dispositions) that professionals have about students and families, their roles in the educational service system, and community participation.
3. *Knowledge barriers*: barriers related to the differences in the levels of knowledge and skills of professionals who represent different roles or agencies, but must work together to achieve common goals for students and families.

As mentioned previously, the cornerstones of collaborative practice are the personal relationships of the individuals involved. Often both the successes and difficulties with the collaborative process can be traced to problems in professional and personal relationships.

Overcoming Organizational, Attitudinal, and Knowledge Barriers

Asking the right *strategic questions*—questions that help define the problem to be addressed through collaboration—helps in selecting the most effective strategies for a collaborative initiative. The following questions represent different collaborative goals for students at different grade levels and for different purposes. What collaborative strategies are needed to help elementary teachers work together to determine how to improve library access for children with disabilities? What collaborative strategies should be used to restructure relationships among secondary general and special education teachers to better support ninth-grade students entering high school from middle school? How can teachers best collaborate to use the results of student assessments to plan curriculum and instruction for student with disabilities in middle school? What collaborative strategies would help middle school teachers and parents work together to improve ongoing communication and participation? How can collaboration help support both general and special education teachers implement positive behavioral supports in the middle school classroom?

Let's return to the four functions of collaboration introduced in Chapter 1 and ask—should the strategy center on collaboration *as discovery, as synthesis, as development of practice, or as building professional community*? Table 6.1 describes the barriers (organizational, attitudinal, and knowledge) to collaboration and system coordination introduced earlier along with strategies for overcoming them.

TABLE 6.1 Barriers to Collaboration and System Coordination

ORGANIZATIONAL BARRIERS

Lack of cooperative processes or agreements to empower school-based and interagency partnerships:
Many within-school and school–community coordination efforts lack formalized processes or agreements. These agreements are crucial to the development of collaborative relationships because they define the local authority for action and define common goals and objectives for the unit or agency.

Problem-solving strategy:
Carefully examine the collaborative processes or cooperative agreement that exists among professionals within the school, or between school and community service agencies. If there is none, then create one and solicit input from all who will be affected by the collaboration. Who are the collaborating partners, the resources available, and the explicit goals of the partnership? Revise the cooperative agreement to make it more flexible and responsive to student needs. Examine the cooperative agreements of other schools and agencies.

Policy and funding barriers:
Different school-based professional groups (e.g., special educators, related services personnel, general educators) and community-based agencies have evolved from separate public laws and funding streams, and therefore have different service requirements and target groups. Coordinating resources or funds among these groups or between schools and community agencies presents a challenge for coordinated services and shared accountability for outcomes.

Problem-solving strategy:
The collaborative leader or interagency coordinator should help personnel to be aware of public laws and local policies that affect the professional groups or key agencies involved in the interagency partnership. Create clear structures by which professional groups regularly meet and develop policies and programs for students in a collaborative manner. Create joint service plans, such as joint IEP/ITPs and IPEs (Individual Plan for Employment Services). If possible, create initiatives in which resources or funds are pooled across agencies.

Legislative shifts and agency priorities:
Changes in legislation and agency priorities mean changes in the way services are organized and delivered (for example IDEA reauthorization and NCLB requirements). Changes that affect a single school unit's services within a collaborative partnership, will affect all cooperating partners.

Problem-solving strategy:
The collaborative leader or interagency coordinator should help personnel to be aware of changes in public laws and local policies that affect the work of professionals within the school and among schools and community agencies. Task interdisciplinary teams to explore how these shifts affect their collaborative roles. This information can be incorporated into orientation and training of staff.

Lack of incentives for coordination:
Personnel in each cooperating unit or agency may be evaluated according to different performance criteria. If coordination activities are not part of the reward system, then not much attention will be devoted to it by the individual partners.

Problem-solving strategy:
Build school-based collaboration or system coordination efforts into the reward systems for each unit or cooperating agency. Be cognizant of the kinds of incentives and disincentives that either encourage or discourage commitment to collaboration. Design special recognition activities for staff of cooperating groups or agencies to show appreciation for their contributions.

Data collection and reporting are inadequate:
Cooperating school-based professional groups and community agencies typically report their performance differently (e.g., services provided, individuals served, etc.) since their missions vary. Some may not report at all. Therefore, each group or agency establishes its own reporting system, monitoring criteria, quality assurance criteria, performance measurement criteria, and annual goals and plans for services.

Problem-solving strategy:
Coordinate unit or interagency efforts to collect and share data on students who need services while in school or as they prepare for transition from high school to college or employment. Develop data collection procedures jointly with cooperating agencies and relate them directly to partnership goals and objectives. Collect a variety of data to obtain a comprehensive picture of student activities and outcomes (school records, baseline data, interviews, observations, surveys of participants).

Aᴛᴛɪᴛᴜᴅɪɴᴀʟ Bᴀʀʀɪᴇʀs

Political pressures and pressure groups:
As economic conditions force agencies to economize, collaborative leaders and system coordinators are increasingly pressured to demonstrate to the school

Problem-solving strategy:
Involve school-based as well as community stakeholder groups in the development of interagency initiatives and in the selection of outcome and performance measures. This involvement

and wider community how school collaboration and interagency linkages can contribute to cost-effective services and student achievement.

will increase the likelihood that the public will support collaborative and service coordination efforts and associated resources. Use research and evaluation data to advocate for the value of service coordination.

Territorialism:

When collaboration is viewed as encroachment of professional groups or agencies on each other's service "territory," it can threaten people and their comfort with traditional ways of operating. Collaborative and system coordination initiatives often result in changes in the way a team or individual agency conducts business.

Problem-solving strategy:

Help personnel to understand the reasons for collaboration and to work to reduce territorialism. Collaborative initiatives often result in changes in the way teachers and other professionals conduct business. It is important to discuss with collaborating personnel their perceptions of individual roles and responsibilities and to encourage them to express fears about the changes that may occur in their roles. Provide opportunities for staff to express concerns about changes in their roles. Educate staff about how the collaboration or coordination will enrich their roles and ultimately benefit students and the organization as a whole.

Staff turnover:

Serious barriers to collaboration and interagency relationships result from high turnover among key personnel. Established relationships, and the emergence of "champions" create leadership and trust, and can accelerate interagency coordination efforts. The loss of a respected "champion" for the partnership can result in the loss of years of progress.

Problem-solving strategy:

Examine staffing arrangement and loads and their potential impacts on opportunities for collaboration. Examine orientation and training programs to determine how well training includes collaborative practices and helps foster collaborative attitudes and communication. Decide if there are adequate career paths or opportunities for increasing responsibility, opportunities for leadership, and promotions. Create a mentor structure to pair new and veteran staff.

KNOWLEDGE BARRIERS

Lack of understanding among personnel about their respective disciplines, unit, or agencies:

It is important that collaborating professionals understand each other's roles and mission and recognize how

Problem-solving strategy:

Develop cross-unit training sessions and share descriptions of unit or department missions, goals, and objectives. Build this information into orientation and training. Create a joint newsletter to share they can improve the service system for all students.

Lack of knowledge about interagency models for collaboration and coordination:

There is a need for new models for school-based collaboration and system coordination and for improvement of collaborative relationships.

information among collaborating groups or coordinating school–community agencies, to highlight accomplishments, and to recognize personnel.

Problem-solving strategy:

Develop common terminology for communication among cooperating departments units or agencies. Define common system coordination activities, and define outcomes and target populations. Share information about interagency models in other districts and states and discuss how they can strengthen the partnership. Examine the structure of the coordination process or interagency agreement, the partners involved, the designated lead unit or agency, the defined outcomes for the relationship, and the process for review of the agreement and for determining how "success" is measured.

What strategies have been shown to be effective in overcoming the organizational, attitudinal and knowledge barriers to collaboration and system coordination? The following sections present these strategies in relation to these three categories while also addressing the collaborative functions: *collaboration as discovery, as synthesis of ideas, as development of practice, and as building professional community.* We will begin with overcoming attitudinal barriers and ask the question: What strategies help people work together effectively?

How Can Knowledge Barriers Be Overcome?

Knowledge barriers refer to the differences in the knowledge and skills of various professionals within a school, or between schools and coordinating community service agencies. The following sections discuss strategies for harnessing and applying knowledge to improve education for all children, including those with disabilities.

Help Personnel Understand How Social Relationships in Schools Affect Student Achievement. Research has demonstrated that effective relationships among school personnel are positively associated with environments that promote student progress and school improvement. *Relational trust* acts as both a foundation for and an agent of school improvement. People work together more effectively when they understand how social relationships affect students and their achievement, and understand the process of improving social relationships among professionals and teams.

Teach Competencies for Effective Collaboration.   Creating and sustaining change on matters of compelling importance in a school or school-linked agency requires a critical mass of personnel within the school who are willing and able to function as change agents. Just about every professional who will be involved with the education and development of children with disabilities needs special preparation for collaboration. The effectiveness of these roles and quality of services depends on the collaborative skills of these professionals in schools and communities. Over the past decade, new performance standards related to collaboration skills have been included in professional development programs for general and special educators and administrators.

The ability to collaborate effectively with others is not innate, but involves complex skills that must be modeled and learned by engaging in collaborative practice. Having *competence* for collaboration means that professionals possess the **knowledge, skills, and dispositions** (attitudes and beliefs) to participate. They must have *knowledge* of the foundational ideas and principles underlying collaboration and coordination. They must learn and practice the *skills* required to participate in and facilitate collaboration. They must also possess the *dispositions*, or beliefs, attitudes, and ethics that are conducive to collaboration and coordination. Examples of dispositions important for collaboration include the following:

1. The belief that *all stakeholders* who are affected by a collaborative change initiative should have a voice (representation) in the process (Hall & Hord, 2001).
2. The belief in the *team lens*—that the combined thinking of people involved in collaboration can lead to superior results and commitment to the process.
3. The belief that disagreement and conflict among collaborators actually *enrich* the process. Critical reflection that requires collaborators to step outside their traditional ways of thinking occurs when they are challenged by the opposing ideas of others (Palmer, 1998).
4. Personal commitment to the goals of the team.
5. Willingness to take reasonable risks.

Specific **competencies for collaboration** and emerging standards that guide professional development are discussed in a later section.

Establish Communities of Practice.   **Communities of practice** (CoP) is an emerging collaborative strategy involving groups of people informally bound together by shared expertise and passion for a joint enterprise (Wenger & Snyder, 2000). The principle output of CoP is extended knowledge, although the CoP impact may transcend organizational boundaries. Communities of practice, formal work groups, teams, and informal networks are useful in complementary ways. Table 6.2 illustrates the characteristics of different types of worker groupings.

Communities of practice share a sense of mission in their work. They draw upon the knowledge that each member brings and their collective ability to link up with a vast outside knowledge network. Communities of practice can greatly accelerate the work of positive change within the school. Let See It in Action, page 167, presents a case illustration of a middle school community of practice.

TABLE 6.2 A Snapshot Comparison

	What's the purpose?	Who belongs?	What holds it together?	How long does it last?
Community of practice	To develop members' capabilities to build and exchange knowledge	Members who select themselves	Passion, commitment, and identification with the group's expertise	As long as there is interest in maintaining the group
Formal work group	To deliver a product or service	Everyone who reports to the group's manager	Job requirements and common goals	Until the next reorganization
Project team	To accomplish a specified task	Employees assigned by senior management	The project's milestones and goals	Until the project has been completed
Informal network	To collect and pass on business information	Friends and business acquaintances	Mutual needs	As long as people have a reason to connect

Source: From *Cultivating Communities of Practice* (p. 142), by E. Wenger, R. McDermott, and W. M. Snyder, 2002, Cambridge, UK: Cambridge University Press. Reprinted with permission.

WHAT ATTITUDES AND BELIEFS (DISPOSITIONS) ABOUT COLLABORATION AND COORDINATION HELP PEOPLE WORK TOGETHER MORE EFFECTIVELY?

Attitudinal barriers, introduced earlier, refer to impediments to collaboration that are rooted in people's beliefs, motivations, and attitudes about students and families, their roles in the educational service system, their colleagues, and their participation in collaborative work. The following sections outline six beliefs that can facilitate collaborative culture in schools and school-linked agencies.

1. *Belief in the human drive for community and growth.* Humans are social beings and they naturally create relationships, networks, and communities (Beyerlein & Harris, 2003; Palmer, 1998). This natural tendency for community can be harnessed and used to improve education for all children. Growth and continuous learning are equally strong motivators. The human brain is a complex information processor that strives to develop greater and increasingly organized knowledge (Stevens, 1998). These beliefs are fundamental to building trust and confidence in the potential of teams for problem solving.

LET'S SEE IT IN ACTION! CASE ILLUSTRATION: A MIDDLE SCHOOL CREATES A CoP

The Sunset Hills Middle School decided to establish an informal CoP, or learning group, to examine ways in which the school could encourage faculty and staff input into the design of a professional development plan aimed at improving support to students with disabilities in general education. The group was formed to include representatives from all faculty disciplines as well as the school guidance counselor, school psychologist, administrative office, instructional development, and support services. The function of the CoP was to create, accumulate, and share understanding about current personnel knowledge and skills and to establish priorities for training in areas of need. Table 6.3 examines the middle school learning group activities in relation to Wenger's functions of the CoP.

TABLE 6.3 Wenger's Functions and the Sunset Hills Middle School Learning Group	
Wenger's Functions for CoPs	**Sunset Hills Middle School Learning Group**
They are nodes or processing locations for the *exchange and interpretation of information*.	The learning group gathered information from various staff groups and brought them to the meetings to exchange and discuss.
They can *retain knowledge* in "living" ways, unlike a database or a manual.	The learning group used the knowledge that they shared in the learning group to discuss training and interests needs with staff in subgroups.
They can *manage competencies* to keep the organization at the cutting edge.	The learning group used the expertise of two of the group members who had been trained in the design of staff development programs to set priorities and help solve the problem of fitting training into staff schedules.
They provide *homes for identities* (Wenger, 1998; Wenger, McDermott & Snyder 2002).	The learning group established its own identity as the "Professional Development Group" and staff began to initiate conversations and bring unsolicited information to the group.

The learning group at Sunset Hills also reflected the five principles for cultivating Communities of Practice:

1. *Design the team for evolution:* They established a 2-year agenda so that they could monitor and assess the effectiveness of the professional development plan and involve additional faculty in the process to improve over time.

2. *Open a dialogue between inside and outside perspectives:* The team held open team meetings and also invited specific personnel to meetings to share their perspectives. They also participated in research to investigate what other schools and districts were doing in professional development to promote the participation of students with disabilities in general education. They even looked for models of full participation outside their state.

3. *Invite different levels of participation:* Some team members signed on for the full 2 years and others for less time.

4. *Develop both public and private community spaces:* The group arranged for private meeting time to discuss issues that may have been sensitive to the school community, such as behavior or discipline policies.

5. *Create a rhythm for the community:* The group shared with the whole school its meeting schedule so that staff would become familiar with the pattern of meetings (Wenger, McDermott, & Snyder, 2002, p. 51).

    2. *Belief in the power of collective vision.* In Chapter 2, the concept of **appreciative inquiry** was introduced and defined as a change strategy that moves people beyond a focus on problems and develops a collective sense of vision and hope for the future (Srivastra & Cooperrider, 1999). Problem-solving approaches focus on deficiencies, whereas appreciative inquiry seeks out strengths within the organization that can be applied in creating a new vision of what is possible. When people practice appreciative inquiry, they experience a cognitive shift. They focus less on what is getting in the way of solving a problem and more on what they can use to move beyond the problem to achieve the desired goal. Those who practice appreciative inquiry value people, diversity, and strengths; they contribute to an environment in which people are intrinsically motivated to achieve, both individually and collectively (Barrett, 1995; Cooperrider, Sorenson, Whetney, & Yaeger, 1999). Collaborative work is strengthened when professionals:

    a. discover what is working well;

    b. identify factors that cause the team and organization to work well;

    c. create a vision of what the team and/or organization is doing in the future that causes it to be successful;

    d. create dialogue that allows honest and open inquiry into all perspectives of the vision;

    e. select the organizational strengths that can be leveraged to create the team or organizational vision;

    f. develop an action plan that uses the leverage points found in these factors of team and organizational strength to create the vision; and

    g. turn the team's language from *depreciative to appreciative as follows:*

- "This won't work here." →   "How can it work here?"
- "We tried that before." →   "How can we do things differently?"
- "We don't have the expertise." → "What would it take to learn what we need to know?"
- "Too many of us are against it." → "What would it take to change attitudes and bring everyone on board?"

    3. *Belief that collaboration is essential for educating the whole child.* Schools and school-linked agencies are finding that the better they work together, the greater improvement they see in student outcomes. Shared approaches to educating and supporting the whole child bring to bear the combined thinking and talents of

LET'S SEE IT IN ACTION! CASE ILLUSTRATION: IRIS IS PUT TO THE TEST

Iris was recently hired as the principal of an inner-city charter school for adolescents who had failed in their base schools and who needed intensive educational and supportive services. She knew that the school and educational program needed a great deal of reform and improvement. She also knew that staff were very suspicious of reformers, having had several come and go over the past decade who had criticized *them* sharply for their failures with the students.

In her first meeting with staff, Iris sensed great anger, distrust, and reluctance to discuss needs for change. There was little constructive participation nor willingness to look to the future and consider possibilities for the reorganization of the school. In the second week, Iris decided to try a new approach (testing the principles of appreciative inquiry that she was learning about in her university program). She began her staff meeting by communicating to staff that she recognized the history of and importance of the school in the community. She recognized the contributions that the current staff had made to the accomplishments of the school over the past 10 years. She reviewed the strengths of the current staff, educational program, and policies that appeared to be working well for the school. Finally, she discussed how she planned to build on these organizational strengths to create a new shared vision for the school and that she wanted the commitment and participation of all of the staff to make it happen.

Iris' "preamble" triggered an outpouring of emotion and sharing of past experiences, grievances, resentments, and painful experiences of the staff. This event changed the climate and, as the meeting closed, many staff thanked Iris for her recognition of them. They told her that she had for the first time in years given them hope, courage, and confidence to go forward.

—Iris, Charter School Principal (Personal communication, 7/25/04)

Scott Cunningham/Merrill

The service coordinator provides the link between the student and the family, and apppropriate services in the school and community, as required by the student's IEP.

many professionals to address the multiple education and support needs of students and families (Conzemius & O'Neill, 2001).

4. *Belief in the value of self-determination.* Educational and human service agencies share a new emphasis on empowering students and families to assume more control over educational decision making and planning. Student participation in personal decision making is associated with positive youth outcomes (Mithaug, Mithaug, Martin, Agran, & Wehmeyer, 2003; Ryan & Deci, 2000). Concern for student self-determination should be placed at the center of collaboration and coordination initiatives.

5. *Belief that systemic change is rooted in individual change and learning.* Effective change processes result in change in each of the professionals who participate in it. Collaborative work of compelling importance requires that professionals reexamine their conventional attitudes, beliefs, knowledge, and assumptions, and be open to confronting new ideas. The process can be chaotic and uncomfortable at times, provoking thoughts and feelings of unnaturalness, frustration, childishness, and incompetence (Herasymowych, 1996). But it can also be exhilarating. Pioneering is never without some anxiety.

6. *Belief in the participation of all who will be affected by change.* Schools and communities have used collaborative work to give voice to people who previously have had little influence in school decision making. Stakeholder involvement—both within schools and between schools and community agencies—increases the likelihood that collaboration and coordination will be sustained over time (Shoshkes, 2004). Let's See It in Action, page 169, describes the experience of a new principal in an urban charter school who must lead her staff out of a very chaotic past.

WHAT PROFESSIONAL DEVELOPMENT CONTENT AND STANDARDS PROMOTE COLLABORATION AND COORDINATION SKILLS?

Learning to work together within a small group, a school, across disciplines, or across agency lines is an acquired set of skills. Unfortunately personnel preparation programs (in-service or preservice) do not adequately prepare teachers, related services personnel, or administrators for effective collaboration. In the United States, most general education teacher training programs include minimal course work and field-based expriences in collaboration with special educators and related services professionals, parents, or community-based personnel. Teachers feel unprepared to include students with disabilities in their classrooms (Epstein, 2001; Katz & Bauch, 1999; Menlove, Hudson, & Suter, 2001; Sanchez, 2005; Study of Personnel Needs in Special Education [SPENSE] 2002). School administrators in training are not required to include course work in special education. Most school counseling programs prepare counselors to work predominantly with a population of children and adolescents *without* disabilities (American School Counseling Association, 2004a).

As a result of these new emphases on serving students with disabilities in the general education curriculum, organizations that develop professional standards now include required collaboration competencies. Standards for special educators, general educators, administrators, and counselors promote teamwork in activities such as student placement decisions, designing differentiated instruction, developing student assessments, providing classroom supports, analyzing student data, working at school improvement, and community collaboration. Although national professional standards can define expectations for collaborative work, change is local and depends on sustained local leadership and commitment.

Standards for the preparation of special education teachers, related service professionals, and special education administrators now include knowledge and skills related to "collaboration and communication" as essential to professional preparation Council for Exceptional Children, 2001a).

Teachers are often the first to identify a child's needs for supportive services. It is important that they be prepared to identify students who need intervention, to develop differentiated instruction to accommodate students with learning problems, to know where to find sources of help for students, to collaborate with specialists, and to view themselves as part of a coordinating team that addresses the needs of the whole student (Boudah & Knight, 1999; Broussard, 2000; Center for Research, Diversity & Excellence, 2003; Evans-Schilling, 1999). The Interstate New Teacher Assessment and Support Consortium (INTASC) has developed national standards that affect the preparation of general education teachers. INTASC, housed at the Council of Chief State School Officers (CCSSO) is a consortium of state education agencies and national educational organizations dedicated to the reform of the preparation, licensing, and continuing professional development of teachers. INTASC's work is guided by the premise that an effective teacher must be able to integrate content knowledge with the specific strengths and needs of students to assure that all students learn and perform at proficient academic levels. State teacher licensing standards represent a state's policy for what all teachers must know and be able to do in order to effectively help all students achieve the K–12 curriculum standards (INTASC, Model Standards for Licensing General and Special Education Teachers of Students with Disabilities, 2001). INTASC standards have incorporated collaboration competencies.

School leaders are essential to the success of school–community partnerships because they help staff view the role of the school in the broader context of community. The school leader helps staff to recognize the complex needs of children and families and the importance of collective support from a variety of sectors—school, mental health, public health, social services, business, and others. The support and involvement of the central office is essential to collaboration and system coordination. Even with the support of a principal, school–community coordination often rises and falls with the engagement and enthusiasm of school faculty and related staff. The principal's support for the involvement of school personnel at the initial stages of a coordination initiative in setting goals and directions can greatly influence the acceptance by others in the school and across the district (Levine, 1998). **Collaborative leaders** nurture leadership in others and reach out to and learn from students or consumers of services. They communicate effectively across organizational boundaries and can negotiate differences among group members (IEL, 2001). Collaborative leaders articulate a strong vision of how organizations, communities, and people work together. They manage and resolve conflicts skillfully and show sensitivity to the pressures group members face. They are honest in their interactions with others, inspiring trust while modeling active listening and problem solving. They encourage group responsibility and model consensus decision making rather than hierarchical decision making. Finally, they are politically savvy, encourage learning among all staff, and use resources strategically (Blank, 2001; Institute for Educational Leadership, 2001).

Summary of Key Points

- There are important connections between the characteristics of adult learners and the development of collaborative practice.
- Genetic and personality dispositions have significant implications for an individual's ability to learn and adopt to changes within the environment; awareness of these dispositions help us understand our behavior and how to become more effective as collaborators.
- Collaborative work must be meaningful and involve matters of compelling importance to the team, school, or community agency.
- Barriers to collaboration and to collaborative practice involve both interpersonal barriers and systemic structural barriers.
- Having *competence* for collaboration means that professionals possess the *knowledge, skills and dispositions* (attitudes and beliefs) to participate.

Key Terms and Phrases

- Adult learner (p. 148)
- Participatory learning (p. 149)
- Self-directed learning (p. 149)
- Transformative learning (p. 149)
- Change agent (p. 155)
- Organizational, attitudinal, and knowledge barriers (p. 160)
- Communities of practice (p. 165)
- Competencies for collaboration (p. 165)
- Knowledge, skills, and dispositions (p. 165)
- Appreciative inquiry (p. 168)
- Collaborative leaders (p. 171)

Questions for Reflection, Thinking, and Skill Building

1. What does it mean to say: Although collaboration involves two or more people, each individual is an essential element in any change process?
2. Describe a collaborative experience you have had and discuss the role of the individual who was considered to be the team leader (even if that was

you)? What strategies did that person use to facilitate team cohesion and effectiveness?

3. How important is effective communication and collaboration to the education of special needs learners? How important is it for the professionals involved?

4. How does personality affect our ability and desire to collaborate with others?

5. Form a team of two or three classmates. Based on the material from the chapter (and any additional resources you desire), construct a simple tool with which you can observe a school team in action and determine how you will score it. The team could be a problem-solving team, a strategy team, a professional development team, a decision-making team, a school improvement team, or other kind of team. Observe the team together using the tool that you have created and score it individually. Discuss your individual scores and any differences among them. Discuss the process and difficulties you had with the process. How would you modify your instrument?

CHAPTER SEVEN

How Do General and Special Educators Collaborate to Coteach Effectively?

We teach to change the world . . . Our dance is the dance of experimentation and risk . . . The habit of critical reflection is crucial for teachers' survival.
—STEVEN BROOKFIELD, 1995

Teacher effectiveness is fundamental to educational reform . . . Collaboration skills are key to teacher effectiveness and teaming . . . Collaboration takes a lot of hard work. You have to have an open mind, listen to others' ideas, give your opinion, and together come to a solution. —O'SHEA, WILLIAMS, & SATTLER, 1999

- Why is collaboration between special and general education teachers important?

- How do special and general education teachers structure their work to collaborate?

- What are the barriers to coteaching and how can teams work together more effectively?

- What professional development content and standards promote collaboration between special and general educators?

PERSPECTIVES

Researcher

A special teacher once told me that her students preferred the special education classroom to the general education classroom. And she said that she could protect them from the rough and tumble nature of the classroom—in other words reality. This is most certainly the bad news and recommends against placement in special classes . . . When students think of themselves as so different that they need to be separated from their peers, we have accomplished our worst fear—and that is students who think, "I don't fit with the others, I am too different." This is an attitude difficult to overcome and one that will not accomplish our goal of inclusion.

—Schwartz, Shanley, Gerver, & O'Cummings, 2003

Parent

After 12 years in special education, Jake will be spending 100% of his time at his base school with no ED (emotional disabilities) classes and will be riding the regular bus. This is an amazing turnaround for the child who for all these years has been just about the most difficult kid in every setting that he has ever attended. His base school has been excellent, providing him with a very careful transition. He is in team taught classes (with general and special educators) and Basic Skills, both of which are definitely helping. It also helps a great deal that he is with other kids without disabilities. Jake himself gets the most credit for getting his life together; there have been no behavior problems at all, and he is determined to free himself entirely from the separate special education system within a year.

—Personal communication with a parent of an adolescent with emotional disabilities, 2004

INTRODUCTION

Since the emergence of the teaching profession, teachers have worked primarily alone, in isolation from one another. As the practice of special education emerged in the 1960s–'70s, it led to the creation of a parallel education system that was disconnected from the regular education system. In the 1990s, while children with disabilities were mainstreamed from separate schools into their base schools, they were still largely taught in separate classrooms with special education teachers. However, over the past 20 years, the proportion of children with disabilities now educated in general education classrooms has greatly increased. Today, as many as 75% of students with disabilities spend 40% or more of their instructional day in general education classrooms (Study of Personnel Needs in Special Education, 2002; U.S. Department of Education, 2004a). More than 25% of all public schoolchildren fall into the categories of students with disabilities and other at-risk populations identified in Chapter 1.

The national priority to promote access to general education for students with disabilities has inspired new models for collaboration between special and general education teachers. The traditional isolation and separation of special and general education teachers is becoming dismantled as the orientation shifts from "those kids" to "our kids." As the perspectives suggest, in a more unified system, general education teachers and administrators are now equally as important for promoting access to general education for special needs students. They are central to achieving greater educational accountability and raising academic standards for all students, including those with disabilities. General education teachers are learning about differentiated instruction, coteaching, and strategies for educating a wide range of special needs learners in their classrooms. Coteaching refers to the *collaboration between general and special education teachers for all of the teaching responsibilities for all students assigned to a classroom* (Gately & Gately, 2001).

Through collaboration between general and special educators as coteachers, the responsibility for achievement and progress of special learners has become a joint mission. Classrooms that successfully include special learners are those that are designed to welcome diversity and to address the individual needs of all students, whether they have identified disabilities or not.

The purpose of this chapter is to examine why the collaboration between special and general education teachers is important for students and teaching. The chapter examines how special and general education teachers collaborate, the barriers they face in their work, and how they can improve collaborative work. Special attention is given to planning for collaboration and coteaching and how to best prepare teachers for the challenges.

WHY IS COLLABORATION BETWEEN SPECIAL AND GENERAL EDUCATION TEACHERS IMPORTANT?

How Do Coteaching Relationships Improve Teaching and Learning?

Research reveals that most general educators have students with disabilities in their classrooms, but few are adequately prepared to address their educational needs. A majority of general educators in the United States report having experience teaching students with disabilities and other special learners, but only 29% expressed feeling very successful instructing them (Study of Personnel Needs in Special Education [SPeNSE], 2002). Upon closer examination, the study data reveal that general educators who received training related to the needs of special learners, and instructional strategies to address them, felt considerably more successful than those who did not receive such training (Ortiz, 2004). In a study by Hudson and Glomb (1997) of about 52% of all general teacher education programs examined, only 9% offered a course on special education or provided students with a separate course or practicum on collaboration (Hudson & Glomb, 1997). However, some progress has been made over the past decade. Although the mandate for collaboration is supported by research, policy, and practical evidence, teacher educators, practitioners, and policymakers remain unclear about the role and importance of collaboration between special and general educators for improving teaching and learning for all students.

Improved Environment for Teaching and Learning. Coteaching relationships yield important benefits for students and professionals, including improved instruction and more collaborative and enriched environments for learning for all students. According to extensive data from the National Study of Personnel Needs in Special Education (SPeNSE, 2002), general educators who collaborate closely with special educators feel considerably more confident in their skills to provide instruction to students with disabilities. Both teachers and administrators appear to be motivated by the increase in shared decision making and power, and report enhanced satisfaction and intellectual stimulation in their jobs (Snell & Janney, 2000). **Collaborative teaching** also reduces the isolation of teachers, improves communication among teachers and related services personnel, and increases professional growth (Kargiannis, Stainback, & Stainback, 1996). Furthermore, when teachers collaborate in their teaching, they are better prepared to support one another's strengths and accommodate weaknesses (Taymans & Lynch, 2004).

Collaborative activities require student teachers to establish new patterns of relationships that run counter to the kind of isolation and independent work characteristic of teachers in our schools (Lambert et al., 1995). These relationships need to be nurtured during the teacher preparation period. The challenge then is to help teachers transfer these patterns to their own workplace and to have an effect on the cultures of their own schools. While some teacher educators are concerned that highly competent new teachers will be bridled by the traditional culture of the school, McLaughlin (2000) concludes that a school's culture is not static. It is in a continual change process in which attitudes, values, and skills continually reinforce each other. In high-performing schools, a nurturing professional community seems to be the container that holds the culture. Teachers feel invigorated, challenged, professionally engaged, and empowered, just because they teach there.

Improved Teaching Approaches. Coteaching creates an atmosphere conducive to successful curriculum integration across subject areas and the development of multimedia environments, through use of hands-on activities, computers, and a variety of teaching strategies. Teachers are more efficient with their time—working together and combining their expertise, their ideas, and their resources. A culture of collaboration promotes faculty innovation and experimentation with new research-based ideas and strategies. Veteran teachers can be mentors to novice teachers and help the process of socialization to the culture of the school (Inger, 1993). Cotaught classes provide "living laboratories" in which teachers can integrate new evidence-based teaching strategies that can be beneficial for all students. Teacher teamwork makes complex tasks more manageable, stimulates new ideas, and fosters continuous learning by teachers that enhances their effectiveness in the classroom (Inger, 1993).

Improved Learning Environments for Students.
Coteaching contributes to positive learning environments for students with and without disabilities. It reinforces a holistic (whole-child) view of and approach to teaching all learners and structuring the learning environment. Education services provided through shared teaching strategies are more effective than those that pull a student out of the classroom (Jorgensen, 1998; Schwartz, Shanley, Gerver, & O'Cummings, 2003; Taymans & Lynch, 2004). Collaboration also reduces isolation of special learners in the school and enhances their social development with typical peers.

Collaborative teaching orients students to expectations such as making responsible choices, working cooperatively, seeking and giving help, setting goals, and using computers and equipment correctly. Shared teaching promotes alternative student assessment as well as strategies that engage students in self-assessment of their own performance and products. Finally, coteaching increases effective integration of technology into the curriculum.

Improved Access to General Education and Coordination of Services.
Coteaching increases the likelihood that students with disabilities can be successfully placed into and benefit from participation in general education classes. Special learners are then more likely to be prepared for and to participate in standardized assessments. Shared decision making between general and special educators results in better decisions on behalf of the students, and general educators are more committed to students' IEPs (Snell & Janney, 2000). It also improves decision making in planning for the multiple transitions of students from elementary to middle school, middle to high school, and high school to postsecondary settings. Finally, the proliferation of coteaching practices has led to joint orientation and training of general and special educators, and has increased the supply of teachers who are skilled in interdisciplinary planning, curriculum adaptations, and collaborative team consultation. Table 7.1 addresses the shift from traditional educational systems to a collaborative, more integrated system.

As Little (1990) observed two decades ago, the complexities introduced by a new curriculum or by the need to revise an existing curriculum are challenging. Teacher teamwork makes these complex tasks more manageable, stimulates new ideas, and promotes coherence in a school's curriculum and instruction. Together, teachers have the organizational skills and resources to attempt innovations that would exhaust the energy, skill, or resources of an individual teacher. The conclusions that can be draw from the experiences of closely orchestrated, task-centered groups in schools are consistent with those drawn from other organizational studies: The accomplishments of a proficient and well-organized group are greater than the accomplishments of an isolated individual (p. 496).

The Let's See It in Action boxes on page 180 and page 181 represent a composite of shared stories from several general and special education teachers who have worked closely together. These case illustrations represent very different sets of conditions for collaboration in the schools today. Collaboration among special and general education teachers for greater access to general education is far more advanced at the elementary level than at the secondary level. There are several reasons for this.

TABLE 7.1 Comparing Traditional Special Education With a Collaborative System	
Traditionally separate educational systems	**Integrated system to promote access to general education and the school community**
• The locus of special educational services is in the segregated special education class or school.	• School districts offer a flexible and responsive continuum of educational placements.
• Educational placements are separated into "regular" and "special" to serve two different "types" of children; students seldom are reintegrated into the general education class once they are removed.	• Initial training (preservice) of general education teachers includes strategies for serving children with special needs.
• General and special education teachers are provided separate professional development that reinforces the orientation to separate systems.	• Continuing education (in-service training) is provided to general and special education teachers in the philosophy and practice of inclusive education and differentiated instruction.
• In their initial preparation, general education teachers are prepared only to serve students without disabilities; they often refer out students with special needs.	• The locus of special educational services and support is shifted to the base school and general education classroom.
• General educators seldom participate in educational planning for students with special needs.	• Educational planning for children with special needs reflects collaboration of general and special educators, related services specialists and appropriate community-based agency personnel.
• Supervision of educational services to general education and special education students is conducted separately.	• Supervision of educational services to general and special needs students is unified.
• Special educational supports in the general education class are unavailable.	• Special education services are provided in the general education classroom, in collaboration with general education teachers.
• Special educators communicate with families of special needs students; general educators with general education students' families.	• General and special educators encourage parent and family involvement through close collaboration.
• Families are informed about special educational services available in special settings.	• Families are informed about the service continuum and educated in the philosophy of inclusive education.

Source: From *Successful Inclusion: Practical Strategies for a Shared Responsibility*, by C. Kochhar, L. West, and J. Taymans, 2000, Englewood Cliffs, NJ: Merrill/Prentice-Hall. Reprinted with permission.

LET'S SEE IT IN ACTION! Case Illustration: Special and General Education Teachers Collaborate for All Elementary Children

Angela Smith teaches fourth grade at Evansville Elementary School. Three days a week, she coteaches the class with Karen Vogel, a special education teacher. Their 25 students include 4 with disabilities who have special learning needs and 2 others who need special help in specific curriculum areas. Each of the students with a disability has an IEP that was developed by a team that included both teachers. The teachers, paraprofessionals, and the school principal believe that these students have a great deal to contribute to the class and that they will be successful in the general education classroom.

All of the school personnel have attended in-service training in collaborative skills for teaming and problem solving. Mrs. Smith and the two paraprofessionals who work in the classroom also received special training on disabilities and on how to create an inclusive classroom environment. The school principal, Peter Butler, had worked in special education many years ago and has received training on the impact of new special education developments and instructional arrangements on school administration. Each year, Mr. Butler works with the building staff to identify areas in which new training is needed. For specific questions that may arise, technical assistance is available through a regional special education cooperative. Mrs. Smith and Miss Vogel share responsibility for teaching and for supervising their two paraprofessionals. In addition to the time they spend together in the classroom, they spend 1 to 4 hours per week planning instruction, and additional time with other teachers and support personnel who work with their students.

The teachers use their joint planning time to problem solve and discuss the use of special instructional techniques for all students who need special assistance. Monitoring and adapting instruction for individual students is an ongoing activity. The teachers use **curriculum-based measurement** to systematically assess their students' learning progress in the context of the curriculum they are learning. They adapt curricula so that lessons begin at the edge of the student's knowledge, adding new material at the student's pace, and presenting it in a manner consistent with the student's *learning style*. For some students, advanced organizers or chapter previews are used to highlight the most important points of the material to be learned; for other students, new vocabulary words are highlighted or reduced reading levels are provided. Some students use special activity worksheets, whereas others learn best by using computer-assisted instruction.

In the classroom, the teachers group students differently for different activities. Sometimes, the teachers and paraprofessionals divide the class, each teaching a small group or tutoring individuals. They use cooperative learning projects to help the students learn to work together and develop social relationships. Peer tutors provide extra help to students who need it. Although the regular classroom may not be the best learning environment for every child with a disability, it is highly desirable for all who can benefit. It provides contact with age peers and prepares all students for the diversity of the world beyond the classroom.

Source: From Including Students with Disabilities in General Education Classrooms, 1993. Reston, VA: Council for Exceptional Children. Adapted with permission.

Questions for Discussion

- What special supports are provided in the classroom to promote full participation of special learners?
- What techniques do Ms. Smith and Ms. Vogel use to share responsibility for instruction and student progress? To differentiate instruction?
- What are the benefits of the general education class to the student with special learning needs?

LET'S SEE IT IN ACTION! Case Illustration: Special and General Education Teachers Collaborate for All Secondary Level Youth

Kali is a special education resource teacher who has 32 students with mild to moderate disabilities on her caseload. The Special Education Department at Chavez High School (CHS) decided 2 years ago to organize by grade level, so most of the students on Kali's case load are in the 10th grade, although she has 2 in the 9th grade and 4 in the 11th. At the end of the last school year, CHS teachers discussed at great length how the school was supposed to become more "inclusive" and how the No Child Left Behind Act might affect secondary special educators.

Although Kali was accustomed to teaching resource classes in English and algebra, her principal just informed her that she will be expected to coteach so that more of her students could be included in general education classes and have their needs met in those classes.

Christian, a general education 10th-grade teacher, also was recently told that he would be coteaching with Kali. It is only a few days before school begins and Christian and Kali find themselves asking the same questions: What exactly is coteaching? How can it be done at the secondary level? What role will, or even should, Kali have in the general education classroom? Is this the same thing as being a glorified aid? Can coteaching really help to meet secondary students' needs?

Source: From "Tips and Strategies for Coteaching at the Secondary Level," by W. Murawsi and L. Dieker, 2004, *Exceptional Children, 5*, pp. 52–58. Copyright 2004 by the Council for Exceptional Children. Reprinted with permission.

Fewer special education students are included in secondary general education classes than in elementary (U.S. Department of Education, 2001a). Secondary schools are organized by subject areas and teachers as subject matter experts have separate professional identities and social communities built around their own disciplines. Working in departments organized by subjects reinforces professional isolation among teachers and impedes their capacity to participate in new forms of collaboration. Furthermore, this separateness is reinforced by the teachers' preparation, state curriculum frameworks, standardized test protocols, textbook design, and teacher licensing requirements (Inger, 1993; McCartney, 1999).

HOW DO SPECIAL AND GENERAL EDUCATION TEACHERS STRUCTURE THEIR WORK TO COLLABORATE?

Coteaching and Collaborative Roles: Aligning Two Systems

Several questions are driving the current movement in the United States for **aligning general and special education** systems to better educate all students: Who is ultimately responsible for special needs learners and students with disabilities in the general education classroom? How can the individualized education model for students with disabilities and the **standards-based curriculum** for all students be aligned? How will special educators' roles change? The balance of this chapter explores models and strategies for achieving such an alignment.

Typically, for each student with a disability who is assigned to an age-appropriate general education class, there is also a special education teacher identified to provide support to that student. The special education teacher is primarily responsible for determining, with the team, the amount and types of support and adaptations required in each subject area in the general education class, for monitoring student progress, and for implementing and evaluating the IEP. The development of instrumental adaptations or classroom accommodations is primarily the responsibility of the special education teacher; however, the general and special education teachers and related services specialists collaborate to develop accommodations that help students to progress in the general education curriculum.

The primary responsibility of general education teachers is to use their skills and content expertise to instruct students in the curricula prescribed by the school system and state. The general education teacher collaborates with the special education teacher to ensure that students' individualized educational priorities are integrated into the daily curriculum and instruction, and that input from specialists is obtained

Scott Cunningham/Merrill

Coteaching makes it possible to individualize instruction for students with disabilities while giving them access to the general education curriculum.

to help with accessing educational technology, modifying and adapting curriculum, and supporting students' social development. The ultimate goal is to help students meet the content standards required of all students.

Special educators' roles and responsibilities may vary depending on the school setting; however, the responsibilities of the special educator usually fall into three categories: (1) preparation and direct teaching, (2) preparation of appropriate reports and other paperwork, and (3) collaboration with other professionals and with parents. Their activities each day will be determined by the children they are teaching, the kinds and severity of disabilities those students have, the children's ages, and the setting in which the teachers work. A high school special education teacher who is **coteaching** a class with a general education teacher, a special education teacher in a self-contained middle school classroom for children with emotional and behavior disorders, and an elementary special education teacher in a resource room who has children coming in and out of the classroom all day will all have very different activities and responsibilities (National Information Center for Children with Disabilities, 1997).

Special education teachers never work completely alone since they are always part of a team. Some schools have established teams to help plan appropriate accommodations and educational interventions for students who are having difficulty in general education classes (Schwartz, Shanley, Gerver, & O'Cummings, 2003). Depending on a child's disability and the school setting, special education teachers also work with speech–language pathologists, school psychologists, occupational therapists, school social workers, and community-based professionals to plan and implement the best education strategies for each child. Special education teachers who coteach or team teach with general education teachers must spend enough time to plan, develop, and implement an educational environment that is challenging and appropriate for all the students in the class, with and without disabilities. Special education teachers who coteach serve as a resource to other staff in the school—teachers, administrators, speech–language pathologists, parents, and others. They also follow up with students throughout the day, wherever they may be. To do all of this effectively, special education teachers need to maintain positive collaborative relationships with the principal, other teachers, and support services personnel. Parents are also an important part of the team. They are the experts on their child and have much to contribute to the educational planning for children with disabilities (National Information Center for Children with Disabilities, 1997).

In the collaborative model, general education and special education teachers each bring their skills, training, and perspectives to the team. Resources are combined to strengthen teaching and learning opportunities, methods, and effectiveness (Ainscow, Booth, & Dyson, 2004; Dettmer, Dyck, & Thurston, 2005; Dieker, 2001). It is in this nexus of classroom-level collaboration that the individualized instructional process for students with disabilities and the standards-based process for all students are brought into alignment.

Models for Coteaching

This section reviews a variety of models for collaboration as it explores the questions: What does coteaching look like? How do teachers structure their work together? Bauwen and Mueller (2000) identified three models of coteaching in common practice today. First is the *complementary instruction* approach in which the classroom teacher is primarily responsible for teaching content while the special educator focuses on providing students with "how-to" skills or strategies for learning content and organizing their work. The second approach is the *team teaching model* in which one teacher delivers curriculum content while the other modifies instruction (clarifies, or uses visual or other learning aids) to help students understand concepts. The third approach is the *supportive learning activities approach* in which the special educator oversees activities such as student group learning or peer tutoring while the general educator teaches content.

Coteaching as Instructional Collaboration for Differentiated Instruction

Coteaching has been described in a variety of ways. Coteaching has been defined as *two or more professionals delivering substantive instruction to a group of students with diverse learning needs* (Cook & Friend, 1995). This approach increases instructional options, improves educational programs, reduces stigmatization for students, and provides support to the professionals involved. Gately and Gately (2001) broadened the definition by defining coteaching as *the collaboration between general and special education teachers for all of the teaching responsibilities of all students assigned to a classroom.* In a cotaught classroom, two teachers, general and special educators, work together to develop differentiated instruction (DI) that meets the needs of a diverse population of students. **Differentiated curriculum and instruction** involves providing accommodations and modifying content, process, and student assessment according to the learning characteristics and interests of the group of students (Tomlinson, 2001). DI is not the same as individualized instruction but requires that teachers be flexible in their approach to teaching and that they offer a variety of instructional strategies to reach all learners. Differentiated instruction may involve content, process, or product. For example, teachers may group students by interest, provide activities at different levels of complexity, or vary products that engage students' preferred learning modalities (auditory, visual, or kinesthetic). Strategies may involve adjusting questions that are targeted toward different levels of ability or readiness, providing alternative activities for students who have already mastered the curriculum, acceleration or deceleration of the pace at which students move through the curriculum, flexible grouping of students, reading or project buddies, independent study projects, learning contracts, and learning centers.

As a result of extensive experience with coteaching over a decade, Gately and Gately (2001) defined eight components of the coteaching classroom that contribute to the development of the collaborative learning environment. In Table 7.2, these have been modified, and two components, transition planning and parent collaboration, have been added to reflect additional aspects of the coteaching relationship that are often overlooked. The eight components have been related to differentiated instruction.

In a cotaught classroom, teachers share the planning, presentation, evaluation (grading), and classroom management in an effort to enhance the learning environment for all students. In this way, the teachers can provide integrated services for students with diverse learning needs (Gately & Gately, 2001). Coteaching is

TABLE 7.2 Components of Coteaching and Differentiated Instruction

Coteaching Component	How It Supports Differentiated Instruction
Interpersonal communication and reflection	Coteachers (special and general education teachers) reflect on their teaching methods and results for all students and work closely together to maximize communication to improve their teaching. Special educators help general educators understand individualized and differentiated instruction through modeling and resource sharing.
Physical arrangements	Coteachers collaborate to identify and facilitate modifications within classroom and community learning environments, whether the student is receiving special education under IDEA or Section 504. In some cases, all students benefit from changes in the classroom arrangement, such as clustering desks to promote collaborative group work.
Familiarity with the curriculum	If the special education teacher is familiar with the general education curriculum, then coteachers can collaborate to modify content and instructional delivery for all students.
Curriculum goals and modifications	Coteachers collaborate to jointly develop goals for students that are appropriate across content areas. They both develop and retain copies of the IEP.
Instructional planning and professional development	Coteachers collaborate to plan for instruction and participate in professional development that strengthens the coteaching process and the differentiated classroom.
Instructional presentation	Coteachers collaborate to modify instructional delivery strategies to match the learning styles and interests of students. Modifications and adaptations include changes in the administration of assignments and tests in the general education classroom, modifications of homework assignments, reducing the reading level of tests or assignments, allowing oral responses for assignments, dividing assignments into small sections, or shortening the number of items on tests and/or classroom assignments.
Classroom management and positive behavioral support	Coteachers combine knowledge and skills to manage classroom behavior and introduce positive behavioral supports for students who need them.
Student assessment and use of data	Coteachers combine knowledge of student learning needs and student assessment to track student progress and develop accommodations for classroom-based and standardized assessments.
Transition planning	Coteachers combine skills in assessing students' transition needs and integrating transition goals into the curriculum.
Parent collaboration	Coteachers collaborate in developing reports to parents on students' progress and jointly meet with parents when needed.

an appropriate instructional model for special needs learners and students with disabilities who can benefit from general education curriculum with the appropriate supports and accommodations. Box 7.1 presents a reflection by an urban special education teacher on the importance of building relationships in the school reform process.

Friend and Cook (2003) have described a variety of coteaching approaches. The *one teach, one observe approach* allows two teachers in a classroom to conduct a detailed observation of students in the learning process and social environment. Such observations are important early in the school year when students experience personal problems or exhibit behavioral challenges. In the *one teach, one drift approach*, one teacher instructs the class while the other provides individual assistance to students as needed.

In the *station teaching* approach, teachers divide the content and the students into groups. They teach the content to one group and then repeat the instruction for the second group. *Parallel teaching* involves the simultaneous teaching of information, using discussions, test reviews, debates, learning games, and other strategies. In the *alternative teaching* approach, one teacher takes responsibility for the majority of the class while the other works with a smaller group that needs support or enrichment. When **team teaching** (tag team teaching) both teachers are delivering the same instruction at the same time. Of all the approaches, most coteachers consider this the most complex yet satisfying way to coteach, but the one that is the most dependent on teachers' styles (Friend & Cook, 2003). These different approaches are reflected in the following descriptions of coteaching team structures in schools.

BOX 7.1   Reflection on Relationships and Reform

Over the past 3 years I have worked as a change leader to improve special education and the school's perception of special education teachers and students. My greatest weakness while working to institute change was that *I did not realize that relationships are the key to reform.* I thought that I could change special education by getting the administrators to start implementing necessary changes with staff. I thought that if I could convince the administration of the urgency of reform and provide them with the strategies to implement my suggestions, they would welcome and support change. Unfortunately, it wasn't that easy. The administration was willing to listen and said that they would support me, but in reality I was on my own.

First, I tried to improve communication between special and general educators. I created a paper communication system in order to keep in touch with all of the teachers who taught special education students. Not surprisingly, new teachers responded to my system, but the veteran teachers did not. What I didn't take into account was that the veteran teachers already had a way of communicating with a senior special education teacher who had been around for many years, and they were perfectly happy with the existing system. I did not see that I needed to honor the old ways of doing things and take pieces of the old system to create the new, before trying to bulldoze the existing system. I also naively thought that I could convince my administrators that we had to start holding general and special education teachers accountable for providing services because it is the law. I did not realize that in order to get people to change their practices, I had to persuade them by *building relationships.* From there, I could teach them the skills they needed to plan lessons collaboratively and improve the performance of students with disabilities. —Kerri Larkin, teacher in an inner city school, by permission.

A Study of Team Structures and Teacher Characteristics

The following descriptions provide visual examples of several types of teams. These descriptions provide a window into different kinds of **structures for collaborative teaching** and are drawn from the extensive research of Schwartz et al. (2003). The following descriptions highlight four of seven teams studied by Schwartz (one, four, five, and six). The teams examined in this study were effective at the selected schools because teaming was an integral part of a school restructuring project to promote inclusion and was central to the school's mission. All schools, elementary, middle, and secondary, served children with mild to moderate disabilities, while one school served children with severe disabilities (Schwartz et al., 2003, by permission).

Team One: Kindergarten and First Grade. Team One included two general education teachers, an assistant teacher, an English as a Second Language (ESL) teacher, and a resource teacher (special educator). One classroom teacher was only in the classroom for half days because she also served as the reading recovery teacher for all kindergarten/first-grade classrooms in the school. The team was developed to meet diverse student needs in two kindergarten/first-grade classrooms. Approximately 40 students were assigned to the team and divided into equal numbers in each classroom. Team members planned and delivered lessons and collaborated with diagnostic specialists to identify children with special needs.

The classrooms were located in pods of four rooms across the hall from each other, allowing frequent interaction and communication between the teams. The two classroom teachers, the ESL teacher, and the special education resource teacher provided instruction in all academic subjects to students in small groups. The small groups were divided by ability for math and reading, but remained grouped according to multiple abilities for science and social studies. One of the classroom teachers and the resource teacher cotaught math, while the ESL teacher and the other classroom teacher were responsible for reading. The assistant teacher taught handwriting and led activities for small groups when they were not engaged in other academic topics. Figure 7.1 depicts this model.

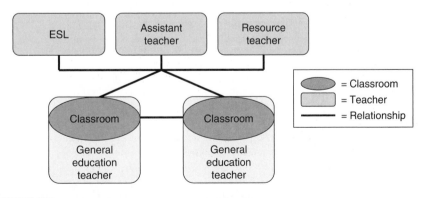

FIGURE 7.1

Team One Model

Source: From A Qualitative Description of Collaborative Teams in Today's Classroom, by A. Schwarz, J. Shanley, M. Gerver, and M. O'Cummings, 2003, Washington, D.C.: Elementary and Middle Schools Technical Assistance Center. Reprinted with permission.

Team Four: Pre-K Through Fifth Grade.   Located in southern Maryland, this elementary school served students from prekindergarten to fifth grade. Four years ago, the school began an effort to restructure the entire school to maintain student groupings according to grade levels. Students with behavioral, cognitive, auditory, and visual disabilities were included in these student groups. The school used various instructional grouping methods to sustain its inclusive environment.

The third-grade team interviewed consisted of four general educators and a resource teacher/special educator. The team provided instruction to approximately 100 students. Different levels of experience among the team allowed for the development of mentoring relationships between seasoned staff and new staff. The team described its primary responsibility as planning and implementing curriculum for all students, including children with disabilities. Team members collaborated to plan and adapt all materials to individualize curriculum to meet student needs. Structured curriculum was used, including thematic units and various types of classroom groupings, to ensure that the instructional needs of all students were being met. While all of the team professionals taught reading, two of the general educators taught math, and two of the general educators taught science and social studies. The resource teacher taught her own reading group and an instructional lab twice a week. The resource teacher provided support to faculty and students in all subjects and followed the progress of students with disabilities in her class. Figure 7.2 depicts this model.

Team Five: Fourth Grade.   The five members of this team, including four general educators (responsible for academic content) and one resource teacher, served 80 to 100 students among the four classrooms. The team used many of the same instructional grouping practices described in the previous section to maintain an inclusive educational delivery setting.

Similar to the third-grade team, Team Five jointly planned and implemented curriculum for all children in an inclusive setting. Through their collaboration, professionals adapted lessons in order to make the curriculum accessible to all of their students. Team members also participated in identifying and evaluating students

FIGURE 7.2
Team Four Model

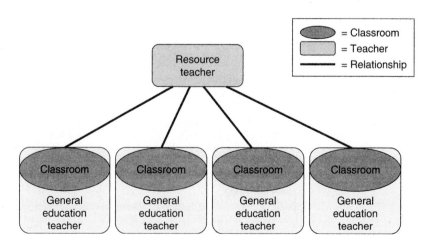

with special needs. Students were grouped in classes heterogeneously, and each class was then divided into groups according to subject. Language arts was the only subject grouped by ability. All of the teachers taught all subjects. When they began, planning occurred jointly across all four classrooms. In the study year, to determine whether the planning process could be more efficient, the team decided to plan in pairs of classrooms rather than as a whole team (all four classrooms). To make instruction more efficient and practical, students with disabilities remained in one of the pairs (two classrooms). This grouping enabled the resource teacher to concentrate her efforts in two classrooms rather than four. Figure 7.3 depicts this model.

Team Six: Middle School.   Team Six served children in grades six through eight from central Virginia. The school was established 9 years ago to implement inclusive practices for children with disabilities through a team approach. Each team was comprised of six general educators and three special educators, all of whom had been working together for 9 years. To facilitate communication, each team was divided into three subteams consisting of two general and one special educator. Most of the students who required special services from the team were identified as having severe learning disabilities and were included in the general education setting for social studies, science, and, if appropriate, for math. However, most of these students received language arts instruction in a self-contained setting.

On the subteam, one of the general educators specialized in math and the other in language arts. All the general educators from all subteams who specialized in math, planned together. There was also a great degree of collaboration and cross-subteam planning by general educators who specialized in language arts, social studies, and science. The subteam also included a special educator who helped plan lessons and discuss student programs. Each subteam was responsible for assessment and instructional delivery. Figure 7.4 depicts this model.

These examples demonstrate the variation in how professionals structure their relationships in collaborative teams to enhance teaching and learning. These models also reflect the four functions of collaboration introduced in Chapter 1: *collaboration as discovery, collaboration as a synthesis of ideas, collaboration as*

FIGURE 7.3
Team Five Model

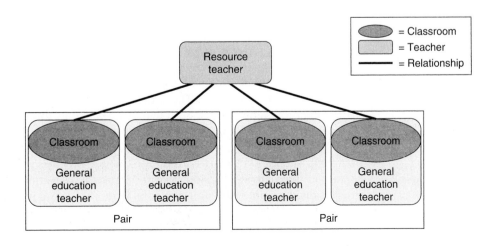

FIGURE 7.4
Team Six Model

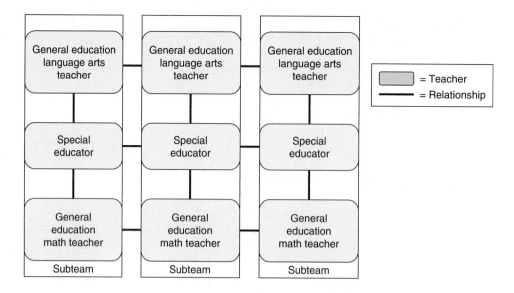

development of practice, and *collaboration as building professional community*. The descriptions reflect how collaboration between general and special education teachers promotes the translation of research to design new practices (*discovery*); promotes the uniting of disciplines and expertise (*synthesis of ideas*) to enhance instruction, understand the needs of children, solve problems, engage parents, and make better decisions for children; advances the *development of practices* and the blending of special and general education teaching strategies to meet the needs of diverse student groups; and advances the development of long-term *professional communities* to support and sustain the improvements in education of all children, and promote continuing professional development.

Box 7.2 presents a tool for assessing readiness for collaborative teaching.

WHAT ARE THE BARRIERS TO COTEACHING AND HOW CAN TEAMS WORK TOGETHER MORE EFFECTIVELY?

There are several barriers and facilitators that affect the special coteaching relationship. Most importantly, effective coteaching practices rely on *effective relationships* among people who work closely together to improve teaching and learning. The team, rather than the individual teacher, becomes the unit of accountability, leadership, and support (Beyerlein & Harris, 2003). To change the way coteachers perform their work, professionals must first change the way they think, believe, or feel about their practices, colleagues, and the students they teach.

Collaboration is an important and powerful instrument for organizing the work of groups, but does far more than simply structure people's work. Collaboration also creates an interpersonal "fusion" that results in the transformation of the efforts of single individuals into one unit, the combination of many perceptions applied to a common problem, and the creation of energy as a result of the "heat and pressure" of a challenging experience.

BOX 7.2   Coteaching Self-Assessment

Right now, the main hope I have regarding this coteaching situation is:

A. My attitude/philosophy regarding teaching special needs learners and students with disabilities in a general education classroom is: _____
_____

B. I would like to have the following responsibilities in a cotaught classroom:
_____
_____

C. I would like my coteacher to have the following responsibilities:
_____
_____

D. The biggest obstacle I expect to have in coteaching is:
_____
_____

E. I think we can overcome this obstacle by:
_____
_____

F. I have the following expectations in a classroom:
   a. regarding discipline: _____
   _____
   _____

   b. regarding class work: _____
   _____
   _____

   c. regarding materials: _____
   _____
   _____

   d. regarding homework: _____
   _____
   _____

   e. regarding planning: _____
   _____
   _____

   f. regarding adaptations and modifications for individual students: _____
   _____
   _____

   g. regarding grading: _____
   _____
   _____

   h. regarding noise level: _____
   _____

   i. regarding cooperative learning: _____
   _____
   _____

   j. regarding giving/receiving feedback: _____
   _____
   _____

   k. regarding parental contact: _____
   _____
   _____

Source: From *Coteaching in the Inclusive Classroom: Working Together to Help All Your Students Find Success (Grades 6–12)* (pp. 36–37), by W. Murawski, 2003, Sharing Hopes, Attitudes, Responsibilities, and Expectations (S.H.A.R.E.) self-assessment tool. Medina, WA: Institute for Educational Development. Reprinted with permission.

Barriers to Effective Coteaching

Improving collaborative practices between special and general educators is not a simple matter. Considerable research has highlighted the challenges that arise when general and special educators attempt to join hands and collaborate (Brownell et al., 2005; Dettmer, Dyck, & Thurston, 2005; DuFour, 2003; Walther-Thomas, 1997b). The art and science of collaboration require additional time, something neither special nor general educators have. The unyielding pressures of the school schedule can result in negative attitudes toward the demands of the inclusive classroom. Many special education teachers are deprived of adequate free time in the school day to make appointments with other staff members or parents; consequently, they may be required to meet outside regular school hours or during lunch or other breaks. Many special education teachers who resign their classroom jobs say they were prompted by lack of time to meet all of their responsibilities on behalf of students (Billingsley, 2003; Kozlesksi, Mainzer, & Deshler, 2000; Soodac, Podell, & Lehman, 1998).

As mentioned earlier, the rise of special education led to the creation of a parallel system for educating students that was separate and disconnected from the regular education system. This traditional structural separation continues to create *organizational, knowledge, and attitudinal barriers* within schools. It impedes professional coordination that is essential for embedding special education and differentiated instruction into the general education framework. In our current model of education, teachers typically maintain a high degree of autonomy and individual decision making (Brownell et al., 2005). Historically, this has been the case for both general and special education teachers. But now, general educators are called upon to teach students with an increasingly diverse range of educational needs, and many feel unprepared to undertake such a responsibility (Harry, 2002; Menlove, Hudson, & Suter, 2001; Monahan, Marino, Miller, & Cronic, 1997). Similarly, there appears to be a growing concern among special educators and parents that the individualized nature of special education is viewed as "diluted" curriculum in the face of higher standards for learning (Sharpe & Hawes, 2003). Collaboration can address this concern by supporting students with disabilities in the general curriculum.

The three categories of barriers introduced in Chapter 6—*organizational, attitudinal, and knowledge*—are applied to the coteaching relationship in Table 7.3.

TABLE 7.3	**Organizational, Attitudinal, and Knowledge Barriers in Coteaching**
Attitudinal barriers	• Professional and personal compatibility problems between coteaching partners, which are critical for the success of coteaching (Zigmond & Rice, 1999). • Entrenched attitudes rejecting inclusive practices and administrators' unwillingness to commit the required time and resources (Zigmond & Rice, 1999). • Traditional teacher autonomy which is grounded in norms of privacy and noninterference, leading most teachers to believe that other teachers' activities are "none of my business" (Friend & Cook, 2003). • Too few teachers who believe that well-implemented coteaching results in academic and social gains for all students and should be regarded as an effective support option for inclusive classrooms (Zigmond & Rice, 1999).
Knowledge barriers	• Lack of awareness of the limitations of teacher and school administrator knowledge about how to implement inclusive practices. • Need for teacher development to understand the goals and effectiveness of inclusive settings for special needs learners and students with disabilities, requirements of the law, accommodations and modifications, instructional strategies, and strategies for coteaching.

	• Need for support in helping typical students understand their peers with disabilities.
	• Lack of technical assistance for collaboration and intensive staff development.
Organizational barriers	• An inadequate theory of collaboration between special and general educators.
	• Need for schoolwide commitment to inclusive principles, differentiated instruction, and coteaching.
	• Too little time for teachers to plan for and learn new skills and practices.
	• Teacher schedules that are constructed before coteaching teams are assigned, causing difficulties with effective collaboration (Gately & Gately, 2001).
	• In secondary schools that are organized by subject matter, most teachers view themselves as subject matter specialists; their capacity to implement new curricular and instructional models is limited by their relative isolation from one another during the school day, but also by subject and departmental boundaries (Friend & Cook, 2003).
	• The separation of vocational and academic education organizationally, physically, educationally, and socially, and the isolation that develops reinforces the separation between vocational and academic teachers (Friend & Cook, 2003).
	• School districts' tendencies toward faddism and quick-fix solutions, so that collaboration initiatives are not sustained.
	• Need for strong school principal and administrator leadership crucial to success in implementing inclusive practices and decreasing barriers to collaboration.
	• Lack of sustained central office support and follow-through for practices and policies that support teacher collaboration.
	• Lack of resources to implement collaborative initiatives and trying to do too much with too little support.
	• Failure to understand and take into account site-specific differences among schools.

Overcoming Barriers to Collaboration Between Special and General Educators

Getting Started in Developing a Coteaching Relationship.   Coteaching has been described as being like an "arranged marriage" (Wald & Boehm, 2002). Commenting on the nature of the coteaching classroom environment, Wald and Boehm say:

> Differences are seen as ordinary in collaboratively taught, inclusive classrooms, and students come to expect that instruction will vary depending on their individual learning needs. One student in the classroom might need instruction in a separate space, for example, and that service is provided; another student might need

enrichment activities, and that service is provided. It's understood by teachers and students alike that there will be a continuum of learning experiences carefully designed to help all students learn the content. (2002, p. 1)

The development of the coteaching relationship proceeds in a series of stages that are helpful for teachers entering into a coteaching partnership.

Stages in the Development of a Coteaching Relationship.

Like any developmental process, the coteaching relationship has stages through which coteachers progress. Gately and Gately (2002) define three developmental stages in the process: *beginning, compromise,* and *collaborative* stages. At each developmental stage, teachers demonstrate varying degrees of interaction and collaboration. These stages mirror the five degrees of collaboration introduced earlier in Chapter 2: communication and networking, cooperation, coordination, collaboration, and integration.

At the *beginning stage* of coteaching, teachers communicate superficially while they develop a sense of boundaries and attempt to establish a professional working relationship. Moving from a social relationship to a professional relationship with a colleague may be difficult for some teachers, and they may experience feelings of intrusion, invasion, detachment, or exclusion. Teachers may move very cautiously as they reshape their roles and create new role expectations. Communication may be polite and guarded. There is a danger that teachers can get stalled in this beginning state, particularly if they have minimal understanding of the developmental nature of the coteaching relationship. It may be that much of the dissatisfaction that is noted in the literature regarding coteaching is expressed by teachers who continue to interact at the beginning level.

In the *compromising stage*, as teachers develop work relationships, their professional communication increases, it becomes more open and interactive, and a sense of compromise prevails as they work to blend their practices. They let go of their traditional roles and move to a more collaborative partnership.

In the *collaborative stage*, open communication, humor, and a high degree of comfort characterizes the coteaching relationship and the collaborative classroom. The teachers' skills and talents complement each other, and it is often difficult for outsiders to discern which teacher is the special educator and which is the general educator.

Coteachers may proceed through these stages rapidly, beginning to collaborate after just a few short weeks, or more slowly, with teachers struggling to communicate and work together. Coteaching is more successful when there is careful planning between special and general education teachers in curriculum design, instructional delivery, classroom management, and assessment and evaluation (Crutchfield, 1997; Friend & Cook, 2003).

Collaborative Planning for Consultation.

Case-centered (individual student focused) **collaborative consultation** is an instructional support strategy in which special and general educators and related services specialists work together to resolve the educational concerns of individual students with special learning needs. It is a problem-solving approach that helps teachers better understand individual children while offering mutual collegial support among two or more teachers. Together the teachers work to create flexible and responsive teaching practices that can be matched to each child's particular learning strengths and needs. The process is interactive, enabling staff members to define problems together and creatively to develop solutions drawing on each teacher's particular expertise (Erchul & Martens, 1997; Palches, 2005).

A school psychologist, behavior specialist, speech–language therapist, or special education teacher might serve as a consultant. Collaborative consultation is not generally considered to be direct service to students, but rather consists of developing accommodations or modifications, providing ongoing progress monitoring, providing general education teachers with instructional strategies and programs, and observing the student in alternate environments. By meeting to identify a problem, systematically developing an intervention, gathering data, and judging the intervention's effectiveness, teachers and consultants can maximize student learning (Friend & Cook, 2003). Examples of this approach include grade-level elementary teams, middle school teams, interdisciplinary or departmental high school teams that meet regularly to discuss curriculum and address problems concerning individual students. The consultation model in the general education classroom can also help in the teaching of complex skills, or help the student practice a recently acquired skill. This model works most effectively with students who require occasional assistance.

Since the special educator's (or other specialists') role is consultative, it is assumed that the general education teacher has the discretion to accept the consultant's recommendations or not. However, since the purpose of the consultation is to improve student functioning, it is important that the special educators be viewed as experts with more than simply an advisory role in which recommendations are made to the general education teacher to accept or reject (Noell & Witt, 1999). Such recommendations should result in actual interventions that will be implemented in the classroom.

Steps for collaborative planning. Murawski and Dieker (2004) outlined a series of **steps for collaborative planning** for coteaching and consultation related to curriculum and instruction. The following steps are partly adapted from their work.

First, collaborating teachers should *establish a rapport* with each other and define their purpose (Why are we doing this? What is the expected outcome of teaching together?) (Bauwen & Mueller, 2000). Before the planning meeting, the general educator should provide the special educators with an overview of content, curriculum, and standards to be addressed. The special educator then provides a snapshot of students' IEP goals, objectives, and needed modifications in the general education class. Next they *discuss how the team can present the content* in a way that maximizes learning and retention for all students, beginning with what will be taught (content goals) and how it will be taught (coteaching strategies and adaptations/modifications).

A coteaching plan book is useful for both special and general educators to distribute tasks and determine how accommodations are to be made for students' learning or behavioral needs. A schedule can be designed to identify the days on which the special educator will take the lead on planning. At the secondary level, the special educators may or may not be able to lead the content, depending on their curricular strengths, but they still can take a lead role in lessons focused on general core content, test-taking strategies, social skills instruction, organizational strategies positive behavior support, or career–vocational lessons related to preparing students for college or future careers.

The next step is to *discuss* **teaching style** *preferences*. If one coteacher is more kinesthetic/tactile and the other is more auditory/visual, these preferences can be integrated into the lesson to assist students with varying learning styles. Students should be given short "brain breaks" to process information and to clear their heads. The teachers can use this time to discuss how the lesson is going and changes that might be needed. Recent brain research indicates that students need a brain break about every 10 to 15 minutes to summarize what they are learning (Jensen, 1998).

A *structured agenda*, which includes the curriculum standards to be addressed, as well as so-called "soft" skills (such as social or study skills that are crucial for students' success) should be posted for the class. These skills are often not an explicit part of the curriculum, but are important goals written into the students' IEPs and may be relevant for all students in the class. A planned agenda helps both coteachers and students remember the objective of the lesson. Middle school and high school students should be encouraged to participate in planning and discussing these objectives.

Although disagreements and discussions about content are important for modeling appropriate communication techniques among adults, it is important to avoid second-guessing or disagreeing with one another about assignments in front of students. Coteachers should work together closely to *assess the link between instruction and student assessment*, and to determine what is working instructionally for the whole class, what areas may need revision, and if there are specific students who may need individual accommodations. Since grading at the secondary level carries primary weight for students' postsecondary goals, discuss the implications of modifying assignments or grades for any students.

Consider a variety of options for assessing students with and without disabilities, to include alternative assessments, products and portfolios, modified assignments, and assessments of students' processes and effort. Discuss how students with IEPs will have their goals and objectives assessed and how individual achievements will be reflected in each student's grade. Provide menus of assignments that allow students to self-select projects or papers that are of interest to them and that best meet their particular learning styles. Create rubrics that will help coteachers define, and help students understand, what knowledge skills are being assessed and how, and share the load by taking turns grading. Finally, *evaluate the coteaching experience* and performance. What would you do differently? What additional resources do you need (adapted from Murawski & Dieker, 2004, by permission)?

Six Strategies for Overcoming Barriers to Coteaching.

Despite the obstacles, meaningful collaborative teaching is taking place in schools. Support for teacher collegiality and collaboration can be viewed in the framework of six dimensions (Dieker, 2002; DiPaola & Walther-Thomas, 2004; Gately & Gately, 2001; Inger, 1993; Murawski & Dieker, 2004). These dimensions will be used to organize this discussion of approaches for overcoming the barriers to collaboration between special and general education teachers.

Dimension 1. Organize assignments and leadership at the school level to support coteaching. School-level reorganization into teams stimulates cooperative work, but does not guarantee it. For teams to be effective, leadership must be broadly distributed among teachers and administrators. In some schools, for example, teachers are given reduced teaching loads in exchange for leading curriculum development work. Planning is also important in selecting the students who will be beneficiaries of the collaborative process. It is important to try to maintain in the classroom the natural proportions of typical students, students identified as being at risk, and students who have been found to have disabilities. Achieving a balanced classroom is easier at the elementary and middle school levels than at the secondary level, where student grouping is affected by course selection (Murawski & Dieker, 2004).

Dimension 2. Give teachers latitude to influence matters of curriculum and instruction. Teachers' investment in team planning rests heavily on the latitude they have for making decisions in areas of curriculum, materials selection, instructional grouping, and student assessment. Teachers need to be engaged in meaningful decisions of importance in the instructional process.

Dimension 3. Provide training and technical assistance. Cooperative work requires task-related training and assistance to help teachers master the specific skills needed for collaboration, develop explicit agreements to govern their work, and gain confidence in their ability to work with one another. Administrators can promote coteaching by providing research-based information about collaborative arrangements, and by encouraging teachers to prepare proactively for this change . . . *before* they actually start the process (Gately & Gately, 2001). In addition, they can team teachers in such a way that more experienced teachers serve as consultants or **coaches** to novice teachers. Staff development opportunities and incentives are important to encourage teachers and administrators to participate in classes, workshops, seminars, and professional conferences on cooperative teaching (Murawski & Dieker, 2004).

Dimension 4. Provide administrative and material support. Principals play an extremely important leadership role in facilitating collaborative efforts by instructional personnel (Murawsi & Dieker, 2004; Surber, 2003). Building-level planning can assist the teams by ensuring that adequate support is in place to sustain collaborative work. Key supports include texts on collaboration strategies, adequate office support and supplies, and adequate space for collaborative meetings.

Dimension 5. Use endorsements and rewards strategically. A **culture of collaboration** is created in schools where principals are attitude leaders who clearly articulate their belief that interdisciplinary instruction serves students better. Principals and other school leaders can promote the culture by communicating the collaborative work of staff, building expectations and incentives into the teacher reward system, and by celebrating collaboration publicly (Arguelles, Hughes, & Schumm, 2000; DiPaola & Walther-Thomas, 2004).

Many educators have applied this framework for teacher support. At the school level, the principal and other administrators are accountable for creating an environment that promotes effective collaboration, or a culture of collaboration. As change agents, they ensure that personnel have the attitudinal leadership, material resources, authority, time, and training to achieve effective collaboration.

Dimension 6. Structure time to support collaborative work. One of the thorniest issues for collaboration is time—for planning, development, and evaluation at the classroom, building, and district levels. Master schedules can either facilitate or place obstacles in the way of collaborative work. School leaders must establish common planning periods for coteachers, regularly scheduled team or subject area meetings, and released time for these activities (Murawski & Dieker, 2004). Administrative support is essential for scheduling common planning periods. For schools on a block schedule, an entire 90-minute period 1 day a week should provide an adequate amount of time to plan 1 to 2 weeks of lessons. In schools where common planning periods are not possible, then substitutes or administrators cover the classes, teachers meet during student activities or have coverage during student assemblies or field trips, or meet during regular lunch or afterschool times. Darling-Hammond and Bramsford (2005) observed the important role of adequate time for collaborative work:

> . . . Since most U.S. teachers have only one 45-minute planning period a day (often less in elementary school), they have very little time to engage in collaborative work. But if collaborative planning and professional development are a priority in school design, it is possible, even on a meager budget, to reallocate resources, organize the schedule, and assign enough staff as teachers so that teachers teach fewer hours during the day and have at least 5 hours a week to work together. Schools in industrialized countries in Asia and in Europe (where per pupil expenses are equal or less than in the United States, but are spent differently), have 20 hours or more per week to plan lessons, to meet with students and parents, and to work together and learn from one another. This collaborative work includes developing curriculum and assessments, observing each other's classes, and participating in study groups and other professional development activities. (Darling-Hammond, 1997; Darling-Hammond & Bransford, 2005)

WHAT PROFESSIONAL DEVELOPMENT CONTENT AND STANDARDS PROMOTE COLLABORATION BETWEEN SPECIAL AND GENERAL EDUCATORS?

A New Era for the Roles of Special and General Educators

Research now confirms strong connections between teacher quality, teacher collaboration, and student achievement (Darling-Hammond, 2001; Wayne & Youngs, 2003). As a result, the roles and professional qualifications for educators are rapidly changing. The new IDEA amendments of 2004 and NCLB call for new relationships between special and general educators and define the new "highly qualified teacher." According to a U.S. Government Accountability Office report (2004c) titled *Special Education: Additional Assistance and Better Coordination Needed Among Education Offices to Help States Meet the NCLB Teacher Requirements*, states are struggling to determine how to assess special educators' qualifications. As of January 2004, no states required secondary special educators teaching core academic subjects to pass a state exam or complete college-level course work in the content area they taught (Education Week, 2004).

Since the IDEA amendments of 2004 adopted the NCLB definition of "highly qualified teacher," there is a unique opportunity to break down existing barriers between special and general education (Ortiz, 2004; Ralabate & Foley, 2003). The

President's Commission on Excellence in Special Education in its publication titled *A New Era: Revitalizing Special Education for Children and Their Families* (2002) anticipated this opportunity:

> Children placed in special education are general education children first. Despite this basic fact, educators and policymakers think about the two systems as separate and tally the cost of special education as a separate program, not as additional services with resultant add-on expense. In such a system, children with disabilities are often treated not as children who are general education students and whose special instructional needs can be met with scientifically-based approaches; they are considered separately with unique costs—creating incentives for misidentification and academic isolation—preventing the pooling of all available resources to aid learning. General education and special education share responsibilities for children with disabilities. They are not separable at any level—cost, instruction, or even identification. (p. 11)

IDEA and NCLB emphasize the importance of collaboration and consultative roles of teachers in (a) helping students progress in the general education curriculum; (b) using coplanning and coteaching methods to strengthen student learning; (c) creating parent partnerships; (d) managing the behavior of students; and (e) working with professionals and referral agencies to identify, assess, and provide services to students with disabilities.

States' solutions to this dilemma for special educators have led to a variety of new structures for collaboration between special and general educators. Special educators who teach core academics may choose to work as special education consultants or gain additional training to meet the requirements for a highly qualified teacher in their content area(s). While this option presents many opportunities for supporting students with disabilities in general education, it also demands knowledge and skills in collaboration for both general and special educators in order to be successful.

General educators require skills and knowledge about children with disabilities, and special educators require greater knowledge about the general education curriculum and standards of learning. Both need to consider the role collaboration will play in implementing the requirements of NCLB and IDEA as they fulfill their individual roles.

IDEA and NCLB also place greater emphasis on the role of the general education teacher in instructing students with disabilities in inclusive settings. Teacher preparation and licensing standards specifically address the nature of the collaborative relationship between general and special education teachers. All general education teachers should know how to effectively teach students with disabilities, with consultation or coteaching support from special educators.

Summary of Key Points

- Collaboration between special and general classroom teachers is essential in order to achieve the goals of IDEA 2004 and NCLB to maximize access to the general education curriculum for all students.
- The traditional isolation and separation of special and general education teachers is changing rapidly, as research demonstrates strong links between teacher collaboration and student achievement.

- Collaboration between special and general education teachers benefits students and their access to appropriate education, teachers' knowledge about students learning needs, and differentiated instructional strategies for all students.
- Teachers use a variety of team structures to support special learners at elementary, middle, and high school.
- The coteaching relationship is developmental and proceeds through stages characterized by varying degrees of interaction and collaboration.
- General educators who receive training in collaboration with special educators and in differentiated instruction feel more successful instructing special learners.

Key Terms and Phrases

- Collaborative teaching (p. 177)
- Curriculum-based measurement (p. 180)
- Aligning general and special education (p. 182)
- Standards-based curriculum (p. 182)
- Coteaching (p. 183)
- Differentiated curriculum and instruction (p. 184)
- Team teaching (p. 186)
- Structures for collaborative teaching (p. 187)
- Collaborative consultation (p. 194)
- Steps for collaborative planning (p. 195)
- Teaching style (p. 196)
- Coaches (p. 197)
- Culture of collaboration (p. 197)

Questions for Reflection, Thinking, and Skill Building

1. Review Let's See It in Action on page 180 and page 181. Discuss how these two case illustrations differ.
2. What are the challenges for aligning the two educational models—*individualized education* for special education students and *standards-based education* for all students? What natural tensions are created? Discuss how they can they be reconciled.
3. What is meant by "coteaching is a developmental process"? What does this mean for collaboration among teachers? What are the implications for preparing teachers for their roles?
4. Discuss the knowledge, skills, and dispositions that special education and general education teachers need to be prepared for collaboration.
5. Reflect and outline your strengths and areas of need as a coteacher or potential coteacher. What can you do to address your areas of need?

6. Think about a coteaching experience you have had or are preparing for. Individually complete the questions in the Coteaching Self-Assessment (Box 7.2) on page 191. Be frank in your responses.

7. After completing the questionnaire individually, share the responses with your coteaching partner by taking turns reading the responses. Jot down thoughts you have regarding your partner's comments. Come back together and begin to share reactions to the responses. Your goal is to (a) agree, (b) compromise, or (c) agree to disagree.

CHAPTER EIGHT

What Is the Role of the Family in School Collaboration and System Coordination?

In Mollie (autistic spectrum disorder), every day there is a new birth. As she learns to discover the world, I am discovering myself. We have suffered, and we have died, and we are looking ahead to a new beginning.

—Patricia Kilbride, parent, 1995

A growing body of knowledge suggests that the presence of a family member with a disability may contribute to the strengthening of the entire family unit, as well as contribute positively to the quality of life of individual members of the family. —Hanline, 1991, p. 53

- Parents as partners: What is the role of families in school collaboration and system coordination?

- What lessons have been learned from research on family collaboration?

- What is the brief history of parent participation in education?

- What family characteristics and stressors impact participation in children's education? A resilience framework

- What are the barriers to effective family collaboration?

- How can the four functions of collaboration be applied to family partnerships?

- What are the principles for family-centered service coordination?

PERSPECTIVES

Teacher

Although it takes time and effort to actively involve many of the parents of my students in regular home–school communication, I have found that setting up a system at the beginning of the year and being consistent is well worth the effort, both in terms of the students' success in school and my effectiveness as a teacher. We can never underestimate the value of the information and influence of a teen's parents and siblings. We cannot afford to leave them out of the process, for long after our involvement with a teen is over, they remain. They are the constants and biggest advocates in a teen's life. Better communication with parents means feeling more connected with the child. Working with Mark and his family is a good example.

—MARK'S TEACHER

Parent

I believe that my son's teachers and school counselor have worked harder with my child because I have reached out and stayed involved. Some parents say—you have to be your child's case coordinator to get the services they need—and they are right. You have to stay involved, reach out, and be a good communicator. My child has many needs, and I have had to work across many agencies—the schools, mental health services, substance abuse, and the courts. Good communication is my responsibility, too, and it gets results. For me, life has rewarded action and a positive attitude. I firmly believe life rewards communication as well. Carrying into the school the baggage of anger, resentment, and weariness will not help that communication.

—CONVERSATION WITH PARENT OF A HIGH SCHOOL STUDENT, 2005

INTRODUCTION

Over the past century, parents and families have been powerful advocates for inclusive education and access to community services for their children with special learning needs. Education and human service workers have long recognized that children do not exist in isolation, but develop as part of a web of relationships among the family, school, and community (Novick, 2001). Educational research has provided evidence that the participation of parents and other family members is the most crucial factor in a child's potential to benefit from education and related services. Parents and families have also been crucial in promoting independence and self-determination for their children. Furthermore, the success of the collaborative process in schools is closely linked to the quality of teacher–family relationships.

This chapter examines (a) the crucial role of parents and families in the collaborative process and their potential to participate as decision makers in the process; and (b) principles and strategies for facilitating family involvement and improving their ability to participate effectively.

Parents as Partners: What Is the Role of Families in School Collaboration and System Coordination?

Creating meaningful parent collaboration that improves student achievement means moving beyond the traditional goals of expanding family involvement training. It begins with the hard work of actively engaging parents in decision making about their children's education. It also begins with programs that prepare teachers for their roles. After two decades of educational reform initiatives and research that affirm the importance of families as partners, parents of students with disabilities are still frequently left out of educational decisions about their children. However, recent change in education legislation is reaffirming the role of parents in education. The IDEA 2004, the NCLB of 2001, and the Higher Education Act Amendments of 1998, all strengthened the role of parents in their children's IEPs and transition plans, in school decision making, and in teacher preparation.

Together, the IDEA 2004 and NCLB set expectations for **parent–professional partnerships** that are unprecedented for the public school system. Parents were given important roles in identifying and evaluating their children with disabilities, and in the development, implementation, and revision of their educational programs. IDEA 2004 encouraged parents to become more involved in their children's education, and additionally, to work in other ways as partners with educators and policymakers (Christie, 2005; Henderson et al., 2003). Parents are encouraged to be involved in policymaking at the state and local levels as members of advisory panels and in developing school improvement plans.

As defined by IDEA 2004, "related services" are supportive services provided to a student with disabilities to assist him or her to benefit from special education (20 USC 1401 (22) and 20 USC 1401 (26)). The law authorizes several types of related services that may be provided directly to the parents of students with disabilities to help their children progress in school. These include counseling of parents regarding hearing loss and audiology services; planning and managing a program of psychological counseling for children and parents; group and individual counseling with the child and family; and parent training (Mountain Plains Regional Resource Center, 2005).

In summary, IDEA and NCLB convey three messages to parents, teachers, and service providers: (1) the importance of the parent–professional partnership in service delivery and improving educational outcomes for children and youth; (2) the inclusion of the family unit (system) as the target for intervention and support by the schools and community agencies; and (3) the importance of strengthening the families' role in decision making and educational improvement. IDEA 2004 and NCLB require schools to transform the traditional notions of parent involvement from signing report cards, reading newsletters, and chaperoning holiday parties, to include activities such as participating in school decision-making processes, providing input to teachers about how to assist their child, and forming meaningful partnerships with the school community.

Family Dynamics and Parent Involvement

There are many kinds of family units with which professionals will develop relationships. Therefore, **family** is defined in the broadest terms, including the following:

- traditional families with a father, mother, and children;
- blended families from previous divorce;
- single-parent families;
- extended families (grandparents, aunts and uncles, cousins);
- families with a grandparent or godparent in a parental role;
- families with an older adult sibling in a parental role;
- same-sex parent families; and
- families of adopted and foster children, including surrogate parents appointed by the courts.

This definition includes blood relatives as well as caregivers who may or may not be legal guardians. Regardless of the form of the family, a common characteristic is that each represents a unit that acts responsibly to protect, care for, and nurture children until they are able to be independent.

Families demonstrate a wide spectrum of abilities and dispositions when they collaborate with school personnel. Some may communicate appreciation as they reach out to teachers and administrators, and others may be suspicious, mistrustful, or simply inexperienced with the expectations of the school system. Some may communicate lack of confidence in professionals or may be frustrated with the performance of their son or daughter. Socioeconomic and cultural differences among families and school personnel are also a source of barriers to parent participation in their children's educational programs (Price, 2005).

Awareness and sensitivity to the pressures, values, and perspectives family members bring to school–family relationships is the starting point for productive parent participation. Sometimes parents may attend a school conference or meeting because they wish to discuss family challenges before focusing on the child's educational goals. The sensitivity of educators and an openness to listen and learn about families' perspectives and life circumstances, beliefs, and needs, form the foundation for parent partnerships. As one parent commented, "There are many people who don't have an understanding of just how difficult it is to parent some children. I'm not just talking about school staff. Other parents can be some of the most unforgiving of children's problems: "Sometimes, I'd love to give them a chance to do a better job raising my son and see how they feel after a couple of months!" (Parent, personal communication, 11/22/05). Let's See It in Action on page 207 shows how both parents and teachers walked a tightrope when it came to new academic testing for students.

In this example, Andrew's parents negotiated carefully and persistently for accommodations in testing for their son. It is a story of competing needs between parents and professionals as well as parents' sometimes unhelpful misperceptions about teachers and schools that can impede constructive collaboration.

Coordination Role of Families

There are many ways that parents participate in the coordination of services, particularly when they have children with disabilities who need extra support services in the classroom. Since most schools do not provide direct help to parents to coordinate services needed outside the school, parents are frequently their own children's "case managers" or "service coordinators." They participate in their child's IEP meetings, learn about the in-school services needed, and take recommendations for external or community-based services.

For example, in the case example of Eric, presented early in Chapter 3, the parents were working among four agencies—county mental health services, private psychological services, substance abuse services, juvenile services and the courts—as well as the school system, to provide multiple services to their son. Their weeks and months that turned into years involved countless hours performing a variety of coordination activities. These included communicating by email and telephone with teachers; contacting and coordinating appointments with agencies; visiting representatives of the agencies involved; tracking and maintaining files related to each agency so as not to duplicate services or evaluations; completing applications and evaluations; participating in team meetings and family counseling sessions; and providing documentation to insurance companies to obtain needed specialized services not provided by the school. Although this is a complex case, parents are often overwhelmed with the complexity of their lives when the needs of a special child must come first in the family's life.

Educators and policymakers have recognized the need to strengthen parent participation in schools as well as increase schools' support of families. It is important that schools be explicit in their communication with parents about the role they are expected to have at all levels. In addition to having strong collaborative relationships in schools and being a full partner in their child's IEP, they should be partners in the policies, program decisions, and reforms. However, to achieve such participation, parents need help with their complex lives.

LET'S SEE IT IN ACTION! CASE ILLUSTRATION: THE IMPORTANCE OF FAMILY ENGAGEMENT

Andrew's mother and father, Michelle and Richard, have felt that since Andrew started at the high school (a small rural school) in a general education class, they have not had the same level of connection with his school program as they had in middle school. The last few IEP meetings have included discussions around transition but they get the sense that the special education teachers really don't think Andrew will be able to achieve a regular diploma. Andrew is maintaining Cs and Ds, and he has great difficulty with the standardized tests. At the last meeting, Andrew's father felt that he had to "get in a few faces" in order to get the accommodations they thought Andrew needed. His mother, of course, tried to smooth things over. She didn't want the school perceiving them as hostile or overly demanding parents. She's been warned by her friend from the autism support group, who also had a son at the high school a few years ago, that if they asked for too much, then they would be labeled with a "reputation for trouble." Everyone seems to be anxious about improving the school's test scores, and more families are becoming concerned.

Attending transition meetings at school is difficult for Andrew's father, Richard. He dropped out of school when his mother died in order to help his father with the family plumbing business. He wasn't upset about that because he didn't like school. He always believed that the teachers were only interested in students who were going to college—the ones from the "good side of town." So school left him with bad memories. He prefers to let his wife go alone, and only when she is really worried about a specific meeting will he attend with her. He doesn't want his children to have the same experiences, and so he is pushing for them to continue their education beyond high school. According to Michelle and Richard, the only person at the school who seems to understand is the young man, Mr. Harris, the transition coordinator, whose job is to make sure that "this thing called transition" happens for Andrew. He dropped by their house last summer before the school year began to talk with them about Andrew's plans and goals for the future. According to Richard, that was where "this crazy idea about going to the community college came from." But as long as Mr. Harris thought Andrew could do college-level work, and if Andrew wanted to try it, then he would support him. The personal home visit by Mr. Harris really convinced him that this could be a possibility for his son.

Andrew and his mother met with Mr. Harris and his resource room teacher. The teachers had recently attended a workshop and learned new strategies to help students with special needs to take the high school exit exam. They offered to meet with Andrew and Michelle to work through some of their concerns and to help them better understand the testing process. The teachers explained to them about the different types of testing accommodations such as having Andrew take the test in a quiet place to reduce distraction. They also shared information about other types of accommodations. They discovered that some of the possible accommodations had not been made available to Andrew when he took and failed the practice I-STEP + (high school exit exam). This process really helped Andrew and his family relieve some of the pressure they were feeling. The family could focus on the next phase of Andrew's life—a job for the summer and a search for the right college with services to accommodate Andrew.

Questions for Discussion

Reflect on the case illustration as you consider the following questions:

- What biases or fears can you identify in the parents about the school and teachers?
- What factors threatened Andrew's high school completion?
- How did teachers engage the parents in helping Andrew prepare for the exit exam?
- What is Andrew's postsecondary goal and how supportive are his parents of the goal?

What Lessons Have Been Learned From Research on Family Collaboration?

There is ample evidence in the United States that parent involvement in education and parent–professional collaboration improve student performance (Ammon & Peretti, 1999; Burts & Dever, 2001; Epstein, 1991; Evans-Schilling, 1999; Katz & Bauch, 1999). It is now widely accepted by the educational community that family involvement in their children's education at school and in the community is an accurate predictor of a student's overall academic achievement. What the family communicates and does is more important to student success than family income or education. More than 30 years of research demonstrate that when families are directly engaged with their children's education, students show increased test scores, higher academic achievement, improved attitudes toward learning, have better social behavior, higher self-esteem, fewer placements in special education, higher school attendance rates, and lower dropout rates (Abrams & Gibbs, 2002; Christenson & Hurley, 1997; Finn, 1998; Newman, 2004; Pena, 2000; Raimondo & Henderson, 2001; Riley, 1997; Wherry, 1998; Zellman & Waterman, 1998). Parents who are actively involved in their children's school also experience better relationships with their children's teachers (Christenson, Hurley, & Renstermacher, 1997a).

Parent activities also shown to help improve student's achievement include teacher-provided strategies for assisting with homework, reading activities, and parent workshops on testing strategies. Parents who monitor their child's out-of-school activities, volunteer time at the school, frequently communicate with their child's teachers, assist their child with homework, and talk to their child about school, are more likely to have children who are academically successful (Abrams & Gibbs, 2002; Berger, 2000; Christenson, Hurley, Sheridan, & Fenstermacher, 1997a; Desimone, 1999; Edwards & Warin, 1999; Finn, 1998; Newman, 2004; Raimondo & Henderson, 2001; Thorkildsen & Stein, 1998; Wandry & Pleet, 2002).

These positive effects of parent involvement on achievement have similar results across economic, ethnic, and cultural backgrounds (Desimone, 1999; Price, 2005). Recognizing the role of parents in the academic future of a child is not a new concept, but it requires more study of how parent involvement can be encouraged in communities where parents are reluctant to become active members of the school community (Valdez-Noel, 2004). Box 8.1 is a reflection on how collaboration can lead to increased parent participation in the school.

One reason for the continuing discrepancy in achievement outcomes between children with and without disabilities in all grade levels is the absence of approaches that promote the students' and families' involvement in developing

BOX 8.1   Improving Parent Participation

When I taught for the Los Angeles Unified School District, I began teaching a class for students with emotional and behavioral disabilities for grades 3–5. This was the only classroom for this population of students within the school. Before I accepted the position, this class remained largely segregated from the rest of the school. For at least 2 years before, they did not have even one parent attend the back-to-school nights or open houses. There had been little to no interaction with parents of the children in this class. In frustration, I created a form called the "Student Success Sheet" that listed all of the class expectations beside a column where I could easily mark whether the student met or did not meet those expectations. In addition, there was plenty of space where I could add comments.

At the end of the day, students were individually called up to my desk to assist me in completing their sheet. Students were often far harder judging their own behavior than I was. They would explain to me why they believed they hadn't met the expectations, while I would point out all that they had done throughout the day to meet those expectations. Together we would write those specific comments on the form, which the students would take home daily for a parent signature. They would then return the form the following day. I would take advantage of opportunities to call the parents to express how well their children were performing and to share their children's achievement. Parents of children with emotional disabilities often hear what their children do wrong, but seldom the progress or success that they regularly achieve.

At the next open house, I had 100% percent parent turnout. Each parent came with a positive outlook for how their children were performing at school. I was pleased to share the students' class work and my plans for the students for the upcoming year. Throughout the year, parents continued to participate in class activities. In addition I was placed in charge of the school's holiday program where, for the first time, students with emotional disturbance were afforded the opportunity to participate and perform in the holiday extravaganza. Approximately 60% of my students' parents came to watch the performance midday as compared to none (0%) in the previous years in which the students had not been invited to participate. The parent involvement experienced within the school setting carried over into the children's homes. Parents regularly responded on the "Student Success Sheet" how they reviewed their children's homework or asked questions about the curriculum. —Kendra Hill, special educator, 2004.

educational goals and services (Calvin et al., 2000; Epstein, Sanders, & Clark, 1999; Minke & Vickers, 1999; Morningstar, Turnbull, & Turnbull, 1996). By encouraging and providing opportunities for meaningful family involvement, schools play a critical role in bridging the divide between home and school (Novick, 2001).

The National Longitudinal Transition Study (Wagner, Newman, Cameto, Garza, & Levine, 2005), sponsored by the U.S. Office of Special Education, surveyed 9,230 parents and guardians of students with disabilities to examine the involvement of families in their children's (ages 13–16) education. This study provides the first national picture of family involvement and its impact on student achievement. The study supports the findings of others that parents' activities in support of their children's education are associated with consistent differences in several achievement domains, independent of disability, functioning, or other differences among youth. Children and youth whose families are more involved in their schools are less far behind grade level in reading, tend to receive better grades, and have higher rates of involvement in organized groups and with individual friendships than those with less family involvement in school. In the domain of independence, children and youth whose families are more involved in their school are more likely than those from less involved families to have had regular paid jobs in the preceding year. Family expectations for the future also help shape the achievements of individuals with disabilities, particularly with regard to academic engagement and achievement (Newman, 2004). These findings support decades of research that have recognized parent and family participation as the most crucial factor in the development and educational success of a child with disability.

A Brief History of Parent Participation in Education

Since the Massachusetts legislature passed the first compulsory school code in 1647, families have been involved in a variety of roles in the schools (Brouillette, 1999). They have directly assisted teachers in classrooms, helped raise funds, and participated in parent–teacher associations (PTA). The Parent Teacher Association (PTA) was first established in 1897 (National PTA, 2003) and has grown to become a powerful organization for parents in partnership with schools.

In the 1960s, the public schools began to systematically address parent involvement in their children's education. At the time parent involvement initiatives were based on the *"deficit" model*—that schools should target parents who lacked the resources, skills, and education needed to help their children academically (Shepard & Rose, 1995). The *deficit model* implied that resources should be used to support parents who needed help and that home cultures were inferior to the school's culture. Programs designed under the deficit model failed to recognize and appreciate the cultural context of the community before forming judgments and labeling families as somehow deficient. Naturally parent involvement efforts based on the deficit model were not well received by the intended audience, and minimal gains were made in parent involvement (Edwards & Warin, 1999; Shepard & Rose, 1995; Valdez-Noel, 2004).

In the 1970s and 1980s, schools shifted their thinking from the *deficit model* to that of the *differential model*. Based on the differential model, schools identified the *difference* in the home culture and the school culture and emphasized building upon the unique characteristics of the home community to help children adjust to the culture necessary for school success (Edwards & Warin, 1999; Shepard & Rose, 1995). In the 1990s, schools entered a more progressive decade for parent involvement through *empowerment*:

> In contrast to deficit or differential models—which often encourage a sense of helplessness and incompetence in parents, *empowerment* interventions view parents as vital sources of information and as having the capacity to make meaningful contributions to their children's lives and their community. (Shepard & Rose, 1995, p. 374)

In the **empowerment model**, collaboration is based on the view of parents as empowered "drivers" of the system of services (Osher & Osher, 2002). Shepard and Rose (1995) describe the empowerment model as having four major components:

1. *Basic communication*: Parents and teachers share reciprocal communication for the purpose of exchanging new information.
2. *Home improvement*: Parents learn to become more engaged through training in parenting skills and at-home learning activities.
3. *Volunteering*: Through volunteer work, parents have more interaction at school which raises their confidence levels and improves relationships with school personnel.
4. *Advocacy*: Parents become knowledgeable of factors that influence educational policies at local and state levels.

Involvement levels differ and are influenced by numerous factors (Hoover-Dempsey & Sandler, 1997). These factors include how well and how much schools inform and involve families. Attitudes and beliefs of teachers about parents affect whether and how much families are engaged in partnerships with professionals (Price, 2005). Berger (2000) outlined seven levels of parent involvement. These levels contain the more traditional approach to family involvement (fund-raising, volunteering in the classroom, assisting with homework) as well as the expanded concept of families as partners with professionals. These expanded roles include the family as active partners and educational leaders at home and school, decision makers on school boards and advisory councils, and community and legislative advocates.

In summary, traditionally, family involvement in schools has meant volunteering in the classroom, helping with homework, and participating in school fund-raising activities—what Christenson and Carroll (2000) call the "big three" forms of involvement. More recent proponents of the empowerment model believe in the contributions of parents and their abilities to be the best advocates for their children (Baer, 1996; Berger, 2000; Corbett & Wilson, 2000; Harry, 1996; Lightfoot, 2001). Empowerment-based programs emphasize the education of parents to help their children as well as to make informed decisions. Today, most school policies related to parent partnerships have embraced the empowerment model, which is also reflected in new requirements of IDEA 2004 and NCLB.

WHAT FAMILY CHARACTERISTICS AND STRESSORS IMPACT PARTICIPATION IN CHILDREN'S EDUCATION? A RESILIENCE FRAMEWORK

Many factors influence the relationship of parents and professionals in their children's schools. These factors include the effect of the disability on the family, the type and severity of the disability and its impact on the school, and the effect of culture on attitudes about disabilities.

The Family System and the Effects of a Disability

Understanding the concept of **family systems** and the stressors on families that influence their active participation in the schools is important for improving relationships. A family is a complex social system in which no member can be viewed in isolation: What affects one family member will affect all family members. Having a child with a disability adds another dimension to the complexity and challenge of raising a family.

It is important to recognize that families of children with disabilities pass through stages of adjustment from the moment they learn of their child's disability. Kubler-Ross (1969) identified several stages an individual passes through when dealing with death. These stages include (1) initial shock, (2) disbelief and denial, (3) anger and resentment, (4) depression and discouragement, (5) bargaining, and finally, (6) acceptance. This model has been extensively applied to families of children with disabilities upon learning of the birth or diagnosis of a disability in their child.

The *Family Systems Model* defined by Turnbull, Brotherson, and Summers (1985) presents a framework for analyzing the strengths and needs families bring to relationships with professionals. The model consists of four family subsystems: (1) the spouse subsystem (husband and wife interactions); (2) the parental subsystem (parent–child interactions); (3) the sibling subsystem (child–child interactions);

and (4) the extrafamilial subsystem (nuclear family interactions with extended family and networks of social, community, and professional support). The presence of these subsystems differs from family to family, as do the resources and strengths within each. For example, the spousal subsystem may be less significant in a single-parent family; in other families, the special needs child may have many siblings who serve as supports and role models.

A Resilience Framework for Family Participation

Caution must be used by professionals when applying coping models such as the Kubler-Ross (1969) "cycle of grief" to family responses to their children's disabilities. Attributions to families, such as "in denial" or "still in the grieving cycle," are often used by professionals to explain a perceived lack of cooperation by these families. Many families find this judgment by professionals to be "condescending and patronizing" (Snow, 2001; Ulrich & Bauer, 2003) and a clear barrier to effective communication and partnership. Although there is certainly a period of adjustment upon learning of a diagnosis, families' needs and conditions evolve over time. Their lives are a series of reactions and adaptations—a series of transitions and readjustments necessitated by their children's developmental stages, year in school, severity of disability, and ongoing medical issues (Carpenter, 2000; Lin, 2000; Perske, 1989; Snow, 2001; Turnbull & Turnbull, 2001). The adjustment process is often cyclical rather than sequential.

It is important, therefore, for teachers and other professionals to view families' adaptations to living with a special needs child as a growth and resilience-building process and seek to recognize the strengths these families bring to that process. More often the disappointment and reevaluation of expectations occurs early on in the adjustment process and becomes intertwined with the task of gaining resilience. Each stage represents natural resilience-building skills that involve knowledge development, self-understanding, empowerment, and, ultimately, enlightenment. Figure 8.1 presents a framework for the stages or tasks of building parent participation in their children's education, based on a **resilience model** of families.

The assumptions upon which the framework is constructed include the following:

1. Parents and family members are the best sources of knowledge about the child and about their own strengths and needs in coping.
2. Parents are under stress and need to be included in the service delivery and support process.
3. Parents possess resilience that may not be immediately appreciable, but should be identified and built upon.
4. Parents are engaged in a continuous adjustment process that can be facilitated if recognized by professionals (Kochhar-Bryant, 2003c).

Let's See It in Action on page 214 offers a window into a family's resilience as they rally to provide support to their daughter with multiple challenges.

It is important for teachers, related services specialists, and administrators to deepen their understanding of the implications of specific disabilities for their own work with families. Parents are among the best sources of information about what works best in support of their children's learning.

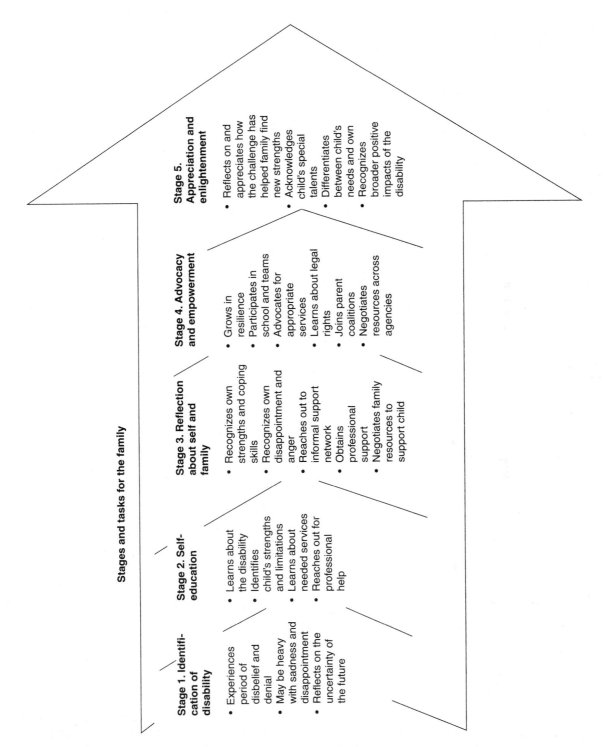

Stages and tasks for the family

Stage 1. Identifi-cation of disability

- Experiences period of disbelief and denial
- May be heavy with sadness and disappointment
- Reflects on the uncertainty of the future

Stage 2. Self-education

- Learns about the disability
- Identifies child's strengths and limitations
- Learns about needed services
- Reaches out for professional help

Stage 3. Reflection about self and family

- Recognizes own strengths and coping skills
- Recognizes own disappointment and anger
- Reaches out to informal support network
- Obtains professional support
- Negotiates family resources to support child

Stage 4. Advocacy and empowerment

- Grows in resilience
- Participates in school and teams
- Advocates for appropriate services
- Learns about legal rights
- Joins parent coalitions
- Negotiates resources across agencies

Stage 5. Appreciation and enlightenment

- Reflects on and appreciates how the challenge has helped family find new strengths
- Acknowledges child's special talents
- Differentiates between child's needs and own
- Recognizes broader positive impacts of the disability

FIGURE 8.1

Resilience Framework: 5 Stages Toward Family Strength

"LET'S SEE IT IN ACTION!" CASE ILLUSTRATION: RESILENCE

Rosa is a 9-year-old in the third grade attending a neighborhood school. Her parents arrived in the United States from Mexico 5 years ago. She is bilingual, speaking both Spanish and English. She has a diagnosis of severe learning disability (SLD) with some fine motor deficits and also has behavior challenges due to an attention deficit and hyperactivity disorder (ADHD). Rosa receives special services 3 hours a week in a pull-out resource room and is supported by a language specialist. Although the IEP team determined that the resource room and use of the language specialist was sufficient to meet Rosa's educational needs, her parents believed that more should be done. Rather than confront the issue at school, they decided to seek extra help at a clinic recommended by a friend. Two afternoons a week her mother picks Rosa up from school and travels 30 miles to the clinic where she is seen by an occupational specialist. On a third afternoon, she takes Rosa to a speech therapist. Rosa's father works two jobs to pay for the extra therapy.

Rosa's family uses a sticker chart system on the refrigerator to manage her behavior. Her older brother practices flash cards with Rosa each night. Her younger sister helps Rosa get ready for bed at night and for school in the morning. Rosa's mother uses the time traveling to the therapists to interact with all three of her children and catch up on their school day.

Weekends are filled with errands, sporting events, and church activities. Rosa's mother and father take turns doing these things with her siblings while the other parent stays with Rosa. Church attendance is a family event, but the parents take separate cars in case Rosa becomes too restless to stay. Sunday afternoon is usually a time for something special that Rosa likes to do (a trip to the playground, a meal at a favorite restaurant) if she has earned the privilege during the week on her chart. Each day is met with challenges for Rosa and her family. Each day they struggle to make things work and find a balance. They work as a team.

Questions for Discussion

- Is there a difference of opinion between the family and the rest of the IEP team about the types and frequency of related services that Rosa needs? Is it resolved within the team process?
- What additional costs was the family bearing for related services not provided by the school?
- What additional stresses are being placed on the family as they access related services?
- What strengths help the family to cope? How have Rosa's siblings contributed to the family functioning?
- What happened after the team meeting in which the school recommended something with which the family did not agree?
- Are there cultural issues involved here that would lead Rosa's family to seek other services rather than work with the school?

Source: From *Learning Modules Series for Building Teacher Preparation Capacity Through Partnerships with Families,* 2006. Orlando, FL: University of Central Florida. Adapted with permission.

Families in the Context of Home and Community Environments

Since each student functions within the wider circle of the family and the family's surrounding community, each student affects these circles and, in turn, is affected by them. He or she brings school concerns home and home concerns to school and often both home and school worries are brought into the community. The outcome may be constructive participation in the community through sports, volunteer work, or projects, or it may involve releasing home–school frustrations through activities that are not constructive.

Along with the type and degree of disability, it is also important to be aware of the onset of the disability and the characteristics of the family's support system. Some children are diagnosed at birth, others when they are 2–5 years old. Still others may not be diagnosed until they are in the second or third grade or later and begin to experience academic difficulties. Some disabilities such as cerebral palsy may require medical intervention and supports. Visual and hearing disabilities require adaptive equipment and accommodations, whereas severe learning disabilities often require intensive remediation once a child enters school. Whatever the disability, the cumulative impact on the family can mount daily. For example, consider the following questions: How does having a child with severe muscle coordination challenges who must rely on the use of a wheelchair affect family outings and vacations? How does having a child with severe emotional disturbance affect the family interactions within the immediate and wider family and with their community of friends? How does having a child with a disability affect the degree of mobility parents have to leave current positions and pursue new work with different employers? How does the family view their child's disability? Are there co-occurring disabilities (two or more disabilities that exist together) that require supplemental services from multiple sources? As teachers and related professionals communicate with parents, it is important that they be cognizant of potential limitations in life style and options for some families of children with disabilities. It is important that professionals remain alert to the variety of coping strategies that many parents demonstrate, such as viewing their child as a source of strength, learning, and appreciation in their lives.

Importance of fathers. Research has demonstrated the importance of fathers in their children's overall development and achievement in school (Baron, Byrne, & Brandscrombe, 2006; Clarke-Stewart, Gruber, & Fitzgerald, 1999; Coleman & Garfield, 2004; Engle & Breaux, 1998; Fagan & Iglesias, 2000; Lambie, 2000; Lewis, 2003). Having a child with a disability can create additional stress on a marriage and is reflected in the high divorce rate among these families. Stepparents particularly face special stresses in coping with a special needs child. While they may have accepted the fact that their new spouse has a child with a disability, they often lack experience with the day-to-day coping (Barnett, Clements, Kaplan-Estrin, & Fialka, 2003).

Blended families. Stepparents may have different ways of coping with stress than do biological parents. Some may internalize their feelings and be unable to openly communicate with their spouses about having a child with special needs. The friction caused by these differences can add stress to the couple's relationship. If the result is a divorce, the stressors facing the single parent can be exacerbated when one or more of the children have a disability. What happens at home can have a profound effect on how a child functions at school. All these factors are interrelated and can affect the educator's relationship with the student and the family (Barnett, Clements, Kaplan-Estrin, & Fialka, 2003). Professionals, however, should also be alert to the fact that many blended families become stronger with the presence of a child with a disability.

Families vary in makeup, stability, socioeconomic levels, and education and have different expectations for their children. Communities also vary in size, history, geography, and socioeconomic levels. Within these communities are entities that care for and have contact with families and students, such as parent resource centers. As Epstein (2001) advises, "Educators need to know the context in which students live, work and play" (p. 5). The whole child must be considered, including all the aspects that affect the child within the home, school, and community.

Responding to Challenging Parent Behavior: Applying the Resilience Framework

Families differ greatly in their strengths and capacities for collaboration with school personnel. Conversely, school professionals vary in their ability to collaborate with families. Some may experience appreciation as they reach out to parents and family members, or they may experience suspicion, mistrust, and avoidance. Awareness and sensitivity to the pressures, values, and perspectives family members bring to the school–family collaboration process is the starting point for productive parent participation. Socioeconomic and cultural differences between families and school personnel can be a source of barriers to parent participation in their children's educational programs. For example, it may be difficult for a family to recognize publicly that their child has a disability because of a cultural stigma that this may carry. Families with fewer resources may be coping with multiple life challenges such as meeting basic needs for their children's education, or for food, shelter, clothing, and safety. Family upheavals such as divorce or remarriage or chronic health problems also affect the emotional ability of parents at any socioeconomic level to deal with their children's educational development. One or several of these factors may cause reluctance to participate in school meetings and activities, or even hostility toward professionals.

Let's examine some parent behaviors that require sensitive collaborative skills on the part of educators. These will be discussed in the context of the resilience framework presented earlier in Figure 8.1 and the stages in the development of family strength:

1. *The parent in denial.* These parents are stuck in Stage 1 (identification of the disability), unable to accept the disability. They may request that evaluations be repeated or that other professionals reassess their child. They may want to have independent evaluations. They may argue for a different kind of diagnosis or placement for their child. *Strategies:* These parents typically need more information about their child's disability and a careful interpretation of the evaluation provided to them. They need to understand more clearly their own attitudes toward disability and to examine their own needs as separate from those of their child. Often group or individual counseling or a parent mentor is indicated for these parents.

2. *The angry parent.* These parents come to meetings with teachers or administrators displaying angry and hostile behavior. They are not open to learning or considering options for their child. They may have rigid ideas about what is needed. They may blame teachers, staff, or inadequacy of services for problems that the child is having in school. They may be stuck in Stage 1, in the process of identification of the disability, and may have a weak understanding of the disability. *Strategies:* The teachers need to display patience and an understanding that the parents may be just beginning to understand their child's diagnosis and have not yet worked through sadness or disappointment. An educational approach will provide important information about the nature of the disability, the assessments of the child, and educational strategies that are effective.

3. *The overwhelmed parent.* These parents present as uncertain and overwhelmed by the discovery of the disability and demonstrate a sense of powerlessness to be good parents. They may be silent in meetings, unable to participate and share their feelings and concerns. Although they may appear indifferent or disinterested or avoid making decisions, they are often in a state of emotional paralysis. They may be stuck in Stage 1, feeling sad and reflecting on the uncertainty of the future of the family with a child with a disability. The uncertainty breeds self-doubt and fear about their ability to cope with the new reality. *Strategies:* Avoid denying the parents' feelings (e.g., "You are seeing things wrong, and you really are good parents."). Instead, acknowledge their feelings of inadequacy. Explain that this is a natural feeling to have and quite common in families. Explain that it is temporary and will fade with knowledge and discovery of strategies and supports for parenting their child. Connect them with other parents who can provide support or to a parent resource center in the community. Offer to refer them for counseling, if appropriate.

4. *The demanding parent.* These parents may be in Stage 2, 3, or 4 in which they are seeking to educate themselves about the disability. They may have conducted their own research and present as knowing more than the professionals. This stance should be viewed not as hostility but as strength in the parents since they are at the stage in which they are willing to become partners with professionals. It is essential at this point that professionals avoid defensiveness and see the parents as eager to learn and valuing knowledge about the disability. Although such parents may be very assertive, they can become strong allies. *Strategies:* Find out how much the parents know and positively reinforce their efforts to educate themselves. Offer to add to their store of knowledge about their child's disability with the most up-to-date information and sources. Invite parents to find out more about particular strategies or programs and share them with the school and with other parents. Connect them with other parents for support or as mentors. Ask them to join a parent advisory team or parent training effort to share their knowledge and experiences. This can channel their energy in a positive direction that is directed less at conflict and more at problem solving.

5. *The parent of limited intellectual ability.* These parents need assistance in understanding the nature of their child's disability and their role and responsibilities for attending team meetings and helping support their child. They may need assistance in all stages in the development of resilience. *Strategies:* Provide the parents with a mentor, ombudsman, or advocate who can support them in meetings, explain jargon, and help them understand the process in concrete terms. Use concrete examples and give them specific strategies that they can carry out with their child. Use videos to help describe processes and strategies because the parents may have weak reading skills. Ask the parents about their experience with the disability their child has and build on that knowledge.

6. *The parent who abuses drugs or alcohol.* Some parents have serious life problems and are unable to help their children with disabilities. Many will make attempts to attend meetings and learn as much as they can, but may be limited in their ability to participate and follow through with recommendations. *Strategies:* These parents will need support throughout the stages of resilience building. If the parents are incapacitated due to obvious substance abuse, a counselor should be brought in for individual consultation with the parents and to discuss the need for referral for additional intervention and support. The parents may not be aware of substance abuse treatment available in the community and may need assistance linking with such services. It is also important to further explore the situation at home to determine if the child is at risk in any way. A school counselor or advocate or parent mentor should be assigned to help parents with obvious substance abuse problems.

For students with special needs, supportive environments in schools depend on positive relationships between teachers and families. The quality of these relationships depends on the preparation of the teachers. Teachers must be prepared to work effectively with families when they graduate from their teacher preparation programs and enter the schools. Professional organizations that develop standards for the preparation of educators have incorporated parent collaboration to varying degrees.

WHAT ARE THE BARRIERS TO EFFECTIVE FAMILY COLLABORATION?

Although there is ample evidence of the positive effects of family involvement, many schools inadvertently discourage family involvement. Public school administrators and teachers concentrate largely on the immediate needs of children, with little time and resources to attend to their family life. Some educators speculate that these circumstances may contribute to lower levels of family involvement (Lightfoot, 2001; National Coalition for Parent Involvement, 2001; North Central Regional Education Laboratory, 2001; Pleet, 2000). Large classes also impede family participation because teachers have minimal time to spend with individual students and to meet with family members outside class, and there are few incentives to do so. Specific barriers to improving parent participation are discussed below.

Ten Barriers to Parent Participation in Their Children's Education

Family members vary in the amount and type of involvement they desire or are able to commit to. A lack of family or parent involvement can be a reaction to a perceived lack of support and respect from school personnel in general. Teachers do not systematically encourage family involvement, and parents do not always participate when they *are* encouraged to do so. This is particularly true in secondary schools, where family involvement is generally more limited than in earlier years (Cohen, 1994; North Central Regional Education Laboratory [NCREL], 2001). Systemic institutional barriers may impede the involvement of parents as their children move into upper elementary, middle school, and high school settings.

1. *Lack of opportunities and resources.* Studies of parents' experiences with schools show a limited range of opportunities for their participation. Parents express frustration with the limited resources available to help them better understand their children's learning and behavioral issues and the rights of their children with disabilities. The literature indicates that the problem is not that parents do not care or are not interested, but may not have appropriate opportunities (Ames & Dickerson, 2004; Desimone, 1999; Edwards & Warin, 1999; Pena, 2000; Porche & Ross, 1999).

2. *Lack of a welcoming environment in the School.* The school climate is the educational and social atmosphere of a school, and in a welcoming school climate, educators treat parents with respect and encourage a wide range of participation. As a result, parents feel accepted, respected, and needed, and they are more likely to become involved in the school (Blank, 2001; NCREL, 2003). Lack of administrator support for parent participation may inhibit family involvement because teachers often need incentives such as administrative recognition before they will extend themselves to family members. A welcoming school climate can be created in several ways:

- Establish flexible policies that encourage parent participation in a variety of activities.
- Permit parents to visit the school during open houses, parent–teacher conferences, art and music events, and athletic and academic programs.
- Provide opportunities for parents to voice their comments and concerns.
- If the parents are not fluent in English, arrange to have a resource person—either a teacher or another parent—communicate with the parents in their first language.
- Create a parent center at the school, staffed by a parent liaison, where parents can congregate, plan school activities, work on classroom projects, and learn about the educational process.
- Provide parent education and support programs (such as parenting classes, seminars for parents on helping children learn at home, and skills improvement classes), publicize parent involvement efforts, and personally thank and honor parents who have volunteered their efforts.
- Provide for ongoing professional development in family participation for all school staff, which should address developing skills in working with parents and families, reducing barriers to parent involvement, communicating with culturally and linguistically diverse families, and improving two-way communication between school and home (NCREL, 2003).

Many of these strategies are being employed in schools across the United States, demonstrating that relationships between home and school are changing in fundamental ways.

3. *Disenfranchised parents.* Many parents feel disenfranchised and alienated and report that they are not more actively involved in their children's education because they believe that school personnel are not interested in them. Some report experiences in which they are denied opportunities to volunteer at their children's schools (Ferguson, 2005; Schribner & Schribner, 2001; U.S. Department of Education, 1998, 1997b).

4. *Lack of well-trained and available staff.* Many school administrators report that levels of parent involvement are linked to adequate numbers of well-trained staff. This includes district administrators with special education backgrounds, school psychologists, and teachers who were not only skilled in working with parents, but also have sufficient time to meet with parents (Henderson, 2002; U.S. Government Accountability Office, 2003).

Few teachers are prepared for the direct participation of parents in school decision making, even though teacher preparation standards address family partnerships. In a study of **national teacher preparation standards**, this author found that teacher and teacher educator competencies related to parent participation in decision making and reform include abilities to conduct the following activities:

    a. Promote direct participation of parents in the development and reforms in the preservice institution, including review of curriculum, participation in program restructuring, parent advisory councils, guest lecturing and coteaching, and participation in student field-based internships involving families.

    b. Promote direct participation in decision making about field-based professional development programs at the state and local levels.

    c. Promote participation of parent advocates and representatives on state advisory councils, the state transition coordinating councils, professional development councils, interagency coordinating councils, and evaluation task forces.

    d. Promote parent participation in local evaluation of services.

    e. Promote participation of parents in local school advisory groups, educational planning, and state and local systemic reforms (Kochhar-Bryant, 2003c).

The goal of improving access and progress of students with disabilities in general education depends on teachers' competence in working closely with parents.

    5. *Communitywide barriers.* Administrators and teachers consistently reported socioeconomic barriers to parent participation, including poverty, lack of transportation, families with multiple jobs, and single-parent households (Ames & Dickerson, 2004). Parents who did not have positive school experiences when they were students may be reluctant to get involved in their children's education. Many students live with extended family members rather than their parents. In many schools, only a few of the students live with both parents, and, overall, 20% of children do not have parents who actively provide care for them (Nord & West, 2001; U.S. Department of Education, 2002a).

    6. *Lack of state and district policies.* NCLB mandates that every Title I school have a written parent involvement policy that includes parents in its development (Education Commission of the States, 2004). Currently, 17 states have grant or award programs that encourage schools or districts to involve parents in their children's education or that recognize those that do so already. Fifteen states have policies that encourage or direct employers to enable parents to attend school activities such as parent–teacher conferences (Christie, 2005).

    7. *Inconsistency in the role of parents in the eligibility determination and IEP process.* Parents report that they are generally not comfortable enough with the IEP process to request changes in the program implementation or goals. In many districts, it is still common for parents to see the IEP for the first time at the IEP meeting and be expected to sign it without necessarily understanding it (Henderson & Mapp, 2002). Within districts, there are wide variations in the level of parent participation in the IEP. Families that expressed reservations about their level of involvement in the individualized education program process were disproportionately from Black, Hispanic, and Asian/Pacific Islander families and from low-income households (Christie, 2005; Epstein, 2001; Henderson & Mapp, 2002).

    8. *Attitudinal barriers.* In a large national study, Study of State and Local Implementation and Impact of IDEA (SLIIDEA, 2003), parents reported that school personnel exhibit attitudinal barriers, including prejudice toward special education students and their parents. These tensions between general education and special education departments over spending for special education can inadvertently be communicated to parents. Another example of discouragement related to mixed messages about parent involvement in advisory councils. Although councils generally welcomed, occasionally administrators felt threatened by parents functioning as an organized group. There are reports in some districts of administrators abolishing parent advisory councils as a way of managing "overly involved" parents. Parents at another site reported that even though they were pleased overall with the quality of services within the district, they often had to push and become very vocal to receive the services their children needed (NCES, 1998; SLIIDEA, 2003; U.S. Government Accountability Office, 2003).

9. *Lack of bilingual resources.* In many school districts that experience an influx of non-English-speaking families, teachers and administrators report that they have difficulty finding printed materials and interpreters who could intervene on behalf of non-English-speaking parents (Ames & Dickerson, 2004; Bernhard, Freire, Pacini-Ketchabaw, & Villanueva, 1998; Brilliant & Duke, 2001; Christie, 2005; Henderson & Mapp, 2002; SLIIDEA, 2003).

10. *Lack of time.* Many teachers are disappointed with the poor turnout of parents at teacher–parent conferences and question their usefulness (Black, 2005). School personnel lack sufficient time to spend with parents, and many are unclear about their role in working with parents of students with special needs (Abrams & Gibbs, 2002; Ames & Dickerson, 2004; Ammon et al, 2000; Berger, 2000).

APPLYING THE FOUR FUNCTIONS OF COLLABORATION TO FAMILY PARTNERSHIPS

Many formal and informal strategies have been identified to strengthen family communication and participation in their children's education and the work of the school. These include traditional activities such as newsletters, phone calls about student progress, surveys, training seminars, and parent resources, as well as non-traditional relationships such as school advisory committees, monitoring and evaluation teams, or study teams. These relationships will be discussed in relation to the four functions of collaboration introduced in Chapter 1: collaboration as *discovery*, *synthesis of ideas*, *development of practice*, and *building professional community*.

Parent Collaboration as Discovery

Parent collaboration as discovery refers to the use of collaboration (or collaborative relationships) to construct new knowledge through action research or team investigation, or to transfer knowledge between and among professionals and parents. Examples of such collaboration include the participation of parents in planning for action research in a classroom, school, or district; inviting parents to provide information to educators through surveys or questionnaires about their child's education or needs or their judgments about the quality of education (Henderson, 2002); and using evaluation tools to assess parent satisfaction and monitor parent/school contact.

Parent Collaboration as Synthesis of Ideas

Parent collaboration as synthesis of ideas refers to the use of collaboration to connect the thinking and knowledge of people in different disciplines or groups within an organization to make team decisions, or to develop new practices, policies, and relationships.

Promoting parent participation in school decision making requires a deeper level of awareness of parents' perspectives and how they can help inform teaching and learning. Teachers need to answer very explicitly for themselves and for parents the questions: Why is it important that parents be key stakeholders in educational decisions for their children and for the school? What can their perspectives add? How can an appreciation of their perspectives empower teachers? How do we turn conflicts that may arise between teachers and parents into constructive interactions and relationships?

Parent Collaboration as the Development of Practice

Parent collaboration as the development of practice refers to efforts to engage parents in developing or improving new practices, processes, and relationships. For example, under both NCLB and IDEA 2004, state and local guidelines for coordination of services emphasize the role of parents in the decision making and coordination efforts in schools.

Henderson and Mapp Study of Strategies to Improve Parent Participation.　In a study of parent participation in schools by Henderson and Mapp (2002), formal school policies generally went beyond mere encouragement of parent participation, often providing guidelines for participation or requirements for school accountability. For instance, the superintendent in one district required that each school increase "meaningful parent participation" in its school improvement plan. Policies required schools to educate parents about their role in their children's education and to encourage their participation in their children's IEP process, evaluation, reevaluation, and placement. They encouraged personnel to negotiate with parents and to bring in mediators over matters of disagreement. Directives to schools encouraged the development of **home–school communication programs** in an effort to develop many forms of parental involvement. Finally, policies required that schools determine how to involve parents who have disabilities, and that at least one trained parent advocate participate in IEP teams in addition to the parent (Henderson & Mapp, 2002).

Additional collaborative strategies that improved parent participation with their children's education and in the work of the school were identified as:

- direct and consistent communication about student progress by telephone or in weekly or quarterly reports;
- use of report cards eight times a year on progress related specifically to IEP goals;
- monitoring and reporting rates of parent participation in the IEP process;
- provision of in-room telephones for classroom teachers to maintain communication with parents;
- workshops for parents of children with disabilities on topics such as IDEA requirements for parent involvement and involvement in the IEP process;
- opportunities to network with other parents of special education students through attendance at **special education parent advisory committees** and other committees;
- distribution of printed materials to parents of children receiving special education services to orient them to their roles and responsibilities related to the IEP;
- guidebooks for parents attending IEP meetings, and encouraging parents who disagree with their children's IEPs to enlist the help of advocates; and

- surveys to parents about their satisfaction with the services of educational specialists and how well related services specialists engaged parents.

Parent evaluations or surveys should be conducted in the student's native language and copies of parent notices provided in several languages.

Home Visiting Programs. Family visits can be extremely important in helping educators understand family circumstances and for reaching out to families to establish relationships. **Home visiting programs**, which involve parents visiting other parents, serving as links between parents and schools, have been effective in including families in the school community. Elements of these programs include (a) paid parent support workers; (b) systematic training, supervision, and support; (c) services which provide information about school programs; (d) services demonstrating positive ways to work with children; (e) services that offer referrals to health and social service agencies; and (f) meetings between teachers and home visitors to exchange information and ideas (Ferguson, 2005; Heleen, 1992).

Kyle and McIntyre (2000) developed guidelines for successful family visit experiences. Prior to visits, the home visitor should (a) make appointments in advance and follow up with reminders; (b) plan to make visits brief, but let families lead on how long to stay; (c) be prepared for unexpected occurrences, such as cancellations, sharing of emotional and troubling information, and views different from the visitor's own. Kyle and McIntyre recommend that to yield the most benefit from a family visit experience, consider that the children, parents, and family members are experts; that personal sharing may be appropriate at times; and that, in addition to asking and answering questions, observing and listening can lead to greater insights. Box 8.2 presents questions to guide discussion in a home visit.

Since 1995, the Southwest Educational Development Laboratory (Henderson & Mapp, 2002) studied 51 parent-related programs that bridge school and home. For example, *family advocates, child and family mentors,* and *child-development assistants* (who are funded by Title 1 of NCLB) can play an important role in bridging home and school and in breaking down barriers that inhibit home–school partnerships. They often provide parenting education and help families access needed health and

---

BOX 8.2   Questions to Guide a Home Visit

Successful home visits have brief agendas, but are flexible and responsive to issues that the family might raise. Good questions to guide discussions, especially during first visits, include the following:

- What are your child's interests and favorite activities?
- What has your child done this summer that was a learning experience?
- What are your child's strengths?
- How does your child handle stress?
- What have you noticed that your child can do now which he or she could not do when school was out (e.g., during summer or long holidays)?

- What do you think your child needs to work on most?
- What does your child want to learn about most?
- How does your child interact with other children?
- What have you helped your child learn?
- What have you discovered about how your child learns best?
- What does your child already know a lot about?
- What are your goals for your child this year?
- Would you like to visit or volunteer in your child's classroom? (Kyle & McIntyre, 2000)

social services. Though typically not certified counselors, advocates work closely with counselors or social workers, as special friends and mentors to children identified as being at risk and needing extra support. They also provide individual consultation and assistance to teachers regarding the students and families they work with, as well as coach teachers in the use of strategies to promote children's social and academic skills. Both training and ongoing support are crucial. When there are a number of family advocates in a district, it is helpful to form a support network that meets on a regular basis. The effectiveness of family advocates is greatly enhanced when they are fully integrated into their school communities (Southwest Educational Development Laboratory, 2003).

Family Literacy Programs. These have been successful in creating home–school collaborative partnerships and in providing enjoyable intergenerational educational experiences. Based on the premise that the family literacy environment is the best predictor of a child's academic success, the goal of family literacy programs is to provide opportunities for children and parents to learn together (National Center for Family Literacy, 2004). Programs may include book giveaways, lending libraries for parents, workshops on storybook reading, early childhood programs, adult basic and parenting education, and coordination with other service providers. Parents are encouraged to see themselves as important teachers, even if they have limited reading skills. For example, parents are encouraged to engage in a variety of enjoyable activities with their children, ask questions and make comments that promote language development, and view storytelling as an important literacy activity that lays the foundation for learning to read. Linguistically diverse parents are encouraged to tell stories, to read to children in their primary language, and to share knowledge of their culture, helping the child to connect their life outside the school with literacy activities (University of Central Florida, 2004).

Parent and Family Resource Centers. These provide training and information to parents and connect children with disabilities to community resources. Each state has at least one **parent resource center**, and states with large populations may have regional centers. There are about 100 parent centers in the United States (Technical Assistance Alliance for Parent Centers, 2001; U.S. Government Accountability Office). At the local level, these centers provide an inviting place where parents can chat with other parents and teachers, watch informational videos, and learn about school activities. In addition, they often provide resources and information about health and social service agencies, adult educational opportunities, child development, school policies and procedures, and how to support their child's education. Most important, family resource centers are a highly effective way to communicate to parents that they are welcome at school.

Parent Collaboration as Building Professional Community

Parent collaboration as building professional community refers to the creative use of collaboration to conduct professional development and to create learning teams to improve practice. This function may also involve the creative use of collaboration for the purpose of embedding research or new knowledge into the practice of teachers, related services personnel, and administrators. Examples of such collaboration include joint teacher–parent training in IDEA requirements or student assessment or involvement of parents and parent advocates in preservice preparation of teachers at a university.

Family-Supportive Schools.   A second strategy for building professional communities to increase parent involvement is to create family-supportive schools that provide a wide range of family services on site. When parents find that their various needs can be met by school-based services they likely will develop a more accepting opinion of the school and be more comfortable with parent involvement activities (NCREL, 2001). Some schools are partnering with family support organizations and offering services under their roofs that historically were available only in state and local social services offices. The community school involves parents at all levels—as partners in planning the school, as members of the parent associations, and as one-on-one partners in their children's education (Blank, Melaville, & Shah, 2003; Harkavy & Blank, 2002; McLaughlin & Blank, 2004).

Parent–Teacher Organizations.   A third strategy for increasing parent involvement in the professional community is through an effective parent–teacher organization. Many schools have a PTA, PTO, or booster club that is operated by parents and provides educational and financial assistance in various ways. The National Parent Teacher Association (PTA) is the largest and most recognized volunteer child advocacy organization in the United States. Its mission is to support and speak on behalf of children and youth in the schools, in the community, and before governmental bodies and other organizations that make decisions affecting children. The PTA also assists parents in developing the skills they need to raise and protect their children and encourages parent and public involvement in the public schools (National Parent Teacher Association, 1999). As part of its promotion of parent and family involvement in schools, the National PTA also has developed national standards for parent/family involvement programs.

PRINCIPLES FOR FAMILY-CENTERED SERVICE COORDINATION

Research has demonstrated that effective parent involvement programs are built on several assumptions: (1) The primary educational environment is the family; (2) parent involvement in a child's education is a major factor in improving school effectiveness, the quality of education, and a child's academic success; (3) the benefits of parent involvement extend from preschool and elementary school through high school; and (4) low-income and language minority children have the most to gain when schools involve parents (Henderson, 1987; Newman, 2004; Raimondo & Henderson, 2001).

It is important to understand the difference between strategies that call for more parent involvement and strategies that are family-centered or aimed at promoting family empowerment and decision making. Current models are taking a **family-centered service coordination** approach in which the service coordinator incorporates family needs assessments into the IFSP (Individual Family Service Plan, ages 0–3), IEP (Individual Education Plan, ages 3–21), and ITP (Individual Transition Plan, age 16 and above). A family-centered perspective and increased coordination between schools and human service agencies are crucial in the move toward service integration (Novick, 2001).

The coordination functions are guided by family support principles, which emphasize *family strengths*, and *principles of family empowerment*, including parents as lead decision makers with their sons/daughters in planning for their educational progress and later for postsecondary life. Family-centered strategies are based on the following principles:

- Informed choice among service options is ensured for the individual and his/her family.
- Services are coordinated around the life of the individual and family, not around the needs of the school or program.
- The ability of ordinary citizens to help people to participate in community life is recognized.
- Parents are children's first teachers and have a lifelong influence on their values, attitudes, and aspirations.
- Children's educational success requires congruence between what is taught at school and values expressed in the home.
- Most parents, regardless of economic status, educational level, and/or cultural background, care deeply about their children's education and can provide substantial support if given specific opportunities and knowledge.
- Schools must take the lead in eliminating, or at least reducing, traditional barriers to parent involvement (Field, Martin, Miller, Ward, & Wehmeyer, 1998a; Fruchter, Galleta, & White, 1992).

As mentioned earlier, family support philosophy emphasizes an *empowerment model* that builds on family strengths and develops home–school relationships that are based on mutual respect and responsibility.

Summary of Key Points

- A family is a complex social system in which no member can be viewed in isolation.
- The strength of teacher–family relationships is tied to the quality of preparation of teachers for such collaboration.
- Changes to IDEA and NCLB reflect a strengthening of the long-standing national commitment to parent involvement in the education of all children.
- Awareness and sensitivity to the pressures, values, and perspectives family members bring to the school–family collaboration process is the starting point for productive parent participation.
- Schools are moving beyond traditional parent involvement strategies to encouraging meaningful participation in school decisions, policies, and improvement of practice.

- Family adaptation to living with a special needs child can be viewed as a growth and resilience development process that builds on the strengths of the family.
- Professional standards for educators and related personnel now address knowledge, skills, and dispositions for working with families.

Key Terms and Phrases

- Parent–professional partnerships (p. 204)
- Family (p. 205)
- Empowerment model (p. 210)
- Family systems (p. 211)
- Resilience model (p. 212)
- National teacher preparation standards (p. 219)
- Home–school communication programs (p. 222)
- Special education parent advisory committees (p. 222)
- Home visiting programs (p. 223)
- Parent resource center (p. 224)
- Family-centered service coordination (p. 225)

Questions for Reflection, Thinking, and Skill Building

1. How have changing demographics affected families and their participation in their children's education?
2. What is the relationship between family participation in education and student achievement? Identify several barriers to family participation in the IEP. Discuss strategies for strengthening participation.
3. In a visual diagram (schematic), present a concept of how parent participation affects the school achievement and adjustment of a special needs child. Include your assumptions and your expected outcomes for improving parent participation.
4. Interview a parent of a child with special needs regarding their beliefs about the strengths and weaknesses of their collaboration with professionals in their schools. Are there barriers to their participation in the IEP? What do they recommend to strengthen family participation in the IEP and to improve overall collaboration with professionals?

CHAPTER NINE

How Does Cultural and Linguistic Diversity Affect School Collaboration and System Coordination?

With Tracy Price

The future calls each of us to become partners in the dance of diversity, a dance in which everyone shares the lead. —HOWARD, 1993, p. 17

■ Why do the needs of culturally and linguistically diverse students demand special attention?

■ Who are culturally and linguistically diverse students and families?

■ What theories about culture are important for understanding culturally and linguistically diverse students?

■ How does cultural and linguistic diversity affect collaboration?

■ How can educators improve collaboration and coordination of services for CLD students with disabilities?

PERSPECTIVES

Special Education Teacher

We sit in child study meetings and discuss dual language assessments that show that for the number of years a student has been in the country the expressive, receptive, and written language skills are not as expected. Still teachers don't understand that it is OK. Language acquisition takes time, but because the student is working below grade level they feel that special education is the only answer.

—SPECIAL EDUCATION TEACHER

Teacher Candidate at the University

When I studied in Mexico, I never imagined classes where you were allowed group projects, class discussions, and, in many instances, the freedom to communicate with the instructor. School for me was a very cold setting, only I didn't know it then. I thought in a box and assumed all other countries ran their school systems the same way. Raising your hand in class was a negative thing to do. When I started college in the United States, I was shocked. When I started teaching and observed learning centers for the first time, I experienced an educational awakening. I must admit, this is a much more conducive way to learn. However, I am still adjusting. I am still afraid to ask questions, and I don't feel comfortable calling professors because in my culture it's considered invasive and rude. It is hard work to reconnect but I already feel it's making me a better person.

—UNIVERSITY STUDENT IN A TEACHER EDUCATION PROGRAM

INTRODUCTION

Previous chapters have discussed the challenges and promise of collaboration and system coordination for improving outcomes for students and families. This chapter introduces another factor in human interaction that makes collaboration and coordination even more complex, yet it also deepens our understanding of the concepts and their importance. That factor is cultural and linguistic diversity (CLD). Every individual is shaped by their cultural environment. All of us are bound by our cultural lenses through which we see the world and interpret the behavior of others. If educators are to help students understand and make meaning of their worlds, they must step outside their own cultural boundaries to view the world from different perspectives. The greater our ability to appreciate perspectives that are rooted in different cultures, the greater our ability to develop collaborative relationships with students, colleagues, and families.

Diversity, broadly defined, includes differences in gender, race, ethnicity, language, nationality, disability, or religion among various groups within a community, organization, or nation. This chapter explores differences in language and in cultural heritage and their implications for human collaboration. For example, even among those who speak English, regional accents and lexicons in states across the United States often create barriers to communication and relationships. Accents and vocabulary can disclose levels of education, social status, personal biases, and a range of other personal characteristics. These differences, however, also add a richness to our experience if we are willing to step outside our own cultural confines. However, for those who are immigrants struggling to learn the English language, the challenge of learning in American schools is enormous. Policymakers and educators have identified several challenges associated with the needs of the rapidly growing numbers of English language learners (ELL), or limited English proficient (LEP) students in schools across the United States, both with and without disabilities.

Cultural diversity is broadly defined as the variety of human cultures in a specific region or nation. Cultural diversity refers to differences among people based on a shared ideology and a valued set of beliefs, norms, customs, and meanings evidenced in a way of life. Cultural and linguistic diversity is reflected in several characteristics by which groups differ, including their concepts of time, personal space concepts, thinking processes, social groupings and relationships, appearance, posture, symbolism, and nonverbal communication (Dahl, 2003). Diverse populations include all groups in the region or nation, including indigenous and immigrant populations.

The purpose of this chapter is to strengthen educators' abilities to establish meaningful collaborative relationships with culturally and linguistically diverse students, parents, and communities. A theoretical framework for understanding diversity and culture is provided, along with principles for working with culturally and linguistically diverse students and parents.

Why Do the Needs of Culturally and Linguistically Diverse Students Demand Special Attention?

Changing Demographics in the United States

The demographics of the United States and the population of students in schools are rapidly changing. Here are some important facts to consider:

- One in five Americans speak languages other than English in the home. Students speak 400 languages across the nation, although students whose native language is Spanish represent 76.9% of students learning English in America (Zehler, Fleischman, Hopstock, Pendzick, & Stephenson, 2003).

- By the year 2010, one in five children will be Hispanic (Center for Research on Education, Excellence and Diversity, 2005), and by 2030, it is estimated that more than 40% of all students in the K–12 population will have culturally and linguistically diverse backgrounds, not of European American heritage (National Symposium on Learning Disabilities in English Language Learners, 2003).

- More immigrants have come to the United States in the last decade (1990–2000) than compared to any other decade (Bureau of U.S. Citizenship and Immigration Services, 2001).

- California has the highest ELL population in the United States with 33%; Texas is second with 12% (California Department of Education, 2004).

- There is a severe shortage of culturally and linguistically diverse (CLD) teachers in the workforce; 45% of U.S. teachers have at least one student with limited English proficiency (LEP) in their classrooms (National Clearinghouse for English Language Acquisition, 2005).

- It is estimated that 9% of all ELL students in U.S. public schools have disabilities (National Symposium on Learning Disabilities in English Language Learners, 2003).

- School personnel have difficulty distinguishing between language acquisition learning difficulties and actual learning disabilities (Zehler et al., 2003); students therefore have difficulty obtaining services from both special education and ESL (English as a Second Language) departments when both are needed.

In the face of NCLB accountability requirements for state testing of students, many school districts are struggling to address the needs of this population in order achieve Annual Yearly Progress (AYP) (McLeod, 2005; Northwest Evaluation Association, 2005; Ruiz-de-Velasco, Fix, & Clewell 2000). States must now provide data on how English language learners (ELL) are performing on state assessments, and ELL students must participate in these assessments (U.S. Department of Education, Biennial Report to Congress on Title III, 2005). The research and education policy community is divided on whether bilingual education or English immersion is best for non-English speakers, and more research is needed (Albus, Lieu & Thurlow, 2002; Albus & Thurlow, 2005; Education Policy Reform Research Institute, 2004).

The needs of culturally and linguistically diverse students (CLD) are currently largely unmet in today's schools, as reflected by two important statistics. First, a disproportionate percentage of Hispanic, Black, and Native American students drop out or do not obtain a high school diploma (Garcia, 2005; National Center for Education Statistics, 2002; U.S. Department of Education, 2005). Second, and equally as important, is the disproportionate percentage of Hispanic, Black, and Native American students placed in special education classes (Cummins, 2001; Northwest Evaluation Association, 2005; Obiakor & Wilder, 2003). Although special education may meet the needs of students with disabilities, it can be inappropriate for students *without* disabilities or who have language acquisition–based learning difficulties. Recent research has demonstrated that improperly placing CLD students in special education can negatively impact their educational outcomes and potential career possibilities (Artiles, 1998; Cummins, 2001; Greene, 2003c; Obiakor & Wilder, 2003; Salend, Garrick-Duhaney & Montgomery, 2002).

These conditions and the growth in diversity of the student population are driving many changes in curriculum and instruction, student assessment, school organizational structure, administration, and personnel preparation. Culturally and linguistically diverse (CLD) students demand a different lens on the educational environment and the needs of the students, particularly if they also have disabilities. IDEA 2004 and NCLB require that in order to properly evaluate a child who may not be proficient in English, schools must assess the child's proficiency in English as well as in his or her native language to distinguish language acquisition needs from learning disabilities. These goals require close collaboration among teachers, ESOL specialists, special educators, and parents.

Children for whom English is not their primary language have numerous challenges to learning that require special responses on the part of teachers and administrators so that all students are given every opportunity to succeed in school. These challenges include (a) language differences that require teachers to understand how students learn to speak and read English when their primary language is different; (b) how the student's immersion in the mainstream language affects academic progress and student assessment; (c) how student and family cultures affect students' learning and progress, and curriculum and instruction; (d) how CLD students are evaluated and referred to special education, so as to avoid overrepresentation or underrepresentation; (e) implications of culture and language for accessing community services; (f) impacts of attitudes and practices that negatively affect ethnic and language diverse student groups; and (g) implications of culture for high school transition planning and employment preparation.

These challenges demand that educators appreciate the complex interaction of language, culture, and professional knowledge and attitudes in the education of culturally and linguistically diverse students. According to many observers, the implications of this new reality are not being fully considered by those advocating or undertaking school reform and improvement (McLeod, 2005, 1996; Zehler et al., 2003). So important are cultural factors in preparing educators, that the Council for Exceptional Children (2002) developed specific content standards for teachers and administrators that address culture and language diversity and the role of families in the educational process. Highly qualified educators, counselors, and administrators must be familiar with the special needs of CLD students with and without disabilities.

Educators are also expected to appreciate the potentially powerful and valuable role of parental participation in the education of their children. Parents provide essential information to educators that cannot be obtained from any other source. They provide an important window into the unique culture of the family and the broader culture of the ethnic community. Active participation of culturally and linguistically diverse parents in the educational decision-making process improves their children's academic achievement (Bernhard, Freire, Pacini-Ketchabaw, & Villanueva, 1998; Brown, 2004; Cummins, 2001; Warger & Burdette, 2000). Culturally and linguistically diverse parents also feel more empowered when they are invited into meaningful collaboration and decision-making processes with educators, and therefore overreferral or underreferral to special education is less likely to occur (Obiakor, Utley, Smith, & Harris-Obiakor, 2002; U.S. Department of Education, 2000a). It is essential, for example, to include parents in prereferral or early intervening processes to ensure that students are receiving every possible support for language acquisition before they are referred to special education.

Let's See It in Action on page 233 provides an illustration of the role of collaboration in addressing the needs of culturally and linguistically diverse students.

LET'S SEE IT IN ACTION! Case Illustration: Creating a System to Improve the Achievement of Culturally and Linguistically Diverse Students

It is April, and Mr. Martin just became the new principal of East Hill Elementary School. He was chosen because of his experience and success at his previous school with a demographically similar population. East Hill Elementary School has a very diverse student population. Forty% of the students receive free and reduced lunches, and 52% come from culturally and linguistically diverse (CLD) backgrounds, speaking 15 different languages. Twenty-three% of the minority students at East Hill Elementary School are in special education, well above the county average of 9%. Mr. Martin knows that minority overrepresentation in special education has complex roots, but he also knows that with proper staff training, resources, collaboration, and coordination of services, CLD students can successfully participate in general education classes, and misidentification can be reduced. One of the primary challenges that Mr. Martin faces is trying to develop the system needed to support the diverse student population at East Hill Elementary School.

Mr. Martin met individually with general education, special education, and ESOL teachers; school counselors; and the school social worker and psychologist. After these conversations, Mr. Martin realized that all of these units in East Hill were functioning as separate entities, widening the gaps in what already was a fragmented system. Teachers were duplicating efforts while some students failed to receive the assistance that they needed to improve their academic success. Collaboration and coordination were needed to produce more effective and efficient results.

A staff meeting was held to discuss the challenges facing staff members as well as the accomplishments that had already been achieved (what's working?). Teachers expressed concerns about language and cultural differences, lack of resources, lack of planning time, and their need for understanding of how cultural and language differences affect learning. These conditions contributed to problems and complicated communication and collaboration with students and parents, particularly in IEP and evaluation meetings. Several accomplishments or strengths from which they could build were identified:

a. a moderate rate of parent and student participation in extracurricular activities such as potluck dinners and movie nights;

b. minimal behavior and discipline problems;

c. teachers' ability to provide needed structure and their commitment to student achievement; and

d. a parent population that was eager to participate and sympathetic to the challenges their children face.

Mr. Martin knew that in order to create a new system within the school, he would have to provide the staff with new tools to work with diverse populations. He knew that encouraging and cultivating CLD parents as resources and decision makers was a crucial factor in the students' and school's success—one that was missing from East Hill. Mr. Martin also knew that change would not be easy and that it would require a major shift in thinking among his teachers.

First, a series of *interactive information sessions* were designed to assess staff knowledge of needs regarding CLD students, the extent of collaboration with CLD parents, and available resources. Next, a *series of training sessions* were developed to help personnel understand the complexities of teaching and supporting CLD students and communicating with their families. Finally, *committees were established* to provide support to staff members throughout the school year.

Blocks of time were then established for collaboration across subject areas and within disciplines. All grade-level teachers met on a regular basis, but so did general education, special education, ESOL, and guidance teachers for each grade level. In order for the collaboration periods to be effective, an outside consultant was brought in to train teachers on strategies for teaching CLD students and of effective collaboration with CLD parents. In a process of continuous peer review (critical friends approach), problems related to collaboration were raised in staff meetings and used as examples for analysis, information sharing, and problem solving by teams. Successful collaboration processes were also highlighted, analyzed, and supported.

Following this, the concept of *shared responsibility* was introduced to staff—the notion that they all shared a common "client." This concept was applied not only to students receiving services, but also to the early intervening services (prereferral intervention) team, the team that decides whether the student needs special education or if the learning problem is related to second language acquisition. It was decided that no decision regarding at-risk students, CLD students, or students receiving multiple services would be made unless it was a team decision involving all relevant service providers. This meant that each teacher became familiar with the functions and expertise of each other's roles while initiating a teaching approach that facilitated the use of language. This approach was designed to prevent duplication of efforts and to ensure the most efficient use of resources. Most importantly, using a multidisciplinary team approach established a unified profile of students based on coordinated information about the student. Such coordination increased the school's ability to implement and evaluate appropriate supports in the classroom before students were prematurely or inappropriately referred for special education.

Teachers were introduced to the concept of *integrated, meaningful, and structured parental participation*. The staff brainstormed how they could engage all parents—not just CLD parents—as *cultural capital* (valued resources) to enhance the learning environment. The first project was an *after-school computer-based writing program* that helped parents compare their own childhood experiences to the childhood experiences of their children. This was a very successful activity and the products were published in a book sold at cost to raise money for future projects. The second project was a series of *parent training sessions* designed to help parents to understand the processes, procedures, and expectations of American schools. One expectation specifically addressed was the responsibility of parents to assist their children with homework and to encourage consistent scheduling of study times at home. The final project in structuring parental participation was a *special education assistance team*, established to assist CLD parents with the special education process to ensure that they have the skills and expertise to be active participants in education decision making. Together, these programs greatly increased the active participation of CLD parents.

A teacher action research team was also established to complete two tasks. The first task was to conduct diversity self-assessments for team members and then to determine how to assess the needs of immigrant students and parents. The team developed a demographic profile of the parent community and then researched strategies used by other schools and organizations to assess the general needs of CLD populations. Next, they sought out several successful programs that serve CLD students and arranged time to observe them and meet with their staff. Based on this research, they compiled a portfolio of general needs and characteristics along with an inventory of successful teaching and collaboration strategies. The product was presented to the staff at an interactive in-service session, and has continued to evolve. Staff plan to develop a Web site to share effective teaching and collaboration strategies.

Finally, it was decided that East Hill students and families needed a *resource center*. School and community agency goals were coordinated to ensure access to the community services necessary to support the needs of students. A survey was sent to families to obtain information that helped in establishing a compatible school-based resource center for East Hill's population.

Questions for Discussion

Consider these questions as you reflect on the case illustration above:

- What made East Hill staff realize that change was needed?
- How would you describe the new kind of collaboration that was needed?
- What strengths were identified that could be built upon?
- What steps did Mr. Martin take to provide staff with new tools to work with a diverse population?
- What collaborative teams were established to create the needed changes?

The rapid change in the East Hill community population, as shown in the case example, signaled to the school that they needed a new kind of response to students and families. The school was unprepared. As the staff assessed the nature of the needs of the students and families, individuals within the system were challenged to create new structures and relationships within the school community. There was no returning to the way things had been in the past; the school had to re-create itself. The challenge of including diverse populations of students extended well beyond ensuring the presence of translators or providing materials in native languages. Staff at East Hill learned that a new kind of collaboration was required that had not previously been experienced. This collaboration took them on a new journey in which understanding and respecting differences in life experiences, worldviews, cultures, mores, and values led to mutual, respectful, collaborative relationships. Ultimately it has led to improved achievement for CLD students of East Hill.

WHO ARE CULTURALLY AND LINGUISTICALLY DIVERSE STUDENTS AND FAMILIES?

CLD families are not a homogeneous group. In order to collaborate effectively with CLD students and families, it is important to consider the spectrum of linguistic possibilities that this population represents, examine the concept of culture, and recognize the importance of acknowledging and respecting native cultures. This understanding is essential to the successful application of the principles presented later in this chapter.

Linguistically diverse students are generally defined as those who speak, or whose families speak, a language other than the dominant language, English (English language learners, ELL). Approximately 15%–20% of students in schools speak a foreign language at home, and this percentage is growing rapidly (Avoke & Wood-Garnett, 2001; National Clearinghouse for English Language Acquisition, 1998). According to the U.S. Department of Education, the percentage of 5- to 24-year-olds who spoke a language other than English in their homes more than doubled between 1979 and 1999 (National Center on Education, 2004). Some are in families that are in or near poverty status, but many are in technical or professional families who earn relatively high incomes. The term non-English speakers is actually more complex than it appears and represent a great range in English language skills. For example, some students and their parents may not speak English at all. Some parents may not speak English, but their children have acquired English to varying degrees even though they may not be fully proficient (limited English proficient, LEP). Many parents and students are bilingual. The possible combinations of language proficiency among students and families from the same linguistic background are numerous, and therefore educators should be careful not to generalize their experiences with non-English speakers to all students and families.

Linguistic Diversity and Literacy

Cultural and linguistic diversity affects collaboration and communication among school professionals, students, and families. When considering the nature of students' diversity, it is important to distinguish between *linguistic diversity, literacy,* and *cultural diversity.* **Literacy** has traditionally been defined as the ability to read and write. Today the definition has been expanded to include the ability to locate, evaluate, use, and communicate using a wide range of information resources including text, visual, audio, and video sources (Fagan, 2001b).

Linguistic abilities can place limitations on how the student becomes literate in both the native and second language. For instance, a parent who only speaks Latvian, the official language of Lithuania, will probably only be fully literate in Latvian. Socioeconomic status and level of education also impact literacy. Some immigrants flee their native countries because of limited resources and poor conditions; therefore, their level of literacy (ability to read and write) may be far below their spoken language ability. Conversely, there are bilingual or multilingual immigrants who have emigrated to work in technical and professional fields in the United States who are literate in several languages.

Cultural diversity is defined as the presence of individuals who are from a variety of cultural backgrounds. There are, however, many definitions of **culture**. Review the definitions listed below and identify themes that emerge:

1. Culture is a body of past human accomplishments that is inherited socially. It is a resource for the lives of current people that live in a specific country or area (Gallego & Cole, 2001).

2. Culture is the aggregate of morals, beliefs, customs, knowledge, laws, art, and any other skill that a person acquires by participating in a social community (Dahl, 2003; Tylor, 1993).

3. Culture is the combined effort of citizens to establish and develop meaning about collective and individual values, beliefs, and actions. Culture is used as a reference point from which people construct their perceptions and reactions to the environment (Dahl, 2003; Slonim, 1991).

The multiple definitions of culture suggest several core themes: Culture is a resource; it embraces beliefs, morals, customs, and values; and it is usually inherited collectively, not individually. Each person's identity is unique, and culture is inextricably tied to personal identity.

Within specific ethnic groups there is a wide variation of culture. As mentioned before, regional differences within the same nation can be significant. For example, imagine two European American families with French heritage whose past five generations have lived in the United States. The only difference is that one has lived in Vermont their entire life and the other in Mississippi. Although surely they will have some elements of their culture that are similar, they also will differ on any number of beliefs, customs, and linguistic patterns. Similarly, differences are also found within the same ethnic groups who emigrate to the United States from other countries. Individuals who may be considered Hispanic or Latino are not all similar. People from El Salvador are very different from people who have emigrated from Honduras, Mexico, Peru, Argentina, or Bolivia. All of them differ from families who have emigrated from Spain.

In the United States, there are individuals from multiple cultures, but an overarching American culture exists which is referred to as the macroculture. The **macroculture** is comprised of numerous **microcultures**, which are the specific cultural practices of individuals within the population (Banks & McGee-Banks, 1992). So, within specific families there may be various combinations of cultural practices. For example, many Latino or Asian families participate in a traditional 4th of July celebration with fireworks and a picnic. Others don't acknowledge the holiday and continue with routine activities. Many immigrant children create traditional Valentine's Day cards, yet their parents and grandparents may not acknowledge the holiday. Obviously, the student or child may be more receptive to new cultural values and norms than a parent or grandparent for whom these practices are unfamiliar. Since many cultures embrace an extended family that actively participates in the family structure, within one household there may be a blending of cultures, both native and American (Midobuche, 2001).

Culture, therefore, is a kaleidoscope of infinite combinations and variations of individual's native and American culture and language. This provides a challenge for collaboration and coordination of services for culturally and linguistically diverse populations (Soodak & Erwin 1995) since no two families or individuals are the same, regardless of their ethnic heritage. Each family is a cultural system within a larger culture, as depicted in Figure 9.1.

Although it is important that educators be very careful not to generalize about people from different regions of the world, it is also important that they understand that some families have left countries in deep poverty or in political conflict. For example, educational systems in some regions of the world are weak, minimal, or nonexistent due to sustained conflict. Even if education is available, many children leave school because of lack of security or economic pressures to go to work to help support the family. Consequently, individuals who have left their countries due to war or poverty may not have experience with or exposure to traditional education. This can place the students and parents at a distinct disadvantage when attending schools in the United States, interacting with educators, and making educational decisions, particularly if they have special learning needs. However, these families may also be very resilient and possess many other resources that enable them to adapt to requirements of the schools. It is the responsibility of the educator to identify these sources of resilience. The illustrations in Boxes 9.1 and 9.2 underscore the diversity of students and families and complexity that they often face in responding to the educational needs of their children.

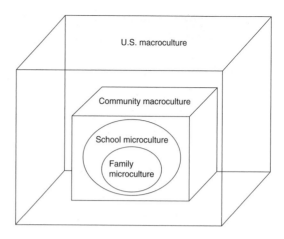

FIGURE 9.1
Embedded Cultures

How can teachers structure parent training sessions so that Juan or other immigrants can begin to understand the U.S. educational system? Box 9.3 continues the story of Juan.

It is important to understand that blind agreement is not collaboration. Juan may have been able to provide valuable assistance to his son at home or valuable

---

BOX 9.1   A Short Story: A Parent Asks, "Where Do I Begin?"

Lilikala Littlebird, a Native American, was referred for a child study to determine her need for special education services. Her grades had dropped markedly in the past two years in the sixth and seventh grades, following the divorce of her parents, and she was showing serious signs of restlessness and inability to pay attention in class. Her mother had moved away from the Cheroke reservation at the time of her divorce three years previously. The child study team concluded from a variety of assessments that Lilikala had auditory processing problems, attention deficits, and depression and also could benefit from speech and language therapy. The team recommended to Mrs. Littlebird (in the presence of a Native American advocate) that she (1) have Lilikala see a counselor or mental health therapist through the county system, (2) seek consultation for ADHD treatment and depression, and (3) seek family therapy to improve support to Lilikala at home. The team also suggested that she seek financial help through her insurance for some of the mental health costs. While Mrs. Littlebird was appreciative of the all the

time, attention, and recommendations of the team, she could not understand how she could possibly locate, arrange, attend, or pay for any of the services recommended. Since her divorce, she has worked two part-time jobs, and she is uncertain what her insurance coverage is, let alone whether it would cover mental heath services. She had only completed 5th grade on the reservation and struggled to understand the terms and labels being used to describe her daughter. She left the team meeting overwhelmed.

It is important for educators to realize that wide differences can exist among people who share a common language and culture. Furthermore, it cannot be assumed that CLD parents and students all have minimal experience with the process of education, but educators should be sensitive and aware of that possibility. Families such as Lilikala's can be overwhelmed with educational recommendations by well-meaning team members. They may have few resources to follow up on recommendations that require them to navigate a complex service system.

BOX 9.2   Coming to America . . . With a Limited View of Schooling

The Story of Juan, Part 1

Juan is an immigrant from the South American country of Bolivia who came to the United States 5 years ago. Like many immigrants, he left his country of birth to seek a better life in the United States. Employment was a major consideration for him, but so was education for his son. In the town where Juan grew up, children only attended school for half a day. Sometimes the teachers would go on strike because they hadn't been paid for weeks and then there would be no school. When classes were held, they were in large rooms that were empty except for desks, a blackboard, and minimal supplies. If children could not pass the yearly end-of-year test, they could retake it, but many eventually would drop out. Sometimes students who misbehaved were forced to kneel in the gravel during recess. There were no programs for students with disabilities. Moderate to severely disabled children were rarely seen in public. The only contact between parents and teachers was the report card. There were no after-school activities, conferences, or PTA. People who had more money could send their children to private schools that were better equipped and provided a more consistent and substantial education. When Juan emigrated to the United States as a teenager, he brought with him his ideas and attitudes about education: bare rooms, minimal supplies, no help in learning, little interaction with teachers, and the belief that quality education is only for the privileged.

BOX 9.3   Living in America . . . Struggling to Participate

The Story of Juan, Part 2

Juan now lives in the United States, and his son attends elementary school. The school contacts him and asks him to come to a local special education screening meeting to discuss some serious learning problems that his son is experiencing in school. It is at this point that Juan begins to try to integrate what he knows about education with his experiences with the American school. Because Juan has minimal education and little understanding of the needs of children with learning problems, he promptly agrees to the diagnostic testing that is recommended by the team. He asks no questions because he has no previous experience with these processes. To Juan, this is obviously better than what might have happened back in Bolivia.

---

information that would provide some insight into the challenges that his son is facing. It is the responsibility of educators to uncover this information, engage the assistance of parents, and begin to establish a meaningful collaborative relationship.

What Theories About Culture Are Important for Understanding Culturally and Linguistically Diverse Students?

Tip of the Iceberg: Layers of Culture

If schools are viewed as systems or collaborative environments, the addition of individuals with different languages and cultures will affect all parts of the system. Difficulties arise when processes and procedures are not modified to accommodate the diverse characteristics and cultural factors that affect student learning. It is important to reflect on the meaning of culture as a factor in understanding collaborative systems.

Students of culture have used the image of an iceberg to explain these many layers of culture (Weaver, 1986). Like an iceberg, depicted in Figure 9.2, part of a culture is "above the water," visible and easy to identify.

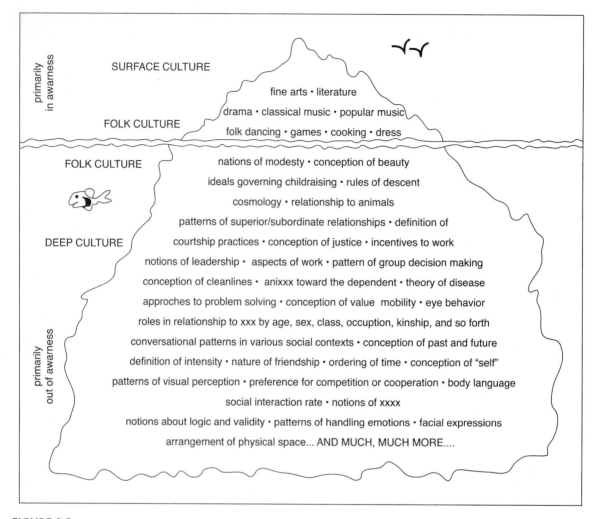

FIGURE 9.2

Culture: Tip of the Iceberg

Source: From "Understanding and Coping with Cross-Cultural Adjustment Stress," by G. R. Weaver 1986. In R. M. Paige (Ed.), *Cross-Cultural Orientation: New Conceptualizations and Applications.* Lanham, MD: University Press of America. Reprinted with permission.

    This part includes surface culture and elements of folk culture, the arts, folk dancing, dress, and cooking—that which typically gets celebrated on school "diversity days." But just as nine-tenths of an iceberg is out of sight below the water, nine-tenths of a culture is also hidden from view. This outside awareness part of culture is termed "deep culture," although it does include some elements of folk culture. Deep culture includes elements such as how individuals in the culture view ideas and concepts such as, for example, the definition of sin, concept of justice, work ethic, definition of insanity, approaches to problem solving, fiscal habits and attitudes, eye contact, approach to interpersonal relationships, and attitudes toward disability (Hanley, 1999; Martinez &

Velazquez, 2000; Paige, 1993; Weaver, 1986). Understanding these elements of deep culture is a part of gaining *cultural competence.* As Jerome Hanley (1999) described it:

> A vital ingredient in cultural competence is experience. One cannot learn about a people or culture exclusively through books, movies, and classes. The Sierra Leone proverb, "a paddle here, a paddle there—the canoe stays still," predicts the outcome of such one-dimensional efforts. The best teacher is firsthand experience with a culture, if not immersion in it. Although the lessons can be painful, you must touch it, try it, make mistakes, apologize, internalize what you have learned, and try again. (Hanley, 1999, p. 10)

Theories About Cultural Difference

Three distinct theories—*ethnocentrism, assimilation,* and the *cultural model perspective*—that influence perspectives on cultural difference are presented here because of the enormous impact that these perspectives can have on collaborative relationships among professionals. As these theories are introduced, keep in mind the principles and concepts discussed previously about effective collaboration and system coordination. Remember that systems are complex, dynamic, and interdependent. They are composed of a network of flexible, mutual relationships.

Ethnocentrism.   **Ethnocentrism** is the belief that one culture is superior to another, that culture and its accompanying actions, values, norms, traditions, and beliefs become the basis on which all other cultures are compared. Within this framework, differences between the dominant culture and other cultures are viewed as deficits.

Deficit Model. Within a **deficit perspective**, people who differ from the dominant cultural patterns are viewed as having deficits or deficiencies (Bernhard et al., 1998; Cummins, 2001; Gallego & Cole, 2001; Harry, 2002; Lee, 2003; Midobuche, 2001; Nieto, 2000; Valencia & Black, 2002). Deficit perspectives justify prejudice, stereotyping, stigmatizing, and distorting culturally different populations. Within this framework learning difficulties are viewed as residing within the student and the environment plays no role (Nieto, 2000). Similarly, if parents do not participate in school activities in a manner similar to that of the dominant culture, they are perceived negatively as uninvolved. Lack of parental involvement is considered to be a deficit (Bernhard et al., 1998). According to Nieto (2000), placing the blame on the student or the parent relieves educators of the daunting task of assessing factors in the school setting that may contribute to parent disengagement or student learning problems. Ethnocentrism can also lead to the belief that children are best taught by teachers of like ethnicity.

Assimilation.   The second perspective, which differs from ethnocentrism, is based on the assumption that in order for culturally different individuals to be successful, they must assimilate into the dominant culture. The goal of **assimilation** is to replace the native culture with knowledge of and behaviors associated with American culture (Gallego & Cole, 2001; Nieto, 2000). Consequently, until those who are different assimilate into the dominant culture, members of the dominant group develop identities that characterize groups in terms of "us" and "them" (Apple, 1996; Cochran-Smith, 2000; Kumashiro, 2001; Valencia & Black, 2002).

Both the ethnocentric and assimilation models attach a stigma to culturally diverse individuals. As Artilles (1998) observed, "The deficit view of minority people might often mediate [the dominant group's] cognitive, emotional, and behavioral reactions to minority individual's phenotypes, interactive styles, language, professions, and worldviews" (p. 33). This stigma of being viewed as deficient makes it difficult for professionals and educators to recognize the strengths and cultural capital (potential contributions) within these populations (Dennis & Giangreco, 1996).

Acculturation, a concept related to assimilation, refers to the process of how individuals adjust, change, or modify their lives as a result of exposure to another culture or society (Fuligni, 2001). The process of acculturation can positively or negatively impact the individual. In the effort to achieve acculturation, individual cultural backgrounds can be viewed as either (a) "mismatched" with the mainstream culture and in need of modifying, or (b) beneficial and complementary to the mainstream culture and viewed as additive.

The **cultural mismatch theory** posits that individuals who are culturally different from the majority population face challenges bridging the gap between the home and school cultures (Delpit, 1995). These individuals do not possess the interaction styles, values, beliefs, and understandings that enable them to easily participate in an environment defined by the dominant culture. Since these cultural challenges impact learning, educators and related service personnel must help students bridge the gap between the native and new culture.

Cultural Model Perspective. The third distinct perspective examined here is similar to acculturation, but more positive. The **cultural model perspective** predicts differences in home and school cultures and is based on the assumption that individuals change in response to exposure to new cultural processes, creating a *shared model* of culture (Edgerton, 1992; Reese & Gallimore, 2000). Educators with this perspective view cultural changes as *additive and beneficial* to the educational setting. Cultural transformation or change is a result of a process that deepens meaning and understanding about cultural differences by students and teachers (Artiles, 2003).

Accommodation is a concept related to the cultural model perspective. Those who embrace an accommodation framework accept cultural differences and recognize different cultures as equal. Within this framework, poor school performance and relationships with parents are altered by making accommodations that try to narrow some of the differences between the home culture and the school culture (Gallego & Cole, 2001). Within the accommodation framework, various interventions or strategies are used to bridge the cultural gap, but all individuals are considered equally valued regardless of their ethnicity.

Culture and Behavior

Although most people are not consciously aware of it, behavior is mostly a result of our cultural experiences. Children born and raised in the United States possess an understanding of interaction styles characteristic of American culture. Sometimes these characteristics are described as "scripts." For example, in the United States, when students are spoken to, they are accustomed to maintaining eye contact, use courtesy markers, and respond (Obiakor & Wilder, 2003). In other cultures, the script may be very different. When addressed, it may be expected that students remain quiet and make no eye contact. What we consider "normal" student behavior may be unfamiliar to students of other cultures. Their behavior is different and, unfortunately, is sometimes perceived by educators as unacceptable. All behavior patterns and expectations are culturally relative.

LET'S SEE IT IN ACTION! Case Illustration: Problems for the Hmong in America

Chou Tans is 13 and lives in a large Hmong community in the Midwest. In the 1970s, her parents fled from a mountain village in Vietnam, through Laos and then came as refugees to the United States. They speak only Hmong in the home, and her parents do not read.

Chou has many friends in the Hmong community and outside, and so she is aware of the differences between Hmong culture and mainstream American culture. It is common for Hmong girls as young as 14 to enter into marriages to men ranging in age from 17 to 35. A 14-year-old wife may have two children by the age of 16 or 17 and will usually not be able to complete high school. Her educational opportunities are often limited. Like many Hmong girls, Chou is also burdened by the heavy responsibilities that are heaped upon her at home. Both her parents work in the evening, often leaving her, the oldest girl, to run the household, preventing her from having a social life.

In the eighth grade, Chou began to suffer from anxiety reactions during school and had to isolate herself from people. Her previously strong grades began to plummet, and she could not pay attention in class or complete homework at home. She agreed to speak to a school counselor who met with her on a weekly basis in school. The counselor had studied Hmong culture and began weekly group counseling sessions with several Hmong girls who were experiencing problems similar to Chou's. In addition, the school counselor matched the girls with older, successful Hmong high school students as mentors for the younger girls (Vignette is a composite of factual information on the Hmong from Lindsay, 2005).

Unfortunately, behaviors that are unfamiliar to teachers can sometimes be misinterpreted as challenging, oppositional, disrespectful, or even indicative of learning or emotional disabilities. Identifying nondisabled CLD students as having emotional disabilities because of behaviors that are rooted in their native culture can have a devastating impact on their education and self-concept. As Let's See It in Action, above, underscores, careful analysis and understanding of culturally different behaviors is critical to properly assess and assist CLD students.

Explicit instruction on expectations and behaviors may be necessary to assist students in developing a repertoire of interaction skills necessary for them to be successful in American schools. Knowing the student is essential.

How Does Cultural and Linguistic Diversity Affect Collaboration?

Cultural differences can potentially impede collaborative relationships among students, families, and school personnel. The most obvious challenge is language. Other differences include style of interaction, notions of acceptable participation, and attitudes toward disability. These differences can be challenging to overcome because cultural characteristics are so integrated into our behavior and identities that often it takes considerable effort to acknowledge and change behavior.

Critical to truly seeing and understanding the children we teach is the courage to face our own biases openly. Recognizing the limits imposed by our embeddedness in our own culture and experience, acknowledging the values and beliefs we cherish, and accepting the influence of emotions on our actions are extraordinary challenges (Balaban, 1995). Sensitivity toward cultural differences provides the foundation on which collaborative relationships can be built.

Cultural Sensitivity: A Powerful Method of Accommodation

One of the first steps teachers can take to become culturally sensitive is to engage in reflective self-analysis to examine their own attitudes toward different ethnic and racial groups and toward gender and social class (Banks, 1996; Banks, Banks, & McGee, 1995; Bohn & Sleeter, 2000; Delpit, 1995). Because our own cultural patterns and language are seldom part of our conscious awareness, we often forget that our taken-for-granted beliefs and values are interpretations, which are culturally and historically specific (Banks, 1996).

Cultural sensitivity, or **cultural competence**, is the ability not only to be aware of and understand an ethnic group's unique norms, values, beliefs, and traditions, but also to appreciate and respect these differences. Those who embrace a culturally sensitive approach to education view differences without value judgment (Gorman & Balter, 1997). Professionals who are culturally sensitive make accommodations to increase such appreciation and respect among different cultural groups.

There are three models that represent levels of cultural sensitivity that schools can incorporate (Gorman & Balter, 1997; Huffman, 2003; Sanchez, Stuckey & Morris, 1998). The first is promoting access through *translated materials*. In many school districts, educational documents for students and parents are translated into the most common languages that are present in that district. Nothing is changed in the practices of the school except the languages that the documents are produced in. The next level of cultural sensitivity is a culturally adapted or **transcultural model**. Schools or programs that adopt this model may provide translated materials, but also incorporate values, norms, or traditions of the target population into the materials. The program maintains its original integrity, but is modified to make it easier for CLD populations to use, access, or participate. Finally, there are *culturally specific models*. These models are designed for a specific cultural population, and the changes in school practices are much more dramatic than in a culturally adapted model (Gorman & Balter, 1997).

According to Kalyanpur and Harry (1999), "awareness of cultural differences provides the scaffolding for building collaborative relationships" (p. 118). Kalyanpur and Harry use the term *cultural reciprocity* to refer to the ways of thinking and behaving that enable members of one cultural, ethnic, or linguistic group to work effectively with members of another. Lynch and Hanson (1997) use the term *cross-cultural competence* (p. 492), which is characterized by (a) awareness of one's cultural limitations; (b) openness, appreciation, and respect for cultural differences, including subtle differences between cultures; (c) avoidance of stereotyping; (d) ability to apply cultural awareness universally to all situations; (e) ability to view intercultural interactions as learning opportunities; (f) skills to use cultural resources in interventions; and (g) empowerment of families and professionals as each learns from the other (Kalyanpur & Harry, 1999; Lynch & Hanson, 1997; University of Central Florida, 2004). Box 9.4 presents a set of guiding questions to assess your own cultural competence.

Family Beliefs About Disability. Members of diverse cultures may vary in child-rearing practices, in their views about disabilities, and in their responses to the authority of the school (Harry, 2002; Valle & Aponte, 2002). A family's cultural

---

BOX 9.4   Assess Your Cultural Competence

The following questions can serve as a guide for assessing your own *cultural competence*.

1. To what extent do you know the demographics, characteristics, and resources within the ethnic communities in your service area?
2. How well are you able to describe the strengths of ethnic groups in your school, district, or service area?
3. Are you familiar with the prevailing beliefs, customs, norms, and values of the major ethnic groups in your service area?
4. Do you attend cultural functions, community forums, interact socially with people of different ethnic groups, patronize businesses, or pursue recreational or leisure activities within ethnic communities?
5. Does your agency work collaboratively with other programs and have linkages with institutions of higher education, civil rights, or human relations groups that provide accurate information concerning ethnic populations?

6. Do staff members use cultural consultants who can help them work more effectively within a diverse cultural context?
7. Does your agency subscribe to publications to stay abreast of ethnic populations, have access to culturally related materials, and maintain a library with cultural resources?
8. Are people of ethnic minority groups on staff in your agency at all position levels?
9. Does the agency discuss barriers to working across cultures?
10. Do personnel use culture-specific assessment instruments for diagnosis, culture-specific treatment approaches, and cultural references or historical accomplishments as a source of empowerment for ethnic populations? (Adapted from Chaisson-Cardenas & Moore, 2003.)

---

beliefs will impact the nature of their participation with professionals and schools, and how they view disabilities.

Family responses to having a child with a disability differ greatly among cultures. In some nations, disabled children are hidden and not presented as part of the family. For example, in Russia, only since the early 1990s have education policies been developed to transfer children with disabilities from institutions into community schools. Still today, the special education program of a major university, ranked first among such institutions in Russia, is called the Institute of Defectology (Moscow State Pedagogical University, 2006).

There are great differences in the way disability is regarded among societies, and the type and severity of a child's disability affect social attitudes toward the disability. Children with mild disabilities are often assimilated into the culture, whereas those with more severe disabilities are often socially isolated and cared for only within the immediate family. For instance, a learning disability or mild cognitive disability might go unnoticed in a developing nation or in a remote rural community that provides limited education and has low levels of literacy. The disability may only be acknowledged if it is readily apparent, either physically or behaviorally. It may be difficult for parents to comprehend the concept of a learning or cognitive disability in a child who functioned adequately within that cultural context of their home country.

Some cultures attribute disability to causes other than biomedical. For example, a study in Papua, New Guinea, showed that 32% of persons with disability and their families attributed disability to sorcery or supernatural causes (Byford & Veenstra, 2004). Some families may attribute their child's disability or developmental delay to something the mother did during her pregnancy or to a family transgression. Another may view an emotional disability in their young teen as the result of a supernatural cause (Kalyanpur & Harry, 1999). These attitudes breed shame about the child's disability and can hinder family participation in school activities. Some cultures place great value on cooperation, cohesiveness, and interdependence—characteristics that differ from many school cultures that emphasize individual achievement and a competitive spirit. For these and other reasons, culturally and linguistically diverse families are sometimes only marginally involved in the education of their children. An understanding of cultural factors is fundamental to implementing educational and related services that are culturally sensitive.

Language. The cultural and linguistic experiences greatly affect the ease with which CLD students can adapt and progress within the mainstream American society. Second language acquisition takes about 5–7 years (to reach content proficiency), but students can reach conversational language proficiency well before that (Winzer & Mazurek, 1998; Zehler et al., 2003). Although parents may appear to fully understand conversations and discussions, it is important that professionals are sensitive to language capabilities.

Unfortunately, language differences often appear to be communication disorders, such as language delays or deficiencies (Obiakor & Wilder, 2003). In many instances, these perceived delays or deficiencies trigger referrals to special education. Once a CLD student is referred to special education, it is likely that he or she will be found eligible (Artiles & Ortiz, 2002; Ysseldyke, Vanderwood, & Shriner, 1997; Zehler et al., 2003). In order to ensure that students are being fairly assessed, collaboration among speech and language therapists, bilingual specialists, and general and special education teachers is essential in the early intervening services stage to determine whether the student is exhibiting a *communication disorder* or *expected language difference.*

Technical language and frequent use of acronyms by school professionals can present obstacles to communication. Special educators are particularly reliant on acronyms that many individuals outside of the field are unfamiliar with (Soodack & Erwin, 1995; Valle & Aponte, 2002)—such as LRE, PTO, PTA, ITP, IFSP, PBS, IEP, and ABA. It may help to develop a list of acronyms and their definitions to distribute to parents in their native language, or to use as a reminder when conversing with individuals whose primary language is not English. Many parents are uncomfortable expressing their lack of understanding and may not ask the questions necessary for them to comprehend and actively participate in a conference or conversation with teachers. It is important to be mindful of the technical language that is used to communicate with all parents, but especially culturally and linguistically diverse families. Box 9.5 continues the story of Juan begun earlier in the chapter. Juan needed help from the special education assistance team to prepare him to be an active participant in this decision-making process. Not only the language of the IDEA statute, but also the spirit and intent of the law, gives Juan the right to be present and to *actively participate* in the meetings and decisions. The presence of a translator alone does not mean active participation because the translator simply translates discussion without interpreting it for Juan.

It is apparent that the inclusion of CLD populations requires the inclusion of different strategies and knowledge for school personnel. A flexible and responsive educational system is designed to recognize the challenges students and parents

---

BOX 9.5   The Story of Juan, Part 3

The day of the special education eligibility meeting is approaching, and Juan is contacted to come to the meeting. Test results are discussed, and a translator is present. The Woodcock Johnson III Test of Achievement and Stanford Binet were used, and numerical scores were presented. Juan dutifully sits through the entire meeting, unable to understand the discussion and overwhelmed and intimidated by the room full of professionals all discussing his child. His son is found eligible for services for learning and emotional disabilities. Juan is passed a paper to sign, and the meeting is over.

---

must overcome and provides them with necessary supports and reasonable time tables to achieve it. At a minimum, most school districts provide translators to minimize language barriers during special education related meetings with families. The availability of translators for other types of meetings varies among school districts, but some schools have engaged parent liaisons who act as translators. Minimally, school districts should have most legal documents translated into the most common languages of the community.

Styles and Beliefs in Interaction.   Different cultures have different styles of interaction, and when these styles clash or are incongruent, they can become barriers to effective collaboration (Harry, 2002). *Interaction style* refers to the body language, spoken language, voice tone, intensity, attitudes about personal space, and role perceptions that make up human interactions. The concept of interaction styles can be applied directly and indirectly to collaboration and coordination of services. Parents who do not access available services for their children may be perceived as uninvolved or neglectful. However, the problem may actually be limited knowledge and experience with community services, pride, or cultural values that reject state-funded assistance (Geenan, Powers, & Lopez-Vasquez, 2001). In some cultures, teachers are considered dominant, and parents have experienced few opportunities to participate in decisions about their child's education (Bernhard, Freire, Pacini-Ketchabaw, & Villanueva, 1998). Culturally and linguistically diverse parents, therefore, may not believe they are entitled to participate in educational decisions and that the school should make such decisions. Different cultural beliefs need to be acknowledged by educators in order to avoid misinterpretation by educators and to facilitate a collaborative relationship.

How Can Educators Improve Collaboration and Coordination of Services for CLD Students with Disabilities?

Coordination to Support English Language Learners (ELL) With Disabilities

Language development should be the shared responsibility of all teachers, not only those in bilingual and ESL (English as a Second Language) classes (Ortiz, 2004). General education teachers provide instruction in the general curriculum, special education teachers help to modify the curriculum or adapt instruction, and ESL/bilingual teachers support second language acquisition. ESL/bilingual teachers understand that **second language acquisition** is not the same as acquiring a first language, and they understand the impact of culture on a child's behavior in class. With an ELL child with disabilities, these teachers must collaborate closely to develop individualized education and supports. McLeod (2005) and others have conducted reviews of strategies related to English language learners (Artiles & Ortiz, 2002; Ortiz, 2004; Yates & Ortiz, 1998). The following sections draw on her synthesis.

Bilingual education is developmental and helps the student develop and maintain proficiency in two languages, English and their native language. *Transitional bilingual* means instruction in the native language while English is used increasingly until the student enters a regular instructional program. When the student has a disability, the special education teacher consults with bilingual teachers to adapt instruction. Other services can be provided through related services personnel. *English as a second language (ESL)* services are now being provided in general education classrooms rather than in pullout settings. Teachers collaborate to employ strategies known to be effective with English learners, such as drawing on their prior knowledge; providing opportunities to review previously learned concepts and teaching them to employ those concepts; organizing themes or strands that connect the curriculum across subject areas; and providing individual guidance, assistance, and support to fill gaps in background knowledge (Artiles & Ortiz, 2002; Yates & Ortiz, 1998).

Differentiating Language Acquisition Problems and Learning Disabilities.

ELL students with disabilities may need to receive both language support services as well as special education services. However, ESL educators and parents are concerned about the overrepresentation of culturally and linguistically diverse students (CLD) in special education services. Once students are classified as individuals with disabilities, schools often strip them of their ESL support. Although reauthorization of IDEA 2004 attempts to provide comprehensive quality services to students with disabilities, lack of language support or bilingual services for ESL students in special education programs is likely to impact ESL teachers when referring a student for special education. Once the student starts receiving special education services, he/she often no longer receives support in language development.

The process of distinguishing between students with language acquisition problems and learning disabilities should begin with several questions. What exposure have these students had to the curriculum? What are their cognitive and learning characteristics? What is their academic experience and background (Garcia & Ortiz, 1988; Ortiz, 2004)? When looking at speech and spelling errors, a question to consider is: Does the child have an auditory or speech problem, or are the difficulties a result of learning two different language systems? Many speech and spelling errors are rooted in language differences between an English language learner's home language and English. These kinds of assessments are essential before a student is placed into special education. In terms of evaluating the language status for non-English speakers and the possible presence of a disability, the following guidelines are offered.

LEP, recent arrival to the United States.   Evaluate the student in the native language. Provide native language instruction or English as a second language instruction (ESL). The IEP should include plans for English language acquisition (bilingual instruction and/or ESL). Special education services should not be provided in English only.

LEP, 1 to 3 years in the United States. Evaluate the student in their native language and in English. Determine language or languages in which special education and related services will be provided—these should be included in the IEP (Albus & Thurlow, 2005; Artiles & Ortiz, 2002).

Long-term LEP, over 3 years in the United States. Evaluate in the native language and English, but do not discontinue language support services.

The appropriate placement does not have to be a self-contained classroom for ELL students. Both bilingual/ESL and special education services can be provided in the general education classroom. Collaboration with bilingual and ESL teachers is essential, especially when general and special educators are not bilingual.

Principles and Strategies

There is no cookbook for working with diverse populations effectively. People need opportunities to share their experiences and cultural views, whether they are part of a teaching team, interdisciplinary planning team, transition team, interagency coordination team, or other collaborative working group. The following sections present eight principles that undergird effective collaborative relationships and service coordination in diverse settings:

Principle 1: It is the responsibility of all citizens in a democratic, multicultural society to promote a collaborative climate that appreciates individuals from all cultures (Bernhard et. al., 1998; Perez & Pinzon, 1997; Swick, Boutte, & Van Scoy, 1999). At its simplest level, multicultural education is a critical forum for reforming schools in ways that support pluralism and equity (Bohn & Sleeter, 2000; Riehl, 2000). Professionals who value a culture of appreciation seek to increase their factual knowledge about diversity while at the same time integrating new information into their worldviews, relationships, and interactions. Through this process they create new personal meaning. Creating new personal meaning means extending our understanding of the world beyond the way we alone have seen it or gaining a new perspective or changing a belief traditionally held, strengthening a personal value, or renewing a commitment to a goal.

The value of appreciating diversity should extend from district to local levels and from administrators to all staff (Dennis & Giangreco, 1996; Swick, Boutte, & Van Scoy, 1999). Improving *students' understanding of cultural diversity* should also be a part of a comprehensive multicultural education program. A greater understanding of diverse patterns of behavior and cultures helps educators to perceive the life experiences of diverse groups more realistically (Bohn & Sleeter, 2000). This understanding, in turn, helps reduce preconceptions and biases and provides a foundation for more effective collaboration.

Principle 2: Personal biases and prejudices must not influence collaborative relationships with diverse individuals. It is useful for educators to examine their position in society in relation to culture and class privilege (Hooks, 1994; Kumashiro, 2001; Nieto, 2000). For example, it is common in many nations for each race to be afforded a specific place among the other races and within the class structure. Often, exploring these issues illuminates discrepancies, disparities, and injustices among individuals that are present in society and contrary to democratic ideals. Once societal positions are explored, this can be a catalyst to foster meaningful discussion related to biases, preconceived stereotypes, and prejudices that negatively impact collaboration.

Principle 3: The collaborative professional acknowledges that CLD families do value education. Many students and families are confronted with insurmountable obstacles to participating in educational processes: language barriers, negative perceptions, exclusionary practices, employment obligations, cultural differences, and failure to understand educational processes and procedures. These factors contribute to behaviors that could be perceived as contradictory to positive, supportive parental participation (Bernhard et al., 1998; Cummins, 2001; Greenan, Powers, & Lopez-Vasquez, 2001; Valencia & Black, 2002). A CLD parent's participation in collaborative interactions should not be judged until every attempt has been made to eliminate or minimize their barriers to such participation.

Principle 4: Actively build collaboration upon cultural and linguistic diversity in the school. Schools and institutions that succeed in empowering students and parents to participate communicate a **continuum of respect for diversity**. They act to marshal diversity to the advantage of everyone when working with culturally and linguistically diverse populations (Bernhard et al., 1998; Nieto, 1994; Warger & Burdette, 2000; Zehr, 2003). The incorporation and respect for diversity can be visualized along an *"additive–subtractive" continuum* (Cummins, 2001). At the positive end of the continuum are educators who acknowledge the benefits of bilingual and bicultural students and parents. In contrast, at the other end of the continuum sit educators whose goal is the complete replacement of native cultures with that of the dominant mainstream. As Figure 9.3 depicts, the positive end of the continuum is empowering, and the negative end is demeaning. *This not to say that the dominant American culture is at the negative end, but rather, that the goal of eliminating native culture is disempowering.*

Parallel to the additive–subtractive continuum is the *collaborative–exclusionary continuum* specifically for working with culturally and linguistically diverse parents. On one end are the educators who unconsciously or consciously want to create an educational system based on equality for all. They actively encourage CLD parents to support the educational progress of their children in the home and school, and they make accommodations to encourage parent participation. At the opposite end of the continuum are educators who perceive themselves solely as *the teacher* and are neutral or negative about parent participation (Cummins, 2001). These educators fail to acknowledge the *cultural capital* and positive impact that diverse parents can have on their child's education.

Principle 5: Create school-based resource centers to promote collaboration with diverse populations. Many schools are creating school-based community resource centers to expand participation of CLD families. Resources fall into two main categories: (1) *family-oriented resources* such as support groups that provide opportunities for families to discuss daily demands, triumphs, and obstacles they encounter (Perez & Pinzon, 1997); and (2) *service-oriented resources* that identify service-based resources for culturally and linguistically diverse students and families. The resource

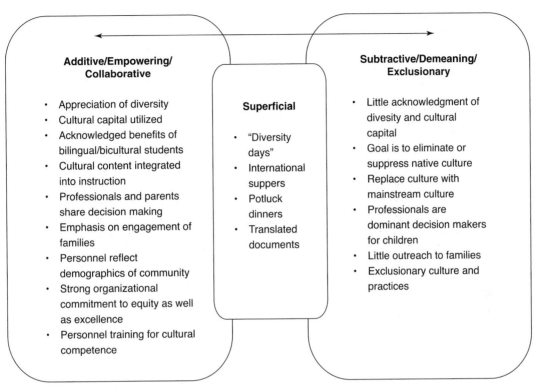

FIGURE 9.3
Continuum of Respect for Diversity

center becomes a logical hub for facilitating frequent and regular participation and linking with school-based and community services (Riehl, 2000). Service-oriented resources include health care options, child care options, coordination of services through mental health facilities or social services, housing, language instruction, economic resources, and other social resources available through public agencies.

Principle 6: Make expectations for participation and collaboration explicit. The hidden curriculum refers to the implicit rules and structures that are associated with the unique culture of the organization or school. "Acceptable" parent participation and collaboration is no exception (Bernhard et al., 1998; Brockett, 1998; Greenan, Powers, & Lopez-Vasquez, 2001; Valdez, as cited in Duran, Duran, Perry-Romero, & Sanchez, 2001). Several strategies have been shown to be effective in communicating expectations for parent collaboration and engagement with the school. It is essential that administrators be committed to improving relationships with families and provide staff development with focus on cultural sensitivity. Hiring bilingual staff and engaging bilingual volunteers can support these goals. Outreach to the community is strengthened by a welcoming environment in the school that includes family-friendly, flexible meeting hours that accommodate families' schedules, and transportation assistance to help families attend meetings. Essential to improving outcomes for CLD students is helping parents understand what "high standards for all children" means.

Principle 7: Acknowledge alternate forms of parental participation and collaboration. CLD parents frequently participate in their child's education indirectly or outside conventional participation activities (Bernhard et al., 1998; Greenan, Powers, & Lopez-Vasquez, 2001; Valencia & Black, 2002). For instance, they may use stories with their children to convey the importance of education. Valencia and Black (2002) found that *consejos*, or advice-giving narratives were a common method that Latino families used to convey their commitment to education to their children. Similarly, "funds of knowledge" or teaching by example are used to communicate values and commitments (Lopez, 2001; Valencia & Black, 2002). It is important to identify, acknowledge, and support these valuable means of participation within a family.

Principle 8: Involve parents in meaningful, structured activities. Culturally and linguistically diverse parents want the best for their children, but they also are constrained by logistics, attitudes, experience, and exposure. Educators need to establish creative means to showcase the cultural capital of students and families while involving them in meaningful educational activities (Perez & Pinzon, 1997). Sometimes, culturally and linguistically diverse parents may need to be shown how to participate in homework and school-related activities (Cummins, 2001).

It is important to differentiate between single events and social activities and meaningful participation designed to empower parents. Potluck dinners and multicultural nights are important social events. International "show and tell" in class can be educational and beneficial to children and families. However, using students or parents from other countries and cultures as "authorities" may appear to be empowering, but must be used with caution because it can be perceived by the students as demeaning and therefore not a meaningful activity. Academic supports for CLD students and administrative resources for parent participation are two examples of activities designed to build long-term capacity to engage parents. Inviting and encouraging parents to serve on committees that support decision making in the school or district is another empowering activity.

Summary of Key Points

- The numbers of CLD students in the United States have risen dramatically in the past decade.
- There are persistent educational performance gaps for many CLD students, and educators have difficulty differentiating between second language acquisition challenges and the presence of a disability.
- Both IDEA 2004 and NCLB have focused on the performance gaps of CLD students and challenged schools to close them.
- Culturally competent teachers and related service personnel appreciate the complex interaction of language, culture, knowledge, and attitudes in the education of culturally and linguistically diverse students.
- Culturally competent personnel recognize diversity as enriching education; they also appreciate the potentially powerful and valuable role of *parental involvement* for improving student achievement and providing a window into the culture of the family.

Key Terms and Phrases

- Culture (p. 236)
- Cultural and linguistic diversity (p. 236)
- Literacy (p. 236)
- Macroculture (p. 237)
- Microcultures (p. 237)
- Assimilation (p. 241)
- Deficit perspective (p. 241)
- Ethnocentrism (p. 241)
- Accommodation (p. 242)
- Acculturation (p. 242)
- Cultural mismatch theory (p. 242)
- Cultural model perspective (p. 242)
- Cultural competence (p. 244)
- Cultural sensitivity (p. 244)
- Transcultural model (p. 244)
- Second language acquisition (p. 247)
- Continuum of respect for diversity (p. 250)

Questions for Reflection, Thinking, and Skill Building

1. Discuss why culture has such a significant impact on interpersonal relationships. How does cultural background affect parent participation in the education of their children?
2. Why are parents considered to be "cultural capital," or valued resources in educating CLD students?
3. Can you identify a time, either personal or professional, when a decision-making process has been negatively affected by different or incongruent cultural beliefs?
4. Explore your personal attitude toward culturally and linguistically diverse populations using the *Assess Your Cultural Competence* tool in Box 9.4 on p. 245. How would you rate your level of cultural competence? Discuss this in a group.
5. How can appreciation for cultural diversity improve teaching? How can it improve you as a professional? How can it improve student learning and student relationships?
6. Review one school's attempt to fully meet the needs and encourage participation of culturally and linguistically diverse populations. How would you judge the effort in terms of strengths and weaknesses? List the positive activities that have been implemented.

INTRODUCTION TO PART THREE

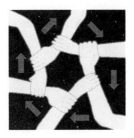

COLLABORATION AND COORDINATION FROM EARLY CHILDHOOD THROUGH POSTSECONDARY TRANSITION

CHAPTER FOURTEEN

How Can School Collaboration and System Coordination Promote Progress of Students in Alternative Education?

CHAPTER FIFTEEN

How Can School Collaboration and System Coordination Promote Transition of Students to Postsecondary Settings?

Children are the living messages we send to a time we will not see.

—John Whitehead

Part 3, Chapters 10 through 15, apply the concepts and processes of collaboration and coordination of services for children, youth, and families along the developmental path from early childhood to young adulthood. This path involves a series of transitions, now viewed as more than a single, brief move from one setting to another. Rather, transition and progress at each stage depend on professional collaboration and coordination of educational services to help students succeed at each stage.

Chapters 10 through 15 examine the spectrum of coordinated responses of educators and related services personnel to children's needs along the developmental continuum. Some responses are similar across the stages and others are developmentally different. Barriers, challenges, and "failures" of these transitions for both students and professionals are also explored. In the case examples, particular emphasis is devoted to seeing the problems and needs through the lens of parents and family members.

Contrary to popular conceptions, the developmental process for children does not occur in a step-by-step linear fashion. Metaphorically, it zigzags side to side and forward and backward, but with a net movement forward, like the child who skips in small circles as he winds his way slowly down the street. Change is a process, not an event, although children are often expected to force fit their zigzag development into the straight lines of grade progression and one-size-fits-all developmental expectations.

Like child development, the development of collaborative relationships among professionals does not develop in a tidy, step-by-step linear fashion. Instead it is messy, complex, and unpredictable. However, in the past 2 decades, research has demonstrated that the challenges and opportunities presented by special learners, in the context of rising academic expectations, have led to close collaboration and unity among personnel who have not previously worked together. Such collaboration has also resulted in new organizational relationships, practices, and policies that were unprecedented for schools but have benefited all students. New patterns of relationships have emerged that are very different from the traditional isolation and independent work that had been characteristic of the teachers, school support staff, and parents in the past. The extent to which our educational systems support children along their developmental pathways ultimately expresses the national will to invest in its future. From the perspective of costs—both school resources and human costs—it is a national imperative that we view successful passages through school as a primary objective for which schools are held accountable.

LET'S SEE IT IN ACTION! Case Illustration: Developmental Nature of Collaboration

Let's look at a "prequel" to the case of Eric in Chapter 3 to explore his earlier life and development. You may want to review the case in Chapter 3 briefly. In an extended interview, the family shared information that is helpful for thinking about the developmental nature of collaboration and coordination needs in the life of a child.

AUTHOR: It seems that you have been serving as a "service coordinator" or "case manager" for your child. How long have you been doing that?

MOTHER: Actually since he was about 5 years old. It began when we noticed how bright Eric was. He walked early and talked early—and never stopped talking after that. We noticed how physically coordinated he was, how accurately he could throw a ball at age 3, and how well he could put things together. His fine motor and gross motor skills were advanced beyond his years. We had him tested at an educational and diagnostic services center and he was given the Wechsler Intelligence Scales for Children (WISC). He scored 148 on the Full Scale IQ, falling into the 99th percentile for his age. Thinking that perhaps this was just a fluke, we had him tested again at age 7 and he scored even higher.

AUTHOR: When did you first identify problems?

MOTHER: I guess actually from the beginning. I had a tough pregnancy, with complications in the first 5 months, and I was put on bed rest for 6 weeks. It was touch and go as to whether he would pull through, but he did and appeared to be fine at birth. But from that point on, my experience with Eric was so different from my experience with my daughter, who is 7 years older than Eric, always self-motivated, highly focused, and a consistent achiever throughout school and into college. Eric on the other hand, did not sleep through the night until age 2. He would not take naps in the day and never seemed to need to rest or sleep until he was exhausted at night. He had boundless energy, and it always seemed as though he was too energetic even to sit in his seat and eat meals with the family, to look people in the eye for any length of time, to have a meaningful conversation, or to follow a simple set of directions when asked (such as "go pick up your shoes and socks and bring them to me").

Eric performed well in kindergarten and was highly social with others. The school was unstructured but stimulating, and there were regular recess breaks. Eric needed to run off his excess energy. During elementary grades, we began to get reports and notes that he would not listen to teachers, not follow directions, would frequently leave his seat, and was generally attention seeking in class. Since he was bright, he performed well, getting all As and Bs in the first and second grades. I didn't put all this together until he was about 10 because, you know, he was a BOY! I thought I just needed to be patient.

AUTHOR: How did you deal with teachers in those early years?

MOTHER: I learned to keep in constant communication with them. They were pretty good at letting me know when he misbehaved or disrupted class. I made sure I went to the parent–teacher conferences early in the year and spoke with the teachers about Eric's problems. I did not demand anything, but only suggested that I would work hard from the family's side to work with Eric, and suggested that perhaps the teacher could give some extra guidance to Eric in class. I walked a fine line, being careful to talk in terms of a partnership with the teacher and that I did not expect the teacher to perform heroics with my child. Some teachers were happy to try small accommodations such as putting Eric in the front of the class for closer attention. Others would allow him to take quizzes standing up because he would fidget too much. The fourth-grade teacher told Eric that if he felt he could not stay in his seat, then it was OK if he went quietly to the back of the room and stood. These were simple, natural accommodations for him.

AUTHOR: Knowing what you know now, do you think you should have requested special education for Eric at that time?

MOTHER: I don't think so. I do regret that I didn't pay more attention in the first 4 years. He clearly was a more intense and energetic child who was easily distracted and had difficulty focusing. But in first grade, while he was showing some behavioral and attention issues, he was keeping up his grades—As and Bs through elementary years—not falling behind his peers. He would not have been eligible for special education, and the truth was that we knew, and the teachers all knew, he could do the work. Often it appeared that he was not paying attention in class, but then he would score an 'A' on the tests. It was not until sixth grade when he was 10 that he began to slide into more serious trouble. The school homework increased in the sixth and seventh grades, and many long-term projects were assigned that required organization and time-management skills.

AUTHOR: So what happened at 10?

MOTHER: I noticed that Eric began to lack interest or motivation to read and had great difficulty with any long-term project that required time management. At age 10, he was diagnosed with attention deficit and hyperactivity disorder, and we arranged for a private tutor to help him get organized at home to complete school projects. He resisted the tutor's visits, did not complete the tasks she asked him to do, and nothing seemed to help improve Eric's progress. This marked the "age of resistance" to every intervention we were to try in the years to come as the problems progressed.

AUTHOR: Did he have difficulty in middle school?

MOTHER: Yes, that's when things became very difficult for Eric. He had to become more responsible for his assignments, for long-term projects, and for generally organizing his work for his classes. The pattern of resistance that we had seen in the early years and his tendency to challenge everything that we wanted him to do intensified. His grades began to plummet in the seventh and eighth grades, even though he scored "advanced proficient" in the state standardized tests. Notes came home about his inattentiveness in class, his drawing attention to himself, failure to turn homework in, and general disorganization. He needed more help and support than we could give him, yet he was not identified as needing special education because his standardized tests showed that he was clearly capable of doing the work. His teachers said he lacked motivation and was disruptive. We were faced with the challenge of figuring out what to do with a child who didn't fit into any of the categories, and none of the professionals were coming forward to help us. I felt as though it would take complete failure on Eric's part before I could get the attention of the system.

AUTHOR: What about his transition to high school?

MOTHER: Of course, we were very anxious as to whether Eric would adjust. We thought perhaps being in the "big school" might trigger some motivation, but our worst fears became a reality. Eric's performance ran right off the tracks, his inattentiveness turned into oppositional behavior, his disruptiveness in class increased, homework was not turned in, and he began to sleep in class and appeared dazed much of the time and frequently refused to go to school. We knew we were all headed for deep trouble. Eric failed ninth grade, isolated himself with pot-smoking friends, stayed out late without calling in, descended into violent behavior at home, and had several incidents in which he was brought home by the police. We had no choice but to follow an interagency team recommendation and place him into an intensive day treatment program—half academic and half therapeutic, combined with substance abuse counseling. At the end of one long, disappointing, and agonizing semester for the family, Eric was determined to need even more structure and was recommended by an interagency team for long-term residential treatment.

Chapter 14 provides the outcome, or "next steps" for Eric.

Children's special needs may or may not show up early in their lives. Some disabilities are plainly identified from the time of birth (e.g., visual, hearing, speech, or physical). Others can develop in the first few years of life (e.g., autism, developmental disabilities, emotional and behavioral disabilities). Many childhood disabilities are not identified as long as the child is at home with strong support of the family but may become evident once the child enters school, with all its social and academic demands (e.g., learning disabilities, ADHD). Even then, the child often has strengths that compensate for his or her disabilities, and the problems may not become serious until the child reaches late elementary or middle school years.

Professionals at each stage of the developmental continuum can best support the student as a team, alert to the needs and the signs of progress. Schools are becoming centers for learning, not only for students but also for families and professionals. The value of collaboration and system coordination has emerged as a central theme in the reform and renewal of our educational institutions as they commit to helping all children succeed.

CHAPTER TEN

How Can School Collaboration and System Coordination Promote Progress of Children in Early Childhood Programs?

If we're ever going to level the playing field so that all kids can succeed in school, our best chance is before they reach the age of five. —Rhode Island Kids Count, 2004

If starting points are dramatically different and the finish line is the same, then equality is a hollow slogan. —Bud Hodgkinson, 2003

- What are developmental services in early childhood education?

- What professional roles support children in early childhood programs?

- What lessons are learned from research on collaboration and coordination in early childhood education?

- What services are mandated for young children with disabilities and their families?

- What are the barriers to collaboration in early childhood education?

- What collaboration and system coordination strategies support young children in early childhood programs?

PERSPECTIVES

Researcher

Working with the early intervention team may serve a functional purpose while parents are still in a stage of grief. To feel that they are doing something constructive, to have goals and activities for their child may be therapeutic for parents. Feeling that they are contributing to their child's development may be a lifeline to parents in the early days of coming to terms with their child's disability (Bridle & Mann, 2000).

Parent

The thing that I resent about the whole business of Nick's infancy/babyhood is that I never actually took the time to just play with him like a baby. I always thought—OK, the most important thing to do was stimulating him and having him sit up . . . instead of just enjoying it. I don't remember just laying on the carpet with him, looking at the sun and blowing on his tummy, just the silly simple things that you remember doing. But I was so exhausted with Nick that I just didn't understand that. I was so busy just dragging him to this appointment, that appointment, staying in hospital, all those things, rather than the things that really matter like, tickling him and looking at him . . . and no one told me that.

INTRODUCTION

Society has come to appreciate the first 5 years of life as a time of profound growth and change for the child, physically, socially, emotionally, and intellectually. Congress has revised educational laws to promote early intervention programs and research, and coordination of services, particularly for children who have disabilities or are at risk for developmental problems. New research and understanding about early child development has led the nation to view early intervention and early childhood education as having profound significance for long-term development (American Academy of Pediatrics Committee on Children with Disabilities, 2001; Bredekamp &

Copple, 1997; Kaplan-Sanoff, Lerner, & Bernard, 2000; U.S. Department of Health and Human Services, 2001c).

Understanding the nature and needs of young children has led to the development of thousands of early intervention programs, nursery schools, and preschools throughout the nation. Early intervention services and early childhood education marks the young child's entrance into the educational development process. Preschools and child care centers aim to nurture children's healthy development, support vulnerable children, strengthen relationships between children and their parents, and connect families to social and emotional support networks in the community. However, there are persistent barriers to the delivery of quality early intervention and early childhood education that remains to be overcome. There is a national awakening to the need to increase investment in these programs. As the expectations for academic performance for children in the K–12 years increase, the early developmental years take on profound significance.

This chapter defines the developmental stages in early intervention and early childhood and explores the legal rights of young children with disabilities and their families during these passages. Key transitions for children through early intervention and early childhood programs are examined, along with the barriers to collaboration in early childhood education. Effective collaboration and system coordination strategies to support young children in early childhood programs and their transition to elementary school are described, as well as the roles of professionals engaged in the process.

WHAT ARE DEVELOPMENTAL SERVICES IN EARLY CHILDHOOD EDUCATION?

The Continuum of Development

As discussed in Chapter 1, system theory explains that a change that occurs in one part of the system affects all other parts. So it is with early development of children. The **continuum of development** in the early years, as depicted in Figure 10.1, includes:

1. early intervention services for infants and toddlers ages 0–3;
2. early intervention and educational services ages 3–5, and transition supports as they move from early intervention into preschool; and
3. educational services and transition supports as children move from preschool into kindergarten, typically at ages 5–7.

Research on the long-term effects of early childhood programs indicates that children who attend high-quality programs, even at very young ages, demonstrate positive outcomes once they enter K–12 schooling, and children who attend poor quality programs show negative effects (Burchinal, 1999; Burchinal, Peisner, Feinberg, Bryant, & Clifford, 2000; National Association for the Education of Young Children, 2003). Children begin to develop a self-concept at birth and awareness of different cultures as early as age 3 (Buckroyd & Flitton, 2004; Reese, 2001; Reese & Gallimore, 2000). During the first few years, children begin to develop their sense of confidence, independence, motivation, curiosity, cooperation, persistence, self-control, and empathy. In these initial years, children begin to develop and to acquire

FIGURE 10.1

Key Transitions in
the Early Years

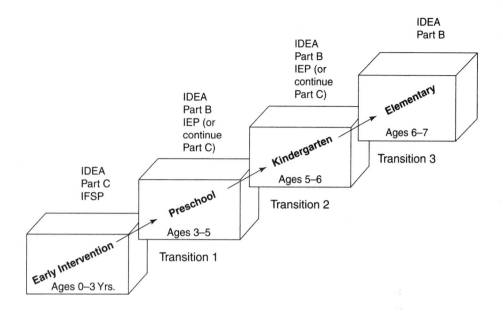

attitudes and values regarding school, self, peers, social groups, family, and adults outside the family.

Early identification of difficulties and intervention in children's academic, personal, and social needs is essential to removing barriers to learning (American School Counseling Association, 2004; Campbell, Ramey, Pungello, Sparling, & Miller-Johnson, 2002; Gallagher & Clifford, 2000; Quinn & McDougal, 1998; Reynolds, Temple, Robertson, & Mann, 2001; Steckbeck, 2004). Furthermore, the experience children have in their transition and early adjustment in kindergarten and elementary school makes a great deal of difference in their attitudes about themselves, learning, and the school environment. Education must be directed to the development of the child's personality, talents, and mental and physical abilities (Lansdown, 2005; United Nations, 2005).

Developmentally Appropriate Practice

Early identification of disability and initiation of services depends upon strong collaboration and communication among families, health professionals, early childhood educators, specialists, and related services professionals. The age of first identification and first services often varies with the child's type of disability. For example, the majority of children with visual impairments or deaf-blindness are identified as having disabilities before age 3 (87%), and almost all children with deaf-blindness also receive their first professional services as infants and toddlers (Schweinhart & Weikart, 1997). Ethnicity is also correlated with age at identification and first services. White students, who tend to be from higher-income families than non-White, are more likely to be identified as having disabilities at younger ages than Hispanic children and less likely to be identified in the older age range than Black or Hispanic children (Schweinhart & Weikart, 1997, p. 18).

Developmentally appropriate practices (DAP) lead to improved achievement. There is ample evidence that children learn and achieve more in programs that employ developmentally appropriate practices. Studies that have examined social and academic development of children in developmentally appropriate and developmentally inappropriate (DAP and DIP) settings have consistently found that children who participated in DAP programs demonstrated more appropriate skills in social settings and received better grades in some academic subjects (Huffman & Speer, 2000; Marcon, 1999a; Schweinhart & Weikart 1997). Schweinhart and Weikart's (1997) longitudinal study reported that children from DAP programs had far fewer emotional difficulties later in life, were less likely to engage in antisocial activities as teenagers and young adults, and showed enhanced personal development (e.g., higher preference for challenge, greater autonomy, higher expectations of success, and less stress in academic situations). DAP programs have generally been shown to have positive effects on children's social and personal development—even for children who are considered at risk in educational settings—and their effects can still be observed as the children approach adulthood (Huffman & Speer, 2000; Marcon, 1999).

From infancy through about age 10, brain cells not only form most of the connections they will maintain throughout life but during this time they retain their greatest malleability (Restak, 2001). *Developmental milestones* are sets of functional skills or age-specific tasks that most children acquire within certain age ranges. Pediatricians and early childhood educators use milestones to help monitor how a child is developing. Although each milestone has an age marker, the actual age by which a typically developing child reaches that milestone can vary quite a bit. Every child is unique (American Academy of Pediatrics Committee on Children with Disabilities, 2001; Bredekamp & Copple, 1997). **Developmental delay** occurs when a child does not reach his or her developmental milestones within expected age ranges. It is an ongoing, major delay in the process of development. If the child is slightly or only temporarily lagging behind, that is not called developmental delay. Delay can occur in one or many areas—for example, motor, language, social, or thinking skills.

The natural environment for a child with a disability is a home or community setting that is natural or typical for a child without disabilities. In the school setting, developmentally appropriate practices (DAP) emphasizes learning as a socially interactive process. Teachers prepare the classroom environment for children to learn through active exploration and interaction with adults, other children, and materials. Developmentally inappropriate practices (DIP) include overuse of individual drill and practice techniques that can stifle interest, creativity, and curiosity and lead to boredom in children. In DIP programs, adult attitudes are not informed by an understanding of how children learn and develop, and there is a lack of appropriate training and support systems for teachers.

Developmentally appropriate practices are based on extensive research about child development and learning and the design of instruction to address the unique needs, strengths, and interests of each child. They are responsive to the cultural and social environments in which each child lives—looking at the whole child (NAEYC, 1996). Children learn when they feel secure and accepted and are encouraged and respected as learners who can initiate, make judgments, and take responsibility.

Classroom practices that are developmentally appropriate tend to be child-initiated and have been shown to be associated with higher levels of cognitive functioning, social skills development, and creativity in comparison to classrooms using traditional didactic teaching methods. Learning activities and materials are concrete and relevant to children's lives (Adams & Edgerton, 1997; Lansdown, 2005).

Collaborative teaching for the younger child takes into account the developmental stage of the child as well as the impact of key transitions in his or her life. Developmentally appropriate practices include any activity involving young children, birth to 8, that is based on knowledge of the stages of child development and an understanding that each child is unique and each child's educational experiences should match his or her developing abilities (Bowman, Donovan, & Burns, 2001; NAEYC, 1997). A developmentally appropriate early childhood program emphasizes:

- active, sensory-based exploration of the environment;
- self-directed, hands-on learning activities balanced with teacher-directed activities;
- a balance between individual and group activities;
- regular and supportive interaction with teachers and peers;
- a balance between active movement and quiet activities; and
- ongoing observation and assessment which informs the program (Lansdown, 2005; NAEYC, 1996; Neuman, Copple, & Bredekamp, 2000).

As mentioned earlier, early childhood professionals rely on three types of information when creating developmentally appropriate practices: (1) What is known about child development and learning; (2) what is known about strengths, interests, and needs of each individual child in the group; and (3) knowledge of the social and cultural context in which children live.

These three types of knowledge identified by the National Association for the Education of Young Children (NAEYC) have several implications for collaboration and coordination among families, educators, and community agency personnel. First, developmentally appropriate practices rely upon the parents' willingness to share information about the development and functional capabilities of the child with school professionals. Educators must engage in regular communication with families, invite parent participation, and, when needed, help families overcome language barriers that may prevent the flow of crucial information. Second, developmentally appropriate practice for diverse children with disabilities requires close coordination among early childhood educators, special educators, bilingual educators, and related services specialists.

Early Intervention Services and Service Plans

Programs that serve infants, toddlers, and preschool-age children with disabilities are an important component of the Individuals with Disabilities Education Act. In **Part C of IDEA 2004, early interventions services** include any supports or services an infant or toddler may need that will support his or her development. Service coordination is a mandated activity of early intervention (EI) programs (IDEA, 2004).

Early intervention (EI) programs provide services to parents that help them identify and link with a variety of community resources necessary to support family functioning (Dunst & Bruder, 2002; National Association of School Psychologists [NASP], 2003). Service coordinators have the complex task of ensuring that families receive all services to which they are entitled. IDEA 2004 gave families the right to early intervention services regardless of income or health care benefits. Family-centered EI services are those that are provided to the child and family based on the strengths and needs identified by the family.

Early intervention programs play a vital role in the lives of families of infants and toddlers with special needs. In these programs, families are eligible to receive a range of services to meet their identified needs and concerns. For example, EI programs provide direct therapeutic and developmental services to children in natural environments such as center-based playgroups or home visits or through consultation to community-based early education programs (Dinnebeil, Hale, & Rule, 1999; NASP, 2003; Shelley-Sireci & Racicot, 2001).

From birth to age 2, children with developmental delays are served by an **individualized family services plan** (IFSP). From age 3 through beginning school age, children with developmental delays are typically served by an individualized education plan (IEP). However, IDEA 2004 included a "Part C option" to allow states to make Part C services available to children after age 3 until they are eligible to enter kindergarten or elementary school (635(c)(1)). The difference between the IFP and IFSP is that the IFSP also provides for direct services and supports for families. The IFSP identifies the services that the child with a disability and their families will receive, and for some children the extension of such family services through to K-1 is essential. The plan is based on the child's developmental needs and outlines specific outcomes for the child. The IFSP must contain:

- the child's present level of development;
- the family's resources, priorities, and concerns as they relate to their child with a disability;
- the major outcomes for the child and his or her family;
- the early intervention services that will be provided;
- the natural environments in which services are provided;
- the dates the services will begin and the family's service coordinator;
- the child's plan to transition to preschool services (IDEA, 2004).

These two kinds of plans define the programs and services that the child and family needs during early childhood, but also defines the kinds of collaboration and coordination needed among professionals and service agencies. Table 10.1 highlights differences between early intervention and preschool special education.

Let's See It in Action on page 268 provides an illustration of a lost opportunity for communication and education between a parent and a physician about a child with early warning signs. When parents like Pete's bring their children to their pediatrician, family physician, or pediatric nurse practitioner, they often leave feeling very unsure about their competence as parents and the decisions they need to make about their toddlers and children. Parents need to know the answers to two questions: (1) How is my baby doing? and (2) how am I doing as a parent? The answer to the first

TABLE 10.1   Differences Between Early Intervention and Preschool Special Education

Item Compared	Early Intervention	Preschool Special Education
Age of child	Birth through 2 years, with option through to K-1	Third birthday to mandatory school age
Administering state agency	Department of health (varies among states)	Department of education
Administering local agency	Community-based organizations	School district
Basis of eligibility	Disability or developmental delay	Documented deficit areas adversely affecting development and function
Service document	Individualized family service plan (IFSP)	Individualized education plan (IEP)
Team members	Family, service coordinator, early intervention specialist, evaluators, service providers, others	(special and regular education) plan psychologist, school district representative, others
Type of placement	Natural environments	Least restrictive environment
Payment	Some services are free, others subject to a sliding fee scale	Free and appropriate public education (FAPE) at no cost to parents

Source: From *First Steps: Early Intervention Services for Infants and Toddlers with Delays or Disabilities*, by Ohio Legal Rights Service, 2004, Columbus, OH: Ohio Legal Rights Service. Reprinted by permission.

question is usually the focus of the visit, but the second is often unheard, unanswered, or ignored. These same two questions are also on the minds of families when they bring their child to an early intervention program or to child care (Brazelton, 1992; Kaplan-Sanoff, Lerner, & Bernard, 2000; Young, Davis, Schoen, & Parker, 1998).

It is imperative that children with special needs be identified as early as possible so that supports can be put into place to prevent future difficulties and potential failure in the school setting. If a family member is concerned about problems at home with a child, then professionals should take notice. Physician referrals for early assessment could greatly assist early identification. Community health departments and school districts are now required by law to make early identification and intervention programs a high priority. Preschool programs are currently being studied at the federal level to identify early intervention curriculum and methods that are effective (Bowman, Donovan, & Burns, 2001; National Institute for Early Education Research, 2004; Study of State and Local Implementation and Impact of the Individuals with Disabilities Education Act [SLIIDEA], 2003).

LET'S SEE IT IN ACTION! Case Illustration: Early Concerns, Little Counsel

It's time for Pete's four-year checkup, and his parents are concerned that he seems to be very active, behaviorally aggressive, and never seems to need sleep. In fact, he didn't sleep through the night until he was 2, and he never took naps. Recently he had shown an increase in biting his mother, Eileen, and other children when he was angry. He cannot sit still long enough to finish a meal with the family, and he cannot seem to focus long enough to complete a simple task such as picking up toys or socks from the floor when asked. This lack of focus also interferes with simple conversations with adults. They worry if he will grow out of this inattentiveness and aggression or if it will become worse later on. They are uncertain whether they should discuss their concerns with Dr. Mann, the pediatrician, who generally rushes through checkups, particularly if the child seems to be generally in good physical health. Dr. Mann's patient education agenda will cover information about injury prevention, maintaining good nutrition, inquiring about sleep and toileting issues, an assessment of general physical development, and a discussion of discipline. All of this will generally take about 15 minutes. There is little chance for additional discussion of concerns.

At this visit, however, Pete decided to assert his will. The doctor's office was his least favorite place in the world, and he was fearful of everyone and everything. He refused to sit on the examining table, screamed when the otoscope was gently placed in his ear, and exhibited so much anxiety during the genital exam that Dr. Mann decided to skip it. She commented to Eileen that Pete seemed to be extraordinarily anxious. Eileen seized this moment to share her concerns about Pete's general hyperactivity, intensity, and inability to focus and its potential impact on his success in school. Dr. Mann responded that at this time Pete had met physical developmental milestones and there was no reason to be overly concerned unless things became much worse. She would see him next year. Eileen was reluctant to argue with the doctor, but left the office with a great sense of disappointment and uncertainty about her own parenting skills and ability to help her son.

Questions for Discussion

- What lost opportunities for education, guidance, and early identification can you identify that might have helped Eileen?
- What kinds of things could Eileen do over the coming year before the next visit?

What Professional Roles Support Children in Early Childhood Programs?

The following sections describe the roles of professionals in early childhood education who collaborate in order to provide needed services for children and their families.

Pediatric Developmental Specialist

Developmental specialists have backgrounds and training in child development, early intervention, special education, child care, social work, counseling, and nursing. The developmental specialist typically provides behavioral and developmental services within a pediatric practice. These roles may include (a) conducting office visits jointly with the pediatric clinician during regular well-child appointments; (b) conducting home visits to support and enhance parent–child interactions and to promote home safety; (c) preventing and helping parents manage common behavioral problems related to early learning (fussiness, sleep, feeding, toilet training, and temper tantrums); (d) checking on children's developmental progress and family health and behavior as part of an office or home visit; (e) facilitating parent groups and staffing a child development telephone information line; and (f) providing referrals and follow-up, as appropriate, to help families make connections within the community. Developmental specialists help parents understand their child's temperament, behavior, and development through observation and discussion of shared experiences (Kaplan-Sanoff et al., 2000).

Service Coordinator/Family Resource Coordinator

Under the Early Intervention program for Infants and Toddlers With Disabilities (Part C) of IDEA, service coordination is defined as activities carried out by a service coordinator to assist and enable an eligible child and the child's family to receive the rights, procedural safeguards, and services that are required to be provided under the state's early intervention program. Under IDEA, the service coordinator is an important member of the early intervention team and is responsible for coordinating all services across agency lines (e.g., preschool, family services, health department) and serves as a single point of contact to help parents obtain the services and assistance they need. The service coordinator assists parents of eligible children to gain access to the early intervention services and other services that are identified in their individualized family service plan (IFSP). They coordinate the early intervention services for the family through development of the IFSP, and work to obtain the services and setting that best supports the child's development. Service coordinators assess service needs of families, monitor delivery of services, and conduct evaluations to improve overall services. Finally, service coordinators facilitate the development of the child's transition plan to preschool services (Hurth, 1998).

The Role of the Preschool Teacher

Collaborative teaching in inclusive settings requires ongoing professional development to expand and update teaching skills and collaborative skills, and to stay connected with current research. Effective early childhood educators have formal training in child development, language acquisition, appropriate instructional and assessment techniques, curricular development, parent involvement, and cultural diversity (Bowman, Donovan, & Burns, 2000; NAEYC, 2003). Though often challenging, the diverse early childhood classroom offers teachers great opportunities to help children develop positive attitudes toward others who are different from themselves and to enable children with diverse needs to achieve all they are capable of (National Association of State Boards of Education [NASBE], 2003). For children placed in inclusive settings, behavioral requirements for successful functioning should be assessed and include the ability to:

- function independently during group instruction,
- follow classroom routines,
- complete tasks within an allotted time period,
- work in the absence of teacher direction,
- demonstrate basic "survival skills" (Carta, Atwater, & Schwartz, & McConnell, 1993; Chadwick & Kemp, 2001, 2002; NAEYC, 2003).

Itinerant Community-Based Teacher

The early childhood itinerant teacher is a special education teacher and inclusion specialist who supports ages 3–5 preschoolers with disabilities in community settings (Dinnebeil, McInerney, Roth, & Ramaswamy, 2001). Itinerant services are offered within these settings as a combination of direct services and collaborative–consultation services (Sadler, 2003). Direct services provided to children include coaching early childhood teachers, providing emotional support and encouragement to classroom staff, consultation on instructional methods and the IEP process, and serving as a resource to teachers (Dinnebeil & McInerney, 2000).

Role of the School Psychologist in Early Childhood Services

School psychologists not only perform roles similar to that of school psychologists working with the school-age population, but must also address the developmental, educational, and mental health needs of young children in a variety of school and community based settings (NASP, 1999). The school psychologist in early childhood settings applies knowledge of culturally and developmentally appropriate assessment practices to design and conduct screenings and individual assessments. They develop accountability systems that enable timely early interventions, as well as assist early intervention teams with the transition of young children from various settings. They work directly with children and families and indirectly with teachers and caregivers to develop, implement, monitor, and evaluate individualized and group interventions for children. School psychologists assist adults in acquiring skills needed to help their children learn. Using research from areas of child development, developmental psychopathology, risk and resilience, and disability prevention, psychologists promote effective instructional practices for children in early childhood programs (NASP, 1999).

WHAT LESSONS ARE LEARNED FROM RESEARCH ON COLLABORATION AND COORDINATION IN EARLY CHILDHOOD EDUCATION?

Rising Participation in Preschool

The number of infants and toddlers served under Part C of IDEA (ages 0–3) has been increasing over the past decade (1990–2000) (OSEP, Data Analysis System, 2002d) and in-home services are on the rise. According to the 2000 child count data,

63% of the children served under Part C were classified as White (non-Hispanic); 17% as Hispanic; 16% as Black (non-Hispanic); 4% as Asian/Pacific Islander; and 1% as American Indian/Alaska Native.

The number of young children attending preschool is also rising, as is the number who have disabilities. Every eighth person in the U.S. population is a preschool child. During the 2000–2001 school year, there were about 19,900 public elementary schools with prekindergarten classes. This represents 35% of all regular and special education public elementary schools in the nation. One national study reported that 10% of students enrolled in public school prekindergarten classes have IEPs, compared with 13% of all public school students (Barnett, Robin, Hustedt, & Schulman, 2003; National Center for Education Statistics [NCES], 2003).

Speech or language impairment was the most prevalent disability category, accounting for 55.2% of all preschoolers served in 2000–01 (NCES, 2003). White (non-Hispanic) preschoolers were overrepresented in the Part B population (older than age 3 and identified as needing special education services). Asian/Pacific Islander and, especially, Hispanic children were underrepresented among the preschoolers served under IDEA (U.S. Office of Special Education, 2002b). Children living in families that are below poverty are less likely to participate in preschool education than children in families living at or above poverty. In 2001, the difference in participation between children from poor and nonpoor families was 12 percentage points (47% versus 59%) (NCES, 2003).

Today, more children than ever are participating in early childhood programs before they enroll in kindergarten. Preschool enrollment of 3–5-year-old children rose by nearly 30% between 1970 and 1998, a larger enrollment increase than for any other age group (Gallop-Goodman, 2000; NCES, 2002). Nearly 65% of children in this age group attend a program such as day care, nursery school, preschool, Head Start, or prekindergarten program. About 51% of these children attend all day, compared to 38% in 1988. There are many reasons for these changes, including an increased number of working mothers, more single-parent families, and desire on the part of parents to ensure that their children are ready for the new demands of kindergarten and elementary school. Furthermore, many lower-income children are able to start their education early because of the federally administered Head Start program (Gallop-Goodman, 2000), which is discussed in greater detail later.

U.S. Department of Education National Study of Early Intervention in the States

The U.S. Department of Education conducted a 5-year series of studies to examine the impact of the 1997 amendments to the Individuals with Disabilities Education Act (Study of State and Local Implementation and Impact of IDEA [SLIIDEA], 2003). One component of the study addressed early intervention and transition. Congress was interested in learning what states, districts, and schools were doing to help young children with disabilities make successful transitions from early intervention services to preschool education and from preschool education to elementary school.

Congress also wanted to know how states, districts, and schools were coordinating services with each other and with preschool services and health and social services. The research found that 92% of the states have coordination plans for early intervention services and 94% have plans for preschool services. Coordination with other agencies is more common for preschool than for early intervention services, and coordination with Head Start is the most common for preschool activities (occurring in 98% of the districts studied). Most states and districts engage in **child-find** activities to identify young children at risk of developmental delay and three-quarters of states (86% of districts) screen preschoolers for vision, hearing, and other problems (SLIIDEA, 2003). These findings indicate that states are giving priority attention to developing outreach and service delivery structures to implement EI services.

Implementing Service Coordination for Early Intervention

Service coordination is a central component in the implementation of Part C (early intervention) under IDEA. Several national studies on early intervention by the Research and Training Center on Service Coordination (RTCSC, 2001) reported great variation in how service coordination is provided in the states. Caseloads for service coordinators ranged from 9 to 70 families and 17 states were in the process of changing their model of service coordination. About 36% of parents surveyed felt that service coordination was very helpful in providing the services and supports their family needed, and 38% believed that service coordination was extremely effective in developing IFSPs that are responsive to their needs. National studies have shown that service coordination needs to be further developed and made available to families as part of early intervention service delivery (RTCSC, 2001).

Study of Factors That Facilitate Collaboration and Service Coordination

Systematic investigation of factors that support or impede collaborative relationships between parents and service coordinators are lacking. The Research and Training Center on Service Coordination (2001) conducted a study of such factors (Dinnebeil, Hale, & Rule, 1999). Two questions were asked of 226 service coordinators and 397 families representing all regions of the United States: (1) Is there anything about the way your early intervention program works that helps collaboration between you and the service coordinator (or parent) with whom you work? (2) Is there anything about the way your early intervention program works that interferes with collaboration between you and the parent (or service coordinator) with whom you work? The results of the survey in five categories included the following:

1. *Program Climate and Philosophy.* The philosophy and principles that guide a program are reflected in its climate. If program personnel truly believe in collaboration and working with families, their behaviors as administrators, individuals, and team members, and the manner in which their programs are organized and operated, will send a message that reflects these basic principles and philosophies. This belief will be translated in the characteristics of the personnel who are hired and in the support and respect that administrators give their staff, all of which affect the individual relationship established with each family.

2. *Service Delivery.* This category addresses the management and delivery of EI services, ranging from staffing and scheduling of programs (i.e., logistics) to the variety of options made available to and developed with families. Families reported that

it was particularly helpful when the service coordinator was also the primary thera-pist; when service coordinators had frequent contact with families; and when coor-dinators were deliberately matched with families based on needs and personalities. Families also identified flexibility in scheduling, service location, and ease of communication with the coordinator as helpful.

3. *Service Delivery Options.* Many responses referred to the ways that EI ser-vices for children and families were delivered and could be accessed by families. Many families appreciated home visits and viewed them as enhancing collaboration (meeting families on their own turf where parents were more relaxed and where it was more comfortable and natural for the children). If home visits were unavailable, then transportation to the centers was helpful.

4. *Team Approach.* Many survey responses referred to the roles and relation-ships of EI team members. Practices that facilitated collaboration included schedul-ing to permit the involvement of all team members; meeting on a weekly basis; open communication among all team members and with parents; including parents in decision making, sharing of resources, and information; keeping all team mem-bers updated on information about the child and needed services; and a balance of both team approaches and one-on-one individual approaches.

5. *Administration and Community Context.* An EI program's ability to provide services in a manner that enhances family/professional collaboration relies on a set-ting that values, rewards, and facilitates collaborative activities. Administrative poli-cies and practices that contribute to collaboration include allowing employees to work on flexible schedules and enabling service coordinators to work on weekends or evenings as needed. Professional development opportunities, ongoing supervi-sion, and mentoring were also considered essential for promoting collaboration, and communicated that collaborative skills were valued by administrators. In addition, administrative trust in the professional capability of the coordinators empowered them. Personnel-related factors that contribute to collaboration included strong com-munication skills, behaviors that reflect a family-centered approach, and friendliness of personnel. Influences of specific agencies and the broader community service sys-tem also impacted the development of collaboration and coordination of EI services, particularly in small communities. Let's See It in Action on page 274 provides an illustration of a countywide system coordination for early intervention services.

Research on Transition to Preschool and Kindergarten

Today's kindergarten is the onset of formal schooling for children—the first time that families, schools, teachers, and communities come together to begin an educa-tional partnership. The transition into kindergarten can be very difficult for a child with disabilities, and complex for the parents. Researchers have demonstrated the importance of collaboration and the formation of a variety of social and information linkages to support children and families during the transition to kindergarten (Pianta & Kraft-Sayre, 2003; RTCSC, 2001).

The Harvard Family Research Project (HFRP) has conducted extensive research on the transition to kindergarten, focusing on promising practices and the role that schools play (Bohan-Baker & Little, 2002). In one study, HFRP interviewed over 200 low-income and ethnically diverse parents whose children were in kindergarten. The parents were mostly mothers from two urban and one rural site in the United

LET'S SEE IT IN ACTION! Case Illustration: Stark County Early Childhood Collaborative Initiative

The Stark County Early Childhood Collaborative Initiative in Stark County, Ohio, focuses on using educational collaboration to engage young children as active learners and to involve parents and families in their children's educational processes. The initiative provides services and programs to children, ages 3–8, including disadvantaged children and children with special needs. The core of the initiative is seven cooperative early childhood education sites, each of which involves community-based services and agencies in planning and delivering programs to young children and families. Two major goals of the Stark County Program are to develop a collaborative planning process for early childhood programs and to develop a primary model that includes transitioning, staff development, parent involvement, technology, appropriate assessment, and the utilization of community linkages. The program sites build upon the neighborhood resources within the community. The Stark County programs include collaboration with 12 school districts, county health department, YMCA, private child care centers, local universities, libraries, Head Start, and the mental health board.

The Stark County initiative is also inclusive of a larger countywide effort that supports parent involvement and family literacy. Stark County schools and Canton City schools, in cooperation with Head Start, are designing organizational structures that support parent volunteers, community services, program and instructional technology, and transitional services to meet individual family needs. The primary building sites will develop wrap-around services that deliver a wide range of community-based services to young children and families. In addition to educational programs, Stark County is a pilot site for the governor's Family and Children First Initiative to develop a county plan that integrates the services of social service agencies and various educational programs. Funding sources for the Stark County initiative include Ohio Department of Education, federal entitlement monies, the Martha Holden Jennings Foundation, East Ohio Gas Company, the Environmental Protection Agency, and local in-kind contributions. The increased use of combined funds allows for quality program expansion and services in the county school systems.

States. About half of the parents participated in the Comprehensive Child Development Program (CCDP), a national early intervention program that offered a menu of family support services such as child care, financial assistance, referrals, a family center, family social activities, and parenting education. The other half did not participate in CCDP. The findings focused on the important role that families play in transition to kindergarten:

- Parents' involvement in school depends in part on how welcomed they feel by the school (Abrams & Gibbs, 2002; Barnard, 2001; U.S. Department of Education, 1997b).
- Early opportunities to visit the school and speak with the teacher may determine how welcomed parents feel (Pianta & Kraft-Sayre, 2003).
- Parents appreciate having someone as a primary contact to help them solve a wide array of problems including transportation, housing, employment, child care, and parenting difficulties.

Sending and receiving teachers (early intervention teachers who send children to kindergarten and kindergarten teachers who receive them) both play important roles in the transition process. Teacher attitudes, instructional priorities, and communication with parents and other members of the transition team determine the quality of the child's transition. Sending and receiving teachers may have different goals and priorities, but they have complementary and collaborative roles in preparing the child for the move from preschool to the general education setting. The sending teacher determines the skills the child will need in order to function adequately in the new setting and implements a program for preparing the child to develop those skills (Bohan-Baker & Little, 2002; Pinkerton, 2004). Sending and receiving teachers will have the continuing role of acting as liaisons between programs and with parents. Good communication and clearly-defined goals will facilitate the preparation for the child's move from preschool to the kindergarten setting (Early, Pianta, Taylor, & Cox, 2001; Jewett, Tertell, King-Taylor, Parker, Tertell, & Orr, 1998).

WHAT SERVICES ARE MANDATED FOR YOUNG CHILDREN WITH DISABILITIES AND THEIR FAMILIES?

Two programs for young children and their families are defined under IDEA of 2004: (1) the Early Intervention Programs for Infants and Toddlers with Disabilities (or Part C, which covers services to children from birth through age two); and (2) the Preschool Program of Part B, which covers services to children ages 3–5. IDEA 2004, however, also included a "Part C option" that permits states to allow families to continue services under Part C after age 3, until the child is eligible to enter kindegarten or elementary school (645(c)(1)). Together these programs represent an important effort to:

1. enhance the development of infants and toddlers with disabilities and to minimize their potential for developmental delay;
2. enhance the capacity of families to meet the special needs of their infants and toddlers with disabilities; and
3. provide financial assistance to increase the ability of state and local agencies to create statewide, comprehensive, coordinated, interagency systems of services for children, birth to age 3 (or older under the Part C option), with disabilities or developmental delays.

As a result of these additions to the legislation, public schools are required to provide special education and related services to young children before they enter first grade. In addition to the IDEA programs, Head Start legislation under No Child left Behind Act, which includes Head Start programs for 3- and 4-year-olds, provides assistance to children and families living below the federal poverty level. These services are aimed at children who are at risk for both significant cognitive delays and poor school readiness.

What Services Must Be Provided?

Early intervention services for children 3 and younger means developmental services are designed to meet the developmental needs of an infant or toddler with a disability in any one or more of the following areas:

- physical development;
- cognitive development;
- communication development;
- social or emotional development;
- adaptive development;
- family training, counseling, and home visits;
- special instruction;
- speech–language pathology and audiology services;
- occupational therapy and physical therapy;
- psychological services;
- service coordination;
- medical services for diagnostic or evaluation purposes;
- early identification, screening, and assessment services;
- health services necessary to enable the infant or toddler to benefit from the other early intervention services;
- social work services;
- vision services;
- assistive technology devices and services; and
- transportation and related costs that are necessary to enable an infant or toddler and the infant's or toddler's family to receive a needed service.

Early intervention services must include a **multidisciplinary assessment** and a written individualized family service plan (IFSP) developed by a multidisciplinary team and the parents. Services provided must be designed to meet the developmental needs of the child and be in accordance with the IFSP. In addition, case management services must be provided for all eligible children and their parents. The personnel who provide services to a family may represent multiple disciplines and agencies, and collaboration among professionals is essential.

Coordination of Services After Age 3

When a child with disabilities nears the age of 3 (or older under the Part C option) he or she must be considered for services beyond early intervention services. These services include special education preschool programs (under Part B of the IDEA), Head Start programs, and public or private preschool programs. At this point, planning for transition services occurs. The purpose of transition services is to ensure that children continue to receive services and support as they move within and between service delivery systems, such as from early intervention to preschool.

Special education preschool programs are available to children with disabilities who are 3 to 5 years old. If a child is eligible for preschool special education services (and is not electing the Part C option), he or she must have an individualized education program (IEP) in place by age 3. All services provided under the IEP must be free to the parents. If a child is not eligible for special education preschool there are other options to consider, such as Head Start, public preschool, or private preschool programs.

The person responsible for ensuring the completion of the transition and service plan is the service coordinator. The service coordinator is required to inform a child's local school district that the child is nearing the age of 3 and must, with the permission of the family, schedule a meeting with the family, other team members, and the local school district representative. The purpose of this meeting, which must be held at least 120 days before the child's third birthday (or later under the Part C option), is to discuss what is needed to determine whether the child is eligible for special education preschool services. A representative of the child's local school district must attend this transition planning conference. Team members review existing evaluations, assessments, and progress reports. If the team determines that it is likely that the child will be eligible for special education preschool services, a multifactored evaluation is completed to determine the areas of documented disability or deficit, and an IEP is then developed.

Interagency Service Coordination Under Part C

Part C early intervention services are operated differently across the United States. In some states Part C services are administered by the health department and in others it is the responsibility of the department of education. Because Part C–eligible families may also be served by other agencies that have service coordination or case management responsibilities, several states have adopted an interagency approach to selecting the person to be designated on the IFSP as the coordinator of Part C services for the family (Danaher, Armijo, & Lazara, 2006; Hurth, 1998; RTCSC, 2001). These agencies may include child health services, mental health services, early intervention providers from various regional agencies, and school personnel. Involving multiple agencies in service coordination provides for local flexibility and family choice.

Use of the Developmental Delay Classification for Children Ages 3–9

Preschool special education is a state and federal mandated program for 3, 4, and 5-year-old children who meet state eligibility criteria for developmental delay. Services are provided through school-based programs and under contracts with Head Start and other local preschool programs. IDEA 1997 expanded the age range to which developmental delay may apply from ages 3–5 to ages 3–9. For children ages 3–9, the phrase "child with a disability" may (at the discretion of the state and the local education agency) include children who are experiencing developmental delays in one or more of the following areas: physical development, cognitive development, communication development, social or emotional development, or adaptive development. Children must meet two criteria in order to receive special education: (1) The child must have one or more of the disabilities listed in IDEA, and (2) he or she must require special education and related services. Not all children who have a disability require special education. Many are able to participate and progress in general education classes without any program modifications or only minor modifications.

States report that using developmental delay to age 9 allows for continuity of services throughout the developmental years without a stigmatizing label associated with a specific disability category (U.S. Government Accountability Office, 2005).

IDEA 1997 and 2004 Strengthened Statewide Provisions to Facilitate Transition into Preschool

Each state is required to develop a statewide system to support transition planning for children and their families and must make sure that children participating in Part C early intervention programs experience a smooth transition into preschool programs (U.S. Government Accountability Office, 2005). The state must develop a state plan with interagency agreements between EI, preschool, and the Head Start program. The state is also required to establish a state interagency coordinating council (SICC) established to advise and assist the state education agency on issues related to the transition from EI to preschool, improving opportunities to children with disabilities, and eliminating barriers to interagency programs. The SICC facilitates the coordination of state resources to ensure that young children with, or at risk for, disabilities and their families receive the early intervention and preschool services and supports that they need. The specific transition requirements include the following:

- The lead agency for young children will notify the local education agency (LEA) that the child is approaching the age of eligibility for preschool services.
- The child's program options will be reviewed for the period from the child's third birthday through the remainder of the school year.
- For children who may be eligible for special education services, the lead agency will convene a transition conference at least 90 days (and up to 6 months) before the child is eligible for preschool services or Head Start.
- The transition conference is to include representatives of the early intervention agency, the early childhood special education agency, and the family. The LEA representative provides information about Part B services and procedures for the referral process.
- The transition conference should result in an *IFSP transition plan*, which includes family involvement, resources, priorities and concerns, agency participation, program options, preparation of the child, child outcomes, and interagency coordination.

The parents and the local education agency are required to participate in transition planning conferences arranged by the designated lead agency. Figure 10.2 provides an illustration of this process in one state.

At the system level, the state is required to create formal interagency agreements that define the financial responsibility of each agency for paying for early intervention services, how disputes will be resolved, and how meaningful cooperation and coordination will be ensured.

Early Childhood Supports Under NCLB

The No Child Left Behind Act has several programs that work in concert with the early intervention requirements under IDEA to promote early development and readiness for formal schooling. Title I services are funded through the U.S.

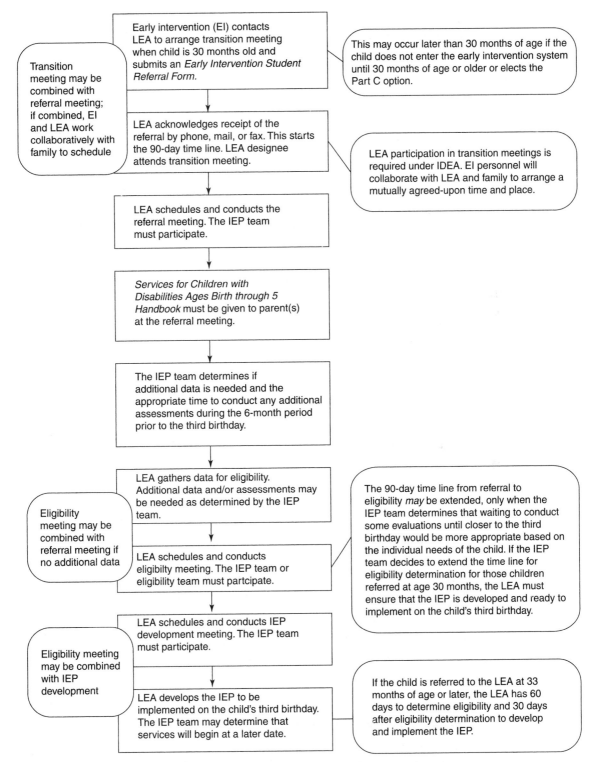

FIGURE 10.2
Early Intervention to K–12 Transition: A State Example.

Department of Education under the Elementary and Secondary Education Act (now NCLB). Title I is the largest federally funded program designed to provide educational services for elementary and secondary students. Many local school districts use a portion of their Title I, Part A funds to provide early childhood services to eligible children.

Head Start has been a pioneer in including special needs children, reaching and serving them before any federal special education mandates existed. Head Start serves children and their families each year in urban and rural areas in all 50 states, the District of Columbia, Puerto Rico, and the U.S. Territories, including many American Indians and migrant children (Fenichel, 2001; Head Start Information and Publication Center, 2001; National Head Start Association, 2002). Head Start and Early Head Start are comprehensive child development programs which serve children ages 0–5, pregnant women, and their families. They are child-focused programs and have the overall goal of increasing the school readiness of young children in low-income families. The Head Start program has a long tradition of delivering comprehensive services designed to foster healthy development in low-income children. Head Start programs provide a range of individualized services in the areas of education and early childhood development; medical, dental, and mental health; nutrition; and parent involvement. The Head Start program is administered by the Head Start Bureau, the Administration on Children, Youth and Families, U.S. Department of Health and Human Services.

Even Start programs are designed to help break the intergenerational cycle of poverty and illiteracy by improving education opportunities for low-income families with limited education. Even Start programs provide an integrated four-component model of family literacy, including early childhood education (for children ages 0–7), adult literacy or basic education, parenting education and support, and interactive literacy activities between parents and their children. Even Start is funded through the U.S. Department of Education under NCLB, Title 1, Part B, Subpart 3 (National Center for Family Literacy, 2004).

Reading First is a component of NCLB that mandates reading proficiency for all children by the third grade. Reading First identifies the five areas of reading instruction that research has shown to be effective in helping children learn to read: (1) phonemic awareness; (2) phonics; (3) vocabulary development; (4) reading fluency, including oral reading skills; and (5) reading comprehension strategies. The *Early Reading First* component is intended to prepare young children to enter kindergarten with the necessary language, cognitive, and early reading skills to prevent reading difficulties and ensure school success. It is hoped that early intervention will reduce the need for special education services in later years (No Child Left Behind Act of 2001).

Preschool Special Education Services is a state and federal-mandated program for 3-, 4-, and 5-year-old children who meet state eligibility criteria for developmental delay. Every school district or special education administrative unit provides special education services to preschool children. The program is funded through a combination of federal funds (under IDEA), state special education funding, and the state's basic school finance formula. Services are provided through school-based programs and under contracts with Head Start and other local preschool programs.

The **_Migrant Education Even Start_** program is a collaborative effort between state departments of education, school districts, and other organizations. The goal of the program is to create comprehensive family literacy services to benefit migrant children and their families for the purpose of breaking the cycle of poverty by increasing literacy and learning. The program supports families with assistance in housing, heath services, early childhood education, employment, transportation, education, and support services to meet their goals on their family action plans.

WHAT ARE THE BARRIERS TO COLLABORATION IN EARLY CHILDHOOD EDUCATION?

Several broad changes have taken place in American society over the last 2 decades that have affected children in their early years. Today 62% of preschool-aged children have working parents and about 70% receive some care outside of their homes before age 3. Only 24% of elementary-aged children who are receiving special education were reported to have disabilities or delays that were identified before age 3. However, fewer than one-third (30%) of these children had participated in early intervention services for infants and toddlers. Among the 65% of children who were younger than age 6 at the time that disability or significant delay was identified, less than half (45%) had received special education services in their preschool years (Kaplan-Sanoff et al., 2000).

Research studies have concluded that, in general, early intervention service systems are fragmented and poorly coordinated resulting in both duplication of efforts and gaps in service delivery (Federal Interagency Forum on Child and Family Statistics, 2003; Shonkoff & Phillips, 2001; U.S. Government Accountability Office, 2005a; U.S. Public Health Service, 2000; Wishman, Kates, & Kaufmann, 2001). Staffing problems also undermine the quality of early childhood programs, with staff turnover ranging from 25%–50% annually. States are finding that they cannot prepare or retain enough qualified individuals, and cannot provide adequate wages or career ladders for them. Implementation challenges and gaps in services are prompting many state and local systems to assess their early intervention services and ask questions such as the following:

1. Is adequate information reaching parents early enough after the birth of a child so that a parent would be aware of and able to look for developmental delays?
2. Are parents informed by hospital personnel, if there are difficulties at the time of birth, about the possible implications of congenital disorders for future development?
3. Are pediatricians and family physicians knowledgeable enough to instruct new parents or to provide resources and referrals if developmental delays are identified in the first year?
4. Are early intervention specialists skilled enough to help young parents to apply EI practices in the home?
5. Is information reaching new parents who may not have the resources to search the Internet for parent information center Web sites?

After friends and family, the pediatrician is the person parents turn to most for guidance on their child's development. Yet, it has been reported that in 60% of all routine well-child visits, the physician ignored parental concerns or provided no developmental or behavioral information or guidance (recall the case example of Pete at the beginning of this chapter) (Kaplan-Sanoff et al., 2000). Similarly, pediatricians frequently spend less than 2 minutes on anticipatory guidance during a visit. Thus pediatric clinicians are missing many opportunities to provide critical information about child development, to interpret child behavior and correct misinterpretations, and to support families as they struggle with the demands of caring for young children and their own feelings of parental competence (Kaplan-Sanoff et al., 2000; Young, Davis, Schoen, & Parker, 1998).

Eligibility and Access Barriers

There is a growing national awareness of the importance of providing early identification and intervention services to children who are at risk for or have delays in social or emotional development. However, access to services may be restricted to children and families based on eligibility criteria, limited funding, diagnostic requirements, and other requirements. Access to high-quality early education programs is elusive for the majority of families, except those with economic means (Helburn et al., 1995; Hofferth, Henke, & West, 1998; National Research Council, 2001; Shonkoff & Phillips, 2001). Program eligibility for more intensive services are restricted to children who are in the most serious need (Center for Evidence-Based Practice [CEBP], 2002a; Infant Mental Health Forum, 2000).

Inadequate Qualifications of Preschool Educators

Training, supervision, and appropriate wages and working conditions are a primary concern in early intervention and early childhood programs. Every state requires a bachelor's degree and teaching certificate for kindergarten teachers although similar standards are not in place for preschool educators. Early childhood educators and clinical staff often lack access to supervision and professional development. High caseloads for preschool educators are a concern, and lower caseloads are correlated with higher-quality services (Barnett, Hustedt, Robin, & Schulman, 2004; National Institute for Early Education Research, 2004).

WHAT COLLABORATION AND SYSTEM COORDINATION STRATEGIES SUPPORT YOUNG CHILDREN IN EARLY CHILDHOOD PROGRAMS?

Elements of **systems of care** that promote young children's social and emotional well-being include comprehensiveness, individualization, family support, collaboration and coordination, eligibility and access procedures, finance policies, and workforce considerations (Smith & Fox, 2003). Individualization refers to the delivery of services and supports in a manner that matches the individual needs of a child and the family. Comprehensiveness refers to the ability of a system to provide a full array of services to meet the individualized needs of children and families. Smith and Fox (2003) proposed several strategies for ensuring individualization and comprehensiveness of services.

First, programs should include prenatal counseling to mothers with an emphasis on parenting, caregiving, and health care. Like health care prevention models, periodic screenings should be conducted to monitor children's growth and development and parent–child interactions. Comprehensive services need to be tailored to the community and settings in which the program operates. Developmentally appropriate practices (DAP) should use content, instruction, and assessment that meets the child's ability to reason, interpret, focus, communicate, and interact both socially and academically. An individualized family service plan (IFSP) is most effective when developed in partnership with the family and addresses family needs. Service coordination to assist families to access services appropriate to individual needs of families is essential.

A Collaborative Process for Creating an Early Childhood Program

The following steps describe a collaborative process for planning and organizing an early childhood program. These steps are synthesized from a variety of research and technical assistance literature:

1. *Create a Task Force.* In the design process, establish a task force that includes teachers, administrators, representatives from agencies that collaborate with programs for children, and representatives from parent education organizations. The task force should help identify best practices in early childhood education and be engaged in decision making about the curriculum, assessment, staff selection, school climate and environment, and parent involvement (North Central Regional Educational Laboratory, 1999). Assess child and family needs for before- and after-school care and for day care during the school holiday periods.

2. *Hire Staff.* Ensure that the teacher–child ratio is appropriate to deliver safe developmentally appropriate instruction and related services. Develop a staff hiring process that is based on quality indicators for staff selection defined by the state and leading national associations concerned with early childhood education (such as the National Association for the Education of Young Children). Typically, teachers and administrators who work with young children should have a background in early childhood education or child development and should have completed supervised training in working with young children. Teachers should have knowledge and skills in (1) theoretical principles of child developmental learning, (2) developmentally appropriate practices, (3) establishing daily schedules for instruction, (4) plans for transition from prekindergarten to kindergarten and primary programs, and (5) parent and family involvement.

Administrators also need knowledge and skills to develop school plans, provide professional development and support to teachers, examine schedules and curriculum to determine if they meet standards for developmentally appropriate practice, establish before- and after-care programs, and provide opportunities for early childhood, kindergarten, and primary grade teachers to discuss transition from one program to another.

3. *Plan the Physical Environment and Curriculum.* The physical environment (including classroom and outdoor setting) should be conducive to the learning styles and special needs of young children in all areas of development. They

should also be accessible for any child with physical or sensory disabilities such as visual impairment. A most important factor in planning for effective early childhood programs is a safe and nurturing environment for all learners. The first step is to evaluate children's learning needs, and if developmental concerns are suspected, perform additional assessments. This information should then be integrated into a developmental curriculum that meets the needs of each child. For children with disabilities, an individualized plan should be developed based on family needs, which may include parenting education, parenting support groups, peer mentors, child care, respite care, home visiting, access to community services, and case management (Bowmen, Donovan, & Burns, 2001; NAEYC, 2003).

4. *Collaboration With Parents.* The influence of the family on the development of the child is particularly powerful throughout the early years. Parents should have opportunities for parent education workshops, classroom participation, and leadership. In some programs, families are assigned family advocates and service coordinators, and are helped to access community services that may be needed for a child with disabilities (evaluations, support services). It is important that families are involved in the planning and evaluation of program services, and serve on policy councils (Administration for Children, Youth and Families, 2001a; Council for Exceptional Children, 2000; Frederick & Smith, 2003; National Head Start Association, 2002; National Research Council, 2001).

5. *Collaboration for Transition to Kindergarten.* Several collaborative strategies have been shown to be effective in supporting children as they make the transition from early childhood programs to kindergarten and elementary school. These include regular meetings between preschool and kindergarten teachers to discuss how to integrate their curricula, encouraging peer relationships that continue from preschool into kindergarten, positive relationships between parents and their children's teachers, and school assessments of the readiness of children in order to gain a better perspective on the strengths and weaknesses of the system of services (Education Week, 2002; Pianta & Kraft-Sayre, 2003; National Association of Early Childhood Specialists, 2002).

The success of transition is ultimately determined by the child's adaptation to the new environment, but also by the receiving teacher's attitude toward and experience with children with disabilities. Teacher attitudes, instructional priorities, collaboration and communication with parents and other members of the transition team determine the quality of the child's transition. The sending teacher needs to gather all available information, both documented and anecdotal, related to the academic and functional skills of the child, present level of performance, and judgments about the anticipated instructional needs of the child in the new setting.

A transition plan with recommendations to the receiving school is essential for designing an appropriate educational plan. The sending teachers should be familiar with the receiving school so they can be knowledgeable about expectations—the skills, levels of performance and behavioral expectations for children, and the responsibilities of families. These expectations include being able to function independently during group instruction, following classroom routines and adapting to change, completing tasks within an allotted time period, and working in the absence of teacher direction. Teaching survival skills as part of the preschool curriculum helps prepare the child for the demands of the general school setting

(Carta, Atwater, Schwartz, & McConnell, 1993; Early, Pianta, Taylor, & Cox, 2001; Pinkerton, 2004).

Strategies for Promoting Adjustment of Students After Transition

The following strategies and ideas, involving collaboration among sending and receiving teachers, and with parents, have been collected from preschool and elementary programs. They are reported as effective in promoting adjustment of students in the passage to the next level (Bohan-Baker & Little, 2002; Early et al., 2001; Education Commission of the States, 2000; Head Start Information and Publication Center, 2001; Jewett, Tertell, King-Taylor, Parker, Tertell, & Orr, 1998; Johnson, 2001; NAEYC, 1997):

1. Play "school" at the end of the preschool year: bring individual desks into the room and arrange them to simulate a first-grade classroom, have children practice raising their hands to speak, introduce them to worksheets, have them line up to go outside, and say the Pledge of Allegiance.

2. Arrange a sending and receiving teacher luncheon so that teachers can get to know each other and participate in a shared staff development activity.

3. Arrange a class field trip to the elementary school. Have the children go to the auditorium where the principal gives a very short welcome. Divide the group into small groups and have third or fourth graders, including students with disabilities, be tour guides to show the children different parts of the school. They could spend short periods of time in the elementary classroom with the teacher, go to the gym for a few minutes, walk through the library, and end up in the cafeteria to have milk and cookies.

4. Arrange kindergarten or elementary parties in which children are invited for one or two hours of activities, ending with lunch in the cafeteria and a meeting with their future teachers.

5. Develop portfolios of children's preschool work to share with the elementary teacher. Include the student's picture, interests, artwork, pictures of favorite things, and other items.

6. Sponsor a parent meeting among families of entering children and those currently in elementary school. Elementary families can share with preschool families information they believe they need to know as their children prepare to go to elementary school.

7. Produce a video that can include pictures of the school, information about screening, parent activities, and other information. In some districts these have been produced by high school media classes.

8. Have a photo album of the new school, including pictures of the front entrance, the school bus (inside and out), the area around the school, and pictures of teachers.

9. Encourage the elementary school teachers to conduct home visits before the start of school. Allow first grade transition days to allow teachers to conduct home visits or parents to make school visits with the children. Or, invite parents to accompany their children the first day or to learn about the school and opportunities for parent participation.

10. Host a summer parent–teacher dinner in which parents are invited to the school to learn about the program and listen to a guest speaker on a topic of interest (e.g., child development, reading, literacy).

11. Once the children make the transition, set up a space for photos of parents and family members that children may "visit" throughout the day. Also include items that reflect the cultural experience of all children to help promote a sense of mutual respect and understanding of diversity. Children need time to adjust to new people and situations. Experience with the new setting can make transition a bit easier, but even with experience, change can still be stressful. Patience and understanding on the part of parents and teachers or caregivers will help children learn how to approach new situations with confidence—a skill that will help them make successful transitions throughout school and in later life.

A Transition Time Line

The Capstone Transition Process (Pinkerton, 2004) is one model that provides clear guidelines for the transition process. The process initiates long-range planning by establishing a time line for children in transition from one level of schooling to another. The time line serves as a guide for accomplishing transition activities and can be set up in chart form to track activities. The Capstone Transition Process addresses specific activities that begin 12 months before the move to a new program. The process includes preparation, implementation, and evaluation activities. The initial steps of the process are designed to prepare the participants for their role in the transition. Steps include notifying and preparing parents and teachers from both the sending and receiving programs. Data on the child's needs are collected or updated. A profile of communication procedures, available services, prerequisite skills, and teacher expectations is developed from existing information. The preparation phase of the process culminates with the development by the transition team of an IEP for use as the basis of educational programming in the new setting. Following the IEP meeting, the time line provides reminders for the transfer of information and records to the receiving program. The final step calls for evaluation of the effectiveness of the process. The school begins with a simple self-assessment for transition, presented in Box 10.1.

Capstone Transition Time Line

1. Develop the transition timeline.
2. Notify appropriate administrators of the student's approaching transition.
3. Inform parent(s) or primary caregiver(s) that the child will be making the transition and collect information on family transition needs.
4. Determine the communication policy of the potential receiving program(s) and obtain a description of the program(s).
5. Obtain information from teacher(s) in potential receiving program(s) regarding the program/classroom overview and skills perceived as important for transition into the classroom.
6. Verify the receipt of transition information or follow-up request for the transition information or additional information.

BOX 10.1   Self Assessment of Transition Supports

Which of the following are provided to support students' transition from preschool to elementary school? Please check all that apply.

- Groups of students visit the school before school starts.
- Personnel from the receiving school come to your preschool to give presentations to students.
- Information is provided to the receiving school about this student (e.g., student performance information, disability awareness).

- Your school staff meet with those from the receiving school specifically about individual students.
- Parents and students are encouraged to meet with staff of the receiving school individually before starting school there.
- Preparatory strategies are developed for individual students who need them (e.g., behavior plans, school scheduling modifications, etc.) (Pinkerton, 2004, by permission).

---

7. Reevaluate: Verify the student's assessment and eligibility.
8. Prepare the parents for the transition planning meeting.
9. Conduct the transition planning meeting.
10. Conduct the IEP meeting, and obtain permission from the parents to release information.
11. Provide information to all transition team participants.
12. Link the parent/primary caregiver of the transitioning child with a parent/primary caregiver of a child already attending the new program.
13. Send the receiving program all pertinent records, and verify the receipt of the records.
14. Provide the receiving program with information about the child's current program.
15. Evaluate the effectiveness of the process after completion.[*]

Improved outcomes for children in early education begin with their successful transition. The process, therefore, cannot be left to chance. Reducing the complexity of the process requires shared solutions and close collaboration among schools, community agencies, and families.

Summary of Key Points

- Early identification and intervention in children's developmental needs are essential to removing barriers to learning.
- Early intervention and early childhood programs are not a specific type of service or setting in which a child can receive services, but rather, is a system of services available to families of infants and toddlers with or at risk for disabilities or developmental delays.

[*]*Source:* From Preparing Children with Disabilities for School, by D. Pinkerton, 1991, Child Development Institute, by Permission.

- As a result of recent amendments to IDEA, public schools are required to provide special education, related services, and service coordination to young children before they enter first grade.
- There is a need to ensure that all children who need services in each state are identified, evaluated, and served thorough a comprehensive, interagency, coordinated system of early intervention services.
- Research has demonstrated that specific early intervention and early childhood education programs cannot operate in isolation from the range of services available to families within a community.
- Services must be flexible and fit the unique and individual needs of the child and family in the context of their culture and community.

Service coordination exists in the context of a relationship between a parent and a service coordinator, and this relationship exists in the context of the early intervention and early childhood program system. It is important that policies and practices of early intervention programs be person centered—that is, that they reflect the needs of families and support the work of early intervention professionals.

Key Terms and Phrases

- Continuum of development (p. 262)
- Early identification (p. 263)
- Developmentally appropriate practices (p. 264)
- Developmental delay (p. 264)
- Part C of IDEA 2004 (p. 265)
- Early intervention services (p. 265)
- Individualized family services plan (p. 266)
- Child find (p. 272)
- Multidisciplinary assessment (p. 276)
- Even Start (p. 280)
- Head Start (p. 280)
- Migrant Education Even Start (p. 281)
- Systems of Care (p. 282)

Questions for Reflection, Thinking, and Skill Building

1. What is developmentally appropriate practice and why is it important? How does it differ from traditional approaches to service delivery?
2. Discuss the difference between Part C and Part B services. Why is transition planning for the move from Part C to Part B services so important?
3. Why is team approach important in early intervention services?

4. Visit a preschool and kindergarten in your community. Interview a preschool teacher and ask them about the transition activities in which they participate before their children move on to kindergarten. In their view, what are the strengths and weaknesses of the process? What recommendations do they have for improving that transition process for special needs children and for all children?

5. In your judgment, based on your visits to the preschool and kindergarten and any available Web site, are there adequate transition supports in place for students? What would you recommend to educators? To policymakers?

CHAPTER ELEVEN

How Can School Collaboration and System Coordination Promote Progress of Children in the Elementary Years?

The pressure to grow up fast, to achieve early is very great in middle-class America. There is no room today for the "late bloomer" . . . Children have to achieve success early or they are regarded as losers. —DAVID ELKIND, *THE HURRIED CHILD* (1988)

The entrance into kindergarten marks children's first interaction with formal schooling, and research shows that success during this first year may predict later school success. —ROBERT C. PIANTA (1999)

School readiness is not a property of a child but is a product of interactions among key settings in which the child participates.
—NATIONAL ASSOCIATION OF EARLY CHILDHOOD SPECIALISTS, 2002

- How do collaboration and system coordination change as the child advances from kindergarten to elementary school?
- What are the barriers to collaboration in the elementary school?
- What collaboration and system coordination strategies support students in the elementary school?
- What professional roles support students in the elementary school?
- What collaboration and system coordination strategies facilitate transition to middle school?

PERSPECTIVES

Elementary Teacher

During my teacher preparation program, I was able to work in an inclusive elementary school. This experience was extremely powerful because I saw proof that students with disabilities and their teachers could all work together successfully to provide equal access for all. I also saw social growth in the students in general education who learned to be compassionate and accept all their peers regardless of their differences.

Parent

Monica has used a wheelchair since she suffered a spinal cord injury. She has always been in the general education class because she remains among the top of her class, and fifth grade is no different for her. However, had the schools not made some structural changes so that Monica could get into the library, the computer lab, the multimedia room, and the cafeteria (which had stairs descending to a half level), I think school would not have been such an inviting place for her. We have been delighted with the inclusive feel of the school and the opportunities for Monica. When I expressed my appreciation one day to the principal, she looked at me quizzically and said, "But . . . isn't that what we are here for?"

INTRODUCTION

The transition from preschool and kindergarten to elementary school can be an exciting time, or it can be daunting for a child and his parents. Recent research indicates that over half of children with special needs demonstrate moderate to serious difficulties with transition to elementary school (Kraft-Sayre & Pianta, 2001). Many are naturally adjusting from part-time schedules to full-time schooling. Close collaboration among professionals and families is essential throughout the elementary years because of the complexity of the changes that the special needs child and the family face. The "3-Cs," depicted in Figure 11.1, apply to several key stakeholders in the

FIGURE 11.1
The 4-Cs: Communication,
Collaboration, Coordination,
and Commitment

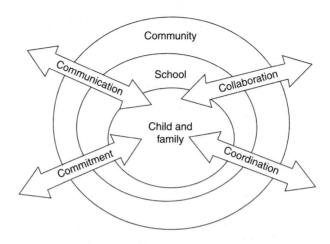

child's ***circle of commitment*** (the 4th "C")—family, school, community, and include parents, siblings, teachers, related services professionals, pediatricians, advocates, and parent resource specialists.

Many stakeholders are involved in a child's circle of commitment as he or she enters formal schooling. Family members, of course, are the primary stakeholders who need to participate actively in the decision making about placement and IEP goals. They are the most knowledgeable about their child's learning needs and behaviors. Siblings can also provide support through teaching, modeling, understanding, and appreciating the child with a disability. Effective educators reach out to family members, viewing them as the primary source of valuable, and often crucial, information about the needs, functioning, and strengths of the child in the home and community. Physicians can be pivotal in the assessment of the child's development and health, and can provide valuable instruction to the parents as well as resources and referrals for additional support. Advocates and parent resource specialists can provide information to families as early as possible in the child's life, and particularly at the crucial transitions in their schooling.

This chapter describes the supports that children need as they make the journey through elementary and prepare for middle school. The implications for collaboration and coordination during these years are explored. Barriers and facilitators to collaboration are examined along with coordination roles that help support elementary school children with disabilities.

HOW DO COLLABORATION AND SYSTEM COORDINATION CHANGE AS THE CHILD ADVANCES FROM KINDERGARTEN TO ELEMENTARY SCHOOL?

Transition Into Elementary School: A Crucial Step

Many parents and teachers take for granted the process of transition from one stage of learning to another. All children are expected to experience some anxiety as their school environment and school schedules change. The entry into preschool from family life can be exciting or traumatic for children, with or without disabilities. Some children who adjusted well to kindergarten may have a different reaction when they transition into a larger, more structured elementary school. No two children are alike—each child will react to the experience in a unique way. Figure 11.2 depicts the key transitions from early intervention to K–12 schooling.

Some children—both with and without disabilities—experience significant anxiety and adjustment reactions upon entry into their elementary schools. These signs of anxiety may include crying, refusing to get out of bed, refusing breakfast, refusing to get on the bus, talking about being afraid, asking to stay home, complaining of feeling sick, or having stomachaches. For these children, the transition proves to be too great, and they are not developmentally ready to make it—unless they receive additional support from the family and the school.

The transition from preschool to elementary school can also be very complex for the parents of a child with a disability. The parents may be uncertain about whether the services their child received in preschool or kindergarten will be continued in elementary school. Collaboration and coordination is extremely important for this transition, for both child and parents. As mentioned earlier, for special needs children, parents and teachers from the sending kindergarten and the receiving elementary school need to be involved in placement, scheduling, and facilitation of the transition. Let's See It in Action on page 294 provides an example of the important role of coordination and support for children who experience adjustment difficulties in the first grade.

There are many causes of anxiety and reluctance to enter elementary school, and there are many degrees of **school readiness** among children. Having a disability, whether it is an obvious physical disability or a less obvious learning or emotional disability, is often a source of anxiety for the child and the family. They may need more time and support than their peers without disabilities to adjust to a new setting.

FIGURE 11.2
Key Transitions in the
Early Years

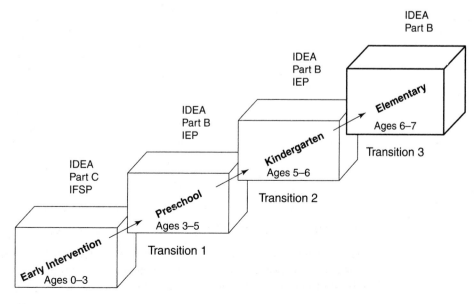

LET'S SEE IT IN ACTION! CASE ILLUSTRATION: THE "LUNCH BUNCH" TO THE RESCUE

Alan was born with learning disabilities and an attention and hyperactivity disorder, and at age 5 scored in the superior range on intelligence tests. He never had trouble in preschool. He cooperated well and loved to be outside and playing with others. We thought that his transition to elementary school would be very easy for him. However, on the first day of first grade, he got dressed, picked at his breakfast, and we sat on the front step to wait for the bus. When it arrived, Alan, with tears in his eyes, was slowly led to the door of the bus. With the assistance of a sympathetic bus driver, Alan was helped to his seat. He put his hand on the window and cried as they drove away. I, too, shed a tear. When he came home, he bounced off the bus and appeared very happy to be home. I believed that we were over the hump, until I found his lunch in his backpack. He hadn't eaten all day. I called the school to see how things had gone during the day.

The next morning, Alan refused to get dressed, refused to eat breakfast, and said that he was scared of school. He was afraid of everyone in the cafeteria and all the noise. The only way I could get him to go was to drive him and walk him into the school. Upon arrival, Mrs. Gooding, the school counselor, met us and walked Alan to his class and returned to speak with me. "Alan is having a little trouble adjusting," she said, "so what I'd like to do is offer some extra support to get him through the first week or two. I have several other students who can also use the support, so I'm going to hold a small group 'lunch bunch' in my conference room during the lunch hour. They will meet with me there daily for a 'special time' away from the big cafeteria, and we can all talk about things until they get more comfortable. I will also keep tabs with the teacher and see how Alan is doing." I felt so relieved and so thankful to have this counselor. She made all the difference in the world for me and for Alan. By the second week, Alan's anxiety about school seemed to have disappeared. The "lunch bunch" was gradually shifted as a group into the cafeteria as Mrs. Gooding phased herself out.

Families and schools have a responsibility to prevent the child from falling behind early in their education. The "lunch bunch" was a brief but effective intervention for a group of students—with and without disabilities—who needed a little extra support and attention in the first few weeks in first grade. Without early support, emotional and academic, the readiness gap that separates children in the kindergarten and elementary years often increases in later years.

New Role for Families at the Elementary Level

Parents serve a variety of new collaboration and coordination roles as their child enters elementary school—as teachers, decision makers, partners, service coordinators, and advocates. They are teacher-collaborators when they reinforce at home the skills acquired in preschool, school partners when they communicate needs with school personnel, and decision makers when they participate in the IEP or evaluation process. They must communicate and collaborate closely with their child's teacher to understand the academic requirements in the elementary school, requirements for homework assignments and projects, and new responsibilities students have for delivering home–school messages and communications. In the elementary school, many parents are committed to participate in the life of the school in order to be closely engaged in and supportive of their children's learning.

Parents are service coordinators, decision makers, and advocates when they participate in the IEP process and help to ensure that their child with special needs receives the support services he or she needs. They take the initiative to understand the laws that have been passed to help them to access and coordinate the supports and service they need. They are informed about the difference between early intervention services and (Part C of IDEA) and early childhood services (Part B of IDEA). Parents provide a vital bridge between preschool programs and elementary school, visiting the new program with their child, helping the child to become familiar with the new setting, and discussing concerns and fears connected with the upcoming change. They can also help bridge the gap by arranging visits with former preschool friends and teachers as well as with new classmates (Pinkerton, 2004). Family members play a pivotal role in providing information about the child's abilities, strengths and weaknesses, and interests and talents. Parental insights complement information obtained from preschool sources and provide a broader picture of the child's capabilities and needs (Pianta & Kraft-Sayre, 2003; Pinkerton, 2004; Wandry & Pleet, 2002).

Let's See It in Action, below, describes a new coordination model that is focused on a child's strengths and a family-centered philosophy and has resulted in great progress in the life of a child with multiple needs.

LET'S SEE IT IN ACTION! CASE ILLUSTRATION: THE INDIVIDUALIZED INTERAGENCY PLAN: WELL WORTH THE EFFORT!

My name is Carolyn, and I live in Minnesota with my husband, Bob, and our seven children. Bob and I have been married for 23 years. In 1990, we became foster parents for Clay County. As a stay-at-home mom for most of those years, we became blessed with four birth children, one adopted daughter, and two permanent foster children. In 1994, our then foster child, Sara, was showing signs of developmental delays, and so began our journey into the world of special services.

At the age of six, when we adopted Sara, she had two diagnoses: attention deficit hyperactivity disorder (ADHD) and fetal alcohol syndrome (FAS). Since then, Sara has also been diagnosed with reactive attachment disorder (RAD) and bipolar disorder. At first we worked with a special education team to develop an IEP that included occupational therapy, adaptive physical education, special education, a support paraprofessional in the classroom, and a pediatrician to coordinate Sara's medications. This process worked well.

As Sara moved into the K–12 education system, the need for home, community, and educational supports increased. I became involved with our local interagency early intervention committee (IEIC) at this time. This committee addresses the needs of children ages 0–7. Our two permanent foster children also have FAS and other complications from premature birth. They required intensive services from birth on and were provided an individual family service plan (IFSP). One of the first things I heard about at the committee meetings was our state's individualized interagency intervention plan (IIIP). Because the IIIP was modeled after the IFSP and was to be phased in by age groups, the interagency early intervention (EI) committee was the first to discuss this document and its implementation. The committee was asked to form a IIIP training team with a parent component to help implement the IIIP process into the local county and school district. The more I learned about the IIIP, I knew this was exactly what Sara needed.

By the time Sara was in third grade, the complications resulting from her psychiatric and subsequent learning disabilities were overwhelming our family. The county stepped in to provide case management services and psychiatric medication monitoring services (for children with mental health diagnoses). The next year we added developmental services through the county, a behavioral specialist, and in-home support. As Sara's mom, it became my full-time job to coordinate communication between agencies, educate staff regarding Sara's mental health issues, and coordinate five different individual care plans under different service agencies. During every meeting or phone call, I was bombarded with comments regarding Sara's manipulative behaviors. She had raging and manic episodes that interfered with her day and with staff's ability to teach her. She was able to "work the system," accepting no accountability for her, behaviors. Sara's strengths were never discussed.

Weekly meetings at school became routine along with many phone calls in between. When Sara began showing signs of another manic episode, it was my job to notify all the professionals with whom we were working, gather input needed for a medication change, and monitor Sara for 24 hours a day to ensure her safety. My husband and I were the only ones who had a complete, comprehensive understanding of Sara's needs. Just getting through the week was exhausting, leaving us with very little time or energy to focus on the needs of our other children.

Our county had recently implemented a "wraparound process," a coordinated team effort to address the needs of high maintenance children. While the team helped with general communication, I continued to coordinate the majority of her services and supports. Our school district was slowly moving forward with the IIIP process, but it would be another year before this new system would be available for Sara's age group.

I approached Sara's special education staff and requested that they consider the IIIP for Sara. It was decided that it was in Sara's best interest to coordinate her care and start addressing her needs using a comprehensive, **strengths-based approach**. So, Bob and I and 15 professionals sat down to write an IIIP for Sara, completing the process in fewer than 2 hours. After years of hearing what Sara couldn't do, we finally had a document that not only addressed her needs and concerns, but also acknowledged her many strengths! Sara was able to learn very quickly, through manipulatives because she was a tactile and kinesthetic learner. She was also very interested in music and art, particularly sculpture. She also excelled in gymnastics. We remain forever grateful for the effort of the team that day.

Sara's progress during that first year on her IIIP was remarkable. We used Sara's strengths to provide her with more accountability for her learning. Her teachers agreed to use her interest in art and sculpture to design class projects. She was also permitted to join the gymnastics team. Most importantly, we were able to develop a behavior plan that encompassed all areas of Sara's life and was consistent in school and home environments. One of Sara's greatest achievements this past year was participating in the regular education classroom for up to 3 hours a day without behavioral supports. Coordinating Sara's care through the IIIP has meant far fewer meetings (reduced to two or three times a year), fewer phone calls, and the development of a cooperative working relationship among staff whose focus is on ensuring that Sara reach her full potential in all environments. Most importantly, I can now be a mom again to Sara and our other children (Minnesota System of Interagency Coordination, 2003, by permission).

Questions for Discussion

As you reflect on the case illustration above, consider the following questions:

- Who had the most complete understanding of Sara's needs?
- Who were the primary case managers?
- How did the focus on strengths make a difference for Sara?

The case illustration shows that the coordination process was shifted to create a shared responsibility within the system for children with disabilities and their families. The new IIIP service model simplified the way in which services were provided. It built a unified, coordinated service system that served Sara's multiple needs and reduced the crushing burden on the family to coordinate services from multiple agencies.

The most important shift was philosophical—moving toward a strengths-based, family and person-centered approach to services. This meant that for Sara, there was a deliberate shift in focus from her disabilities (problem-focused) to a focus on her strengths, assets, and abilities. It represents a move away from traditional service delivery approaches to a more family-centered model of care. While the traditional approaches focus on deficits (what's wrong with the child so we can "fix" it), the new focus asks: What is working well and what strengths and capacities can be drawn upon to help Sara manage her own difficulties? As a result, the IIIP reflected the full range of Sara's assets & strengths.

What Are the Barriers to Collaboration in the Elementary School?

Despite 2 decades of research about the importance of structured transition planning and support in elementary school, this process is still left largely to chance. The assumption that all children are expected to make the changes "naturally" as a normal part of childhood contributes to professional "blind spots." Since movement from one level of schooling to another is viewed as natural or automatic, then specific interventions to ease the transition are not always considered necessary.

Roadblocks to Smooth and Seamless Transition Into First Grade

While researchers and policy highlight the importance of effective professional collaboration to support transition into elementary school, the most common practices do not match the needs of children and families. One study of 3,600 teachers reported that 52% of children have a successful entry into kindergarten, whereas 48% have moderate or serious problems (Kraft-Sayre & Pianta, 2001; Pianta, 1999). One of the primary barriers to progress in the elementary years are children's skills at entry. Table 11.1 presents teachers' reports of elementary students who enter with specific needs.

Of 11 practices examined by Pianta and others, over 50% of teachers reported that they had not used half of the practices. Over half of teachers (57%) reported having had regular meetings with first-grade teachers to discuss continuity of the curriculum between kindergarten and first grade. Just over half of these teachers (56%) reported arranging for their class to visit a first-grade class. Less than 25% of teachers reported attending transition meetings, sending parents information on how placements are made, attending meetings to plan transitions for individual children, or planning activities for children with special needs (Early, Pianta, Taylor, & Cox, 2001; Kraft-Sayre & Pianta, 2001; 2000; Pianta & Kraft-Sayre, 1999). Also, teachers are more likely to talk to other teachers about transition than they are to parents, revealing a lack of communication and coordination between school and home.

TABLE 11.1	Teachers' Report of Needs of Students Entering Elementary School
Following directions	46% (of teachers)
Academic skills	36%
Home environment	35%
Working independently	34%
Formal preschool experience	31%
Working in a group	30%
Immaturity	20%
Communicating	14%

Source: From "Transition Practices: Findings from a National Survey of Kindergarten Teachers," by D. M. Early, R. C. Pianta, L. C. Taylor, and M. V. Cox, 2001. *Early Childhood Education Journal, 28*, p. 201. Reprinted by permission.

The implications of the findings are that children have little facilitated contact with their first-grade teachers. Contact is even less frequent in schools with a high minority representation and in schools in high poverty areas. Kindergarten-to-first-grade transition practices are essential to promote children's adjustment and success in first grade (Early, Pianta, Taylor, & Cox, 2001).

The most common coordination practice for transition is talking with parents in the weeks after school begins and arrangement of open houses early on. Teachers in schools with the highest concentrations of poverty rely more heavily on activities that occur after the school year begins than do teachers in other settings. Some of the problems that teachers have identified with the transition process and during the school year include the following:

a. They do not get student class lists until a week or two before school begins.

b. They lack adequate time before school begins in the fall to arrange meetings and establish relationships with families that can provide for continuity between kindergarten and elementary school.

c. Teachers don't get paid in the summer, so transition planning activities remain voluntary.

d. There is a need to develop school policies to define the transition plan and what is expected of teachers.

e. One-quarter of kindergartners either leave or enter during an academic year, creating constant change in the environment.

f. Less than a quarter of teachers receive either specific training or information about ways to enhance transitions for children and families (Abrams & Gibbs, 2000; Blackorby & Wagner, 2002; Kraft-Sayre & Pianta, 2001; La Paro & Pianta, 2000; Pianta et al, 2001; Pianta & Cox, 1999).

Whereas the studies discussed above center on schools and classrooms, the practice of transition to elementary school encompasses a much broader context, including

---

BOX 11.1   Turned Away

Perhaps no high-ranking education official better exemplifies the changing face of special education—or is a more fervent advocate for including students with disabilities in regular classrooms—than Judy Heumann, who has used a wheelchair since contracting polio as an infant. Her firsthand experiences began in the 1950s when her parents tried to enroll her in kindergarten at the public elementary school in her middle-class Brooklyn neighborhood. Because of her wheelchair, she was turned away. The district sent a teacher to her home for a few hours each week. "If you were lucky, you were getting a little home instruction," Heumann, now in her 50s, recalls of the climate in the New York City schools at the time.

Fourth grade was the first time she saw the inside of a classroom, after her parents navigated a tough admissions screening for a special class for students with cerebral palsy. The class was in the basement of the local elementary school, completely separate from the classes for other youngsters. At the time, no student in the special class had ever entered high school. Heumann, however, went on to attend a public high school and later graduated from Long Island State University with a bachelor's degree and earned a master's degree from the University of California, Berkeley. She also went on to found the World Institute on Disability, which she says was the first research institution devoted entirely to disability issues. In 1993, she joined the U.S. Department of Education as the Assistant Secretary for Special Education and Rehabilitative services (Sack, 1999).

---

the roles of parents and siblings, school leaders, pediatricians, parent resource personnel, and policymakers. Box 11.1 presents the remarkable story of a well-known educator with a disability who faced extraordinary challenges as her parents tried to enroll her in kindergarten at the public elementary school.

WHAT COLLABORATION AND SYSTEM COORDINATION STRATEGIES SUPPORT STUDENTS IN THE ELEMENTARY SCHOOL?

New Expectations at the Elementary Level

First grade is the beginning of "big school" as many children and families refer to it. Six- or seven-year-olds have reached the age when they can sit still for longer periods of time, exhibit reasonable self control, and are learning to read and write. They are also expected to respond appropriately to teachers and peers in the class, organize materials and books, and be responsible for their behavior. They are beginning to gain a new sense of independence and self-confidence as they go to school on the bus alone, eat lunch with classmates in the cafeteria, take home their report cards, and participate in school choruses and plays. They also begin to participate in sports, clubs, and field trips.

In comparison to preschool, elementary school is a more structured and challenging academic environment for all children, including for those with disabilities. Children with disabilities in the general education classroom are held to the same expectations for performance as their peers. They are expected to join in activities and field trips with their peers.

Collaboration for Instructional Teaming and Support

Introduced in Chapter 10, **developmentally appropriate practice** is based on knowledge about how children develop and learn (National Association for the Education of

Children with disabilities interact with other elementary students on a field trip to the fire station.

Laima Druskis/PH College

Young Children [NAEYC], 1996). The inclusion of special needs students in the general elementary classroom demands educational planning and **instructional teaming**. For example, addressing the teaching and learning needs of an elementary student with learning disabilities and a speech disorder may require the combined expertise of the general education teacher, special education teacher, speech and language therapist, school counselor, and assessment specialist. Figure 11.3 depicts the variety of professionals who might be involved in an instructional teaming relationship.

Instructional teaming often relies on collaboration with other staff members such paraprofessionals, teaching assistants, and volunteers. Another important, and often "unsung," member of the instructional team is the school librarian or technology resource room specialist. Library services and technology services are now expected to be integrated into instruction and student learning, and, therefore, these roles are crucial to collaborative teaming. Adequate support from these staff members can help achieve appropriate student–teacher ratios (2 to 25 for elementary age children without disabilities, as recommended by the NAEYC, 1997). Additional staff and smaller group sizes may be necessary when children with disabilities are part of the class.

Collaboration for Universal Design and the Inclusive Curriculum

Classrooms that successfully include special needs students are designed to welcome diversity and to address the individual needs of all students, whether they have disabilities or not. Such a curriculum emphasizes the strengths, but accommodates the

FIGURE 11.3

Instructional Teaming

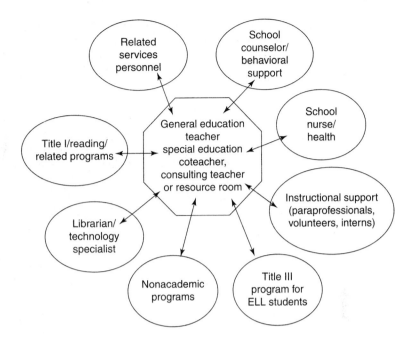

needs of all children—including children with disabilities or developmental delays, children at risk for falling behind, and children for whom English is not their primary language.

As a new paradigm for teaching, learning, assessment, and curriculum development, **universal design for learning** (UDL) means creating structures that accommodate the widest spectrum of students (users) possible. Universally designed teaching materials or curricula address the diverse needs of special populations, and usability for everyone increases. UDL shifts old assumptions about teaching and learning in four fundamental ways:

1. Students with disabilities fall along a continuum of learner differences and do not constitute a separate category.
2. Teacher adjustments for learner differences should occur for all students, not just those with disabilities.
3. Curriculum materials should be varied and diverse including digital and online resources, rather than centering on a single textbook.
4. Instead of remediating students so that they can learn from a set curriculum, curricula should be made flexible to accommodate learner differences (Center for Applied Special Technology, 2004).

The central premise of UDL is not that instruction should be individualized but that a curriculum should include alternatives to make it accessible and appropriate for individuals with different backgrounds, learning styles, abilities, and disabilities in widely varied learning contexts. The "universal" in universal design reflects a recognition that each learner is unique and learns differently. Let's See It in Action on p. 302 illustrates the power and potential of collaborative teaming for universal design in the general education classroom.

LET'S SEE IT IN ACTION: CASE ILLUSTRATION: COLLABORATION FOR INSTRUCTIONAL TEAMING AND UNIVERSAL DESIGN

Mary Jo Callahan teaches fourth grade at Green Spring Elementary School. Three days a week, she coteaches the class with James Ralston, a special education teacher. Their 20 students include four who have special educational needs, two students for whom English is not the primary language, and two others who currently need special help in the areas of math and English. The students with disabilities have IEPs that were developed by a team that included both teachers. The teachers, paraprofessionals, parents, and the school principal believe that these students have a great deal to contribute to the class and that they will achieve their best in the environment of a general education classroom.

All of the school personnel have attended inservice training designed to develop collaborative skills for teaming and problem solving in the general education classroom. Mary Jo Callahan and the two paraprofessionals who work in the classroom also received special training on disabilities and on how to create an **inclusive classroom environment**. The school principal, Alan Browning, had coordinated special education in an elementary school many years ago and has received additional training on the implications of new special education developments and on universal design. Each year, Mr. Browning identifies training that is needed for building personnel and has arranged for ongoing technical assistance through the regional special education cooperative center and the Parent Training Institute.

Ms. Callahan and Mr. Ralston share responsibility for teaching and for supervising their two paraprofessionals assigned to the class. In addition to the time they spend together in the classroom, they spend 1–4 hours per week planning instruction, and additional planning time with other teachers and support personnel who work with their students. These support personnel include the physical therapist, speech therapist, school counselor, and nurse. The teachers use their joint planning time to problem solve and to discuss the use of special instructional techniques and how they can be used with all of the students who need special assistance. Monitoring and adapting instruction for individual students is a continuing activity.

The teachers use curriculum-based measurement to systematically assess their students' learning progress based on what the curriculum requires. They adapt curricula so that lessons build upon existing student knowledge, adding new material at the student's pace, and presenting it in a manner that is consistent with the student's learning style. For some students, advanced organizers or chapter previews are used to bring out the most important points of the material to be learned. For other students, new vocabulary words are highlighted, or reduced reading levels are used. Some students may use supplemental activity worksheets, while others may learn best by using media or computer-assisted instruction.

In the classroom, the teachers group students differently for different activities. Sometimes, the teachers and paraprofessionals divide the class, each teaching a small group or tutoring individuals. They use cooperative learning projects to help the students learn to work together, develop social relationships, and reinforce use of language. Peer tutors provide extra help to students who need it. Students without disabilities have become much more than willing to help their friends who have disabilities because they have come to know them better and realize that these students are much like them, but with differences in learning. They realize that their strengths can be combined to complement and support one another. Also, the collaborative relationship among the professional staff models teamwork for students and attests to the power of combining strengths.

Models for Supporting Children With Disabilities in Elementary Grades

There are several comprehensive models for supporting children with disabilities in the elementary years which emphasize collaboration and coordination and a shared responsibility among parents, schools, and the community. These models reflect research on effective practices, including developmentally appropriate practice, child-centered planning, instructional teaming, inclusive curriculum, and a collaborative environment. A few examples are highlighted below.

A Caring Community of Learners: Creating a Protective Shield. Caring communities are defined as places where teachers and students care about and support each other, actively participate in and contribute to important decisions, feel a sense of belonging and identification, and have a shared sense of purpose and common values (Lewis, Schaps, & Watson, 1996). The caring community concept differs sharply from the "factory model" school that emphasizes competition among students and hierarchical authority, and still exerts a strong influence on our educational system. Schools organized as caring communities foster a shared sense of responsibility for teaching and learning. In comparison with traditional schools, they are characterized by student self-direction and a strong motivation to learn, experimentation, reduced absenteeism, greater social competence, respect for individual differences, and higher educational expectations and academic performance of students (Clark & Astuto, 1994; Lewis et al., 1995).

A central goal of such a **community of learners** is to create a positive school climate by carefully attending to interactions and relationships between teachers and children and among children. Along with families, all members of the school community contribute to the care and education of young children. Caring community schools recognize that emotional competence is learned through interactions with peers and adults (Villa & Thousand, 1999). School personnel emphasize the crucial role they play as models of attitudes and behaviors. Children are also helped to reflect on their own feelings and are required to increase their awareness of others' feelings.

WHAT PROFESSIONAL ROLES SUPPORT STUDENTS IN THE ELEMENTARY SCHOOL?

Many professional roles collaborate to provide services for children and their families throughout the elementary years. These roles are introduced at length in this chapter and are similar at the middle and high school settings. In the latter chapters, only differences that are relevant for older children and adolescents will be highlighted.

These roles are integral to instructional teaming and for creating a caring community for all learners. The first point of coordination is the **school evaluation team** which typically is made up of educational resource center staff, school psychologist, speech and language specialist, general education teachers, administrators, and parents. The evaluation team meets to determine the course of action to be taken with students who have been referred for possible assessment for special education. The team makes recommendations about needed assessments and special services or placements, and can serve as a resource to staff and families.

The second point of coordination is the *IEP team* which involves special and general education teachers, parents, administrator, counselors, related services personnel, and others who are appropriate for educational planning. These professionals work initially to develop an appropriate educational plan and revisit the IEP when revisions are needed.

Essential Role of Administrators in Creating Collaborative Environments for Learning

Collaborative teaming for inclusive learning environments requires the unconditional support and strong leadership of school administrators. Administrative commitment is essential to support elementary teachers who are implementing developmentally appropriate practices and inclusive curriculum based on universal design principles. School leadership is also essential in supporting and inviting parents and families to engage in school activities and decision making.

School administrators are also responsible for strategic use of professional development to promote collaboration and school–community coordination. Collaborative teaching in inclusive settings requires ongoing professional development to develop and update both teaching and collaborative skills and to stay connected with current research.

The Nonadministrative Roles

General Educator. Elementary school teachers play a vital role in the development of all children. What children learn and experience during their early years can shape their views of themselves and the world and can affect their later success or failure in school, work, and their personal lives. Most elementary school teachers instruct one class of children in several subjects. In some schools, two or more teachers collaborate as a team and are jointly responsible for a group of students in at least one subject. In other schools, a teacher may teach one special subject—usually music, art, reading, science, arithmetic, or physical education—to a number of classes. A small but growing number of teachers instruct multilevel classrooms with students at several different learning levels (U.S. Department of Labor, 2004a).

The general education teacher collaborates with the special education teacher to (1) design differentiated instruction, (2) ensure that individualized educational priorities specific to the student get integrated into the daily curriculum, and (3) make sure that input from specialists is obtained to help with accessing educational technology, modifying and adapting curriculum, and supporting students' social development.

Special Educator. Typically, for each student with a disability who is assigned to a general education class, there is also a collaborating special education teacher. The special education teacher determines, with the team, the amount and types of support and adaptations required in each subject area in the general education class. The special education teacher also monitors the development, implementation, and evaluation of the IEP. Though development of adaptations is primarily the responsibility of the special education teacher, the general and special education teachers and related services specialists all collaborate in their development. Responsibilities of the special educator usually fall into three categories:

- instructional preparation and direct teaching,
- preparing appropriate reports and other paperwork, and

- collaborating with general elementary teachers, related services professionals and parents.

Special education teachers never work completely alone, since they are always part of a team. Some elementary schools have established teams to help plan appropriate adaptations and educational interventions for students who are having difficulty in general education classes (Schwartz, Shanley, Gerver, & O'Cummings, 2003). Not only do they teach their students when they are in the classroom, but they also follow up with them throughout the day wherever they may be (National Information Center for Children and Youth with Disabilities, 1997). Special education teachers who work in inclusive settings or who coteach with elementary general education teachers must spend enough time to adequately plan, develop, and implement an educational environment that is challenging and appropriate for all the students in the class, those with disabilities and those without.

School Psychologist. School psychologists are professionals, specializing in both mental health and education, who provide services that help students succeed academically, emotionally, and socially. They are trained to identify and address a wide range of student barriers to school and community success, including learning disabilities, cognitive deficits, behavioral difficulties, and emotional stressors. Students often experience mental health and health-related problems that can limit their ability to learn, participate in activities, socialize, concentrate, or even attend school. Through collaboration with other mental health providers as well as medical professionals, school psychologists help youngsters develop resilience, competence, self-control, and self-esteem, and can facilitate integration of services between home and school. School psychologists are often the only school-based mental health professionals trained in child psychology, learning, and development, as well as school systems and classroom environments.

School psychologists address a variety of health-related problems that affect elementary student achievement, behavior and/or mental health status, including chronic child illness (e.g., diabetes, asthma, severe allergies, cancer), obesity and eating disorders, violence and aggression, attention deficit/hyperactivity disorder (ADD/ADHD), suicidal thoughts and risk, vision and hearing impairments, and mental health disorders.

School psychologists serve general education students through consultation, direct intervention, and referral. Schools are mandated to address health issues as part of special education disability determination under IDEA. School psychologists play essential roles in assisting IEP teams to identify and provide needed services for students with health-related disabilities. In addition to coordination of services through collaboration with parents and school and community healthcare providers, school psychologists support children with health-related problems through (a) consultation to assure consistency between home, school, and community providers; (b) observations and performance feedback to physicians monitoring the effects of medications and therapies on student's school performance; (c) assessments to help determine student strengths and weaknesses as part of determining eligibility for special education and/or need for accommodations or modifications of instructional program; (d) diagnostic assessments that assist parents, physicians, and psychiatrists to address conditions such as ADHD and depression appropriately; (e) risk assessments regarding potential for suicide and violence; (f) specific student skills training (e.g., social skills, organization skills, study skills); (g) individual or group counseling around relevant issues (e.g., chronic illness, sibling or parent illness, substance abuse prevention, etc.); and (h) in-service and parent education programs regarding mental health and learning issues related to medical conditions (e.g., attention deficit disorder, eating disorders dealing with a terminally ill parent).

Elementary School Counselor.   Elementary school counselors set the tone for developing knowledge, attitudes, and skills necessary for children to become competent and confident learners. By providing education, prevention, early identification, and intervention, school counselors help children achieve academic success. Counselors are professional educators with a mental health perspective who understand and respond to the challenges that students face in their lives, their communities, and families. Elementary school counselors don't work in isolation, but rather are integral to the total educational program. They are pivotal collaborators for engaging all stakeholders in the delivery of programs and services to help students achieve in school (American School Counselor Association, 2004a).

Elementary school counselors design individual student academic programs; interpret cognitive, aptitude, and achievement tests; counsel students with excessive absenteeism and disciplinary problems; collaborate with teachers to present information about mental health and social skills development; interpret student records; provide teachers with suggestions for classroom management or hall management; maintain student records in accordance with state and federal regulations; and assisting the school principal to identify and resolve student issues (American School Counselor Association, 2004; Schmidt, 2004).

Counselors are impeded in carrying out their responsibilities when their role is poorly understood by school personnel and teachers. Counselors are often taken away from essential counseling tasks to perform noncounseling activities such as registering students, administering achievement tests or standardized tests, signing excuses for tardy students, teaching classes when teachers are absent, supervising study halls, or clerical record keeping. Through a comprehensive developmental school counseling program, counselors work as a team with the school staff, parents, and the community to create a caring and positive climate for development and learning.

Mental Health Team.   In some elementary schools, a mental health team is available that is made up of experienced professionals whose duties include crisis intervention, special education assessment, conflict management, community liaison, affective education in the classrooms, individual student support, parent support and resource, teacher support and resource, and child advocate representatives. The team leaders typically facilitate support groups on a regular basis. These groups help children learn about and deal with their individual challenges related to social skills, family changes, study skills, death and loss, and behavior concerns.

Education/Behavior Consultant.   The education/behavior consultant provides direct and consultative services to students with behavioral disorders that interfere with learning and require intervention in school. Behavior consultants also collaborate closely with teachers and related services professionals to develop positive behavioral plans and develop interventions in the classroom. The consultant typically has experience in working with students on social and behavioral issues. The delivery models include individual direct services to students, small group work, classroom groups, parent support, teacher support, and special education assessment.

Child Development Specialist.   The child development specialist provides individual and group counseling for academic, personal, and social concerns of elementary school children. Also, they provide consultation to parents, guardians, and staff members and make appropriate referrals to community agencies. Child development specialists may also chair consultation teams. These are proactive and collaborative teams of professionals who consult with parents, guardians, teachers, and students to implement interventions and strategies that address the needs of the student.

School Nurse.   The school nurse assesses and identifies health-related problems and may help identify disabilities. She provides recommendations and follow-up in regard to identified health problems. She promotes preventive health care through health education and serves as a resource person and consultant to faculty, students, family, or the student's health care provider. She also provides professional development to staff. The nurse cares for students in the event of accidents and illness in cooperation with the parents or guardians.

Reading Specialist.   The reading specialist is becoming a more common resource and collaborator in elementary schools since early reading competence has become a priority under IDEA and the No Child Left Behind Act. The reading specialist assesses students who are referred for reading difficulties and is available for consultation with teachers, teacher's assistants, and parents. The reading specialist typically works with small groups of first and second graders who are below their grade level in reading. The reading specialist may also be involved with schoolwide or statewide reading initiatives which may include more intensive one-on-one reading programs with children with disabilities and those who are at risk for falling behind.

Occupational and Physical Therapists.   From preschool through high school, occupational therapists (OTs) help children with motor, neurological, or sensory difficulties reach their potential in the school environment. OTs help students perform everyday tasks and regain physical and cognitive abilities. OTs provide services for children who have cognitive and learning disabilities, developmental delays, and other conditions that affect school performance. Specific areas that OTs target include grasp and manipulation of objects, computer access, use of school tools (pencil use, scissors, etc.), lunchroom skills, sensor processing, and positioning in the classroom to optimize learning.

Physical therapists (PTs) work with children who have been injured or have a disease or disability to help them regain functioning and independence. PTs assist children from preschool through high school by providing services for children with severe physical disabilities such as spina bifida, traumatic brain injury, developmental delays, and a variety of other neurological or orthopedic disabilities. PTs assist with standing, walking, use of wheelchairs and other assistive orthopedic devices, and safe, efficient travel in the school setting.

There is a difference between the OT and the PT roles. Physical therapy deals with the realm of movement, ambulation, and range of muscle motion. Occupational therapy concentrates on activities that occupy people—for children than means school and learning activities. In additional to concentrating on a student's physical well-being, occupational therapists address psychological, social, and environmental factors that impede independent functioning in all aspects of life.

Educational Resource Center Specialist.   Students who qualify for special education assistance in reading, writing, or math are eligible to receive services from the school's educational resource center. The staff of the ERC provide supplemental instruction to students, particularly students with disabilities and those for whom English is not their primary language. ERC staff provide supplemental instruction to students.

Speech and Language Pathologist.   Speech and language services are provided to students with communication disorders such as articulation, fluency, voice, or language difficulties. These impairments must have a significant impact on the student's academic performance in order to qualify for direct consultative services of an SLP. The speech–language pathologist diagnoses and provides intervention for those students who are eligible for service based on state eligibility criteria.

Vision Specialist and Audiologist.   Students identified with vision and/or hearing needs may receive services from district specialists within the general education setting. Services may include assessments, direct interventions, or consultation. The educational audiologist is responsible for the identification, evaluation, provision of auditory habilitation, and counseling and guidance of students, parents, teachers about hearing loss.

Adaptive Physical Education Specialist.   Adaptive P.E. services are provided for students who cannot safely and successfully participate in the regular physical education program. The adaptive P.E. teacher works with students who have orthopedic impairments, cognitive impairments, autism, or a variety of other disabilities.

The following two scenarios in Box 11.2 illustrates how these roles described above work in concert with one another to support students with disabilities and complex needs in a specialized elementary school.

What Collaboration and System Coordination Strategies Facilitate Transition to Middle School?

Transition From Elementary to Middle School

Transition from elementary school typically occurs in the sixth grade, but in some schools it can occur in the fifth grade as students move on to middle school for their sixth, seventh, and eighth years. Once again, the child must adjust to a very different environment, new set of expectations, and a new set of peers. For most children, their elementary experiences have prepared them to manage the adjustment within a few days or weeks, and they quickly grow comfortable with the new demands. However, many children—both with and without disabilities—may not be adequately prepared in advance for these changes in the educational setting before they enter middle school.

BOX 11.2   Learning, Behavioral, and Developmental Disabilities in the Elementary School: Ages 5–10

The elementary program, located at the Jerusalem Avenue School in North Bellmore provides a dynamic preacademic or academic educational program for students, grades K–5, who have learning, behavioral, or developmental disabilities that interfere with their abilities to succeed in general education. Remedial, supportive, and related services are available as needed. Class ratios are 6:1 or 9:1 and are determined by student need. The program is aligned with the New York State standards for learning.

Classrooms, staffed by caring, certified special education teachers and paraprofessionals, provide a highly individualized learning environment where reading, language arts, math, science, social studies, and health curriculums are adapted to meet students' cognitive levels and learning styles. Social and emotional objectives are integrated into classroom activities. Teachers develop social learning skills throughout the curriculum by eliciting socially appropriate responses and encouraging students to reflect on their behavior (choices) to determine if they are socially appropriate. Within the classroom, students work as a team to support each other in social growth. Psychologists and social workers also work closely with students in individual sessions to support the development of positive social skills.

Computers are provided in the classroom to promote student involvement and curriculum reinforcement. Classroom instruction is supplemented in the learning center which offers a distraction-free setting for different types of individualized instruction. Learning center staff work closely with classroom teachers to align and supplement classroom materials.

A schoolwide growth recognition program includes a specific plan for each child developed by the child's teacher, psychologist, and social worker. The plan is tied to classroom goals and uses a point system for earning rewards, such as purchases at the school store. Students regularly evaluate themselves to determine where they have succeeded and where they need to improve. As students progress, they set new goals.

In the Health and Community Awareness (HCH) program, students meet with a teacher who uses a curriculum that involves simulation of home and community activities. Safety and health issues are explored, and social skills are developed. Library activities encourage students to develop good reading habits, gain additional knowledge, and function independently. Music

helps students develop creativity, self-expression, and language. Auditory and perceptual skills and sensory-motor functions are also enhanced through the music program.

Psychologists and social workers support, reassure, and assist students through individual and group activities and are available to parents on a group or individual basis. Social workers offer biweekly parent workshops. Occupational and physical therapies assist students in meeting educational goals. Physical therapists work with students individually or in small groups to develop coordination, muscle control, and fine and gross motor skills. Occupational therapists develop fine motor skills and sensory integration for students with major deficits in this area.

Speech and language services are designed to increase students' learning potential. Receptive and expressive difficulties are addressed. Different modes of communication are used to meet the needs of individual students. The collaborative classroom, created through an innovative model pairing a speech teacher and a special education teacher in a team-teaching approach, is an important part of the program's speech and language services. The model creates an interactive learning environment where two classes are linked together to develop speech and language skills while addressing academic goals. Language skills such as vocabulary, grammar, critical thinking, and auditory comprehension are developed.

Through adaptive physical education, students develop awareness and control of their bodies within their environment. They engage in a variety of enjoyable yet challenging activities that improve physical fitness and visual–motor coordination. Supplemental activities include many different enrichment experiences, such as creative performances. Field trips and outdoor education provide activities in the community to bring classroom learning into the larger world.

The elementary program now provides the intensive support program (ISP) through a collaborative program developed by Nassau BOCES (Board of Cooperative Educational Services) and the North Shore Child & Family Guidance Center for students with significant emotional difficulties. Services of the ISD program address the emotional and behavioral issues that interfere with the achievement of educational goals. Additionally, the elementary program has developed a specialized program

(Continued)

BOX 11.2   (Continued)

for those students with significant behavioral issues and who require a more experiential approach to academic learning. The primary focus of these classes is to promote teamwork, develop pro-social skills, improve peer interaction, and instill a sense of belonging.

Parents are encouraged to be active partners in the education of their child by reinforcing at home what the child learns in school, and parent education is offered to help them do this. Progress reports and report cards keep parents informed about their youngster's success.

Source: From "A Description of Support Services at the Jerusalem Avenue School, North Bellmore, NY," 2004. Nassau, NY: Board of Cooperative Education Services. Reprinted with permission.

During these years, parents, teachers, administrators, and support personnel play a crucial role in helping students develop a positive self-image and the skills they need to cope with the changes in their learning environment and the new demands and pressures they face. Their ability to communicate and collaborate as a team to address the individual needs of youth in the middle school can make the essential difference for the child in the transition and for the remainder of their school years.

Strategies for Effective Transition Into Middle School.
The **transition to middle school** is a crucial pathway toward graduation that must be successfully navigated. The National Association of Elementary School Principals (2004), along with the National Middle School Association have called upon schools at both levels to adopt early transition plans to help youth to achieve a sense of belonging in their new school. Teachers and counselors at the elementary and middle level are beginning to work together to share information about students with special needs before they make the passage to the next level. And parents are not just encouraged to find out about the program at the next level, but are being helped by professionals to engage in the process. The old practice of inducing parents to take the initiative in finding out about middle school is shifted toward supportive practices involving communication, information sharing, and direct assistance in the process. The following collaborative activities represent a synthesis of those used in elementary and middle schools across the United States to support transition for special needs students:

- In the sixth grade (or fifth grade if the first middle school year is sixth grade) teachers fill out a transition plan which includes information on reading and math levels; writing ability; IEPs; students' strengths, interests, and special talents; counseling needs, home support, learning styles; behavior problems; and organizational problems. These forms are used to guide placement.
- The middle school counselor meets with students in each rising elementary class to give a presentation about middle school, homework, organization, scheduling, typical day, teachers, school activities, clubs, and athletics.
- Middle school "ambassadors," including students with special needs, are sent to the elementary schools to speak to the fifth-grade students.
- Short videos are used to introduce students to the schools; these can even be produced by middle school students as special projects under the guidance of teachers.

- Middle school students are paired with rising elementary students for a day at the middle school. The "shadows" attend classes and take notes on what they experience. Then they share their experiences with their home elementary classmates.
- Parent question-and-answer nights are hosted; these include the principal or assistant principal, a member of one of the middle school teachers teams, and a counselor in the school that the children will be attending.
- Tours of the middle school are arranged for students and parents in which discipline rules and regulations are reviewed.
- An assembly or round table mixer is held in the gym to allow rising elementary students to mix with middle school students.
- Rising elementary students write their top questions that they would like answered about middle school. Middle school students then write back or videotape their responses.
- The last two or three classroom guidance sessions for rising elementary students are devoted to answering questions and easing fears about transition.
- A list is developed of rising elementary students who are identified as possibly needing extra support in the adjustment to middle school. An "early bird" group is established that meets a week before the start of the school year (the invitation, however, should go out to all students). The early bird students get their lockers and schedules, practice opening their lockers, review daily procedures such as getting lunch tickets, checking out library books, and other tasks. This group could continue occasionally during the first few months of school to monitor how students are adjusting and if they need continued support.

These strategies formalize transition planning and support for students with special needs and their families, as illustrated in Box 11.3. Such activities must be structured into the work of schools.

BOX 11.3 Helping Casey Make the Transition

Postella, who teaches visually impaired students for the San Mateo (California) Office of Education was working with a student named Casey. Casey, a visually impaired fifth grader who used braille, wasn't ready for middle school. She talked with her supervisor about beginning a program for students going into middle school and then developed a proposal. Teachers at the California School for the Blind got on board and with no outside funding, the Middle School Preparation Program began with five students. Casey was one of them.

The Middle School Preparation Program stresses life skills as well as academics. Teachers follow an expanded core curriculum that includes braille, special living skills, and assistive technologies. Teachers work one-on-one with the students, focusing on the skills those students need to improve. They learn skills they will need to live independently as they grow older: how to travel independently, make phone calls, go shopping and pay for items, eat out in restaurants, and ride buses. Teachers also work on developing study skills such as organizational and note-taking skills, navigating the Internet for research (using talking computers), exploring career options, and using assistive technologies such as braille note takers, which they will use for taking notes in middle school classes.

Casey and another student both made successful transitions to middle school and, in the second year, seven students enrolled in the program. We've added a mainstream component in which students go to a local middle school to take one or two classes (Steele-Carlin, 2001).

Many stakeholders are involved in ensuring the success of children as they negotiate the often fragile passage from part-time preschool to formal schooling. Systematic teamwork among professionals and parents is directly related to children's adjustment and progress in the elementary years and beyond.

Summary of Key Points

- The entrance into elementary school marks children's first interaction with formal schooling, and research shows that success during this first year may predict later school success.
- As a new paradigm for teaching, learning, assessment and curriculum development, universal design for learning (UDL) means creating structures that accommodate the widest spectrum of students (users) possible in the general education classroom.
- Despite 2 decades of research about the importance of structured transition planning and support in elementary school, this process is still left largely to chance.
- As more research is conducted on larger numbers of children, we are learning that the transitions from one educational level to another are far more important than previously recognized.

Key Terms and Phrases

- Circle of commitment (p. 292)
- School readiness (p. 293)
- Strengths-based approach (p. 296)
- Developmentally appropriate practice (p. 299)
- Instructional teaming (p. 300)
- Universal design for learning (p. 301)
- Inclusive classroom environment (p. 302)
- Community of learners (p. 303)
- School evaluation team (p. 303)
- Transition to middle school (p. 310)

Questions for Reflection, Thinking, and Skill Building

1. Identify at least three key findings from national research studies on transition from kindergarten into elementary school. How does elementary school differ from preschool? What changes in professional roles are suggested by these findings?

2. What is developmentally appropriate practice and why is it important to educators?

3. Interview one or more elementary school teachers and ask them about the transition activities that they participate in as they prepare children to make the move to kindergarten. In their views what are the strengths and weaknesses of the process? Have there been changes in the process instituted over the past few years? What recommendations do they have for improving the transition process for children with disabilities and for all children?

4. Visit an elementary school in your community. Examine the literature that is given out to elementary school students and families. How much helpful information is there about school support services and community services for children with disabilities and their families? Ask about the provisions for preparing students for the transition into elementary school and for the transition to middle school. If possible, visit an urban/suburban and rural school and compare both.

5. Visit the Web site for your public schools and examine the information available for educators, parents, and the general public. How much helpful information is there about school support services in the elementary school for children with disabilities? Is there information about legal rights and responsibilities for children with disabilities, preparation for the transition into elementary school, and opportunities for parent participation? What would you recommend to educators?

CHAPTER TWELVE

How Can School Collaboration and System Coordination Promote Progress of Middle School Children?

I urge the next generation of middle school educators to help save the ninth grade. The middle school concept has, too often, not been able to fulfill its announced intention to make the transition to high school a smooth and successful experience. In fact, the transition to high school has never been more treacherous nor the consequences more personally disastrous for so many. All over America, thousands and thousands of ninth graders are and have been painfully failing. . . . We can no longer allow all the good work you do in middle schools to evaporate in the first 6 weeks of high school. —George, 1999

- What are the special needs of middle school students?

- What service coordination roles support middle school students?

- What are the barriers to collaboration and coordination between school and home?

- What collaboration and system coordination strategies promote success in middle school?

- What system coordination strategies support transition from middle to high school?

PERSPECTIVES

Student

Looking back, elementary school was much easier for me because everything was in the same place every day and I had just one teacher to work with. She liked me, and I liked her, and I didn't mind coming to school every day. When I graduated to seventh grade and changed schools, I had much bigger classes, and I felt like some of the teachers didn't like me. A couple of teachers had been in the elementary school and didn't like teaching middle school. I felt I didn't belong, and I think I needed someone—an adult—to help me feel better about myself in the new school. A friend of mine in another school said they had groups for kids to talk about their feelings, and so I asked my teacher about it. My school had a pretty OK counselor who let me join a leadership group. After that I started feeling a lot better and made some good friends.

INTRODUCTION

Who are middle school students? They are part children, carefree and ebullient, and part adolescents, restless and intense. They are in transition from the protection and support of the smaller elementary environment to the greater demands of their family and a larger school and wider world. While most families celebrate this passage to a new stage in the child's development, some students and parents may harbor great apprehension about the move, uncertain about how prepared they are for the new demands. Some children adjust well but others, both with and without disabilities, need extra support.

The middle years represent major transformations in the educational environment, and expectations and needs of students at this stage are complex. Students experience change in the new setting—new social demands, demands for homework and time-management skills, new expectations for independence and personal responsibility, multiple classrooms, and a cadre of teachers. At the same time, these children are experiencing physical and emotional changes as they enter adolescence.

The combination of these changes can be both exciting and stressful, which for some students proves too great and they may call out for help. They may react to the stress by exhibiting behaviors or changes in personality that are quite different from their behavior in the elementary years. For example, they may for the first time exhibit fearfulness about school, disengagement from learning and general apathy toward schooling, loss of interest in home activities, resistance to completing or turning in homework, uncooperative or aggressive behavior, and even depression. Students with disabilities are more likely than their nondisabled peers to experience these problems and are twice as likely to drop out of school in middle and high school (Blackorby & Wagner, 1996; Christenson & Thurlow, 2004b).

For these reasons, the transition from elementary to middle school for special needs students—indeed for all students—should be made as smooth, seamless, and supportive as possible, and parents, teachers, and support personnel must remain vigilant in their watch for the signs of stress. Open and continuous communication among professionals and with families is particularly important during these years because of the complexity of the changes the child and the family face. Attention to processes of transition into middle school from elementary school and from middle school to high school is essential to sustain the progress children have made in the early years.

This chapter discusses the change that special needs students experience as they advance from the elementary to middle school years. It examines the barriers and challenges to coordination of services in the middle school and explores collaboration and system coordination strategies that are effective in supporting middle school students with disabilities. Finally, the chapter examines the role of the service coordinator in the middle years. The terms *middle school* and *junior high school* will be used interchangeably in this chapter, although in some localities middle school refers to the seventh and eighth grades and junior high may include sixth through eighth.

What Are the Special Needs of Middle School Students?

Middle School Students at Risk

There is a growing attention to the unique needs and experiences of middle school students in the United States. Just when many young adolescents feel most vulnerable, they leave their self-contained elementary classrooms, their relationships with a single teacher and a small group of peers, and shift to a large, often impersonal middle school. Here they attend up to six or seven different classes with seven sets of students, taught by a variety of teachers with different personalities and expectations. They have important choices to make about courses and curriculum and extracurricular activities. Students are assigned lockers that may be located in a far corner of the building, out from under adult watch, and locker combinations must be memorized. They must organize their books and materials and transport them from class to class. Daily class schedules may vary throughout the week, and students must record and track their homework assignments daily or over a period of weeks. The transformations of adolescence, compounded by the change that the move to middle school brings, leave many students particularly vulnerable to alienation and dropout.

The dropout rate for students with disabilities is approximately twice that of general education students and peaks at the late middle and early secondary levels

(Blackorby & Wagner, 1996; Christenson & Thurlow, 2004a). Students with emotional disabilities are particularly vulnerable during the transition to middle school. A 2001 report from the U.S. Surgeon General estimates that 21% of young people in the United States, ages 9 to 17 (about 15 million children) have diagnosable emotional or behavioral health disorders, but fewer than a third get help for these problems (Olbrich, 2003; U.S. Department of Health and Human Services, 2001e). These young Americans—fully one-quarter of adolescents, ages 9 to 17—may be at risk of failing to achieve productive adult lives.

Results of a large youth risk behavior survey (Simeonsson, McMillen, McMillen, & Lollar, 2002) indicated that students with disabilities were more likely to report (a) engaging in risky behaviors that result in injuries (not wearing seatbelts or bicycle helmets, riding with a drinking driver, carrying weapons, fighting); (b) feeling depressed or considering suicide; (c) using alcohol, tobacco, marijuana, and other drugs; and (d) engaging in unhealthy weight loss behaviors. Students with disabilities were also more likely to report having had property stolen or damaged at school, a low quality of life, and poor health status (Frank Porter Graham Child Development Institute, 2002). In 2000–01, 12% of all students in alternative schools and programs for at-risk students were special education students with an individualized education plan (Bear, Quinn, & Burkholder, 2001). This number excludes those who fail to qualify for special education services, but are failing in the school setting (Bazelon Center for Mental Health Law, 2003).

Increased concerns about the dropout problem are also emerging because of state and local education agency experiences with high-stakes accountability and standardized testing. A growing number of students are having difficulty with these assessments (Thurlow, Sinclair, & Johnson, 2002). The use of high-stakes tests have been associated with higher dropout rates—6 to 8 percentage points higher just between eighth and tenth grades (Center for Education Statistics, 1999b; Huebert & Hauser, 1999; Warren & Edwards, 2001). A variety of dropout prevention strategies, therefore, are now targeted at students in middle school, where the pressures of schooling related to a more complex curriculum, a less personal environment, and the growing need for peer acceptance pose a danger to students who are already disadvantaged (Alspaugh, 1998; Anderman, Maehr & Midgley, 1999; Butler & Hodge, 2004; Elias, 2001).

Many middle school students have hidden disabilities such as a learning, emotional and behavioral, ADD/ADHD, or language and sensory integration dysfunctions. These groups represent 95% of all students with disabilities. Many go undiagnosed, particularly those with learning and emotional disabilities and ADHD, and do not receive services until school age, many not until the middle school years (Blackorby & Wagner, 2002). The following defines sensory integration:

> Sensory integration is the ability to take in information through the senses and integrate and organize this information in the brain. Children with sensory integration dysfunction may be hyperreactive to stimuli in the environment, impulsive, distractible, have difficulty planning tasks and adjusting to new situations. Others may react with frustration, anger, aggression, or withdrawal when they encounter failure. (DiMatties & Sammons, 2003),

Estimates of students with ADD/ADHD range from 3% to 7.5% of all school-aged children (National Institute of Mental Health, 2003). It is not unusual for

ADD/ADHD students with high intellectual abilities to go undiagnosed until middle school since they can learn how to compensate enough to "get by" in elementary grades (Goldstein & Goldstein 1992; Wagner, Marder, & Cardoso, 2002). Often impairments are not manifested until the demands of middle school become too great, and then students may be labeled as inattentive, lazy, bored, alienated, oppositional, or behaviorally or conduct disordered. Furthermore, fewer students with disabilities in general education classes receive accommodations at the middle and secondary levels than in elementary grades, which undermines learning and test taking (Blackorby & Wagner, 2002).

Middle schools are undergoing reforms to become more developmentally appropriate for young adolescents, building in greater collaboration and coordination among educators, parents, students, and outside agencies. Promptness in identifying possible disabilities is essential for preventing more serious, and perhaps lifelong problems.

Transition to Middle School: A Sudden Event

Researchers and educators have come to view early adolescence as a unique period of development in all domains—cognitive, social–emotional, and physical (Ames & Miller, 1994; Billig, 2001; Collins, 1996; Doyle & Moretti, 2000; Steinburg & Baier, 2003; Stoffner & Williamson, 2000). Two of the nation's leading educational organizations—National Association of Elementary School Principals (NAESP, 2002) and the National Middle School Association (NMSA, 2004), as well as a variety of disability associations, have called for a collaborative partnership among parents, teachers, principals, counselors, and students to support them as they change from childhood to adolescence and move from elementary to middle school.

With the exception of infancy, early adolescence is the time when a child's body and brain grows and changes faster than in any other phase of life. The student is in a process of change from child to adolescent, yet the change in environment from elementary to middle school is a sudden event. Since most children are developing at different rates, some come into middle school ready for the changes, others struggle to keep up, and still others fall behind. As with all school transitions, the **transition to middle school** occurs as a "one-size-fits-all" event that all children are expected to adapt to at the same time.

Recent brain research also reveals that during the teen years up to age 15, the areas in the middle and back of the brain associated with associative thinking and language reach their peak growth rates (Wilson & Horch, 2004). The growth spurt is most predominant just before puberty in the prefrontal cortex, the part of the brain crucial to information synthesis. The prefrontal cortex is the area of the brain that controls planning, working memory, organization, and mood modulation. Brain researchers have observed that this area of the brain is not mature until about 18 years of age (Spinks, 2002). The prefrontal cortex appears to be the last region of the brain to mature (Casey, Giedd, & Thomas, 2000), undergoing major changes throughout puberty. These recent findings about adolescent brain development have major implications for classroom practices and student supports. Only recently have educational researchers and practitioners begun to relate new brain research to learning. The challenge for middle school teachers and administrators, however, it to integrate this research in classroom practice and organization of middle schools for all students, including special needs learners (Brandt & Wolfe, 1998; Hough, 2003).

During the middle school years, relationships with parents, peers, and other adults can become very challenging for adolescents. There are conflicting influences—pushes and pulls from the family, school, and peers. These pushes and pulls often send mixed messages about what is expected of them. Young people are caught in a vortex of physical, psychological, and social growth. They constantly feel competing demands for how and with whom they should invest their time, how to improve their status with peers and adults, how to relate to authority figures, and how to define themselves. Yet, in the midst of all this change, young people, particularly those who are special learners, need stability and people on whom they can rely. The adults in their families and schools, acting in partnership, must fill these critical needs (Billig, 2001; Mizelle & Mullins, 1997; Mullins, 1997; Roeser, Eccles, & Sameroff, 2000; Stoffner, 2000).

Let's See It in Action on page 320 illustrates how communication and collaboration between teachers and parents in the middle school years can make a great difference in the life of a young adolescent. This example continues from the story of Eric introduced in Chapter 3.

What can we learn about this case? First, Eric's experience of change in his educational environment placed great stress on his coping skills. He was predisposed to being at risk of poor adjustment to the new demands of middle school. He had not received professional help during his elementary years because he was bright and able to compensate for his learning challenges. Eric also had no one with whom to share his feelings and fears. Second, Eric's parents had little communication from the middle school teachers about Eric's behavior, so they missed many opportunities to intervene at home. While the teachers may have been well-meaning in "hoping" and giving Eric a chance to "change on his own," they inadvertently contributed to his deterioration. Opportunities were lost to intervene early, to provide supports in school, and to help Eric overcome his sense of failure and defeat.

A serious and gathering situation was diffused, however, due to the persistence of Eric's mother, the support of an astute and caring school counselor, and the willingness of ninth-grade teachers to coordinate and provide support. Close collaboration around Eric's needs was achieved. Without such a response on the part of the school, Eric may well have deteriorated further in ninth grade and have become a dropout statistic. Eric's case mirrors that of a growing number of middle school students who may or may not be diagnosed as having disabilities, yet are at significant risk for alienation, academic failure, and dropout.

Why Are There Middle Schools?

The middle schools are a relatively new model in the history of education in the United States. In the 1960s, four of five graduates had attended junior high schools, which was the primary mode of schooling for adolescents. However, the effectiveness of the junior high school model came under criticism as simply a replication of high school that could not meet the social, intellectual, and physical needs of young adolescents (Krouscas, 1997).

Recently, reformers have recommended a new "middle school" model that would serve children in grades 6–8 and have several components that rely on collaboration and coordination: a comprehensive curriculum plan, student mentor/

LET'S SEE IT IN ACTION! Case Illustration: Saving Eric

ERIC: When I started at Waymans Middle School, I was afraid, but I didn't want anyone to know. There was so much pressure. Things were easy at my other school because I only had one teacher and one classroom and I always kept my books and papers in one desk. Now I have a locker, a combination to remember, and a bunch of classes to get to with so little time. I have to keep all my subjects organized, my papers and stuff organized, get different homeworks in to different teachers, prepare for lots of different tests on different days, and there's so many big projects. I have trouble with organization and remembering things, and no one gave me help with this. I started falling behind slowly day by day and feeling worse and worse about myself. After a few months, I just gave up.

ERIC'S
MOTHER: Eric was always a very active child and had trouble with attention. Conversations were difficult with him because his mind was always flitting away like a butterfly. During elementary years this high activity level and lack of attention created difficulty, but he was very bright and could always compensate. We didn't have him diagnosed because he seemed to find a way to keep up. He was never identified as needing special education because he could perform average or better. Each year, though, his teachers reported problems with minor disruptions in class, disorganized behavior, and trouble paying attention. Because I had good relationships and continuous communication with his elementary teachers, I could stay on top of the problems and provide supports at home. When Eric was 10, he was diagnosed with attention deficit and hyperactivity disorder (ADHD).

Once Eric hit seventh grade, though, everything changed. He had to develop organizational skills for homework assignments, subjects, schedule of classes, teachers, long-term projects, and papers. Organization was his Achilles' heel. He began to change, became distant, hung out with friends who I was very concerned about. I thought at first this was Eric just being a preteen, but by the end of the year his grades had plummeted, and by the end of eighth grade, he was nearly failing every subject. More frequently, he was refusing to go to school, and we had to start using structured behavioral strategies. During the seventh grade, no teachers had attempted to communicate with me about his situation, and no one provided any extra help to Eric to organize himself. When I went to the back-to-school night, I expressed my concerns and one teacher said, "In middle school we expect them to manage independently. This isn't elementary, and they have to take more responsibility for themselves." I asked, "What if they have difficulty with this and need extra help? What if they fall too far behind?" The teacher responded, "Well, if they're in the general education class, we treat everyone alike. No special treatment." Eric did pass eighth grade by a small margin, and I feared for the following year when he shifted to ninth grade.

HIGH SCHOOL
COUNSELOR: Eric's mother made an appointment to talk to me just before the end of his eighth-grade year. She was very concerned about her son's experience in seventh and eighth grades and worried about his near failure and what that

meant for the coming year. Unfortunately, I have a caseload of 300 students, so it's hard for me to spend much time with each child. But, I was interested in this case and appreciated the mother's concern and involvement. I pulled his file and found that, yes indeed, Eric had nearly failed all of his classes. Yet, what was amazing was that he had taken the state assessment tests in eighth grade and had scored "advanced proficient" on all of them. Moreover, he had early psychological tests that showed that he was a very bright kid. How could he be failing his grades yet scoring "advanced proficient"? Something was terribly wrong.

I spoke with some of his teachers in middle school, and they reported that Eric was known to sleep in class, routinely failed to turn in homework, and often showed disruptive and attention-seeking behavior in class. I asked if any of the teachers had let his parents know about this behavior or had provided any extra support for Eric, and they all said no. They believed Eric could do the work, could pass the tests, but was just unmotivated. They did not believe he needed special education. They were reluctant to report on his behavior because they wanted to "give him every chance to make the changes on his own." Furthermore, the special education screening team refused to evaluate Eric for services because of his SOL scores and teacher reports. And so, in my opinion—and in his mother's—we had failed him in the middle school. This student clearly needed help and was at particular risk of academic failure in ninth grade. His marginal adjustment in middle school and growing sense of isolation had left him even more vulnerable to the pressures and demands of high school.

I met and talked with Eric about his feeling of being overwhelmed with the work and promised to get him some help with organization and time management during the year. We set up a time to visit the high school and meet with a few of the teachers and classrooms. I discussed what he could expect in terms of schedule and workload and other expectations. I also stayed in close touch with his mother for the balance of the year to give suggestions about how she might provide extra support at home and prepare him for the transition at the end of summer. During ninth grade we held a teacher's roundtable with Eric and his mother and the high school counselor to discuss progress at midyear and share what supports were being used in his classes. By the middle of the year, Eric's grades had improved from failing to Bs and Cs and his attitude toward school was improving. The frequency of disruptive and attention-seeking behavior began to decline.

Questions for Discussion

- How did middle school teachers characterize middle school expectations for Eric? How were these expectations different from those in elementary school?
- How does Eric characterize the new demands placed on him?
- Why was Eric not screened for special education services in the elementary years even though he was diagnosed with ADHD?
- How did the school counselor intervene and provide support to Eric and his mother?

advisory plan, continuous progress arrangements, team planning and teaching, a variety of instructional plans, adequate health and physical education programs, and planning and evaluation systems (McEwin, Dickinson, & Jenkins, 1996).

Over 40 years have passed since the introduction of the concept of the middle school, and there are wide variations in **middle school structure**. While there is consensus that the elementary school is "nurturing," "child centered," and "self-contained," descriptions of middle school learning environments are inconsistent. Middle schools may implement supportive practices, such as interdisciplinary teaching, thematic units, flexible scheduling, and flexible grouping to address student needs. On the other hand, many middle schools mirror traditional high school departmentalization, 50-minute classes, and ability groupings. Some middle schools are organized to create a gradual transition from self-contained to departmental configuration. For example, the fifth grade may be self-contained, the sixth grade may have two-person teams, the seventh may have two- to three-person teams with larger blocks of time, and the eighth grade may have four or more teachers, each specializing in a subject area. There is a great variety of middle school configurations (McEwin, Dickenson, & Jacobson, 2004).

Despite variations across the United States, the **middle school concept** today is based on the following components:

1. *Educators Committed to Young Adolescents.* Teachers and professionals are trained to understand and teach young adolescents, including those with special needs, and have a passion to deal with the unique characteristics of the middle school student.

2. *Interdisciplinary Teams Are Formed.* A team of teachers work together, with other support professionals, to help educate the same group of youngsters. Interdisciplinary teams plan their own schedule and build a sense of community with their core of students.

3. *An Adult for Every Student.* Each student is given the opportunity to connect with at least one adult. This typically occurs within the context of a teacher mentor/advisory program.

4. *Exploratory Curriculum.* The curriculum is structured so that all students, including those with disabilities, have the opportunity to explore their various hidden abilities.

5. *Integrative Curriculum.* Connections are made among content areas, and students are able to identify those connections (McEwin, Dickenson, & Jacobson, 2004).

Because middle school students want to and need to be involved in their own learning, teachers in effective middle schools make every attempt to actively involve all students (National Middle School Association, 2004).

What Service Coordination Roles Support Middle School Students?

A variety of professionals collaborate and coordinate services for middle school adolescents and their families. These roles were introduced in Chapter 11, but the distinct activities at the middle school level are summarized next.

Middle School Teachers

Middle school teachers understand the developmental needs of young adolescents and are prepared to collaborate with counselors and related services professionals to provide support to students with disabilities. They help students delve more deeply into subjects introduced in elementary school and expose them to more information about the world. Middle school teachers specialize in a specific subject, such as English, Spanish, mathematics, history, or biology. They also can teach subjects that are career oriented. Vocational education teachers, also referred to as career and technical education teachers, instruct and train students to work in a wide variety of fields, such as health care, business, auto repair, communications, and, increasingly, technology. They often teach courses that are in high demand by area employers, who may provide input into the curriculum and offer internships to students. Many vocational teachers play an active role in building and overseeing these partnerships. Often general education teachers collaborate closely with special educators and vocational educators to integrate academic and career–vocational content.

Special Education Teachers

Many middle school students receive direct support in each general education classroom through the presence of the special education teacher. Through a collaborative coteaching model, students receive indirect service through collaborative planning between the general education teacher and the special education teacher. In middle school classes, special educators employ special educational strategies and techniques during instruction to improve the development of sensory- and perceptual-motor skills, language, cognition, and memory. They work with general educators to modify the general education curriculum, confer with other staff members to plan and schedule lessons promoting learning, following approved curricula. They confer with parents, school counselors, psychologists, and administrators in order to resolve students' behavioral and academic problems. Special educators with specialized training in positive behavioral supports help general educators establish and enforce rules for behavior and develop behavioral intervention plans in the classroom.

The middle school special educators' activities each day will be determined by the children they are teaching, the kinds and severity of disabilities those students have, the children's ages, and the setting in which the teachers are working. A middle school special education teacher who is coteaching a class with a general education teacher, a special education teacher in a self-contained middle school classroom for children with emotional and behavior disorders, and a special education teacher in a resource room who has students entering the classroom all day will all have very different activities and responsibilities. But regardless of the setting, special education teachers' responsibilities usually fall into three categories: direct teaching (and preparing for it), preparing reports and individualized plans, and collaborating with other professionals and parents.

School Counselors and Guidance Counselors

Middle school counselors are professional educators with a mental health perspective whose work is integral to the total educational program. They develop and implement comprehensive, developmental, and systematic school counseling programs. In middle or junior high schools, counselors collaborate with a variety of other school professionals to help identify the developmental and learning needs of students. Active participation in sound counseling programs contributes to creating a safe environment in which students can explore and develop resiliency skills necessary to cope with the pressures they face (Dahir & Eby, 2001). The following functions of the school counselor are developmental and impact all grade levels:

- *Academic improvement and individual planning* includes participation in the special education process, selection of a course of study for students, placement in appropriate courses and programs, assistance to improve attendance, and study skills development.
- *Collaboration with teachers* includes assistance with students' academic plans, classroom guidance on study skills and career development, learning style assessment, identification of at-risk students, implementation of interventions, and parent communication.
- *Collaboration with administrators* on school climate, behavioral management plans, schoolwide needs assessments, student data and student assistance team building.
- *Personal/social growth* includes counseling in self-esteem, communication skills, decision making and relationship skills, as well as conflict resolution and reduction of prejudice.
- *Crisis intervention services* include counseling students in crises such as suicide, child abuse, pregnancy, and substance abuse; counselors are integral to a **crisis intervention** team.
- *Transition support services* orient students as they move between grades as well as between school buildings.

Mary Kate Denny/Photo Edit Inc.

School counselors are trained to address the developmental needs of adolescents and their families, to strengthen students' resilience to pressures they face, and to contribute to safer learning environments.

- *Parent support* includes referral to services, individual conferences, and group meetings with parents centered on the academic and personal growth of their children.
- *School guidance and career/life planning* increases students' awareness of the career and educational planning process and instills in students the values and attitudes necessary to successfully contribute to their families and community. Counselors assist with career and postsecondary planning.
- *Consultation and teacher support* includes serving as a reference and resource for students, parents, and school staff (American School Counselor Association, 2004a).

Middle school counselors enhance learning and promote academic achievement.

School Psychologist

In the middle school, the services of the psychologist include psycho-educational testing for students suspected of having educational disabilities, and evaluation, including individualized intelligence testing, achievement testing, assessments of visual perception, and motor and social/emotional disabilities. School psychologists also provide consultation in educational planning, make instructional recommendations, and make recommendations to teachers and parents for restructuring students' schedules within the school. Psychologists also explore appropriate educational placements outside the school for students with severe disabilities. When needed, school psychologists provide short-term or crisis counseling in situations in which students or families are experiencing significant changes. They also provide information and referrals to community service agencies for parents who are pursuing outside evaluations or counseling services.

Speech/Language Therapist

The middle school speech–language clinician provides diagnostic and therapeutic services for all students who exhibit an educational disability related to speech/language. In some cases, a program of intervention is offered for students who require speech improvement services.

School Nurse/Teacher

Most middle schools have nurses who also have educational responsibilities to provide ongoing health information in the nurse's office for students and parents who have medical concerns. They are also a resource for teachers who are covering class topics related to anatomy, physiology, health maintenance, sex education, substance abuse, and safety. They may also provide classroom support in teaching first aid during certain consumer education units such as baby sitting and home safety. School nurses also offer a program of health services for students at the middle school level. School nurses communicate health needs to other school personnel and clarify the impact of medical issues upon the participation of students within the full range of school activities.

School Assistance Counselors and Resource Officers

Many middle schools employ middle school student assistance counselors who provide prevention/intervention services for students who may be at risk for substance abuse or dangerous behaviors. The student assistance counselor serves as a member of the overall student personnel team and assists in the identification of at-risk students. Student assistance counselors provide individual and group counseling in school, as well as follow up communication with families. They serve as a resource for identifying outpatient and treatment facilities to assist children and families in securing appropriate community-based assistance. The school resource officer (SRO) provides a police presence at the school and assists in ensuring a safe school environment. The purpose for having the presence of an SRO in the middle school is to identify and address potentially unsafe situations proactively.

Middle School Advisors or Mentors

Research on successful middle schools highlights the importance of advisory programs for adolescents. There is no one single design for advisory programs because they need to be adapted to fit the population. The underlying assumption of middle school advisory programs is that every adolescent can benefit from having an adult serve as a mentor, guide, and advocate. This individual, who may also be a teacher, would get to know them well, and work with them closely in a supportive and non-judgmental way as they negotiate their way through to high school (Ayers, 1994; Miller, 1999). Box 12.1 provides an example of the roles of middle school coordinators or advisors in a school district.

WHAT ARE THE BARRIERS TO COLLABORATION AND COORDINATION BETWEEN SCHOOL AND HOME?

Research has demonstrated that young adolescents with special needs are particularly vulnerable and need extra support in middle school. In the middle school, partnerships among professionals, parents, and students are typically not as strong as they were at the elementary level. Yet they are needed more.

BOX 12.1   Middle School Coordinators for Drug Prevention and School Safety

Nine middle schools in Imperial County are benefiting from additional manpower in the form of middle school coordinators through a grant funded by the U.S. Department of Education. The primary objective of the five middle school coordinators was to assess and identify incidences of school violence, bullying, absenteeism, truancy, discipline referrals, expulsions, suspensions, use of alcohol and other drugs, and any other factors that affect academic performance. Middle school coordinators identified research-based strategies and curriculum to address the problems and needs of each school. This initiative resulted in increased grade point averages, improved attendance, assignment completion, and achievement scores while decreasing discipline referrals and the proportion of students repeating a grade (U.S. Department of Education, 2003e).

The Changing Environment From Elementary to Middle School

In middle school, the environment changes dramatically for all students, including those with disabilities who are included in the general education class for a majority of the day. The school is typically much larger and more impersonal than the elementary school that they have known and they have a wider group of new friends. Unlike elementary teachers, middle school teachers typically do not remind students to turn in homework, and students who have cognitive difficulties with organization and attention may have trouble managing their work. A large, noisy, and bustling cafeteria must be negotiated each day, and lunch money managed. Students must also arrange transportation with their families to participate in after-school activities or use public transportation. For most students, these changes are adjusted to within the first few weeks of school, and they quickly grow comfortable with the new demands. For some, however, these changes are challenging without extra support.

Challenging Behaviors in Middle School. Middle schools can also be breeding grounds for the emergence of adolescent aggression and violence, requiring closer collaboration among teachers, administrators, and counselors. In most middle schools, there are great differences in students' size, height, and weight. Larger students may use their size to bully others or intimidate them. Behind-the-locker bullying may be a frequent occurrence for some children. Approximately one-quarter of students ages 13–17 are physically attacked or involved in fights at school (U.S. Department of Education, 2003b). For example, bigger students may pressure or physically threaten smaller ones, or those with disabilities, to purchase extra lunch items for them with their own money. Or they may simply bully them into handing over lunch money or lunch card ID numbers. Students may be afraid to report these situations to adults because of the fear of retribution. These are very stressful situations for seventh- and eighth-grade students, particularly if they feel incapable of defending themselves or insecure that adults can protect them.

Few students are prepared in advance for these changes in the educational setting before they enter middle school. Few are ever prepared for this kind of problem solving. While a majority of middle school children are not bullies and are not aggressive, these behaviors are more common at the onset of adolescence (Abrams, 2002; Haugaard, 2000). Bullying behavior peaks in middle school—for students with and without disabilities—and the impacts of these behaviors on students can be devastating (Hoover & Stenhjem, 2003). When young people feel physically or socially unsafe, schools become a breeding ground for ridicule and attack (Brendtro, 2001).

Peer Influences. Greater academic demands come at a time when students are experiencing physical changes, becoming interested in the opposite sex, and becoming independent (individuating) from their parents. These changes necessitate close communication between teachers and parents. Peers become very powerful influences on them, and they may resist their parents' rules and limits in a way that they have not done before. As a result, conflicts within the home may develop, and both the parents and child must renegotiate their relationships. How these conflicts are resolved can have a profound impact on the child's adjustment in middle school. Some students throw their effort into their work and strive to achieve to please the adults in their world. Others may rebel. This complicated period of transition has often been associated with a decline in academic achievement, motivation, and self-perceptions, and a time of experimentation with at-risk behaviors (Elias, 2001; Hough, 2003; National Association of Elementary School Principals, 2002; National Middle School Association, 2002).

Rethinking the Middle School Model. Middle schools that mirror high school environments have been blamed for the increase in student behavior problems and cited as the cause of teens' alienation, disengagement from school, and low achievement. These conditions have recently prompted some educators to question the middle school model. The RAND Corporation conducted a nationwide assessment of the middle school and found that there is ample evidence suggesting that separate schools and the transitions they require can cause problems that negatively affect students' developmental and academic progress. The RAND Corporation study recommends that, over the coming years, states and school districts consider alternatives to the sixth- through eighth-grade structure to reduce multiple transitions for students and allow schools to better align their goals across grades K–12 (Felner et al., 1997; McCombs et al., 2004; Williamson & Johnston, 1999).

Summary of Barriers to Collaboration and Coordination

The strength of school–family partnerships decline with each grade level, beginning with kindergarten, and show the most dramatic decrease at the point of transition into the middle grades (Alspaugh, 1998; Anderman, et al., 1999; Elias, 2001; Henderson & Raimondo, 2002). There are several barriers or roadblocks to collaboration among professionals and between professionals and parents in the middle years.

Parent Involvement Changes in Middle School. First, the type of parent involvement desired by adolescents changes as they develop. Many parents report that they are no longer able to help their children at this time, either because their children, now entering preadolescence, begin to reject their help or because they feel that they lack the education and parenting skills. Many parents feel able and comfortable assisting their children with school work in the elementary years, but at middle school and high school levels may not believe that they have adequate knowledge to help. Since almost one out of five students lives in homes in which English is not spoken, and with parents who may not have completed high school, their ability to assist their children with academic work may be limited.

Change in Parent–Child Relationships. Second, preadolescents (ages 9–12) begin to push their parents away, and peers take on greater importance in their lives. For example, in the elementary years, the student may have been proud to have his mother or father as a school volunteer. But now, in middle school, having his mother's presence in the school can be "embarrassing" for some students, or viewed as "spying" or undermining their independence. Students want their parents to be less visible and less active in school settings. As a result, students often discourage their parents from volunteering to help in school, and sometimes even from attending parent–teacher conferences (Billig, 2001, 1995; Rutherford, Barry, & Billig, 1995; Sadowski, 2003; Sanders & Epstein, 2000; U.S. Department of Education, 2000a). Although many parents would like to maintain their involvement during the middle school years, only a small percentage receive guidance from schools on how to help their children. Often, families lack information on courses, curriculum choices, grading procedures, testing and assessments, and many other aspects of middle school.

Homework Resistance and Communication. Homework is frequently a challenge for students with disabilities because they must manage new tasks and their time at home without the structure of the classroom or teacher. Parents and teachers often report that students are not aware of assignments, have left books or homework at school, or completed work is not returned or submitted for grading (Bos, Nahmias, & Urban, 1999). If the parents are able to help them with structure and support, the challenge may be met. Homework, however, is often at the center of a lot of home–school communication and collaboration. Responses to homework represent important behavior in a child, and problems that surround it should be taken very seriously. Homework demands and challenges are often a lightening rod for parent–adolescent conflict and is often a good measure of how a student is adjusting to the demands of middle school and of increasing personal responsibility. Fears and power struggles over homework can alert teachers to potential difficulties that the child is experiencing in general and his or her need for extra support. Homework resistance is often the way children communicate their anxiety about school. With standards-based educational models in place, homework is more likely now to count significantly toward the overall course grade. If left unattended, homework resistance leads to disappointment and frustration of parents, erosion of motivation in school, a sense of failure for the child and ultimately, grade retention or academic failure. Students with learning and emotional disabilities are particularly vulnerable to homework resistance.

Homework also means longer and more complex, project-based assignments that require time management over several days or weeks to complete (discussed later in the chapter). The project may require a multimedia presentation that requires Internet research, reading, writing, artwork, or construction with materials, and an oral presentation.

Students are typically expected to manage project-based work with some help from parents, but many students have great difficulty with time management and great anxiety about these kinds of projects, even though they may not talk about it. Such anxiety can lead to significant homework resistance that should be closely observed. Such resistance can mean that the child is trying to communicate a deeper problem. He or she may fear the oral presentation in front of class, particularly if there is a speech or language or physical disability. Or they may simply feel overwhelmed with the scope of the project and unable to break it up into pieces so they can manage it over time. The teacher should work with the parent to carefully assess the nature of the homework problem and avoid jumping to the conclusion that the student "just doesn't want to do homework." Together they should provide extra support, structure, and guidance during the project period, or make adjustments in the assignment. Often giving students greater choice and decision making in an assignment can be used as a strategy for overcoming anxiety and resistance surrounding more complex and lengthy projects.

Through home–school collaboration, parents can learn about homework policies and their role (Bos, Nahamius, & Urban, 1999), what to expect in terms of the amount of homework, how to communicate weekly through checklists and folders, strategies for monitoring homework completion, and strategies for overcoming resistance to completing homework. Teachers can learn about home schedules and routines and, through close communication, can learn if difficulties are arising around homework. Teachers can also learn about the capacity of the parents or guardians to assist with homework. If interventions are put in place early, they can prevent deeper problems.

Communication Between Schools and Families.   Communication between schools and families during middle and high school years is often one way—from the school to the family. Except for parent–teacher conferences, families are seldom asked about their children or for suggestions to improve communication. When a family is contacted it is often because their child has been in trouble for some time. In many schools, when young adolescents face social, academic, and personal problems, there is seldom a coordinated or well-organized effort by families, schools, and community agencies to address the problems (George, 1999; Hines, 2001; Swaim, 2003). Ensuring such coordination reduces the mixed messages that are received by families and adequate help can be provided before the problem has grown too large. The case illustration at the beginning of this chapter demonstrates many of the points listed above. There are many collaborative strategies that have been shown to be effective in overcoming these barriers and supporting students in their passage through middle school.

WHAT COLLABORATION AND SYSTEM COORDINATION STRATEGIES PROMOTE SUCCESS IN MIDDLE SCHOOL?

Middle school reforms to improve the success of special needs students—and all students—include many strategies that are explored in the following sections. These reforms include (1) elementary to middle school transition supports; (2) reshaping the middle school environment; (3) collaboration between home and school; (4) interventions and supports for at-risk behaviors; (5) academic and career–technical curriculum blending; (6) interdisciplinary teaching teams with shared planning; and (7) activities that bring middle school and high school educators together. These reforms are based on decades of research on the developmental needs and capacities of young adolescents and explorations of how middle schools might be restructured for a better match. Each of these reforms involves collaboration among professionals and coordination of services.

Supporting Students Through Middle School

Many schools are doing more than "tinkering around the edges" with classroom structure, developing more comprehensive approaches to supporting students with disabilities in general and special education (Swaim, 2003). First, such comprehensive approaches reflect a commitment to collaboration and team approaches involving partnerships among educators, parents, students, and community professionals. Second, such collaborative approaches support the view that transition is not a simple movement from one setting to another, but rather a process of change and adjustment that may last a full year. The responses of the school, therefore, must begin at the opening of the school year and remain in place throughout (Hines, 2001; Ritter, Michel, & Irby, 1999; Swaim, 2003). Third, the comprehensive approach also means focusing on student strengths as well as their needs—asking "what's working in the life of the student and what are his or her strengths and talents?"

Collaboration Structures in Middle School

The structure of most middle school programs facilitates professional collaboration and peer support, important ingredients for successful inclusion. Interdisciplinary team organization is a distinguishing characteristic and foundation of the effective middle level school. Interdisciplinary teaming allows the same group of teachers to work with the same group of students. This gives the team of teachers the flexibility and autonomy to create the most efficient learning environment for each student. Middle school educators claim that teaming offers students an opportunity to maximize learning (Walther-Thomas, Korinek, McLaughlin, & Williams, 1997b, 2000).

During these middle years, teachers and parents play a crucial role in helping young adolescents develop a positive self-image and the skills they need to deal with the changes in their learning environment and the new demands and pressures they face. Their ability to communicate and collaborate with each other can make the essential difference for the child in the transition and for the remainder of their school years.

Collaboration Strategies for the Developmentally Responsive Middle School

Effective middle schools provide a strong academic program that is developmentally responsive to the unique needs of young adolescents. In the **developmentally responsive middle school**, welcoming activities may include orientation to the school for students and families, meetings between parents at both levels, assignment of a peer mentor and adult advisor, orientation to the year's curriculum, orientation to new expectations for student behavior and responsibility, and information about available supports. During the year, supportive activities for special needs students "wrap around" the youth during the school day. Such activities include mentors or peer partners for support during the first visitation days and throughout the year, help with lockers and schedules, ongoing advising to choose extracurricular activities, drop-in problem-solving sessions for dealing with peer problems or homework assistance, peer mediation, and parent support groups.

According to the National Middle School Association's (NMSA) report, *This We Believe: Developmentally Responsive Middle Level Schools* (1995), an adult advocate is a key feature of a developmentally responsive middle school. Middle school students need assistance in resolving both educational and personal issues they face during these transitional years. The National Middle School Association's report is based on decades of research on what works. The report describes 12 characteristics of an effective, student-supportive school:

1. Educators committed to young adolescents
2. A shared vision
3. High expectations for all
4. An adult advocate for every student
5. Family and community partnerships
6. A positive school climate
7. Curriculum that is challenging, integrative, and exploratory
8. Varied teaching and learning approaches
9. Assessment and evaluation that promote learning
10. Flexible organizational structure
11. Programs and policies that foster health, wellness, safety
12. Comprehensive guidance and support services. (National Middle School Association, p. 16)

These 12 characteristics provide a framework for what middle schools should and can be, according to NMSA (Hough, 2003; NMSA, 1995; Swaim, 2003). Specific strategies that middle schools use to address the developmental needs of middle school youth are discussed below.

Focus on Students' Strengths. Often parents and teachers of adolescents focus on the problems and needs and fail to ask—what is right with this teen? What is working in their lives? What are their special talents and interests? The answers to these questions—which involve asking the youth—can often serve as essential levers for motivating adolescents during the delicate passage through the middle years. The developmentally appropriate curriculum for middle school students builds upon the student's strengths and experiences and continues to be personalized and responsive to each individual's development and learning patterns. This is achieved with small classes and low student/teacher ratios. Students benefit from these small classes and multiage groupings, learning from their peers and at their own pace. **Strength-based student assessment** directs professionals to identify and build upon the existing strengths and skills that the child and family presents (Epstein & Rudolph, 2004; Friedman, Leone, & Friedman, 1999).

Interdisciplinary Teaming for Developmentally Appropriate Curriculum and Instruction. Schools engaged in interdisciplinary teaming have a more positive school climate, have more frequent contact with parents, have high job satisfaction among teachers, and report higher student achievement scores than non-teaming schools (Flowers, Mertens, & Mulhall, 1999). During the middle years, several factors related to curriculum and instruction are important for helping young adolescents who are special needs learners adjust to the changes and new demands placed on them. These factors include the way in which curriculum is organized, how instruction is delivered, the way decisions are made about course selection.

Several strategies have been associated with student achievement in middle schools—for all students. When teachers are engaged in teams with fewer students (90 or fewer), they can participate more frequently in team activities, particularly curriculum coordination and coordination of student assignments. Teachers and counselors need frequent common planning time when students have learning difficulties (National Middle School, 2004; Rottier, 2001). In order to assess the effectiveness of their strategies, teachers should document the teaching and learning approaches used within their classes and should document student results. Administrators are pivotal in helping teachers appreciate the value of their teaming in creating a positive climate, particularly for special needs learners, and for improving their relationships with students, parents, and other professionals (Flowers et al., 1999; Mertens, Flowers, & Mulhall, 1998).

Classroom Strategies Compatible With Adolescent Development.

As research has indicated earlier, there is a disconnect between expectations of the standardized general educational environments on the one hand and, on the other, the nonstandard, individual, highly variable social, cognitive, and physical changes that occur during early adolescence (Carnegie Council on Adolescent Development, 2000; Haugaard, 2000; National Educational Research Policy and Priorities Board, 2000; Urdan & Klein, 1998).

Neuropsychologists agree that the prefrontal cortex of the brain is where memory and attention undergo changes during adolescent development. They also agree that the way to hold attention in young adolescents is to engage the senses and emotions and to combine this with problem-based learning (Casey, Giedd, & Thomas, 2000; Kwon & Lawson, 2000; Montgomery & Whiting, 2000; Wilson & Horch, 2004; Wolfe, 2001). Teachers encourage students to ask questions that interest them after they are introduced to a problem in a unit. Using essential questions to frame the unit, incorporating the senses and emotions to focus the learning, and then facilitating students as they find multiple ways to solve problems can focus adolescent learning while building complex neuron connections within the brain (Wilson & Horch, 2004).

Classroom Activities Compatible With Attention and Memory in Adolescents.

These activities are problem based and situated in real-world experiences and contexts. This means that students learn as they are engaged in working together to examine real-life issues relevant to them and solve problems using all their senses. They are also expected to take responsibility for directing their own work and for team participation. In project-based units of study, students are asked overarching questions and then develop their own projects to find the answers, such as interviewing people who have experienced the Great Depression or the Holocaust. Simulations are engaging and involve students in understanding various perspectives on a topic or in discussing complex ethical issues. Playing music can link memory to specific learning tasks to facilitate young adolescents' sensorimotor connections.

Having students write reflectively can help reinforce and consolidate learning. Posing visual and word problems or puzzles to challenge thinking demonstrate to students that there are many ways to solve a problem or puzzle. This type of thinking strengthens neural connections and gives students more confidence in their abilities to tackle problems. Physical challenges can also be used as a context for solving problems and building collaboration. Low ropes courses and other physical/mental problem solving involve the mind and body in learning and team building.

Involving students in real-life apprenticeships allow students to shadow workers in various jobs or to learn skills in a short internship that either connects to an area of study or helps them understand one of the problems they have posed themselves. Using peer collaboration or cooperative learning helps broaden students' understanding and promotes group problem solving. Students work as partners and in small groups, and use self-assessment and peer assessment. They may be involved in the process of reporting to parents, creating learning improvement plans, and developing integrated homework notebooks. These activities create an environment where it is "cool" to do well because they rely on the real interests and talents of adolescents.

In addition, more middle schools are establishing subschools and adopting a small team-based model of student management and support. The team-based model establishes home groups and rooms and provides a supervised make-up room with flexible timetables (Sousa, 2001; Tileston, 2000; Wilson & Horch, 2004; Wolfe, 2001).

Teaming for Exploratory Curriculum.   Developmentally responsive middle schools provide an inviting, challenging, and **exploratory curriculum** that connects subject areas. An exploratory curriculum balances attention to academic basics and students' need to explore a wide variety of interests and experiences. Exploratory classes in areas of art, music, drama, technology, foreign languages, and others offer students opportunities to explore their interests (National Middle School Association, 2004).

Developmentally appropriate curriculum involves interdisciplinary teams that consist of two or more teachers from different subject areas and the group of students they commonly instruct. Team teachers plan, coordinate, and evaluate curriculum and instruction across academic areas. Teams cultivate meaningful and regular communication with families. Teams often share the same schedule and the same area of the building. For teachers, teams provide a collaborative and supportive work group, and for students of all abilities, teams offer stable relationships with teachers and peers (Jackson & Davis, 2000). Seventy-nine percent of principals in middle level schools report that they had teams in 2000, up from 57% in 1992 (National Middle School Association, 2004; Valentine, Clark, Hackman, & Petzko, 2002). The team of teachers make possible small communities of learners which enhance personal relationships among students and teachers.

Practices such as these are recommended in middle schools for young adolescents, particularly those with disabilities, because they connect the content of the curriculum and the teaching strategies with the personal experiences of students. Such connection and its ability to motivate students demonstrates in practice what brain research hypothesizes. Box 12.2 describes the advantages of a middle school within a K–8 structure.

Cordova Primary and Middle Schools are separate entities within a K–8 school, with separate principals for its K–3 and 4–8 programs. The unusual arrangement enables the middle school program to develop and use middle-level instructional strategies. Both schools operate on block schedules designed to provide quality reading time for the primary grades as well as an uninterrupted block of time for core classes for middle school students. The schedules also provide time for both programs to be served by the school's music, art, and physical education teachers. In the middle school schedule, elective blocks are reserved for the first and last periods of the school day. This allows students to have a continuous block of time, interrupted by only a 30-minute lunch break, for science, social studies, math, reading, and language classes. The primary grade students benefit from an uninterrupted reading block for the first part of the day.

The middle school schedule allows students proficient in the core subjects to explore and enhance their talents and skills in other areas. They can use both of the schedule's elective blocks for band, chorus, or art. Or they may prefer something a little different, like library science, computer technology, peer mediation, or acting as student assistants. The student assistants serve as mentors at all grade levels, providing them with opportunities to enhance their leadership skills while supporting academic success for others. Middle school students who are not performing well in the core subjects are allowed to choose an elective in one block, using the other block for remedial assistance in language arts and/or math. While Cordova's primary and middle schools share the same campus, middle-level approaches like common planning time, elective enrichment programs, and building student leadership have helped provide diverse adolescents, including those with special learning needs, with the type of instruction and the support they need within a K–8 setting. —Karen Williams, Principal, Cordova Middle School, Phoenix, Arizona, 2002, by permission of the National Association of Elementary School Principals

Renewing Middle School Instruction to Support Students With Disabilities: The Coral Springs Middle School Experience

Recently, researchers have been interested in closely examining the process schools undergo when they collaborate to restructure middle schools to address the diverse developmental needs of students with and without disabilities. For example, Kilgore, Griffin, Sindelar, and Webb (2001) conducted in-depth qualitative studies of several middle schools in the process of changing their classroom practices to support inclusive classrooms. The following describes the process and strategies used by one middle school faculty at Coral Springs Middle School.

Using the Coalition of Essential Schools' (CES) principles for school reform (Blank, Melaville, & Shah, 2003), school faculty held workshops, faculty meetings, retreats, and summer training at a collaborating university. Faculty adopted the assumption that children are natural learners and that it was the teacher's responsibility to find strategies that work for individual children. They realized that placing at-risk students and students with disabilities in every class forced every teacher to abandon old methods that worked well in homogeneous classes, but no longer worked in diverse classrooms. In team meetings, teachers shared strategies that worked or failed with particular children. Teachers offered their colleagues weekly workshops on innovative instructional strategies. Coalition study groups read and discussed articles on teaching and learning. Special education teachers ran workshops describing specific learning disabilities and shared accommodation suggestions.

Teachers came to believe that the strategies that helped children with special needs helped all children in the classes and that good teachers did not have one best teaching method, but rather an arsenal of approaches appropriate in different circumstances. Teachers told us they were becoming better teachers. As one teacher put it, "When you teach kids with special needs, you do a better job of teaching in general." Some teachers realized that there were problems with the traditional curriculum that they were delivering with new methods. The material did not motivate students they found hardest to reach and teach. Teachers recrafted parts of the curriculum to build in interdisciplinary lessons and organized the teaching of concepts across the curriculum. Teachers adopted a variety of instructional strategies, including cooperative learning and peer tutoring in which students were grouped so that advanced students could assist their less advanced classmates. More teachers began using computers to increase student motivation and productivity, supplement instruction, and enhance the curriculum.

Teachers invited colleagues in to observe their classes and held weekly professional development sessions. Coteachers modeled teaching strategies with their teams. Teachers looked for authentic and alternative assessment practices that would help them monitor and document student performance. To respond to some students who still lagged behind, teachers expanded their teaching strategies to make better use of coteachers, modify assignments, provide one-to-one instruction or small group instruction, use more explicit forms of instruction, and provide alternative forms of testing. Students with reading difficulties received specialized instruction (Kilgore et al. 2001, 44–51; Kilgore & Webb [and the faculty and staff of Coral Springs Middle School] 1997, by permission).

These strategies reflect the four functions of collaboration introduced in Chapter 1: collaboration as discovery, as synthesis of ideas, as development of practice, and as building professional community. The research of Kilgore et al. (2001) suggests that inclusive classroom are most likely to be accepted and supported by faculty and staff when schools alter traditional cultures, transform themselves into learning communities, and develop the capacity for continual professional growth (Senge, 1994; Wenger, McDermott, & Snyder, 2002). Several factors were instrumental in the transformation of the school culture at the middle school as faculty and staff worked together to implement inclusive education: a system of democratic governance, a culture of collaboration, commitment to and capacity for professional growth, strong supportive leadership, and concern about equity and the success and well-being of individual students.

Collaboration to Prevent At-Risk Behavior: Positive Behavioral Intervention

As middle schools undergo reforms to become more developmentally appropriate for young adolescents, they are building in greater collaboration and coordination among educators, parents, students, and outside agencies. Home–school collaboration is crucial for students with disabilities, and the information that parents provide makes a difference in teachers' effectiveness with students (Ammon & Peretti, 1999; Anderson, Christenson, & Lehr, 2004; Bos, Nahamias, & Urban, 1999; Braddock, Hemp, Parish, & Rizzolo, 2000; Chavkin, Gonzalez, & Rader, 2002; Reese & Gallimore, 2000).

Schools are increasing their efforts to engage parents in assessment of behavioral needs and development of behavior plans. With the IDEA 2004 reauthorization, parent involvement is required in all stages of assessment, identification, and the development of behavior plans. Whereas parents have always been included as participants on their child's multidisciplinary and individualized education program (IEP) teams, they must now have input during early intervening services and eligibility meetings and to plan positive behavioral interventions (interventions for dealing with behavioral challenges of students with disabilities). Parents have much to offer, whether it be information about a child's medical, developmental, and educational history; assessments of behavior and attention levels; or information about interests and rewards that can be used to reinforce students' behavior. When a behavior concern is identified, the use of a problem-solving process that is based on parent–teacher collaboration can make all the difference to the student (Catalano, Arthur, Hawkins, Berglund, & Olson, 1998; Chalfant & Pysh, 1989; DiNatale & Shore, 2000; Ryan, 2001). In cases in which the students become involved in high risk behaviors, such as substance abuse and criminal activity, substance abuse counselors, sponsors, or probation officers may become a part of a school team.

Most students with disabilities, at some time in their middle school years, will require additional related services from community-based agencies in order to successfully participate in their academic programs. Let's See It in Action below, describes a coordinated team approach to support middle school students with emotional and behavioral disabilities.

Collaboration for Career Education

Career education is an important element in the curriculum for both middle and high school, particularly for students with special needs who have employment as their postsecondary goal. In the middle school, adolescents are beginning to learn about careers, and some participate in service learning (unpaid work experiences) in their communities. Career education has been defined as the totality of experience through which one learns to live a meaningful, satisfying work life (Sitlington, Clark, &

LET'S SEE IT IN ACTION: CASE ILLUSTRATION: A COORDINATED TEAM APPROACH FOR MIDDLE SCHOOL

The intensive support program (ISP) is provided through a collaborative program developed by Nassau BOCES (Bureau of Cooperative Education Services) and the North Shore Child and Family Guidance Center for students with significant emotional difficulties. Services of the ISP program address the emotional and behavioral issues that interfere with the achievement of educational goals. The North Shore clinical staff, who include licensed clinical social workers and psychiatrists, work with Nassau BOCES educational staff which include administrators, psychologists, teachers, and teacher aides, to provide a coordinated team approach. ISP services include support in the school setting such as individual, group, and family treatment; crisis intervention; coordination of family services; and medication management.

Our middle school program firmly believes in the team approach to education and provides many schoolwide incentives to assist students in the development of social skills. A schoolwide behavior system based on positive behavior intervention supports (PBIS) increases our capacity to educate our students by using clearly defined outcomes, research validated practices, supportive administrative systems, and information for effective problem solving. The behavior management system reaches out to students experiencing behavioral problems and offers positive supports and strategies for success. Students in crisis are assisted in problem solving and learn to take responsibility for their actions as they acquire a repertoire of acceptable and appropriate school behaviors. In providing a well-rounded educational environment, occupational education such as woodshop and food trades are provided, as well as art and music, which makes learning a positive experience (Northshore Families Helping Families, 2003).

Kolstoe, 2000). Career education provides the opportunity for youth to learn, in the least restrictive environment possible, the academic, daily living, personal–social and occupational knowledge, and specific vocational skills necessary for attaining their highest levels of economic, personal, and social fulfillment. The individual can obtain this fulfillment through work (both paid and unpaid) and in a variety of other social roles and personal lifestyles, including his or her pursuits as a student, citizen, volunteer family member, and participant in meaningful leisure time activities (Altman, 1997; Bailey, 2001; Brown, 2000; Council for Exceptional Children [CEC], 1997; Eisenman, 2001; Gordon, 1973; Sarkees-Wircenski & Scott, 2003).

Individualized appropriate education for children with disabilities includes the opportunity for every student to achieve his or her highest level of career potential through career education experiences. Career education is viewed as an integral part of the total curriculum and the entire school program. Career education is infused throughout the curriculum by knowledgeable teachers who integrate career development goals with subject matter goals, in collaboration with career assessment specialists, special educators, and transition specialists. For example, in a math class, the teacher might include a discussion about the variety of careers in which mathematics is a central component.

Career education involves the blending of academic and vocational curriculum with community-based work experiences. Therefore, career-oriented learning requires collaboration among general educators, special educators, guidance counselors, vocational assessment personnel, vocational rehabilitation counselors, and business–industry personnel. Educators work together to blend the curriculum and ensure the appropriate accommodations and supports are available in the career–vocational classroom and work-based setting. Guidance counselors assist the student in planning and preparing to achieve postsecondary goals. Vocational assessment and rehabilitation personnel assess career strengths, needs, and interests, and determine accommodations or supports needed in the employment setting. All of these professionals collaborate with parents to guide career education planning and set postsecondary goals.

What System Coordination Strategies Support Transition From Middle to High School?

Bringing Middle and High School Educators Together

Underlying successful high school transition programs are activities that bring middle school and high school administrators, counselors, and teachers together to collaborate and learn about the programs, courses, curriculum, and requirements of their respective schools and to plan for transition. Transition from middle to high school is not the sole responsibility of the middle school or the high school, but their shared responsibility. Recognition of shared responsibility means that educators must work together to design a seamless process. Activities that create a mutual understanding of curriculum requirements at both levels, and of the adolescent learner and his or her needs, will enable middle school educators to better prepare students for high school.

Do Middle and High School Educators Agree on What Youth Need?

Two university researchers, Hertzog and Morgan (1999)—a former middle school principal and a former high school assistant principal—conducted a 4-year study of transition from middle to high school. Initially, 17 middle schools and 14 high schools were involved, but the study was expanded to include all of the school systems in the states of Georgia and Florida (97 middle schools and 56 high schools). They asked the questions: When high school people criticize middle schools for failing to adequately prepare students to succeed academically in ninth grade, how do you react? Is this legitimate criticism? What should principals and teachers from both sides be doing to better ensure a successful transition? The responses were eye-opening and revealed the tensions—and sometimes resentments—between educators at both levels in terms of how they view the role of the school, the needs of adolescents, and the responsibilities of educators.

The Hertzog and Morgan study found that some schools (middle and high) conducted only a building tour and followed that with the high school counselor assisting the eighth grade students in high school registration. These schools had the highest dropout and retention rates. The bottom line was that the more extensive the transition program, the lower the dropout rate and retention rate (ninth grade). Schools that have increased their transition support practices have lowered their retention rates in ninth grade and lowered their dropout rates at the high school.

Strategies for Coordinating Transition to High School

Several strategies have been successful in helping educators and parents collaborate to support students as they prepare for the journey into high school. MacIver (1990) first clustered high school transition activities into three groups: (1) those that provide students and parents with information about the high school; (2) those that provide students with social support during the transition; and (3) those that bring middle and high school personnel together to learn about curriculum and requirements. The following strategies, many of which begin in middle school and carry over into high school, have been synthesized from a variety of studies on middle school transition (Alspaugh & Harting, 1997; Dahir & Eby, 2001; Elias, 2001; Hertzog & Morgan, 1999; Hertzog, Morgan, Diamond, & Walker, 1996; Hough, 2003; MacIver, 1990; McAdoo, 1999; Mizelle, 1999; Mizelle & Mullins 1997; Phelan, Davidson, & Yu, 1998; Sanders & Epstein, 2000; Vars, 1998).

Information Sharing for Students and Parents. There are many ways of sharing information to support transition to high school. Ninth-grade students, teachers, or counselors can share information in visits to groups of eighth-grade students. Parents should be involved in decisions that rising eighth-grade students are asked to make about courses of study they will choose in ninth grade. Students can shadow a high school student for a day to learn about the setting, or attend a function at the high school. They can create a project to examine the high school Web page to learn about the school, activities, clubs, sports, and courses of study, or attending a presentation by a high school student or panel of students.

Providing Social and Academic Supports. Some high schools are redesigning their structure to allow freshmen to stay with the same group of teachers for the ninth and tenth grades, remaining somewhat separate from older high school students. This permits more intensive relationships and support services as students make the adjustment to secondary school. Supportive advisory groups or "Big Sister/Brother" programs that begin in eighth grade and continue through ninth grade can help bridge the transition year. Summer programs provide responsive remediation for students who need more preparation for the secondary course of study. Finally, writing programs in which eighth-graders correspond with high school students can help students build connections with secondary students and the school.

Bringing Middle and High School Personnel Together. Continuing professional preparation in adolescent development is essential for both middle and high school teachers. Middle and high school personnel can also be strategically joined through curriculum planning meetings, teacher or administrator visitations, observations, and teaching exchanges. Activities such as these, unfortunately, are often the first to be cut as budgets recede in local school systems, and parents, educators, and students must advocate for them. Advocacy for effective middle school transition is most effective when sound data is maintained on positive results for educators and students.

Summary of Key Points

- For students with disabilities, transition into, through, and out of middle school requires the collaboration of the middle school and high school communities.
- A significant number of children show changes in academic performance, perceptions about school, and self-perceptions as they make the transition to middle school.
- Students in the United States are most at risk for failure at the time of their transition from eighth to ninth grade; schools with extensive transition support programs for students entering middle school have significantly reduced dropout rates.
- Academic rigor and a nurturing environment are not mutually exclusive, but are mutually supportive and should be each teacher's, school's, and educational level's dual mission.
- The developmentally responsive middle school provides peer mentors and adult advocates and orients students to new expectations for student behavior and responsibility.
- Career education and postsecondary planning is viewed as an integral part of the total curriculum.

Key Terms and Phrases

- Transition to middle school (p. 318)
- Middle school concept (p. 322)
- Middle school structure (p. 322)
- Crisis intervention (p. 324)
- Middle school reforms (p. 330)
- Developmentally responsive middle school (p. 331)
- Strength-based student assessment (p. 332)
- Exploratory curriculum (p. 334)
- Developmentally appropriate curriculum (p. 334)
- Career education (p. 337)

Questions for Reflection, Thinking, and Skill Building

1. What is transition planning in middle school? Why are transition supports in and out of middle school so important?

2. Why is it important for schools to coordinate closely with parents in the middle school years? What key professionals are important for student development and support?

3. For young adolescents in transition from elementary to middle school, discuss the behaviors or reactions that educators should be alert for as signs of the need for additional supports.

4. Pair up with a classmate. Discuss your own experiences with the move from elementary to middle school. Do recall how you felt? What do you remember as the main differences between the schools? Can you remember what it was that most helped you to adjust to the new environment? Who was involved in providing that help? Were there supports you wish had been in place?

5. Interview a seventh-grade teacher (or teacher teaching first-year middle school students). Ask him or her about the transition activities in which they participate before they receive a new group of students from elementary. In their view what are the strengths and weaknesses of the process? What recommendations do they have for improving the transition process for children with disabilities and for all children?

6. Visit a middle school in your community. Examine the literature provided to middle school students and families. How much helpful information is there about school support services and community services for students with disabilities? Ask about the provisions for preparing students for the transition into middle school and for the transition to high school. In your judgment, are there adequate transition supports in place for students? What would you recommend to educators?

CHAPTER THIRTEEN

How Can School Collaboration and System Coordination Promote Progress of High School Students?

With Robert Baer

Many high school students have no idea where they want to be tomorrow, let alone where they may want to be as an adult living in a world where they will be making personal decisions, working to support themselves, and adding value to the world. Transition should start in the early years with educators and families making children aware of choices, possibilities, and allowing them to dream. Exploration and preparation for transition should be developed during the middle and high school years. —Colorado Department of Education, 2003

- Who decides about high school curriculum for students with and without disabilities? A historical perspective

- What are the legal requirements to prepare high school students for transition?

- What coordination roles and competencies promote progress of students in high school?

- What planning strategies are effective for high school students with special needs?

- What collaboration and system coordination strategies promote progress for secondary students?

- What is the school or district level interagency transition team?

- How can interagency agreements overcome barriers to system coordination? The Ohio Experience

PERSPECTIVES

High School Student

I was asked to lead my own IEP meeting where we talked about transition and my plans for graduation. My teacher helped me plan for it and what to expect. It made me feel like I was in charge of my own future and that everyone would be listening to what I wanted and what I was interested in. For so long, I have been the one who couldn't learn, and now I was leading something important. And that's the way it should be.

—HIGH SCHOOL STUDENT

Parent

My daughter could not have finished her tenth grade without a lot of help from her teachers and school counselor. She needed special education supports in the general classroom in reading and mathematics, speech and language services, and group counseling services for an anxiety disorder. Without the collaboration among teachers and school professionals, and the interagency agreement they had with outside agencies, we would not be here.

—MOTHER OF A HIGH SCHOOL STUDENT WITH MULTIPLE DISABILITIES

INTRODUCTION

Many have characterized the high school years as requiring a **transition perspective** for education of youth with disabilities (Baer et al., 1996; Clark & Patton, 1997; Halpern, 1999; Johnson et al., 2000; Kohler, 1998; Lueking & Certo, 2004; Martin et al., 1996; Michaels, 1994; Ward & Wehmeyer, 1995). Kochhar-Bryant and Bassett (2002b) referred to transition as a "unifying framework" for aligning standards-based education (state-defined common learning standards for all) and transition services and supports for students with disabilities. Transition planning, therefore, is the foundation concept that integrates the four building blocks of individualized education—standards, outcomes in multiple life domains, opportunities to learn (accommodations and supports), and curriculum options. This definition and the associated planning processes are used as the defining characteristics of collaboration at the secondary level. They describe both individual and systems level interventions that have been successful in encouraging collaboration among key stakeholders and assure that secondary education is meaningful and designed to prepare students to enter the adult environments of their choosing.

Societal interest in career awareness, career choice, graduation pathways, and adjustment to adult roles has emerged as a new subfield within education. Preparation for transition from school to adult life involves changes in the self-concept, motivation, and development of the individual, and is a fragile passage for the adolescent seeking to make difficult life choices (German, Martin, Marshall, & Sale, 2000; Michaels, 1994). This passage is even more delicate for youth with disabilities who need additional support and preparation to make the journey. For professionals seeking to help students on this journey, the process involves forming linkages among education and other human service agencies, including employment and training, adult services, and rehabilitation.

This chapter begins with a historical perspective on curriculum choice and planning for high school youth as a context for understanding the relationship between academic and career–vocational preparation in today's standards-based environment. Basic legal requirements for preparing students for transition are summarized along with coordination roles that promote the progress of high school students with disabilities. Collaboration and coordination strategies that support instruction in the secondary setting are presented, including local interagency transition teams and their role in supporting students to prepare for transition to postsecondary settings.

WHO DECIDES ABOUT HIGH SCHOOL CURRICULUM FOR STUDENTS WITH AND WITHOUT DISABILITIES? A HISTORICAL PERSPECTIVE

Historical context is important for understanding the relationship between academic and career–vocational preparation in today's standards-based educational environment. While career development for children, youth, and adults of all exceptionalities has been evolving since the turn of the century, the concepts of high school transition and career education have only emerged since the 1950s. More recently, educators and policymakers are recognizing the need to understand the role of career and vocational development, and high school diploma options, within the overall framework of adolescent development. There is a growing concern in the United States about identifying interventions believed to be positively associated with improved graduation rates and transition of youth with disabilities from school to employment and adult life roles.

History of the Debate Over Academic and Occupational Education

Philosophers from the Aristotelian era to modern day have disputed the role of career and vocational preparation in the educational development of children and youth. Aristotle, like Plato, distinguished between liberal education and technical training, viewing the liberal arts as enlarging a person's horizons, consciousness, and choices, and viewing vocational training as an interference with intellectual development (Ornstein & Levine, 1997). The debate about the concept of career development and vocational choice and their roles in the social and educational development of children and youth continues today. Educational historians have observed that as the public schools emerged in the United States over the past 200 years, they mirrored this schism, breaking the curriculum into academic subjects and separating it from vocational or career-oriented learning. Different pathways to graduation and diploma options emerged as students made forced choices between college and trade or career. Furthermore, concerns about the image of vocational education and differences of opinion about which students belong in the programs have plagued policymakers and educational practitioners since the emergence of the first vocational education programs. Two examples include (1) whether students with disabilities should be "tracked" into vocational education and (2) whether vocational education should be destigmatized by renaming it career–technical education and including more technical courses in it? By separating the concept of academic education from that of career development, educators perpetuated the dichotomy between learning and work, intellectual pursuit and manual activity, individual achievement and social responsibility. Statesmen and leading educators such as Ben Franklin, Horace Mann, and John Dewey have spoken against this artificial dichotomy since before the beginning of this century (Dewey 1916; Mann, 1957; Spring, 1988).

Origins of Career–Vocational Education

Career, vocational, technological, or practical arts education has a history spanning centuries. In Europe at the time of the onset of the industrial revolution in England, Denis Diderot (1713–1784) and Jean-Jacques Rousseau (1712–1778) began to stimulate a wider interest in the mechanical arts in France. In his *Discourse on the Sciences and Arts of 1750*, Rousseau criticized the arts and sciences (especially the arts in the luxury trades) for their undesirable effects on social values. His essay described the detrimental effects of the arts and sciences on civilization, criticizing urban high society and its self-serving promotion of the arts and sciences. Diderot wanted to elevate the status of the mechanical arts by systematizing the arts and helping craftsmen work in a manner similar to the liberal arts and sciences. One of his purposes was to promote among the literate a better understanding and appreciation for craftsmen and their work and their contributions to technological progress. He also believed that his work would benefit craftsmen by helping them to think more critically about their craft through more systematic and analytical reflection (Pannabecker, 1995, 2004). These two philosophers contributed greatly to the development of technological education. Elements of the differences between Diderot and Rousseau are still part of the mix in contemporary technological education and will continue to be a part of future patterns in curriculum and instruction (p. 21).

Manual Arts Enters the Public School Curriculum

The shop system, based on the early theories of Rousseau, Diderot, and others, remains a central part of vocational–technical education today. In the United States, career and vocational education is rooted in the old apprenticeship system in which adolescents lived with their masters who would teach them a craft and, also, how to be responsible members of society. In that system, career and life were intimately connected. The manual arts movement emerged in the late 1800s when several vocal educators advocated to increase the availability of manual training to all students as part of the public schools (Walter, 1993). Manual arts training signaled a shift away from the belief that college preparatory curriculum should be the sole purpose of high school to a belief that it should be broadened to prepare students for a variety of career paths (Gordon, 1999).

During the 1830s and 1840s vocational training was introduced into orphanages and reform schools. As a result, vocational education became stigmatized and viewed as education for the "poor, the backward, deficient, incorrigible, or otherwise subnormal" (Federal Board for Vocational Education, 1917; Meers, 1980, 1993). The industrial revolution also accelerated the decline of the apprenticeship system by introducing fragmented, specialized, and standardized production lines that eroded the connection between craft and preparation for responsible life (Spring, 1988). The apprenticeship program lost its most important characteristics, the personal guidance and instruction by a master (Gordon, 1999). However, in 1937, the Fitzgerald Act was passed which established a program of apprenticeship in the United States and standards for employing and training apprentices. According to Gordon, apprenticeship in America today has grown into a governmental credentialing system for developing and recognizing specific skills, competencies, and accomplishments and where training takes place under close supervision of a skilled and experienced craft worker.

Many social and economic forces have influenced the rise of vocational and technical education. The mass production, automation, and technological explosion that occurred during the late 1800s and the early 1900s accelerated the expansion of vocational and technical educational opportunities for youth. The federal government has had an important role in this expansion with the creation of the Commission on National Aid to Vocational Education (1914) and passage of the Smith-Hughes Act (P.L. 64–347, 1917) which provided the basis for the vocational education movement. Vocational rehabilitation programs for individuals with disabilities were also built into this Act (Meers, 1980, p. 9).

Career Education Becomes a National Priority and Includes Disadvantaged Populations

The **career education movement** in the United States gained additional momentum in the 1960s when it became a high priority of the then U.S. Office of Education's Bureau of Adult, Vocational, and Technical Education (Halpern, 1985, 1999). In 1963, the Vocational Education Act (P.L. 88–210) was passed to maintain, extend, and improve upon existing programs of vocational education, as well as to use funds for persons who have academic, socioeconomic, or other disadvantages that prevent them from succeeding in regular vocational education (Gordon, 1999). In 1971, career education was proclaimed as a major educational reform by the U.S. Commissioner of Education, Sidney Marland, Jr. Marland believed that the high dropout rate in the United States was due in part to the failure of the educational system to provide students with a relevant education that was aligned with their future goals and potentials (Kokaska & Brolin, 1985). Students with disabilities were not included in the initiative originally, but in 1977, the Career Education Implementation Incentive Act (P.L. 95–207) was passed to help states infuse career education into school curricula. Students with disabilities were included as a target population (Michaels, 1994). The Perkins Vocational Education Act of 1984 (P.L. 98–524) named for House Representative and civil rights supporter Carl D. Perkins, and still bears his name. Career development under the Perkins Act, and transition systems under IDEA have remained enduring concepts and instruments in federal policy over the past half century to improve secondary education and postsecondary outcomes for youth with disabilities.

What Are the Legal Requirements to Prepare High School Students for Transition?

According to the IDEA 1997, by age 14, the individual education program (IEP) for students with disabilities was required to assure that they have access to educational and career–vocational programs congruent with their postschool goals. The IDEA amendments of 2004 revised the language to begin transition services at age 16, with the local option to begin earlier. The 2004 amendments define **transition** as a coordinated set of activities for a student with a disability that:

- Is designed to be within a results-oriented process, that is focused on improving the academic and functional achievement of the child with a disability to facilitate the child's movement from school to postschool activities, including postsecondary education; vocational education; integrated employment (including supported employment); continuing and adult education; adult services; and independent living or community participation;
- Is based on the individual child's needs, taking into account the child's strengths, preferences, and interests; and
- Includes instruction, related services, community experiences, the development of employment and other postschool adult living objectives and, when appropriate, acquisition of daily living skills and functional vocational evaluation. (Sec. 602, 20 USC 1400)

The IEP must include a statement, beginning no later than the first IEP in effect when the student is 16 and updated annually, of "appropriate measurable postsecondary goals based on age-appropriate transition assessments related to training, education, employment, and independent living skills." The IEP must also include transition services, including courses of study needed to assist in reaching the postsecondary goal (IDEA, 2004).

Greene and Kochhar-Bryant (2003) identified four broad courses of study or transition pathways leading to four general postschool goals. These were (1) fully integrated into academics leading to a 4-year college or university, (2) integrated academics leading to a community college or vocational-technical school, (3) general and life skills education for competitive employment and semi-independent living, and (4) community and life skills education for supported employment and supervised living. Many states are defining different graduation options or pathways that result in several diploma options (Johnson & Thurlow, 2003).

For a student to choose from among different options or pathways such as these requires the involvement of special and general educators, counselors, and vocational educators who can explain the requirements of each pathway; advise students on their feasibility; and explain the course of study required to complete the pathway. It also requires the involvement of adult service and related service providers who can provide supports along the way. Students must be engaged in the planning process to ensure that the pathway best fits their goals and interests. Figure 13.1 illustrates the variety of professionals involved in a transition collaboration for a student with a disability entering high school.

Collaboration at Key Transition Points

If local school districts exercise the option of beginning transition planning much earlier than age 16 (as IDEA 2004 permits), the first transition point might occur between the middle school and high school. Collaboration between middle school and high school teachers and related professionals becomes essential. The second transition point for secondary students with disabilities is the transition from school

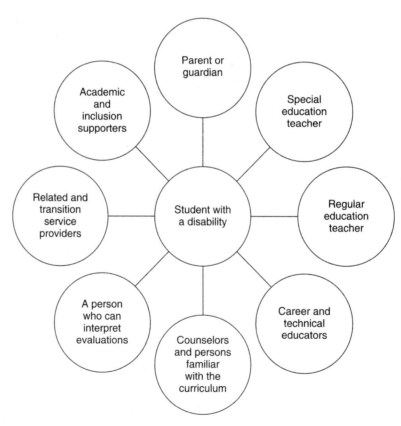

FIGURE 13.1
Collaboration for the Student Entering High School

to adult settings. This requires another form of collaboration to assure that these students plan for and acquire the necessary supports and linkages to move into their desired postsecondary environments. Collaboration at this stage requires a team able to provide the range of transition services identified in IDEA including instruction, related services, community experiences, development of employment, and adult living objectives, acquisition of daily living skills, functional vocational evaluation, and interagency linkages. Figure 13.2 provides an example of the type of collaboration that would be required for the transition from high school to postsecondary environments.

Generally, the formation of a collaborative team has been an important consideration in the development of an effective IEP and transition plan for a secondary student with a disability. Team members should be selected in consultation with the student and the family (Aspel, Bettis, Quinn, Test, & Wood, 1999; Bremer, Kachgal, & Schoeller, 2003; O'Brien, 1987) because they often have informal networks that can aid in achieving graduation and postschool goals. In fact, outcome studies have found that self–friend–family networks accounted for more than 80% of the jobs

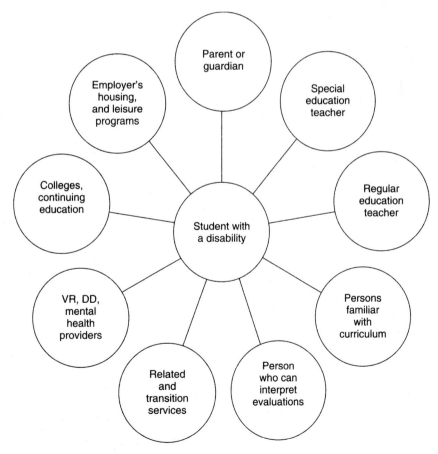

FIGURE 13.2
Collaboration for a Student Who Is in High School

obtained by students after graduation (Hazasi, Gordon, & Roe, 1985; Storms, O'Leary, & Williams, 2000b; Wagner & Blackorby, 1996). The selection of the team should also include representatives from high school and postsecondary environments desired by the students, so that the student and the family can establish contacts and become familiar with the requirements of the programs they want to enter. In addition to the core members included in Figures 13.1 and 13.2, individual students may have specific needs or preferences that require the involvement of other members. These include, but are not limited to, (a) work–study coordinators, (b) vocational rehabilitation counselors, (c) adult service providers, (d) postsecondary education providers, (e) employers, and (f) advocates.

What Coordination Roles and Competencies Promote Progress of Students in High School?

Key roles important in promoting progress of students in high school are presented below. Related services roles were described in Chapter 12.

Special Education and General Education Teachers in High School

As in middle school, special education teachers develop an individualized education program (IEP) for each special education student. The IEP sets personalized goals for each student, including the academic course of study, and is tailored to the student's individual learning style and ability. In the high school, the program includes a transition plan outlining specific steps to prepare special education students for life after high school. Teachers review the IEP with the student's parents, related services specialists, counselors, school administrators, and the student's general education teacher. Teachers work closely with parents to share their child's progress and suggest techniques to promote learning at home. Preparing special education students for daily life after graduation is an important aspect of the job. Teachers provide students with career counseling or help them learn routine skills, such as maintaining a bank account and a checkbook.

Since high schools are becoming more inclusive, special education teachers and general education teachers are increasingly working together in general education classrooms. Special education teachers help general educators adapt curriculum materials and teaching techniques to meet the needs of students with disabilities. They coordinate the work of teachers, teacher assistants, and related personnel, such as therapists and social workers, to meet the requirements of inclusive special education programs. They also consult with general educators on accommodations and preparation for students to take standardized exit exams or alternative tests.

High School Counselor

High school counselors are professionals who have a mental health perspective and who are integral to the total educational program for youth in high school. High school counselors implement counseling programs for high school students by providing a variety of supports. Classroom guidance involves helping students develop academic skills, including organizational, study and test-taking skills. They assist with postsecondary planning and college applications. Counselors help students with individual planning by guiding them to develop academic plans, career plans, and transition plans. They provide responsive services that include individual and small-group counseling, individual/family/school crisis intervention, peer facilitation, consultation and collaboration, and referrals to community service agencies. Counselors provide system supports through professional development, consultation and teaming, program management and operation (American School Counselor Association, 2004a).

Role of the Service Coordinator and Transition Specialist

A taxonomy, or set of categories for transition services, was first developed by Kohler (1998) and has been expanded and revised through a CEC review process of the Council for Exceptional Children. The taxonomy included best practices recommended by transition experts and derived from the findings of empirical studies. These best practices were clustered and rated by another group of transition professionals on their level of importance. From this work, Kohler developed a **taxonomy of transition planning and services** that includes (a) student development, (b) student-focused planning, (c) collaboration, (d) family involvement, and (e) program structure and attributes. The category of student development emphasizes activities that include development of self-determination skills, learning strategies, accommodations, social skills, vocational skills, and career goals. The student-focused planning category emphasizes the importance of developing measurable postschool transition goals, relevant educational activities, vocational objectives, student participation in IEP planning, and ongoing monitoring of services.

Within the category of collaboration, are included the development of system-level interagency teams, consultation with regular and career–vocational educators,

Liz Moore/Merrill

Student engagement in developing work skills is vital to their preparation for postsecondary employment or further education.

and coordination of student assessment. The family involvement category addresses the importance of promoting family participation in IEP planning, family knowledge of school and postschool options, and individualized consideration of parent roles in the transition process. Lastly, the category of program structure and attributes stresses the importance of developing outcome-based programs, flexible curricula, integrated learning settings, identification of student outcomes and postschool needs, and development of transition resources.

Kohler's research established the foundation for defining the service coordination and collaboration competencies needed by secondary educators. This work led the Council for Exceptional Children's (CEC) Subcommittee on Knowledge and Skills and the CEC Division of Career Development and Transition (DCDT) to identify the need for individuals trained in these skills, known as the **transition specialist**, who is defined as:

> . . . an individual who plans, coordinates, delivers, and evaluates transition education and services at the school or system level, in conjunction with other educators, families, students, and representatives of community organizations. (CEC, 1998c, p. 1)

Transition specialists in many local districts have separate school-based roles, and in other districts (particularly rural regions), the special educator has these activities embedded into teaching and consultation roles. The CEC Division on Career Development and Transition (DCDT) specialist competencies were organized according to the competency areas for special educators as delineated in What Every Special Educator Must Know (CEC, 2004).

WHAT PLANNING STRATEGIES ARE EFFECTIVE FOR HIGH SCHOOL STUDENTS WITH SPECIAL NEEDS?

Backward Planning

The common characteristic of collaboration at the secondary level is the shift from a focus on developmental and academic progress to a focus on achieving specific quality postschool outcomes (Turnbull, Turnbull, Wehmeyer, & Park, 2003). Therefore, planning at this level must begin with the end in mind and should use a process known as **backward planning** (Steere, Wood, Pancsofar, & Butterworth, 1990; Wiggins & McTighe, 2005). Traditionally, IEP planning has tended to pursue developmental milestones based on progress that the student has made in the past with a focus on remediating student disabilities (Stowitschek, Laitinen, & Prather, 1999). Consequently, the traditional IEP process has used forward planning. In contrast, backward planning uses future goals to identify current and future student performance needs. This process is therefore proactive and pragmatic with a focus on developing the most direct route to desired postschool outcomes by using students' strengths and support systems (rather than developmental milestones) to achieve their postschool quality-of-life outcomes.

Figures 13.3 and 13.4 show examples of how backward planning can be used to assure that students, one with a severe disability and one with a learning disability, have the services and opportunities to achieve supported employment or college upon graduation. In these examples, the students are established in desired **postschool environments** before graduation to assure that the necessary supports

FIGURE 13.3
Backward Planning
Worksheet 1

Name: Kevin Short

Postsecondary Goal: Supported employment in a clerical setting

Current Age: 18

Age to Graduate: 19

Needed Transition Service	Age 16	Age 17	Age 18	Age 19
1. Supported employment in a clerical setting			X	X
2. Follow-along support			X	X
3. Job placement services and job club		X	X	
4. Transportation training	X	X		
5. Develop social security work incentive plan		X		
6. Vocational education in clerical skills	X	X		
7. Work experience during the school year		X		
8. Summer jobs	X	X		
9. Job shadowing	X	X		
10. Guidance counseling	X			
11. Employability skills training	X	X		
12. Apply for social security benefits			X	
13. Referral vocational rehabilitation	X			
14. Referral for MR/DD services	X			

are in place and that no interruption of services occurs. Figure 13.3A shows a backward plan in which the student is actually participating in supported employment in the final 2 years before graduation.

The backward planning requires that the students receive job placement services 3 years prior to graduation, and transportation training, appropriate referrals to adult services, and benefits planning at 4 years to graduation. This process can be continued backward to the student's current year in school and be used for other postschool transition goals such as postsecondary education, residential living, or community participation. For students with milder disabilities, the steps are larger and have less overlap in services, but the principles are the same.

Backward planning is important because it is based on the expectation that students can achieve their desired postschool outcomes through early planning and a

FIGURE 13.4
Backward Planning
Worksheet 2

Name: Nancy Kessler

Postsecondary Goal: Community college, nursing assistant program

Current Age: 18

Age to Graduate: 19

Needed Transition Service	Age 16	Age 17	Age 18	Age 19
1. Supported employment in a clerical setting				
2. Follow-along support			X	X
3. Job placement services and job club				
4. Transportation training				
5. Develop social security work incentive plan				
6. Vocational education in health care services program	X	X		
7. Work experience during the school year		X		
8. Summer employment in local hospital	X	X	X	
9. Job shadowing				
10. Guidance counseling	X	X		
11. Employability skills training				
12. Apply for social security benefits				
13. Referral vocational rehabilitation		X		
14. Referral for MR/DD services				

team commitment to immediate action. This provides teams with a sense of urgency in regard to taking concrete action steps to help students achieve their postsecondary goals. However, transition coordinators should be aware that the focus of backward planning—on high expectations, long-term commitment, and flexibility in achieving postschool goals—is incompatible with traditional IEP planning approaches. Traditional approaches have limited goals, year-to-year commitments, and little flexibility (Aspel et al., 1999; Storms et al., 2000a; Stowitschek & Kelso, 1989). For reasons, it may be necessary to conduct backward planning as part of person-centered planning or informal planning outside of the IEP, allowing the team to set high expectations and be creative without fear of administrative and legal complications.

Developing Career Goals

Effective backward planning starts with clear career goals which in turn require greater involvement of career counselors and representatives of postschool, community, and adult service providers. A number of outcome-oriented strategies may be used to support the development of career goals for a student with a disability, which can be generally categorized as (a) person-centered planning, (b) self-determination approaches, and (c) career development strategies. These approaches may be used individually or collectively to support the backward planning process. Care must be used in the selection of these strategies because students with disabilities will have widely varying needs, support systems, and levels of career maturity (Menchetti & Piland, 1998). It should be emphasized that no single planning strategy will work effectively for the entire population of students with disabilities.

Person-Centered Planning. **Person-centered planning** approaches have been used effectively with students with severe disabilities who have difficulty reading and understanding language (O'Brien & Mount, 2005). These approaches were developed in the mid-1980s to involve individuals with disabilities and their natural supporters in solving problems related to moving these individuals into integrated, productive, and rewarding roles in the community (O'Brien & O'Brien, 2002). The person-centered approach relies on organizing individualized, natural, and creative supports to achieve meaningful goals based on the individual's strengths and preferences. Planning is not based on the services available, but rather creates a team of people who know and care about the individual with a disability. They come together to develop and share a dream for the person's future, and work together to organize and provide the supports necessary to achieve those goals.

Person-centered planning approaches have generally involved a neutral facilitator who leads a student and a family-selected team to answer questions regarding student's (a) history, (b) dreams, (c) nightmares, (d) relationships, (e) abilities, and (f) plans of action. Person-centered planning approaches typically have taken longer than traditional planning, have been held outside the agency, have involved the family and supporters, and have used visuals in which the ideas are depicted both in pictures and words to aid students in understanding and taking a leadership role in the planning process. Some common person-centered planning approaches have included:

- *Personal Futures Planning* (Kincaid & Fox, 2002; Mount & Zwernick, 1988). Personal futures planning focuses on what the team can do to address the themes or issues identified within a personal profile or other person-centered process. In personal futures planning, the team identifies an appropriate time frame for achieving a futures plan that specifically addresses themes in five areas (home, school, community, choices and preferences, and relationships).
- *MAPS* (Pearpoint, Forest, & O'Brien, 1996). MAPS (making action plans) is a person-centered planning process that brings together the key players in a child's life to identify a "roadmap" for working toward and achieving goals for the focus child. The assumptions underlying and guiding the MAPS process include integration, individualization, teamwork and collaboration, and flexibility.

- *PATH* (Kincaid & Fox, 2002; Pearpoint, Forest, & O'Brien 1996). PATH (planning alternative tomorrows with hope) is an effective process for bringing together a team that may already know a child well and has made a commitment to supporting the child in the future. PATH evolved from the MAPS process and uses information gathered in MAPS to develop a strategic plan of action. The team asks the person to choose where he or she wants to live and with whom, where he or she will be working, and how he or she will be involved in the community, including friendships, recreation, and transportation. The individual's preferences and choices become the basis for a clearly defined series of steps to make that dream come true. This process results in a strong commitment on the part of the team members to take specific actions now to help the individual progress along his\her path to the future. The process provides time lines for achieving goals and breaks them into achievable, measurable steps. It also identifies individuals on the team who are responsible for each action step (Kincaid & Fox, 2002).
- *Essential Lifestyle Planning* (Smull, Sanderson, & Harrison, 1996). This is a guided process for learning how someone wants to live their life and developing a plan to help make it happen.
- *COACH* (Giangreco, Cloninger, & Iverson, 1998) (choosing outcomes and accommodations for children) is an assessment and planning tool designed for students ages 3–21 with significant disabilities. Its purpose is to create a program for implementation in an inclusive setting based on individually determined quality-of-life outcomes.

Self-Determination Strategies.

Self-determination strategies are another important means of helping students develop career goals with emphasis on student participation and decision making. Person-centered planning approaches are rooted in the philosophy of "normalization" (Wolfensberger, 1972) and the principle that persons with disabilities should have the right to as "normal" a life as possible, including the exercise of choice (Nirje, 1972). The U.S. Department of Education began promoting self-determination for students with disabilities in 1989 when it held a national conference on self-determination that emphasized student-directed IEP planning (Ward, 1996). This led to legislative changes in the IDEA of 1990 which required that students be invited to IEP meetings in which their transition to adulthood was discussed (Sec. 300. 344) and in the IDEA of 1997 which transferred IDEA rights to the student with a disability upon reaching the age of majority (Sec. 300. 347).

The **self-determination** initiative led to the development of numerous self-determination approaches that have been categorized as those (a) that are focused on providing choices and (b) that focus on goal setting and attainment (Martin, Marshall, & DePry, 2001). Overall, self-determination approaches improve students' ability to (a) self-advocate, (b) make decisions, (c) develop goals, (d) demonstrate leadership, and (e) take an active role in the IEP meeting (Martin et al., 2001). Self-determination approaches include the following:

- *Choicemaker* (Martin & Marshall, 1996) is a curriculum focused on choosing goals, expressing goals (or self-directed IEP), and taking action (i.e., making goals happen). The self-determination transition assessment tool assesses both the students' skills and the students' opportunity to learn, practice, and express these skills in their environment.

- *Whose Future Is It Anyway?* (Wehmeyer & Kelchner, 1995) is a student-directed transition process with a curriculum that is designed for middle school and high school–aged students with mild to moderate intellectual, developmental, or learning disabilities.
- *Next Step* (Halpern et al., 1997) is a student transition and educational planning tool.
- *I Plan* (Van Reusen, Bos, Schumaker, & Preschler, 2002; Van Reusen & Bos, 1990) is a process for helping students communicate in planning conferences.
- *Take Charge* (Powers et al., 2001) includes two curricula intended for students ages 12–15 considered to be at risk due to health challenges, physical/learning/emotional disabilities, and/or family/community stresses.

Career Development and Planning.   **Career development and planning** approaches have included a large number of theoretical frameworks developed over the years for persons with and without disabilities. These approaches have been more career-oriented rather than a person-centered or a self-determination approach, but have not worked well for students with limited language or limited career maturity because performance norms have not been developed for students with disabilities (Menchetti & Piland, 1998). Two exceptions are the popular Life Centered Career Education (Brolin, 1989) and the Transition Planning Inventory (Clark & Patton, 1997), both of which were developed for students with disabilities. Care should be used in applying other career development strategies to students who have limited work experiences or decision-making skills, and career assessments should be administered by persons qualified to do so. Career planning approaches do have advantages because they are (a) systematic, (b) developmental, (c) focused on self-awareness, and (d) oriented to a wide range of occupations. Some common career planning approaches have included:

- *Life Centered Career Education* (LCCE) (Brolin, 1989)
- *What Color Is Your Parachute?* (Bolles, 1999)
- *Transition Planning Inventory* (Clark & Patton, 1997)
- *The Self-Directed Search* (Holland, 1985)
- *The Career Development Index* (Super, Thompson, Lindeman, Joordan, & Myers, 1981)
- *The Career Maturity Inventory* (Crites, 1978)

Combining Approaches.   It should be emphasized that these planning approaches can be used in combination. Person-centered planning approaches can lay a good foundation for other planning approaches and tend to encompass other aspects of the student's life that are not addressed in most career planning and self-determination approaches. Self-determination strategies can enhance the student's ability to make choices and preferences known and therefore supplement person-centered and career development approaches. Generally, person-centered planning approaches have been used for students with the most significant disabilities. Self-determination approaches have generally been applied for students with language skills, though some new computerized approaches can facilitate choice making through pictures. Career development approaches (with the exception of

LCCE and the Transition Planning Inventory) have tended to be more successful with students with milder disabilities who have more advanced language skills and career maturity.

What Collaboration and System Coordination Strategies Promote Progress for Secondary Students?

Formal and Informal Assessments to Inform Individualized Planning

The first step in implementing collaboration for secondary students with disabilities relates to gathering information. This includes information that will help the student and the family make informed choices regarding postsecondary goals. Assessments should include a range of strategies and should generally focus on student strengths since remediation of deficits becomes less likely as graduation approaches. **Informal assessments** include information gathered from the student, the family, and other persons working closely with the student. Student history is one of the best predictors of what the student will do in the future and should include both work and nonwork experiences. Hobbies, how the student spends free time, personal achievements, and things the student has not liked to do in the past can be very useful in making informed choices about future environments.

Standardized assessments can be useful or damaging. Such assessments must (a) be valid for the particular student being tested, (b) address student strengths, (c) be understandable, and (d) provide accommodations for students with disabilities. Research indicates that standardized assessment procedures often lack validity for students with disabilities because they do not consider the effects of supports, technology, and training on student performance (Menchetti & Piland, 1998). Standardized assessment procedures may have little validity with students with severe disabilities, since they lack experience with the pressures, cues, sights, and sounds of the environments in which students will have to perform (Greene, 2003b; Hagner & Dileo, 1993). Assessment experts advocate strongly for the use of **situational assessments**, or assessments that are conducted in the authentic environments in which the student is expected to perform. The following list includes the types of assessments that may be useful for a high school student with a disability (Clark & Patton, 1997):

- Parent and student interviews
- Computer interest inventories
- Surveys of student needs and preferences
- Curriculum-based assessments
- Social histories
- Situational assessments (home, work, etc.)
- Adaptive behavior tests
- Life skills inventories
- Aptitude tests
- Social skills inventories
- Vocational skills assessments

- Medical assessments
- Psychological assessments
- Occupational and physical therapy assessments
- Speech and vision assessments
- College entrance examinations
- Career portfolios
- Work samples

The IEP/Transition Meeting

Before the IEP/transition meeting, it is advisable for the teacher and other IEP team members to review service needs identified by assessments with the student and the family to develop consensus on (a) appropriate postsecondary goals, (b) the student's course of study, and (c) the types of transition services needed. The teacher should develop a meeting agenda with time specifically allotted at the beginning of the meeting for the student and the family to lead discussion. The meeting agenda should specify meeting activities, the amount of time allotted for each activity, and desired outcomes. At the start of the IEP/transition meeting, there should be time for all transition team members to introduce themselves, identify their role, and state how they know the student. Figure 13.5 provides a sample two-hour IEP/transition team meeting agenda.

Times and agenda items may vary depending on the number of meeting participants, student transition service needs, and the level of consensus among team members prior to the meeting. The meeting should allot 2 hours in order to leave time for backward planning. A meeting of this duration should be considered at the start of high school and anytime thereafter as warranted by the student's change of goals or lack of sufficient progress toward those goals.

As can be seen from the order of the meeting agenda in Figure 13.5, the meeting facilitator can employ backward planning in developing the IEP in which transition is discussed. The agenda should therefore start with the vision and develop postschool goals first. The present level of functioning is then contrasted with postschool goals to yield (a) the student's high school course of study and (b) transition objectives the student will need to achieve prior to graduation. These transition objectives can then be defined for each year leading up to graduation starting with the final year first, 2 years from graduation, and so on.

The person assigned responsibility for coordinating the IEP/transition plan should schedule follow-up contacts so that IEP and transition activities are completed on schedule. The general rule of follow-up activities is to "inspect what you expect." This means that the plan coordinator should contact responsible parties at least a month prior to the due date for activities to assure that they are being provided as planned.

Career Portfolio Assessment Tool

It is advisable for the student and teacher to monitor and record the process through the development of a **career portfolio**. The career portfolio is an important tool for assessing competencies, especially during the transition years. The career

FIGURE 13.5
Sample Meeting
Agenda

IEP Meeting for Jane Dove
5/2/2008
10:00 AM to 12:00 PM
Community Center

Meeting called by:	Jane Dove, student	Type of meeting:	IEP and transition meeting
Facilitator:	Julie Downs, teacher	Timekeeper:	Jane Dove, student
Invited Attendees:	Jane Dove, student; Sarah Dove, mother; Julie Downs, teacher; Fred Simpson, regular education teacher; Jack Johnson, psychologist; Jim Waters, vocational special educator; Brenda Gill, vocational rehabilitation counselor; Bill Williams, employer; Carrie Fields, mobility specialist; Jill Rettick, friend		
Please bring:	Assessments, ideas, and samples of work		

—— Agenda Topics ——

Introductions	Student and Family	5
Overview of meeting rules	Teacher	5
Present student vision	Student and family	15
Identify specific postschool goals	Student and teacher	10
Discuss present levels of function	Teacher	10
Identify student's needed course of study	Student and teacher	10
Identify transition objectives 1 year to graduation	Student and teacher	5
Identify transition objectives 2 years to graduation	Student and teacher	5
Identify transition objectives 3 years to graduation	Student and teacher	5
Identify transition objectives for the current year	Student and teacher	5
Identify other IEP objectives for current year	Student and teacher	10
Assign responsibilities and timelines	Teacher and team	10
Establish follow-up plan	Student and teacher	10

portfolio may serve several functions. It can provide a standardized form of assessment that can be used for all students, including students with the most severe disabilities. It may also help students in job matching and job interviews by providing documentation of skills desired by employers (Bostaph & Vendelend, 2000; Powell & Jankovich, 1998; Sarkees-Wircenski & Wircenski, 1994).

The career portfolio documents a set of competencies that can be applied to student high school experiences and activities. The student has demonstrated these competencies in a number of environments including the home, the school, work, and the community. Documentation of competencies includes examples of the student's work, photographs, supervisor comments and evaluations, and even videotapes. The assessment of the career portfolio may be conducted by the teacher in collaboration with family members, other educators, related service providers, adult service providers, or employers.

WHAT IS THE SCHOOL- OR DISTRICT-LEVEL INTERAGENCY TRANSITION TEAM?

In the course of planning with individual students, it may become clear that adult services, related services, or career-vocational education are unavailable or are subject to barriers. Often these collaborative issues cannot be resolved at the individual level and require an interagency coordination strategy. Research indicates that school-level interagency collaborations are significantly correlated with transition policy compliance, best practices, and student outcomes (Baer, Simmons, & Flexer, 1997; McMahan & Baer, 2001). Typically, a school-level collaboration involves a variety of transition stakeholders in a discussion about barriers and issues facing transition-age youth and then develops a plan to address these issues. These stakeholders include educators, adult service providers, parents, students, employers, administrators, vocational educators, general educators, and related service providers.

Improving Transition Services at Individual and System Levels

School-level collaborations may approach the problem of improving transition services from either an individual case study or systems planning approach. In the case study approach, the collaborative team reviews the transition issues facing selected students to identify areas in which transition services should be developed, improved, or scaled back. The advantage of this approach is that team members feel genuine concern about problems that affect individual students and are therefore more likely to remain engaged and committed to solving these problems. The disadvantage of this approach is that the problem-solving efforts tend to be a short-term "fix" that may lack any systemwide coherency.

Using a systems planning approach, the school-level collaborative team examines transition service utilization, quality, and outcomes for all students using various forms of data including (a) projected and actual utilization of school and adult service transition services, (b) stakeholder satisfaction surveys, and (c) postschool outcome studies. The advantage of this approach is that the school-level collaborative team can take a "big picture" approach that identifies underlying systemic problems such as lack of collaboration, resources, or expertise. The disadvantage of systems planning approaches is that they require data collection, sophisticated knowledge of the system, and can lose members who lack interest or expertise in dealing with broader systems issues.

The authors recommend a combined approach that examines and interprets system issues in relation to individual case studies. These approaches might be combined by identifying a particular systems issue and then obtaining case studies that relate to this issue (Baer, Martonyi, Simmons, Flexer, & Goebel, 1994). The collaborative team may then approach the issue either by working the case or by working the system or both. This design provides flexibility in the team's approach to transition issues and is most suitable for a team that consists of consumers, practitioners, and administrators.

Group Development Process

The development of the **school-level interagency transition team** requires some knowledge of the group development processes. It has been the author's experience that many so-called "groups" are actually a series of meetings that are sporadically attended by members with little or no commitment to an outcome. Often members are selected using a "Noah's Ark" approach by simply enlisting representatives of targeted subgroups such as parents, students, employers, teachers, related service providers, and so on. This approach often presents difficulties for the coordinator for two reasons. First, studies indicate that the effectiveness of groups drops when the group size exceeds 12 members. Second, simply enlisting members based on their subgroup can result in the selection of individuals who have limited time or commitment to the purposes of the group. It is therefore the authors' view that groups should begin with a core of committed members representing three major categories: (a) consumers, (b) influential experts, and (c) decision makers.

Once the core group has been gathered, the process of group development can begin. Tuckman and Jensen (1977) suggest that groups pass through five basic **stages of group development:** (1) forming, (2) storming, (3) norming, (4) performing, and (5) adjourning. Tuckman and Jensen's model can be summarized as follows:

1. *Forming.* In this stage, the leader needs to address issues of trust while trying to gain commitment from potential members. Additional members may be added at this stage of group development.
2. *Storming.* In this stage, the leader needs to downplay criticism while trying to elicit ideas and suggestions. This is the fun and creative phase of the group where everyone needs to become involved in submitting any and all ideas.
3. *Norming.* In this stage, the leader needs to help group members fit in while trying to establish general rules and procedures on how the group is to function and what it is to do. This is a critical stage where the group makes a commitment to a mission and group objectives.
4. *Performing.* In this stage, the leader needs to mobilize leadership within the group and assign responsibilities, establish time lines, and obtain successes critical to maintenance of group morale. The successful group encounters and overcomes challenges from the outside.
5. *Adjourning.* In this stage, the leader needs to either recognize and adjourn the group, or re-form the group around new tasks. This is the stage where members celebrate accomplishments and recognize individual contributions.

The Forming Phase of the School-Level Interagency Collaboration.   It should be noted that each community will have a different set of agencies and transition

stakeholders. Therefore, persons developing interagency teams need to examine their own community and make choices accordingly, being sensitive to stakeholder groups that are traditionally overlooked in community organization projects. It is important to meet with agency directors to discuss the need for an interagency team before staff are recruited. Parents and students may best be represented by members of advocacy groups (e.g., the ARC or Learning Disabilities Association) who can represent a wide range of disability issues. To promote involvement of all agencies, no particular disability type should be emphasized in presenting the need.

Once agency directors have agreed to the need for an interagency team, it is then possible to begin recruiting representatives from their agencies. Generally, job developers and employment specialists are preferred recruits; however, it is important to get an agreement from the director about their participation on the team, and the extent to which representatives can make decisions for the agency. If the director decides to appoint a representative, suggest a person with experience in employing persons with disabilities.

After representatives have been recruited from all agencies, an orientation meeting should be held and participants' contact information collected. At this meeting, representatives should introduce themselves and discuss what they are doing, goals of their agencies, populations served, and barriers they have encountered relative to employment of persons with disabilities. The leader should then present a brief overview of the role of the school-level interagency collaborative team. A discussion of scheduling and the location of subsequent meetings can then follow.

The Storming Phase of the School-Level Interagency Collaboration.   During the storming phase, discussion should focus on identifying (a) postschool outcomes that are generally desired by students with disabilities, (b) transition activities that promote these outcomes, (c) barriers that hinder these outcomes, and (d) ideas for enhancing successful transition activities or for removing barriers. Each of these issues should be posed in the form of a question (e.g., What postschool outcomes are generally desired by students with disabilities?) The purpose of "brainstorming" is twofold. First, this process will generate novel ideas and viewpoints that may provide a new way of thinking about transition services. Second, brainstorming will group members' ownership and commitment to the issues that emerge. Table 13.1 illustrates a specific brainstorming establish process that has been used with school-level teams.

The Norming Phase of the School-Level Interagency Collaboration.   The norming phase formalizes the work of a collaborative team by establishing the mission, identifying the issues to be addressed, and assigning important issues to subcommittees. These can be drawn from the brainstorming phase with the mission being derived from the question: What outcomes do students with disabilities desire? In the mission statement, it is necessary for service providers to come to some kind of agreement as to why this collaborative team has been formed and what it will do. It is suggested that a participation agreement be drawn up in conjunction with the mission statement. The participation agreement and the mission statement can be taken back to agency directors for their approval. This can be helpful in maintaining agency involvement if there is a new director, or if turf battles emerge.

Once the mission of the interagency team has been specified, service goals should be prioritized. It is suggested that the collaborative team focus on only 2 to 4

TABLE 13.1   **Brainstorming Procedures**

1. In a small or large group, select a leader, a recorder, and a timekeeper.
2. Distribute Post-it® Notes and marker pens to participants.
3. Write each question to be brainstormed on the large Post-it® "tabletop" pads (one question per pad). Post the first question to be discussed in front of the participants.
4. Set up the rules for the session: Let the leader have control; allow everyone to contribute; ensure that no one will insult, demean, or evaluate another participant or his/her response; and state that no answer is wrong.
5. Set a time limit for brainstorming for each question (10–15 minutes). Ask the timekeeper to indicate when time is up.
6. Start the brainstorming. The leader should (a) recognize participants and have them state their ideas, (b) restate participant ideas, and (c) instruct them to write them on the small Post-it® notes in short phrases in large writing. The recorder will collect and post these ideas as generated.
7. Put Post-it® note ideas on table-top Post-it® pads for each question. Put ideas that don't fit under a question to the side on a table-top Post-it® pad marked "parking lot." These items can be dealt with later.
8. (Optional) Once you have finished brainstorming, go through the results and begin evaluating the responses. Some initial qualities to look for when examining the responses include: group like concepts together; move responses that do not fit to the "parking lot"; discuss "parking lot" ideas and decide how to use them.
9. Once ideas are grouped, develop categories or names for each grouping. If time permits, allow members to vote on most important categories or ideas (e.g., give each member five votes to distribute as they like.)

of the highest priority goals or objectives so that its energies are not spread too thinly. It is also suggested that the collaborative team develop a referral process whereby problems encountered by students with disabilities can be referred to the team for consideration. By dealing with individual referrals, the team can measure the impact of its activities on the day-to-day problems of students with disabilities.

The Performing Phase of the School-Level Interagency Collaboration.   In the performing, stage the leader needs to mobilize the group members by maintaining open lines of communication, monitoring time lines for assigned activities, heading off failure through problem solving, recognizing successes, and maintaining group morale. The first step in this process is to keep regular and precise meeting minutes and to distribute them in a timely manner.

Student referrals should be reviewed as part of each meeting agenda. After determination that traditional approaches have been unsuccessful in serving a referral, that individual can be considered for action by the collaborative team. The team may also want to add other items to the agenda. If individual members have concerns about agency services, they should be discussed as part of the regular meeting. If subcommittees have been formed by the interagency team, their reports should also be reviewed at each meeting. During meetings, handle old business before new to ensure that closure is reached on existing projects before taking on additional responsibilities.

The Adjourning Phase of the School-Level Interagency Collaboration.

Though the school-level collaborative team needs to be an ongoing effort to continuously improve transition services, the leader should provide the opportunity for members to complete their service and for new members to be taken in. Most ongoing boards or teams deal with this issue by staggering the terms of team members over 3 years so that only a third of the team is replaced or renewed at a time.

The adjourning phase of the team is typically an annual meeting where it is possible to recognize the achievements of the team, celebrate victories, and provide recognition for team members who have provided exemplary service. This meeting can also be a time when new members (or renewing members) are announced. This adjourning phase of the team's development can therefore be seen as both an end and a beginning of a planning cycle. For nonrenewing members, it provides closure and confirms that their time and efforts were valued. For renewing and new members, it will establish a new commitment to the goals of the team and will mark the forming phase of the next planning cycle. The case illustration below describes one state's efforts to improve system coordination.

LET'S SEE IT IN ACTION! Case Illustration: The Interagency Agreement

In 1994, the U.S. Office of Special Education and Rehabilitation Services (OSERS) awarded Ohio a transition systems change grant as part of a national effort to reorganize a fragmented system of services for youth with disabilities entering adulthood (Baer, 1996). In this proposal, Ohio identified six objectives that could be accomplished through **interagency agreements** and that could address multiple barriers to system coordination. These were:

1. a single service coordination (case management) process for transition services;
2. a reciprocal assessment, eligibility, and referral process across all agencies involved in transition services;
3. a single planning process that encompasses the individualized plans of multiple agencies;
4. cross-training for consumers, parents, and professionals;
5. cross-agency coordination, cooperation, funding, and service delivery; and
6. coordinated youth/consumer management information and follow-up system.

How Can Interagency Agreements Overcome Barriers to System Coordination? The Ohio Experience

A single service coordination process is one objective that could be pursued through an interagency agreement. In Ohio's past, transition service coordination for youths with disabilities occurred through a patchwork of adult service coordinators (case managers) and school transition specialists. Some students were be eligible for multiple case management services whereas others were eligible for none. Some family participants recounted being overrun with service coordinators and planners; others reported being lost in the system with no support at all. Ohio participants were in agreement that the current system was actually a "nonsystem" of duplication, gaps, and lack of shared information. Additionally, participants noted that the current system disempowered consumers by tying service coordination to agency services, leaving consumers with little information or opportunity to explore services outside the agency or school providing service coordination (Baer, 1996).

A second area that may be addressed through interagency agreements is reciprocal assessment, eligibility, and referral. In a March 1995 needs assessment, Ohio respondents identified lack of communication and the maze of paperwork and bureaucracy as a major barrier to providing effective transition services for youth with disabilities. They listed confidentiality issues and a lack of reciprocal agreements as the two biggest barriers to information sharing and noted that differing definitions of disability made referrals and shared eligibility determinations difficult. Respondents reported that agencies used a range of tests to determine eligibility including (a) the Ohio Eligibility Determination Instrument (OEDI), (b) the DSM-IV (Diagnostic and Statistical Manual), (c) the multifactored evaluation (MFE), (d) financial means tests, (e) categorical eligibility determination, (f) medical histories, (g) legal histories, and (h) employment histories (Baer, 1996).

A third area that may be addressed through interagency agreements is coordinated planning. Ohio's needs assessment identified the need for coordinated long-range planning for youth with disabilities preparing for transition from high school. Respondents noted that barriers to unified planning included different agency accreditation standards, policies, philosophies, and agency missions. While participants acknowledged that the IEP was the primary planning tool for youth with disabilities, they reported that schools were hesitant to list agency services in the IEP for fear of being required to provide the service if it was not provided by the agency as planned. Respondents also noted that that there were not enough staff to attend both IEP and interagency planning.

A fourth area that may be addressed through an interagency agreement is cross-training on transition for agencies, schools, and families. Ohio's needs assessment identified turf issues, lack of money, and time as three major barriers to transition cross-training for families and professionals. Needs assessment respondents reported that school training funds could only be spent on special educators and not on adult service agencies, and they noted a general lack of communication among agency and school staff development personnel. In addition, school representatives reported limited time available for teacher training due to a lack of substitutes and a lack of professional development time. Parent–consumer representatives reported that parent involvement in daytime training was difficult due to work and family obligations (Baer, 1996).

Collaborative service delivery is a fifth area that may be addressed by an interagency agreement. For example, students with developmental disabilities may benefit through collaborative service programs where developmental disability (DD) agencies assign some of their job specialists to select schools for the purpose of developing community-based work experiences. Students with other disabilities may benefit by jointly staffed or funded programs with Vocational Rehabilitation, Mental Health, Work Incentive Act, and other collaborations that develop an overlap between school services and adult services in the last few years of school.

A sixth area that may be addressed through an interagency agreement is a coordinated effort to follow up or follow along youth who have exited schools. This information could be used to identify programs that were highly related to desired postschool outcomes for youths with disabilities. A coordinated information system would involve schools collecting data on transition service utilization and then working with adult service agencies to predict postschool service needs. Data collection on postschool outcomes would allow schools and agencies to identify transition services that appear to result in improved outcomes for students with disabilities.

These are only a few of the issues that may be addressed through interagency agreements. The development of interagency agreements may require parallel efforts at the local, regional, and state offices so that local agreements are in accord with state and regional agreements. An additional problem in implementing interagency agreements is that the constant reform of education and adult service programs often renders such agreements obsolete when agency priorities, procedures, or policies change. This explains why a school-level interagency collaborative team is vital to continuously update these agreements.

The appendix at the end of this chapter provides a sample 'Bill of Rights' for students in Transition.

Summary of Key Points

- While career development for children, youth, and adults of all exceptionalities has been evolving since the turn of the century, the concepts of high school transition and career education have emerged only since the 1950s.
- Secondary education should focus on the student's postschool goals and reflect a "transition perspective" of education.
- The 2004 amendments implied that collaboration for transition from middle to high school should focus on developing a student's course of study or career path, while high school collaboration and coordination should focus on identifying and securing the student's desired postschool outcomes.
- Backward planning for transition uses future goals to identify future student performance needs and is based on the expectation that students could achieve their desired postschool outcomes through early planning and a team commitment to immediate action.
- State and local interagency agreements are demonstrating success in overcoming barriers to system coordination.
- Assessments should include a range of strategies and should generally focus on student strengths since remediation of deficits becomes less likely as graduation approaches.

Key Terms and Phrases

- Transition perspective (p. 343)
- Career education movement (p. 346)
- Transition (p. 347)
- Taxonomy of transition planning and services (p. 351)
- Backward planning (p. 352)

- Postschool environments (p. 352)
- Transition specialist (p. 352)
- Person-centered planning (p. 355)
- Self-determination (p. 356)
- Career development and planning (p. 357)
- Informal assessments (p. 358)
- Situational assessments (p. 358)
- Standardized assessments (p. 358)
- Career portfolio (p. 359)
- School-level interagency transition team (p. 362)
- Stages of group development (p. 362)
- Interagency agreements (p. 365)

Questions for Reflection, Thinking, and Skill Building

1. Give examples of (a) a person-centered planning approach; (b) self-determination training approach; (c) a career development approach.
2. Identify two possible uses of interagency agreements for secondary students with disabilities.
3. In a small group, discuss the impacts of the change in IDEA 1997 to IDEA 2004 moving the age for initiating transition services from 14 to 16. What implications does this change have for coordination between middle and high schools?
4. How would the IEP meeting differ for a student entering high school from that of a student who is nearing graduation?
5. How would you prepare and support a student and the family for meaningful participation in the IEP meeting in which transition is discussed?
6. Examine the role of an adult service agency that might be involved in an interagency agreement for transition from secondary school to the adult world. Develop a profile that outlines the role of that agency in planning for the student.

APPENDIX
A SUMMARY OF MY RIGHTS AND RESPONSIBILITIES

Rights of High School Students Receiving Special Education Services

I need to balance exercising my rights. . . .

- I have the right to know what my disability is and how it affects my ability to learn, live independently, and be a part of a lifelong learning system.
- I have the right to be provided information regarding assessment, services, and my Individualized Education Program (IEP) in a language and format that I understand.
- I have the right to participate in my IEP meetings.
- When I am 18, I will have the right to accept or refuse services.
- When I am 18, I will have the right to disagree with my IEP and to receive help in writing a complaint or requesting mediation or a due process hearing.

Responsibilities of High School Students Receiving Special Education Services

. . . with accepting my responsibilities.

- I have the responsibility to ask questions, request help, or seek self-advocacy training and peer support so that I can learn more about my disability and advocate for my needs.
- I have the responsibility to ask questions until I understand.
- I have the responsibility to attend all IEP meetings and actively participate in planning for my adult life.
- I have the responsibility to invite people (i.e., friend, parent, grandparent, coach, teacher) I trust and know well.
- I have the responsibility to understand that refusing services may affect my school/work program, and that I may not get these services back.
- I have the responsibility to follow through and be cooperative with any process that I request.

Source: Adapted with permission from the Minnesota Department of Children, Families and Learning IDEA '97 Transition Requirements: A Guide.

CHAPTER FOURTEEN

HOW CAN SCHOOL COLLABORATION AND SYSTEM COORDINATION PROMOTE PROGRESS OF STUDENTS IN ALTERNATIVE EDUCATION?

With Renee Lacey

Come to the edge, you won't fall. Come to the edge, you won't fall. I came to the edge, they pushed me, and I flew. —GUILLAUME APOLLINAIRE

- Why is alternative education becoming a national concern?

- Who is the student likely to enter alternative education?

- What are the characteristics of students with disabilities in alternative education programs?

- What laws and state policies affect student placement in alternative education?

- What models and collaborative practices promote student progress in alternative education?

- What is the role of the student in exercising personal decision making in life planning?

PERSPECTIVES

Counselor

Kyle, a 14-year-old with a learning disability and a behavioral disorder, lives with his maternal grandparents who have had him since he was 7. While Kyle is very bright, articulate, and athletic, he is getting into more trouble with his family, in school, and in the community. His grandparents report that he has become secretive at home, refusing to tell them where he is after school, staying out long past curfew, arguing about everything, and beginning to be destructive at home. His grades have plummeted, he sleeps in class, is truant more often, and is becoming a disciplinary problem at school. He has been banished from the local supermarket for theft and is using marijuana frequently with his friends. He has been returned home by the police for being found smoking marijuana under a bridge in the neighborhood. Kyle has a lot of strengths but will need help from a variety of agencies to overcome his difficulties.

Researcher

Adolescents and young adults who are unsuccessful in traditional schools or are behaviorally at-risk or delinquent have complex needs. In order for these young people to succeed when they leave the traditional school or return to the community from residential and juvenile correctional facilities, systematized collaborative support must be provided by a host of professionals and community members (Lehman, Wolford, Kellys, & Stuck, 1998, p. 5).

Alternative Education Student

Schools are trying to help kids if they have problems and get in trouble, but you can't make kids use the help if they don't want it. You might force the horse to the water and you might even force it to drink, but it might not swallow. Some kids just have to go through the hard stuff. The only thing you can do is be there all the way along. Be there for when we are ready to come back.

—GRADUATE OF AN ALTERNATIVE HIGH SCHOOL

INTRODUCTION

Although transition through adolescence and into adult roles is difficult for all youth, it is especially challenging for youth with either visible or hidden disabilities such as a learning, emotional and behavioral, ADD/ADHD, and language and sensory integration dysfunction. These groups represent 95% of all students with disabilities. These students are among those most at risk of poor school attendance, dropout, delinquency, unemployment, and failure to transition to adult independence. About one-quarter of all students drop out of the K–12 educational system before receiving their high school diploma and 41.1% of students ages 14 and older with disabilities drop out. In some states these figures reach 60% for students with disabilities (U.S. Department of Education, 2003b).

Dropout rates for students with disabilities vary by type of disability; however, more than one-half of all students with emotional and behavioral disabilities (51.4%) drop out of school (U.S. Department of Education, 2002e). As high school graduation rates have declined over the past 10 years, the rate at which American children have been turning to alternative education has more than doubled. Many observers contend that traditional schools are failing to engage a significant number of such students and to meet their complex and multiple needs. States report that they are now more likely to rely on alternative placements for students with learning and behavioral problems, particularly in response to the pressure of new student achievement accountability requirements (Lehr, 2004).

Research has shown that quality long-term alternative education programs can have positive effects on school performance, attitudes toward school, and self-esteem (Leone & Drakeford, 1999; White, 2005). The alternative school or programs include public, private, and interagency but are more commonly becoming part of the middle or high school program, and students typically are chronically underachieving and deficient in credits to graduate or to be with their same age peers. They may have been placed into the alternative school by the court system, but they desire to stay in school and gain their diplomas. A review of legislation on alternative schools in 48 states indicated they were most frequently defined as nontraditional settings that serve students at risk of school failure (Lang & Lanners, 2004; Lehr, 2004). Long-term alternative schools and programs (more than 5 days) have also emerged as one educational option for students with and without disabilities who have a history of failure and are at risk of dropout from traditional public schools (Aron, 2003; National Governors Association, 2002).

This chapter provides a picture of students—both with and without disabilities—who are placed into alternative education because they (1) are at risk of failure in the traditional school setting and need a nontraditional learning environment; (2) are disruptive, violent, or have been involved in juvenile crime; or (3) have violated school discipline codes. The chapter addresses students with and without disabilities for several reasons. First, in the United States, an increasing number of students without disabilities, as well as those with IEPs or Section 504 plans, are being placed in alternative settings as a result of new discipline policies in schools that affect all students (Kauffman & Brigham, 2000).

Second, many students with hidden disabilities go undiagnosed and do not get the special educational services and supports they need early enough, increasing their chances of school failure and behavior that places them at risk. A study conducted by the National Council on Disability (2000c) on federal monitoring and enforcement of IDEA found that almost every state was out of compliance with some IDEA requirements and that in some states the lack of compliance has persisted for years. Lack of resources and weak compliance can lead to systematic underidentification of students and lack of access to needed services.

Third, many students with emotional and behavioral disorders are at risk of school failure, but fall into diagnostic categories that make them ineligible for special education under IDEA (e.g., conduct disorder, substance abuse, or social maladjustment). This group, which represents a growing number of youth in alternative education programs, will be discussed in greater detail later in the chapter.

The chapter also explores the need to connect services within the school and between school and community agencies, placing students at the center of responsible decision making for their future. Barriers to school collaboration and service coordination are examined, as well as implications for students who are not protected under IDEA.

WHY IS ALTERNATIVE EDUCATION BECOMING A NATIONAL CONCERN?

The subject of alternative education is very timely for communities across the nation who face staggering social and economic costs resulting from the growing numbers of alienated, undereducated, and poorly socialized youth and young adults. After operating for decades on the fringes of public education, alternative schools are now receiving serious attention.

Alternative Education Is Not a New Concept

Alternatives in education have existed from the birth of public education in the United States, and their forms have continued to evolve into the present. The term **alternative education** has been used to describe various programs and approaches for students who, for a variety of reasons, have been unsuccessful in their home schools. Since compulsory and tax-supported education was initiated in 1837 by Horace Mann, the first Secretary of Education, challenges to the notion of standardized, one-size-fits-all public education have been part of the educational discourse. While the "normal" schools, or government common schools, opened the doors of public education to more Americans and immigrants, they were designed to standardize curriculum and regulate teacher training. Many groups within the nation, including Native Americans, religious groups, and others who mistrusted the paternalism of the state, wanted their rights to choose alternatives to the government controlled system protected. The search for alternatives has been evolving ever since (White & Kochhar-Bryant, 2004).

Alternatives that have emerged over the past few decades—free schools, open schools, schools without walls, schools within schools, and multicultural schools, learning centers, and magnet schools—have advanced the idea that a singular, inflexible system of education that alienated or excluded major segments of the population would not be accepted (Raywid, 1994). Alternative schools have responded to groups of students who have not been served successfully or have not progressed in the "regular" school programs. In short, not all students learn best in the same educational setting. Raywid (1999) has also suggested that unsuccessful students need a good education a lot more than do youngsters who manage to succeed under virtually any circumstance.

Alternative Education Programs on the Rise

Long-term alternative education programs (more than 5 days) are proliferating in an attempt to meet the needs of students who are not progressing in traditional school settings. For decades, national legislation and state policies have promoted school collaboration and interagency service coordination for students receiving special education services. The No Child Left Behind Act of 2001 strengthened the responsibility of the school system to address students who require the coordination of multiple services to achieve school success, but who may not necessarily be eligible for special education. Increasingly, students who are not succeeding in a traditional school due to academic or behavior problems are turning to alternative programs designed to address their specific needs (Peterson & Smith, 2002). The National Center for Education Statistics (2002) and U.S. Government Accountability Office (2003a) report the following statistics regarding the status of alternative education:

- Overall, there were 10,900 public alternative schools and programs for at-risk students in the nation during the 2000–01 school year; 39% of all school districts in the United States administered at least one alternative school or program during the 2000–01 year.

- In 2000–01, 12% of all students in alternative schools and programs for at-risk students were special education students with an individualized education plan.

- As of October 1, 2000, 612,900 students, or 1.3% of all public school students, were enrolled in public alternative schools or programs for at-risk youth.

- Fifty-nine percent (6,400) of all public alternative schools and programs for at-risk students were housed in separate facilities (not in a regular school) during the 2000–01 school year.

- Urban districts, large districts (those with 10,000 or more students), districts in the Southeast, districts with high minority student enrollments, and districts with high poverty concentrations were more likely than other districts to have alternative schools and programs for at-risk students during the 2000–01 school year.

- Of districts with 5% or fewer of minority students, only 26% percent had alternative schools or programs. However, 62% of districts with more than 50% minority enrollment had alternative programs, indicating that minority students are more likely to be referred to alternative education.

- About one-third (33%) of districts with alternative schools and programs for at-risk students had at least one such school or program that had reached capacity during the 1999–2000 school year. This was more likely to be the case for large and moderate-sized districts than for small ones (43% and 39% compared with 25%).
- Fifty-four percent of districts with alternative schools and programs for at-risk students reported that within the last 3 years there were cases where demand for enrollment exceeded capacity. These districts reported employing a variety of procedures in such cases. Putting students on a waiting list was the most common procedure of districts where demand exceeded capacity (83%) (National Center for Education Statistics, 2001, p. iii).

Let's See It in Action, p. 376, provides strategies for effective school collaboration and interagency service coordination, placing the student at the center of personal decision making.

The Target Population and Outcomes for Youth With Disabilities

Most youth with disabilities experience poor outcomes in comparison with their nondisabled peers, including higher absenteeism, lower grade point averages, high dropout rates, low rates of enrollment in postsecondary education, low employment rates, and poor adult adjustment. These disabilities are not just school disabilities, but life disabilities. Lack of basic academic skills, career guidance, and preparation affect all other areas of life. Teenage high school dropouts, specifically from low-income families, and those with disabilities, face the most difficult challenges in finding employment opportunities and are more likely to generate other social costs including incarceration and welfare (Benz, Lindstrom, & Yovonoff, 2000; Izzo, Cartledge, Miller, Growick, & Rutkowski, 2000; Madison & Ankemy, 2000; Neubert, 2000; Sitlington, Clark, & Kolstoe, 2000).

Adolescents with emotional and behavioral disabilities (EBD) have only a 41.9% graduation rate and the highest dropout rate of any disability category (U.S. Department of Education, 2001b). Relatively small numbers of students with EBD go on to a postsecondary degree (Rogers & Rogers, 2001). Three years after graduating from high school, none of the youth with EBD in one study met the criterion for successful adult adjustment and at least 40% were not engaged in either part-time or full-time work (Carson, Sitlington, & Frank, 1995). For those who decide to leave school, 10% of youth with EBD are living in a correctional facility, halfway house, drug treatment center, or on the street—twice as many as students with other disabilities (Leone, Quinn, & Osher, 2002; Wagner, Cameto, & Newman, 2003). Overall, parents report that about one-third of students ages 13–17 with disabilities have been suspended or expelled and 18.9% of students ages 10–12 years (U.S. Department of Education, 2003).

Youth in the Juvenile Justice System. Youth with disabilities are substantially over-represented in the juvenile justice system (Rutherford, Quinn, Leone, Garfinkle & Nelson, 2002). Youth with specific learning, emotional, or behavioral disabilities are

LET'S SEE IT IN ACTION! CASE ILLUSTRATION: AN ALTERNATIVE PATHWAY LEADS TO HIGH SCHOOL COMPLETION

Tommy is a 17-year-old white male who had to overcome tremendous obstacles so that he could succeed both academically and socially. Tommy's mother was diagnosed with bipolar disorder, and his father was clinically depressed. When Tommy was 14 his father committed suicide. Shortly thereafter, his mother took an overdose of pills, and Tommy was the one who found her. After her death, Tommy went to live with a family friend who connected him with counseling services through the local community services board (CSB). Tommy presented the classic symptoms of an individual with bipolar disorder and depression which included disrupted sleep patterns. He was placed on medication but only took it sporadically. Eventually, Tommy stopped going to counseling and refused to take the medication. As a result, he began to exhibit inappropriate behaviors in school, his grades plummeted, and he dropped out of school.

Tommy moved in with his brother who is 3 years older and who also did not complete high school. Shortly after moving in, he met a young lady who had a profound and positive impact on his life and his future. She encouraged him to return to school and to finish his high school education. Reluctantly, because of his fear of failure, he enrolled in his base school and was referred to an alternative school program that could provide the level of support for someone facing his challenges in his life. There he met the transition coordinator, Mr. Moody. After exploring his academic record with the school guidance counselor, Tommy found that he needed only three Carnegie units to graduate. Mr. Moody also discussed Tommy's past history and quickly recognized that this young man would need an inordinate amount of support to successfully achieve his goal of high school graduation. The story of Tommy will be continued later in this chapter. (See page 393.)

---

more vulnerable to alternative placement outside their base school or in juvenile or adult corrections than youth not identified as disabled. Rutherford, Quinn, Leone, Garfinkle, and Nelson (2002) found that 46% of youth with a disability in corrections had a primary diagnosis of a specific learning disability, and 45% were identified with an emotional disturbance.

While it is not well understood why individuals with disabilities are so highly represented in the juvenile justice system, some evidence suggests that police officers, attorneys, judges, corrections staff, and probation officers are typically unaware of characteristics associated with youths with disabilities (Leone, Quinn, & Osher, 2002; Rutherford et al., 2002). Adolescents may be more vulnerable to involvement in the juvenile or criminal justice system when poorly developed reasoning ability, inappropriate affect, and inattention are misinterpreted by professionals as hostility, lack of cooperation, and other inappropriate responses. This phenomenon has several implications. Youth placed at risk for involvement in the juvenile justice system, including students with disabilities, must receive support and preventative services to minimize their vulnerability. Early identification and intervention can reduce chances of incarceration and long-term dependence.

Ethnic minorities are dramatically overrepresented in the population of young offenders. A study conducted from 1988–1997 of youth held in public and private juvenile detention, correctional, and shelter facilities revealed that more than three-quarters (86.5%) of the 105,000 juveniles studied were young men from ethnic minority backgrounds (40% Black and 18.5% Hispanic) ranging in age from 13 to 17 years old. Although young women make up a smaller number of incarcerated youths, they tend to be younger in age than their male counterparts. About 21.4% of incarcerated females are 13 years of age.

Youth in Institutional Settings. NCLB addresses the needs of at-risk youth in institutional settings. The prevention and intervention programs for children and youth who are neglected, delinquent, or at-risk provides financial assistance to educational programs for youths in state-operated institutions, correctional, or community day programs. This program makes students returning from correctional facilities a priority for local educational agencies. The school district program is required to focus primarily on the transition and academic needs of students returning from correctional facilities. Often, there is a disconnect between the programs of local schools and correctional facilities, which results in low student achievement. As students transition from correctional facilities back to their local schools, follow-up services can ensure that their education continues and that they can meet the same challenging state standards required of all students. The NCLB program for at-risk youth responds to research affirming widespread neglect of students who are failing in public schools.

Challenges to Serving Youth With Disabilities in Alternative Education

Alternative schools are gradually becoming viewed as a positive choice for students with disabilities whose needs cannot be met in the regular school setting. However, challenges to quality education for students with disabilities remain. In some cases, students are pushed out of traditional school in a subtle or overt manner, with school officials suggesting alternative schools as an option. The IEP may be continued, modified, or may not systematically follow the student from their previous school. Many questions need to be answered regarding the quality of services in place for students with disabilities, the quality and availability of staff licensed in special education, and the degree to which alternative schools are appropriate settings for students with disabilities (Lehr, 2004; Lehr, Lange, & Lanners, 2004).

Once a student with a disability enrolls in an alternative school, several scenarios may occur. In some alternative schools, procedures may be in place to ensure a review of the IEP and a level of services similar to that which the student received in the past. In other alternative schools, the IEP may be rewritten to reflect more limited special education and related services. If the IEP is rewritten, it may or may not be closely monitored. In other cases, parents or students (once they reach the age of majority) may no longer request special education upon entrance into the alternative school.

State directors suggest several factors that can influence the degree to which the IEP is implemented. First, alternative school educators may believe that the student's needs can be met through the existing alternative program (rather than through special education) given the smaller student–teacher ratio and more individualized programming. The alternative school may not have certified special education teachers available, and the small size of the school can limit available services and resources. In some school districts, tensions exist between special educators and alternative school educators who believe that students with disabilities should not take up the slots reserved for at-risk youth because they have funding in the regular school setting (Lehr, 2004). Furthermore, many teachers in programs that serve the most challenging students lack the requisite skills and experience necessary to provide appropriate instruction to achieve student success. As a result, these students frequently fall through the cracks.

Researchers examining school dropout over the past decade are concerned that high-stakes testing and the resulting retention will cause the dropout problem to increase 50% by 2015 (Bridgeland, Dilulio, & M. Schargel, 2003; National Dropout Prevention Center, 2003). High dropout rates reflect a breakdown of collaboration and coordination systems among professionals and agencies within a school or district. Since it is highly unlikely that the dropout population will diminish or disappear in the next decade, it is imperative that schools and community agencies form effective partnerships through collaboration and interagency coordination to address the varied needs of students at risk.

Who Is the Student Likely to Enter Alternative Education?

There is no standard definition for the **student at risk** of needing alternative education. Although the term has been defined in a variety of ways, it typically refers to students who are in school but at-risk of school failure; those who have dropped out of high school or are seeking a general education diploma (GED); and those who have experienced an unstable family life, family poverty, single parent homes, divorce, physical abuse, and substance abuse (Hallahan & Kauffman, 2003; Kidscount, 2003b; Smith, Polloway, Patton, & Dowdy, 2001; Vaughn, Bos & Schumm, 2003). Students considered at risk often exhibit antisocial behaviors toward adults and their peers, which causes them to fall behind academically. They come from every socioeconomic, religious, and ethnic group. They may or may not be eligible for special education services, yet they are in need of special learning strategies, interventions, or supports to be successful in school (Smith, et al., 2001). These **risk factors** and their influence on learning demand nontraditional learning environments, increased supports, and close collaboration among professionals providing supportive services.

Multiple studies have identified additional risk factors that can be attributed to school failure as early as the third grade. These factors include (1) reading below grade level, (2) math ability that is 2 years below grade level, (3) limited English proficiency, (4) at least 1 year grade retention, and (5) having a parent who has not completed high school (Abrams, 2002; Blechman, Fishman, & Fishman, 2004; Brendtro & Shahbazian, 2003; Huffman & Speer, 2000). Because these students typically have a long history of failure, they are often faced with a negative academic climate, teachers who have low expectations of them, and teachers who are not sensitive to their unique circumstances.

How Does Poverty Contribute to Student Risk?

The child poverty rate is perhaps the most widely used measure to identify the health and well-being of children. According to Smith et al. (2001), "poverty is a social condition associated with many different kinds of problems. Poverty has been related to crime, physical abuse, learning problems, behavior problems, and emotional problems" (p. 355). While the number of poor children living in families totally dependent on welfare has actually fallen since 1985, the number living in families earning an income (no income from public assistance) increased from 4.4 million in 1976 to 6.9 million in 2000 (Kidscount, 2003a). Despite the wealth in the United States, the rate of poverty among children in the United States is higher than in any other developed country. Elders (2002) observes that children of the "Five H Club"—hungry, healthless, homeless, hugless, and hopeless—have difficulty concentrating on schoolwork, which often leads them to mask learning difficulties by exhibiting acting out behaviors.

Does Divorce Contribute to Student Risk?

Research estimates that about half of new marriages will end in divorce. As a result, divorce forces children to live in single-parent homes. The research supports that a female heads the vast majority of these households. Further, the Decennial Census (U.S. Census Bureau, 2000) showed that about 40% of children in female-headed families were poor in 2000, compared to only 8% of children in households of married couples. Divorce often creates problems for many children as they struggle to reorganize their lives. Children respond in different ways to divorce—from guilt to anger, grief, anxiety, hopelessness, and antisocial behaviors. Although divorce has different effects on different children, the separation destroys continuity in the family unit, and the instability affects learning.

How Does Abuse Contribute to Student Risk?

Child abuse can occur at every socioeconomic level, ethnic background, and religion. The literature describes two major types of abuse—emotional and physical. Thompson and Kaplan (1999) suggest that emotional abuse can be defined as excessive demands placed on children by parents, peers, and siblings and the failure of parents to provide an emotional support system. Students who have experienced emotional abuse may exhibit a low self-esteem, thoughts of suicide, depressions, antisocial behaviors, and difficulty initiating and maintaining relationships with adults and peers, which are characteristics of many students who attend alternative programs.

Children who are physically abused are more likely to become discipline problems than children who do not experience abuse. These students have difficulty forming relationships with their peers, and exhibit physically aggressive behaviors and social skills deficits. Research further suggests that deficits in cognitive functioning are greater in students who are abused (National Center for Education Statistics, 2001; U.S. Department of Health and Human Services, 2003).

Does Substance Abuse Impact Student Risk?

The illegal use of drugs and alcohol, and abuse of prescription drugs, is on the rise nationwide (Volkow, 2005). Even after aggressive substance abuse education, the use of drugs and alcohol has not decreased among school-aged youth. The National Center for Education Statistics (2001) reports that students who abuse substances have a difficult time keeping up with their peers academically. Substance abuse not only affects students' academic achievement, but also may result in poor attendance, difficulty concentrating, apathy, impulsivity and disordered behavior, and sleeping in class, which greatly impact cognition and thinking patterns.

WHAT ARE THE CHARACTERISTICS OF STUDENTS WITH DISABILITIES IN ALTERNATIVE EDUCATION PROGRAMS?

Although schools in many states are making great gains in achieving their overall education goals, research shows that states are experiencing rising dropout rates. Six states (Georgia, Mississippi, Nevada, Alabama, Louisiana, and Florida) graduate fewer than 25% of students with special needs (Orfield, 2004; U.S. Department of Education, 2003b). Furthermore, in the 2000–01 school year, more than 91,000 special education students were removed from their educational settings for disciplinary reasons (U.S. Government Accountability Office, 2003). In three states studied by GAO, special education students who were removed for longer than 10 days were primarily placed in alternative schools or homebound placements (2003). States report that anywhere from 19% to 60% of alternative education students have disabilities (whether they were or were not identified before placement), and a majority has learning and emotional/behavioral disabilities, most often co-occurring (Lehr, Lange, & Lanners, 2004). Based on a study of 49 state directors of special education, approximately 12% of all students in alternative education were special education students with IEPs, and many students are unidentified (Lehr, 2004). The number of students with mental health problems, conduct disorders, and traumatic brain injuries attending alternative schools is also increasing.

Students Who Don't Qualify for Special Education

Typically, students in alternative education programs may be characterized as having poor grades, truancy, disruptive behavior, pregnancy, suspension, or any factors that are associated with an exit from school before completion of a course of study leading to a diploma. Many students considered at risk and placed in alternative education programs do not qualify for special education services although their behaviors and school performance may seriously impede their ability to learn and succeed in a traditional school environment (Smith et al., 2003). Although these students may have attended class in the mainstream, unlike some students with disabilities, they have often been disassociated from their peers due to problem behaviors and social relationships. The students often have difficulty learning basic skills and keeping up with their peers. As a result, these students may be referred to an alternative school program, typically located in a separate facility from the traditional school.

Educators and other service providers have expressed concerns about placing at-risk students into more restricted alternative settings because they may have unidentified disabilities and will lack the protection and benefits provided under IDEA 2004. Many of these students are labeled as **socially maladjusted** and exhibit behaviors associated with oppositional defiant disorder and conduct disorder and may also have the co-occurring diagnosis of substance abuse. These disorders are *not* included in the definition of disability under IDEA, and therefore, students are ineligible for services (American Psychiatric Association 2000; Bazelon Center for Mental Health Law, 2003). Students, however, may qualify for accommodations under Section 504 of the Vocational Rehabilitation Act of 1973 (Public Law 93–112) (see Chapter 4).

Another population participating in alternative education programs is youth who are in contact with the juvenile justice system. A number of these individuals may have received educational services through correctional settings or may be reintegrating back to their communities after a period of detention. Educational programs in juvenile detention centers or less secure detention facilities, provide a spectrum of services including basic academic skill instruction, remedial and tutorial services, high school courses with Carnegie credits, general education diploma (GED) preparation, special education, pre-employment training, and programs focused on cognitive, social, and life skills development (Meisel, Henderson, Cohen, & Leone, 2000).

The primary goal of most alternative programs is to meet the needs of students who would benefit from nontraditional approaches to learning. Although Raywid (1994) describes three types of alternative programs, the majority of alternative placements have been created to address the chronically disaffected group of students at risk. Many programs are therapeutic, working to change or modify behaviors in order to assist students with successful assimilation into a mainstream environment (Raywid, 1998). However, the majority of these placements are temporary; students who succeed or improve in such alternative schools are permitted to return to the mainstream. Not all do, and many of these schools are understood to be permanent placements. Also, because of their disassociation from the mainstream, students are usually reluctant to participate in any decisions that impact their lives. Regardless of the reasons for alternative placement, these students require special supports to meet their unique needs.

What Laws and State Policies Affect Student Placement in Alternative Education?

Changes in IDEA 2004, NCLB, and new state laws now make long-term alternative settings more likely options for a growing number of youth who may be subject to a growing number of disciplinary violations. IDEA allows greater discretion for school personnel to remove students with disabilities who violate codes of conduct (Sec. 665, Interim Alternative Education Settings, Behavioral Supports, and Systemic School Interventions). In addition, NCLB provides more parental options for transfer or removal of their children from "failing schools" that are not making adequate yearly progress (AYP). Although this provision applies also to alternative education schools, guidance from the U.S. Department of Education (2004b) states that students/families can be denied their right to transfer if the placement is involuntary (for disciplinary reasons or court order).

The two terms **interim alternative placement** and *alternative education program* are not synonymous. Under IDEA, school personnel "may remove a student" to an appropriate interim alternative educational setting for not more than 45 "school" days ("school" days replaces calendar days), without regard to whether the behavior is determined to be a manifestation of the child's disability when the student either carries or possesses a weapon on school premises; or knowingly possesses, sells, or uses illegal drugs on school premises; or inflicts serious bodily injury upon another person on school premises. IDEA requires that any child removed from the current placement must continue educational services, participate in the general education curriculum, progress toward meeting IEP goals, and receive a functional behavioral assessment, behavioral intervention, and modifications to address the behavior violation to prevent reoccurrence (IDEA, Sec. 665).

Both laws, along with the federal **Safe and Drug Free Schools legislation**, state "Safe Schools Reporting" and policies related to "Arrests for Reportable Offenses" (children ages 5–22), also require school reporting of statistics on discipline, crime, and violence. Reportable offenses include abduction, arson, kidnapping, manslaughter, maiming, rape, robbery, robbery with a deadly weapon, carjacking or armed carjacking, sexual offenses, use of a handgun in commission of a felony, assault, carrying a handgun or dangerous weapon or chemical device with intent to injure.

Coordination between schools and law enforcement agencies is growing closer. For example, in 1999 Maryland passed Senate Bill 391/House Bill 907 which addressed the growing problem of violence in schools by providing further protections designed to promote the safety of Maryland's public school students and employees. The state has added new offenses to those offenses committed by a child (an individual under the age of 18 years) that a law enforcement agency must report to the superintendent of schools of the school system in which the child is enrolled as soon as possible after an arrest. New reportable offenses include (1) various controlled dangerous substance offenses beyond minor possession offenses and (2) offenses relating to destructive devices. Under current law, reportable offenses by a child that a law enforcement agency is required to disclose to a local superintendent include crimes of violence, serious crimes for which a child over the age of 16 years may be tried as an adult, and certain handgun and weapons violations.

The bills also expand the existing prohibition against molesting or threatening with bodily harm a student, employee, administrator, agent, or any other individual who is lawfully on school property to include those who are in a school vehicle, at an activity sponsored by a school that is held off school property, or on property that is owned by a county board and is used for administrative or other purposes. The legislation further prohibits a person from threatening with bodily harm any employee of any institution of elementary, secondary, or higher education at home by any means, including in person, by telephone, or by electronic mail.

Today, a fist fight between two 16-year-olds can get a student recommended for expulsion with little option but alternative placement. These policies may explain why the national survey of parents reported that about one-third of students ages 13–17 with disabilities and 18.9% of those ages 10–12 have been suspended or expelled (U.S. Department of Education 2003b).

State Zero-Tolerance Policies Promote Long-Term Alternative Settings

Alternative education is also proliferating because schools across the nation are raising the stakes for student behavior and conduct in schools—expanding the use of **zero-tolerance** and **school safety and security policies**, redefining "dangerous" behavior, and expanding the range of behaviors that are subject to citations or suspensions or recommendations for alternative education placements (National Governors Association, 2005). For example, in 2002–03, Virginia alone reported 344,184 incidents of discipline, crime, and violence, which included disorderly conduct (75% of all violations), threats/intimidation, cigarette violations, trespassing, toy look-alike gun, battery with no weapon (fighting), bullying, drug and alcohol offenses, vandalism, sexual offenses, and breaking and entering (Virginia Department of Education, 2004). By 2000 at least 21 states had enacted new laws related to alternative education. Data from the Education Commission of the States (2004) revealed the following about these shifts in state policies:

- increased requirements that schools develop alternative education plans;
- expansion of definition of "dangerous behavior" or the types of behavior or conduct that meet conditions for removing students from their base schools;
- clarification or expansion of the authority of school superintendents, principals, and school boards to suspend, expel, or change the placement of pupils for conduct;
- lowering of the age by which certain students may attend alternative education and expanding alternative education opportunities to middle school and elementary students;
- protection of students from being "pushed out" due to poor test scores (in response to evidence of increasing practices);
- clarification of requirements to provide appropriate education to students who are suspended;
- provision of alternative settings for students in schools with high dropout rates (Education Commission of the States, 2004).

Need for Coordination and Policies for Dropout Prevention Policies in School Districts

The SSLIIDEA Study (Study of State and Local Implementation and Impact of the Individuals With Disabilities Education Act, 2003), revealed that across 17 districts examined, 5 had no formal **dropout prevention** policies in place. Respondents in some of these districts said they did not need to focus on dropouts because such education programs as career education, alternative placements, and teacher–student counseling were enough to keep students in school. Others implemented policies they believed would tangentially impact dropouts—such as attendance and suspension policies. One district, for example, implemented an attendance policy that required students to repeat a grade if they were absent more than 26 days in any single year. In another district, middle school administrators said their strict suspension policy served as a "wake-up call" for students at risk for dropping out.

Finally, two districts were taking the most aggressive stand on dropout prevention by adopting an individualized approach to dropouts, emphasizing high expectations for all students and creative problem solving involving teachers, students, and parents. Educators in these districts reportedly made an exceptional effort to keep students in school.

Consistent with their policies, some districts had few or no dropout prevention activities in place, while others offered a wider range of practices. In K–6 elementary school districts, where few policies were in place, the practice of placing students in alternative settings was one of the only options available for students at risk. In contrast, other districts offered specific activities designed to reduce dropouts, including adjustment counselors, behavior plans, flexible and block scheduling, individual tutoring, vocational education, IEP adjustments, alternative placements, and practices to encourage parent involvement.

What appears to work for youth who have dropped out of school and who have contact with the juvenile justice system is a reorientation of services offered by the variety of agencies and organizations that exist in every community to serve youth. Education, juvenile justice, mental health, child welfare, and recreation services may all have a role to play in the life of these youth and their families. Too often, however, youth—particularly "difficult" youth with a variety of challenges, including cognitive and behavioral disabilities—have difficulty effectively using these services. Youth may get shuttled around between agencies that often do not communicate with one another. It is all too easy for these youth and their families to fall through the cracks of already stressed systems (Leone, Quinn, & Osher, 2002).

Wʜᴀᴛ Mᴏᴅᴇʟs ᴀɴᴅ Cᴏʟʟᴀʙᴏʀᴀᴛɪᴠᴇ Pʀᴀᴄᴛɪᴄᴇs Pʀᴏᴍᴏᴛᴇ Sᴛᴜᴅᴇɴᴛ Pʀᴏɢʀᴇss ɪɴ Aʟᴛᴇʀɴᴀᴛɪᴠᴇ Eᴅᴜᴄᴀᴛɪᴏɴ?

There is emerging evidence that high-quality alternative schools that are smaller than traditional high schools engage at-risk students more actively in learning than do traditional education and build on students' strengths and interests (Knight & Stallings, 1998; Lehr, Lang, & Lanners, 2004; Leone & Drakeford, 1999). Even among traditional high school systems, the creation of smaller schools-within-schools is producing positive outcomes. For example, a study of 820 high schools in the National Education Longitudinal Study (NELS) found that schools that had restructured to personalize education and develop collaborative learning processes produced significantly higher achievement gains and that the gains were more equitably distributed (Darling-Hammond, Ancess, & Ort, 2002; Lee & Smith, 1995; U.S. General Accounting Office, 2002).

Open and continuous communication and collaboration among professionals and families are essential in alternative education settings because of the complexity of the challenges the student and the family face. In addition, close collaboration and coordination are crucial for supporting students' transition from their base schools into alternative settings and back.

Models of Alternative Programs

The most common form of alternative school operating today to serve at-risk youth is designed to be part of a school district's comprehensive dropout prevention program (Cash, 2004; Raywid, 1998). The alternative program is usually part of the middle or high school program, and students typically are underachieving and deficient in credits. In many communities, alternative schools also offer special programs for teenage mothers desiring to graduate from high school, but who are unable to attend the traditional high school. Hefner-Packer (1991, 1995) studied these models and has described five models of alternative schools:

1. the *alternative classroom*, designed as a self-contained classroom within a traditional school, simply offering varied programs in a different environment;

2. the *school-within-a-school*, housed within a traditional school, but having semiautonomous or specialized educational programs;

3. the *separate alternative school*, separated from the traditional or base school and having different academic and social adjustment programs;

4. the *continuation school*, developed for students no longer attending traditional schools, such as street academies for job-related training or parenting centers; and

5. the *magnet school*, a self-contained program offering an intensified curriculum in one or more subject areas such as math or science.

In many districts, alternative schools fall under the auspices of educational alternatives that also include charter schools, magnet programs, distance learning programs, and private schools. Some of these options have much in common; each has distinct features, as well. However, alternative schools for at-risk youth are usually distinguished from charter or magnet programs, which typically seek academically high-performing students. Some alternative schools, however, are seeking "charters," but still aim to serve students who are at risk or have disabilities and cannot be served in the traditional school setting.

In smaller alternative settings, students receive support and guidance to overcome barriers to learning and develop resilience in coping with life challenges.

Findings from research conducted by the Alternative Schools Research Project (Lehr et al., 2004) describe alternative schools across the United States. Alternative schools are designed to meet a variety of needs including preventing students from dropping out of school, providing another educational option, serving as a disciplinary consequence, or providing academic and behavioral remediation. They are generally described as having small enrollments (i.e., 25–75 students) and are designed for high school–aged students, although many states have schools that are serving younger students. Students enter alternative schools either by direct application, agency referral, or as a result of suspension or expulsion from their base school. Such schools typically serve students either on a short-term basis with the goal of returning to the sending school, or a long-term placement through to graduation. Most schools offer educational programs that include individual instruction, a focus on basic academic skills, social services or counseling, and community work-based learning.

Principles and Elements of Effective Programs

High-quality alternative education programs are generally known for their adherence to **youth development principles**. These principles include (1) physical and psychological safety (e.g., safe facilities, safe ways to handle conflicts between youth); (2) appropriate structure (limit setting, clear rules, predictable structure to the program and routines); (3) supportive relationships (warmth and closeness with adults and peers); (4) opportunities to belong (meaningful inclusion); (5) positive social norms (expectations for behavior); (6) empowering youth through a challenging environment with opportunities for leadership; (7) opportunities for skill building (e.g., learning about social and communication skills, media literacy, habits of the mind); and (8) integration of family, school, and community efforts (National Governors' Association, 2001; National Research Council, 2001; Smith & Fox, 2003).

While there are numerous models for serving students with disabilities in alternative programs, there are seven essential elements of effective programs:

1. *Functional Assessment.* Assessment of student needs forms the basis for developing educational and treatment plans. Functional assessment procedures identify student strengths and skills deficits that interfere with educational achievement and social and emotional adjustment.

2. *Functional Curriculum.* A functional education curriculum allows the program to meet a student's individual academic, career, social, and behavioral needs. Such a curriculum focuses on the student's general curriculum and their IEP goals. In addition to academic skills, this curriculum can include developing functional job-related skills, coping and daily living skills, and social skills. Effective alternative programs provide opportunities for part-time employment and access to career training in the community. The student's IEP team should review and revise the IEP to include goals that directly target the behaviors that triggered the placement into the alternative setting. These goals should be based on a functional behavioral assessment and should lead to a positive behavior intervention plan.

3. *Effective and Efficient Instruction.* Functional instruction uses positive and direct student-centered instructional strategies. Instruction should address the short-term objectives in the student's IEP as well as the standards in the general education curriculum. Effective instruction can also involve behavioral strategies to teach acceptable replacement behaviors and reduce inappropriate behaviors.

4. *Comprehensive systems.* Comprehensive systems provide coordinated special educational services, including direct instruction and therapeutic programs. If the program has separate treatment and education components, then it is important that staff develop common goals and objectives for student success. In addition, coordinated and comprehensive linkages must be developed among the public schools, the alternative education program, the student's family, and community service agencies.

5. *Appropriate staff, resources, and procedural protections for students with disabilities.* In view of the expansion of alternative educational options, serious attention is needed to the quality of these programs and the professionals who teach in them. At-risk youth have complex needs and require an intensive educational and support program. It is the obligation of school systems to ensure that as alternative placements proliferate, appropriate educational services, including special education, are extended to students who need them (Quinn, Rutherford, & Osher, 1999).

It is important that education staff with special education certification be available, and support staff should have extensive training in how to serve students with disabilities. Multidisciplinary education and treatment teams are essential for serving students with emotional and behavioral disabilities Special education services include instruction in academics, independent living skills, social skills, and work-related skills. Procedural protections should be assured, including parental notification of evaluation and parental involvement in the review and revision of IEPs.

6. *Supportive climate.* Effective alternative programs create safe, productive, caring environments. Everyone is treated with respect, and problem behavior is viewed as an opportunity to teach new skills (Quinn, Osher, Hoffman, & Hanley, 1998; Quinn & Rutherford, 1998; Rutherford & Quinn, 1999).

7. *Transition.* Both IDEA and NCLB focus on transition support to youth in alternative settings, including correctional facilities, and the need to align transition supports with access to the general education curriculum. Teachers possess competencies related to transition planning into the alternative setting and out, accessing academic and social–behavioral information from previous settings, connecting students with community agency services, and providing academic guidance to ensure that students can complete required academic credits to complete their regular diplomas. Many students in alternative education require services from multiple agencies (e.g., mental health, substance abuse, family services, social services), and therefore coordination strategies are essential. It is important to begin setting postschool goals and planning for transition as soon as the student enters the alternative setting, whether the student will return to the base school or enter a postsecondary setting (Kochhar-Bryant & Lacey, 2005; Quinn, Rutherford, & Osher, 1999).

Facilitating School Collaboration in Alternative Programs

The alternative program is responsible for establishing a team of professionals who will help the student ease the transition to the new placement. The person responsible for this transition of the student, whether it is the guidance counselor, the administrator, or the transition coordinator, begins the preparation for the movement to the new placement once the student is recommended for placement in an alternative program or school. Quinn and Rutherford (1998) recommend that the transition coordinator or specialist who is located at the alternative program or school should be the point of coordination among the parent, school, and community to facilitate the appropriate educational setting and supports. As an advocate for the student, the transition coordinator monitors student progress and facilitates parent and agency involvement.

Establishing a team of school professionals to advocate for the student is the first step in the collaboration process. Because alternative programs are unique, various individuals in alternative programs may assume the leadership role. Once the team is established, the student should be assigned an adult mentor who will provide support and guidance during their period in the program. The student support team typically includes the student, the parent, an administrator, a guidance counselor, and when available, a social worker and psychologist. These professionals share equally in the decisions regarding the implementation of the **alternative education plan** (AEP).

In most alternative education programs, the majority of students do not have an individualized education plan (IEP). A majority of these students have undiagnosed emotional or behavioral problems, conduct disorder, or have been considered "socially maladjusted"; they have not been considered eligible for special education under IDEA. However, many alternative programs have adapted the IEP to create an alternative education plan. All school services needed by the student should be clearly stated in the AEP. The student should be able to define the services that he or she requires in order to prepare for a successful transition back to the base school or to a postschool setting.

Most alternative placements and programs offer an array of services although the coordination of these services is frequently disjointed. There are few **full-service programs** (Lehr, 2004). Since student behavior is often the primary cause for placement in alternative education, other services typically offered are those of the guidance counselor, social worker, or school psychologist. These individuals frequently provide part-time services to the program largely due to inadequate funding of the program. Often counseling is provided through group sessions at the alternative placement.

Coordinating Nonschool Services in Alternative Programs

Failure in educating at-risk youth is usually a failure of coordination of needed services, both within and outside the school. The majority of students attending an alternative education program require support services, not only from their school, but also through other providers such as social services, transportation, court services, and mental health. Raywid (1998) observed that, "An alternative [program] must have broad aims, making its concern the full development of each youngster—character and intellect, personal and social development, as well as academic achievement. It is concerned with the person, not just with the person's academic achievements" (p. 27).

The need for coordination of services is paramount for the overall achievement of the student at risk. The type of collaboration most widely reported by districts with alternative schools and programs for at-risk students was with the juvenile justice system (84%) (National Center for Education Statistics, 2001). Seventy-five percent of districts collaborate with community mental health agencies while 70% collaborate with police or sheriff's departments. Sixty-nine percent collaborate with child protective services. Districts were least likely to report collaboration with parks and recreation departments (23%).

Coordination of services combines the expertise of many professionals to help the student achieve success in all aspects of his or her life. Since the reasons for placement in an alternative program vary from chronic behavior problems, to substance abuse, disruptive behavior, and mental health problems, the need for a full- service approach to service delivery is paramount. The conditions that place students at risk are typically so complex that schools alone cannot intervene in the multiple problems that interfere with student success (Vaughn et al., 2003, p. 314). A team of professionals is able to offer more knowledge and experiences to respond to the varied needs of the student. Each team member, including the student, is held accountable for the success of the collaboration; the student, therefore, is also an integral member of the team. Through participation in the interdisciplinary team process, students are encouraged to practice the skills of self-determination (Wehmeyer & Sands, 1998).

A member of the **student support team** usually facilitates the coordination of the nonschool professionals to form a multidisciplinary team to provide a holistic approach to service delivery. The interdisciplinary team provides a safety net against individual errors in judgment. The coordination of services also ensures that there is a continuation of services for the student regardless of any future transition that the student may make. In many local districts or counties, a central student tracking system, shared by many agencies (e.g., the school, mental health agency, family services, juvenile courts, probation and parole, substance abuse system, and others) ensures that student information is centrally maintained.

The need to set goals and plan ahead is crucial for the student in an alternative education placement. Regrettably, by the time many students enter an alternative program, the base school has relinquished its responsibility for the student, and parents are either unable to cope with their child or have given up. Thus, student support at home may be compromised. Once the student has entered his or her new placement, it is important that the teacher(s) make the connection with various providers to ensure that support needs of students are met.

System Coordination and Young Offenders

Until recently, educational services for young offenders in correctional facilities has been notoriously weak across the United States. Similarly, coordination during the transition from correctional facilities to employment, postsecondary education, and the community have been fragmented, inefficient, and disconnected. Coordinated systems of support are now being developed in most states to increase the likelihood of successful youth transition and reentry into the community (National Center on Education, Disability and Juvenile Justice, 2004). Effective transition practices for youth released from correctional facilities involve close coordination among correctional education personnel, the public schools, and community-based agencies such as mental health and social services. Transition coordination can increase the likelihood that incarcerated youth will be reenrolled in their home school, complete high school, and become gainfully employed in their communities (Stephens & Arnette, 2000).

Studies of service coordination strategies for young offenders have shown that these services can improve positive adjustment, decrease negative behaviors, and reduce the likelihood of reincarceration (Bullis & Cheney, 1999; Chamberlain & Weinrott, 1990; Stephens & Arnette, 2000). However, there are several obstacles to effective transition services for youth in juvenile correctional facilities. Related and transition services are seldom considered in the IEP or provided to ensure that students benefit from their educational program (Meisel, Henderson, Cohen, & Leone, 1998). Service providers often receive inadequate professional development and specialized training to provide transition services. This can result in a significant lack of communication, coordination, and commitment among agencies that serve at-risk and delinquent youth. Given the fragmentation of many systems and agencies, it is often impossible to provide continuous, integrated services to juveniles with disabilities. Transition planning is often delayed due to difficulty obtaining educational records. Furthermore, institutional records are not systematically forwarded to educational or community aftercare programs once youth return to the community. The lack of family involvement often undermines successful transition for young offenders. Research on promising transition practices indicates a strong need for strategies to strengthen family involvement (Correctional Education Association, 2001; National Center on Education, Disability and Juvenile Justice, 2004).

Several promising practices are being implemented in many states to overcome the obstacles identified above. Cooperative contractual agreements among local agencies that provide transition services to juveniles are being established in order to maintain a seamless continuum of care. Such linkages result in increased postrelease options for youth leaving corrections. A consistent transition planning process, curricula to support transition planning, databases to track and monitor student progress, and a planned sequence of services after release are the key ingredients of successful transition. Individualized wraparound service models that focus on the strengths of the individual and his or her family are also being established. Finally, there is evidence that juveniles who receive prerelease training in social skills, career exploration, and career education are more likely to succeed after release from juvenile correctional facilities (National Center on Education, Disability and Juvenile Justice, 2004; Stephens & Arnette, 2000). Successful transition between correctional facilities and schools requires integrated and coordinated prerelease strategies developed and implemented collaboratively by all agencies involved in providing facility-based and aftercare services to youth and their families (Office of Juvenile Justice and Delinquency Prevention, 2000). Coordinated aftercare and follow-up can make the difference for youth and prevent their return to detention.

WHAT IS THE ROLE OF THE STUDENT IN EXERCISING PERSONAL DECISION MAKING IN LIFE PLANNING?

Students identified as at risk often exhibit antisocial behaviors which impede their ability to achieve academically and socially. They often have difficulty communicating about their needs. As a result, students considered at risk are not usually actively involved in personal decision making or in their educational planning, which often leaves them unprepared for employment or postsecondary education.

Students in alternative education programs must be provided the opportunity and directly taught the skills needed to participate actively in decisions regarding their education and life plans. Their involvement is an integral part of their overall development. Wehmeyer (1999) defines self-determination as "acting as the primary causal agent in one's life and making choices and decisions regarding one's quality of life free from undue external influence or interference" (p. 24). As the causal agent, the student is the initiator of change in his or her life (Wehmeyer & Sands, 1998). The authors summarize four key characteristics of persons who exhibit self-determined behaviors: (1) act autonomously; (2) self-regulate their own actions; (3) initiate and respond to events in a psychologically empowered manner; and (4) act in a self-realizing manner (p. 7).

The commonly accepted view of many students at risk, and for that matter any students with disabilities, is that they do not have the capacity or competency to make life decisions. The student typically has a history of failing to engage actively in personal decision making and in planning educational goals. As a result, teachers and administrators create plans and present them to students who remain passive players in the process.

Self-determination skills prepare students to be self-advocates, expressing their needs, interests, and desires that further lead to greater independence. People who are self-determined take control of their lives; make choices and decisions based on their interests, abilities, and preferences; and take responsibility for their lives (Wehmeyer & Sands, 1998). Self-advocacy occurs when students have the ability to understand their strengths and limitations and are able to communicate their needs, interests, and desires effectively (Vaughn et al., 2003). Learning activities that promote goal setting and self-monitoring of achievements help students to be involved in planning for their future.

Developing the Alternative Education Plan With the Student

Before being placed in an alternative education school or program, the student, along with the parent, school, and appropriate service providers, should review the student's skills, abilities, and interests to create an alternative educational plan for the high school program and for transition to postsecondary education or work. Although there are emerging alternative middle school programs across the United States, most students are placed in alternative settings during the early high school years (Lehr et al., 2004).

Since IDEA mandates the active involvement of the student in the development of his or her IEP, students at risk should have the same opportunity to be major contributors to their alternative education plans (AEP). The student should be encouraged to participate in the development of the plan that will eventually have lifelong effects on the student. The AEP, usually created in a student support meeting, should include (1) student academic performance data (i.e., test scores on standardized measures and letter/numeric grades for the end of grading periods), (2) student academic goals, (3) student personal goals, (4) student behavioral goals, (5) student interests, and (6) student learning style. Through coaching and encouraging and providing the appropriate tools, the student can learn to be the major driver of the AEP. The following strategies contribute to effective school collaboration and coordination of services, placing the student at the center of personal decision making:

1. The school establishes a student support team of professionals within the school who will identify and address the unique needs of the student. This team should include the parent, the student, the counselor, a mentor, an administrator, and a social worker or a psychologist, as appropriate.

2. A team leader is designated, and can be any member of the team who will act as an advocate for the student. This individual schedules meetings and facilitates all coordination within and outside of the school setting. The team leader ensures that all decisions are documented for the student record. This individual should be willing to explore creative ways to deliver appropriate services to the student.

3. The team leader or the mentor will ensure that the student is actively engaged in each process by providing contacts for the students and coaching the student in how to follow through.

4. The student should be supplied with a planner to track all appointments, classes, and assignments and given specific tasks and responsibilities to complete and record.

5. The team leader meets, at least weekly, with the student to establish and review goals and accomplishments. This fosters student responsibility and accountability.

Each member of the student support team is open to taking the necessary time to explore creative ways of providing services and support to the student.

WHAT WORKED FOR TOMMY?

Let's See It in Action, p. 393, revisits the case of Tommy, a student in the midst of learning the skills of personal decision making as school personnel formed a collaborative support team and coordinated services to help him achieve success. He has just entered the alternative school program.

The case of Tommy presents an example of successful, intensive school collaboration, interagency collaborative effort, and a lot of dedication. The transition coordinator was willing to expand the traditional role of ensuring successful movement from one placement to another to work extensively with a student on a personal level. With direction from the guidance counselor, the school support team explored and created nontraditional strategies for fulfilling graduation requirements and was willing to provide the necessary supports that would facilitate Tommy's success. The community agency realized the need to work with the student in an alternative location to ensure his access to services. The school administration supported the child support team by allowing them the latitude to make creative decisions that would respond to the unique needs of the student. Finally, Tommy was willing to accept assistance, direction, and guidance. As a result, he learned to navigate the system and advocate for himself, taking control of personal decision making in his life.

LET'S SEE IT IN ACTION! CASE ILLUSTRATION: TOMMY GAINS CONTROL OF HIS LIFE

Once Tommy entered the alternative program, Mr. Moody formed a school support team to address his specific needs. The team concluded that Tommy's personal needs, as well as his academic needs, had to be addressed. Continual monitoring of Tommy's progress would be an important event since there were multiple concerns. Mr. Moody had met Tommy earlier at the initial placement conference and had formed a relationship, thus he appointed himself as his mentor. At their initial meeting, they explored his academic record and found that he needed only three Carnegie units of credit to graduate. The AEP was developed and agreed to by all participants. Due to his mental health challenges, Mr. Moody, with the assistance of the guidance counselor, quickly determined that Tommy would need an inordinate amount of support to achieve his goal of high school graduation.

In a world of high-stakes testing, a primary concern for school district administrators is whether or not students pass statewide standardized assessments. For students at risk of school failure, academic needs cannot be adequately met until their social and emotional needs are addressed. As time progressed, it was evident that Tommy lacked the self-determination skills necessary to access the services and supports he needed to succeed—obtain assessment of his mental health needs, set goals, and properly communicate his needs. Research suggests that these skills must be taught while students are in school (Wehmeyer & Sands, 1998). Getting Tommy involved in his educational planning meant more than merely having him participate in the process. It meant connecting him to his education by immersing him in his educational experiences. Mr. Moody supplied Tommy with phone numbers and contact persons at the community mental health center. In order to build his self-confidence and teach and enforce self-advocacy, he would often have him make contacts from his office so that he could serve as a coach. Mr. Moody held Tommy accountable by having him self-monitor, maintaining a daily record of his progress. Each day he touched base with Tommy to review his follow through.

After a few weeks of regular meetings and follow-up with his teachers, Mr. Moody noticed a drop in Tommy's attendance and grades. Tommy still suffered from depression and the sleep disorders, so it was obvious that these areas needed special attention. Even with the smaller number of students in the class, Tommy seemed to have difficulty interacting with his teachers and participating in class. The child support team reconvened to modify the AEP.

Members of the school support team and the counselor from the mental health center met with Tommy to review his plan. To maintain the student's engagement takes positive attitude and effort across multiple contexts and environments to give them the skills, opportunities and support required (Wehmeyer & Sands, 1998, p. 43). First, the team listed Tommy's strengths, limitations, and his interests. They identified the academic supports and where they could be obtained. Since Tommy had difficulty waking to attend early morning classes, Mr. Moody contacted a private alternative school in the area that operated on a flexible schedule using a trimester concept. He coached Tommy through the process of contacting the school and requesting an appointment to discuss enrollment in the program. With Tommy's input, as well as the counselor's from mental health, the team discussed the feasibility of Tommy attending the private school. It was determined that this change in schedule allowed for him to attend school later in the morning 4 hours twice a week for one of the classes he needed for graduation. The base school used the funds from the per-pupil allocation to pay for his enrollment at the private school.

Second, Tommy was not keeping his appointments with the mental health center because he lacked transportation and was not diligent about taking his medication. The mental health counselor was amenable to meeting Tommy weekly at the school during his lunch period to ensure he kept his appointments. Tommy kept a journal of his meetings with the mental health counselor to monitor his progress. As he became more comfortable with the mental health counselor, he trusted his advice that taking the medication was important to his success. Tommy began recording his medication to make sure he did not miss any doses.

Third, Tommy's major concern was securing employment since he was responsible for providing for himself. He had recently obtained a job busing tables at a restaurant in the area. The school support team suggested to Tommy that he regulate his schedule at school before starting his new job. The team agreed that there had been many changes in Tommy's life and he needed time to adjust. After several weeks with his new school schedule, Tommy was able to begin his new job. The school support team was concerned about his specific plans to maintain his schedule since he was relying on others for his transportation needs. Although the team found that he had a good support system of friends to take him to school, at times that support was unreliable. To remedy this situation, the team supplied Tommy with public transportation tokens. Finally, he was supplied with a planner to keep track of all appointments, classes, and assignments. Tommy chose to graduate from the private school rather than returning to his base school. He is currently pursuing his dream of working in a music studio and recording his own music.

Summary of Key Points

- The primary purpose of public and private alternative programs is to provide an educational option designed to meet the individual needs of students who would benefit from a nontraditional approach to learning, or who need a combined therapeutic and academic program.
- Although students at risk require special supports to succeed academically, many do not qualify for special education services under IDEA.
- Students considered at risk are not usually actively involved in personal decision making or in their educational planning which often leaves them unprepared for employment or postsecondary education.
- It is essential that the school establish a support team within the school to advocate for the student.
- A growing body of research demonstrates that students who have been labeled failures, troublemakers, or dropouts in traditional schools can thrive and succeed in smaller, more individualized settings.

Key Terms and Phrases

- Alternative education (p. 373)
- Risk factors (p. 378)
- Student at risk (p. 378)

- Socially maladjusted (p. 381)
- Interim Alternative placement (p. 382)
- Safe and Drug Free Schools legislation (p. 382)
- Dropout prevention (p. 383)
- School safety and security policies (p. 383)
- Zero tolerance (p. 383)
- Youth development principles (p. 386)
- Alternative education plan (p. 388)
- Full-service programs (p. 388)
- Student support team (p. 389)

Questions for Reflection, Thinking, and Skill Building

1. What characteristics of alternative education programs make them effective in addressing the needs of at-risk youth?

2. How does the alternative education plan (AEP) contribute to successful collaboration of services within the school? How does the AEP contribute to successful coordination of services with the multiagency team?

3. What types of classroom interventions did Tommy need to experience success? What services inside the school setting did Tommy need? What services outside of the school setting did Tommy need?

   - How did the school support team collaborate to find solutions for Tommy's challenges?

   - How did the transition coordinator build self-determination in Tommy?

   - What barriers did Tommy face that could have been handled differently to achieve a more successful collaborative effort?

4. Visit an alternative school or alternative program in your school district or area. Inquire about how they support school collaboration and multiagency collaboration for their students and families. Find out the agencies with which they coordinate.

CHAPTER FIFTEEN

HOW CAN SCHOOL COLLABORATION AND SYSTEM COORDINATION PROMOTE TRANSITION OF STUDENTS TO POSTSECONDARY SETTINGS?

For most students, participation in post-secondary education is not limited to being physically present in a lecture hall. It is the possibility to ask questions, to discuss ideas with classmates, to have a critical conversation with professors about papers, to reflect upon readings, to explore the library, to have access to information in accessible formats at the same time as their non-disabled classmates, to work on a research project, to have coffee with friends, to participate at campus social and cultural events, and really take part in the college experience.

—NATIONAL COUNCIL ON DISABILITY, 2003a

- What do we know about the participation of graduates with disabilities in postsecondary education?

- What changes as the student moves from the secondary to the postsecondary world?

- What laws promote collaboration for participation in postsecondary education and employment?

- What service coordination roles support the transition of youth to postsecondary settings?

- What system coordination strategies support graduates preparing for postsecondary settings?

- What are the barriers to participation in postsecondary education?

- What do we know about youth employment after high school?

- What are barriers to employment for youth with disabilities?

- What system coordination strategies support high school graduates in their transition to employment?

PERSPECTIVES

College Student

I have a hidden disability—a learning disability—and so I had a much harder time proving to professors that I really had a disability and needed help.

Professor

I have had many students with disabilities in my classes, including those who are deaf, have visual disabilities, use wheelchairs, have recovered from traumatic brain injuries, and have speech and learning difficulties. I work with them in any way I can to help them overcome their disadvantages. In my 20 years as a professor, I have not yet met a student with a disability who was malingering or asking for unreasonable accommodations. For the most part, I have found them to be extraordinarily hard working, ambitious, grateful for the opportunity to be at the university, and untiring in their pursuit of higher education. They are model students.

INTRODUCTION

Americans throughout history have recognized the power of education to transform the lives of all people and to advance our democratic way of life. Rapid changes in the employment market have made a postsecondary education (2- and 4-year college) essential for career advancement and success in many fields. In response, a national investment in youth development is assisting students to access education and employment preparation programs and increase social and economic independence. Interest in career development and transition to postsecondary education and employment is greater than it has ever been in the past, both in the

United States and in other nations. Successful transition from secondary school to the adult world is becoming recognized as a chief indicator of the effectiveness of our educational system for preparing youth and young adults for employment, post-secondary education, military service, and adult independence (Johnson, Sharpe & Stodden, 2000).

This chapter describes collaboration and system coordination strategies for students as they move from the secondary to postsecondary setting. The chapter examines disability laws that affect young people in postsecondary institutions and employment settings. A variety of coordination activities are described along with the professional roles in schools and communities that help young people at the crossroads of high school graduation.

What Do We Know About the Participation of Graduates With Disabilities in Postsecondary Education?

Postsecondary Options for Youth With Disabilities

The point of transition from high school to the postsecondary world is a challenging crossroads for all young people. They have to make choices about what college they will choose, what they will study, where they will live, whether they will work while they study, and how they will pay for their living expenses. If they choose to enter employment directly, they may be concerned about the kind of job for which they should interview, whether they have the skills and can work the long hours, how they will save and budget their earnings, and how they will juggle all of life's demands.

There are many postsecondary options for youth with disabilities in the United States. Four-year colleges and universities offer bachelor of arts or bachelor of science degrees. Some also offer graduate and professional degrees. Community colleges are public, 2-year colleges that typically serve people in their immediate communities and offer academic, technical, and continuing education courses. The programs often lead to a license, a certificate, or associate of arts or science degrees that are aligned with 4-year college curriculum. Community colleges often operate under an open admissions policy, and admissions requirements may vary. Some community colleges offer programs for individuals with cognitive disabilities, autism, and other disabilities and are focused on developing functional, independent living, and employment skills.

Vocational and technical colleges offer a variety of options, including associate degrees, certificates, and work apprenticeships. Associate degree programs prepare students for technical occupations (e.g., accountant, dental hygienist, computer programmer). Technical diploma programs meet the needs of businesses and industry and provide employees with required certification for employment (e.g., automotive maintenance, accounting assistant, pharmacy technician). Apprenticeships are geared toward those interested in working in industrial or service trades (e.g., carpentry, plumbing, machining). Military service can also help young people achieve their career goals; however, the military branches are not required to accommodate individuals on the basis of disability (Brown 2000; HEATH Resource Center, 2006). Finally, assistance with employment in competitive jobs or supported work settings is available to youth.

At the time of transition to college life, individuals with disabilities have the same choices to make as their nondisabled peers, but have on their plate many additional considerations that add to the uncertainty and stress. Many ask: What colleges have the support services, accommodations, and assistive technology I need, and will the disability support services office need proof of my disability? Will I get into a dorm with my disability, and will I make friends in my classes? Will professors help accommodate me if I cannot finish the tests on time due to my reading disability, or will they be suspicious of my motives? Will there be counselors if I run into difficulty and need help? Will the campus be accessible for my wheelchair? Will people accept me as an equal in my new job? Because these additional uncertainties place extraordinary demands on the young adult, supportive services are often (though not always) needed to help in the transition and adjustment to the college or work setting. Box 15.1 describes a college program for individuals with significant disabilities.

Participation in and Outcomes of Postsecondary Education

Young adults with disabilities who complete a college degree are as likely to become employed as their peers without disabilities; however, they are much less prepared or likely to enroll or to complete college (National Center for Secondary Education and Transition, 2004; Blackorby & Wagner, 1996).

Preparation for Postsecondary Settings.   Many youth with disabilities are not adequately prepared in high school to meet the entrance requirements and academic rigor of postsecondary institutions. Students with disabilities are less likely than their peers without disabilities to complete a full secondary school academic curriculum, especially in math and science curriculum areas. Furthermore, many are not encouraged in high school to extend their education beyond secondary school. Secondary students with disabilities have minimal involvement in their IEP meetings and therefore are unprepared with a postsecondary transition plan or to self-advocate for their needs (National Council on Disability, 2000b; Storms, O'Leary, & Williams, 2000b). When ranked according to qualifications for college admission, students

---

BOX 15.1   LIFE Program Provides Postsecondary Education for Young Adults With Severe Challenges

Over the past few years, some 2- and 4-year colleges and universities are providing innovative independent living programs and courses to students with disabilities. For example, the Helen A. Kellar Institute for Human disAbilities at the George Mason University, outside Washington, D.C., has launched a new program to prepare students with disabilities for careers and independent living. The program blends functional instruction with academics to prepare young adults with significant disabilities for employment and independent living in their communities. The Learning Into Future Environments (LIFE) program, the first of its kind at a public 4-year university, allows these students to obtain a postsecondary education in a supportive, inclusive environment. At the same time, the program provides Mason students majoring in disciplines such as education, psychology, assistive technology, and social work with practical experience in working with individuals with disabilities (George Mason University, Helen A. Kellar Institute for Human disAbilities 2006, by permission).

with disabilities were less likely than their peers to be even minimally qualified, based on an index score of grades, class rank, National Education Longitudinal Study (NELS) composite test scores, and SAT/ACT scores (National Center for Education Statistics [NCES], 1999).

Increased Number of Students in College Who Report Disabilities. The number of postsecondary students (all types of institutions) reporting a disability has increased dramatically, climbing from 2.6% in 1978, to 9.2% in 1994, 19% in 1996 (Blackorby & Wagner, 1996), and 20% in 2002. This increase is partly due to changes in the Higher Education Act, Section 504 of the Rehabilitation Act and Americans With Disabilities Act that require institutions of higher education (2- and 4-year colleges and universities, career and technical schools) to provide reasonable accommodations for students with disabilities. Since 1990, there has been a 90% increase in the number of colleges, universities, technical institutions, and career technical centers offering opportunities for persons with disabilities to continue education (Pierangelo & Crane, 1997).

Long-Term Outcomes of Participation in College. Substantial federal and state investments in creating a "seamless" transition for students with disabilities have not had a significant impact on the enrollment and completion of postsecondary programs by students with disabilities in comparison with their nondisabled peers (Blackorby & Wagner, 2002; Gilmore, Bose, & Hart, 2002). Studies have found that only 27% of students with disabilities enroll in postsecondary education as compared to 68% of students without disabilities. More than 26% of freshmen with disabilities at 4-year colleges do not return for their sophomore year (Izzo, Hertzfeld, Simmons-Reed, & Aaron, 2001). Students with disabilities who enroll in postsecondary institutions are less likely to complete a bachelor' s degree (16% and 27% for students with and without disabilities, respectively). Students with disabilities who earn a bachelor's degree do almost as well with employment as do those individuals without a disability (67% of youth with disabilities with a bachelor's degree were working full time compared with 73% for persons with disability holding the same degree) (National Center for Education Statistics, 2000; U.S. Department of Education, 2001). Nonetheless, the enrollment of people with disabilities in postsecondary institutions is still 50% lower than enrollment among the general population (Getzel, Stodden & Briel, 2001; Vreeberg-Izzo, Hertzfeld, Simmons-Reed, & Aaron, 2001; Roessler & Rumrill, 1998; Sharpe & Johnson, 2001). This gap in educational attainment effects long-term employment prospects, and there is a great distance to go to close it.

What Changes As the Student Moves From the Secondary to the Postsecondary World?

According to the National Council on Disability (2003a), students with disabilities and their parents need to be better informed about the differences in the rights and responsibilities of schools and students as they move from high school to higher education. The result is that students are often harshly surprised rather than prepared for the disparity between the two levels of education (2003, p. 8). In secondary school, the teachers and other school professionals share the responsibility for the educational success with the student, but in higher education it is up to the individual. Students must have the skills to advocate for their needs in college or on the job, skills they may not have learned in high school.

Self-Advocacy Skills Needed for Postsecondary Participation: It's Up to the Student.

Only one-half of secondary schools have specific curriculum to teach secondary students **self-advocacy and self-determination skills** (Study of State and Local Implementation and Impact of the IDEA, 2004; U.S. Government Accountability Office, 2003d). However, most states are now emphasizing transition services and are working to ensure that students with disabilities who need such services are provided with adequate planning and support.

Postsecondary school is different from secondary school in many ways. Class schedules are flexible, class offerings are varied, classes may be located in different buildings, and books and tuition can be very costly. Students are expected to take full responsibility for their progress and to spend much more time and effort on independent study. For students living on campus, there is a wide variety of social and special interest opportunities, and often a great sense of freedom from parental supervision. Success is now up to the student.

Laws Governing Secondary and Postsecondary Settings Are Different.

For students with disabilities, the laws governing special assistance in the **postsecondary setting** are different and change students' experiences in several ways:

1. While high school decision making is parent driven, students in postsecondary settings are responsible for identifying their disability, providing documentation, and requesting assistance (student driven).

2. Disability services personnel make decisions about services based on the "reasonable accommodations" requirements of the Americans With Disabilities Act (ADA) and Section 504 of the Rehabilitation Act, and not on services prescribed by the Individuals With Disabilities Education Act (IDEA).

3. Students make decisions about the services available; there is no professional team to decide for them.

4. Students with disabilities often have to repeat the process of requesting services and accommodations each year (National Center for Secondary Education and Transition, 2003).

Under Section 504 of the Rehabilitation Act, it is not mandated that all postsecondary students with disabilities receive services and supports, but rather services are based on whether (1) the individual is determined to be eligible for the services, and (2) whether the accommodation does not result in a change in content or standards expected for all students. In the postsecondary setting, supports are based on what is "reasonable," rather than what is "appropriate" and "least restrictive," as mandated by IDEA. Therefore, support services and accommodations are aimed at providing access to content and reducing barriers to learning, rather than on promoting achievement. For example, a postsecondary school is more likely to provide a notetaker than a tutor.

Let's See It in Action, p. 402, presents a central question for students with disabilities who plan to seek admission to postsecondary education after graduation from high school.

LET'S SEE IT IN ACTION! Case Illustration: What Accommodations Can I Expect in College?

QUESTION: I am a high school senior with a learning disability, and I have just been admitted to the college of my choice. Will the accommodations that were provided to me in high school under my IEP automatically be provided to me in college?

ANSWER: First of all, NO accommodations will be provided to you unless and until you identify yourself to be a student with a disability and provide documentation of your disability. Once the proper administrator has been notified, under Section 504 of the Rehabilitation Act, and under the Americans with Disabilities Act, the college must provide reasonable accommodations and academic adjustments that specifically address your known disability. By providing such accommodations, they afford you an equal opportunity to participate in the institution's programs, courses, and activities. However, the college is not required to provide accommodations just because they appear in your IEP, though that information can certainly be very helpful to disability support service (DSS) coordinators as they develop your personal accommodations plan. In fact, DSS personnel may determine that some accommodations you received in high school substantially alter aspects of the curriculum, and are therefore not reasonable. They were actually "modifications" to the curriculum. In short, it will be useful to refer to your IEP when discussing possible accommodations for college-level work, yet be prepared to consider alternative accommodations or adjustments in the event that some in the IEP are no longer available to you (HEATH Resource Center, 2005).

What Laws Promote Collaboration for Participation in Postsecondary Education and Employment?

Despite the challenges of entering a "different world" of postsecondary education, recent laws have greatly improved access and support of youth with disabilities. Most postsecondary institutions are responding to the mandates and are developing greater capacity to recruit and include students with disabilities.

How Does IDEA 2004 Promote Collaboration for Postsecondary Participation?

Collaboration and the Summary of Performance.   The IDEA 2004 included a new requirement to assist students to make the transition from high school to postsecondary education or employment. Under IDEA 2004 local, educational agencies must provide a students with a summary of the child's academic achievement and functional performance (**summary of performance** or SOP), which includes recommendations on how to assist the child in meeting their postsecondary goals (IDEA, 2004, Section 300.305 (e) (3)). The SOP also provides **documentation of disability** which is necessary, under Section 504 of the Rehabilitation Act and the

Americans with Disabilities Act, to help establish a student's eligibility for reasonable accommodations and supports in postsecondary settings. It is also helpful in the vocational rehabilitation comprehensive assessment process to determine eligibility for VR services. Developing the SOP may be the responsibility of the special educator or school psychologist, but coordination and participation of teachers, counselors, and related services professionals is essential to gathering and summarizing relevant information on the student.

Postsecondary educational institutions do not typically accept an individualized education program (IEP) from a high school as documentation of a disability or an academic accommodation (HEATH, 2006). However, colleges may use high school testing results, documented in the summary of performance if the information is current and disability specific. For example, after consultation with the college, a student with a learning disability might submit the psycho-educational evaluation from 11th grade as documentation of the learning disability. It is very important that students collect and maintain their high school records and their summary of performance for the purposes of disability documentation (Hart, Zafft, & Zimbrich, 2001; Kochhar-Bryant & Vreeburg, 2006; Shaw, 2006; Shaw & Dukes, 2001).

Collaboration at the Age of Majority.   **Age of majority** refers to the age at which a young person acquires all the rights and responsibilities of being an adult. In most states, the age is 18. IDEA outlined a procedure for the transfer of parental rights to the student when he or she reaches the age of majority. Collaboration and communication between school professionals and parents is essential. Schools must now notify the student and both parents about the student's rights when he or she reaches the age of majority. One year before the student reaches the age of majority under state law, the IEP must include a statement that he or she has been informed of the rights that transfer to the students once she reaches the age of majority. This transfer of rights is an enormous step toward the student's independence and participation in the decision making for further education and future planning (Bremer, Kachgal, & Schoeller, 2003; Eisenman & Chamberlin, 2001).

Collaboration and Section 504 of the Vocational Rehabilitation Act

The 1998 **Rehabilitation Amendments** (P.L. 102–569) strengthened the collaboration and coordination among secondary schools, postsecondary schools, and rehabilitation agencies to support transition to employment or postsecondary settings. For students eligible for vocational rehabilitation (VR) services, state interagency agreements transferred responsibility for transitioning students from the state education agency to the state unit providing VR services. This provision links the IEP and the individual written rehabilitation plan (IWRP) in accomplishing rehabilitation goals prior to high school graduation.

Vocational rehabilitation provides funds for eligible students with disabilities to attend postsecondary education or technical education programs. VR assists persons with cognitive, sensory, physical, or emotional disabilities to attain employment, postsecondary education, and increased independence. Students with disabilities are entitled to accommodations to help them succeed in the postsecondary program, but students are responsible for disclosing their disabilities and asking for the accommodations they need. VR services typically last for a limited period of time and are based on an individual's rehabilitation plan.

The 1998 Amendments to the Rehabilitation Act also require rehabilitation agencies to make information about services and providers available to students in their final 2 years of high school. Rehabilitation services such as early assessment for eligibility for services, vocational assessments, and counseling in work behaviors are now available to students in their final years of high school and after graduation. Close collaboration between secondary personnel and rehabilitation counselors after the student reaches age 16 is vital to linking the student with VR services and engaging parents in planning.

Collaboration and the Higher Education Act

The **Higher Education Act** of 1998 (HEA, P.L. 105–244) is designed to assist individuals to participate in postsecondary education, including students with disabilities. HEA encourages collaborative partnerships between institutions of higher education (IHEs) and secondary schools, particularly those that serve low-income and disadvantaged students. HEA encourages collaboration among IHEs, businesses, labor organizations, community-based organizations, and private and civic organizations to improve accessibility and support in higher education. The act also promotes collaboration between IHEs, schools, and other community agencies for outreach to students with disabilities for the purposes of reducing barriers that prevent participation of individuals with disabilities within their community. The HEA aims to improve college retention and graduation rates for low-income and first-generation college students with disabilities and to encourage programs that counsel students about financial aid and support services.

Coordination and the Americans With Disabilities Act in Postsecondary Institutions and Employment

The **Americans with Disabilities Act** of 1990 is a civil rights law that prohibits discrimination in work settings, job training programs, and postsecondary schools. ADA does not guarantee anyone a job or admission to postsecondary education, but it does require employers and colleges to make reasonable accommodations for persons with disabilities. The ADA promotes collaboration to provide accommodations in both public and private organizations, including public and private schools, colleges and universities, postsecondary career–technical schools, employer-based training programs, and other private training programs. According to ADA regulations, reasonable accommodations at the postsecondary level include modifications to a postsecondary education admission procedure to enable individuals to be considered for admission, modifications in classrooms, test taking, and instructional modifications that would help the student participate in and learn in the college setting. Through antidiscrimination provisions, the ADA encourages postsecondary institutions to consider applicants with disabilities in their recruitment of teachers, professors, and support personnel.

In most colleges and universities, students can expect to apply for and receive services from an office with a title such as "student support services" or "office of

Anthony Magnacca/Merrill

Good communication with faculty helps students self-advocate for accommodations in the college setting but also requires faculty knowledgeable about their role and responsibilities.

disability services." While a student may not have an IEP or 504 plan in college, postsecondary institutions are required under ADA and the Higher Education Act of 1998 to provide reasonable accommodations (Brinkerhoff, McGuire, & Shaw, 2002; Ekpone & Bogucki, 2002; HEATH, 2003). Often students have **support service plans** that are similar to 504 plans since they specify the kinds of accommodations that the student is to receive in classrooms and in nonacademic activities. A support services counselor helps the student determine the kinds of accommodations that will be needed on campus. The counselor will help schedule interpreters and assist instructors in providing materials in alternative formats, such as audiotape or braille. It is the student's responsibility to inform his or her instructors of the need for accommodations (PACER Center, 2001). Accommodations that can be requested in postsecondary education include testing accommodations, physical accommodations, adaptations of technology, special software for large print, notetakers, supplemental online tutorials, extensions of time for papers and homework, tutors, and groups support sessions. If students plan to use telecommunications equipment as part of the educational program or in their work on campus, then accommodations for sensory deficits must be made.

ADA in Employment.   The Americans With Disabilities Act (ADA) prohibits discrimination by employers against "qualified individuals with disabilities (visible or hidden)"—those who possesses the skills, experience, education, and other job-related requirements of a position and who, with or without **reasonable accommodations**, can perform the essential functions of the job. This antidiscrimination provision covers all aspects of employment, including application, testing and medical examinations, promotion, hiring and layoffs, assignments and termination, evaluation and compensation, disciplinary actions and leave, and training and benefits.

Examples of reasonable accommodations include job restructuring; modified work schedules; reassignments of position; modifications to equipment; modifications of examinations, training materials, or policies; and provision of readers or interpreters (Dixon, Kruse, & Van Horn, 2003). Employers are not required to guarantee jobs or to lower their standards to make such accommodations, nor are they required to provide accommodations if they impose "undue hardships" on the business through actions that are very costly or disruptive of the work environment (National Information Center for Children and Youth with Disabilities, 1999). However, most accommodations cost less than $500. Box 15.2 provides examples of accommodations worked out through discussions between employees and employers in consultation with the Office of Disability Employment Policy's Job Accommodation Network (JAN) (2005).

Ticket to Work and Work Incentive Improvement Act

In late 1999, the Congress enacted the **Ticket to Work and Work Incentive Improvement Act** (TWWIIA, P.L. 106–170). The Social Security Administration (SSA) administers the Act and the Department of Health and Human Services administers the health care component. Under the voluntary Ticket to Work Program, individuals with disabilities can obtain job-related training and placement assistance from an

---

BOX 15.2   Simple Accommodations for Workers With Disabilities

Situation: A bowling alley worker with mental retardation and finger dexterity problems in both hands was having difficulty wiping the bowling shoes that had been returned by customers. **Solution:** A local job coach service provider fabricated a device that allowed the individual to roll the shoes in front of a brush rather than run a brush over the shoes. Cost: no cost as scraps of wood that were left over from other projects were used to make the device.

Situation: A high school guidance counselor with attention deficit disorder was having difficulty concentrating due to the school noise. **Solution:** The school replaced the bell on his phone with an electric light bulb device that lights up when the phone rings, soundproofed his office, and provided a floor fan for white noise. Cost: under $600.

Situation: A machine operator who developed arthritis had difficulty turning the machinery control switches. **Solution:** The employer replaced the small machine tabs with larger cushioned knobs and provided the employee with nonslip dot gripping gloves that enabled him to grasp and turn the knobs more effectively and with less force. Cost: approximately $130.

Situation: A 25-year veteran warehouse supervisor whose job involved managing and delivering company supplies was having difficulty with the physical demands of his job due to fatigue from cancer treatment. **Solution:** The employer provided the employee with a three-wheeled scooter to reduce walking and enable him to manage the warehouse. The employer also rearranged the layout of supplies in the warehouse to reduce climbing and reaching. Cost: $3,000.

Situation: A part-time college instructor had a learning disability—specifically, auditory discrimination difficulties. This was causing problems for her during meetings and in class and prevented her from meeting time lines for projects. **Solution:** The employee was permitted to take notes during staff meetings and to provide written responses to all attendees on the questions raised during the meeting within a time frame agreed upon by the meeting participants. The employee also received a copy of meeting agendas and project expectations in advance of the face-to-face meetings and was thereby able to ask questions or provide follow-up responses in writing. Cost: $0.

approved provider of their choice. For example, youth in transition to work can receive employment services, vocational services, or other services to help them enter employment. Employment Networks are private organizations or government agencies that have agreed to work with SSA to provide employment services to persons with disabilities at no cost. The second measure expands health care coverage so that individuals with disabilities will be able to become employed without fear of losing their health insurance (U.S. Department of Labor, 2001b). The Ticket to Work program has helped many young people make the transition into employment in their communities.

What Service Coordination Roles Support the Transition of Youth to Postsecondary Settings?

The following sections describe several service coordination roles that assist youth to navigate a transition from high school to postsecondary settings successfully.

Secondary Transition Coordinator: Bridge to the Postsecondary World

Secondary transition specialists typically begin work with students when they reach the age at which they are eligible for services and planning (16 under IDEA 2004, with option to begin earlier if needed). The coordinator works with the student to identify preferences and goals. He or she collaborates with general educators to recommend a course of study through high school to prepare for careers and independent living in either college or employment settings. The coordinator arranges opportunities for the student (or a group of students) to learn about different careers through videos, job shadowing, visits to work environments, and hands-on work activities that allow the student(s) to try out jobs. Finally the coordinator makes connections with the adult service system, identifies the support services or accommodations the student may need in the postsecondary setting, and assists students in assembling portfolios of academic records, job experiences, resumes, and postsecondary recommendations. **Transition coordinators** may follow up with the student and continue their support services for a period of time after the student has graduated. Recent research on the role of transition coordinators shows that 94% of states also employ one or more at the state level (Jackson, 2003; Schiller et al., 2003; U.S. Department of Education, 2003b).

School Guidance Counselor

At the high school level, guidance counselors are concerned with educational and career guidance while they also focus on the personal development of the students. High school counselors help students choose school courses and activities that relate to their interests and will prepare them for life after high school. They also show students how to apply for college or for job-training programs. At the postsecondary level, academic advisors provide information about college entrance requirements, financial aid programs, and entry-level job opportunities in the areas where they might be attending school.

Disability Support Specialist

The **disability support specialist** in the postsecondary institution provides consultation and ongoing support to enable students to make full use of opportunities at the college or university. The DSS director often serves as liaison with college faculty, staff and administrators, vocational rehabilitation counselors, and other social service agencies. DSS serves as the central point of contact for information on physical and programmatic access, specific accommodations, resolution of complaints and problems, faculty and staff concerns, and identification of available services. In addition, the DSS office can provide training, consultation, and information regarding disability issues. The coordinator of the disability support center also fulfills the role of 504 coordinator and helps provide for reasonable accommodations.

Vocational Rehabilitation Counselor

The vocational rehabilitation counselor is often involved in a student's transition planning while the student is still in school. Upon graduation, the VR counselor works with the student to assist with access to and support in employment or postsecondary education. The rehabilitation counselor typically works for the state's vocational rehabilitation (VR) agency, helping people with disabilities prepare for and find employment. For students who are eligible for VR, services may include evaluation of the person's interests, capabilities, and limitations; job training; transportation; aids and devices; job placement; support to begin postsecondary education; and job follow-up. Priority in services is given to individuals with significant disabilities.

Job Development Specialist

A job development specialist works for either a school system or an adult service agency such as the vocational rehabilitation agency or a supported employment agency. As the job title suggests, the primary role is to find jobs for people with disabilities. The job developer visits employers to inquire about available positions and may offer the employer services such as placement of individuals into jobs; training the employee on job tasks and appropriate workplace behavior; talking with supervisor(s) and coworkers about disability awareness; providing long-term support to the employee on the job; and helping to promote interaction between the employee and his or her coworkers (PACER Center, 2001; Thuli & Hong, 1998).

What System Coordination Strategies Support Graduates Preparing for Postsecondary Settings?

Postsecondary Planning in the Last Year of High School

IDEA legislation mandates transition supports for youth preparing for graduation. Information about the requirements for entering postsecondary institutions or employment should be obtained and that information used through "backward planning" to map students' secondary course of study. The classes that secondary students take in their final years—both academic and career–technical—should not only meet requirements for graduating from secondary school, but also for entering postsecondary education or employment. The IEP team identifies and explores supports and accommodations that the student will need in postsecondary environments and plans for ways to prepare the student to transition to these supports (National Center on Secondary Education and Transition, 2004).

In the final year of high school, the student, in consultation with parents and guidance counselors, should identify potential colleges that (a) they can qualify for, (b) have programs that match their interests and abilities, (c) have student support services available, and (d) have a strong record of supporting students with disabilities. If the student is planning to enroll in a 2- or 4-year college or technical school, he or she can ask their guidance counselor to help them select colleges, apply and negotiate for support services, find information on how to access campus resources, discuss interview techniques, discuss self-advocacy techniques and ways to promote one's strengths, and the advantages and disadvantages of self-disclosure of the disability. There are several important questions that youth with disabilities should ask when preparing to apply for disability support services:

- Who is responsible for coordinating services for students with disabilities?
- What is the size of the disability support services counselor's caseload?
- How many students are served by the disability support services office?
- What documentation of my disability will the college need? What should I make sure I take with me from high school?
- Is there anyone to help me coordinate academic and other support services? Will I have an advocate or mentor?
- Is there ongoing professional supervision of support service providers such as tutors, peer mentors, counselors, and other specialists?
- Is a program representative available to answer all my questions clearly and thoroughly?
- Do students have to pay for support services? Are these charges considered in the school's financial aid packet?

In the last year of high school, with the support and involvement of the family and transition team, each student should make sure the IEP includes transition plans and a summary of performance, now required under IDEA 2004. Finally, students should learn to discuss their disability and to describe accommodations that are necessary and effective. If appropriate, they should contact the vocational rehabilitation (VR) agency and/or the Social Security Administration at age 18 or in the last year of school to determine eligibility for benefits (Kochhar-Bryant & Vreeburg-Izzo, 2006).

Coordination With Community Service Agencies in the Last Year of High School

Adult service agencies provide a comprehensive system of services responsive to the needs of individuals with emotional disabilities, cognitive disabilities, physical disabilities, and multiple disabilities. These services typically include mental heath, developmental disabilities, employment, and independent living services. Examples of employment services include supported and sheltered employment and competitive employment support for those who need minimal assistance. Examples of adult and independent living services include service coordination to access and obtain local services, therapeutic recreation, day activities, respite care, and residential services (group homes and supervised apartments).

IDEA 2004 requires school-linked human service agencies to support students' transition from school to postsecondary education and employment. While the school system is required by law to provide the services that are written into the IEP, organizations that provide supportive services are expected to share the responsibility for transition support services. For example, if the student needs medical services, they can be sought and provided from Medicaid, public health agencies, private insurance, early periodic screening, and diagnosis and treatment programs. If transition support services are needed, they may be sought and provided from vocational rehabilitation agencies, employment services, adult service agencies, job training programs, Workforce Investment Act programs, or supported employment projects.

The student's IEP should contain a statement of interagency responsibilities or any linkages required to ensure that the student has the transition services needed from outside agencies and that representatives from those agencies are invited to attend IEP meetings. This requirement for interagency services means that there must be formal interagency agreements between schools and cooperating agencies.

Social Security Administration

The Social Security Administration operates the federally funded program that provides benefits for people of any age who are unable to perform substantial work and have a severe mental or physical disability. Several programs are offered for people with disabilities, including Social Security Disability Insurance (SSDI), Supplemental Security Income (SSI), Plans to Achieve Self-Support (PASS), Medicaid, and Medicare. Examples of employment services include cash benefits while working (e.g., student-earned income), Medicare or Medicaid while working, help with extra work expenses the individual has as a result of the disability, and assistance to start a new line of work (discussed later). Postsecondary services generally include financial incentives for further education and training.

What Are the Barriers to Participation in Postsecondary Education?

Many college students with and without disabilities are faced with challenging physical and social environments. These adjustments are compounded for students with disabilities because they are faced with architectural barriers and attitudinal misperceptions about their skills and abilities by faculty, staff, and their nondisabled peers (Justesen & Justesen, 2000). Youth face several barriers as they prepare for and participate in postsecondary school education.

Lack of Identification of the Disability in Early School Years

Many students with disabilities are not appropriately identified and provided special education and related services during childhood and adolescent years. For example, in one study, 31% of national survey respondents with specific learning disabilities (SLD) indicated that their disability was first identified at the postsecondary level (National Center for the Study of Post-Secondary Education Supports, 2002). When declaring a primary disability, 44% of participants with an attention deficit disorder (ADD) indicated that their disability was first identified at the postsecondary level (Izzo, 2003). Delayed identification prevents students from benefiting from years of needed services. More schools are making efforts to identify disabilities in the early years (Bradley, Danielson, & Hallahan, 2002; Steckbeck, 2004).

Lack of Access to Guidance Counseling

As mentioned earlier, dropout rates and receipt of alternative diplomas are much higher for youth with disabilities than for their nondisabled peers. At the high school level, many youth with disabilities are pulled out of content classes and placed into special education classes and as a result may not meet the entry requirements of many postsecondary schools. Others face barriers to tests and assessments, such as the SAT, which may require testing accommodations. Finally, many academic and career counselors lack the necessary skills to provide guidance to students with disabilities. Secondary students are often left with inadequate guidance due to poor coordination among teachers and counseling staff (Stodden, Galloway, & Stodden, 2003; Stodden, Jones, & Chang, 2002). Schools across the United States are more carefully examining the role of the guidance counselor in assisting youth with disabilities to prepare for postsecondary education (National Council on Disability, 2004).

Lack of Financial Support Through College

Individuals with disabilities are more likely to face financial barriers during post-secondary education than their nondisabled peers. Individuals with disabilities are more than twice as likely to live below the poverty line as individuals without disabilities (National Council on Disability, 2003a). At the same time, research has shown that few students with disabilities are accessing disability benefits that are available to them in postsecondary study. As one study shows, only 8.3% of post-secondary students with disabilities participate in SSI and SSDI disability programs. In general, postsecondary students with disabilities, when compared to nondisabled peers, receive less financial aid and are unable to participate in assistance programs due to lack of awareness about SSI or SSDI disability benefits, or work incentive programs (Berry & Jones, 2000). Policymakers and postsecondary educators are carefully examining the problems of financial support for students with disabilities (National Council on Disability, 2004; U.S. Government Accountability Office, 2003d).

Attitudes and Stigma

Many youth who attend college experience negative self-concept, under developed socialization skills, anxiety, and professors who are reluctant to help (Chadsey & Sheldon, 1998; Wolanin & Steele, 2004). Students with disabilities often choose to remain invisible because they may be concerned about the stigma of accommodations, believing that: "Teachers and other students think I'm getting away with something when I'm given accommodations" (National Center for Study of Postsecondary Educational Supports, 2000b, p. 11). While these experiences are still widespread, there is a growing awareness on college campuses of the need and value of creating a welcoming attitude toward all students (Taymans & West, 2001).

Barriers for Culturally and Linguistically Diverse Students

Entering postsecondary education from high school can be an overwhelming process for students with disabilities. These gaps are even greater for students with significant disabilities and who are culturally and linguistically diverse (CLD). Compared with their non-CLD peers, CLD students with disabilities are more likely to face language and social barriers, the negative effects of having grown up in poverty, and have difficulty processing "standard English" oral and written information, all of which may contribute to their risk of school failure (Greene & Nefsky, 1999). Furthermore, students with disabilities who are from diverse cultures are less likely to disclose their disability and receive support services in postsecondary schools (Flowers & Edwards, 1996; Hart et al., 2001; Hasnain, 2001; Stodden & Dowrick, 2001; Stodden, Jones, & Chang, 2002). These conditions point to the need for greater assistance to culturally and linguistically diverse postsecondary students, as illustrated in Let's See It in Action, page 413.

Gap in Technology Access

Lack of access to technology impedes students' ability to achieve to their potential in high school and to use technology in the postsecondary environments. Only 28.4% of Americans with disabilities have access to the Internet at home or work, compared to 56.7% of those without disabilities. Almost 60% of Americans with disabilities have never even used a personal computer, compared to fewer than 25% of Americans without disabilities (Kaye, 2000; National Organization on Disability, 2000). When students with disabilities do have access to technology in high school, it is more than likely that they will not be able to take the technology with them after graduation (Gaylord, Johnson, Lehr, Bremer, & Hasazi, 2004). Greater opportunities are becoming available on college campuses to assist students with disabilities to access technology (Burgstahler, 2002; Malouf, 2000).

Inadequate Preparation of College Faculty

An important factor that affects students' persistence and retention is the lack of awareness of faculty members of the disability needs of students, available supports on campus, and their responsibility for making accommodations. Furthermore, poor preparation to make needed accommodations may invite further misunderstanding

LET'S SEE IT IN ACTION! Case Illustration: Circle of support at the University of Hawaii

Fasy ("Faz-ee") grew up in a small island country in the Pacific Ocean. He became paralyzed as a teenager when he fell from a cliff and suffered a serious spinal injury. Unable to walk, he learned to use a wheelchair. Neither the schools nor other government services provided much in special services for people like Fasy. However, with his determination and academic capabilities, he earned entry to the University of Hawaii at Manoa. A number of support services were available to him there. Due to the seriousness of his disability, Fasy required assistance to get around campus and take care of his basic needs, but extensive aide services were not available. Fortunately, in keeping with the family orientation of his Pacific Island culture, some of his family members were able to come to Hawaii specifically to support him to reach his postsecondary education goals. During much of his academic career, one or two of his brothers were always at his side, and when they were not available, other family members assisted him. With the support of his family, Fasy earned his bachelor's degree and then two master's degrees, one in history and the other in Pacific Islands studies. The challenges presented by his disability, as well as cultural and language differences, resulted in his taking several extra years to complete his studies. However, his own efforts, the supports provided by his family, and supports provided by the university, were successful, and now, in his late 30s, he is the director of one of the four campuses of his country's national university.

This case study illustrates how a cultural strength (individuals giving priority to the success of the family as a whole) can be built upon to support a CLD student with severe disabilities to achieve postsecondary educational success. What is notable in this case is the ready and coordinated participation of the entire family. This "collectivist" orientation contrasts with the more "individualistic" orientation of mainstream American society, and should be taken into account when addressing the support needs of persons with disabilities from collectivist cultural backgrounds (Leake & Cholymay, 2003, by permission).

or conflict that could lead to dropping out or to adversarial relationships with the institution (National Council on Disability [NCD], 2003b). Recent initiatives by universities, with support from the U.S. Department of Education, are improving faculty preparation and resources for accommodating students with disabilities in their classrooms (Izzo, Hertzfeld, Simmons-Reed, & Aaron, 2001).

What Do We Know About Youth Employment After High School?

Researchers have consistently documented that large gaps still exist between young people with disabilities and the remainder of the population with regard to education, transition, economic, and independent living outcomes. Despite decades of federal and state initiatives to improve employment outcomes for youth with disabilities, they continue to reflect the widest gulf between youth with disabilities and the general population (Blanck, 2000). According to the Census Bureau (McNeil, 2000), only 3 in 10 working-aged people with disabilities are employed full-time, compared to 8 in 10 people in the rest of the population. Fabian, Lent, and Willis (1998) found that 3–5 years after high school only about half (50%) of young people with disabilities were employed, compared to 69% of their peers. Currently, only 27% of students in special education who complete high school are enrolled in postsecondary education compared to 68% of the general student population. And, 3–5 years after high school, only a little more than half become employed compared to 69% of their peers (Fabian, Lent, & Willis, 1998; McNeil, 2000). Many barriers to employment persist for people with disabilities.

What Are the Barriers to Employment for Youth With Disabilities?

Lack of Career-Related Course Work

Students with disabilities who choose to enter directly into employment after completing high school are not adequately prepared to reach their goals. Students with disabilities are less likely than students without disabilities to complete courses in high school that prepare them to succeed in skilled employment. Preparation must begin in the early school years to ensure that students participate in appropriate career development courses. Schools can bridge the gap by providing work experiences, career and academic counseling, job coaching, and mentoring opportunities while encouraging students to enroll in the kinds of academic courses that will prepare them to succeed in work and college.

Work-Based Learning Experiences in School

Over the past 15 years, **work-based learning** experiences have become more available to youth with disabilities (Wagner, Cadwallader, & Marder, 2003). According to parents' reports, almost 60% of youth with disabilities were employed during a 1-year period in high school, some at work–study jobs, but the vast majority at nonschool-related jobs (Cameto, Marder, Wagner, & Cardoso, 2002). Approximately 15% of youth with disabilities held work–study jobs in a given year (6 percentage points more than in 1987); increases of 14–18 percentage points were significant for youth with cognitive disabilities, emotional disturbance, or multiple disabilities. The most common work–study placements are in food service (19%), maintenance (16%), and clerical jobs (15%).

More than 90% of youth in work–study jobs receive school credit and/or pay for their work. Older youth are more likely than younger youth to have work–study jobs. Work–study employment rates are approximately 10% for youth 15 years of age or younger, 15% for 16-year-olds, and 19% for 17-year-olds. The percentage of youth with work–study jobs varies for youth in different disability categories. Youth with speech impairments or learning disabilities are the least likely to have work–study jobs (7% and 10%, respectively). In contrast, approximately 30% of youth with significant cognitive disabilities, autism, multiple disabilities, or deaf-blindness hold work–study jobs. Participation in work-based learning is associated with successful outcomes for youth with disabilities.

What System Coordination Strategies Support High School Graduates in Their Transition to Employment?

Two federally funded studies published in 2000 (Bruyere, 2000; Loprest & Maag, 2001) show that much remains to be done to improve access to employment for persons with disabilities. Key national and local initiatives are needed in the areas of preparation, education, and training of persons with disabilities; outreach by the employment community to recruit persons with disabilities; a better understanding of reasonable accommodation in the workplace; and a concerted effort to break through the attitudinal barriers that are so detrimental to full integration of people with disabilities into the employment arena (Justesen & Justesen, 2000).

Initiatives to Promote Employment and Self-Support for Individuals With Significant Disabilities

An increasing number of youth apply for Supplemental Security Income (SSI) or Social Security Disability Income (SSDI) each year, despite significant federal, state, and local investments in special education; about 60,000 between ages 18–24 come on the rolls annually (Berry & Jones, 2000; U.S. Social Security Administration Annual Statistics, 2004), and less than 1% ever leave. An increasing number of young people with disabilities apply for SSI or SSDI each year.

To provide incentives for young people to enter the workforce, the Social Security Administration developed the plan for achieving self-support (PASS) to help individuals make the transition without losing disability benefits (U.S. Department of Labor, 2004). A **PASS plan** lets the young worker use his or her income or other assets to reach work goals. For example, a young graduate could set aside money to go to school to get specialized training for a job or to start a business. The job that the individual wants should allow them to earn enough to reduce or eliminate the need for benefits provided under both the Social Security and Supplemental Security Income (SSI) programs. A plan is designed to help the individual to obtain services, items, or skills that are needed to reach their employment goals.

Three requirements are needed to qualify for a PASS plan: (1) desire to work, (2) currently receiving SSI (or can qualify for SSI by having this plan) because the person is disabled or blind, and (3) have other income or resources to get a job or start a business (U.S. Department of Labor, 2004b). Under previous SSI rules, any income that the individual earned reduced the SSI payment for disability. But, with an approved PASS plan, the individual can use that income to pay for the items needed to reach their work goal. Money that is set aside toward work-related goals is not counted under this plan when the SSI payment amount is determined. Money set aside can be used for transportation to and from work; tuition, books, fees, and supplies needed for school or training; child care; attendant care; employment services, such as job coaching and resume writing; supplies to start a business; equipment and tools to do the job; or uniforms, special clothing, and safety equipment. If the plan is approved, the coordinator/specialist will stay in contact to make sure that the plan is followed and the goals are being met. Let's See It in Action, page 416, illustrates how the PASS plan can open doors for individuals with disabilities transitioning to employment.

LET'S SEE IT IN ACTION! CASE ILLUSTRATION: THE PASS PLAN FOR SELF-SUPPORT

Dana Simpkins likes spending time in front of the computer. As an e-mail specialist for the Gap, Inc., in Columbus, Ohio, that's his job. But Dana has spinal muscular atrophy and relies on a wheelchair. There was a time when he didn't know the joy of job satisfaction. Supplemental Security Income (SSI) helped make ends meet, but he wanted to work. "My PASS (Plan for Achieving Self-Support) was what allowed me to work," Dana remembers. The PASS let him keep his SSI while he went to work. He used his SSI to meet his basic needs, and his wages were saved in a special PASS account to help meet his goal of getting a van modified for wheelchair transportation. Now, with his modified van, Dana no longer needs the help of SSI. "My advice to those who are considering work is to simply go for it. Don't be afraid to try and fail. The feeling I got cashing that first paycheck was sweeter having overcome greater challenges than most" (U.S. Social Security Administration, 2004).

Becoming Employed After High School

The next section examines the types of employment opportunities available for young men and women with significant disabilities, including competitive, supported, and sheltered employment.

Competitive Employment. **Competitive employment** means a "mainstream" full-time or part-time job with competitive wages and responsibilities. Typically, competitive employment means that no long-term support is provided to the employee to help him or her learn the job or continue to perform the job. The absence of ongoing or long-term support distinguishes competitive employment from both supported employment and sheltered employment (described below). A variety of jobs are considered competitive employment—restaurant service worker, mechanic, teacher, secretary, factory worker, file clerk, or computer programmer. The amount of education or training a person needs will vary depending on the type of job.

Supported Employment. **Supported employment** is a program to assist people with the most significant disabilities to become and remain successfully and competitively employed in integrated workplace settings. Supported employment is designed for people with the most significant disabilities for whom competitive employment may not be feasible, has been interrupted or is intermittent because of the disability, or who, because of the severity of their disability, need intensive or extended support services to work competitively (U.S. Department of Labor, 2005). Supported employment models include the following:

1. *Individual Placement.* The individual obtains employment independently and then contacts the supported employment providers to get assistance or support, as needed.

2. *Agency Supported.* A rehabilitation or community services agency places the individual in a job and provides or coordinates the ongoing support services needed to help assist him or her to retain the job.

3. *Entrepreneurial.* The individual is supported by the rehabilitation or community services agency to obtain the services and supports needed to successfully run his or her own business.

Supportive services may include job development and placement; intensive - job-site training; facilitation of natural supports; special skills training; supplementary assessment; contact with employers, parents, family members, and advocacy organizations; and teaching compensatory workplace strategies. *Job development* means locating jobs for people with disabilities through networking with employers, businesses, and community leaders. The use of business advisory councils is an excellent way to develop contacts that lead to employment for people with disabilities. An Employment Specialist/Consultant (Job Coach) is typically employed by a job training and placement organization serving people with disabilities who matches clients with jobs, provides necessary supports during the initial employment period, and then facilitates the transition to natural workplace supports while reducing his or her role.

Sheltered Employment. With **sheltered employment** individuals with disabilities work in a separate, self-contained center and are not integrated with nondisabled workers. This type of employment is generally supported by federal or state funds. The type of training that workers receive varies among programs, as does the type of work. Typical tasks include boxing and packaging materials, putting together materials in envelopes for mailing, or collating papers. In the past, segregated employment was thought to be the only option available for individuals with significant cognitive disabilities such as mental retardation or autism. Today, many individuals with significant disabilities can work in community settings when provided with adequate support.

Summary of Key Points

- Successful transition to postsecondary education and employment is a process that requires the active participation of the youth in their future planning.
- Since 1990, there has been a 90% increase in the number of colleges, universities, technical institutions, and vocational technical centers offering opportunities for persons with disabilities to continue their education.
- IDEA mandates transition services for youth preparing for graduation.
- Local interagency collaborative teams are effective in helping students with disabilities make the transition to postsecondary education and employment.
- Postsecondary services are not mandated by law as they are for students with disabilities in high school. College disability services personnel make decisions about services based on the "reasonable accommodations" requirements of the Americans With Disabilities Act (ADA) and Section 504 of the Rehabilitation Act, and not on services prescribed by the Individuals With Disabilities Education Act (IDEA).
- Employment outcomes continue to reflect the widest gulf between youth with disabilities and the general population.

Key Terms and Phrases

- Postsecondary setting (p. 401)
- Self-advocacy and self-determination skills (p. 401)
- Documentation of disability (p. 402)
- Summary of performance (p. 402)
- Age of majority (p. 403)
- Rehabilitation Amendments (p. 403)
- Americans With Disabilities Act (p. 404)
- Higher Education Act (p. 404)
- Reasonable accommodations (p. 405)
- Support service plan (p. 405)
- Ticket to Work and Work Incentive Improvement Act (p. 406)
- Transition coordinators (p. 407)
- Disability support specialist (p. 408)
- Work-based learning (p. 414)
- Competitive employment (p. 415)
- PASS plan (p. 415)
- Supported employment (p. 416)
- Sheltered employment (p. 417)

Questions for Reflection, Thinking, and Skill Building

1. Discuss the key difference between the secondary and postsecondary environments for students with disabilities in terms of their rights and responsibilities.
2. How does the "age of majority" impact youth with disabilities as they prepare for transition from high school?
3. Why is documentation of the disability important in the postsecondary setting?
4. Discuss several key barriers to access to postsecondary education and employment for youth with disabilities.
5. Have you met or had a friendship with someone with a disability while you were in college or university? What do you remember about the special barriers that he or she had to overcome?
6. Have you met or had a friendship with someone with a disability while you were in an employment setting? What do you remember about the special barriers that he or she had to overcome?
7. Discuss examples of accommodations for individuals with disabilities in the workplace.
8. Research on the Internet for standards for accessibility on postsecondary campuses. In a team of two or more, take a tour of a local college or university campus and assess the accessibility of the campus in general for individuals

with disabilities using the standards that you researched. Design a template or checklist to record your assessment. Discuss your findings.

9. With their prior permission and approval, interview a student with a disability and ask if they have encountered barriers to participation in their education in the following areas: physical accessibility, course taking, test taking, use of technology, communication with faculty, homework assignments or projects, or issues with peers. Ask what particular supports or conditions have helped make a positive difference in their lives and participation in postsecondary education. To what do they attribute their persistence and success in achieving access to and success in postsecondary education?

REFERENCES

Abbot, J. (2001). *The unfinished revolution: Learning, human behavior, community and political paradox.* Alexandria, VA: Association for Supervision and Curriculum Development.

Abdal-Haqq, I. (1993). *Integrated services: New roles for schools, new challenges for teacher education.* ERIC Clearinghouse on Teacher Education. Washington, DC. (ED355197)

Abery, B., & Stancliffe, R. (1996). The ecology of self-determination. In D. J. Sands & M. L. Wehmeyer (Eds.), *Self-determination across the life span: Independence and choice for people with disabilities* (pp. 111–146). Baltimore: Paul H. Brookes.

Abrahams, D., Boyd, S., & Ginsburg, G. (2001). *Fair labor standards handbook for states, local governments and schools.* Washington, DC: Thompson Publishing Group.

Abrams, L., & Gibbs, J. (2000). Planning for school change: School–community collaboration in a full-service elementary school. *Urban Education, 35*(1), 79–103.

Abrams, L. S. (2002). Rethinking girls 'at-risk': Gender, race, class intersections and adolescent development. *Journal of Human Behavior in the Social Environment, 6*(2), 47–64.

Abrams, L. S., & Gibbs, J. T. (2002). Disrupting the logic of home–school relations: Parent participation and practices of inclusion and exclusion. *Urban Education, 37*(3), 384–407.

Abt Associates, Inc. (2003, November). *Study of state and local implementation of IDEA, final interim report (1999–2000 school year).* Cambridge, MA: Author.

Academy for Educational Development. (1999). *Positive youth development: AED makes young people a priority.* Washington, DC: Author.

Access Board. (2004). *Community rehabilitation program.* Washington, DC: The Access Board. Retrieved May 12, 2006, from http://www.access-board.gov/

Adams, G., Gullotta, T., & Montemayor, R. (1992). *Adolescent identity formation.* Newbury Park: Sage Publications.

Adams, L., & Edgerton, S. (1997, April 17). *Assessment in early childhood education.* Mid-West Association for the Education of Young Children Annual Conference, Grand Rapids, MI.

Adelman, H., & Taylor, L. (1997). Addressing barriers to learning: Beyond school-linked services and full service schools. *American Journal of Orthopsychiatry, 67*(3), 408–421.

Adelman, H. S., Taylor, L., Bradley, B., & Lewis, K. D. (1997). Mental health in schools: Expanded opportunities for school nurses. *Journal of School Nursing, 13*(3), 6–12.

Adelsheim, S., Carrillo, K., & Coletta E. (2001). Developing school mental health in a rural state: The New Mexico school mental health initiative. *Child & Adolescent Psychiatry, 10*(1), 151–159.

Administration for Children and Families. (2000). *Celebrating cultural and linguistic diversity in Head Start.* Washington, DC: U.S. Department of Health.

AECT Council on Systemic Change. (1999). *Characteristics of a system.* Bloomington, IN: Author.

Aiello, J., & Bullock, L. M. (1999). Building commitment to responsible inclusion. *Preventing School Failure, 43*(3), 99–102.

Ainscow, M., Booth, T., & Dyson, A. (2004). Understanding and developing inclusive practices in schools: A collaborative action research network. *International Journal of Inclusive Education, 8*(2), 125–139.

Alabama State Department of Education. (2004). *Early intervention to LEA transition process.* Montgomery: Alabama State Education Agency,.

Alberta Teacher Association. (1998, February 24). TD Baker School: Collaboration in action. *The ATA News, 32*(13), 7–8.

Albus, D., Lieu, K., & Thurlow, M. (2002, April). *Large scale assessment participation and performance of limited English proficient students with disabilities: What public data reports tell us.* Roundtable presentation at the annual meeting of the American Educational Research Association, New Orleans, LA.

Albus, D., & Thurlow, M. (2005). *Beyond subgroup reporting: English language learners with disabilities in 2002–2003 online state assessment reports (ELLs with Disabilities Report 10).* Minneapolis: University of Minnesota, National Center on Educational Outcomes.

Alee, V. (2001). 12 principles of knowledge management. *American Society for Training and Development.* Retrieved April 10, 2005, from http://www.astd.org/astd/Resources/performance_improvement_community/principles.htm

Algozzine, B., Browder, D., Karvonen, M., Test, D.W., & Wood, W. M. (2001). Effects of interventions to promote self-determination for individuals with disabilities. *Review of Educational Research, 71*(2), 219–277.

Allen, C., & Bekoff, M. (1995). Cognitive ethnology and the intentionality of animal behavior. *Mind and Language, 10,* 313–328.

Alper, S., Ryndak, D., & Schloss, C. (2001). *Alternate assessment of students with disabilities in inclusive settings.* Boston: Allyn & Bacon.

Alspaugh, J. W. (1998). Achievement loss associated with the transition to middle school and high school. *The Journal of Educational Research, 92*(1), 20–25.

Alspaugh, J. W., & Harting, R. D. (1997). Effects of team teaching on the transition to middle school. *ERS Spectrum, 15*(1), 9–14.

Altman, J. H. (1997). Career development in the context of family experiences. In H. S. Farmer (Ed.), *Diversity and women's career development: From adolescence to adulthood* (pp. 229–242). Thousand Oaks, CA: Sage.

American Academy of Pediatrics Committee on Children with Disabilities. (2001). Developmental surveillance and screening of infants and young children (RE0062). *Pediatrics, 108*(10), 192–196.

American Association of School Administrators. (2001). *Building tests to support instruction and accountability.* Washington, DC: Commission on Instructionally Supportive Assessment (AASA, NAESP, NASSP, NEA, and NMSA).

American Federation of Teachers. (2001). *Making standards matter 2001: Fifty state report on efforts to implement a standards-based system.* Retrieved August 20, 2005, from http://www.aft.org/pubs-reports/downloads/teachers/msm2001.pdf.

American Federation of Teachers. (2001). *The many names of school vouchers.* Retrieved August 20, 2005, from http://www.aft.org/topics/nclb/downloads/QAonNCLB.pdf

American School Counselor Association. (2004a). *The professional school counselor and students with special needs: Position statement.* Alexandria, VA: Author.

American School Counselor Association. (2004b). *Ethical standards for school counselors.* Alexandria, VA: Author.

American Youth Policy Forum. (2002). *Twenty-five years of educating children with disabilities: The good news and the work ahead.* Washington, DC: Center on Education Policy.

Americans With Disabilities Act. (ADA), Pub. L. 101-336, 42 U.S.C., § 12101 *et seq.* (1990).

Ames, N., & Dickerson, A. (2004). Five barriers to parent involvement. *Middle Matters, 13*(1), 6–10.

Ames, N., & Miller, E. (1994). *Changing middle schools: How to make schools work.* San Francisco: Jossey-Bass.

Ammon, M., Chrispeels, J., Safran, D., Sandy, M., Dear, J., & Reyes, M. (2000). *Preparing educators for partnerships with families. Report of the advisory task force on educator preparation for parent involvement.* Sacramento: California Commission on Teaching Credentialing. (ERIC Document Reproduction Service No. 437369)

Ammon, M. S. (1990, April). *University of California project on teacher preparation for parent involvement* (Report I). Conference and initial follow-up. Berkeley: University of California.

Ammon, P., & Peretti, D. (1999). Preparing constructivist teachers for parent involvement: The developmental teacher education program. In M. S. Ammon (Ed.), *Joining hands: Preparing teachers to make meaningful home–school connections* (pp. 16–36). Sacramento, California Department of Education.

Ancess, J. (2000). The reciprocal influence of teacher learning, teaching practice, school restructuring, and student learning outcomes. *Teachers College Record, 102*(3), 590–619.

Anderman, E. M., Maehr, M. L., & Midgley, C. (1999). Declining motivation after the transition to middle school: Schools can make a difference. *Journal of Research and Development in Education, 32*(3), 131–147.

Anderson, A. R., Christenson, S. L., & Lehr, C. A. (2004). Promoting student engagement to enhance school completion: Information and strategies for educators. In A. Canter, S. Carroll, L. Paige, & I. Romero (Eds.), *Helping children at home and school II: Handouts from your school psychologist* (pp. 65–68). Washington, DC: National Association of School Psychologists.

Anderson, A. R., Christenson, S. L., Sinclair, M. F., & Lehr, C. A. (2004). Check & Connect: The importance of relationships for promoting engagement with school. *Journal of School Psychology, 42*(2), 95–113.

Anderson, J., & Wright, E. (2005). *DAWN sixth annual project evaluation study.* Bloomington: Indiana Consortium for Mental Health Research.

Anderson, M. E., Minnema, J. E., Thurlow, M. L., & Hall-Lande, J. (2003). *Confronting the unique challenges of including English language learners with disabilities in statewide assessments.* Minneapolis, MN: National Center on Educational Outcomes. Retrieved August 15, 2005, from http://education.umn.edu/NCEO/OnlinePubs/ELLsDisReport9.html

Antil, L., Jenkins, J., Wayne, S., & Vadasy, P. (1998). Cooperative learning: Prevalence, conceptualizations, relation between research and practice. *American Educational Research Journal, 35*(3), 419–454.

Antunez, B. (2003). *English language learners in great city schools: Survey results on students, languages and problems.* Washington, DC: Council of Great City Schools.

Apple, M. W. (1996). *Cultural politics and education.* New York: Teachers College Press.

Apples4theteacher.com. (2006). *Including students with disabilities in general education classrooms.* Retrieved May 21, 2006, from http://www.apples4theteacher.com/resources/modules

Apps, J. (1994). Leadership for the emerging age: Theory and context. *Journal of Special Education, 32*(1), 32–37.

Arat, Z. (1991). *Democracy and human rights in developing countries.* London: Lynne Reiner Publishers.

Arguelles, M., Hughes, M., & Schumm, J. (2000). Co-reaching: A different approach to inclusion. *Principal, 7*(4), 48, 50–51.

Aron, L. (2003). *Towards a typology of alternative education programs: A compilation of elements from the literature.* Washington, DC: The Urban Institute.

Arowosafe, D. S., & Irvin, J. E. (1992). Transition to a middle level school: What kids say. *Middle School Journal, 24*(2), 15–19.

Artiles, A. J. (1998). The dilemma of difference: Enriching the disproportionality discourse with theory and context. *Journal of Special Education, 32*(1), 32–36.

Artiles, A. J. (2003). Special education's changing identity: Paradoxes and dilemmas in views of culture and space. *Harvard Educational Review, 73*(2), 164–202.

Artiles, A. J., & Ortiz, A. (2002). *English language learners with special needs: Identification, placement, and instruction.* Washington, DC: Center for Applied Linguistics.

Asante, S. (1997). *When spider webs unite: Challenging articles and essays on community, diversity and inclusion.* Toronto, ON, Canada: Inclusion Press.

Aspel, N., Bettis, G., Quinn, P., Test, D., & Wood, W. (1999). A collaborative process for planning transition services for students with disabilities. *Career Development for Exceptional Individuals, 22*(1), 21–42.

Aspel, N., Bettis, G., Test, D., & Wood, W. (1998). An evaluation of a comprehensive system of transition services. *Career Development for Exceptional Individuals, 21*(2), 203–222.

Aspen Energy Policy Forum. (2003). *Market, technology and policy drivers.* Queenstown, MD: Aspen Institute Policy Office.

Asselin, S. B., Hanley-Maxwell, C., & Syzmanski, E. (1992). Transdisciplinary personnel preparation. In F. R. Rusch, L. DeStefano, J. Chadsey-Rusch, L. A. Phelps, & E. Syzmanski (Eds.), *Transition from school to adult life* (pp. 265–283). Sycamore, IL: Sycamore.

Association for Career and Technical Education. (2005). *Conference Priorities related to the Carl D. Perkins Vocational and Technical Education Act,* H.R. 366, S. 250. Alexandria, VA: Association for Career and Technical Education.

Association for Persons in Supported Employment. (2000). *Supported employment quality indicators.* Richmond: VA: Author.

Association for Retarded Citizens. (2003). *Individual service coordination for individuals with mental retardation.* Retrieved May 25, 2005, from http://www.thearc.org/faqs/caseqa.html

Astuto, T., Clark, D. L., Read, A., McGree, K., & Fernandez, L. (1993). *Challenges to dominant assumptions controlling educational reform.* Andover, MA: Northeast Regional Laboratory for Educational Improvement.

Astuto, T., Clark, D. L., Read, A., McGree, K., & Fernandez, L. (1994). *Roots of reform: Challenging the assumptions that control change in education.* Bloomington, IN: Phi Delta Kappa Educational Foundation.

Atherton, J. (1999). *Problem-based learning, learning and teaching.* Retrieved August 22, 2005, from http://www.dmu.ac.uk/~jamesa/learning

Avoke, S., & Wood-Garnett, S. (2001, March/April). Language minority children and youth in special education. *Teaching Exceptional Children, 33*(4).

Axelrod, R. (1997). *The complexity of cooperation.* Princeton, NJ: Princeton University Press.

Ayres, L. (1994). Middle school advisory programs: Findings from the field. *Middle School Journal, 25*(3), 8–14.

Axelrod, R., & Cohen, M. (1999). *Harnessing complexity: Organizational implications of a scientific frontier.* New York: The Free Press.

Axelrod, R., & Dion, D. (1988). The further evolution of cooperation. *Science, 242,* 1385–1390.

Bachrach, L. L. (1986). The challenge of service planning for chronic mental patients. *Community Health Journal, 22*(3), 170–174.

Badcock, C. (1991). *Evolution and individual behavior: An introduction to human sociobiology.* Oxford: Basil Blackwell.

Baer, R. (1996). *The Summit County L.I.F.E. Project: Linkages for individual and family empowerment* [Report]. Kent, OH: Kent State University, Center for Innovation in Transition and Employment.

Baer, R., Martonyi, E., Simmons, T., Flexer, R., & Goebel, G. (1994). Employer collaboration: A tri-lateral group process model. *Journal of Rehabilitation Administration, 18*(3), 151–163.

Baer, R., Simmons, T., & Flexer, R. (1996). Transition practice and policy compliance in Ohio: A survey of secondary special educators. *Career Development for Exceptional Individuals, 19*(1), 61–72.

Bailey, L., & Stadt, R. (1973). *Career education: New approaches to human development* (pp. 346–347). Bloomington, IL: McKnight.

Bailey, L. J. (2001). *Working: Learning a living* (3rd ed.). Cincinnati, OH: South-Western/ITP.

Baker, F., & Intagliata, J. (1982). Quality of life in the evaluation of community support systems. *Evaluation and Program Planning, 5,* 69–79.

Baker, J. M., & Zigmond, N. (1995). The meaning and practice of inclusion for students with learning disabilities: Themes and implications from the five case studies. *Journal of Special Education, 29*(2), 163–180.

Baker, M. (2000). *Evaluation of the truancy reduction demonstration program: Interim report.* Denver: Colorado Foundation for Families and Children.

Baker, M., Sigmon, J., & Nugent, M. E. (1999). *Truancy reduction: Keeping kids in school.* Washington, DC: Office of Juvenile Justice and Delinquency Prevention, U.S. Department of Justice.

Bakken, T., & Kortering, L. (1999). The constitutional and statutory obligations of schools to prevent students with disabilities from dropping out. *Remedial and Special Education, 20,* 360–366.

Balaban, N. (1995). Seeing the child, knowing the person. In W. Ayers (Ed.), *To become a teacher: Making a difference in children's lives* (pp. 49–58). New York: Teachers College Press.

Ballard, L. B. (1996). *Services for adolescents at risk (STAR): Final program review for the 1995–1996 school year.* Alexandria City Community Policy Management Team and Virginia Commonwealth Comprehensive Services Act. Alexandria, VA: Alexandria City Public Schools.

Ballen, J., & Moles, O. (1994). *Strong families, strong schools.* Washington, DC: U.S. Department of Education.

Bandura, A. (1973). *Aggression: A social learning analysis.* Englewood Cliffs, NJ: Prentice Hall.

Bandura, A. (1977). *Social learning theory.* New York: General Learning Press.

Banks, J., Banks, A., & McGee, C. (Eds.). (1995). *Handbook of research on multicultural education.* New York: Macmillan.

Banks, J., & McGee-Banks, C. A. (1992). *Multicultural Education: Issues and perspectives* (2nd ed). Boston: Allyn & Bacon.

Banks, J. A. (Ed.). (1996). *Multicultural education, transformative knowledge and action: Historical and contemporary perspectives.* New York: Teachers College Press.

Bantlinger, E. (1997). Using ideology: Cases of nonrecognition of the politics of research and practice in special education. *Review of Educational Research, 67,* 425–459.

Barkow, J. H., Cosmides, L., & Tooby, J. (Eds.) (1992). *The adapted mind: Evolutionary psychology and the generation of culture.* New York: Oxford University Press.

Barlas, C., Kasl, E., Kyle, R., MacLeod, A., Paxton, D., Rosenwasser, P., & Sartor, L. (2000). Collaborative inquiry as a facilitator for perspective transformation. In C. Weissner, S. Meyer, & D. Fuller (Eds.), *Challenges of practice: Transformative learning in action* (3rd International Transformative Learning Conference Proceedings, October 26–28) (pp. 51–56). New York: Teachers College, Columbia University.

Barnard, W. M. (2001). *Early intervention, parent involvement in early schooling and long-term school success.* Unpublished doctoral dissertation, University of Wisconsin, Madison.

Barnett, C., & Monda-Amaya, L. E. (1998). Principals' knowledge and attitudes toward inclusion. *Remedial and Special Education, 19,* 181–192.

Barnett, D., Clements, M., Kaplan-Estrin, M., & Fialka, J. (2003). Building new dreams: Supporting parents' adaptation to their child with special needs. *Infants & Young Children, 16*(3), 184–200.

Barnett, D. W., Lentz, F. E., Bauer, A. M., Macmann, G., Stollar, S., & Ehrhardt, K. E. (1997). Ecological foundations of early intervention: Planned activities and strategic sampling. *The Journal of Special Education, 30,* 471–490.

Barnett, M. F. (1995). *Strengthening partnerships by reaching out to families.* Paper for the National Council of Teachers of English annual spring conference, Minneapolis, MN (pp. 16–18). (ED 388 412)

Barnett, S., Hustedt, J., Robin, K., & Schulman, K. (2004). *The state of preschool: 2004 state preschool yearbook.* New Brunswick, NJ: National Institute for Early Education Research, Rutgers.

Barnett, S., Robin, K., Hustedt, J., & Schulman, K. (2003). *The state of preschool: 2003 state preschool yearbook.* New Brunswick, NJ: National Institute for Early Education Research, Rutgers.

Barnett, W. S. (1995). Long-term effects of early childhood programs on cognitive and school outcomes. *The Future of Children, 5*(3), 25–50.

Baron, R. A., Byrne, D., & Brandscombe, N. R. (2006). *Social psychology* (11th ed.). Boston: Allyn & Bacon.

Baron-Cohen, S. (1995). *Mindblindness: An essay on autism and theory of mind.* Cambridge, MA: MIT Press.

Barone, C., Aguirre-Deandreis, A. I., & Trickett, E. J. (1991). Mean-ends problem-solving skills, life stress, and social support as mediators of adjustment in the normative transition to high school. *American Journal of Community Psychology, 19*(2), 207–225.

Barrett, F. (1995). Creating appreciative learning cultures. *Organizational Dynamics, 24*(1), 36–49.

Barton, D., Hamilton, M., & Ivanic, R. (2000). *Situated literacies: Reading and writing in context.* London: Routledge.

Barton, P. E. (1996). *Cooperative education in high school: Promise and neglect.* Princeton, NJ: Educational Testing Service. Policy Information Center.

Barton, P. E. (2001). *Facing the hard facts in education reform.* Princeton, NJ: Educational Testing Services.

Bassett, D., & Kochhar-Bryant, C. (2002). Future directions for transition and standards-based education. In C. A. Kochhar-Bryant & D. S. Bassett (Eds.), *Aligning transition and standards-based education: Issues and strategies* (pp. 187–201). Arlington, VA: Council for Exceptional Children.

Bassett, D., & Underwood, L. (1999). Systems change and its effect on student involvement: One school's approach to creating resources. *Journal of Vocational Special Needs Personnel, 21*(3), 27–32.

Bauwens, J., & Hourcade, J. J. (1995). *Cooperative teaching: Rebuilding the schoolhouse for all students.* Austin, TX: PRO-ED, Inc.

Bauwens, J., & Mueller, P. (2000). Maximizing the mindware of human resources. In R. Villa & J. S. Thousand (Eds.), *Restructuring for caring and effective education, piecing the puzzle together* (2nd ed., pp. 328–359). Baltimore: Brookes Publishing.

Bazelon Center for Mental Health Law (2003). *Failing to qualify: The first step to failure in school?* Washington, DC: Author.

Beamon, G. W. (1997). *Sparking the thinking of students, ages 10–14: Strategies for teachers.* Thousand Oaks, CA: Corwin.

Becker, H. J., & Epstein, J. L. (1992). Teacher practices of parent involvement: Problems and possibilities. *Elementary School Journal, 83*, 103–113.

Bekoff, M., & Allen, C. (1997). Cognitive ethology: Slayers, skeptics, and proponents. In R. Mitchell, N. S. Thompson, & H. L. Miles (Eds.), *Anthropomorphism, anecdote and animals.* Albany, NY: SUNY Press.

Belcher, D. C., & Hatley, R. V. (1994). A dropout prediction model that highlights middle level variables. *Research in Middle Level Education, 18*(1), 67–78.

Bemak, F. (2000). Transforming the role of the counselor to provide leadership in educational reform through collaboration. *Professional School Counselor, 3,* 323–331.

Bendor, J. (1993). Uncertainty and the evolution of cooperation. *Journal of Conflict Resolution, 37,* 709–734.

Bendor, J., & Mookherjee, D. (1990). Norms, third-party sanctions, and cooperation. *Journal of Law, Economics, and Organization, 6,* 33–63.

Bennis, S., & Biederman, P. (1997). *Organizing genius: The secrets of creative collaboration.* Reading, MA: Addison-Wesley.

Benson, P. L. (1997). *All kids are our kids.* San Francisco: Jossey-Bass.

Benz, M., & Kochhar, C. (1996). School-to-Work Opportunities Act: A position statement. *Career Development for Exceptional Individuals, 19*(1), 31–48.

Benz, M., Lindstrom, L., & Yovonoff, P. (2000). Improving graduation and employment outcomes of students with disabilities: Predictive factors and student perspectives. *Exceptional Children, 6*(4), 509–529.

Berger, E. H. (2000). *Parents as partners in education* (5th ed.). Upper Saddle River, NJ: Merrill Prentice Hall.

Berger, P., & Luckmann, T. (1966). *The social construction of reality: A treatise in the sociology of knowledge.* New York: Doubleday.

Bergstrom, A., Clark, R., Hogue, T., Perkins, D., & Slinski, M. (1995). *Collaboration framework: Addressing community capacity.* Columbus, OH: The National Network for Collaboration.

Bernhard, J. K., Freire, M., Pacini-Ketchabaw, V., & Villanueva, V. (1998). A Latin-American parent's group participates in their children's schooling: Parent involvement reconsidered. *Canadian Ethnic Studies, 30*(3), 77–99.

Bernheimer, L. P., Gallimore, R., & Weisner, T. S. (1990). Ecocultural theory as a context for the individual family service plan. *Journal of Early Intervention, 14*(3), 219–233.

Berry, H., & Jones, M. (2000). *Social Security Disability Insurance and Supplemental Security Income for undergraduates with disabilities: An analysis of the National Postsecondary Student Aid Survey* (NPSAS 2000). Honolulu, HI: National Center for the Study of Postsecondary Education Supports.

Berry, J., & Hardman, M. L. (1998). *Lifespan perspectives on the family and disability.* Boston: Allyn & Bacon.

Beyerlein, M., McGee, C., Klein, G., Nemiro, J., & Broedling, L. (Eds.). (2003). *Critical success factors in team-based organizing.* San Francisco: John Wiley & Sons.

Beyerlein, M. M., & Harris, C. (2003). Guiding the journey to collaborative work systems: A strategic design workbook. San Francisco: Jossey-Bass.

Bicchieri, C. (1990). Norms of cooperation. *Ethics, 100,* 838–861.

Bickman, L., & Rog, D. (1997). *Handbook of applied social research methods.* Thousand Oaks, CA: Sage Publications.

Biggs, D., & Colesante, R. (2000, April 24–28). *The Albany approach to urban youth development.* Presented at the annual meeting of the American Education Research Association. New Orleans, LA.

Billig, S. (2001). Meeting the challenges of family involvement in the middle grades. *Middle Matters, 10,* 3–4.

Billingsley, B. S. (2003). Special education teacher retention and attrition: A critical analysis of the literature (COPSSE Document No. RS-2E). Gainesville: University of Florida, Center on Personnel Studies in Special Education.

Bing Nursery School. (2005). *The program for young children.* Stanford, CA: Child Development Research & Training. Retrieved December 5, 2005, from http://www.stanford.edu/dept/bingschool/program.htm

Birnbaum, W. (2003). *Introduction to strategic planning.* Costa Mesa, CA: Birnbaum Associates.

Black, R. S., Smith, G., Chang, C., Harding, T., & Stodden, R. (2002). Provision of educational supports to students with disabilities in two-year postsecondary programs. *Journal on Vocational Special Needs Education, 24*(2), 3–17.

Black, S. (2005). Rethinking parent conferences. *American School Board Journal, 192*(10). Retrieved April 1, 2006, from http://www.asbj.com/2005/10/1005research.html

Black, S. E., & Lynch, L. M. (2003). The new economy and the organization of work. In D. C. Jones (Ed.), *New economy handbook.* London: Elsevier Science Academic Press.

Blackorby, J., Newman, L., & Finnegan, K. (1998, July). *Integrated services, high need communities, and special education: Lessons and paradoxes.* Menlo Park, CA: SRI International.

Blackorby, J., & Wagner, M. (1996). Longitudinal post-school outcomes of youth with disabilities: Findings of the National Longitudinal Transition Study. *Exceptional Children, 62,* 399–413.

Blackorby, J., & Wagner, M. (2002). *Special Education Elementary Longitudinal Study.* Menlo Park, CA: SRI International.

Blackorby, J., Wagner, M., Cadwallader, T., Cameto, R., Levine, P., & Marder, C. (with Giacalone, P.) (2002). *Behind the label: The functional implications of disability.* Menlo Park, CA: SRI International.

Blanchard, K., & Bowles, S. (2001). *High five: The magic of working together.* New York: Harper Collins Publisher.

Blanck, P. D. (Ed.). (2000). *Employment, disability, and the Americans With Disabilities Act: Issues in law, public policy, and research.* Evanston, IL: Northwestern University Press.

Blank, M. (2001). *School-community partnerships in support of student learning.* Washington, DC: Institute for Educational Leadership, Coalition for Community Schools.

Blank, M., Melaville, A., & Shah, B. (2003). *Making the difference: Research and practice in community schools.* Washington, DC: Institute for Educational Leadership, Coalition for Community Schools.

Blank, M. J., & Melaville, A. I. (1999). Creating family-supportive schools: Taking the first steps. *America's Family Support Magazine, 18*(3), 37–38.

Blechman, E., Fishman, D., & Fishman, D. (2004). *Caregiver alliances for at-risk and dangerous youth.* Champaign, IL: Research Press.

Bloir, K. (1997, November). *Parenting that promotes resilient urban African American families: Scholars describe the characteristics of their parents' parenting behaviors.* Paper presented at the annual conference of the National Council on Family Relations, Arlington, VA. (ED 419 596)

Blustein, D. L. (1997). A context-rich perspective of career exploration across the life roles. *Career Development Quarterly, 3,* 260–274.

Blyth, D. A., Simmons, R. G., & Bush, D. (1978). The transition into early adolescence: A longitudinal comparison of youth in two educational contexts. *Sociology of Education, 51*, 149–162.

Blyth, D. A., Simmons, R. G., & Carlton-Ford, S. (1983). The adjustment of early adolescents to school transition. *Journal of Early Adolescence, 3*, 105–120.

Blyth, T., Allen, D., & Powell, B. (1999). *Looking together at student work.* New York: Teachers College Press.

Bochner, A. P., & Eisenberg, E. (1987). Family process: System perspectives. In C. Berger & S. Chaffee (Eds.), *Handbook of communication science* (pp. 540–563). Newbury Park, CA: Sage Publications.

Bogdan, R. (1999). *Building stronger communities for all: Thoughts about community participation for people with developmental disabilities.* Syracuse, NY: Center on Human Policy, Syracuse University.

Bohan-Baker, M., & Little, P. (2002). *The Transition to kindergarten: A review of current research and promising practices to involve families* [Harvard Family Research Project]. Cambridge, MA: Harvard University Press.

Bohn, A. P., & Sleeter, C. (2000). Multicultural education and the standards movement: A report from the field. *Phi Delta Kappan, 82*(2), 156–159.

Bolles, R. N. (1999). *What color is your parachute?* Berkeley, CA: Ten Speed Press.

Bondy, E., & Brownell, M. T. (1997). Overcoming barriers among partners-in-teaching. *Intervention in School and Clinic, 33*(2), 11–15.

Bonner-Thompkins, E. (2000, October). Well-being and school achievement: Using coordinated services to improve outcomes among students. *Gaining Ground Newsletter.* Washington, DC: Council of Chief State School Officers.

Borman, G., & Hewes, G. (2002). The long-term effects and cost-effectiveness of success for all. *Educational Evaluation and Policy Analysis, 24*(4), 243–266.

Bos, C., Nahamias, M., & Urban, M. (1999). Targeting home–school collaboration for students with ADHD. *Teaching Exceptional Children, July/August,* 4–11. Arlington, VA: Council for Exceptional Children.

Bos, C. S. (1999). Home–school communication. In C. Jones, H. R. Searight, & M. A. Urban (Eds.), *Parent articles for ADHD.* San Antonio, TX: Communication Skill Builders.

Bostaph, C., & Vendeland, R. (2000). *The employment portfolio: Identifying skills, training, accomplishments, and references for the job seeker.* Upper Saddle River, NJ: Prentice Hall.

Boston Plan for Excellence in the Public Schools. (2002). *Introduction to collaborative coaching and learning.* Retrieved April 15, 2006, from http://www.bpe .org/pubs/ccl/getting%20started%20CCL.pdf

Boston Plan for Excellence in the Public Schools. (2002). *PD with purpose: Coaching in Boston's schools,* [Video]. Available from Boston Plan for Excellence, 6 Beacon St, Boston, MA 08.

Boudah, D., & Knight, S. L. (1999). Creating learning communities of research and practice: Participatory research and development. In D. Byrd & J. McIntyre (Eds.), *Research on professional development schools: Teacher education yearbook VII* (pp. 97–114). Thousand Oaks, CA: Corwin Press.

Bourgeois, J., & Rakic, P. (1993). Changes of synaptic density in the primary visual cortex of the macaque monkey from fetal to adult stage. *Journal of Neuroscience, 13*(7), 2801–2820.

Bowe, F. (2005). *Making inclusion work.* Upper Saddle River, NJ: Merrill/Prentice Hall.

Bowman, B. T., Donovan, M. S., Burns, M. S. (Eds.). (2000). *Eager to learn: Educating our preschoolers.* Washington, DC: National Academies Press.

Boyd, B. (2000). *Youth for community action: Leadership for inner-city youth.* College Station, TX: Texas A&M University.

Boyer, E. L. (1990). *Scholarship revisited.* Princeton, NJ: Carnegie Foundation for the Advancement of Teaching.

Boyer, E. L. (1995). *The Basic School.* Princeton, NJ: Carnegie Foundation for Advancement of Teaching.

Boykin, A. W. (2000). A talent development model of schooling. *Journal of Education for Student Place At-Risk, 5*, 3–25.

Braddock, D., Hemp, R., Parish, S., & Rizzolo, M. C. (2000). Growth in state commitments for community services: Significance of the Medicaid Home and Community-Based Services Waiver. *Mental Retardation, 38*, 186–189.

Bradley, D. F., King-Sears, M. E., & Tessier-Switlick, D. M. (1997). *Teaching students in inclusive settings.* Needham Heights, MA: Allyn & Bacon.

Bradley, D. F., & Switlick, D. M. (1997). From isolation to cooperation in teaching. In D. F. Bradley, M. E. King-Sears, & D. Tessier-Switlick (Eds.), *Teaching students in inclusive settings: From theory to practice* (pp. 109–128). Boston: Allyn & Bacon.

Bradley, R., Danielson, L., & Hallahan, D. (Eds.). (2002). *Identification of learning disabilities: Research to practice.* Mahwah, NJ: Lawrence Erlbaum Associates.

Bradshaw, J. (2003). *Paige releases principles for reauthorizing the Individuals with Disabilities Education Act (IDEA).* Washington, DC: U.S. Department of Education.

Brandt, R. (1998). *Powerful learning.* Alexandria, VA: Association for Supervision and Curriculum Development.

Braxton, B. (1999). Philip's transformation. *Rethinking Schools, 13*(2), 11.

Bray, J., Lee, J., Smith, L. L., & Yorks, L. (2000). *Collaborative inquiry in practice.* Thousand Oaks, CA: Sage Publications.

Brazelton, T. B. (1992). *Touchpoints, the essential reference: Your child's emotional and behavioral development.* New York: Addison-Wesley.

Bredekamp, S., & Copple, C. (l997). *Developmentally appropriate practice in early childhood programs.* Washington, DC: National Association for Education of Young Children.

Bremer, C., Clapper, A., Hitchcock, C., Hall, T., & Kachgal, M. (2002). Universal design: A strategy to support student's access to general education curriculum. *Information Brief, 1*(3).

Bremer, C., Kachgal, M., & Schoeller, K. (2003). Self-determination: Supporting successful transition. *Research to Practice Brief: Improving Secondary Education and Transition Services Through Research, (2)*, 91.

Brendtro, L. (2001). Worse than sticks and stones: Lessons from research on ridicule. *Reclaiming Children and Youth: Journal of Strength-Based Interventions, 10*(1), 47–49.

Brendtro, L., & Shahbazian, M. (2003). *Troubled children and youth: Turning problems into opportunities.* Champaign, IL: Research Press.

Briar-Lawson, K., & Lawson, H. (1997a). School-linked comprehensive services: Promising beginnings, selected lessons learned, and future challenges. *Social Work in Education, 19*, 136–148.

Briar-Lawson, K., & Lawson, H. (1997b). Collaboration and integrated, community-based strategies for individuals and families in rural areas. In S. Jones & J. Zlotnick (Eds.), *Preparing helping professionals to meet community needs: Generalizing from the rural experience* (pp. 111–126). Alexandria, VA: Council on Social Work Education.

Briar-Lawson, K., & Lawson, H. (2001). *Family-supportive policy and practice: International perspectives.* New York: Columbia University Press.

Bridgeland, J. M., Dilulio, J. J., & Morison, K. B. (2006). *The silent epidemic: Perspectives on high school dropout.* Washington, DC: Peter D. Hart Research Associates, for the Bill & Melinda Gates Foundation.

Bridle, L., & Mann, G. (2000). Mixed feelings— A parental perspective on early intervention. In *Proceedings of the Early Childhood Intervention Australia National Conference, July 1–3, 2000* (pp. 59–72). Melbourne, Australia: RMIT Publishing.

Briggs, J., & Peat, D. (1999). *Seven lessons of chaos: Timeless wisdom from the science of change.* New York: Harper Collins Publishers.

Brilliant, C., & Duke, G. (2001). Parental involvement in education: Attitudes and activities of Spanish-speakers as affected by training. *Bilingual Research Journal, 25*(3), 251–274.

Brinckerhoff, L. C., McGuire, J. M., & Shaw, S. F. (2002). *Postsecondary education and transition for college students with learning disabilities.* Austin, TX: PRO-ED.

Brockett, D. (1998). Reaching out to immigrant parents. *Education Digest, 63*(8), 29–32.

Brolin, D. E. (1989). *Life-centered career education: A competency-based approach.* Reston, VA: The Council for Exceptional Children.

Bronfenbrenner, U. (1979). *The ecology of human development.* Cambridge, MA: Harvard University Press.

Bronfenbrenner, U. (1986). The ecology of the family as a context for human development: Research perspectives. *Developmental Psychology, 22*, 723–742.

Bronfenbrenner, U. (1995). Developmental ecology through space and time: A future perspective. In P. Moen, G. H. Elder, Jr., & K. Luscher (Eds.), *Examining lives in context: Perspectives on the ecology of human development* (pp. 619–647). Washington, DC: APA Books.

Bronfenbrenner, U., & Ceci, S. J. (1994). Nature–nurture reconceptualized: A bio-ecological model. *Psychological Review, 101*(4), 568–586.

Bronfenbrenner, U., McClelland, P., Wethington, E., Moen, P., & Ceci, S. J. (1996). *The state of Americans: This generation and the next.* New York: The Free Press.

Bronfenbrenner, U., & Morris, P. A. (1998). The ecology of developmental processes. In W. Danon (Series Ed.), & R. M. Lerner (Vol. Ed.), *Handbook of Child Psychology, 1, Theory* (5th ed.). New York: Wiley.

Brookfield, S. (1987). *Developing critical thinkers: Challenging adults to explore alternative ways of thinking and acting.* San Francisco: Jossey-Bass.

Brookfield, S. (1995). *Becoming a critically reflective teacher.* San Francisco: Jossey-Bass.

Brookfield, S. (2001). *The skillful teacher.* New York: John Wiley & Sons.

Brouillette, M. (1999). *School choice in Michigan: A primer for freedom in education.* Midland, MI: Mackinac Center for Public Policy.

Broussard, A.C. (2000). Preparing teachers to work with families: A national survey of teacher education programs. *Equity and Excellence in Education, 33*, 41–49.

Brown v. Board of Education, 347 U.S.C. 483 (1954).

Brown, C. (2004). Reducing the over-referral of CLD students for language disabilities. *NABE Journal of Research and Practice, 2*(1), 225–43.

Brown, D. S. (2000). *Learning a living: A guide to planning your career and finding a job for people with learning disabilities, attention deficit disorder, and dyslexia.* Bethesda, MD: Woodbine House.

Brown, M. T., Lum, J. L., & Voyle, K. (1997). Roe revisited: A call for the reappraisal of the theory of personality development and career choice. *Journal of Vocational Behavior, 51*(2), 283–294.

Brown, W., Denton, E., Kelly, P., & Neal, S. (1999). Reading recovery effectiveness: A five-year success story in San Luis Coastal Unified School District. *ERS Spectrum: Journal of School Research and Information, 17*(1), 3–12.

Brownell, M. T., Bishop, A. M., Gersten, R., Kingner, J. K., Dimino, J., Haager, D., Menon, S., Penfield, R., & Sindelar, P. T. (2005). *Defining and assessing the quality of beginning special education teachers: First steps, conclusions drawn and challenges encountered.* Gainesville: Center on Personnel Studies in Special Education, University of Florida.

Brownell, M. T., Yeager, E., Reinells, M., & Riley, T. (1997). Teachers working together: What teacher educators and researchers should know. *Teacher Education and Special Education, 20*(4), 340–359.

Bruner, J. (1966). *Toward a theory of instruction.* New York: Norton.

Bruner, J. (1990). *Acts of meaning.* Cambridge, MA: Harvard University Press.

Bruno, B. (2001). Student assistance at East Hartford H.S. *Issues in Education,* July, 2001, pp. 1–2. Accessed August 13, 2006, from http://www.snet.net/features/issues/articles/2001/07130101.shtml

Bruns, E. J., Walrath, C., Glass-Siegal, M., & Weist, M. D. (2004). School-based mental health services in Baltimore: Association with school climate and special education referrals. *Behavior Modification, 28*(4), 491–512.

Bruyere, S. (2000). *Disability employment policies and practices in private and federal sector organizations.* Ithaca, NY: Cornell University, Program on Employment and Disability, School of Industrial and Labor Relations, Extension Division. Retrieved August 18, 2005, from http://dsl.snet/features/issues/rticles/2001/07130101.shtml

Bryk, A. S., & Schneider, B. L. (2002). *Trust in schools: A core resource for improvement.* New York: Russell Sage Foundation.

Buckroyd, J., & Flitton, B. (2004). The measurement of self-concept in children with complex needs. *Emotional Behavioral Difficulties, 9,* 31–139.

Bullis, M., & Cheney, D. (1999). Vocational and transition interventions for adolescents and young adults with emotional or behavioral disorders. *Focus on Exceptional Children, 32,* 1–24.

Bunch, G., Lupart, J., & Brown, M. (1997). *Resistance and acceptance: Educator attitudes to inclusion of students with disabilities.* (AN410713). Wolfville, NS, Canada: Acadia University.

Burchinal, M. R. (1999). Child care experiences and developmental outcomes. *The Annals of the American Academy of Political and Social Sciences, 563,* 73–97.

Burchinal, M. R., Peisner-Feinberg, E., Bryant, D. M., & Clifford, R. (2000). Children's social and cognitive development and child-care quality: Testing for differential associations related to poverty, gender, or ethnicity. *Applied Developmental Science, 4,* 149–165.

Burgstahler, S. (2002). *Bridging the digital divide in postsecondary education: Technology access for youth with disabilities.* Minneapolis, MN: National Center on Secondary Education and Transition.

Burgstahler, S., Crawford, L., & Acosta, J. (2001). Transition from two-year to four-year institutions for students with disabilities. *Disability Studies Quarterly, 21*(1). Retrieved July 3, 2005, from http://www.cds.hawaii.edu/dsq/_articles_html/2001/Winter/dsq_2001_Winter_05.html

Burnim, I., & Mathis, J. (2000). After Olmstead v. L.C.: Enforcing the integration mandate of the Americans with Disabilities Act. *Clearinghouse Review, 33* (11/12), 633.

Bursuck, W. D., Rose, E., Cowen, S., & Yahaya, M. A. (1989). Nationwide survey of postsecondary education services for students with learning disabilities. *Exceptional Children, 56,* 236–245.

Burt, M. R., Resnick, G., & Novick, E. R. (1998). *Building supportive communities for at-risk adolescents: It takes more than services.* Washington, DC: American Psychological Association.

Burts, D. C., & Dever, M. T. (2001). Engaging teacher education students in an authentic parent education project. *Journal of Early Childhood Teacher Education, 22,* 59–62.

Butler, R., & Hodge, S. (2004). Social inclusion of students with disabilities in middle school. *Research in Middle Level Education On Line, 27*(1). Retrieved December 8, 2005, from http://www.nmsa.org/Publications/MiddleSchoolJournal

Byford, J., & Veenstra, N. (2004). The importance of cultural factors in the planning of rehabilitation services in a remote area of Papua New Guinea. *Disability and Rehabilitation, 26*(3), 166–175.

Caine, R. N., & Caine, G. (1994). *Making connections: Teaching and the human brain.* Menlo Park, CA: Innovative Learning Publications.

Caine, R. N., & Caine, G. (1997). *Education on the edge of possibility.* Alexandria, VA: Association for Supervision and Curriculum Development.

California Department of Education. (1999). *Healthy Start works: A statewide profile of Healthy Start sites.* Retrieved August 3, 2005, from http://www.cde.ca.gov/healthystart/eval/evalworks.htm

California Department of Education. (2001). *California School to Work Interagency Transition Partnership, transition to adult living: A guide for secondary education.* Sacramento: Author.

California Department of Education. (2004). *Text from January 29th CAPA training of trainers.* Retrieved May 15, 2005, from http://www.cde.ca.gov/sp/se/sr/webcsto129.asp

California School Redesign Network. (2005a). *Design features: Democratic decision making.* Stanford: Author.

California School Redesign Network. (2005b). *Collaborative planning and professional development.* Stanford: Author.

California Wellness Foundation. (2001). *Reflections on capacity building.* Woodland Hills: Author. Retrieved March 15, 2004, from http://www.tcwf.org/reflections/2001/april/pages/definition of_capacity_building.htm

Calvin, E., Fenton, R., Lee, A., Pattison, B., Warner-King, K., & Purbaugh, J. (2000). *Make a difference in a child's life: A manual for helping children and youth get what they need in school.* Seattle, WA: Team Child and Casey Family Programs. Retrieved January 30, 2005, from htp://www.washingtonstatecasa.org

Cameto, R., Marder, C., Wagner, M., & Cardoso, D. (2003). Youth employment: NLTS2 Data Brief. *Report from the National Longitudinal Transition Study, 2*(2), 1–3.

Campbell, E. (2000). Professional ethics in teaching: Towards the development of a code of practice. *Cambridge Journal of Education, 30*(2), 203–221.

Campbell, F. A., Ramey, C. T., Pungello, E. P., Sparling, J., & Miller-Johnson, S. (2002). Early childhood education: Young adult outcomes from the Abecedarian Project. *Applied Developmental Science, 6,* 42–57.

Campeau, P., & Wolman, J. (1993). *Research on self-determination in individuals with disabilities.* Palo Alto, CA: American Institutes for Research.

Campos, P. (2002). *Technical assistance help. Research consultation, coaching, and technical assistance.* Retrieved April 12, 2005, from http://www.prndata.com/services.htm

Caplan, J., Hall, G., Lubin, S., & Fleming, R. (1997). *Parent involvement: Literature review of school–family partnerships.* Naperville, IL: North Central Regional Educational Laboratory. Retrieved August 15, 2005, from: http://www.ncrel.org/sdrs/pidata/pi0over.htm

Capra, F. (1996). *The web of life: A new scientific understanding of living systems.* New York: Anchor/Doubleday.

Carl D. Perkins Vocational and Applied Technology Education Act Amendments of 1998, Pub. L. No. 105–332, § 112 Stat. 3076. *Federal Register, 65*(10), 2463–2489.

Carnegie Council on Adolescent Development. (2000). *Turning Points 2000: Educating adolescents in the 21st century.* Washington, DC: Author.

Carnegie Task Force on Learning in the Primary Grades. (1996). *Years of promise: A comprehensive learning strategy for America's children.* New York: Carnegie Corporation of New York.

Carpenter, B. (2000). Sustaining the family: Meeting the needs of families of children with disabilities. *British Journal of Special Education, 27*(3), 135.

Carrizosa, K., & Sheppard, S. (2000). *The importance of learning styles in group design work.* Kansas City, MO: 30th ASEE/IEEE Frontiers in Education Conference, T2B-12.

Carson, R., Sitlington, P., & Frank, A. (1995). Young adulthood for individuals with behavioral disorders: What does it hold? *Behavioral Disorders, 20,* 127–135.

Carta, J. J., Atwater, J. B., Schwartz, I. S., & McConnell, S. R. (1993). Developmentally appropriate practices and early child special education: A reaction to Johnson and McChesney Johnson. *Topics in Early Childhood Special Education, 13*(3), 243–254.

Casey, B. J., Giedd, J. N., & Thomas, K. M. (2000). Structural and functional brain development and its relation to cognitive development. *Biological Psychology, 54,* 241–257.

Casey Family Programs. (2001). *Starting early starting smart.* Seattle, WA: Author.

Cash, T. (2004). Alternative schooling. In J. Smink & F. P. Schargel (Eds.), *Helping students graduate: A strategic approach to dropout prevention.* Larchmont, NY: Eye on Education.

Caspar, B., & Leuchovius, D. (2005, April). Universal design for learning and the transition to a more challenging academic curriculum: Making it in middle school and beyond. *The National Center on Secondary Education and Transition (NCSET) Parent Brief,* 1–5.

Catalano, F., Arthur, M., Hawkins, J., Berglund, L., & Olson, J. (1998). Comprehensive community and school-based interventions to prevent antisocial behavior. In R. Loeber & D. Farrington (Eds.), *Serious and violent juvenile offenders: Risk factors and successful interventions*, 248–283. Thousand Oaks, CA: Sage Publications, Inc.

Center for Applied Special Technology. (2004). *Universal design for learning.* Wakefield, MA: CAST. Retrieved August 25, 2005, from http://www.cast.org/about/index.cfm?i=231

Center for Evidence-Based Practice. (2002a). *Young children with challenging behavior: Research synthesis on effective intervention procedures.* Tampa, FL: Author.

Center for Research on Education, Diversity & Excellence. (2003, January). *National study of school effectiveness for language minority students' long-term academic achievement.* Berkeley, CA: University of California: Author.

Center for Universal Design. (1997). *What is universal design?* Retrieved April 22, 3005, from http://www.design.ncsu.edu/cud/univ_design/ud.htm

Center for Universal Design. (1998). *History: Ronald L. Mace, FAIA, 1941–1998.* Retrieved May 4, 2005, from http://www.design.ncsu.edu/cud/center/history/ronmace.htm

Center for Workforce Development. (2003). *Rising to the Challenge.* Washington, DC: Author.

Center on Education Policy. (2003). *From the capitol to the classroom: State and federal efforts to implement the No Child Left Behind Act.* Washington, DC: Author.

Center on Education Policy. (2005). *From the capitol to the classroom: State and federal efforts to implement the No Child Left Behind Act*, March. Washington, DC: Author.

Center on Personnel Studies in Special Education. (2003). *Special education teacher retention and attrition: A critical analysis of the literature.* Gainesville: University of Florida, Center on Personnel Studies in Special Education. (COPSSE Document No. RS-2E)

Center for Educational Research and Innovation. (1998). *Coordinating services for children and youth at risk: A worldview.* Paris: Organization for Economic Co-operation and Development.

Chadwick, D., & Kemp C. (2001). Essential skills for survival in a mainstream kindergarten classroom. *Special Education Perspectives, 9*(2), 27–41.

Chadwick, D., & Kemp, C. (2002). Critical factors of successful transition to mainstream kindergarten for children with disabilities. *Australasian Journal of Special Education, 26*, 50–68.

Chaisson-Cardenas, J., & Moore, E. (2003). *What do you mean by diversity? Developing cultural competency skills across professional and community lines.* Iowa City: National Resource Center for Family Centered Practice, University of Iowa.

Chamberlain, P., & Weinrott, M. (1990). Specialized foster care: Treating seriously emotionally disturbed children. *Children Today, 19*(1), 24–27.

Chambers, J., Parrish, T., & Harr, J. (2002). *What are we spending on special education services, 1999–2000?* Washington, DC: U.S. Department of Education, Office of Special Education.

Chavkin, N. (1991). *Family lives and parental involvement in migrant students' education.* Charleston, WV: ERIC Clearinghouse on Rural Education and Small Schools. (ERIC Document Reproduction Service No. ED335174)

Chavkin, N. F., Gonzalez, J., & Rader, R. (2002). A home–school program in a Texas–Mexico border school: Voices from parents, students, and school staff. *The School Community Journal, 10*(2), 127–37.

Chavkin, N. F., & Williams, D. L. (1988). Critical issues in teacher training for parent involvement. *Educational Horizons, 66*, 87–89.

Cheney, D. (1998). Using action research as a collaborative process to enhance educators' and families' knowledge and skills for youth with emotional or behavioral disorders. *Preventing School Failure, 42*, 88–93.

Chesapeake Institute. (1997). *Research finding frameworks: A compendium of cross-project findings.* Washington, DC: Author.

Chik, L. (2000). *Partnering with parents of youth with disabilities in the transition.* Annual conference of the National Transition Alliance. Champaign: Transition Research Institute at Illinois, University of Illinois.

Child Trends. (2000). *School readiness: Helping communities get children ready for school and schools ready for children.* Washington, DC: Author.

Children's Behavioral Alliance. (2003). *Children and adults with attention deficits/ hyperactivity disorder: In the best interests of all?* A position paper. Washington, DC: Author.

Children's Defense Fund. (2003). *Leave no child behind.* Washington, DC: Author.

Chrispeels, J., Strait, J., & Brown, J. (1999). The paradoxes of collaboration: What works? *Educational Leadership, 29*(2), 16–19.

Christenson, S. L., & Carroll, E. B. (2000). Strengthening the family school partnership through Check and Connect. In E. Frydenberg (Ed.), *Learning to cope: Developing as a Person in Complex Societies*, 248–273. London: Oxford University Press.

Christenson, S. L., Hurley, C. M., Hirsch, J. A., Kau, M., Evelo, D. L., & Bates, W. (1997b). Check and Connect: The role of monitors in supporting high-risk youth. *Reaching Today's Youth: The Community Circle of Caring Journal, 2*(1), 18–21.

Christenson, S. L., Hurley, C. M., Sheridan, S. M., & Fenstermacher, K. (1997a). Parents' and school psychologists' perspectives on parent involvement activities. *School Psychology Review, 26*(l), 111–130.

Christenson, S. L., & Sheridan, S. M. (2001). *Schools and Families: Creating essential connections for children's learning.* New York: Guilford Press.

Christenson, S. L., Sinclair, M., Evelo, D., & Thurlow, M. (1995). *Tip the balance: Policies and practices that support or alienate youth with disabilities at high risk for dropping out of school.* Minneapolis: University of Minnesota, Institute on Community Integration.

Christenson, S. L., Sinclair, M. F., Lehr, C., & Godber, Y. (2001). Promoting successful school completion: Critical conceptual and methodological guidelines. *School Psychology Quarterly, 16*(4), 468–484.

Christenson, S. L., Sinclair, M. F., Lehr, C. A., & Hurley, C. M. (2000). Promoting successful school completion. In D. Minke & G. Bear (Eds.), *Preventing school problems—promoting school success: Strategies and programs that work.* Bethesda, MD: National Association of School Psychologists.

Christenson, S. L., Sinclair, M. F., Thurlow, M. L., & Evelo, D. (1999). Promoting student engagement with school using the Check & Connect model. *Australian Journal of Guidance & Counseling, 9*(1), 169–184.

Christenson, S. L., & Thurlow, M. L. (2004a). School dropouts: Prevention, considerations, interventions, and challenges. *Current Directions in Psychological Science, 13*(1), 36–39.

Christenson, S. L., & Thurlow, M. L. (2004b). Keeping kids in school: Efficacy of Check & Connect for dropout prevention of high-risk students. *Communique, 32*(6), 37–40.

Christie, K. (2005). Changing the nature of parent involvement. *Phi Delta Kappan, 86*(9), 645–646.

Christman, J. (2001). *Powerful ideas, modest gains: Five years of systemic reform in Philadelphia middle schools.* Philadelphia: Consortium for Policy Research in Education, University of Pennsylvania.

Christman, J., & Rhodes, A. (2002). *Civic engagement and urban school improvement: Hard to learn lessons from Philadelphia.* Philadelphia: The Consortium for Policy Research in Education. Retrieved July 4, 2005, from http://www.cpre.org/publications/children 07.pdf

Chynoweth, J. K. (1994). *A guide to community-based, collaborative strategic planning.* Washington, DC: Council of Governors' Policy Advisors.

Clark, D. L., & Astuto, T. A. (1994). Redirecting reform: Challenges to popular assumptions about teachers and students. *Phi Delta Kappan, 75*(7), 512–520.

Clark, G. M., & Patton, J. R. (1997). *Transition planning inventory: Administration and resource guide.* Austin, TX: PRO-ED.

Clark-Stewart, K., Gruber, C. P., & Fitzgerald, L. M. (1994). *Children at home and in day care.* Hillsdale, NJ: Lawrence Erlbaum Associates.

Clay, M. M. (1985). *The early detection of reading difficulties* (3rd ed.). Auckland, New Zealand: Heinemann.

Cleary, L. M., & Peacock, T. W. (1998). *Collected wisdom: American Indian education.* Boston: Allyn & Bacon.

Coalition for Community Schools. (2001). *Community schools: Partnerships for excellence.* Washington, DC: Author. Retrieved from http://www.community schools .org/partnershipsforexcellence.pdf

Cobb, B., & Johnson, D. (1997). The statewide systems change initiative as a federal policy mechanism for promoting educational reform. *Career Development for Exceptional Individuals, 20*(2). Reston, VA: Council for Exceptional Children.

Cochran-Smith, M. (2000). Blind vision: Unlearning racism in teacher education. *Harvard Educational Review, 70*(2), 157–190.

Code of Federal Regulations. (2001a). Title 34, 34CFR Part 361.1, *State Vocational Rehabilitation Services Program.* Revised as of July 1, 2001, U.S. Government Printing Office via GPO Access.

Code of Federal Regulations. (2001b). Title 45, CFR Part 46, *Federal Policy for the Protection of Human Subjects.* Department of Health And Human Services, National Institutes of Health, Office for Protection from Research Risks, December 13.

Cohen, E. (Ed.). (2004). *Teaching cooperative learning: The challenge for teacher education.* Albany: State University of New York Press.

Cohen, M. (2001). *Transforming the American high school: New directions for state and local policy.* Washington, DC: Aspen Institute.

Cohn, L. D., Macfarlane, S., Yanez, C., & Imai, W. K. (1995). Risk perception: Differences between adolescents and adults. *Health Psychology, 14,* 217–222.

Cole, C. M., & McLeskey, J. (1997). Secondary inclusion programs for students with mild disabilities. *Focus on Exceptional Children, 29*(6), 1–15.

Coleman W. L., & Garfield, C. (2004). Fathers and pediatricians: Enhancing men's roles in the care and development of their children. *Pediatrics, 113*(5), 1406–1411.

Collins, P. (1998). *Improving the quality of community-based services and supports in California for persons with developmental disabilities: A report of the Senate Select Committee on Developmental Disabilities and Mental Health.* Sacramento, CA: Senate Publications.

Collins, W.A. (1996). Parent–child relationships in the transition to adolescence: Continuity and change in interaction, affect, and cognition. In R. Montemayer, G. R. Adams, & T. P. Gullota (Eds.), *From childhood to adolescence: A transitional period? Advances in adolescent development* (p. 2). Thousand Oaks, CA: Sage Publications.

Colorado Department of Education Special Education Services Unit. (2003). *Colorado options, a handbook of post-secondary education services for students with disabilities.* Denver: Author.

Comer, J. P. (1997). *Waiting for a miracle: Why schools can't solve our problems and how we can.* New York: Dutton.

Comer, J. P., Haynes, N., Joyner, E., & Ben-Avie, M. (1996). *Rallying the whole village: The Comer process for reforming education.* New York: Teachers College Press.

Conchas, G. Q. (2001). Structuring failure and success: Understanding the variability in Latino school engagement. *Harvard Educational Review, 71*(3), 475–504.

Condelucci, A. (1995). *Interdependence: The route to community.* Winter Park, FL: GR Press.

Connell, B. R., Jones, M., Mace, R., Mueller, J., Mullick, A., & Ostroff, E. (1997). *The principles of Universal Design.* Retrieved April 22, 2005, from http://www.design.ncsu.edu:8120/cud/univ_design/princ_overview.htm

Consortium for Citizens with Disabilities. (2001). *Principles for the Individuals with Disabilities Education Act (IDEA).* Washington, DC: Author.

Conzemius, A., & O'Neill, J. (2001). *Building shared responsibility for student learning.* Alexandria, VA: Association for Supervision and Curriculum Development.

Cook, J., & Jonikas, J. (2002). Self-determination among mental health consumers/survivors: Using lessons from the past to guide the future. *Journal of Disability Policy Studies, 13*(2), 87–95.

Cook, L., & Friend, M. (1995). Co-teaching: Guidelines for creating effective practices. *Focus on Exceptional Children, 28*(3), 1–16.

Cooperrider, D. L., & Dutton, J. (Eds.). (1998). *No limits to cooperation: The organization dimensions of global change.* Newbury Park, CA: Sage Publications.

Cooperrider, D. L., Sorensen, P., Whitney, D., & Yaeger, T. (Eds.). (1999). *Appreciative inquiry: Rethinking human organization toward a positive theory of change.* Champaign, IL: Stipes Publishing, LLC.

Cooperrider, D. L., & Whitney, D. (1998). When stories have wings: How 'relational responsibility' opens new options for action. In S. McNamee & K. Gergen (Eds.), *Relational responsibility.* Thousand Oaks, CA: Sage.

Corbett, D., & Wilson, B. (2000). *I didn't know I could do that!: Parents learning to be leaders through the Commonwealth Institute for Parent Leadership.* Lexington, KY: Commonwealth Institute for Parent Leadership.

Corbett, N. L. (1996). *Project PART interns' plans and decisions for students who are hard to teach and manage.* Unpublished doctoral dissertation, University of Florida.

Correctional Education Association. (2001). CEA releases preliminary findings of multi-state recidivism, education study. *Correctional Education Bulletin, 4*(4), 4–6.

Cosmides, L., & Tooby, J. (1992). Cognitive adaptations for social exchange. In J. Barkow, L. Cosmides, & J. Tooby (Eds.), *The Adapted Mind,* 163–228. New York: Oxford University Press.

Cosmides, L., & Tooby, J. (1997). *Evolutionary psychology: A primer.* Santa Barbara: Center for Evolutionary Psychology, University of California.

Cosmides, L., & Tooby, J. (2000). *What is evolutionary psychology?: Explaining the new science of the mind.* New Haven, CT: Yale University Press.

Costa, A. L., & Kallick, B. (Ed.). (2000). *Habits of mind: A developmental series.* Alexandria, VA: Association for Supervision and Curriculum Development.

Council for Exceptional Children. (1993). *Including students with disabilities in general education classrooms.* Reston, VA: Council for Exceptional Children. (ERIC Document Reproduction Service No. ED358677)

Council for Exceptional Children. (1997). *Council for Exceptional Children Policy Manual: 1997.* Reston, VA: Author.

Council for Exceptional Children. (1998a). *DEC position on services for children birth to age eight.* Division for Early Childhood, Arlington, VA: Author.

Council for Exceptional Children. (1998b). *What every special educator must know: International standards for the preparation and licensure of special educators.* Reston, VA: Author.

Council for Exceptional Children. (2000a). *Council for Exceptional Children performance-based standards for transition specialist.* Reston, VA: Author.

Council for Exceptional Children. (2000b). *DEC position on addressing preventive measures for disabilities.* Division for Early Childhood. Reston, VA: Author.

Council for Exceptional Children. (2001a). *Content standards for all beginning special education teachers* (pp. 14–17). Arlington, VA: Author.

Council for Exceptional Children. (2001c). *Policy and practice to ensure high quality teachers for children and youth with disabilities.* National Symposium, June 8–10, 2001, Washington, DC: Author.

Council for Exceptional Children. (2002). President's Commission Report receives mixed reviews. *CEC Today, 9*(4), 6.

Council for Exceptional Children. (2004a). *What every special educator must know: Ethics, standards, and guidelines for special education* (5th ed.). Upper Saddle River, NJ: Merrill/Prentice Hall.

Council for Exceptional Children. (2004b). *The new IDEA: Summary of significant changes.* Arlington, VA: Author.

Council for Exceptional Children, Division for Early Childhood. (1999). *DEC concept paper on the identification of and intervention with challenging behavior.* Arlington, VA: Author.

Council for Exceptional Children, Division of Career Development and Transition. (1998). *Transition specialist competencies.* Retrieved August 4, 2005, from http://dcdt.org/pdf/trans_educators.pdf

Council of Administrators of Special Education. (1999). *Section 504 and the ADA promoting student access: A resource guide for educators* (2nd ed.). Albuquerque, NM: Author.

Council of Chief State School Officers. (1996). *Interstate School Leaders Licensure Consortium (ISLLC) standards for school leaders.* Washington, DC: Author.

Council of Chief State School Officers. (1999). *Policy statement on early childhood and family education.* Washington, DC: Author.

Council of Chief State School Officers. (2000). *Next steps: Moving toward performance-based licensing in teaching.* Washington, DC: Author.

Council of Chief State School Officers. (2001). *Model standards for licensing general and special education teachers of students with disabilities.* Interstate New Teacher Assessment and Support Consortium (INTASC) Special Education Sub-Committee, May. Washington, DC: Author.

Council of Chief State School Officers. (2002). *State systems of technical assistance delivery in special education: Key survey findings.* Washington, DC: Author.

Counts, G. (1932). *Dare the school build a new social order?* Carbondale: Southern Illinois University Press.

Court TV. (2003). *Safe passage: Voices from the middle school.* New York: Courtroom Television Network LLC.

Covey, S. (2004). *The seven habits of highly effective people.* New York: The Free Press.

Cox, S., & Osguthorpe, R. T. (2003). How do instructional design professionals spend their time? *Tech Trends, 47,* 45–47.

Crawford, V. (2002). *Embracing the monster: Overcoming the challenges of hidden disabilities.* Baltimore, MD: Paul H. Brookes.

Crigal, M. (1998). The time–space continuum: Using natural supports in inclusive classrooms. *Teaching Exceptional Children, 30*(6), 44–51.

Crites, J. (1978). *The career maturity inventory.* Monterey, CA: CTB/McGraw-Hill.

Crockett, L. J., Petersen, A. C., Graber, J. A., Schulenberg, J. E., & Ebata. A. (1989). School transition and adjustment during early adolescence. *Journal of Early Adolescence, 9,* 181–210.

Crowson, R., & Boyd, J. (1993). Coordinated services for children: Designing arks for storms and seas unknown. *American Journal of Education, 101,* 140–179.

Crutchfield, M. (1997). Who's teaching our children with disabilities? *NICHY News Digest, 27,* 1–32.

Cuban, L., & Usdan, M. (2002). *Powerful reforms with shallow roots: Getting good schools in 6 cities.* New York: Teachers College Press.

Cummins, D., & Allen, C., (Eds.). (1998). *The evolution of mind.* Oxford: Oxford University Press.

Cummins, J. (2001). Empowering minority students: A framework for intervention. *Harvard Educational Review, 71*(4), 656–676.

Cushman, K. (1996). Looking collaboratively at student work: An essential toolkit. *Horace, 13*(2), 1–42.

Cushman, K. (1998). Teacher renewal: Essential in a time of change. *Horace, 14*(4), 1–5.

da Costa, J. L., Marshall, J. L., & Riordan, G. (1998, April). *Case study of the development of a collaborative teaching culture in an inner city elementary school.* Paper presented at the annual meeting of the American Educational Research Association, San Diego, CA. (AN 420630)

Dahir, C., & Eby, L. (2001, Winter). Building resiliency: The role of the school counselor in the middle grades. *Middle Matters,* 5–6.

Dahl, S. (2003). *Communications and culture transformation: Cultural diversity, globalization and cultural convergence.* Luton, UK: University of Luton.

Dana, R. H., Behn, J. D., & Gonwa, T. (1992). A checklist for the examination of cultural competence in social service agencies. *Research on Social Work Practice, 2*(2), 220–233.

Danaher, J., Armijo, C., & Lazara, A. (Eds.). (2006). *Part C updates: Selected aspects of the early intervention program for infants and toddlers with disabilities, (Part C) of IDEA.* Chapel Hill, NC: National Early Childhood Technical Assistance Center.

Danaher, J., Kraus, R., Armijo, C., & Hipps, C. (2005). *Section 619 profile* (13th ed.). National Center for Early Development and Learning, January. Chapel Hill, NC: FPG Child Development Institute.

Darling, N. (1999). Parenting style and its correlates, *ERIC Digest.* Champaign: ERIC Clearinghouse on Elementary and Early Childhood Education, University of Illinois. Retrieved August 2, 2005, from http://ericeece.org/pubs/digests/1999/darlin99.html

Darling-Hammond, L. (1997). *The right to learn: A blueprint for creating schools that work.* San Francisco: Jossey-Bass.

Darling-Hammond, L. (2001a). *Policy and practice to ensure high quality teachers.* Keynote speech before the National Symposium of the National Clearinghouse for Professions in Special Education, Council for Exceptional Children. June 8–10, 2001, Mayflower Hotel, Washington, D.C.

Darling-Hammond, L. (2001b). *The research and rhetoric on teacher certification: Response to a teacher certification reconsidered.* Washington, DC: National Commission on Teaching for America's Future.

Darling-Hammond, L. (2002). *The factory model schools.* Stanford, CA: Stanford School Redesign Network, Stanford University. Retrieved December 2, 2005, from http://www.schoolredesign.com/srn/server

Darling-Hammond, L., Ancess, J., & Faulk, B. (1995). *Authentic assessment in action: Studies of schools and students at work.* New York: Teachers College Press.

Darling-Hammond, L., Ancess, J., & Ort, W. (2002). Reinventing high school: Outcomes of the Coalition Campus Schools Project. *American Educational Research Journal, 39*(3), 639–673.

Darling-Hammond, L., & Bransford, J. (2005). *Preparing teachers for a changing world: What teachers should learn and be able to do.* San Francisco: Jossey-Bass.

Darling-Hammond, L., Lieberman, A., & McLaughlin, M. (1995). *Practices and policies to support teacher development in an era of reform.* New York: National Center for Restructuring Education, Schools and Teaching.

Daro, D. A., & Harding, K. A. (1999). Healthy families America: Using research to enhance practice. *The Future of Children, 9*(1), 152–176.

Davies, D. (1994). But these parents just aren't interested: The League of Schools reaching out challenges an old assumption. *Family Resource Coalition Report, 13*(1,2), 9–11.

Davis, G. (2001). There is no four-object limit on attention. *Behavioral and Brain Sciences, 24*(1), 120.

Day, S. (1998, May). *New administrators in old organizations: What to do before redesign.* ARISE Conference, The George Washington University, Washington, DC.

De Acosta, M. (1996). A foundational approach to preparing teachers for family and community involvement in children's education. *Journal of Teacher Education, 47,* 9–15.

Deal, T., & Peterson, K. (1999). *Shaping school culture: The heart of leadership* [Jossey-Bass Educational Series]. San Francisco: Jossey-Bass.

De Bellis, M. D., Keshavan, M. S., Beers, S. R., Hall, J., Frustaci, K., Masalehdan, A., et al. (2001). Sex differences in brain maturation during childhood and adolescence. *Cerebral Cortex, 11*(6), 552–557.

DeBoer, A. (1996). *Working together: The art of consulting and communication.* Denver, CO: Sopris West.

Deci, E. L., & Ryan, R. M. (1985). *Intrinsic motivation and self-determination in human behavior.* New York: Plenum.

Deci, E. L., & Ryan, R. M. (2000). The "what" and "why" of goal pursuits: Human needs and the self-determination of behavior. *Psychological Inquiry, 11,* 227–268.

Deci, E. L., & Ryan, R. M. (Eds.). (2006). *The handbook of self-determination research.* Rochester, NY: University of Rochester Press.

Deery, H. (1999). Hazard and risk perception among young novice drivers. *Journal of Safety Research, 30*(4), 225–236.

DeFur, S., & Patton, J. (1999). *Transition and school-based services: Interdisciplinary perspectives for enhancing the transition process.* Austin, TX: PRO-ED.

DeFur, S., & Williams, B. (2002). Cultural considerations in the transition process and standards-based education. In C. A. Kochhar-Bryant & D. S. Bassett (Eds.), *Aligning transition and standards-based education: Issues and strategies,* (pp. 104–124). Arlington, VA: Council for Exceptional Children.

Delpit, L. (1995). *Other people's children: Cultural conflict in the classroom.* New York: The New Press.

Deming, W. E. (1982). *Out of the crisis.* Cambridge, MA: MIT Press.

Dempster, N., & Berry, V. (2003). Blindfolded in a minefield: Principals' ethical decision making. *Cambridge Journal of Education, 33*(3), 457–477.

Dennis, R. E., & Giangreco, M. F. (1996). Creating conversation: Reflections on cultural sensitivity in family interviewing. *Exceptional Children, 63*(1), 103–116.

Deshler, D. D., Schumaker, J. B., & Woodruff, S. K. (2004). Improving literacy skills of at-risk adolescents: A school-wide response. In D. S. Strickland & D. E. Alvermann (Eds.), *Bridging the literacy achievement gap grades 4–1,* 86–104. New York: Teachers College Press.

Desimone, L., (1999). Linking parent involvement with student achievement: Do race and income matter? *Journal of Educational Research, 93*(1), 11–31.

DeStefano, L. Hazasi, S., & Trach, J. (1997). Issues in the evaluation of a multi-state federal systems change initiative. *Career Development for Exceptional Individuals, 20*(2). Reston, VA: Council for Exceptional Children.

DeStefano, L., Heck, D., Hazasi, S., & Furney, K. (1999). Enhancing the implementation of the transition requirements of IDEA: A report on the policy forum on transition. *Career Development for Exceptional Children, 22*(1), 85–100.

Dettmer, H. W. (1997). *Goldratt's theory of constraints: A systems approach to continuous improvement.* Milwaukee, WI: Quality Press.

Dettmer, P., Dyck, N., & Thurston, L. P. (2005). *Consultation, collaboration, and teamwork for students with special needs* (5th ed.). Boston: Allyn & Bacon.

Dettmer, P., Thurston, L., & Dyck, N. (2001). *Consultation, collaboration and teamwork for students with special needs* (4th ed.). Boston: Allyn & Bacon.

Deutsch-Smith, D. (1998). *Introduction to special education: Teaching in an age of challenge.* (3rd ed.). Needham Heights, MA: Allyn & Bacon.

Developmental Disabilities Assistance and Bill of Rights Act of 2000, P.L. 106-402, sec. 152 (d), 42 U.S.C. § 15062 (2000).

Dewey, J. (1938). *Experience and education.* New York: Macmillan.

Dewey, J. (1916). *Democracy and education.* New York: Macmillan.

Dick, B. (1999). *Action research activities.* Retrieved January 5, 2005, from http://www.scu.edu.au/schools/gcm/ar/whatisar.html

Dieker, L. A. (2001). What are the characteristics of 'effective' middle and high school co-taught teams for students with disabilities? *Preventing School Failure, 46*(1), 14–23.

Dieker, L. A., & Murawski, W. W. (2003). Co-teaching at the secondary level: Unique issues, current trends, and suggestions for success. *High School Journal, 86*(4), 1–13.

DiMatties, M., & Sammons, J. (2003, May). *Understanding sensory integration.* Arlington, VA: Council for Exceptional Children. (ERIC EC Digest #E643)

DiNatale, N., & Shore, H. (2000). *Life works: Behavioral health in the classroom.* Doylestown, PA: Foundations of Behavioral Health.

Dinnebeil, L., Hale, L., & Rule, S. (1999). Early intervention program practices that support collaboration. *Topics in Early Childhood Special Education, 19*(4), 225–235.

Dinnebeil, L., & McInerney, W. (2000). Supporting inclusion in community-based settings: The role of the 'Tuesday morning teacher.' *Young Exceptional Children, 4*(1), 19–26.

Dinnebeil, L., McInerney, W., Roth, J., & Ramaswamy, V. (2001). Itinerant early childhood special education services: Service delivery in one state. *Journal of Early Intervention, 24,* 35–44.

DiPaola, M. F., & Walther-Thomas, C. S. (2004). *Principals and special education: The critical role of school leaders.* Gainesville: The Center for Personnel Studies in Special Education, University of Florida.

The Disabled Persons Rehabilitation Act, Public Act 92-0452, Illinois Compiled Statutes, 20 ILCS 2405/Public Acts 92nd General Assembly, Illinois State Legislature, Springfield. (2001).

Dixon, K. A., Kruse, D., & Van Horn, C. E. (2003). *Restricted access: A survey of employers about people with disabilities and lowering barriers to work.* New Brunswick, NJ.: John J. Heldrich Center for Workforce Development. Retrieved August 15, 2005, from www.heldrich.rutgers.edu

Dolan, R. P., & Hall, T. E. (2002). Universal design for learning: Implications for large-scale assessment. *Perspectives: The International Dyslexia Association, 27*(4), 22–25.

Doll, E., Sands, D., Wehmeyer, M. L., & Palmer, S. (1996). Promoting the development and acquisition of self-determined behavior. In D. J. Sands & M. L. Wehmeyer (Eds.), *Self-determination across the life span: Independence and choice for people with disabilities* (pp. 65–90). Baltimore: Paul H. Brookes.

Doner, K. (1996). My teacher hates me. *Working Mother, 19*(9), 46–48.

Donham, J. (1999). Collaboration in the media center: Building partnerships for learning. *NAASP, 83,* 20–26.

Donohew, L., Zimmerman, R., Cupp, P. S., Novak, S., Colon, S., & Abell, R. (2000). Sensation seeking, impulsive decision making, and risky sex: Implications for risk-taking and design of interventions. *Personality and Individual Differences, 28,* 1079–1091.

Dorfman, D., & Fisher, A. (2002). *Building relationships for student success: School–family–community partnerships and student achievement in the northwest.* Portland, OR: Northwest Regional Education Laboratory.

Doyle, A., & Moretti, M. (2000). *Attachment to parents and adjustment in adolescence: Literature review and policy implications.* Montreal, QE, Canada: Center for Research in Human Development.

Drucker, P. (2002). *Meeting the collaboration challenge workbook: Developing strategic alliances between nonprofit organizations and businesses* (Peter F. Drucker Foundation for Nonprofit Management). San Francisco: Jossey-Bass.

Dryfoos, J. G. (1998). *Safe passage: Making it through adolescence in a risky society.* New York: Oxford University Press.

Dryfoos, J. G. (2002). *Evaluation of community schools: Findings to date.* Washington, D.C: Coalition for Community Schools, Institute for Educational Leadership.

Dryfoos, J. G. (1994). *Full service schools: A revolution in health and social services for children, youth, and families.* San Francisco: Jossey-Bass.

DuFour, R. (2003). Leading edge: 'Collaboration lite' puts student achievement on a starvation diet. *Journal of Staff Development, 24*(3), 1–3.

DuFour, R. (2004). What is a 'professional learning community?' *Educational Leadership, 61*(8), 6–11.

DuFour, R., & Eaker, R. (1998). *Professional learning communities at work: Best practices for enhancing student achievement.* Alexandria, VA: Association for Supervision and Curriculum Development.

Dunst, C., & Bruder, M. (2002). Valued outcomes of service coordination, early intervention, and natural environments. *Exceptional Children, 68*(3), 361–375.

Dunst, C. J., & Trivette, C. M. (1988). Toward experimental evaluation of the family, infant and preschool program. In H. B. Weiss & F. H. Jacobs (Eds.), *Evaluating family programs* (pp. 315–346). New York: Aldine De Gruyter.

Dunst, C. J., Trivette, C. M., & Deal, A. G. (Eds.). (1994). *Supporting and strengthening families: Methods, strategies and practices,* Cambridge, MA: Brookline Books.

Duran, R., Duran, J., Perry-Romero, D., & Sanchez, E. (2001). Latino immigrant parents and children learning and publishing together in an after-school setting. *Journal of Education for Students Placed at Risk, 6*(1&2), 95–113.

Early, D. M., Pianta, R. C., Taylor, L. C., & Cox, M. J. (2001). Transition practices: Findings from a national survey of kindergarten teachers. *Early Childhood Education Journal, 28,* 199–206.

Easton, D., & Schelling, C. (1991). *Divided knowledge: Across disciplines, across cultures.* Newbury Park, CA: Sage Publications.

Eastwood, K., & Louis, K. S. (1992). Restructuring that lasts: Managing the performance dip. *Journal of School Leadership, 2*(2), 213–224.

Eaton, H., & Coull, L. (1998). *From transitions to postsecondary learning: Student work guide.* Vancouver, Canada: Eaton Coull Learning Group.

Eccles, J. S., Lord, S., & Midgley, C. (1991). What are we doing to early adolescents? The impact of educational contexts on early adolescents. *American Journal of Education, 99*(4), 521–543.

Eccles, J. S., & Midgley, C. (1989). Stage-environment fit: Developmentally appropriate classrooms for young adolescents. In C. Ames & R. Ames (Eds.), *Research on motivation in education: Goals and cognitions* (pp. 139–186). New York: Academic Press.

Eccles, J. S. Wigfied, A., Reuman, D., & Mac Iver, D. (1987, April). Changes in self perceptions and values at early adolescence. In C. Midgley (Ed.), *Early adolescence: Schooling psychological, and social transitions.* Symposium conducted at the annual meeting of the American Education Research Association, Washington, DC.

Ede, L., & Lunsford, A. (2000, December). *Creative collaboration: Alternatives to the adversarial academy,* Presidential Forum, 2000, Modern Language Association Meeting, Washington, DC.

Education for All Handicapped Children Act, P. L. No. 94-142, 20 U.S.C. § 1401 *et seq.* (1975).

Education for All Handicapped Children Act, 1983 Amendments, P. L. 98-199 (1983).

Education Commission of the States. (2000). *Easing the transition to kindergarten.* Denver, CO: Author.

Education Commission of the States. (2004a). *Parental involvement policy.* Retrieved December 4, 2005, from http://www.publiceducation.org/pdf/nclb/parental_involvement.pdf

Education Commission of the States. (2004b). *Report to the nation: State implementation of the No Child Left Behind Act.* Retrieved August 15, 2005, from http://www.ecs.org/ecsmain.asp?page=/html/special/nclb/reporttothenation/reporttothenation.htm

Education Policy Reform Research Institute. (2004). *Ensuring accountability for all children in an era of standards-based reform: Alternate achievement standards.* Arlington, VA: Author.

Education Week. (2002). *Quality counts: Building blocks for success: State efforts in early childhood education.*

Retrieved July 21, 2006, from http://counts.edweek .org/sreports

Education Week. (2004). *Quality counts 2004 count me in: Special education in an era of standards.* Retrieved December 3, 2004, from http://counts .edweek.org/sreports/qc04

Edwards, A., & Warin, J. (1999). Parent involvement in raising the achievement of primary school pupils: Why bother? *Oxford Review of Education, 25*(3), 325–342.

Edwards, S. W. (2002). *Creating the climate for positive school change.* Retrieved August, 1, 2005, from http://monroemiddleschool.org/articles/50/docs/ Rochester2002.pdf

Eick, C., Ware, F., & Jones, M. (2004). Coteaching in a secondary science methods course: Learning through a coteaching model that supports early teacher practice. *Journal of Science Teacher Education, 15*(3), 197–209.

Eilem, G., & Shamir, B. (2005). Organizational change and self-concept threats: A theoretical perspective and a case study. *The Journal of Applied Behavioral Science, 41*(4), 399–421.

Eisenman, L. T. (2000). Characteristics and effects of integrated academic and occupational curricula for students with disabilities: A literature review. *Career Development for Exceptional Individuals, 23*, 105–119.

Eisenman, L. T. (2001). Conceptualizing the contribution of career-oriented schooling to self-determination. *Career Development for Exceptional Individuals, 24*, 3–17.

Eisenman, L. T., & Chamberlin, M. (2001). Implementing self-determination activities: Lessons from schools. *Remedial and Special Education, 22*, 138–147.

Eisenman, L. T., & Wilson, D. (2000). Making the link: Implementing integrated curricula for all. *Journal of Vocational Special Needs Education, 22*(3), 38–48.

Ekpone, P. M., & Bogucki. R. (2003). *Students with psychiatric disabilities in postsecondary education.* Washington, DC: The George Washington University HEATH Resource Center.

Elbaum, B., & Vaughn, S. (1999, May). *Can school-based interventions enhance the self-concept of students with learning disabilities? A research synthesis.* Document prepared for Keys to Successful Learning: A National Summit on Research in Learning Disabilities held by the National Center for Learning Disabilities, Washington, DC.

Elders, J. (2002, March). *Keynote address.* Presented at the 57th Annual Conference of the Association for Supervision and Curriculum Development, San Antonio, TX.

Elias, M. (2001, Winter). Middle school transition: It's harder than you think. *Middle Matters,* 1–2.

Eliot, T. (1928). Should courts do case work? *The Survey, 60*, 601–603.

Elkind, D. (1988). *The hurried child: Growing up too fast too soon.* New York: Addison-Wesley.

Elliot, D., & McKenney, M. (1998). Four inclusion models that work. *Teaching Exceptional Children, 30*, 54–58.

Elmore, R. (2002a). *Bridging the gap between standards and achievement: Report on the imperative for professional development in education.* Washington, DC: Albert Shanker Institute.

Elmore, R. (2002b, January/February). The limits of change. *The Harvard Education Letter,* 1–2.

England, J. (1996). Teaching team concept helps Missouri district's inclusion effort. *Inclusive Education Programs, 4*(4), 6–7.

Engle, P. L., & Breaux, C. (1998). Fathers' involvement with children. *Social Policy Report, 12*(1), 1–21.

Entwisle, D. R. (1995). The role of schools in sustaining early childhood program benefits. *The Future of Children, 5*(3), 133–144.

Epstein, J. L. (1998). Effects on students' achievement of teacher practices and parent involvement. In S. Silvern (Ed.), *Advances in reading language research, 5. Literacy through family, community, and school interaction,* (pp. 261–276). Greenwich, CT: JAI Press.

Epstein, J. L. (2001). *School, family, and community partnerships: Preparing educators and improving schools.* Boulder, CO: Westview Press.

Epstein, J. L., Coates, L., Salinas, K., Sanders, M., & Simon, B. (1997). *School, family, and community partnerships: Your handbook for action.* Thousand Oakes, CA: Corwin Press.

Epstein, J. L., Sanders, M., & Clark, L. (1999). *Preparing educators for school–family professional partnerships.* [Report no. 34]. Baltimore: Center on School, Family and Community Partnerships, Johns Hopkins University.

Epstein, M. H., Rudolph, S., & Epstein, A. A. (2000). Using strength-based assessment in transition planning. *Teaching Exceptional Children, 32*(6), 50–54.

Epstein, M. H., & Sharma, J. (1998*). Behavioral and emotional rating scale: A strength-based approach to assessment.* Austin, TX: PRO-ED.

Erchul, W. P., & Martens, B. K. (1997). *School consultation: Conceptual and empirical bases of practice.* New York: Plenum Press.

Ettling, D. (2002). The praxis of sustaining transformative change. *Teachers College Record,* Retrieved August 6, 2005, from http://www.tcrecord.org

Ettling, D., & Guilian, L. (2001). *Collaborators as mid-wives of transformation.* Paper presented at the Transformative Learning Conference, San Antonio, TX.

Evaluation Associates. (2002). *Evaluation of collaboration in the higher education sector.* Bristol, UK: Higher Education Funding Council.

Evans, D. (1993). Restructuring special education services. *Teacher Education and Special Education, 16,* 137–145.

Evans-Schilling, D. (1999). Preparing educational leaders to work effectively with families: The parent power project. In M. S. Ammon (Ed.), *Joining hands: Preparing teachers to make meaningful home-school connections* (pp. 16–36). Sacramento: California Department of Education.

Fabian, E. S., Lent, R. L., & Willis, S. P. (1998). Predicting work transition outcomes for students with disabilities: Implications for counselors. *Journal of Counseling & Development, 76,* 311–315.

Fagan, J., & Iglesias, A. (2000). The relation between fathers' and children's communication skills and children's behavior problems: A study of Head Start children. *Early Education and Development, 11*(3), 307.

Fagan, W. T. (2001a). *The literacy maze: Practice without policy.* St. John's, Canada: University of Newfoundland.

Fagan, W. T. (2001b). *Writing FOR the workplace: Writing process with workplace content.* St. John's, Canada: Memorial University.

Family Resource Coalition of America. (1999). *How are we doing? A program self-assessment toolkit for the family support field.* Chicago: Author.

Federal Board for Vocational Education. (1917). *Statement of Policies, Bulletin No. 1* (p. 17). Washington, DC: Government Printing Office.

Federal Interagency Forum on Child and Family Statistics. (2003). *America's children: Key national indicators of well-being 2003.* Washington, DC: Author.

Feidler, C. (2000). *Making a difference: Advocacy competencies or special education professionals.* Boston: Allyn & Bacon.

Feinburg, E., Beyer, J., & Moses, P. (2002). *Beyond mediation: Strategies for appropriate early dispute resolution in special education.* A Briefing Paper from the Consortium for Appropriate Dispute Resolution in Special Education, Washington, DC.

Felner, R. D., Jackson, A. W., Kasak, D. Mulhall, P., Brand, S., & Flowers, N. (1997). The impact of school reform for the middle years: Longitudinal study of a network engaged in turning points-based comprehensive school transformation. *Phi Delta Kappan, 78*(7), 528–550.

Fenichel, E. (Ed.). (2001). Infant mental health and early Head Start: Lessons for early childhood programs. *Zero to Three, 22*(1), 1–81.

Fenzel, L. M. (1989). Role strains and the transition to middle school: Longitudinal trends and sex differences. *Journal of Early Adolescence, 9,* 211–226.

Fenzel, L. M. (1992). The effect of relative age on self-esteem, role strain, GPA, and anxiety. *Journal of Early Adolescence, 12,* 253–266.

Ferguson, C. (2005). *Reaching out to diverse populations: What can schools do to foster family–school connections?* Austin, TX: Southwest Educational Development Laboratory, National Center for Family and Community Connections.

Ferrara, M. M. (2000). Capturing conversations of change: The polylog. *Action in Teacher Education, 22*(2), 55–62.

Festinger, L. (1957). *A theory of cognitive dissonance.* Stanford, CA: Stanford University.

Fetterman, D. M. (1996). *Empowerment evaluation: An introduction to theory and practice.* In D. M. Fetterman, R., Kaftarian, S., & Wandersman, A. (Eds.). *Empowerment evaluation: Knowledge and tools for self-assessment and accountability* (pp. 1–46). Thousand Oaks, CA: Sage Publications.

Feuerstein, A. (2001). School characteristics and parent involvement: Influences on participation in children's schools. *Journal of Educational Research, 94*(1), 27–40.

Feurstein, R. (1990). The theory of structural cognitive modifiability. In B. Z. Presseisen, *Learning and thinking styles: Classroom interaction* (pp. 68–134). Washington, DC: National Education Association.

Feurstein, R., Klein, P., & Tannenbaum, A. (1991). *Mediated learning experience: Theoretical psychosocial and learning implications.* London: Freund.

Field, S., Hoffman, A., & Spezia, S. (1998). *Self-determination strategies for adolescents in transition.* Austin, TX: Pro-Ed.

Field, S., Martin, J., Miller, R., Ward, M., & Wehmeyer, M. (1998a). *A practical guide for teaching self-determination.* Reston, VA: Council for Exceptional Children, Division on Career Development and Transition.

Field, S., Martin, J., Miller, R., Ward, M., & Wehmeyer, M. (1998b). *Self-determination for persons with disabilities: A position statement of the Division on Career Development and Transition.* Arlington, VA: Council for Exceptional Children.

Finger, J. A., & Silverman, M. (1966). Changes in academic performance in the junior high school. *Personnel and Guidance Journal, 45,* 157–164.

Finn, J. (1998). Parent engagement that makes a difference. *Educational Leadership, 55*(8), 20–24.

Finnan, C. (2000, April). *Implementing school reform models: Why is it so hard for some schools and easy for others?* Paper presented at the meeting of the American Educational Research Association, New Orleans. (ED446356)

Fishbaugh, M. (2000). *The collaboration guide for early career educators.* Baltimore: Paul H. Brookes.

Fisher, T. A., & Griggs, M. B. (1994, April). *Factors that influence the career development of African-American and Latino youth.* Paper presented at the annual meeting of the American Educational Research Association, New Orleans. (ED 380 532)

Fix, M., & Passel, J. (2001). *U.S. immigration at the beginning of the 21st Century.* Testimony before the Subcommittee on Immigration and Claims Hearing on The U.S. Population and Immigration, Committee on the Judiciary U.S. House of Representatives.

Fix, S. (2000). *Innovative principal turns school around with student's help.* Retrieved August, 17, 2005, from http://archives.charleston.net/news/education/innovat0430.htm

Fixsen, D., Powell, D., & Dunlap, G. (2003). *Pathways to service utilization: A synthesis of evidence relevant to young children with challenging behavior.* Tampa, FL: Center for Evidence-Based Practice, Young Children with Challenging Behavior. Retrieved July 30, 2005, from www.challengingbehavior.org

Flanagan, B. (2001). Parents' views of and participation in the special education process (Doctoral dissertation, Virginia Polytechnic Institute, 2001). (VTEDT dissertations, etd-03132001-103550)

Flecha, R. (2000). *Sharing words: Theory and practice of dialogic learning.* Lanham, MD: Rowman & Littlefield.

Fleming, T. (2002, January 27). Habermas on civil society, lifeworld and system: Unearthing the social in transformation theory. *Teachers College Record.* Retrieved August 18, 2005, from http://www.tcrecord.org (ID Number: 108770)

Flexer, R., Simmons, T., Luft, P., & Baer, R. (2001). *Transition planning for secondary students with disabilities.* Upper Saddle River, NJ: Merrill/Prentice Hall.

Flowers, C. R., Edwards, D., & Pusch, B. (1996, July–September). Rehabilitation cultural diversity initiative: A regional survey of cultural diversity within CILs. *Journal of Rehabilitation,* 22–27.

Flowers, N., Mertens, S., & Mulhall, P. (1999). The impact of teaming: Five research-based outcomes of teaming. *Middle School Journal, 31*(2), 57–60.

Fogg, C. D. (1994). *Team-based strategic planning: A complete guide to structuring, facilitating and implementing the process.* New York: AMACOM.

Ford, D., & Lerner, R. (1992). *Developmental systems theory: An integrative approach.* Newbury Park, CA: Sage Publications.

Forest, M., & Lusthaus, E. (1989). Promoting educational equality for all students: Circles and maps. In S. Stainback, W. Stainback, & M. Forest (Eds.), *Educating all students in the mainstream of regular education.* Baltimore, MD: Paul H. Brookes.

Forest, M., & Pearpoint, J. (1997). *Inclusion! The bigger picture.* Retrieved July 15, 2005, from http://www. inclusion.com.tools.html

Forness, S. R., Serna, L. A., Nielsen, E., Lambros, K., Hale, M. J., & Kavale, K. A. (2000). A model for early detection and primary prevention of emotional or behavioral disorders. *Education and Treatment of Children, 23,* 325–345.

Fosnot, C. (1992). Constructing constructivism. In T. M. Duffy & D. H. Jonassen (Eds.), *Constructivism and the technology of instruction: A conversation* (pp. 167–176). Hillsdale, NJ: Lawrence Erlbaum Associates.

Foster, A., & Mantle-Bromley, C. (2000). *First-year teacher study: Executive summary of new teachers' study.* Fort Collins, CO: Research and Development Center for the Advancement of Student Learning.

Fowler, S., Donegan, M., Lueke, B., Hadden, S., & Phillips, B. (2000). Evaluating community collaboration in writing interagency agreements on the age 3 transition. *Exceptional Children, 67*(1), 35–50.

Fox, N., Leone, P., Rubin, K., Oppenheim, J., Miller, M., & Friedman, K. (1999). *Final report on the Linkages to Learning program and evaluation at Broad Acres Elementary School.* College Park: University of Maryland, Department of Special Education.

Frank Porter Graham Child Development Institute. (2002). *Youth Risk Behavior Survey: Risk behaviors among middle school students with and without disabilities. The North Carolina Middle School YRBS.* Chapel Hill: University of North Carolina.

Fraser, B. J., & Fisher, D. L. (1983). Student achievement as a function of person–environment fit: A regression surface analysis. *British Journal of Educational Psychology, 53,* 89–99.

Freschi, D. (1999). Guidelines for working with one-to-one aides. *Teaching Exceptional Children, 31*(4), 42–47.

Frick, T. (1993). A systems view of restructuring education. In C. Reigeluth, B. Banathy, & J. Olson (Eds.), *Comprehensive systems design: A new educational technology* (pp. 260–271). Berlin: Springer-Verlag.

Friedman, K. A., Leone, P. E., & Friedman, P. (1999). Strengths-based assessment of children with SED:

Consistency of reporting by teachers and parents. *Journal of Child and Family Studies, 8,* 169–180.

Friend, M. (1995). *The power of two: Including students through co–teaching* [videotape]. Bloomington, IN: Elephant Rock Productions. Distributed by the Council for Exceptional Children, Reston, VA.

Friend, M. (2000a). *Complexities of collaboration.* Bloomington, IN: Elephant Rock Productions.

Friend, M. (2000b). Myths and misunderstandings about professional collaboration. *Remedial and Special Education, 21,* 130–132, 160.

Friend, M. (2000c). *Accessing the general curriculum.* Presentation for National Association of State Directors of Special Education Satellite Conference Series, December, 2000, Alexandria, VA.

Friend, M., & Bursuck, W. D. (1996). *Including students with special needs: A practical guide for classroom teachers.* Boston: Allyn & Bacon.

Friend, M., & Bursuck, W. (2002). *Including students with special needs: A practical guide for classroom teachers* (3rd ed.). Boston: Allyn & Bacon.

Friend, M., & Cook, L. (1992). The new mainstreaming. *Instructor, 101*(7), 30–36.

Friend, M., & Cook, L. (2000). *Interactions: Collaboration skills for school professionals* (3rd ed.). White Plains, NY: Longman.

Friend, M., & Cook, L. (2003). *Interactions: Collaboration skills for school professionals.* Boston: Allyn & Bacon.

Friere, P. (1989). *Learning to question: A pedagogy of liberation.* New York: Continuum Publishing.

Friere, P. (1993). *Pedagogy of the oppressed.* New York: Continuum Publishing.

Friere, P. (1994). *Paulo Friere on higher education.* Albany: State University of New York Press.

Friere, P. (1995). *Teachers as cultural workers: Letters to those who dare teach.* Boulder, CO: Westview Press.

Friesen, B., & Poertner, J. (Eds.) (1997). *From case management to service coordination for children with emotional, behavioral or mental disorders: Building on family strengths.* Baltimore, MD: Paul H. Brookes.

Fromm, E. (1941). *Escape from freedom.* New York: Farrar & Rinehart.

Fruchter, N., Galletta, A., & White, J. L. (1992). *New directions in parent involvement.* Washington, DC: Academy for Educational Development.

Fry, R., & Lowell, L. (2002). *Work or study: Different fortunes of U.S. Latino generations.* Washington, DC: Pew Hispanic Center.

Fuchs, D., Fuchs, L. S., Mathes, P. G., & Simmons, D. C. (1997). Peer-assisted learning strategies: Making classrooms more responsive to diversity. *American Educational Research Journal, 34*(1), 174–206.

Fuligni, A. (2001). A comparative longitudinal approach to acculturation among children from immigrant families. *Harvard Educational Review, 71*(4), 566–578.

Fullan, M. (1999). *Change forces: The sequel.* London: Routledge Falmer.

Furney, K., & Salembrier, G. (2000). Rhetoric and reality: A review of the literature on parent and student participation in the IEP and transition planning process. In D. R. Johnson & E. J. Emmanuel (Eds.), *Issues influencing the future of transition programs and services in the United States* (pp. 111–126). Minneapolis: University of Minnesota, Institute on Community Integration, National Transition Network. Retrieved August 17, 2005, from http://ici.umn.edu/search/productsearch.taf?_

Future Education Funding Council. (2002). *Strategic planning: Analysis of institutions' plans 1999–2000 to 2001–02.* Cardiff, Wales: Author.

Gable, R. A., & Manning, M. L. (1999). Interdisciplinary teaming: Solution to instructing heterogeneous groups of students. *The Clearing House, 72,* 182–185. Retrieved on December 8, 2003, from Wilson Web online database on the World Wide Web: http://library.valdosta.edu

Gajar, A. (1998). Postsecondary education. In F. Rusch & J. Chadsey (Eds.), *Beyond high school: Transition from school to work* (pp. 383–405). Belmont, CA: Wadsworth Publishing.

Gallagher, J., & Clifford, R. (2000). The missing support infrastructure in early childhood. *Early Childhood Research and Practice, 2*(1). Retrieved August 15, 2000, from http://ecrp.uiuc.edu/v2n1/gallagher.html

Gallego, M., & Cole, M. (2001). Classroom cultures and cultures in the classroom. In V. Richardson (Ed.), *The fourth edition of the handbook of research on teaching.* Washington, DC: American Education Research Association.

Gallop-Goodman, G. (2000). You're never too young. *Forecast, 20*(10), 3–4.

Garbarino, J. (1995). *Raising children in a socially toxic environment.* San Francisco: Jossey-Bass.

Garcia, D. (2000, April). *Exploring connections between teacher efficacy and parent involvement: Implications of practice.* Paper presented at AERA, New Orleans.

Garcia, E. (1998). Collaboration in support of diversity: A dean's reflections. *On Common Ground, 8,* 16, 31.

Garcia, E. (2005). *NCLR Escalera Project: Taking steps to success.* Washington, DC: National Council for La Raza, Division of Workforce and Economic Development.

Garcia, S., & Ortiz, A. (1988). *Preventing inappropriate referrals of language minority students to special education*. Washington, DC: National Clearinghouse for Bilingual Education.

Gardner, H. (1983). *Frames of mind*. New York: Basic Books.

Gardner, S. (1993). The ethics of collaboration. *Georgia Academy Journal, 1*(1), 2–4.

Gardner, S. (2003). *Cities, counties, kids, and families: The essential role of local government*. Lanham, MD: University Press of America.

Garmston, R., & Wellman, B. (1999). *The adaptive school: A sourcebook for developing collaborative groups*. Norwood, MA: Christopher-Gordon Publishers.

Garry, E. M. (1996). *Truancy: First step to a lifetime of problems* [Bulletin]. Washington, DC: U.S. Department of Justice, Office of Justice Programs, Office of Juvenile Justice and Delinquency Prevention.

Gartner, A., & Lipsky, D. (2001). *Inclusion: A service, not a place. A whole school approach and inclusion and school reform: Transforming America's classrooms*. Port Chester, NY: National Professional Resources.

Gately, S., & Gately, F. (2001, March/April). Understanding co-teaching components. *Teaching Exceptional Children*, 40–44.

Gaylord, V., Johnson, D. R., Lehr, C. A., Bremer, C. D., & Hazasi, S. (Eds.). (2004). *Impact: Feature issue on achieving secondary education and transition results for students with disabilities, 16*(3). Minneapolis: University of Minnesota, Institute on Community Integration.

Gaynor, A. (1998). *Analyzing problems in schools and school systems: A theoretical approach*. Mahwah, NJ: Lawrence Erlbaum Associates.

Gazzaniga, M. S. (Ed.). (2000). *The new cognitive neurosciences*. Cambridge, MA: MIT Press.

Geenen, S., Powers, L. E., & Lopez-Vasquez, A. (2001). *Parents as partners: Understanding and promoting the multicultural aspects of parent involvement in transition planning*. Portland, OR: Oregon Health Sciences University, Center on Self-Determination.

George Mason University. *Mason Life Program*. Fairfax, VA: Kellar Institute. Retrieved August 15, 2006, from http://masonlife.gmu.edu/

George, P. S. (1999). *A middle school—If you can keep it: Part II* [Midpoints Occasional Papers]. Columbus, OH: National Middle School Association.

Gerlach, P. (2003). *Who's really running your life?* (2nd ed.). Lincoln, NE: Stepfamily Association of America.

German, S., Martin, J., Marshall, L., & Sale, H. (2000). Promoting self-determination: Using 'Take Action' to teach goal attainment. *Career Development for Exceptional Individuals, 23*(1), 27–38.

Getzel, L. Stodden, R. A., & Briel, L. (2001). Pursuing postsecondary education opportunities for individuals with disabilities. In P. Wehman (Ed.), *Life beyond the classroom: Transition strategies for young people with disabilities* (3rd ed). Baltimore: Paul H. Brookes.

Giangreco, M. F., Cloninger, C. J., & Iverson, V. S. (1993). *Choosing options and accommodations for children: A guide to planning inclusive education*. Baltimore: Paul H. Brookes.

Giangreco, M. F., Cloninger, C. J., & Iverson, V. S. (1998). *Choosing outcomes and accommodations for children (COACH): A guide to educational planning for students with disabilities* (2nd ed.). Baltimore: Paul H. Brookes.

Giangreco, M. F., Edelman, S. W., Luiselli, T. E., & MacFarland, S. Z. C. (1997). Helping or hovering? Effects of instructional assistant proximity on students with disabilities. *Exceptional Children, 63*, 7–17.

Giedd, J. N., Vaituzis, A. C., Hamburger, S. D., Lange, N., Rajapakse, J. C., Kayssen, D., et al. (1996). Quantitative MRI of the temporal lobe, amygdala and hippocampus in normal human development: Ages 4–18 years. *Journal of Comparative Neurology, 366*(2), 223–230.

Gillies, R., & Ashman, A. (2000). The effects of cooperative learning on students with learning difficulties in lower elementary school. *Journal of Special Education, 34*, 19–27.

Gilmore, D. S., Bose, J., & Hart, D. (2002). Postsecondary education as a critical step toward meaningful employment: Vocational rehabilitation's role. *Job Training & Placement Report, 26*(3), 1–3.

Giroux, H. A. (1988). *Schooling and the struggle for public life: Critical pedagogy in the modern age American culture, 1*. Minneapolis: University of Minnesota Press.

Giroux, H. A. (1992). *Border crossings: Cultural workers and the politics of education*. New York: Routledge.

Glance, N., & Huberman, B. (1994, March). The dynamics of social dilemmas. *Scientific American, 270*, 76–81.

Glatthorn, A., & Craft-Tripp, M. (2000). *Standards-based learning for students with disabilities*. Larchmont, NY: Eye On Education.

Golan, S., Wagner, M., Shaver, D., Wechsler, M., & Williamson, C. (1996). *From principles to action: Local implementation of California's Healthy Start School Linked Services Initiative*. Menlo Park, CA: SRI International.

Goldberg, M. (2000, September). Leadership for change: An interview with John Goodlad. *Phi Delta Kappan, 82*(1), 82–85.

Goldratt, E. (1992). *The goal.* Great Barrington, MA: North River Press.

Goldsmith, H. H., Lemery, K. S., Aksan, N., & Buss, K. A. (2000). Temperamental substrates of personality development. In V. J. Molfese & D. L. Molfese (Eds.), *Temperament and personality development across the lifespan,* 1–32. Mahwah, NJ: Lawrence Erlbaum Associates.

Goldstein, L. (1993). Discipline split at heart of IDEA overhaul debate. *Education Week, 22*(1), 18.

Goldstein, L. (2003). Disabled by paperwork? Special educators vexed by amount of time spent on student documentation. *Education Week, 22*(1), 23.

Goldstein, S., & Goldstein, M. (1992). *Hyperactivity: Why won't my child pay attention?* New York: John Wiley and Sons.

Golman, D. (1995). *Emotional intelligence: Why it can matter more than IQ.* New York: Bantam Books.

Gonzalez, R. (2002). *Issue Brief 8–The No Child Left Behind Act: Implications for local educators and advocates for Latino students, families, and communities.* Washington, DC: National Council of La Raza.

Goodlad, J. (1984). *A place called school.* New York: McGraw-Hill.

Goodman, J., Sutton, V., & Harkavy, I. (1995). The effectiveness of family workshops in a middle school setting: Respect and caring make the difference. *Phi Delta Kappan, 76*(9), 694–700.

Goodman, R. M., & Wandersman, A. (1994). FORECAST: A formative approach to evaluating community coalitions and community-based initiatives. *Journal of Community Psychology,* [Monograph Series-CSAP Special Issue], 625.

Goodman, S., & Cook, M. (1997). *IDEA and discipline. Assistive Technology Funding & Systems Change Project (ATFSCP).* Retrieved June 15, 2005, from http://www.ucpa.org/html/innovative/atfsc_index.html

Gordon, D. (2004). *Fuel for reform: The importance of trust in changing schools.* Chicago: College of Education, University of Illinois at Chicago. Retrieved October 11, 2004, from http://www.smallschools workshop.org/who1.htm

Gordon, E. (1973). Broadening the concept of career education. In D. McClure & M. Buan, *Essays on career education.* Portland, OR: Northwest Regional Educational Laboratory.

Gordon, H. (1999). *History and growth of vocational education in America.* Needham Heights, MA: Allyn & Bacon.

Gorman, J. C., & Balter, L. (1997). Culturally sensitive parent education: A critical review of quantitative research. *Review of Educational Research, 67*(3), 339–370.

Graf, J., & Jahier, R. (2001). Analysis of the Workforce Investment Act: Implications for persons with disabilities, postsecondary education and life-long learning opportunities. *Disability Studies Quarterly, 21*(1), 151–169.

Greenberg, P. (1990). Why not academic preschool? *Young Children, 45*(2), 70–80.

Greene, G. (2002). Pathways to successful transition for youth with disabilities. In C. A. Kochhar-Bryant & D. S. Bassett (Eds.), *Aligning transition and standards-based education: Issues and strategies.* Arlington, VA: Council for Exceptional Children.

Greene, G. (2003a). *Transition pathways.* In G. Greene & C. A. Kochhar-Bryant (Eds.), *Pathways to successful transition for youth with disabilities* (pp. 199–229). Upper Saddle River, NJ: Merrill/Prentice Hall.

Greene, G. (2003b). Pathways to successful transition for youths with disabilities. In C. A. Kochhar-Bryant & D. S. Bassett (Eds.), *Aligning transition and standards-based education: Issues and strategies.* Arlington, VA: Council for Exceptional Children.

Greene, G., & Kochhar-Bryant, C. (Eds.). (2003). *Pathways to successful transition for youth with disabilities.* Upper Saddle River, NJ: Merrill/Prentice Hall.

Greene, G., & Nefsky, P. (1999). Transition for culturally and linguistically diverse youth with disabilities: Closing the gaps. *Multiple Voices for Ethnically Diverse Exceptional Learners, 3*(1), 15–24.

Greene, M. (1973). *Teacher as stranger: Educational philosophy for the modern age.* Belmont, CA: Wadsworth Publishing.

Greene, M. (1978). *Landscapes of learning.* New York: Teachers College Press.

Greene, M. (1995). *Releasing the imagination: Essays on education, the arts, and social change.* San Francisco: Jossey-Bass.

Greenwood, G., & Hankins, A. (1989). *An analysis of professional knowledge content base commonalities among ten teacher certification exams.* Unpublished manuscript, College of Education, University of Florida, Gainesville.

Greenwood, G. E., & C. W. Hickman. (1991). Research and practice in parent involvement: Implications for teacher education. *Elementary School Journal, 91*(3), 279–288. (EJ 429 060)

Griffin, D. (1982). *Animal mind—human mind.* Berlin: Dahlem Konferenzen.

Grissmer, D., Flanagan, A., Kawata, J., & Williamson, S. (2000). *Improving student achievement: What state NAEP test scores tell us.* Santa Monica, CA: RAND.

Gronna, S. S. (1998). *Effects of grade school transition and school characteristics on eighth-grade achievement:*

A multilevel analysis. Unpublished doctoral dissertation, University of Hawaii, Oahu.

Grover, R. (Ed.). (1996). *Collaboration.* [Lessons learned series]. Chicago, IL: American Association of School Librarians and American Library Association.

Guy, B., Goldberg, M., McDonald, S., & Flom, R.A. (1997). Parental participation in transition systems change. *Career Development for Exceptional Individuals, 20*(2), 165–177.

Habermas, J. (1976). *Communication and the evolution of society.* Cambridge, UK: Polity Press.

Habermas, J. (1984). *The philosophical discourse of modernity.* Cambridge, UK: Polity Press.

Habermas, J. (1987). *The theory of communicative action* (Vol. 2). Boston: Beacon Press.

Hagebak, B. R. (1992). *Getting local agencies to cooperate.* Baltimore, MD: University Park Press.

Hagner, D., & Dileo, D. (1993). *Working together: Workplace culture, supported employment, and persons with disabilities.* Cambridge, MA: Brookline Books.

Haimson, L. (2000). Class size matters: What the research on class size reduction tells us. *Management Information: School Information and Research Service, 25,* 5–6.

Haladyna, T., & Thomas, G. (1979). The attitudes of elementary school children toward school and subject matters. *Journal of Experimental Education, 48,* 18–23.

Hall, A. S., Kelly, K. R., Hansen, K., & Gutwein, A. K. (1996). Sources of self-perceptions of career-related abilities. *Journal of Career Assessment, 4*(3), 331–343. (EJ 528 957)

Hall, G., & Hord, S. (2001). *Implementing change: Patterns, principles and potholes.* Needham Heights, MA: Allyn & Bacon.

Hallahan, D. P., & Kauffman, J. M. (2003). *Exceptional learners, introduction to special education* (9th ed). Needham Heights, MA: Allyn & Bacon.

Halperin, S. (Ed.). (2001). *The forgotten half revisited: American youth and young families, 1988–2008.* Washington, DC: Youth Policy Forum.

Halpern, A. (1985). Transition: A look at the foundations. *Exceptional Children, 51,* 497–486.

Halpern, A. (1999). *Transition: Is it time for another rebottling?* Paper presented at the 1999 Annual OSEP Project Directors' Meeting, Washington, DC.

Halpern, A. S., Herr, C. M., Doren, B., & Wolf, N. K. (2000). *Next S.T.E.P.: Student transition and educational planning.* Austin, TX: PRO-ED.

Halpern, A. S., Herr, C. M., Wolf, N. K., Lawson, J. D., Doren, B., & Johnson, M. D. (1997). *Next S.T.E.P.:*
Student transition and education. Austin, TX: PRO-ED.

Halvorsen, A. T., & Nearny, T. (2001). *Building inclusive schools: Tools and strategies for success.* Needham Heights, MA: Allyn & Bacon.

Hamaguchi, P. M. (2001). *Childhood speech, language & listening problems: What every parent should know* (2nd ed.). New York: John Wiley & Sons.

Hamer, D., & Copeland, P. (1998). *Living with our genes: Why they matter more than you think.* New York: Doubleday.

Hamilton-Pennell, C., Lance, K. C., Rodney, M. J., & Hainer, E. (2000). Dick and Jane go to the head of the class. *School Library Journal Online.* Retrieved July 3, 2005, from http://www.slj.com/articles/20000401_7475.asp

Hammerstein, P. (Ed.). (2003). *Genetic and cultural evolution of cooperation.* Cambridge, MA: MIT Press.

Hammond, S. (1998). *Appreciative inquiry* (2nd ed.). Plano, TX: Thin Book Publishing.

Hanley, J. (1999). Beyond the tip of the iceberg: Five stages toward cultural competence. *Reaching Today's Youth, 3*(2), 9–12

Hanline, M. F. (1991). Transitions and critical events in the family life cycle: Implications for providing support to families of children with disabilities. *Psychology in the Schools, 28,* 53–59.

Hansen, V., Hooper-Briar, K., & Pinder-Cook, S. (1994). *School-linked integrative services: A replication guide.* Miami: Institute on Children and Families at Risk, Florida International University.

Hanson, L., Deere, D., Lee, C. A., Lewin, A., & Seval, C. (2001, Spring). *Key principles in providing integrated behavioral health services for young children and their families: The Starting Early Starting Smart Experience.* Washington, DC: Casey Family.

Harbin, G., McWilliam, R. A., Shaw, D., Buka, S. L., Sideris, J., & Kochaek, T. T. (1998). *Implementing federal policy for young children with disabilities: How are we doing?* Chapel Hill, NC: Early Childhood Research Institute on Service Utilization.

Harbin, G., & Salisbury, C. (2000). Recommended practices in policies, procedures, and systems change. In S. Sandall, M. E. McLean, & B. J. Smith (Eds.), *DEC recommended practices in early intervention/early childhood special education.* Longmont, CO: Sopris West.

Harcourt, A. (1992). Cooperation in conflicts: Commonalities between humans and other animals. *Politics and the Life Sciences, 11,* 251–259.

Hargreaves, A. (Ed.). (2000). *Learning to change: Teaching beyond subjects and standards.* San Francisco: Jossey-Bass.

Harkavy, I., & Blank, M. (2002). Community schools: A vision of learning that goes beyond testing. *Education Weekly, 21*(31), 58.

Harley, D. A., Donnell, C., & Rainey, J. A. (2003). Interagency collaboration: Reinforcing professional bridges to serve aging populations with multiple service needs. *Journal of Rehabilitation, 69*(2), 32–37. Retrieved March 12, 2005, from www.findarticles.com

Harrington, M., Perez-Johnson, I., Meckstroth, A., Bellotti, J., & Love. J. M. (2000). *Protecting children from substance abuse:Lessons learned from Free to Grow Head Start partnerships.* Princeton, NJ: Mathematica Policy Research.

Harry, B. (1996). *Cultural diversity, families, and the special education system: Communication and empowerment.* New York: Teachers College Press.

Harry, B. (2002). Trends and issues in serving culturally diverse families of children with disabilities. *The Journal of Special Education, 36*(3), 131–138.

Harry, B., Allen, N., & McLaughlin, M. (1995). Communication versus compliance: African American parents' involvement in special education. *Exceptional Children, 61*(4), 364–377.

Harry, B., Kalyanpur, M., & Day, M. (1999). *Building cultural reciprocity with families.* Baltimore: Paul H. Brookes.

Hart, D., Zafft, C., & Zimbrich, K. (2001). Creating access to postsecondary education for all students. *The Journal for Vocational Special Needs Education, 23*(2), 19–30.

Hart, D., Zimbrich, K., & Ghiloni, C. (2001). Interagency partnerships and funding: Individual supports for youth with significant disabilities as they move into postsecondary education and employment options. *Journal of Vocational Rehabilitation, 16*, 145–154.

Hart, D., Zimbrich, K., & Whelley, T. (2002). *Challenges in coordinating and managing services and supports in secondary and postsecondary options.* [Issue Brief, 1(6)]. Minneapolis, MN: National Center for Secondary Education and Transition.

Hart, M. (1995). *Guide to sustainable community indicators.* OLF/Atlantic Center for the Environment. Princeton, NJ: Mathematica Policy Research.

Harter, S., Whitesell, N. R., & Kowalski, P. (1992). Individual differences in the effects of educational transitions on young adolescents' perceptions of competence and motivational orientation. *American Educational Research Journal, 29*, 777–808.

Harvard Civil Rights Project. (2004). *No Child Left Behind: A federal, state, and district-level look at the first year.* Retrieved August 10, 2005, from http://www.gse.harvard.edu/news/features/orfield02092004.html

Harvard Family Research Project. (1997). *New skills for new schools: Preparing teachers in family involvement.* Cambridge, MA: Harvard Family Research Project.

Hasazi, S., Furney, K., & DeStefano, L. (1999). Implementing the IDEA transition mandates. *Exceptional Children, 65*(4), 555–566.

Hasazi, S. B., Gordon, L. R., & Roe, C. A. (1985). Factors associated with the employment status of handicapped youth exiting high school from 1979 to 1983. *Exceptional Children, 51*, 455–469.

Hasnain, R. (2001). *Entering adulthood with a disability: Individual, family, and cultural challenges.* Unpublished doctoral dissertation, Boston University, Boston.

Haugaard, J. J. (2000). *Problematic behaviors during adolescence.* New York: McGraw-Hill.

Hausslein, E. B., Kaufman, R. H., & Hurth, J. (1992). From case management to service coordination: Families, policymaking and Part H. *Zero to Three, 12*(3), 10–12.

Havelock, R. (1995). *The change agent's guide* (2nd ed.). Englewood Cliffs, NJ: Educational Technology Publications.

Hawaii State Improvement Grant. (2004). *Interagency Team Demonstration Project.* Retrieved May 12, 2005, from http://www.sig.hawaii.edu/demonstration_project/demo.htm

Hayden, P., Frederick. L., & Smith, B. (2003). *A roadmap for facilitating collaborative teams.* Longmont, CO: Sopris West.

Haynes, N. M. (2002). Addressing students' social and emotional needs: The role of mental health teams in schools. *Journal of Health Social Policy, 16*(1–2), 109–123.

Head Start Information and Publication Center. (2001). *Easing the transition from preschool to kindergarten: A guide for early childhood teachers and administrators.* Washington, DC: Head Start Bureau.

HEATH Resource Center. (2005). *Frequently asked questions.* Washington, DC: George Washington University. Retrieved July 21, 2006, from http://www.heath.gwu.edu/usefulanswers.htm

HEATH Resource Center. (2006). *Counselor's toolkit: Advising high school students with disabilities on postsecondary options.* Washington, DC: George Washington University.

Hebbeler, K., Wagner, M., Spiker, D., Scarborough, A., Simeonsson, R., & Collier, M. (2001). *A first look at *the characteristics of children and families entering early intervention services.* Menlo Park, CA: SRI International.

Hefner-Packer, R. (1991). *Alternative education programs: A prescription for success* [Monographs in Education]. Athens: The University of Georgia.

Hefner-Packer, R. (1995). *Alternative education programs: A prescription for success.* Athens: The University of Georgia.

Hegel, G. (1807). *The phenomenology of mind.* Translated by J. B. Baillie, 2nd edition, 2003. Mineola, NY: Dover Publications.

Heleen, O. (1992). Is your school family friendly? There are a number of ways to effectively link schools with families and communities. *Principal, 72*(2), 5–8.

Henderson, A. T. (1987). *The evidence continues to grow: Parent involvement improves student achievement.* Columbia, MD: National Committee for Citizens in Education.

Henderson, A. T., & Berla, N. (1994). *A new generation of evidence: The family is critical to student achievement.* Washington, DC: Center for Law and Education. (ERIC Document Reproduction Service No. ED375968). Retrieved February 12, 2005, from http//www.edrs.com/Webstore/Detail.asp?q1+@MetaPubID%20391384

Henderson, A. T., Mapp, K., Jordan, C., Orozco, E., Averett, A., Donnelly, D., et al. (2003). *A new wave of evidence: The impact of school, family, and community connections on student achievement.* Austin, TX: Southwest Educational Development Laboratory.

Henderson, A., & Raimondo, B. (2002). Every child counts: Citizens tackle school district's achievement gap. *Middle Ground: The Magazine of Middle Level Education, 5*(4), 1–3.

Henderson, C. (1999). *College freshmen with disabilities: Statistical year 1998.* Washington, DC: American Council on Education.

Henderson, C. (2001). *College freshmen with disabilities: A biennial statistical profile.* Washington, DC: American Council on Education.

Henderson, K. (2002). *Study of state and local implementation and impact of the Individuals with Disabilities Education Act, Final Report on Focus Study I,* July 22, 2002. Washington, DC: U.S. Department of Education, Office of Special Education Programs.

Henderson, K. (2003). *Study of state and local implementation and impact of the Individuals with Disabilities Education Act, Final Report on Selected Findings.* Washington, DC: U.S. Department of Education, Office of Special Education Programs.

Herasymowych, M. (1996). Building learning organizations: Managing change means managing learning. *Infomine, 3*(3), May–June, 1–4.

Herasymowych, M., & Herasymowych, S. (2000). The new sciences and the learning organization: Old brains at work. *InfoMine, 7*(2), 1–2.

Heron, J., & Reason, P. (2001). The practice of co-operative inquiry: Research 'with' rather than 'on' people. In P. Reason & H. Bradbury (Eds.), *Handbook of Action Research.* London: Sage Publications.

Herring, R. (1998). *Career counseling in schools: Multicultural and developmental perspectives.* Washington, DC: American Counseling Association.

Herzog, C., & Morgan, P. (1999). Breaking the barriers between middle school and high school: Developing a transition team for student success. *NASSP Bulletin, 82*(597), 94–98.

Hertzog, C. J., Morgan, P. L., Diamond, P. A., & Walker, M. J. (1996). Transition to high school: A look at student perceptions. *Becoming, 7*(2), 6–8.

Hesselbein, F., Goldsmith, M., & Somerville, I. (2001). *Leading for innovation and organizing for results.* San Francisco: Jossey-Bass.

Heubert, J., & Hauser, R. (1999). *High stakes: Testing for tracking, promotion and graduation.* National Research Council. Washington, DC: National Academy Press.

Hiatt-Michael, D. (2000). *Parent involvement as a component of teacher education programs in California.* Paper presented at the annual meeting of the American Educational Research Association, New Orleans.

Higher Education Act of 1965, Pub. L. 89–329, § 79 Stat. 1219.

Higher Education Act Amendments of 1998, Pub. L. No. 105–244, 20 U.S.C. § 1001 *et seq.* [Title II, Section 201. Teacher Quality] (1998).

Higher Education Funding Council of England. (2002). *Evaluation of collaboration in the higher education sector.* Bristol, England: Author.

Higher Education Funding Council of England. (2003). *Evaluation of collaboration between HEIs and FECs to increase participation in higher education.* Staffordshire, UK: Institute for Access Studies, Staffordshire University.

Hiltenbrand, D. (n.d.). *Collaboration for interagency coordination.* Unpublished paper, George Washington University, Washington, DC.

Himmelman, A. (1992). *Communities working collaboratively for a change* [Monograph]. Minneapolis, MN: The Himmelman Consulting Group.

Himmelman, A. (1996). Collaboration and the three T's: Time, trust and turf constraints. *Health Systems Leader, 3*(10), 13–16.

Hinde, E. (2003). Reflections on reform: A former teacher looks at school change and the factors that shape it. *Teachers College Record*, August 3, 2003. Retrieved August 6, 2005, from http://www.tcrecord.org (ID Number: 11183)

Hinde, E. R. (2002). *Switching classes: Teachers' conceptualizations of change in their professional lives.* Unpublished doctoral dissertation, Arizona State University, Tempe.

Hinde, R., & Groebel, J. (Eds.). (1991). *Cooperation and prosocial behavior.* Cambridge: Cambridge University Press.

Hines, R. (2001). *Inclusion in middle schools.* Champaign, IL: ERIC Clearinghouse on Elementary and Early Childhood Education.

Hines, R. A., & Johnston, J. H. (1996). Inclusive classrooms: The principal's role in promoting achievement. *Schools in the Middle, 5*(3), 6–11.

Hinton, C., Weil, M., Rounds, K., & Zipper, I. (1993). *Family-centered service coordination: A manual for parents.* Newton Upper Falls, MA: Brookline Books.

Hipp, K., & Huffman, J. (2002, April). *Documenting and examining practices in creating learning communities: Exemplars and non-exemplars.* Paper presented at the annual meeting of the American Educational Research Association, New Orleans.

Hirsch, B. J., & Rapkin, B. D. (1987). The transition to junior high school: A longitudinal study of self-esteem, psychological symptomatology, school life, and social support. *Child Development, 58*, 1235–1243.

Hitchcock, C. (2001). Balanced instructional support and challenge in universally designed learning environments. *Journal of Special Education Technology, 16*(4), 23–30.

Hitchcock, C., Meyer, A., Rose, D., & Jackson, R. (2002). *Technical brief: Access, participation, and progress in the general curricula.* Peabody, MA: National Center on Accessing the General Curricula. Retrieved May 20, 2005, from http://www.cast.org/ncac/index.cfm?i=2830

Hoagwood, K., Burns, B., Kiser, L., Ringeisen, H., & Schoenwald, S. (2001). Evidence-based practice in child and adolescent mental health services. *Psychiatric Services, 52*(9), 1179–1189.

Hocutt, A. M., McKinney, J. D., Montague, M. (2002). The impact of managed care on efforts to prevent development of serious emotional disturbance in young children. *Journal of Disability Policy Studies, 13*(1), 51–60.

Hodgkinson, B. (2003). *Leaving too many children behind: A demographer's view on the tragic neglect of American's youngest children.* Washington, DC: Institute for Educational Leadership.

Hoey, P. (2001). *Examination arrangements for students with disabilities—A guide for institutions of higher education.* Dublin: AHEAD Education Press.

Hoff, D. (2000). *Access for all: A resource manual for meeting the needs of one-stop customers with disabilities.* Boston: National Center on Workforce and Disability, Institute for Community Inclusion.

Hofferth, S. L., Henke, R. R., & West, J. (1998). *Characteristics of children's early care and education programs: Data from the 1995 National Household Education Survey.* Washington, DC.: U.S. Department of Education, National Center for Education Statistics.

Hogue, T., Perkins, D., Clark, R., Bergstrom, A., & Slinski, M. (1995). *Collaboration framework: addressing community capacity.* Columbus, OH: National Network for Collaboration.

Holland, J. L. (1985). *Manual for vocational preference inventory.* Odessa, FL: Psychological Assessment.

Hooks, B. (1994). *Teaching to transgress: Education as the practice of freedom.* New York: Routledge.

Hooper-Briar, K., & Lawson, H. (1994). *Serving children, youth and families through inter-professional collaboration and service integration: A framework for action.* Oxford, OH: The Danforth Foundation and the Institute for Educational Renewal at Miami University.

Hoover, J. & Stenhjem, P. (2003). Bullying and teasing of youth with disabilities: Creating positive school environments for effective inclusion. National Center on Secondary Education and Transition, *Issue Brief, 2*(3), 1–5. Available at http://www.ncset.org/publications/printresource.asp?id=1332

Hoover-Dempsey, K., & Sandler, H. (1997). Why do parents become involved in their children's education? *Review of Educational Research, 67*(1), 3–42.

Hoover-Dempsey, K., Walker, J., Jones, K., & Reed, R. (2000, April). *Teachers involving parents (TIP): An inservice teacher education program for enhancing parental involvement.* Paper presented at the annual meeting of the American Education Research Association, New Orleans.

Hord, S. M. (1980). *Distinguishing between cooperation and collaboration: A case study approach to understanding their relative requirements and outcomes.* Presented at the annual meeting of the American Educational Research Association, Boston.

Hord, S. M. (1997). Professional learning communities: What are they and why are they important? *Issues About Change, 6*(1), 1–8. Retrieved July 15, 2005, from http://www.sedl.org/pubs/

Horn, L., & Berktold, J. (1999). *Students with disabilities in postsecondary education: A profile of preparation, participation, and outcomes.* Washington, DC: National Center for Education Statistics, U.S. Department of Education. (NCES #1999–187)

Horn, R. (2001, September). *The Workforce Investment Act (WIA): Creating opportunities for youth with disabilities.* Teleconference, National Center for Secondary Education and Transition, Minneapolis.

Horne, R., & Morris, S. (1998). Transition of youth with disabilities. *Liaison Bulletin, 28*(4), Alexandria, VA: National Association of State Directors of Special Education.

Hough, D. L. (1997). A bona fide middle school: Programs, policy, practice, and grade span configurations. In J. L. Irwin (Ed.), *What current research says to the middle level practitioner* (pp. 285–294). Columbus, OH: National Middle School Association.

Hough, D. L. (2003). *Research, rhetoric, and reality: A study of studies addressing NMSA's 21st century research agenda.* Columbus, OH: National Middle School Association.

Hough, D. L., & Irwin, J. L. (1997). Research in middle level education. In J. L. Irwin (Ed.), *What current research says to the middle level practitioner* (pp. 3–11). Columbus, OH: National Middle School Association.

Howard, G. (1993). Whites in multicultural education: Rethinking our role. *Phi Delta Kappan, 75*, 36–41.

Hudson, P., & Glomb, N. (1997). If it takes two to tango, then why not teach both partners to dance? Collaboration instruction for all educators. *Journal of Learning Disabilities, 30*, 442–448.

Huffman, L. R., & Speer, P. W. (2000). Academic performance among at-risk children: The role of developmentally appropriate practices. *Early Childhood Research Quarterly, 15*, 167–184.

Huffman, T. (2003). A comparison of personal assessments of the college experience among reservation and non-reservation American Indian students. *Journal of American Indian Education Abstracts, 42,*(2), 1–16.

Hume, D. (1921). *An enquiry concerning human understanding.* London: Keynes, J. (Original work published 1748)

Hunt, P. (2000). 'Community' is what I think everyone is talking about. *Remedial and Special Education, 21*(5), 305.

Hunter, R. (1905). *Poverty.* New York: Harper & Row.

Hurth, J. (1998). *NECTAS service coordination caseloads in state early intervention systems.* Chapel Hill, NC: NECTAS.

Husock, H. (1993). *Democracy and public management cases.* Cambridge, MA: Fellows of Harvard College, John F. Kennedy School of Government.

Husted, S. W., Mason, R. E., & Adams, E. (2003). *Cooperative occupational education.* Upper Saddle River: Prentice Hall.

Husu, J. (2001). Teachers at cross-purposes: A case-report approach to the study of ethical dilemmas in teaching. *Journal of Curriculum and Supervision, 17*(1), 67–89.

Hutt, M., Stafford, E., Walker, B., & Heingen, P. (2000). Case study: Defining the social network of a strategic alliance. *Sloan Management Review, 41*(2), 51–62.

Ianacone, R. N., & Kochhar, C. A. (1996). Great expectations: Perspectives on transition policy and practice in the context of social change. *Career Development for Exceptional Individuals, 19*(1), 177–200.

Idol, L., & Nevin, A., & Paolucci-Whitcomb, P. (1994). *Collaborative consultation* (2nd ed.). Austin, TX: PRO-ED.

Illback, R. J., Cobb, C. T., & Joseph, H. M. (Eds.). (1997). *Integrated services for children and families: Opportunities for psychological practice.* Washington, DC: American Psychological Association.

Imel, S. (1999). Focusing groups in adult learning: Theory and practice. *Journal of Continuing Education in the Health Professions, 19*(1), 54–61.

Independent Living Resource Center. (2005). *Independent Living Services.* Retrieved February 12, 2005, from http://www.ilrcks.org/do.html

Individuals With Disabilities Education Act, P. L. 105–17. Final Rules and Regulations, 34 C.F.R. § 300.533 *et seq. Federal Register, 64*(48) (March 12, 1999).

Individuals With Disabilities Education Act Amendments, 20 U.S.C. 1400 (1997).

Individuals With Disabilities Education Act of 1990, P. L. 101–476, 20 U.S.C. § 1400 *et seq.*

Individuals With Disabilities Education Act of 1997, S. Rep. (to accompany S. 717) No. 46, 105th Cong., 1st Sess. (1997).

Individuals With Disabilities Education Act Amendments of 1997, P. L. 105–17, 20 USC § 1400 *et seq.*

Individuals With Disabilities Education Act Amendments of 2004, P.L. 108–446, 20 USC β 1400 *et seq.*

Infant Mental Health Forum. (2000, October). *A commitment to supporting the mental health of our youngest children.* Arlington, VA: Author.

Information Today. (1996, November/December). Caught in the middle, U.S. middle schools on the Web. *MultiMedia Schools.* Medford, NJ: Author.

Inger, M. (1993). *Teacher collaboration in secondary schools.* Berkeley, CA: National Center for Research in Vocational Education.

Ingram, D., Bloomberg, L., & Seppanen, P. (1996). *Collaborative initiatives to develop integrated services for children and families: A review of the literature.* Minneapolis: Center for Applied Research and Educational Improvement, University of Minnesota.

International Association of Facilitators. (2004). *Statement of values and code of ethics for facilitators.* St. Paul, MN: Author.

International Reading Association. (1995). *Learning disabilities—A barrier to literacy instruction.* Washington, DC: Author.

Interstate New Teacher Assessment and Support Consortium. (2001, May). *Model standards for licensing general and special education teachers of students with disabilities.* Washington, DC: Special Education Sub-Committee, Council of Chief State School Officers.

Interstate School Leaders Licensure Consortium. (1996). *Interstate School Leaders Licensure Consortium Standards for School Leaders,* (pp. 13–14). Washington, DC: Council of Chief State School Officers.

Institute on Community Integration. (1994). *Competencies for interdisciplinary collaboration and interagency coordination in early intervention, transition from school to adult life, and children's mental health services.* Minneapolis: University of Minnesota.

Institute on Community Integration. (1998). A person-centered planning with youth and adults who have developmental disabilities. *Impact, 11*(2). Minneapolis: College of Education & Human Development, University of Minnesota.

Institute for Educational Leadership. (1994). *Preparing collaborative leaders: A facilitator's guide.* Washington, DC: Author.

Institute for Educational Leadership. (2001). *Leadership for student learning: Recognizing the state's role in public education* (p. 23). Washington, DC: Author.

Institute for Educational Leadership. (2003). *The thin book of appreciative inquiry, and lessons from the field: Applying appreciative inquiry.* Washington, DC: Author.

Intagliata, J. (1982). Improving the quality of community care for the chronically disabled: The role of case management. *Schizophrenic Bulletin 1982, 8*(4), 655–674.

Izzo, M., Hertzfeld, J., Simmons-Reed, E., & Aaron, J. (2001). Promising practices: Improving the quality of higher education for students with disabilities. *Disability Studies Quarterly, 21*(1), Winter, 1–18.

Jackson, A., & Davis, G. (2000). *Turning Points 2000: Educating adolescents in the 21st century* (pp. 24–25). New York: Teachers College Press.

Jackson, T. (2003). *Secondary transition coordinators at the state level.* Project Forum Brief. Alexandria, VA: National Association of State Directors of Special Education.

James, W. J., Osguthorpe, R. T., & Hite, S. J. (2002). A framework for increasing reflection in the instructional design process. *Journal of Educational Research, Theory, and Practice in East Africa, 3*(2), 30–33.

Janney, R., & Meyer, L. (1990). *Child centered educational consultation to assist schools in serving students with disabilities and severe behavior problems in integrated settings.* New York: Syracuse University, Division of Special Education and Rehabilitation.

Jarvela, S., Lehtinen, E., & Hamalainen, S. (1997, August). *Turning towards a joint task: Goal-oriented teacher–student interaction and reciprocal understanding.* Paper presented at the symposium: Technologies and social tools for apprenticeship and perspective taking: Research emerging on various fronts. 7th European Conference for Research on Learning and Instruction, Athens, Greece.

Jarzabkowski, L. (2001, December). *The social dimensions of teacher collegiality.* Paper presented at the annual conference of the Australian Association of Research in Education, Notre Dame University, Perth. (JAR01124)

Jenkins, J., Jewell, M., Leicester, N., O'Connor, R. E., Jenkins, L., & Troutner, N. M. (1994). Accommodations for individual differences without classroom ability groups: An experiment in school restructuring. *Exceptional Children, 60*(4), 344–359.

Jenni, R., & Mauriel, J. (2004). Cooperation and collaboration: Reality or rhetoric? *International Journal of Leadership in Education, 7*(2), 181–195.

Jennings, J. (2003a). *From the capitol to the classroom: State and federal efforts to implement the No Child Left Behind Act.* Washington, DC: Center on Education Policy.

Jennings, J. (2003b). *A tale of three cities: Urban perspectives on special education.* Washington, DC: Center on Education Policy.

Jensen, E. (1998). *Teaching with the brain in mind.* Alexandria, VA: Association for Supervision and Curriculum Development.

Jersild, A. (1955). *When teachers face themselves.* Columbia University: Teachers College Press.

Jewett, J., Tertell, L., King-Taylor, M., Parker, D., Tertell, L., & Orr, M. (1998). *Four early childhood teachers reflect on helping children with special needs make the transition to kindergarten.* Washington, DC: American Psychological Association.

Job Training Improvement Act of 2005, H.R. 27, 109th Cong. (2005).

Johns Hopkins University. (2000, April/May). *Focusing on middle schools: Johns Hopkins develops new whole school reform mode.* Baltimore, MD: Center for Social Organization of Schools.

Johnson, C. (2001). *Supporting families in transition between early intervention and school age programs.* Denver, CO: Hands & Voices International.

Johnson, D. (2005, January 15). *National standards for secondary education and transition for all youth.* Teleconference transcript, National Center on Secondary Education and Transition, Minneapolis, MN.

Johnson, D. R., & Sharpe, M. (2000). *Analysis of local education agency efforts to implement the transition services requirements of IDEA of 1990.* Minneapolis: University of Minnesota, Institute on Community Integration.

Johnson, D. R., Sharpe, M., & Sinclair, M. (1997). *Evaluating state and local efforts to implement the Part B transition service requirements of the Individuals with Disabilities Education Act.* Minneapolis: University of Minnesota, Institute on Community Integration.

Johnson, D. R., Stodden, R. A, Emanuel, E. J., Luecking, R., & Mack, M. (2002). Current challenges facing secondary education and transition services: What research tells us. *Exceptional Children, 68*(4), 519–531.

Johnson, D. R., & Thurlow, M. L. (2003). *A national study on graduation requirements and diploma options for youth with disabilities* [Technical Report No. 36]. Minneapolis: University of Minnesota, National Center on Educational Outcomes.

Johnson, D. W., & Johnson, R. T. (1998). Cooperative learning and social interdependence theory. In R. Tindale, L. Heath, J. Edwards, E. Posavac, F. Bryant, Y. Suzrez-Balcazar, et al. (Eds.), *Theory and research on small groups: Vol. 4. Social psychological applications to social issues* (pp. 9–36). New York: Plenum.

Johnson, D. W., Johnson, R. T., & Stanne, M. B. (2000). *Cooperative learning methods: A meta-analysis.* Minneapolis: University of Minnesota.

Johnson, L. J., Cook, M., & Yongue, C. P. (1990). *Capstone transition process.* Unpublished manuscript, University of Alabama, Tuscaloosa.

Johnson, L. J., Zorn, D., Tam, B., Lamontagne, M., & Johnson, S. A. (2003). Stakeholders' views of factors that impact successful interagency collaboration. *Exceptional Children, 69*(2), 195–209.

John-Steiner, V., Weber, R. J., & Minnis, M. (1998). The challenge of studying collaboration. *American Educational Research Journal, 35*(4), 773–83.

Johnston, M. (1997). *Contradictions in collaboration: New thinking on school–university partnerships.* New York: Teachers College Press.

Jones, R. (2001). Involving parents is a whole new game: Be sure you win! *Education Digest, 67*(3) 36–44.

Jones, T. A., Klintsova, A. Y., Kilman, V. L., Sireyaag, A. M., & Greenough, W. T. (1997). Induction of multiple synapses by experience in the visual cortex of adult rats. *Neurobiology of Learning and Memory, 68*(1), 13–20.

Jonikas, J. A., & Cook, J. A. (2004). *This is your life! Creating your self-directed life plan.* [NRTC Self-Determination Series]. Chicago: National Research & Training Center on Psychiatric Disability, University of Illinois at Chicago.

Jordan, W., Lara, J., & McPartland, J. (1998). *Exploring the complexity of early dropout causal structures, in school expulsions, suspensions, and dropouts.* Bloomington, IN: Phi Delta Kappa International.

Jorgensen, C. M. (Ed.). (1998). *Restructuring high schools for all students: Taking inclusion to the next level.* Baltimore: Paul H. Brookes.

Joyce, B. (1990). *Changing school culture through staff development.* Alexandria, VA: American Society for Curriculum Development.

Justesen, T. R., & Justesen, T. R. (2000). *Helping more students with disabilities prepare for college: A review of research literature and suggested steps GEAR UP grantees can take.* Washington, DC: U.S. Department of Education, Office of Postsecondary Education, Gaining Early Awareness and Readiness for Undergraduate Programs (GEAR UP).

Kagan, J. (2003). Biology, context, and developmental inquiry. *Annual Reviews in Psychology, 15*(49), 7.2–7.20.

Kalyanpur, M., & Harry, B. (1997). A posture of reciprocity: A practical approach to collaboration between professionals and parents of culturally diverse backgrounds. *Journal of Child and Family Studies, 6,* 73–76.

Kalyanpur, M., & Harry, B. (1999). *Culture in special education: Building reciprocal family–professional relationships.* Baltimore: Paul H. Brookes.

Kagan, S. L. (1994, April). *Defining America's commitments to parents and families: An historical–conceptual perspective.* New Haven, CT: Yale University Press.

Kagan, S. L., & Neuman, M. J. (1998). Lessons from three decades of transition research. *The Elementary School Journal, 98*(4), 365–379.

Kagan, S. L., & Neville, P. (1993). *Integrating services for children and families: Understanding the past to shape the future.* New Haven, CT: Yale University Press.

Kame'enui, E. J., Carnine, D. W., Dixon, R. C., Simmons, D. C., & Coyne, M. D. (2002). *Effective teaching strategies that accommodate diverse learners* (2nd ed.). Upper Saddle River, NJ: Merrill/Prentice Hall.

Kampwith, T. (1998). *Collaborative consultation in the schools: Effective practices for students with learning and behavior problems.* Upper Saddle River, NJ: Merrill/Prentice Hall.

Kaplan-Sanoff, M., Lerner, C., & Bernard, A. (2000). New roles for developmental specialists in pediatric primary care. *Zero to Three, 21*(2), 17–23.

Kargiannis, A., Stainback, S., & Stainback, W. (1996). Rationale for inclusive schooling. In S. Stainback & W. Stainback, *Inclusion: A guide for educators.* Baltimore, MD: Paul H. Brookes.

Kasl, E., & Yorks, L. (2002, January). An extended epistemology for transformative learning theory and its application through collaborative inquiry. *Teachers College Record,* 1–12. Retrieved August 6, 2005, from http://www.tcrecord.org (ID 10878)

Kasl, E., & Yorks, L. (2004). Collaborative inquiry for adult learning. In L. Yorks & E. Kasl (Eds.), Collaborative inquiry as a strategy for adult learning: Creating space for generative learning. *New Directions for Adult and Continuing Education* (p. 94). San Francisco: Jossey-Bass.

Katz, L., Aidman, A., Reese, D., & Clark, A. (1996). *How can we prevent and resolve parent–teacher differences?* ERIC Clearinghouse on Elementary and Early Childhood Education. Washington, DC: National Library of Education, Office of Educational Research and Improvement, U.S. Department of Education.

Katz, L., & Bauch, J. P. (1999). The Peabody family involvement initiative: Preparing preservice teachers for family/school collaboration. *The School Community Journal, 9*, 49–69.

Katz, L. G. (1995). Mothering and teaching: Significant distinctions. In L. G. Katz, *Talks with teachers of young children: A collection.* Norwood, NJ: Ablex. (ED 380 232)

Katz, L. G. (1996). Building resilience: Helping your child cope with frustrations at school. *Instructor, 106*(3), 95–98.

Katz, M., Miller, M., & Peters, K. (2002). Academic democracy: Pursuing faculty involvement. *Collegiate Governance, Planning and Changing, 34*(1&2), 15–30.

Katzman, L., Gandhi, A., Harbour, W., & LaRock, J. (Eds.). (2005). *Special education for a new century.* Cambridge, MA: Harvard Education Press.

Kauffman, J. M., & Brigham, F. J. (2000). Zero tolerance and bad judgment in working with students with emotional or behavioral disorders. *Behavioral Disorders, 25*, 277–279.

Kaufman, D. (1980). *Systems one: An introduction to systems thinking.* Minneapolis, MN: The Innovative Learning Series, Future Systems.

Kaye, H. S. (2000). Computer and Internet use among people with disabilities. *Disability Statistics Report, 13.* Washington, DC: U.S. Department of Education, National Institute on Disability and Rehabilitation Research.

Kendziora, K., Bruns, E., Osher, D., Pacchiona, D., & Mejia, B. (2001). *Systems of care: Promising practices in children's mental health, Series* (p. 1). Washington, DC: Center for Effective Collaboration and Practice, American Institutes for Research. Retrieved May 12, 2005, from http://cecp.air.org/AIRMonograph.pdf

Kennedy, C. H., & Itkonen, T. (1994). Some effects of regular class participation on the social contacts and social networks of high school students with severe disabilities. *Journal of the Association for Persons with Severe Handicaps, 19*, 1–10.

Kennedy, M. M. (1984). How evidence alters understanding and decisions. *Educational Evaluation and Policy Analysis, 6*(3), 207–226.

Kerka, S. (1989). *Cooperative education: Characteristics and effectiveness.* (ERIC Digest Report No. 91). Columbus, OH: ERIC Clearinghouse on Adult Career and Vocational Education. (ERIC Document Reproduction Service No. ED312455)

Kerka, S. (1998). *Adults with learning disabilities: Definitions and issues.* Washington, DC: National Adult Literacy and Learning Disabilities Center. (ED414434)

Kerka, S. (1999). *New directions for cooperative education.* Columbus, OH: ERIC Clearinghouse on Career and Vocational Education. (ERIC Document Reproduction Service No. EDO-CE-99-209)

Kerka, S. (2000). *Parenting and career development.* Columbus, OH: ERIC Clearinghouse on Adult Career and Vocational Education. (ERIC Document Reproduction Service No. 214)

Ketterson, T. U., & Blustein, D. L. (1997). Attachment relationships and the career exploration process. *Career Development Quarterly, 46*(2), 167–178. (EJ 562 308)

Kidscount. (2003a). *Percent of children in poverty.* Washington, DC: Center for Effective Collaboration and Practice, American Institutes for Research. Retrieved December 12, 2002, from http://www.aecf.org/kidscount/kc2002/summary.htm

Kidscount. (2003b). *Percent of families with children headed by a single parent.* Retrieved October 15, 2003, from http://www.aecf.org/kidscount/kc2002/summary.htm

Kilgore, K. L., Griffin, C. C., Sindelar, P. T., & Webb, R. B. (2001). Restructuring for inclusion: A story of middle school renewal (Part I). *Middle School Journal, 33*(2), 44–51.

Kilgore, K. L., & Webb, R. B. (1997). Making shared decision making work. *Middle School Journal, 28*(5), 3–13.

Kim-Rupnow, W. S., Dowrick, P. W., & Burke, L. S. (2001). Improving access and outcomes for individuals with disabilities in postsecondary distance education. *American Journal of Distance Education, 15*(1), 25–40.

Kincaid, D., & Fox, L. (2002). Person-centered planning and positive behavior support. In S. Holburn & P. Vietze (Eds.), *Person-centered planning: Research, practice, and future directions* (pp. 29–49). Baltimore: Paul H. Brookes. Retrieved May 13, 2005, from http://www.findarticles.com/p/articles/mi_m0NQM/is_1_41/ai_90190487/pg_1

King, A. (2002). Structuring peer interaction to promote high level cognitive processing. *Theory Into Practice, 41*(1), Winter, 265–267.

King-Sears, M. E. (1997). Best academic practices for inclusive classrooms. *Focus on Exceptional Children, 29*(7), 1–22.

Kirst, M. (1994, September). *School-linked services: Appraisal, financing, and future directions.* Paper prepared for the AERA/OERI Conference on School Linked Services, Leesburg, VA.

Kirst, M., & Jehl, J. (1995). *Getting ready to provide school-linked, integrated services.* Oak Brook, IL: North Central Regional Educational Laboratory.

Kline, S. A., Simpson, R. L., Blesz, D. P., Myles, B. S., & Carter, W. J. (2001). School reform and multicultural learners with emotional and behavioral disorders: Issues, challenges, and solutions. In C. A. Utley & F. E. Obiakor (Eds.), *Special education, multicultural education, and school reform: Components of quality education for learners with mild disabilities* (pp. 118–129). Springfield, IL: Charles C. Thomas.

Knapp, M. S. (1995). How shall we study comprehensive, collaborative services for children and families? *Educational Researcher, 24*(5), 5–16.

Knight, D., & Wadsworth, D. (1999). Is the development of family/school partnerships promoted in the nation's special education teacher preparation programs? *Contemporary Education, 70*(2), 22–28.

Knight, S. L., & Boudah, D. (2003). Using participatory research and development to impact student outcomes. In D. Wiseman & S. Knight (Eds.), *The impact of school–university collaboration on K–12 student outcomes.* Washington, DC: American Association of Colleges of Teacher Education.

Knight, S. L., & Stallings, J. (1998). Increasing the academic and social success of children, youth, and families: Case study of an alternative program. In D. van Veen, C. Day, & G. Walraven (Eds.), *Multi-service schools: Integrated services for children and youth at risk* (pp. 99–114). Leuven/Apeldoorn, The Netherlands: Garant Publishers.

Knitzer, J. (2000). Early childhood mental health services: A policy and systems development perspective. In J. P. Shonkoff & S. J. Meisels (Eds.), *Handbook of early childhood intervention second edition* (pp. 416–438). Cambridge: Cambridge University Press.

Knoff, H. M. (2002). Best practices in facilitating school reform, organizational change, and strategic planning. In A. Thomas & J. grimes (Eds.), *Best practices in school psychology-IV* (pp. 235–254). Washington, DC: National Association of School Psychologists.

Knott, L., & Asselin, S. B. (1999). Transition competencies: Perception of secondary special education teachers. *Teacher Education and Special Education, 22,* 55–65.

Knowledge Works Foundation. (2002). *Ohio education matters: Schools as centers of community: 2001–2002 poll.* Cincinnati, OH: Author.

Knowles, M. (1998). *The adult learner: The definitive classic in adult education and human resource development.* Burlington, MA: Gulf Professional Publishing.

Kochan, F. K., Bredeson, P. V., & Riehl, C. (2002). Rethinking the professional development of school leaders. *Yearbook of the National Society for the Study of Education, 101*(1), 289–306.

Kochhar, C. (1995). *Training for interagency, interdisciplinary service coordination: An instructional modules series.* Des Moines, IA: Iowa State Department of Education and the Mountain Plains Regional Resource Center, Drake University.

Kochhar, C. A. (1998a). *Literature synthesis on alternative schools and programs for violent, chronically disruptive and delinquent youth.* Washington, DC: Hamilton Fish Institute on School and Community

Violence, The George Washington University, Institute for Educational Policy Studies.

Kochhar, C. A. (1998b). Analysis of the special populations provisions in the 1998 Carl D. Perkins Vocational Technical Education Act Amendments. *Journal for Vocational Special Needs Education, 21*(1), 3–20.

Kochhar, C. A. (1998c). New vocational rehabilitation law revitalizes transition services. *Journal for Vocational Special Needs Education, 20*(2), 3–11.

Kochhar, C. A. (1999). *Synthesis of state needs and barriers to systemic reform in the 1998 special education state improvement grants.* Washington, DC: Academy for Educational Development.

Kochhar, C., & Gopal, M. (1997). The concept of full participation in promoting sustainable educational development. In J. Lynch, C. Modgil, & S. Modgil (Eds.), *Education and development: Concepts, approaches and assumptions.* London: Cassell Publishers.

Kochhar, C., & West, L. (1995). Future directions in federal legislation affecting transition services for individuals with special needs. *Journal of Vocational Special Needs Education, 17*(3), 85–93.

Kochhar, C., & West, L. (1996). *Handbook for successful inclusion.* Rockville, MD: Aspen Publishers.

Kochhar, C., West, L., & Taymans, J. (2000). *Successful inclusion: Practical strategies for a shared responsibility.* (2nd ed.). Upper Saddle River, NJ: Merrill/Prentice Hall.

Kochhar-Bryant, C. (2000). *Reflection and teacher education* [Bridging Papers Series]. Washington, DC: George Washington University.

Kochhar-Bryant, C. (2002a). Coordinating systems and agencies for successful transition. In G. Greene & C. Kochhar-Bryant, *Pathways to successful transition for youth with disabilities,* (pp. 108–153). (2nd ed.). Upper Saddle River, NJ: Merrill/Prentice Hall.

Kochhar-Bryant, C. (2002b). Implementing interagency agreements for transition. In G. Greene & C. Kochhar-Bryant, *Pathways to successful transition for youth with disabilities,* (pp. 314–379). (2nd ed.). Upper Saddle River, NJ: Merrill/Prentice Hall.

Kochhar-Bryant, C. (2003). *The quality of state standards for preparing teachers for partnerships with families* [Briefing Paper 2]. Orlando: University of Central Florida.

Kochhar-Bryant, C., & Bassett, D. (Eds.). (2002a). *Aligning transition and standards-based education: Issues and strategies.* Arlington, VA: Council for Exceptional Children.

Kochhar-Bryant, C., & Bassett, D. (2002b). Challenge and promise in aligning transition and standards-based education. In C. A. Kochhar-Bryant & D.S. Bassett (Eds.), *Aligning transition and standards-based education: Issues and strategies* (pp. 1–24). Arlington, VA: Council for Exceptional Children.

Kochhar-Bryant, C., & Lacey, R. (2005). *Alternative education as a quality choice for youth: Preparing educators for effective programs.* Proceedings of the Persistently Safe Schools Conference. Washington, DC: Hamilton Fish Institute on School and Community Violence.

Kochhar-Bryant, C., & Vreeburg-Izzo, M. (Eds). (2006). *Access to post-high school services: Transition assessment and the summary of performance. Special Issue.* Career Development for Exceptional Individuals, Division on Career Development and Transition. Austin, TX: PRO-ED.

Kofman, F., & Senge, P. (1993). Communities of commitment: The heart of learning organizations. *Organizational Dynamics, 22*(2), 5–23.

Kohler, P. D. (1998). Implementing a transition perspective of education: A comprehensive approach to planning and delivering secondary education and transition services. In F. R. Rusch & J. G. Chadsey (Eds.), *Beyond high school: Transition from school to work* (pp. 179–205). New York: Wadsworth Publishing.

Kohler, P. D. (2003). *Taxonomy for transition programming: Worksheet for interagency collaboration practices.* Kalamazoo, MI: Department of Educational Studies, Western Michigan University.

Kohler, P. D., & Hood, L. K. (2000). *Improving student outcomes: Promising practices and programs for 1999–2000. A directory of innovative approaches for providing transition services for youth with disabilities.* Champaign: Transition Research Institute, University of Illinois.

Kokaska, C., & Brolin, D. (1985). *Career education for handicapped individuals.* Upper Saddle River, NJ: Merrill/Prentice Hall.

Kolb, B. (2000). Experience and the developing brain. *Education Canada, 39*(4), 24–26.

Kolb, D. A. (1984). *Experimental learning: Experience as the source of learning and development.* Englewood Cliffs, NJ: Prentice Hall.

Kordalewski, J. (1999). *Incorporating student voice into teaching practice.* New York: ERIC Clearinghouse on Teaching and Teacher Education. (Digest Number 1999–4)

Koskinen, P. S., Blum, I. H., Bisson, S. A., Phillips, S. M., Creamer, T. S., & Baker, T. S. (2000). Book access, shared reading, and audio models: The effects of supporting the literacy learning of linguistically diverse students in school and home. *Journal of Education Psychology, 92*(1), 23–36.

Kowalski, P. S., Harter, S., & Whitesell, N. (1986, March). *Self-perceptions in the transition to seventh grade.* Paper presented at the biennial meeting of the Society for Research on Adolescence, Madison, WI.

Kozleski, E., Mainzer, R., & Deshler, D. (2000). *Bright futures for exceptional learners: An action agenda to achieve quality conditions for teaching and learning.* Arlington, VA: Council for Exceptional Children.

Kracke, B. (1997). Parental behaviors and adolescents' career exploration. *Career Development Quarterly, June, 45*(4), 341–350. (EJ 555 154)

Kraft-Sayre, M. E., & Pianta, R. C. (2000). *Enhancing the transition to kindergarten: Linking children, families, and schools.* Charlottesville: University of Virginia, National Center for Early Development & Learning.

Kraft-Sayre, M. E., & Pianta, R. C. (2001). Enhancing the transition to kindergarten: Connecting families and elementary schools. *Dimensions of Early Childhood, 29*(1), 25–29.

Kroth, R. L., & Edge, D. (1997). *Strategies for communicating with parents and families of exceptional children.* Denver, CO: Love Publishing.

Krouscas, J. (1997). *History of middle schools.* Falls Church: Virginia Middle School Association.

Kubler-Ross, E. (1997). *On death and dying.* New York: Touchstone.

Kumashiro, K. (2001). Posts' perspectives on anti-oppressive education in social studies, English, mathematics, and science classrooms. *Educational Researcher, 30*(3), 3–12.

Kwon, Y., & Lawson, A. E. (2000). Linking brain growth with the development of scientific reasoning ability and conceptual change during adolescence. *Journal of Research in Science Teaching, 37*(1), 44–62.

Kyle, D., & McIntyre, E. (2000). *Family visits benefit teachers and families—and students most of all.* Louisville: University of Kentucky, Center for Research on Education, Diversity, and Excellence.

La Paro, K. M., Pianta, R. C., & Cox, M. J. (2000a). Kindergarten teachers' reported use of kindergarten to first grade transition practices. *Elementary School Journal, 101*(1), 63–78.

La Paro, K. M., Pianta, R., & Cox, M. J. (2000b). Teachers' reported transition practices for children transitioning into kindergarten and first grade. *Exceptional Children, 67,* 7–20.

Lagemann, E. (2000). *An elusive science: The troubling history of educational research.* Chicago: University of Chicago Press.

Lambert, L. (1997). *Who will save our schools: Teachers as constructivist leaders.* Thousand Oaks, CA: Corwin Press.

Lambert, L. (1998). *Building leadership capacity in schools.* Alexandria, VA: ASCD.

Lambert, L. (2003). *Leadership capacity for lasting school improvement.* Alexandria, VA: ASCD.

Lambert, L., Walker, D., Zimmerman, D., Cooper, J., Lambert, M., Gardner, M., & Slack, P. (1995). *The constructivist leader.* New York: Teachers College Press, Columbia University.

Lambie, R. (2000). *Family systems within educational contexts.* Denver, CO: Love Publishing.

Lance, K. C., & Rodney, M. J. (1999). *Proof of the power: A look at the results of the Colorado study . . . and more!* Retrieved July 23, 2005, from http://www.lrs.org/html/about/school_studies.html

Lansdown, G. (2005). *The evolving capacities of the child.* Florence: UNICEF Innocenti Research Centre.

Laufgraben, J., & Shapiro, N. (2004). *Sustaining and improving learning communities.* San Francisco: Jossey-Bass.

Lawrence-Lightfoot, S. (1978). *Worlds apart: Relationships between families and schools.* New York: Basic Books.

Lawson, H. (1998). Collaborative educational leadership for 21st century school communities. In D. van Veen, C. Day, & G. Walraven (Eds.), *Multi-service schools: Integrated services for children and youth at risk* (pp. 173–193). Leuven/Apeldoorn, The Netherlands: Garant Publishers.

Lawson, H. (1999, Fall). Two frameworks for analyzing relationships among school communities, teacher education, and interprofessional education and training programs. *Teacher Education Quarterly,* 9–29.

Lawson, H. (2002). Strengthening democracy by expanding the boundaries of school reform and developing caring school communities for children, youth, and their families. In W. Sailor (Ed.), *Whole-school success and inclusive education: Building partnerships for learning, achievement, and accountability* (pp. vii–xii). New York: Teachers College Press.

Lawson, H., & Briar-Lawson, K. (2001). Family-supportive community schools: Thirteen strategies. In P. Senge & N. Cambron-McCabe (Eds.), *Schools that learn* (pp. 534–536). New York: Doubleday Currency.

Lawson, H., & Hooper-Briar, K. (1994). *Expanding partnerships: Involving colleges and universities in interprofessional collaboration and service integration.* Oxford, OH: Danforth Foundation and Institute for Educational Renewal, Miami University.

Lawson, H., & Sailor, W. (2000). Integrating services, collaborating, and developing connections with schools. *Focus on Exceptional Children, 33*(2), 1–22.

Leake, D., & Cholymay, M. (2003). *Addressing the needs of culturally and linguistically diverse students with disabilities in postsecondary education.* Manoa, HI: CLD Transition Research Project, Center on Disability Studies, University of Hawaii.

Leconte, P. J. (1994). Vocational appraisal services: Evolution from multidisciplinary origins and applications to interdisciplinary practices. *Vocational Evaluation and Work Adjustment Bulletin, 27*(4), 119–127.

Leconte, P. J. (1999). Vocational evaluation. In S. H. deFur & J. R. Patton (Eds.), *Transition and school-based services for enhancing the transition process* (pp. 387–417). Austin, TX: PRO-ED.

Leconte, P. J., & Neubert, N. A. (1997). Vocational assessment: The kick-off point for transition. *Alliance, The Newsletter of the National Transition Alliance, 2*(2), 1, 3–4, 8.

Lee, M. Y. (2003). A solution-focused approach to cross-cultural clinical social work practice: Utilizing cultural strengths. *Families in Society, 84*(3), 385–398.

Lee, P. C., Statuto, C. M., & Kedar-Voivodas, G. (1983). Elementary school children's perceptions of their actual and ideal school experience: A developmental study. *Journal of Educational Psychology, 75,* 838–847.

Lee, V. E., & Smith, J. B. (1995). Effects of high school restructuring and size on early gains in achievement and engagement. *Sociology of Education, 68*(4), 241–270.

Lehman, C. M., Wolford, B., Stuck, E. M., Jr., & Kelly, R. E. (1998). Introduction. In *Building collaboration between education and treatment for at-risk and delinquent youth: An interdisciplinary approach with action plan* (pp. 1–6). Richmond, KY: National Juvenile Detention Association.

Lehr, C. A. (2004). Alternative schools and students with disabilities: Identifying and understanding the issues. *Information Brief, 3*(6). Minneapolis: National Center on Secondary Education and Transition, University of Minnesota.

Lehr, C. A., Hansen, A., Sinclair, M. F., & Christenson, S. L. (2003). Moving beyond dropout towards school completion: An integrative review of data-based interventions. *School Psychology Review, 32*(3), 342–364.

Lehr, C. A., Lang, C., & Lanners, E. (2004). *Alternative schools: Findings from a national survey of the states, Research Report 2.* Minneapolis: Institute on Community Integration, University of Minnesota.

Lehr, C. A., Sinclair, M. F., & Christenson, S. L. (2004). Addressing student engagement and truancy prevention during the elementary years: A replication study of the Check & Connect model. *Journal of Education for Students Placed At-Risk, 9*(3), 279–301.

Leone, P., & Drakeford, W. (1999). Alternative education: From a 'last chance' to a proactive model. *The Clearing House, 77,* 86–88. Washington, DC: The Helen Dwight Reid Educational Foundation.

Leone, P., Quinn, M., & Osher, D. (2002). *Collaboration in the juvenile justice system and youth serving agencies: Improving prevention, providing more efficient services, and reducing recidivism for youth with disabilities.* Washington, DC: American Institutes for Research. Retrieved December 10, 2005, from http://cecp.air.org/juvenilejustice/docs/Collaboration

Leuchovius, D., Hazasi, S., & Goldberg, P. (2001). *A survey of federally funded parent centers.* Minneapolis, MN: PACER Center, Technical Assistance on Transition and Rehabilitation Act.

Levin, P. F. (1999). Preparing teachers to connect home and school: Learning about the sociocultural contexts of teaching and learning. In M. S. Ammon (Ed.), *Joining hands: Preparing teachers to make meaningful home–school connections* (pp. 16–36). Sacramento: California Department of Education.

Levine, C. (1998, June). A lasting collaboration is more than a two-step dance. *School Administrator,* 1–3.

Levine-Coley, R., Chase-Lansdale, P. L., & Li-Grining, P. (2001). Child care in the era of welfare reform: Quality, choices and preferences. *Welfare, Children & Families, Policy Brief, 01–4.*

Lewis, C. (2003). Fathers' influences on children's development: The evidence from two-parent families. *European Journal of Psychology of Education, 18*(2), 211–228.

Lewis, C., Schaps, E., & Watson, M. (1995). Beyond the pendulum: Creating caring and challenging schools. *Kappan, 76,* 547–554.

Lewis, C., Schaps, E., & Watson, M. (1996, September). The caring classroom's academic edge. *Educational Leadership,* 16–21

Lieberman, A. (1995a). Practices that support teacher development: Transforming conceptions of professional learning. *Phi Delta Kappan, 76*(8), 591–596.

Lieberman, A. (1995b). Restructuring schools: The dynamics of changing practice, structure, and culture. In A. Lieberman (Ed.), *The work of restructuring schools: Building from the ground up* (pp. 1–17). New York: Teachers College Press.

Lieberman, A., & Grolnick, M. (1997). Networks, reform and the professional development of teachers. In A. Hargreaves (Ed.), *Rethinking educational change with heart and mind* (pp. 192–215). Alexandria, VA:

Association for Supervision and Curriculum Development.

Lightfoot, S. L. (2001). *Partnerships with families: The presence of parents can transform the culture of a school*. Portland, OR: Northwest Regional Educational Laboratory. Retrieved August 15, 2003, from http://www.nwrel.org/cfc/frc/beyus12.html

Lin, S. (2000). Coping and adaptations in families of children with cerebral palsy. *Exceptional Children, 66*, 201–218.

Lindsay, J. (2005). *Tragedy of the Hmong*. [Web page]. Retrieved August 25, 2005, from http://www.jefflindsay.com/Hmong_tragedy.html#young

Link, B. G., & Phelan, J. C. (2001). Conceptualizing stigma. *Annual Review of Sociology, 27*, 363–385.

Link, B. G., Phelan, J. C., Bresnahan, M., Stueve, A., & Pescosolido, B. A. (1999). Public conceptions of mental illness: Labels, causes, dangerousness, and social distance. *American Journal of Public Health, 89*, 1328–1333.

Linz, M., McAnally, P., & Wieck, C. (1990). *Case management: Historical current and future perspectives*. Newton Upper Falls, MA: Brookline Books.

Lipton, L., & Wellman, B. (2000). *Pathways to understanding: Patterns and practices in the learning-focused classroom* (3rd ed.). Sherman, CN: MiraVia.

Lipton, L., & Wellman, B. (2003). *Mentoring matters: A practical guide to learning-focused relationships* (2nd ed.). Sherman, Connecticut, MiraVia.

Little, J. W. (1990). The persistence of privacy: Autonomy and initiative in teachers' professional relations. *Teachers College Record, 91*(4), 509–536.

Little, P. (1998). *Family involvement in early childhood programs: How to choose the right program for your child. Early Childhood Digest*. Cambridge, MA: Harvard Family Research Project, Harvard University.

Little, P., & Lauver, S. (2005). Engaging adolescents in out of school time programs: Learning what works. *The Prevention Researcher, 12*(2), 7–10.

Liu, K., Thurlow, M., Barrera, M., Guven, K., & Shyyan, V. (2005). *Graduation exam participation and performance (2000–2001) of English language learners with disabilities* (ELLs with Disabilities Report 3). Minneapolis: University of Minnesota, National Center on Educational Outcomes. Retrieved July 11, 2005, from http://education.umn.edu/NCEO/Online Pubs/ELLsDisReport3.html

Livingston, S. (2003, November 4). *High stakes tests and deaf students*. Rochester, NY: Northeast Technical Assistance Center.

Locke, J. (1690). *An essay concerning human understanding*. P. H. Nidditch (Ed.) (Clarendon, 1989)

Lockwood, A., Stinnette, L., & D'Amico, J. (2004). *Collaborating for the common good. Leadership for learning* [Essay Series]. North Central Regional Educational Laboratory. Retrieved May 15, 2005, from http://www.ncrel.org/cscd/pubs/lead21/2-1b.htm

Lockwood, A. T. (1997). *Conversations with educational leaders: Contemporary viewpoints on education in America*. Albany: State University of New York Press.

Loeber, R., & Farrington, D. (2000). Young children who commit crime: Epidemiology, developmental origins, risk factors, early interventions, and policy implications. *Development and Psychopathology, 12*(4), 737–762.

Longo, P. (2003). Standards, transition, post-secondary goals, and the individualized education plan: One state's efforts at integration. In C. A. Kochhar-Bryant & D. S. Bassett (Eds.), *Aligning transition and standards-based education: Issues and strategies*. Arlington, VA: Council for Exceptional Children.

Loprest, P., & Maag, E. (2001, January). *Barriers and supports for work among adults with disabilities: Results from the NHIS-D*. Washington, DC: The Urban Institute.

Lorenz, K. (1974). *On aggression*. New York: Harcourt Brace.

Louis, K. S., & Kruse, S. D. (1995). *Professionalism and community: Perspectives on reforming urban schools*. Thousand Oaks, CA: Corwin Press.

Lourie, I. S., Stroul, B. A., & Friedman, R. M. (1998). Community-based systems of care: From advocacy to outcomes. In M. H. Epstein, K. Kutash, & A. Duchnowski (Eds.), *Outcomes for children & youth with behavioral and emotional disorders and their families: programs & evaluation best practices* (pp. 3–19). Austin, TX: PRO-ED.

Love, J. M., Kisker, E. E., Ross, C. M., Schochet, P. Z., Brooks-Gunn, J., & Paulsell, D. (2002). *Making a difference in the lives of infants and toddlers and their families: The impacts of early Head Start, executive summary*. Washington, DC: U.S. Department of Health and Human Services, Administration for Children and Families.

Lueking, R., & Certo, N. (2002). Integrating service systems at the point of transition for youth with significant disabilities: A model that works. *Addressing Trends and Developments in Secondary Education and Transition, 1*(4), 1–3. Retrieved April 12, 2005, from www.ncset.org

Luecking, R. G., Fabian, E. S., & Tilson, G. P. (2004). *Working relationships: Creating career opportunities for job seekers with disabilities through employer partnerships*. Baltimore: Paul H. Brookes.

Lustberg, M. (1999). *Partnering with parents to foster learning at home*. Morristown, NJ: Geraldine R. Dodge Foundation. Retrieved April 25, 2003, from http://eric-eb.tc.columbia.edu/npinpdfs/lustberg.pdf

Lynch, E. W., & Hanson, M. J. (Eds.). (1997). *Developing cross-cultural competence: A guide for working with children and families* (p. 492). Baltimore: Paul H. Brookes.

Lynch, J. (1994). Provision for children with special education needs in the Asia region. *The World Bank Technical Paper Number 261*. Asia Technical Department, Population and Human Resources Division.

Mac Iver, D. J. (1990). Meeting the needs of young adolescents: Advisory groups, interdisciplinary teaching teams, and school transition programs. *Phi Delta Kappan, 71*(6), 458–464. (EJ 402 385)

Mack, M., & Wiltrout, D. (1999). *Standards-based educational reform: A strategy to improve educational outcomes for all learners*. Minneapolis: National Transition Network, University of Minnesota.

Maeroff, G. I. (1993). Building teams to rebuild schools. *Phi Delta Kappan, 74*(7), 512–519.

Mahdi, L., Christopher, N., & Meade, M. (Eds.). (1996). *Crossroads: The quest for contemporary rights of passage*. Chicago: Open Court Press.

Malmgren, K., Edgar, E., & Neel, R. S. (1998). Postschool status of youths with behavioral disorders. *Behavioral Disorders, 23*, 257–263.

Malouf, D. (2000). Understanding and using technology. In J. M. Taymans, L. L. West, & M. Sullivan (Eds.), *Unlocking potential: College and other choices for people with LD and AD/HD* (pp. 232–242). Bethesda, MD: Woodbine House.

Mamlin, N. (1999). Despite best intentions: When inclusion fails. *The Journal of Special Education, 33*(1), 36–49.

Mandlawitz, M. (2006). *What every teacher should know about IDEA 2004*. Boston: Allyn & Bacon.

Manzo, A. (1997). *Content area literacy: Interactive teaching for active learning* (2nd ed.). New York: Wiley Publisher.

Mapp, K. L. (1997). Making the connection between families and schools. *The Harvard Education Letter, 13*(5), 1–3.

Marcon, R. A. (1999a). Differential impact of preschool models on development and early learning of inner-city children: A three-cohort study. *Developmental Psychology, 35*, 358–375.

Marcon, R. A. (1999b). Positive relationships between parent school involvement and public school inner-city preschoolers' development and academic performance. *School Psychology Review, 28*(3), 395–412.

Marcuse, H. (1964). *One dimensional man*. Boston: Beacon Press.

Marder, C., Wagner, M., & Sumi, C. (2003). The social adjustment of youth with disabilities. In M. Wagner, C. Marder, J. Blackorby, R. Cameto, L. Newman, P. Levine, & E. Davies-Mercier (with M. Chorost, N. Garza, A. Guzman, & C. Sumi), *The achievements of youth with disabilities during secondary school. A report from the National Longitudinal Transition Study-2 (NLTS2)*. Menlo Park, CA: SRI International.

Marsick, V., & Mezirow, J. (2002, January 25). New work on transformative learning. *Teachers College Record*. Retrieved August 1, 2005, from http://www.tcrecord .org (ID Number: 10876)

Martin, J. E. (2002). The transition of students with disabilities from high school to post-secondary education. In C. A. Kochhar-Bryant & D. S. Bassett (Eds.), *Aligning transition and standards-based education: Issues and strategies*. Arlington, VA: Council for Exceptional Children.

Martin, J. E., & Marshall, L. H. (1996). *ChoiceMaker: Self-determination transition assessment*. Longmont, CO: Sopris West.

Martin, J. E., Marshall, L. H., & Depry, R. L. (2001). Participatory decision making. In R. Flexer, T. Simmons, P. Luft, & R. Baer (Eds.), *Transition planning for secondary students with disabilities*. Upper Saddle River, NJ: Merrill/Prentice Hall.

Martin, J. E., & Marshall, L. H. (1995). ChoiceMaker: A comprehensive self-determination transition program. *Intervention in School and Clinic, 30*, 164–169.

Martin, J. E., & Marshall, L. H. (1996). Infusing self-determination instruction into the IEP and transition process. In D. J. Sands & M. L. Wehmeyer (Eds.), *Self-determination across the lifespan: Independence and choice for people with disabilities* (pp. 215–236). Baltimore: Paul H. Brookes.

Martin, J. E., Marshall, L., & De Pry, R. (2002). Participatory decision making: Innovative practices that increase student self-determination. In R. Flexer, T. Simmons, P. Luft, & R. Barr (Eds.), *Planning transition across the life span*. Upper Saddle River, NJ: Merrill/Prentice Hall.

Martin, J. E., Mithaug, D. E., Oliphint, J. H., Husch, J. V., & Frazier, E. S. (2002a*). Choose and take action: Finding the right job for you*. Longmont, CO: Sopris West.

Martin, J. E., Mithaug, D. E., Oliphint, J. H., Husch, J. V., & Frazier, E. S. (2002b). *Self-directed employment: A handbook for transition teachers and employment specialists*. Baltimore: Paul H. Brookes.

Martinelli, F. (2002). *Strategic planning*. Madison, WI: Learning Institute for Nonprofit Organizations

Collaboration, Center for Community Economic Development, University of Wisconsin Extension.

Martinez, D. (2004). *Opening the door to post-secondary education for all: Accessing the Higher Education Act.* Washington, DC: HEATH, The George Washington University.

Martinez, Y. G., & Velazquez, J. A. (2000*). Involving migrant families in education.* National Parent Information Network. Retrieved August 1, 2004, from http://npin.org/library/2002/n00644/n00644.html

Martinson, K. (1999). *Literature review on service coordination and integration in the welfare and workforce development systems.* Washington, DC: Urban Institute.

Marx, C. (1844). *Economic and philosophical manuscripts.* Penguin Books, 1983.

Marzano, R. (2003). *What works in schools: Translating research into action.* Alexandria, VA: ASCD.

Maslow, A. (1954). *Motivation and personality.* New York: Harper.

Maslow, A. (1968). *Toward a psychology of being.* New York: Van Nostrand.

Mason, J. L. (1995). *The cultural competence self–assessment questionnaire: A manual for users.* Portland, OR: Portland Research and Training Center.

Mattessich, P. N., & Mansey, B. R. (1992). *Collaboration: What makes it work: A review of the research literature on factors influencing successful collaboration.* St. Paul, MN: Amherst H. Wilder Foundation.

Maxwell, J. (2004). *Qualitative research design: An interactive approach (applied social research methods).* Thousand Oaks, CA: Sage Publications.

McAdoo, M. (1999). Studies in transition: How to help adolescents navigate the path to and from middle school. *Middle Ground, 2*(3), 21–23.

McBride, B. (1990). *Preservice teachers' attitudes toward parental involvement.* Athens: University of Georgia.

McCabe, K., Houser, D., Ryan, L., Smith, V., & Trouard, T. (2001). A functional imaging study of cooperation in two-person reciprocal exchange. *Proceedings of the National Academy of Science, 98*(20), 11832–11835.

McCabe, K., & Smith, V. (2000). A comparison of näive and sophisticated subject behavior with game theoretic predictions. *Proceedings of the National Academy of Sciences 97,* 3777–3781.

McCartney, E. (1999). Barriers to collaboration: An analysis of systemic barriers to collaboration between teachers and speech and language therapists. *International Journal of Language and Communication Disorders, 34*(4), 421–440.

McCombs, J. S., Kirby, S. N., Barney, H., Darilek, H., & Magee, S. J. (2004). *Achieving state and national literacy goals: A long uphill road: A report to Carnegie Corporation of New York.* Santa Monica, CA: Rand Corporation.

McCord, J., Spatz Widom, C., Bamba, M., & Crowell, N. (Eds.). (2000). *Education and delinquency: Summary of a workshop.* Panel on Juvenile Crime: Prevention, Treatment, and Control, Commission on Behavioral and Social Sciences and Education, National Research Council and the Institute of Medicine. Washington, DC: National Academy Press.

McCormick, L., Noonan, M., Ogata, V., & Heck, R. (2001). Co-teacher relationship and program quality: Implications for preparing teachers for inclusive preschool settings. *Education and Training in Mental Retardation and Developmental Disabilities, 36*(2), 119–32.

McDermott, P., & Rothenberg, J. (2000). Why urban parents resist involvement in their children's elementary education. *The Qualitative Report, 5*(3/4). Retrieved July 3, 2005, from http://www.nova.edu/ssss/QR/QR5-3/mcdermott.html

McDonnell, L. M., McLaughlin, M. J., & Morison, P. (1997). *Educating one & all: Students with disabilities and standards-based reform.* National Research Council. Washington, DC: National Academy Press.

McEwin, C. K., Dickinson, T. S., & Jacobson, M. G. (2004). *Programs and practices in K–8 schools: Do they meet the educational needs of young adolescents?* Westerville, OH: National Middle School Association.

McEwin, C. K., Dickinson, T. S., & Jenkins, D. M. (1996). *America's middle schools: Practices and progress: A 25-year perspective.* Columbus, OH: National Middle School Association.

McGahee, M., Mason, C., Wallace, T., & Jones, B. (2001). *Student-led IEPS: A guide for student involvement.* Arlington, VA: Council for Exceptional Children.

McGuire, J. M., Norlander, K. A., & Shaw, S. F. (1990). Postsecondary education for students with learning disabilities: Forecasting challenges for the future. *Learning Disabilities Focus, 5,* 69–74.

McInturff, J. (1997). *Collegial coaching, special needs, and the nontraditional classroom.* (ERIC Document Reproduction Service No. ED405722 EC305446)

McIntyre, T., & Battle, J. (1998). The traits of 'good teachers' as identified by African-American and white students with emotional and/or behavioral disorders. *Behavioral Disorders, 23,* 134–142.

McKenzie, J. (1998). The information literate school community. *From Now On: The Educational Technology Journal, 8*(1), 1–4.

McKenzie, J. (2000). *Beyond technology: Questioning, research and the information literate school.* Bellingham, WA: FNO Press.

McKeon, R. (1947). *Introduction to Aristotle.* New York: Random House.

McKinney, J. D., & Hocutt, A. M. (1982). Public school involvement of parents of learning disabled children and average achievers. *Exceptional Education Quarterly, 3*(2), 64–73.

McLaughlin, M. (2000). *Community counts: How youth organizations matter for youth development.* Washington, DC: Public Education Fund Network.

McLaughlin, M., & Blank, M. (2004). Creating a culture of attachment. *Education Week,* November 10, 34–35.

McLaughlin, M. L., Nolet, V., Rhim, L. M., & Henderson, K. (1999). Integrating standards including all students. *The Council for Exceptional Children, 3*(3), 66–71.

McLaughlin, M. W., & Talbert, J. E. (2001). *Professional communities and the work of high school teaching.* Chicago: University of Chicago Press.

McLeod, P. (1996). *School reform and student diversity: Exemplary schooling for language minority students.* Santa Cruz: University of California, National Center for Research on Cultural Diversity and Second Language Learning, Retrieved August 20, 2005, from http://lmri.ucsb.edu/addres/2/ncrcdsll/summary.txt

McLeod, P. (2005). *Instructional strategies for English learners with disabilities.* Washington, DC: Council of Chief State School Officers.

McMahan, R., & Baer, R. (2001). IDEA transition policy compliance and best practice: Perceptions of transition stakeholders. *Career Development for Exceptional Individuals, 24*(2), 169–184.

McMillen, M., Kaufman, P., & Whitener, S. (1994, September). *Dropout rates in the United States: 1993.* Washington, DC: U.S. Department of Education, National Center for Education Statistics. (NCES 94-669)

McNeil, J. M. (2000). *Employment, earnings and disability.* Paper prepared for the 75th Annual Conference of the Western Economic Association International, Vancouver, BC, Canada.

McNeal Jr., R. B. (1997). Are students being pulled out of high school? The effect of adolescent employment on dropping out. *Sociology of Education, 70,* 206–220.

McTighe, J., & Wiggins, G. (1999). *Understanding by design handbook.* Alexandria, VA: Association for Supervision and Curriculum Development.

Mead, G. (1934). The nature of reflective intelligence. In C. W. Morris (Ed.), *Mind, self and society from the standpoint of a social behaviorist* (pp. 90–100). Chicago: University of Chicago.

Mead, G. H. (1982). *The individual and the social self.* Chicago: University of Chicago Press.

Medrich, E., Ramer, C., & Merola, L. (2000). *School-to-work progress measures: A Report to the National School-to-Work Office.* Washington, DC: U.S. Department of Labor.

Meers, G. (1980). Introduction to special vocational needs education. Rockville, MD: Aspen Publications, Inc.

Meers, G. (1993). On their own: Preparing disabled students for independent living and productive careers. *Vocational Education Journal, 68*(8), 30–31.

Meier, D., & Schafran, A. (1999). Strengthening the preschool-to-kindergarten transition: A community collaborates. *Young Children, 54*(3), 40–46.

Meisel, S., Henderson, K., Cohen, M., & Leone, P. (1998). Collaborate to educate: Special education in juvenile correctional facilities. In R. Rutherford, M. Nelson, and B. Wolford (Eds.), *Building collaboration between education and treatment for at-risk and delinquent youth* (pp. 59–72). Richmond, KY: Eastern Kentucky University, National Juvenile Detention Association.

Meisel, S., Henderson, K., Cohen, M., & Leone, P. (2000). *Collaborate to educate: Special education in juvenile correctional facilities.* College Park, MD: University of Maryland, National Center on Education, Disability and Juvenile Justice. Retrieved December 30, 2003, from http://www.edjj.org/Publications/pub01_17_00.html

Meisels, S. (1999). Assessing readiness. In R. C. Pianta & M. J. Cox (Eds.), *The transition to kindergarten* (pp. 39–66). Baltimore, MD: Paul H. Brookes.

Mekos, D. (1989, April). *Students' perceptions of the transition to junior high: A longitudinal perspective.* Paper presented at the biennial meeting of the Society for Research in Child Development, Kansas City, MO.

Melaville, A. (1993). *Critical issue: Linking at-risk students and schools to integrated services.* Washington, DC: North Central Regional Education Library.

Melaville, A. I., Blank, M. J., & Asayesh, G. (1993). *Together we can: A guide for crafting a profamily system of education and human services.* Chevy Chase, MD: PrismDAE.

Menchetti, B. M., & Piland, V. C. (1998). A person-centered approach to vocational evaluation and career planning. In F. R. Rusch & J. Chadsey (Eds.), *Beyond high school: Transition from school to work* (pp. 319–339). Belmont, CA: Wadsworth Publishing.

Menlove, R., Hudson, P., & Suter, D. (2001). A field of IEP dreams: Increasing general education teacher participation in the IEP development process. *Teaching Exceptional Children, 33*(5), 28–33.

Mertens, S. B., Flowers, N., & Mulhall, P. (1998). *The middle start initiative, phase 1: A longitudinal analysis of Michigan middle-level schools.* Urbana: University of Illinois.

Meszaros, P. S. (1993, Fall). The 21st century imperative: A collaborative ecological investment in youth. *Journal of Home Economics,* 11–21.

Meyer, D., Madden, D., & McGrath, D. (2004). *English language learner students in U.S. public schools: 1994 and 2000.* Washington, DC: Education Statistics Services Institute (ESSI), National Center for Educational Statistics.

Meyer, L. (2000). Standards for school leaders. *The NTA Resource Bulletin,* April, 1–6. Retrieved August 14, 2005, from http://ici.umn.edu/ncset/publications/nta/bulletins/april_2000.html

Mezirow, J. (1978). Perspective transformation. *Adult Education, 28*(2), 100–110.

Mezirow, J. (1991). Transformative dimensions of adult learning. San Francisco: Jossey-Bass.

Mezirow, J. (1994). Understanding transformation theory. *Adult Education Quarterly, 44*(4), 222–232.

Mezirow, J. (1997). Transformative learning: Theory to practice. In P. Cranton (Ed.), *Transformative learning in action. New directions for adult and continuing education* (p. 74). San Francisco: Jossey-Bass.

Mezirow, J. (2000a). *Learning as transformation.* San Francisco: Jossey-Bass.

Mezirow, J. (2000b). Learning to think like an adult: Core concepts of transformative learning theory. In J. Mezirow, (Ed.), *Learning as transformation* (pp. 3–34). San Francisco: Jossey-Bass.

Michaels, C. (1994). *Transition strategies for persons with learning disabilities.* San Diego, CA: Singular Publishing.

Midgley, C., & Feldlaufer, H. (1987). Students' and teachers' decision-making fit before and after the transition to junior high school. *Journal of Early Adolescence, 7,* 225–241.

Midobuche, E. (2001). More than empty footprints in the sand: Educating immigrant children. *Harvard Educational Review, 71*(3), 529–535.

Midura, D. W. & Glover, D. R. (2003). *Essentials of team building: Principles and practices.* Champaign, IL: Human Kinetics Publishers.

Miedel, W. T., & Reynolds, A. J. (1999). Parent involvement in early intervention for disadvantaged children: Does it matter? *Journal of School Psychology, 37*(4), 379–402.

Miles, P., & Franz, J. (2001). *Foundations of wraparound: Values, practice patterns and essential ingredients.* Boston: Federation for Children With Special Needs.

Miller, A., Valasky, W., & Melloy, P. (1998). Learning together: The evolution of an inclusive class. *Active Learner, 3*(2), 14–16.

Miller, H. (1999, Spring). Making the most of advisory programs: Teaching, mentoring, or just killing time? *Middle Matters,* 1–7.

Mills, C. (2001). *Principles for individual and family self-determination partnerships.* OHSU Center on Self-Determination. Retrieved May 14, 2005, from http://cdrc.ohsu.edu/selfdetermination/indivprin

Mills v. Board of Education, 348 F. Supp. 866 (D. DC 1972).

Miner, C., & Bates, P. (1997). The effects of person-centered planning activities on the IEP/transition planning process. *Education and Training in Mental Retardation and Developmental Disabilities, 32,* 105–112.

Minke, K. M., & Vickers, H. S. (1999). Family-school collaboration. In S. Graham & K. R. Harris (Eds.), *Teachers working together: Enhancing the performance of students with special needs* (pp. 117–150). Cambridge, MA: Brook Line.

Minnesota Department of Children, Families and Learning. (2002). *Five-step process.* St. Paul: Author.

Minnesota Governors Council on Disabilities. (2002). *Service coordination: Partners in policymaking.* St. Paul, MN: Governor's Council on Disabilities. Retrieved on May 4, 2005, from http://www.partnersinpolicymaking.com/curriculum/curriculum3.htm

Minnesota System of Interagency Coordination Communication Project. (2003, Fall). Service coordination: What's it all about? *Newsletter of the Minnesota System of Interagency Coordination.* Minneapolis: University of Minnesota, Institute on Community Integration.

Mintzberg, H. (1994). *Rise and fall of strategic planning.* New York: Free Press.

Mithaug, D., Wehmeyer, M. L., Agran, M., Martin, J., & Palmer, S. (1998). The self-determined learning model of instruction: Engaging students to solve their learning problems. In M. L. Wehmeyer & D. J. Sands (Eds.), *Making it happen: Student involvement in educational planning, decision making and instruction* (pp. 299–328). Baltimore: Paul H. Brookes.

Mithaug, D. E. (2000). *Learning to theorize: A four-step strategy.* Thousand Oaks, CA: Sage Publications.

Mithaug, D. E., Mithaug, D. K., Martin, J. E., Agran, M., & Wehmeyer, M. L. (2003). *Self-determined learning theory: Construction, verification, and evaluation.* Mahawah, NJ: Lawrence Erlbaum.

Mizelle, N. B. (1995, April). *Transition from middle school into high school: The student perspective*. Paper presented at the annual meeting of the American Educational Research Association, San Francisco.

Mizelle, N. B. (1999). Helping middle school students make the transition into high school. *LD Online*. Retrieved August 1, 2005, from http://www.ldonline.org/ld_indepth/transition/middle_school_transition.html

Mizelle, N. B., & Mullins, E. (1997). Transition into and out of middle school. In J. L. Irvin (Ed.), *What current research says to the middle level practitioner* (pp. 303–313). Columbus, OH: National Middle School Association.

Mogharreban, C., & Branscum, S. (2000). Educare: Community collaboration for school readiness. *Dimensions of Early Childhood, 28*(1), 21–28.

Monahan, R. G., Marino, S. B., Miller, R., & Cronic, D. T. (1997). *Rural teachers', administrators', and counselors' attitudes about inclusion* [Report No. 021000]. Greenwood, SC: ERIC. (ERIC Documentation Reproduction Service No. 406099)

Montgomery County Public Schools. (2003). *Achievement gains by at-risk students on 2003 CTBS prompt implications for continued local, national improvements: Report to the board of education*. Rockville, MD: Author.

Montgomery, L., & Whiting, D. (2000, February 8–12). *Teachers under construction—incorporating principles of engaged and brain based learning into a constructivist "technology in education" program* (pp. 1–3). Society for Information Technology & Technology Education International Conference: Proceedings of SITE 2000, San Diego, CA.

Montgomery, W. (2003). Creating culturally responsive, inclusive classrooms. In K. L. Freiberg (Ed.), *Annual Editions, Educating Exceptional Children 02/03*(4), 20–25.

Montiel-Overall, P. (2005). *Toward a theory of collaboration for teachers and librarians*. Chicago: American Library Association.

Morley, R. E. (1991). Alternative education. Dropout prevention research reports. Clemson, SC: National Dropout Prevention Center. (ERIC Document Reproduction Service No. 349 652)

Morningstar, M. (2002). The role of families of adolescents with disabilities in standards-based reform and transition. In C. A. Kochhar-Bryant & D. S. Bassett (Eds.), *Aligning transition and standards-based education: Issues and strategies*. Arlington, VA: Council for Exceptional Children.

Morningstar, M. E., Turnbull, A., & Turnbull, N. R. (1996). What do students with disabilities tell us about the importance of family involvement in the transition from school to adult life? *Exceptional Children, 62*, 249–260.

Morrill, W. A. (1992). Overview of service delivery to children. *The Future of Children: School Linked Services, 2*(1), 32–43.

Morris, V. G., & Satomi, I. T. (1998). Alleviating barriers to family involvement in education: The role of teacher education. *Teaching and Teacher Education, 14*, 219–231.

Morrissette, D., & Morrissette, P. (1999). Rethinking parent participation in special education. *International Electronic Journal For Leadership in Learning, 3*(14). (ISSN 1206-9620)

Morse, A. B., Anderson, A. R., Christenson, S. L., & Lehr, C. A. (2004). Promoting school completion. *Principal Leadership, 4*(6), 9–13.

Morse, A. B., Christenson, S. L., & Lehr, C. A. (2003). *Staying in school: A guide to keeping students actively engaged in school*. Minneapolis: Check and Connect Project, University of Minnesota. Retrieved July 4, 2005, from http://www.teachersandfamiliescom/open/parent/engage5.cfm

Morse, A. B., Christenson, S. L., & Lehr, C. A. (2005). Promoting student engagement to enhance school completion: Information and strategies for parents. In A. Canter, S. Carroll, L. Paige, & Romero, I. (Eds.), *Helping children at home and school: Handouts from your school psychologist*. Washington, DC: National Association of School Psychologists.

Moscow State Pedagogical University. (n.d.). *Contemporary Educational Programmes*. Retrieved July 15, 2006, from http://www.cep.ru/mspu.shtml

Moses, B. (1998). *Career intelligence: The 12 new rules for work and life success*. San Francisco: Berrett-Koehler.

Mount, B., & Zwernik, K. (1988). *It's never too early, it's never too late: A booklet about personal futures planning* (pp. 88–109). St. Paul, MN: Governor's Planning Council on Developmental Disabilities. (Publication No. 421)

Mountain Plains Regional Resource Center. (2005). *The parent counseling and training services guide: A primary for parents*. Arlington, VA: LRP Publications.

Moxley, D. (1997). *Case management by design: Reflections on principal and practices*. Belmont, CA: Wadsworth Publishing Company.

Mullins, E. R. (1997). *Changes in young adolescents' self-perceptions across the transition from elementary to middle school*. Unpublished doctoral dissertation, University of Georgia, Athens.

Mullins, E., & Irvin, J. (2000). What research says: Transition into middle school. *Middle School Journal, 31*(3), 57–61.

Murawski, W. (2003). *Co-teaching in the inclusive class-room: Working together to help all your students find success (Grades 6–12)* (pp. 36–37). Medina, WA: Institute for Educational Development.

Murawski, W., & Dieker, L. (2004). Tips and strategies for co-teaching at the secondary level. *Teaching Exceptional Children, 5,* 52–58. Arlington, VA: Council for Exceptional Children.

Murawski, W. W., & Swanson, H. L. (2001). A meta-analysis of co-teaching research: Where are the data? *Remedial and Special Education, 22*(5), 258–267.

Murphy, S. (2002). Substance abuse and child welfare systems collaboration: Use of the family group conferencing model. *Issues of Substance, 7*(1), 1, 3, 5. Washington, DC: NASW Publications.

Mutchler, S., & Pollard, R. (1994). *Linkages among education, health and human services in states that are creating new governance structures.* Paper presented at the Annual Meeting of the American Educational Research Association (New Orleans, LA, April 4–8, 1994).

Nahmias, M. L. (1995). Communication and collaboration between home and school for students with ADD. *Intervention in School and Clinic, 30,* 241–247.

National Adult Literacy and Learning Disabilities Center. (1995, Summer). *Adults with learning disabilities: Definitions and issues.* Washington, DC: Academy for Educational Development.

National Association for the Education of Young Children. (1996). *Statement of the position Developmentally appropriate practice in early childhood programs serving children from birth through age 8.* Washington, DC: Author.

National Association for the Education of Young Children. (1997). *A good preschool for your child.* Washington, DC: Author.

National Association for the Education of Young Children. (1999). *NAEYC position statement: Developing and implementing effective public policies to promote early childhood and school-age care program accreditation.* Washington, DC: Author.

National Association for the Education of Young Children. (2003). *Preparing early childhood professionals: NAEYC's standards for programs.* Washington, DC: Author.

National Association of Early Childhood Specialists. (2002, Summer). Preschool to kindergarten: A new model for the transition process. *Primary Interest, 9*(3), 1–3.

National Association of Elementary School Principals. (2004). *When schools and families work in partnership, students benefit: Strengthening the connection between school and home.* Alexandria, VA: Author.

National Association of School Psychologists. (1998). *Position statement on early childhood care and education.* Bethesda, MD: Author.

National Association of School Psychologists. (1999). *Position statement on early intervention services.* Bethesda, MD: Author.

National Association of School Psychologists. (2002). *IDEA reauthorization: Challenging behavior and students with disabilities.* Bethesda, MD: Author.

National Association of School Psychologists. (2003). *Position statement on early intervention services.* Bethesda, MD: Author.

National Association of State Boards of Education. (2003). *Creating a unified, comprehensive system of early childhood education: Early Childhood Education Network, Final Report.* Alexandria, VA: Author.

National Association of State Directors of Special Education. (2002a). *Legislative priorities.* Alexandria, VA: Author. Retrieved June 13, 2005, from http://www.nasdse.org/government_relations/legislative_priorities.htm

National Association of State Directors of Special Education. (2002b). *Mental health, schools and families working together for all children and youth: Toward a shared agenda.* Alexandria, VA: Author.

National Board for Professional Teaching Standards. (2001a, March). *Early childhood through young adulthood/exceptional needs specialist standards.* Arlington, VA: Author.

National Board for Professional Teaching Standards. (2001b, March 9–10). *Early childhood/generalist standards, middle childhood/generalist standards, early adolescence/generalist standards, and early childhood through young adulthood/exceptional needs specialist standards.* Arlington, VA: Author.

National Center for Children in Poverty. (2001a). *Improving the odds for the healthy development of young children in foster care.* New York: Author. Retrieved July 15, 2005, from www.nccp.org

National Center for Children in Poverty. (2001b). *Building services and systems to support the healthy emotional development of young children: An action guide for policymakers.* New York: Author. Retrieved July 15, 2005 from www.nccp.org

National Center for the Dissemination of Disability Research. (1996). *A review of the literature on dissemination and knowledge utilization.* Austin, TX: Southwest Regional Education Laboratory. Retrieved June 16, 2005, from http://www.ncddr.org/du/products/litreview.pdf

National Center for Early Development and Learning (2005). *Data from the Section 619 profile* (13th ed.). Chapel Hill, NC: FPG Child Development Institute.

National Center for Education Statistics. (1998). *Parent involvement in children's education: Efforts by public elementary schools.* Washington, DC: U.S. Department of Education. (NCES Number: 98032)

National Center for Education Statistics. (1999a). *Students with disabilities in postsecondary education: A profile of preparation, participation and outcomes.* Washington, DC: U.S. Department of Education.

National Center for Education Statistics. (1999b). *Dropout rates in the United States: 1998.* Washington, DC: U.S. Government Printing Office. (NCES No. 2000-022)

National Center for Education Statistics. (2000). *Trends in educational equity for girls and women.* Washington, DC: U.S. Government Printing Office. (NCES No. 2000-030)

National Center for Education Statistics. (2001). *Public alternative schools and programs for students at risk of education failure: 2000–2001.* Washington, DC: U.S. Department of Education.

National Center for Education Statistics. (2002). *The condition of education.* Washington, DC: U.S. Department of Education, Office of Education Research and Improvement.

National Center for Education Statistics. (2003). *Common core of data 2000–2001, local education agency survey: School year 2000–2001.* Washington, DC: U.S. Department of Education, National Center for Education Statistics, unpublished tabulations. (NCES No. 2002–360).

National Center for Education Statistics. (2004). *The condition of education 2004, 6*(1/2). Washington, DC: U.S. Department of Education, National Center for Education Statistics, unpublished tabulations.

National Center for Family Literacy. (2004). *Stories of impact: Improving parent involvement through family literacy in the elementary school.* Louisville, KY: Author.

National Center for Policy Analysis. (1996). *Many Texas students 'at risk.'* Retrieved April 6, 2005, from http://www.ncpa.org

National Center for the Study of Postsecondary Educational Supports. (2000a). *Technical report: Postsecondary education and employment for students with disabilities: Focus group discussion on supports and barriers to lifelong learning.* Honolulu, HI: Author.

National Center for the Study of Postsecondary Educational Supports. (2000b). *Technical report:*

National survey of educational support provision to students with disabilities in postsecondary education settings. Honolulu, HI: Author.

National Center for the Study of Postsecondary Educational Supports. (2000c). *Quarterly summary report, October 1–December 31, 2000.* Honolulu, HI: Manoa Center on Disability Studies, University of Hawaii.

National Center for the Study of Postsecondary Educational Supports. (2001). *Quarterly summary report: October 1, 2001–December 31, 2001.* Honolulu, HI: University of Hawaii at Manoa, Center on Disability Studies.

National Center for the Study of Postsecondary Educational Supports. (2002, July 8). *Preparation for and support of youth with disabilities in postsecondary education & employment: Implications for policy, priorities and practice.* Proceedings and Briefing Book for the National Summit on Postsecondary Education for People with Disabilities, Washington, DC.

National Center on Education, Disability and Juvenile Justice. (2004). *Transition planning and services.* College Park, MD: University of Maryland.

National Center on Outcomes Research. (2001). *Practice guidance for delivery outcomes in service coordination.* Towson, MD: Author.

National Center on Secondary Education and Transition. (2002a). Integrating services systems at the point of transition for youth with significant disabilities: A model that works. *NCSET Information Brief, 1*(4). Minneapolis, MN: Author.

National Center on Secondary Education and Transition. (2002b). *Youth with disabilities and the Workforce Investment Act of 1998, 1*(2). Minneapolis, MN: Author.

National Center on Secondary Education and Transition. (2004, November 17). *Preparing for post-secondary education.* [NCSET Topics]. Minneapolis, MN: Author.

National Clearinghouse for English Language Acquisition. (1998). *Summary report of the survey of the states' limited English proficient students and available educational programs and services, 1996–1997.* Retrieved February 25, 2004, from http://www.ncbe.gwu.edu/ncbepubs/seareports/96-97/a12.htm

National Clearinghouse for English Language Acquisition. (2005). *Biennial report to Congress on the implementation of Title III, Part A of ESEA.* Washington, DC: The George Washington University.

National Coalition for Parent Involvement in Education. (2001). *Institute for Responsive Education Promoting*

Family and Community Involvement in Education, NCPIE Update. Fairfax, VA: Author.

The National Coalition of Educational Equity Advocates. (1994). *Educate America: A call for equity in school reform.* Chevy Chase, MD: The Mid-Atlantic Equity Consortium.

National Council for Accreditation of Teacher Education. (1994, September). Program standards for initial and advanced programs in early childhood education. *National Association for the Education of Young Children (NAEYC),* 10–12.

National Council for Accreditation of Teacher Education. (2000). *State partnership board adopted NCATE performance-based policy principles.* Washington, DC: Author.

National Council for Accreditation of Teacher Education. (2001a, January). *Professional standards for the accreditation of schools, colleges, and departments of education* (pp. 12–13). Washington, DC: Author.

National Council for Accreditation of Teacher Education (NCATE). (2001b). *Standards for professional development schools.* Washington, DC: Author.

National Council on Disability. (2000a). *Back to school on civil rights: Advancing the federal commitment to leave no child behind.* Washington, DC: Author.

National Council on Disability. (2000b). *Transition and post-school outcomes for youth with disabilities: Closing the gaps to postsecondary education and employment.* Washington, DC: Author.

National Council on Disability. (2003a). *People with disabilities and postsecondary education.* Washington, DC: Author.

National Council on Disability. (2003b, January 24). *Youth Advisory Committee to the National Council on Disability.* Record of personal meeting, teleconference, Washington, DC.

National Council on Disability. (2004). *Improving educational outcomes for students with disabilities.* Washington, DC: Author.

National Early Childhood Technical Assistance System. (2001). *Evaluation highlights: Client feedback from 1991–2000.* Chapel Hill, NC: Author.

National Educational Research Policy and Priorities Board. (2000, July 24–25). *Papers and proceedings from the National Conference on Curriculum, Instruction and Assessment in the Middle Grades: Linking Research and Practice.* Washington, DC: U.S. Department of Education.

National Educators Association. (1998). *Promoting quality in early care and education: Issues for schools.* Washington, DC: Author.

National Governors Association. (2005). *Graduation counts: A report of the national governors association task force on state high school graduation data.* Washington, DC: Author.

National Governors Association, Center for Best Practices. (2001). Setting high educational standards in alternative education. *Issue Brief, Employment and Social Services.* Washington, DC: Author.

National Head Start Association. (2002). *National Head Start Association 2002 policy agenda.* Alexandria, VA: Author. Retrieved on July 23, 2005, from www.nhsa.org

National Information Center for Children and Youth With Disabilities. (1997). Who's teaching our children with disabilities? *News Digest,* 27, 2–25.

National Information Center for Children and Youth With Disabilities. (1999a). Helping students with cognitive disabilities find and keep a job. *Technical Assistance Guide 3 (TA3).* Washington, DC: Author.

National Information Center for Children and Youth With Disabilities. (1999b). Child outcomes when child care center classes meet recommended standards for quality. Early Child Care Research Network. *American Journal of Public Health, 89*(7), 1072–1077.

National Information Center for Children and Youth with Disabilities. (2002a). *A student's guide to the IEP* (2nd ed.). Washington, DC: Author.

National Information Center for Children and Youth with Disabilities. (2002b). *Technical assistance guide: Helping students develop their IEPs* (2nd ed.). Washington, DC: Author.

National Institute for Early Education Research. (2004). *The State of Preschool: 2004 State Preschool Yearbook.* New Brunswick, NJ: Rutgers.

National Institute of Mental Health. (2001). *Blueprint for change: Research on child and adolescent mental health.* Washington, DC: National Advisory Council's Workgroup on Child and Adolescent Mental Health Intervention Development and Deployment, National Institute of Mental Health,

National Institute of Mental Health. (2003). *Attention deficit and hyperactivity disorder.* Washington, DC: Author.

National Mental Health Association. (1998). *Cultural competency in mental health systems.* Washington, DC: Author. Retrieved June 3, 2005, from www.nmha.org

National Mental Health Association. (2000). *The use of psychotropic medication to treat children's mental health needs.* Washington, DC: Author. Retrieved June 3, 2005, from www.nmha.org

National Middle School Association. (2003). *This we believe: Developmentally responsive middle level schools.* Columbus, OH: Author.

National Middle School Association. (2004). *Supporting students in their transition to middle school.* Position paper jointly adopted by the National Middle School Association and the National Association of Elementary School Principals, Westerville, OH.

National Organization on Disability. (2003, September 15). *People with disabilities and post-secondary education, [position paper].* Washington, DC: Author.

National Organization on Disability/Louis Harris & Associates, Inc. (2000). *Harris survey of Americans with disabilities.* New York: Author.

National Parent Teacher Association. (1999). *National PTA mission.* Washington, DC: Author. Retrieved May 16, 2005, from http://www.pta.org/apta/fastfcts.htm

National Parent Teacher Association. (2003). *PTA milestones along the way (1897–1899).* Washington, DC: Author. Retrieved August 20, 2003, from http://www.pta.org/aboutpta/history/mile1890.asp

National Research Council. (1993). *Losing generations: Adolescents in high-risk settings.* Panel on High-Risk Youth, Commission on Behavioral and Social Sciences and Education, National Research Council. Washington, DC: National Academy Press.

National Research Council. (2001). *Suicide prevention and intervention.* Summary of a workshop, committee on pathophysiology and prevention of adolescent and adult suicide Board on Neuroscience and Behavioral Health, Institute of Medicine. Washington, DC: National Academies Press.

National Research & Training Center. (2002). *Self-determination framework for people with psychiatric disabilities.* Chicago: University of Illinois at Chicago. Retrieved July 18, 2005, from http://www.psych.uic.edu/UICNRTC/sdframework.pdf

National State Boards of Education. (2003). Creating a unified, comprehensive system of early childhood education. Alexandria, VA: Author.

National Task Force on School Readiness. (1991). *Caring communities: Supporting young children and families.* Alexandria, VA: National Association of State Boards of Education.

National Transition Alliance. (2000, April 25). *Partnering with parents of youth with disabilities in the transition process.* Conference call presentation, Washington, DC.

Nee-Benham, M., & Cooper, J. (2000). *Indigenous educational models for contemporary practice: In our mother's voice.* New York: Lawrence Erlbaum.

Nerdrum, L., & Erikson, T. (2001). Intellectual capital: A human capital perspective. *Journal of Intellectual Capital, 2*(2), 127–135.

Neubert, D. A. (2000). Transition education and services guidelines. In G. M. Clark, P. Sitlington, & O. P. Kolstoe. *Transition education and services for adolescents with disabilities* (3rd ed., pp. 39–69). Boston: Allyn & Bacon.

Neubert, D. A., & Moon, M. S. (1999). Working together to facilitate the transition from school to work. In S. Graham, & K. R. Harris (Eds.), *Teachers working together: Enhancing the performance of students with special needs* (pp. 186–213). Cambridge, MA: Brookline Books.

Neuman, S. B., Copple, C., & Bredekamp, S. (2000). *Learning to read and write: Developmentally appropriate practices for young children.* Washington, DC: National Association for the Education of Young Children.

Newman, L. (2004). *Family involvement in the educational development of youth with disabilities.* A Special Topic Report of the National Longitudinal Transition Study (NLTS2). Menlo Park, CA: SRI International.

Newmann, F. M. (1993). Beyond common sense in educational restructuring: The issues of content and linkage. *Educational Researcher, 22*(2), 4–13, 22.

Newmann, F. M., & Wehlage, G. G. (1995). *Successful school restructuring: A report to the public and educators.* Madison, WI: Center on Organization and Restructuring of Schools.

New Mexico Department of Health and Department of Education. (2001). *Facilitating smooth and effective transition for children and families in New Mexico: A guidance document for transition from early intervention to other services and supports.* Santa Fe, NM: Author.

New York Board of Cooperative Education Services. (2004). *Jerusalem Avenue School Elementary Program.* Garden City, NY: Nassau BOCES.

New York State Office of Mental Health. (2001). *2001–2005 statewide comprehensive plan for mental health services.* Rochester, NY: Author.

Nichols, J. D. (1996). The effects of cooperative learning on student achievement and motivation in a high school geometry class. *Contemporary Educational Psychology, 21*(4), 467–476.

Nichols, S., & Good, T. (2004). *America's teenagers—myths and realities: Media images, schooling, and the social costs of careless indifference.* Mahwah, NJ: Lawrence Erlbaum Associates.

Nicholson, N. (1998). How hardwired is human behavior? *Harvard Business Review, 76*(4), 134–147.

Nielsen, A., & Gerber, D. (1979). Psychosocial aspects of truancy in early adolescence. *Adolescence, 14,* 313–326.

Nielsen, L. E., & Finkelstein, J. M. (1993). A new approach to parent conferences. *Teaching PreK–8, 24*(1), 90–92. (EJ469327)

Nieto, S. (1994). Lessons from students on creating a chance to dream. *Harvard Educational Review, 64*(4), 392–426.

Nieto, S. (1996). *Affirming diversity* (2nd ed.). New York: Longman.

Nieto, S. (2000). Placing equity front and center: Some thoughts on transforming teacher. *Journal of Teacher Education, 51*(3), 180–187.

Nirje, B. (1972). The right to self-determination. In W. Wolfensberger (Ed.), *The principle of normalization in human services* (pp. 176–193). Toronto, ON, Canada: National Institute on Mental Retardation.

Nirje, B. (1976). The normalization principle. In R. B. Kugel & A. Hearer (Eds.), *Changing patterns in residential services for the mentally retarded* (Rev. ed.; pp. 231–240). Washington, DC: President's Committee on Mental Retardation. DHEW No. 76-21015

Nishio, H., Kasuga, S., Ushijima, M., & Harada, Y. (2001). Prenatal stress and postnatal development of neonatal rat's sex-dependent effects on emotional behavior and learning ability of neonatal rats. *International Journal of Developmental Neuroscience, 19*(1), 37–45.

Nissani, H. (1999, Fall). Family support in our nation's schools: The charge and the challenges. *America's Family Support Magazine,* 25–27.

No Child Left Behind Act of 2001, P. L. No. 107-110 § 115 Stat. 1425 [Section 501, Innovative Programs and Parental Choice Provisions] (2002).

No Child Left Behind Act of 2001, P. L. 107-220, 20 U.S.C. § 6301 *et seq.* (2002).

Noell, G., & Witt, J. (1999). When does consultation lead to intervention implementation?: Critical Issues for Research and Practice. *Journal of Special Education, 33(1),* 29–35.

Nord, C. W., & West, J. (2001). *Fathers' and mothers' involvement in their children's schools by family type and resident status.* Washington, DC: U.S. Department of Education, National Center for Education Statistics.

North Central Regional Educational Laboratory. (1993). Stark County Early Childhood Collaborative Initiative. *NCREL Policy Briefs,* report 3: *Integrating community services for young children and their families.* Oak Brook, IL: Author.

North Central Regional Educational Laboratory. (1996). Human services coordination: Who cares?! *NCREL Policy Briefs,* report 1. Naperville, IL: NCREL, Evaluation and Policy Information Center (EPIC).

North Central Regional Educational Laboratory. (1999). *Critical issue: Organizing for effective early childhood programs and practice.* Retrieved August 12, 2006, from http://www.ncrel.org/sdrs/areas/issues/students/earlycld/ea100.htm

North Central Regional Educational Laboratory. (2001). *Urban parent involvement overview.* Naperville, IL: Author. Retrieved June 23, 2004, from http://www.ncrel.org/sdrs/

North Central Regional Educational Laboratory. (2003). *Critical issue: NCLB option—Choosing to change schools.* Retrieved August 14, 2006, from http://www.ncrel.org/sdrs/areas/issues/envrnmnt/famncomm/pa600.htm

North Central Regional Educational Laboratory. (2004). *Promising school-linked services initiatives.* Retrieved May 11, 2005, from http://www.ncrel.org/cscd/pubs/lead21/2-1k.htm/

Northshore Families Helping Families. (2003). *Review of families helping families centers.* Covington, LA: Author. Retrieved August 17, 2005, from http://www.fhfla.org/nfhf/contact_us.php

Northwest Evaluation Association. (2005, April). *Impact of NCLB on student achievement and growth: 2005 education research brief.* Lake Oswego. OR: Author.

Northwest Regional Educational Laboratory. (1999, March). *Parent partners: Using parents to enhance education.* Portland, OR: Author.

Northwest Regional Educational Laboratory. (2001). *School improvement project.* Portland, OR: Author. Retrieved August 15, 2003, from http://www.nwrel.org/scpd/ote/impact.shtml

Novick, R. (2001). *Family involvement and beyond: School-based child and family support programs.* Portland, OR: Northwest Regional Education Laboratory.

Nowak, M., & Sigmund, K. (1998). Evolution of indirect reciprocity by image scoring. *Nature, 393,* 573–577.

Obiakor, F. E. (1999). Teacher expectations of minority exceptional learners: Impact on 'accuracy' of self-concept. *Exceptional Children, 66,* 39–54.

Obiakor, F. E., Utley, C., Smith, R., & Harris-Obiakor, P. (2002). The comprehensive support model for culturally diverse exceptional learners: Intervention in an age of change. *Intervention in School & Clinic, 38*(1), 14–27.

Obiakor, F. E., & Wilder, L. K. (2003). Disproportionate representation in special education. *Principal Leadership, 4*(2), 16–22.

O'Brien, C. L., & O'Brien J. (2002). The origins of person-centered planning. In S. Holburn & P. M. Vietze (Eds.), *Person-centered planning.* Baltimore: Paul H. Brookes.

O'Brien, J. (1987). A guide to life-style planning: Using the activities catalogue to integrate services and natural support system. In G. T. Bellamy & B. Wilcox (Eds.), *A comprehensive guide to the activities catalogue: An alternative curriculum for youth and adults with severe disabilities* (pp. 175–190). Baltimore: Paul H. Brookes.

O'Brien, J., & Mount, B. (2005). Make a difference: *A guidebook for person-centered support*. Toronto, ON, Canada: Inclusion Press.

Office of Juvenile Justice and Delinquency Prevention. (2000, February). From the courthouse to the schoolhouse: Making successful transitions. *Juvenile Justice Bulletin*, xx–xx.

O'Hare, M., & Printz, P. (2003). *Collaboration in New Hampshire: A look at service integration between Early Head Start and family-centered early supports and services*. Newton, MA: Education Development Center, Inc.

Ohio Legal Rights Service. (2004). *First steps: Early intervention services for infants and toddlers with delays or disabilities*. Columbus, OH: Ohio Legal Rights Service.

Olson, L. (2000). Policy focus converges on leadership. *Educational Week, 19*(17), 1, 16.

O'Neil, J. (1995). On schools as learning organizations. *Educational Leadership, 52*(7), 20–23. (ERIC Document Reproduction Service No. EJ 502 905)

Oregon Department of Human Services. (2002). *Department of Human Services integrated client database, services integration program*. Portland, OR: Author.

Orfield, G. (2004). *Dropouts in America: Confronting the graduation rate crisis*. Cambridge, MA: Harvard Education Press.

Orkwis, R., & McLane, K. (1998). *A curriculum every student can use: Design principles for student access.* [ERIC/OSEP Topical Brief.] Reston, VA: Council for Exceptional Children. (ED423654) Retrieved March 25, 2005, from http://www.cec.sped.org/osep/udesign.html

Ornstein, A., & Levine, D. (1997). *Foundations of education*. Boston: Houghton Mifflin.

Ortiz, D. (2004). *NCLB & IDEA 2004: A reexamination of the 'highly qualified teacher' definition & a consideration of the impact in the field of special education*. Unpublished paper, George Washington University.

Osguthorpe, R. T. (2000). Lessons from a school–university partnership. *Liberal Education, 86*(2), 38–45.

Osguthorpe, R. T. (2002). A framework for examining collaborative relationships in international educational partnerships. *International Journal of Educational Policy, Research and Practice, 3*(1), 69–78.

Osguthorpe, R. T., Osguthorpe, R. D., Jacobs, W. J., & Davies, R. (2003). The moral dimensions of instructional design. *Educational Technology, Research and Development, 43*(2), 19–23.

Osguthorpe, R. T., & Patterson, R. S. (1998). *Balancing the tensions of change: Eight keys to collaborative educational renewal*. Thousand Oaks, CA: Corwin Press.

O'Shaughnessy, T. E., Draper, K., Christenson, S. L., Miltich, A., Waldbart, A., & Gabriel, S. (2004). *Preventive intervention for kindergarten children at risk for school failure: Efficacy of a sustained early literacy-school engagement procedure*. Minneapolis: Institute on Community Integration, University of Minnesota.

O'Shea, D. J., Lee, W. A., & Sattler, R. O. (1999). Collaboration across special education and general education: Preservice teachers' views. *Journal of Teacher Education, 50*(2), 147–157.

O'Shea, D. J., & O'Shea, L. J. (1997). Collaboration and school reform: A twenty-first century perspective. *Journal of Learning Disabilities, 30*(4), 449–462.

O'Shea, D. J., O'Shea, L. J., Algozzine, R., & Hammitte, D. J. (2001). *Families and teachers of individuals with disabilities: Collaborative orientations and responsive practices*. Boston: Allyn & Bacon.

Osher, D., & Osher, T. (2002). The paradigm shift to true collaboration with families. *Journal of Child and Family Studies, 11*(10), 47–60.

Osipow, S. H. (1997). Roe revisited: Why? *Journal of Vocational Behavior, 51*(2), 306–309. (EJ 551 606)

O'Sullivan, E. (2003). Bringing a perspective of transformative learning to globalized consumption. International. *Journal of Consumer Studies, 27*(4), 326–330.

Otterbourg, S. D. (2003). *Investing in partnerships for student success: A basic tool for community stakeholders to guide educational partnership, development and management*. Washington, DC: Partnership for Family Involvement in Education. Retrieved August 15, 2005, from http://www.ed.gov/pubs/parents/pfie.html

Overton, S. (2005). *Collaborating with families: A case study approach*. Upper Saddle River, NJ: Merrill/Prentice Hall.

PACER Alliance. (2001). *Survey of families and IDEA*. Project of National Significance: Building Teacher Preparation Capacity through Partnerships with Families: Improving Teacher Quality. Orlando: University of Central Florida.

PACER Center. (2001). *Transition and beyond. . . now what?* Minneapolis, MN: Author.

Paige, M. (Ed.). (1993). *Education for the intercultural experience.* Yarmouth, ME: Intercultural Press.

Palches, A. (2005). *Collaborative consultation: Strategies for supporting the learning of all children within the classroom.* Perspectives, September/October. Massachusetts Association for Supervision and Curriculum Development.

Palmer, P. (1998). *The courage to teach: Exploring the inner landscape of a teacher's life.* San Francisco: Jossey-Bass.

Palmer, P. (2000). *Let your life speak: Listening for the voice of vocation.* San Francisco: John Wiley & Sons.

Pannabecker, J. R. (1995). Rousseau in the heritage of technology education. *Journal of Technology Education, 6*(2), 40–52.

Pannabecker, J. R. (2004). Inventing industrial education: The Ecole d'Arts et Métiers of Châlons-sur-Marne, 1807–1830. *History of Education Quarterly, 44*(2), 222–249.

PARC (Pennsylvania Association for Retarded Children) vs. Commonwealth of Pennsylvania, 334 Supp. 1257 (E. D. PA 1972).

Parents Engaged in Educational Reform. (2001). *Parents guide to special education.* Boston: Federation for Children with Special Needs.

Parrish, T. (2000). *Understanding the costs of special education.* The State Education Standard: Innovations in School Finance, Summer, Vol. 1 (3, 1–17). Alexandria, VA: National Association of State Boards of Education.

Pathways Mapping Initiative: School Readiness Pathway. (2004). *Project on effective intervention.* Cambridge, MA: Harvard University.

Patton, J., & Trainor, A. (2003). Utilizing applied academics to enhance curricular reform in secondary education. In C. A. Kochhar-Bryant & D. S. Bassett (Eds.), *Aligning transition and standards-based education: Issues and strategies.* Arlington, VA: Council for Exceptional Children.

Patton, J. R., & Blalock, G. (1996). *Transition and students with disabilities.* Austin, TX: PRO-ED.

Paulson, A. (2003, October 28). No parent left behind. *Christian Science Monitor,* 1–2.

Pavri, S., & Monda-Amaya, L. (2000). Loneliness and students with learning disabilities in inclusive classrooms: Self-perceptions, coping strategies, and preferred interventions. *Learning Disabilities Practice and Research, 15,* 23–34.

Payne, E. (2004). *New teacher toolkit.* Austin, TX: Texas Adult Education Agency, Texas State University–San Marcos, Center for Initiatives in Education.

Pearpoint, J., Forest, M., & O'Brien, J. (1993). *PATH: Planning possible positive futures.* Toronto, ON, Canada: Inclusion Press.

Pearpoint, J., Forest, M., & O'Brien, J. (1996). MAPs, Circles of Friends, and PATH: Powerful tools to help build caring communities. In S. Stainback & W. Stainback (Eds.), *Inclusion: A guide for educators* (pp. 67–86). Baltimore: Paul H. Brookes.

Peck, M. S. (1978). *The road less traveled: A new psychology of love, traditional values and spiritual growth.* New York: Simon & Schuster.

Pena, D. (2000). Parent involvement: Influences factors and implications. *Journal of Educational Research, 94*(1), 42–55.

Perez, M. A., & Pinzon, H. L. (1997). Latino families: Partners for success in school settings. *Journal of School Health, 67*(5), 182–185.

Perske, R. M. (1989). *Hope for the families: New directions for persons with retardation.* Nashville, IN: Abingdon Press.

Peter F. Drucker Foundation for Non-Profit Management. (2002). *Meeting the collaboration challenge: Developing strategic alliances between nonprofit organizations and businesses.* San Francisco: Jossey-Bass.

Petersen, A. C., & Crockett, L. (1985). Pubertal timing and grade effects on adjustment. *Journal of Youth and Adolescence, 14,* 191–206.

Peterson, K., & Brietzke, R. (1994). *Building collaborative cultures: Seeking ways to reshape urban schools.* [Urban Monograph Series]. Oak Brook, IL: North Central Regional Educational Laboratory.

Peterson, R., & Smith, C. (2002). *Dealing with behaviors perceived as unacceptable in schools: The interim alternative education setting solution* (pp. 13–22). Arlington, VA: Council for Children With Behavior Disorders.

Phelan, P., Davidson, A., & Yu, H. (1998). *Adolescents' worlds: Negotiating family, peers, and school.* New York: Teachers College Press.

Phelan, P., Yu, H. C., & Davidson, A. L. (1994). Navigating the psychosocial pressures of adolescence: The voices and experiences of high school youth. *American Educational Research Journal, 31*(2), 415–447.

Piaget, J. (1964). Development and learning. *Journal of Research in Science Teaching, 2*(3), 176–186.

Piaget, J. (1985). *The equilibrium of cognitive structures: The central problem of intellectual development.* Chicago: University of Chicago Press.

Piaget, J., & Inhelder, B. (1971). *The psychology of the child.* New York: Basic Books.

Pianta, R., & Kraft-Sayre, M. E. (2003). *Successful kindergarten transition: Your guide to connecting children, families and schools.* National Center for Early Development and Learning. Baltimore: Paul H. Brookes.

Pianta, R. C., & Hamre, B. K. (2001). *Students, teachers, and relationships support (STARS).* Lutz, FL: Psychological Assessment Resources.

Pianta, R. C., Cox, M. J., Taylor, L., & Early, D. (1999). Kindergarten teachers' practices related to the transition to school: Results of a national survey. *The Elementary School Journal, 100*(1), 71–86.

Pianta, R. C., & Kraft-Sayre, M. E. (1999). Parents' observations about their children's transitions to kindergarten. *Young Children, 54*(3), 47–51.

Pianta, R. C., Rimm-Kauffman, S. E., & Cox, M. J. (1999). *The transition to kindergarten.* Baltimore: Paul H. Brookes.

Pianta, R. C., Steinberg, M. S., & Rollins, K. B. (1995). The first two years of school: Teacher–child relationships and deflections in children's classroom adjustment. *Development and Psychopathology, 7*(2), 295–312.

Pianta, R. C., & Walsh, D. J. (1996). *High-risk children in schools: Constructing sustaining relationships.* New York: Routledge.

Pierangelo, R., & Crane, R. (1997). *Complete guide to special education transition services.* West Nyack, NY: Center for Applied Research in Education.

Pierce, N. (2003). *Community schools: Is it their time?* Retrieved August 20, 2005, from http://www.postwritersgroup.com/archives/peir0519.htm

Pindus, N., Koralek, R., Martinson, K., & Trutko, J. (2000). *Coordination and integration of welfare and workforce development systems* (p. 4). Washington, DC: Urban Institute. Retrieved May 7, 2005, from www.urban.org/welfare

Pinker, S. (2002). *The blank slate: The modern denial of human nature.* New York: Penguin Putnam.

Pinkerton, D. (1991). *Preparing children with disabilities for school.* Arlington, VA: Council for Exceptional Children. (ED340147)

Pinkerton, D. (2004). *Preparing children with disabilities for school.* Orange, CA: Child Development Institute.

Pleet, A. (2000). *Partnering with parents of youth with disabilities in the transition.* Annual Conference of the National Transition Alliance, Transition Research Institute, University of Illinois at Champaign.

Polgar, M., & Cabassa, L. (2001). Continuity of mental health care for young adults. *Focal Point, 15*(1), 11–12.

Polister, B., Blake, E., Prouty, R., & Lakin, K. (1998). *Reinventing quality: The 1998 sourcebook of innovative programs for the quality assurance and quality improvement in community services* [Report #52]. Minneapolis: Institute on Community Integration, University of Minnesota.

Porche, M., & Ross, S. (1999). *Parent involvement in the early elementary grades: An analysis of mothers' practices and teachers' expectations.* Paper presented to AERA Conference, Montreal, QE, Canada. Harvard Graduate School of Education.

Pounder, D. (1999). Opportunities and challenges of school collaboration. *UCEA Review, xl*(3), 1–3, 9–10.

Powell, K. S., & Jankovich, J. L. (1998, December). Student portfolios: A tool to enhance the traditional job search. *Business Communication Quarterly, 61*(4), 72–82.

Powers, L. E. (1996, June). *Promoting self-determination in transition planning: What does it take?* Presentation at the 11th Annual Transition Project Directors Meeting, Washington, DC.

Powers, L. E., Sowers, J., Turner, A., Nesbitt, M., Knowles, A., & Ellison, R. (1996). A model for promoting self-determination among adolescents with challenges. In L. E. Powers, G. H. Singer, & J. E. Sowers (Eds.), *On the road to autonomy: Promoting self-competence for children and youth with disabilities* (pp. 69–92). Baltimore: Paul H. Brookes.

Powers, L. E., Turner, A., Matuszewski, J., Wilson, R., Ellison, R., Westwood, D., & Phillips, A. (2001). TAKE CHARGE for the future: A controlled field-test of a model to promote student involvement in transition planning. *Career Development for Exceptional Individuals, 24*(1), 89–104.

Powers, L. E., Wilson, R., Matuszewski, J., Phillips, A., Rein, C., Schumacher, D., & Gensert, J. (1996). Facilitating adolescent self-determination: What does it take? In D. J. Sands & M. L. Wehmeyer (Eds.), *Self-determination across the life span: Independence and choice for people with disabilities* (pp. 257–284). Baltimore: Paul H. Brookes.

President's Commission on Excellence in Special Education. (2002). *A new era: Revitalizing special education for children and their families.* Washington, DC: U.S. Department of Education, Office of Special Education.

Price, T. (2005). *Development of an instrument to measure dispositions of teachers toward culturally and linguistically diverse families.* Unpublished dissertation, George Washington University, Washington, DC.

Primavera, J. (2000). Enhancing family competence through literacy activities. *Journal of Prevention and Intervention in the Community, 20*(1–2), 85–101.

Pritchard, I. (2000). Reducing class size, what do we know? *Management Information: School Information and Research Service, 25,* 13–23.

Pugach, M. C., & Johnson, L. J. (1999). *Collaborative practitioners, collaborative schools.* Denver, CO: Love Publishing.

Putnam, R. (2004, March). Bowling together. *OECD Observer.*

Quinn, K. P., & Epstein, M. H. (1998). Characteristics of children, youth, and families served by local interagency systems of care. In M. H. Epstein, K. Kutash, & A. Duchnowski (Eds.), *Outcomes for children and youth with behavioral and emotional disorders and their families* (pp. 81–114). Austin, TX: PRO-ED.

Quinn, K. P., & McDougal, J. L. (1998). A mile wide and a mile deep: Comprehensive interventions for children and youth with emotional and behavioral disorders and their families. *School Psychology Review, 27,* 191–203.

Quinn, M. M., Osher, D., Hoffman, C. C., & Hanley, T. V. (1998). *Safe, drug-free, and effective schools for ALL students: What works!* Washington, DC: Center for Effective Collaboration and Practice, American Institutes for Research.

Quinn, M. M., & Rutherford, R. B. (1998). *Alternative programs for students with social, emotional, and behavioral problems.* Reston, VA: Council for Children with Behavioral Problems.

Quinn, M. M., Rutherford, R. B., & Osher, D. M. (1999). *Special education in alternative education programs.* Reston, VA: Council for Exceptional Children.

Radcliffe, B., Malone, M., & Nathan, J. (1994). *Training for parent partnership: Much more should be done.* Minneapolis: Center for School Change, Hubert Humphrey Institute of Public Affairs, University of Minnesota.

Rado, G., Hamner, D., & Foley, S. (2004). State agency systems collaboration at the local level: Gluing the puzzle together. The staff perspective. *Research to Practice, 10*(1). Retrieved August 2, 2005, from http://www.communityinclusion.org/publications/pub.php?page=rp34

Raimondo, B., & Henderson, A. (2001). Unlocking parent potential. *Principal Leadership, 2*(1), 26–32.

Ralabate, P. F., & Foley, B. (2003). *IDEA and ESEA: Intersection of access and outcomes.* Washington, DC: National Education Association.

Ramey, C. T., & Ramey, S. L. (1999). Beginning school for children at risk. In R. C. Pianta & M. J. Cox (Eds.), *The transition to kindergarten.* Baltimore: Paul H. Brookes.

RAND Corporation. (2000). *Improving student achievement: What state NAEP test scores tell us (2000).* Santa Monica, CA: RAND Education.

Random House. (2001). *Webster's unabridged dictionary* (2nd ed.). New York: Author.

Raywid, M. A. (1994). Synthesis of research: Alternative schools. The state of the art. *Educational Leadership, 52*(1), 26–32.

Raywid, M. A. (1998). The journey of the alternative schools movement: Where it's been and where it's going. *The High School Magazine, 6*(2), 12–15.

Raywid, M. A. (1999). History and issues of alternative schools. *Education Digest, 64*(9), 47–51.

Reason, P. (1999). General medical and complementary practitioners working together: The epistemological demands of collaboration. *Journal of Applied Behavioural Science, 35*(1), 71–86.

Reese, B. (2001). Diversity and conflict resolution: Historical antecedents and future challenges. *ACResolution, 9*(1), 28.

Reese, L., & Gallimore, R. (2000). Immigrant Latinos' cultural model of literacy development: An evolving perspective on home-school discontinuities. *American Journal of Education, 108,* 103–134.

Rehabilitation Act Amendments of 1998, P. L.102–569, § 504 (29 U.S.C. Sec. 794).

Reihl, C. J. (2000). The principal's role in creating inclusive schools for diverse students: A review of normative, empirical, and critical literature on the practice of educational administration. *Review of Educational Research, 70*(1), 55–81.

Relave, N. (2002). Improving collaboration between welfare and workforce development agencies. *Welfare Information Issue Notes, 6*(4). Retrieved December 8, 2004, from www.financeprojectinfo.org/Publications/improvingcollaborationIN.htm

Reschly, D. J., & Ysseldyke, J. E. (1995). School psychology paradigm shift. In A. Thomas & J. Grimes (Eds.), *Best practices in school psychology III.* Bethesda, MD: National Association of School Psychologists.

Research and Training Center on Service Coordination. (2001). *Data report: Service coordination policies and models.* Farmington, CT: University of Connecticut Health Center, Research and Training Center on Service Coordination, Division of Child and Family Studies.

Restak, R. (2001). *The secret life of the brain.* Washington, DC: National Academies Press.

Reyes, E. I. (1999). Parents, families and communities ensuring children's rights. *Bilingual Review, 24*(1–2), 49–56.

Reynolds, A., Temple, J., Robertson, D., & Mann, E. (2001). Long-term effects of an early childhood intervention on educational achievement. *Journal of the American Medical Association, 285*, 2339–2346.

Rhode Island Kids Count. (2004). *Rhode Island kids count factbook.* Providence, RI: Author.

Rice, D., & Zigmond, N. (2000). Co-teaching in secondary schools: Teacher reports of developments in Australian and American classrooms. *Learning Disabilities Research and Practice, 15*(4), 190–197.

Rice, D., & Zigmond, N. (2001). Co-teaching in secondary schools—Teacher reports of developments in Australian and American classrooms. *Learning Disabilities Research and Practice, 15*(4), 190–197.

Richardson, J. (2001, February). Student work at the core of teacher learning. *Results Newsletter.* Oxford, OH: National Staff Development Council.

Ridley, M. (1998). *The origins of virtue: Human instincts and the evolution of cooperation.* New York: Penguin Books.

Ridley, S. (2002). *Cumberland County school readiness assessment.* Chapel Hill: Frank Porter Graham Child Development Institute, University of North Carolina.

Riehl, C. J. (2000). The principal's role in creating inclusive schools for diverse students: A review of normative, empirical, and critical literature on the practice of educational administration. *Review of Educational Research, 70*(1), 55–81.

Riley, R. (1994, February 15). *State of American education.* Prepared remarks for presentation at Georgetown University. Washington, DC: U.S. Department of Education.

Ripley, S. (1997). *Collaboration between general and special education teachers.* Washington, DC: ERIC Clearinghouse on Teaching and Teacher Education. (ED409317 SP037495)

Ripley, S. (2000). *Partnering with parents of youth with disabilities in transition.* Annual Conference of the National Transition Alliance, Transition Research Institute at Illinois, University of Illinois, Champaign.

Risko, V. J., & Bromley, K. (2001). *Collaboration for diverse learners.* Newark, DE: International Reading Association.

Ritter, C. L., Michel, C. S., & Irby, B. (1999). Concerning inclusion: Perceptions of middle school students, their parents and teachers. *Rural Special Education Quarterly, 18*(2), 10–17. (EJ 607 015)

Rivard, J. C., Johnson, M. C., Morrissey, J. P., & Starrett, B. E. (1999). The dynamics of interagency collaboration: How linkages develop for child welfare and juvenile justice sectors in a system of care demonstration. *Journal of Social Service Research, 25*, 61–82.

Rivera, C., Collum, E., Shafer, L., & Sia, J. K. (2004). *Analysis of state assessment policies regarding the accommodation of English language learners, 2000–2001.* Arlington, VA: George Washington University, Center for Equity and Excellence in Education.

Roach, A. (1999). Leadership giftedness: Models revisited. *Gifted Child Quarterly, 43*(1), 13–24.

Robbins, H. (1995). *Why teams don't work: What went wrong and how to make it right.* Princeton, NJ: Pacesetter Books.

Robinson, V., & Timperley, H. (2000). The link between accountability and improvement: The case of reporting to parents. *Peabody Journal of Education, 75*, 66.

Roeser, R. W., Eccles, J. S., & Sameroff, A. J. (2000). School as a context of early adolescents' academic and social–emotional development: A summary of research findings. *The Elementary School Journal, 100*(5), 443–471.

Roessler, R. T., & Rumrill, P. D. (1998). Self-advocacy training: Preparing students with disabilities to request classroom accommodations. *Journal of Postsecondary Education and Disability, 13*(3), 20–31.

Rogers, C. (1994). *Freedom to learn* (3rd ed.). Upper Saddle River, NJ: Merrill/Prentice Hall.

Rogers, E. L., & Rogers, D. C. (2001). Students with EB/D transition to college: Make a plan. *Beyond Behavior, 11*(1), 42–49.

Rose, D. H., & Meyer, A. (2000). Universal design for learning. *Journal of Special Education Technology, 15(1),* Winter, 67–70.

Rose, D. H., & Meyer, A. (2002). *Teaching every student in the digital age: Universal design for learning.* Baltimore: Association for Supervision & Curriculum Development. Retrieved August 5, 2005, from http://www.cast.org/teachingeverystudent/ideas/tes

Rosenblatt, A., & Woodbridge, M. (2003). Deconstructing research on systems of care for youth with EBD: Frameworks for policy research. *Journal of Emotional and Behavioral Disorders, 11*(1), 25–35.

Rosenblum, L., Dicecco, M. B., Taylor, L., & Adelman, H. S. (1995). Upgrading school support programs through collaboration: Resource coordinating teams. *Social Work in Education, 17,* 117–124.

Rosenfeld, S. J. (2005). *Section 504 and IDEA: Basic similarities and differences* (pp. 1–8). Hollywood, FL: Edlaw.

Rosenkoetter, S. E., Whaley, L. T., Hains, A. H., & Pierce, L. (2001). The evolution of transition policy for young children with special needs and their families: Past, present, and future. *Topics in Early Childhood Special Education, 21*(1), 3–15.

Rosman, E., McCarthy, J., & Woolverton, M. (2001). *Interagency coordination.* Washington, DC: Georgetown Child Development Center.

Rossi, P., Freeman, H., & Lipsey, M. (1999). *Evaluation: A systematic approach.* (6th ed.). Thousand Oaks, CA: Sage Publications.

Rothstein, R. (2002, April 10). Lessons, schools, accountability and a sheaf of fuzzy math. *New York Times,* Sec. B, 9, Col. 1.

Rottier, J. (2001). *Implementing and improving teaming: A handbook for middle level leaders.* Westerville, OH: National Middle School Association.

Rous, B., & Hallam, R. A. (1998). Easing the transition to kindergarten: Assessment of social, behavioral and functional skills in young children with disabilities. *Young Exceptional Children, 1*(4), 17–27.

Rous, B., Schuster, J., & Hemmeter, M. L. (1999). Evaluating the impact of the STEPS model on the development of community-wide transition systems. *Journal of Early Intervention, 22*(1), 38–50.

Rousseau, J. (1968). *The Social Contract* (M. Cranston, Trans.). New York: Penguin Classics.

Rueda, R., & Kim, S. (2001). Cultural and linguistic diversity as a theoretical framework for understanding multicultural learners with mild disabilities. In C. A. Utley & F. E. Obiakor (Eds.), *Special education, multicultural education, and school reform: Components for quality education for learners with mild disabilities* (pp. 74–89). Springfield, IL: Charles C. Thomas.

Ruiz-de-Velasco, J., Fix, M., & Clewell, B. (2000). *Overlooked and underserved: Immigrant students in U.S. secondary schools.* Washington, DC: Urban Institute Press. Retrieved August 10, 2005, from http://www.urban.org/UploadedPDF/overlooked.pdf

Rural Inclusion Project. (2001). *Training rural educators in Kentucky, role and responsibility changes in inclusive schools.* Lexington: University of Kentucky.

Russell, W. (2002). High quality technical assistance. *Benchmarks, Spring, 3*(2), 1–10. Washington, DC: National Clearinghouse for Comprehensive School Reform. Retrieved February 20, 2005, from http://www.goodschools.gwu.edu/pubs/bench/benchsp02.pdf

Rutherford, B., & Billig, S. (1995a). *Parent, family and community involvement in the middle grades.* Urbana IL: ERIC Clearinghouse on Elementary and Early Childhood Education.

Rutherford, B., & Billig, S. (1995b). Eight lessons of parent, family and community involvement in the middle grades. *Phi Delta Kappan, 77*(1), 64–68.

Rutherford, R., Magee-Quinn, M., Leone, P., Garfinkle, L., & Nelson, C. (2002). *Education, disability and juvenile justice: Recommended practices* (pp. 11–13, 28–29). Arlington, VA: Council for Children with Behavioral Disorders.

Rutherford, R. B., Jr., & Quinn, M. M. (1999). Special education in alternative education programs. *The Clearing House, 73*(2), 79–81.

Ryan, A. (Ed.). (2001). *Strengthening the safety net: How schools can help youth with emotional and behavioral needs complete their high school education and prepare for life after school.* Burlington, VT: School Research Office.

Ryan, R. M., & Deci, E. L. (2000). Self-determination theory and the facilitation of intrinsic motivation, social development, and well-being. *American Psychologist, 55*, 68–78.

Saab, T. D., & Gamble, M. J. (2003). *Accommodations: The five-step process to job success.* St. Augustine, FL: Training, Inc.

SABE USA. (2000). *The history of the developmental disabilities assistance and the bill of rights act.* New Fairfield, CT: Self Advocates Becoming Empowered (SABE). Retrieved July 28, 2005, from http://www.sabeusa.org/actdda.html

Sabornie, E., & DeBettencourt, L. (1997). *Teaching students with mild disabilities at the secondary level.* Upper Saddle River, NJ: Merrill/Prentice Hall.

Sack, J. (1999, January). Bringing special education students into the classroom. *Education Week on the Web.* Retrieved August 8, 2005, from http://www.edweek.org/ew/vol-18/20inclus.h18

Sadler, F. (2003). The itinerant special education teacher in the early childhood classroom. *Teaching Exceptional Children, 35*(3), 8–15. Arlington, VA: Council for Exceptional Children.

Sadowski, M. (Ed.). (2003). *Adolescents at school: Perspectives on youth, identity, and education.* Cambridge, MA: Harvard Education Publishing Group.

Sailor, W. (2002). Devolution, school/community/family partnerships, and inclusive education. In W. Sailor (Ed.), *Whole-school success and inclusive education: Building partnerships for learning, achievement, and accountability.* New York: Teachers College Press.

Saint-Laurent, L., Dionne, J., Giasson, J., Royer, E., Simard, C., & Pierard, B. (1998). Academic achievement effects of an in-class service model on students with and without disabilities. *Exceptional Children, 64,* 239–253.

Salend, S. J. (2001). *Creating inclusive classrooms: Effective and reflective practices.* Upper Saddle River, NJ: Merrill/Prentice Hall.

Salend, S. J., & Duhaney, L. G. (1999). The impact of inclusion on students with and without disabilities and their educators. *Remedial and Special Education, 20*(2), 114–127. (EJ 585 702)

Salend, S. J., Garrick-Duhaney, L. M., & Montgomery, W. (2002). A comprehensive approach to identifying and addressing issues of disproportionate representation. *Remedial and Special Education, 23*(5), 289–300.

Sanchez, J., Stuckey, M., & Morris, R. (1998, Winter). Distance learning in Indian country: Becoming the spider on the web. *Journal of American Indian Education, 37*(3), 1–20.

Sanchez, S. (2005). *Study of the perceptions of general educators of their ability to teach students with disabilities in their classrooms: A secondary analysis of the National Longitudinal Survey of Schools (NLSS).* Unpublished doctoral dissertation, George Washington University, Washington, DC.

Sandall, S., McLean, M. E., & Smith, B. J. (2000). *DEC recommended practices in early intervention/early childhood special education.* Longmont, CO: Sopris West.

Sanders, M. G., & Epstein, J. (1998). *School–family–community partnerships in middle and high schools: From theory to practice (CRESPAR Report 22).* Baltimore: Johns Hopkins University, Center for Research on the Education of Students Placed At Risk.

Sanders, M. G., & Epstein, J. L. (2000). Building school–family–community partnerships in middle and high schools. In Sanders, M. G. (Ed.), *Schooling students placed at risk: Research, policy, and practice in the education of poor and minority adolescents* (pp. 339–361). Mahwah, NJ: Lawrence Erlbaum Associates.

Sands, D. J., & Doll, B. (1996). Fostering self-determination is a developmental task. *The Journal of Special Education, 30,* 58–76.

Saphier, J., & Gower, R. (1997). *The skillful teacher: Building your teaching skills* (5th ed.). Acton, MA: Research for Better Teaching.

Sarkees-Wircenski, M., & Scott, J. L. (2003). *Special populations in career and technical education.* Homewood, IL: American Technical Publishers, Inc.

Sarkees-Wircenski, M., & Wircenski, J. (1994). Transition planning: Developing a career portfolio for students with disabilities. *Career Development for Exceptional Individuals, 17,* 203–214.

Sartorius, N. (2005). *Families and mental disorders: From burden to empowerment.* Hoboken, NJ: Wiley.

Sax, C., & Thoma, C. (2002). *Transition assessment: Wise practice for quality lives.* Baltimore: Paul H. Brookes.

Scales, P. C., & Gibbons, J. L. (1996). Extended family members and unrelated adults in the lives of young adolescents. A research agenda. *Journal of Early Adolescence, 16*(4), 365–389.

Schargel, F. (2003). *Strategies to help solve our school dropout problem.* Larchmont, NY: Eye on Education.

Schein, E. (1993, Winter). How can organizations learn faster? The challenge of entering the green room. *Sloan Management Review, 34*(2), 85–92.

Schemo, D. (2002). Schools face new policy on transfers. *New York Times,* December 9, 2002, A26.

Schiller, E., Burnaska, K., Cohen, G., Douglas, Z., Joseph, C., Johnston, P., et al. (2003). *Study of state and local implementation and impact of the Individuals with Disabilities Education Act—Final report on selected findings.* Bethesda, MD: Abt Associates.

Schmidt, J. (2004). *A survival guide for the elementary and middle school counselor.* San Francisco: Jossey-Bass.

Schmidt, M., & Harriman, N. (1998). *Teaching strategies for inclusive classrooms: Schools, students, strategies and success.* New York: Harcourt Brace.

Schmoker, M. (2001). *Results fieldbook.* Alexandria, VA: ASCD Publications.

Schoenwald, S. K., & Hoagwood, K. (2001). Effectiveness, transportability, and dissemination of interventions: What matters when? *Psychiatric Services, 52*(9), 1190–1197.

Schon, D. A. (1983). *The reflective practitioner.* New York: Basic Books.

Schon, D. A. (1987). *Educating the reflective practitioner.* San Francisco: Jossey-Bass.

School to Work Opportunities Act of 1994, P. L. 103-239, 20 U.S.C. § 6101 *et seq.*

Schribner, A. P., & Schribner, J. D. (2001). *High performing schools serving Mexican–American students: What they can teach us.* (ERIC Document Reproduction Service No. ED459048)

Schulenberg, J. E., Asp, C. E., & Petersen. A. C. (1984). School from the young adolescent's perspective: A descriptive report. *Journal of Early Adolescence, 4,* 107–130.

Schultz, T., Lopez, E., & Hochberg, M. (1995). *Early childhood reform in seven communities: Front–line practice, agency management, and public policy.* Washington, DC: U.S. Department of Education.

Schwandt, D., & Marquardt, M. (2000). *Organizational learning: From world-class theories to global best practices.* Boca Raton, FL: Lucie Press.

Schwartz, A., Shanley, J. Gerver, M., & O'Cummings, M. (2003). *A qualitative description of collaborative teams in today's classroom.* Washington, DC: Elementary and Middle Schools Technical Assistance Center.

Schweinhart, L. J., & Weikart, D. P. (1997). The High/Scope preschool curriculum comparison study through age 23. *Early Childhood Research Quarterly, 12*, 117–143.

Sefa Dei, G. J., Massuca, J., McIsaac, E., & Zine, J. (1997). *Reconstructing 'drop-out': A critical ethnography of the dynamics of 'black students' disengagement from school.* Toronto, ON, Canada: University of Toronto Press.

Semmel, M., Abernathy, T., Butera, G., & Lesar, S. (1991, September). Teacher perceptions of the regular education initiative. *Exceptional Children, 58*(1) 9–23.

Senge, P. (1994). *The fifth discipline: The art and practice of the learning organization.* New York: Doubleday.

Senge, P., Cambron-McCabe, N., Lucas, T., Kleiner, A., Dutton, J., & Smith, B. (2000). *Schools that learn: A fifth discipline fieldbook for educators, parents, and everyone who cares about education.* New York: Doubleday/Currency.

Senge, P. M., Kleiner, A., Roberts, C., Ross, R., & Smith, B. (1994). *The fifth discipline fieldbook.* New York: Doubleday.

Sergent, M. T., Carter, R. T., Sedlacek, W. R., & Scales, W. R. (1988). A five-year analysis of disabled student services in higher education. *Journal of Postsecondary Education and Disability, 6*, 21–27.

Sergiovanni, T. J. (1994). *Building community in schools.* San Francisco: Jossey-Bass.

Sevenson, R. (2003, March). Wraparound services: A community approach to keep even severely disabled children in local schools. American Association of School Administrators, *The School Administrator Web Edition.* Retrieved July 10, 2005, from http://www.aasa.org/publications/sa/2003_03/stevenson.htm

Shapiro, H. (1990). Society, ideology and the reform of special education: A study of the limits of educational change. *Educational Theory, 30*(3), 237–250.

Shapiro, I. (1980). *Social justice in the liberal state.* New Haven, CT: Yale University Press.

Shapiro, J., & Stefkovich, J. (2001). *Ethical leadership and decision making in education: Applying theoretical perspectives to complex dilemmas.* Mahwah, NJ: Lawrence Erlbaum Associates.

Sharpe, J. (1997). *Communities of practice: A review of the literature.* Retrieved April 20, 2005, from http://www.tfriend.com/cop-lit.htm

Sharpe, M., & Hawes, M. (2003). *Collaboration between general and special education: Making it work,* [Issue Brief, 1(2)]. Minneapolis, MN: National Center for Secondary Education and Transition.

Sharpe, M., & Johnson, D. R. (2001). A 20/20 analysis of postsecondary support characteristics. *Journal of Vocational Rehabilitation, 16*(3/4), 169–177.

Shartrand, A., Weiss, H., Kreider, H., & Lopez, M. (1997). *New skills for new schools: Preparing teachers for family involvement, Harvard Family Research Project.* Cambridge, MA: Harvard Graduate School of Education.

Shaw, S., Kochhar-Bryant, C., Izzo, M., Benedict, K., & Parker, D. (2005). *A model template for the summary of performance.* Stors, CT: National Transition Documentation Summit, University of Connecticut.

Shaw, S. F. (2006). Legal and policy perspectives on transition assessment and documentation. Special Issue, Career Development for Exceptional Individuals, *Journal of the Division on Career Development and Transition, 29*(2), Fall.

Shaw, S. F., & Dukes, L. L. (2001). Program standards for disability services in higher education. *Journal of Postsecondary Education and Disability, 14*(2), 81–90.

Shaw, S. F., McGuire, J. M., & Brinckerhoff, L. C. (1994). College and university programming. In P. J. Gerber & H. B. Reiff (Eds.), *Learning disabilities in adulthood: Persisting problems and evolving issues* (pp. 141–151). Austin, TX: PRO-ED.

Shelley-Sireci, L. M., & Racicot, L. (2001). Are natural environments unnatural? A survey of early intervention service providers. *NHSA Dialog: A Research to Practice Journal for the Early Intervention Field, 4*(1), 123–147.

Shepard, R., & Rose, H. (1995). The power of parents: An empowerment model for increasing parental involvement. *Education, 115*(3), 373–377.

Shinn, G. (1996). *The miracle of motivation: The action guide to happiness and success.* Carol Stream, IL: Tyndale House Publishers.

Shonkoff, J. P., & Phillips, D. A. (Eds.). (2001). *From neurons to neighborhoods: The science of early development.* Washington, DC: National Academy Press.

Shore, R. (1998). *Ready schools: A report of the Goal 1 Ready Schools Resource Group.* Washington, DC: The National Education Goals Panel.

Shors, T. J., Chua, C., & Falduto, J. (2001). Sex differences and opposite effects of stress on dendritic spine density in the male versus female hippocampus. *Journal of Neuroscience, 21*(16), 6292–6297.

Shoshkes, E. (2004). *Creating communities of learning: Schools and smart growth.* Trenton, NJ: Education Law Center.

Shrage, M. (1990). *Shared minds.* New York: Random House.

Siegel, L., & Senna, J. (1997). *Juvenile delinquency* (6th ed.). St. Paul, MN: West Publishing.

Sigmon, J. N., Nugent, M. E., & Engelhardt-Greer, S. (1999). *Abolish chronic truancy now diversion program: Evaluation report.* Alexandria, VA: American Prosecutors Research Institute.

Sileo, T. W., & Prater, M. A. (1998). Preparing professionals for partnerships with parents of students with disabilities: Textbook considerations regarding cultural diversity. *Exceptional Children, 64*(4), 513–528.

Sileo, T. W., Sileo, M., & Prater, M. A. (1998). The role of parents in the education of children with disabilities. *Teaching Exceptional Children, 32*(1), 8–13.

Silver, A. A., & Hagin, R. A. (1990). *Disorder of learning in childhood.* New York: Wiley.

Simeonsson, R., McMillen, B., McMillen, J., & Lollar, D. (2002). *Risk behaviors among middle school students with and without disabilities: The North Carolina middle school YRBS.* Chapel Hill: Frank Porter Graham Child Development Institute, University of North Carolina.

Simmons, D. C., & Kame'enui, E. J. (1996). A focus on curricula design: When children fail. *Focus on Exceptional Children, 28*(7), 1–16.

Simmons, E. (2002). The impact of home/school/community collaboration on student achievement: An analysis of reading renaissance. *Action Research Exchange, 1*(1), 1–2. Retrieved August 3, 2005, from http://chiron.valdosta.edu/are/Litreviews/vol1no1/simmons_litr.pdf

Simmons, R. G., & Blyth, D. A. (1987). *Moving into adolescence: The impact of pubertal change and school context.* Hawthorne, NY: Aldine de Gruyter.

Simmons, R. G., Blyth, D. A, VanCleave, E. F., & Bush, D. M. (1979). Entry into early adolescence: The impact of school structure, puberty, and early dating on self-esteem. *American Sociological Review, 44*, 948–967.

Simmons, R. G., Burgeson, R., Carlton-Ford, S., & Blyth, D. (1987). The impact of cumulative change in early adolescence. *Child Development, 58*, 1220–1234.

Simmons, R. G., Carlton-Ford, S., & Blyth, D. (1987). Predicting how a child will cope with the transition to junior high school. In R. Lerner & T. Foch (Eds.), *Biological–psychological interactions in early adolescence: A life-span perspective.* Hillsdale, NJ: Lawrence Erlbaum Associates.

Simmons, R. G., Rosenberg, F., & Rosenberg, M. (1973). Disturbance in the self-image at adolescence. *American Sociological Review, 38*, 553–568.

Simpson, J., Jivanjee, P., Koroloff, N., Doerfler, A., & Garcia, M. (2001). *Promising practices in early childhood mental health. Systems of care: Promising practices in children's mental health, 2001 series, Volume III.* Washington, DC: Center for Effective Collaboration and Practice, American Institutes for Research.

Sinclair, M. F. (2000, April). *Check & connect: Replication of a data-based student engagement/school completion model.* Paper presented at the annual meeting of the American Educational Research Association, Division H, New Orleans, LA.

Sinclair, M. F., Christenson, S. L., Evelo, D. L., & Hurley, C. M. (1998). Dropout prevention for high risk youth with disabilities: Efficacy of a sustained school engagement procedure. *Exceptional Children, 65*(1), 7–21.

Sinclair, M. F., Christenson, S. L., Lehr, C. A., & Anderson, A. R. (2003). Facilitating student engagement: Lessons learned from check & connect longitudinal studies. *The California School Psychologist, 8*(1), 29–42.

Sinclair, M. F., Christenson, S. L., & Thurlow, M. L. (2005). Promoting school completion of urban secondary youth with emotional or behavioral disabilities. *Exceptional Children, 71*(4), 465–482.

Sinclair, M. F., Christenson, S. L., Thurlow, M. L., & Evelo, D. L. (1994). *Are we pushing students in special education to drop out of school?* Washington, DC: National Institute on Disability and Rehabilitation Research. (ERIC Document 370325)

Sinclair, M. F., Christenson, S. L., Thurlow, M. L., & Evelo, D. L. (1996, December). On a collision course? Standards, discipline, and students with disabilities. *Policy Research Brief, 8*(4), 1–13. Minneapolis MN: University of Minnesota, Institute on Community Integration.

Sinclair, M. F., Hurley, C., Christenson, S., Thurlow, M., & Evelo, D. (2001). Connections that keep kids coming to school. In R. Algozzine & P. Kay (Eds.), *Preventing problem behaviors* (pp. 162–182). Thousand Oaks, CA: Corwin Press.

Sinclair, M. F., & Lehr, C. A. (2000, September). *Dakota county: Check & connect early truancy prevention programs: Summative program evaluation report.* Minneapolis: University of Minnesota, Institute on Community Integration.

Sinclair, M. F., Thurlow, M., Christenson, S., & Evelo, D. (1995). Check and connect partnership for school success: Project evaluation 1990–1995. In H. Thornton (Ed.), *Staying in school: A technical report of three dropout prevention projects for middle school students with learning and emotional disabilities.* Minneapolis: University of Minnesota, Institute on Community Integration.

Sindelar, P. (1995). Full inclusion of students with learning disabilities and its implications for teacher education. *Journal of Special Education, 29*(2), 234–244.

Singer, P. (2000). *A Darwinian left: Politics, evolution and cooperation.* New Haven, CT: Yale University Press.

Sippanen, P., Bloomberg, L., Ingram, D., & Hirsch, J. (1996). *Collaborative initiatives to develop integrated services for children and families: An outcome evaluation resource manual.* Minneapolis, MN: Center for Applied Research and Educational Improvement (CAREI).

Sitlington, P. L., Clark, G. M., & Kolstoe, O. P. (2000). *Transition education & services for adolescents with disabilities* (3rd ed.). Boston: Allyn & Bacon.

Sitlington, P., Neubert, D., & Leconte, P. (1997). Transition assessment: The position of the Division on Career Development and Transition. *Career Development for Exceptional Individuals, 20,* 69–79.

Sitlington, P. L., Neubert, D. A., Begun, W., Lombard, R. C., & LeConte, P. J. (1996). *Assess for success: Handbook on transition assessment.* Reston, VA: Council for Exceptional Children.

Slater, L. (2004). Collaboration: A framework for school improvement. *International Electronic Journal for Leadership in Learning, 8*(5), 1–11.

Slavin, R. (1995). *Neverstreaming: Ending learning disabilities before they start.* Baltimore: Johns Hopkins University, Center for Research on the Education of Students Placed at Risk.

Slavin, R. E. (1996). Research on cooperative learning and achievement: What we know, what we need to know. *Contemporary Educational Psychology, 21*(1), 43–69.

Slavin, R. E., Madden, N. A., & Wasik, B. A. (1996). Roots and wings. In S. Stringfield, S. Ross, & L. Smith (Eds.), *Bold plans for school restructuring: The new American schools development corporation designs* (pp. 207–231). Mahwah, NJ: Lawrence Erlbaum Associates.

Slonim, M. (1991). *Children, culture, and ethnicity.* New York: Garland.

Smith, B., & Fox, L. (2003). *Systems of service delivery: A synthesis of evidence relevant to young children at risk of or who have challenging behavior.* Sarasota: Center for Evidence-Based Practice, Young Children with Challenging Behavior, University of South Florida.

Smith, B., Miller, A. W., Archer, T., & Hague, C. (1996). *Working with diverse cultures.* Retrieved from http://www.ag.ohio-state.edu/~ohioline/bc-fact/0014.html

Smith, D. S., McLeskey, J., Tyler, N., & Saunders, S. (2002). *The supply and demand of special education teachers: The nature of the chronic shortage of special education teachers.* Unpublished manuscript, University of Florida, Gainesville.

Smith, D. S., Pion, G., Tyler, N. C., Sindelar, P., & Rosenberg, M. (2001). *The study of special education leadership personnel: With particular attention to the professoriate.* Nashville, TN: Vanderbilt University Press.

Smith, P., & Bell, C. H. (1996). *Structure-construction of a coalition.* Columbus: Ohio State University. Retrieved July 15, 2005, from http://www.ag.ohio-state.edu/~ohioline/lines/kids.html#COALI

Smith, R., & Knight, S. (1997). Collaborative inquiry: Teacher leadership in the practice of creative intelligence. In R. Sinclair & W. Ghory (Eds.), *Reaching and teaching all children* (pp. 39–60). New York: Corwin.

Smith, S. C., & Scott, J. J. (1990). *The collaborative school: A work environment for effective instruction.* Eugene: University of Oregon, ERIC Clearinghouse of Educational Management.

Smith, T. E. C., Polloway, E., Patton, J. R., & Dowdy, C. A. (2001). *Teaching students with special needs in inclusive settings* (3rd ed.). Boston: Allyn & Bacon.

Smith, T. E. C., Polloway, E., Patton, J. R., & Dowdy, C. A. (2003). *Teaching students with special needs in inclusive settings* (4th ed.). Boston: Allyn & Bacon.

Smith-Davis, J. (1991). *Planned change for personnel development: Strategic planning and the CSPD.* Lexington: Mid-South Regional Resource Center, University of Kentucky.

Smull, M. W., Sanderson, H., & Harrison, S. B. (1996). *Reviewing essential lifestyle plans: Criteria for best plans.* Kensington, MD: Support Development Associates.

Snell, M. E., & Janney, R. (2000). *Teacher's guides to inclusive practices: Collaborative teaming.* Baltimore: Paul H. Brookes.

Snow, K. (2001). *Disability is natural.* Woodland Park, CO: Braveheart Press.

Soodac, L. C., & Erwin, E. J. (1995). Parents, professionals, and inclusive education: A call for collaboration.

Journal of Educational and Psychological Consultation, 6(3), 257–276.

Soodac, L. C., Podell, D. M., & Lehman, L. R. (1998). Teacher, student and school attributes as predictors of teachers' responses to inclusion. *The Journal of Special Education, 31*(1), 480–497.

Sousa, D. (2001). *How the brain learns: A classroom teacher's guide.* Thousand Oaks, CA: Corwin.

Sparks, D. (2003). *National Staff Development Council's theory of change.* Retrieved June 10, 2005, from http://www.nsdc.org/library/publications/results/res9-03spar.cfm

Spinks, S. (2002). *Adolescent brains are works in progress: Here's why.* Retrieved August 2, 2005, from http://www.pbs.org/wgbh/pages/frontline/shows/teenbrain/work/adolescsent.html

Spring, J. (1988). *Conflicts of interest: Politics of American education.* White Plains, NY: Longman.

Srivastra, S., & Cooperrider, D. (1999). *Appreciative management and leadership: The power of positive thought and action in organizations.* Euclid, OH: Williams Custom Publishing.

Sroufe, L. A., & Fleeson, J. (1986). Attachment and construction of relationships. In W. Hartup & Z. Rubin (Eds.), *Relationships and development* (pp. 51–71). Hillsdale, NJ: Lawrence Erlbaum Associates.

Stainback, S., & Stainback, W. (1996). *Inclusion: A guide for educators.* Baltimore: Paul H. Brookes.

Stainback, W., Stainback, S., & Moravec, J. (1992). Using curriculum to build inclusive classrooms. In S. Stainback & W. Stainback (Eds.), *Curriculum considerations in inclusive classrooms: Facilitating learning for all students* (pp. 65–84). Baltimore: Paul H. Brookes.

Standards for Professional Development Schools (2001, Spring). *National Council for Accreditation of Teacher Education,* 12.

Starr, T. (2002). *Creating and sustaining collaborative relationships among teachers.* Retrieved July 9, 2005, from http://www.educ.uvic.ca/epls/faculty/storey/Starr.htm

Steckbeck, P. (2004). Early literacy and language identification and intervention: A team approach. *The ASHA Leader, 2,* 6–7.

Steele-Carlin, S. (2001). California School for the Blind Pioneers Program. *Education World.* Retrieved August 30, 2005, from http://www.education-world.com/a_curr/curr339.shtml

Steere, D. E., Wood, R., Panscofar, E. L., & Butterworth, J. (1990). Outcome-based school-to-work transition planning for students with severe disabilities. *Career Development for Exceptional Individuals, 13*(1), 57–70.

Stehli, A. (1995). *Dancing in the rain: Stories of exceptional progress by parents of children with special needs.* Westport, CT: Georgiana Organization, Inc.

Steinburg, P., & Baier, S. (2003). *Alderwood Middle School makes a difference.* Seattle, WA: New Horizons for Learning.

Steiner, G. (1997). *Strategic planning.* Carmichael, CA: Touchstone Books.

Stephens, R. D., & Arnette, J. L. (2000). *From the courthouse to the schoolhouse: Making successful transitions.* Washington, DC: U.S. Department of Justice, Office of Juvenile Justice and Delinquency Prevention.

Stevens, T. (1998). *You can choose to be happy: Rise above anxiety, anger, depression.* Seal Beach, CA: Wheeler-Sutton Publisher.

Stevenson, R. (2003, March). Wraparound services: A community approach to keep even severely disabled children in local schools. *The School Administrator Web Edition.* Retrieved January 15, 2005, from http://www.aasa.org/publications/sa/2003_03/stevenson.htm

Stodden, R. A. (2001). Postsecondary educational supports for students with disabilities: A review and response. *The Journal for Vocational Special Needs Education, 23*(2), 4–11.

Stodden, R. A., & Dowrick, P. W. (2001). Postsecondary education and employment of adults with disabilities. *American Rehabilitation, 25*(3), 19–23.

Stodden, R. A., Galloway, L. M., Stodden, N. J. (2003). Secondary school curricula issues: Impact on postsecondary students with disabilities. *Exceptional Children, 70*(1), 9–25.

Stodden, R. A., Jones, M. A., & Chang, K. (2002). *Services, supports and accommodations for individuals with disabilities: An analysis across secondary education, post-secondary education and employment.* Honolulu: Center on Disability Studies, University of Hawaii at Manoa. Retrieved February 15, 2005, from http://www.rrtc.hawaii.edu/capacity/papers/StoddenJones_formatted.htm

Stodden, R. A., & Welley, M. (2002). *Post-secondary supports for individuals with disabilities: Latest research findings.* Honolulu: National Center for the Study of Postsecondary Educational Supports, Center on Disability Studies, University of Hawaii at Manoa.

Stodden, R. A., Whelley, T., Harding, T., & Chang, C. (2001). Current status of educational support provision to students with disabilities in post-secondary education. *Journal of Vocational Rehabilitation, 16,* 1–10.

Stoffner, M. F., & Williamson, R. D. (2000). Facilitating student transitions into middle school. *Middle School Journal, 31*(4), 47–51.

Storms, J., O'Leary, E., & Williams, J. (2000a). *The Individuals with Disabilities Education Act of 1997 transition requirements: A guide for states, districts, schools, universities and families.* Minneapolis: National Transition Network Institute on Community Integration, University of Minnesota.

Storms, J., O'Leary, E., & Williams, J. (2000b). *Transition requirements: A guide for states, districts, schools, universities and families.* Minneapolis: Western Regional Resource Center, National Network Institute on Community Integration, University of Minnesota.

Stowitschek, J., & Lovitt, T. (2000). Contrasting profiles of collaboration in two urban high schools, *Journal of Vocational Special Needs Education, 22*(2), 6–19.

Stowitschek, J. J., & Kelso, C. A. (1989). Are we in danger of making the same mistakes with ITPs as were made with IEPs? *Career Development for Exceptional Individuals, 12*(2), 139–151.

Stowitschek, J. J., Laitinen, R., & Prather, T. (1999). Embedding early self-determination opportunities in curriculum for youth with developmental disabilities using natural teaching incidents. *Journal for Vocational Special Needs Education, 21*, 15–26.

Strage, A. A., & Brandt, T. S. (1999). Authoritative parenting and college students' academic adjustment and success. *Journal of Educational Psychology, 91*(1), 146–156.

Strain, P. S., & Timm, M. A. (2001). Remediation and prevention of aggression: An evaluation of the Regional Intervention Program over a quarter century. *Behavioral Disorders, 26*(4), 297–313.

Straus, D. (2002). *How to make collaboration work.* San Francisco: Berrett-Koeler Publishers.

Stroul, B. (1993). *Systems of care for children and adolescents with severe emotional disturbances: What are the results?* Washington, DC: Georgetown University Child Development Center, CASSP Technical Assistance Center.

Study of Personnel Needs in Special Education. (2002). *General education teacher's role in special education.* Gainesville: University of Florida. Retrieved April 7, 2005, from http://ferdig.coe.ufl.edu/spense/gened11-29.pdf

Study of State and Local Implementation and Impact of the Individuals With Disabilities Education Act. (2003). *Highlights from the 1999–2000 School Year—Year 1 Data Collection.* Bethesda, MD: Abt Associates.

Stuhlman, M., Hamre, B., & Pianta, R. (2002, Fall). Building supporting relationships with adolescents. *Middle Matters,* 1–3.

Stump, C. S. (2004). *Collaboration in education.* San Francisco: San Francisco State University.

Substance Abuse and Mental Health Services Administration. *Starting early starting smart (SESS): The collaboration essentials.* Rockville, MD: Author.

Sugai, G., & Tindal, G. (1993). *Effective school consultation, an interactive process.* Pacific Grove, CA: Brooks/Cole.

Super, D. E., Thompson, A. S., Lindeman, R. H., Joordan, J., & Myers, R. A. (1981). *Career development inventory.* Palo Alto, CA: Consulting Psychologists Press.

Surber, J. (2003, March). Flexible service delivery. *The School Administrator Web Edition.* Retrieved June 12, 2005, from http://www.aasa.org/publications/sa/2003_03/stevenson_surber.htm

Sussman, T. (2000). Interagency collaboration and welfare reform. *Welfare Information Network: Issue Note, 4*(1). Retrieved January 15, 2005, from http://www.welfareinfo.org/crosscuttingtara/htm

Sutherland, J. (1973). *A general systems philosophy for the social and behavioral sciences.* New York: George Braziller.

Swaim, S. (2003, Winter). What middle schools should and can be. *Middle Matters,* 4–6.

Swartz, S. (2004). *Working together: A collaborative model for the delivery of special services in general classrooms.* San Bernardino, CA: Foundation for Comprehensive Early Literacy Learning. Retrieved October 11, 2004, from http://www.stanswartz.com/collaboration.html

Swick, K. J., Boutte, G., & Van Scoy, I. (1999). *Families and schools: Building multicultural values together.* [Annual Editions, Multicultural Education, 98/99]. Guilford, CT: Dushkin Publishing Group.

Sykes, C. J. (1995). *Dumbing down our kids: Why America's children feel good about themselves but can't read, write, or add.* New York: St. Martin's Press.

Sylwester, R. (2003). *A biological brain in a cultural classroom: Enhancing cognitive and social development through collaborative classroom management* (2nd ed.). Thousand Oaks, CA: Corwin.

Sztompka, P. (1999). *Trust: A sociological theory.* Cambridge: Cambridge University Press.

Talbot, P. (1998). *Critical beginnings: Creating school community for all children and families.* Virginia Tech Electronic Theses and Dissertations. Blacksburg: Virginia Polytechnic Institute and State University.

Tanaka, G. (1996). What's health got to do with it? A case for health programs in middle level schools. *Midpoints, 6*(1), 1–12.

Tannenbaum, L. G. (2001). *Parent/professional perceptions of collaboration when viewed in the context of Virginia's Comprehensive Services Act System of Care.* [Virginia Tech Electronic Theses and Dissertations]. Blacksburg: Virginia Polytechnic Institute and State University.

Tashie, C., Shapiro-Barnard, S., Dillon, A. D., Schuh, M., Jorgensen, C., & Nisbet, J. (1993). *Changes in latitudes, changes in attitudes: The role of the inclusion facilitator.* Concord: Institute on Disability, University of New Hampshire.

Tate, M. (2004). *Sit and get won't grow dendrites: 20 professional learning strategies that engage the adult brain.* Thousand Oaks, CA: Sage Publications.

Taylor, E. (1998). *The theory and practice of transformative learning: A critical review.* Information Series No. 374. Columbus: Ohio State University, ERIC Clearinghouse on Adult, Career, and Vocational Education.

Taylor, L., & Adelman, H. (2000). Toward ending the marginalization of mental health in schools. *Journal of School Health, 70,* 210–215.

Taylor, L., & Adelman, H. (2001). Enlisting appropriate parental cooperation and involvement in children's mental health treatment. *The Mental Health Desk Reference, 31,* 219–224.

Taylor-Powell, E., Rossing, B., & Geran, J. (1998). *Evaluating collaboratives: Reaching the potential.* Madison: University of Wisconsin, Cooperative Extension.

Taymans, J., & Lynch, S. (2004). Developing a unit planning routine. In B. Lenz, D. Deshler, & B. Kissam, *Teaching content to all: Evidence-based inclusive practices in middle and secondary schools.* Boston: Allyn & Bacon.

Taymans, J., & West, L. (2001). *Selecting a college for students with learning disabilities of attention deficit hyperactivity disorder (ADHD).* Arlington, VA: Council for Exceptional Children.

Taymans, J. M., West, L. L., & Sullivan, M. (Eds.). (2000). *Unlocking potential: College and other choices for people with LD and AD/HD.* Bethesda, MD: Woodbine House.

Technical Assistance Alliance for Parent Centers. (2001). Developing parent leadership: A grant writing manual for community parent resource centers. Minneapolis, MN: Author.

Texas Education Agency. (1996). *Career pathways toolbook* (pp. 143–144). Austin, TX: Author.

Thagard, P. (1992). *Conceptual revolutions.* Princeton, NJ: Princeton University Press.

Thagard, P. (1997). Collaborative knowledge. *Nous, 31,* 242–261.

Thoma, C. A. (1999). Supporting student voices in transition planning. *Teaching Exceptional Children, 31*(5), 4–9.

Thomas, C., Correa, V., & Morsink C. (2001). *Interactive teaming: Enhancing programs for students with special needs* (3rd ed). Upper Saddle River, NJ: Merrill/Prentice Hall.

Thompson, A.E., & Kaplan, C. A. (1999). Emotionally abused children presenting to child psychiatry clinics. *Child Abuse and Neglect, 23,* 191–196.

Thompson, J. R., Fulk, B. M., & Piercy, S. W. (2000). Do individualized transition plans match the postschool projections of students and parents? *Career Development for Exceptional Individuals, 23,* 3–26.

Thompson, S., Thurlow, M., Parson, L., & Barrow, S. (2000). *Initial perceptions of educators as they work toward including students with disabilities in Minnesota's High Standards, Report 25.* Minneapolis, MN: National Center on Educational Outcomes.

Thorkildsen, R., & Scott Stein, M. R. (1998). *Is parent involvement related to student achievement? Exploring the evidence* (Research Bulletin No. 22). Bloomington, IN: Phi Delta Kappa, December (22), 17–20.

Thorn, C. A. (2001). Knowledge management for educational information systems: What is the state of the field? *Education Policy Analysis Archives, 9*(47).

Thousand, J. S., & Villa, R. S. (1990). Sharing expertise and responsibilities through teaching teams. In S. Stainback & W. Stainback, *Inclusion: A guide for educators.* Baltimore: Paul H. Brookes.

Thuli, K. J., & Hong, E. (1998). *Employer toolkit.* Washington, DC: National Transition Alliance for Youth with Disabilities, Academy for Educational Development.

Thurlow, M. L., Anderson, M. E., Minnema, J. E., & Hall-Lande, J. (2005). Policymaker perspectives on the inclusion of English language learners with disabilities in statewide assessments. In *English Language Learners With Disabilities Report 8.* Minneapolis: University of Minnesota, National Center on Educational Outcomes.

Thurlow, M. L., Christenson, S., Sinclair, M., & Evelo, D. (1995). *Staying in school: Strategies for middle school students with learning and emotional disabilities.* Minneapolis: University of Minnesota, College of Education and Human Development, Institute on Community Integration.

Thurlow, M. L., Christenson, S. L., Sinclair, M. F., & Evelo, D. L. (1997). Wanting the unwanted: Keeping those 'out of here' kids in school. *Beyond Behavior, 8*(3), 10–16.

Thurlow, M. L., Minnema, J. E., & Treat, J. E. (2004). *A review of 50 states' online large scale assessment policies: Are English language learners with disabilities considered?* [Report 5]. Minneapolis: University of Minnesota, National Center on Educational Outcomes.

Thurlow, M. L., Sinclair, M. F., & Johnson, D. R. (2002). *Students with disabilities who drop out of school: Implications for policy and practice. Issue Brief, 1*(2), 1–7. Minneapolis: University of Minnesota, Institute on Community Integration, National Center on Secondary Education and Transition.

Thurlow, M. L., Thompson, S., & Johnson, D. (2002). Traditional and alternative assessments within the transition process and standards-based education. In C. Kochhar-Bryant & D. S. Bassett (Eds.), *Aligning transition and standards-based education: Issues and strategies.* Arlington, VA: Council for Exceptional Children.

Tileston, D. W. (2000). *10 best teaching practices: How brain research, learning styles, and standards define teaching competencies.* Thousand Oaks, CA: Corwin.

Tinbergen, N. (1970). *Signals for survival.* Gloucestershire, UK: The Clarendon Press.

Tindle, K., Leconte, P., Buchanan, L., & Taymans, L. (2004). *Community mapping as a tool for teachers and students.* Minneapolis: National Center for Secondary Education and Transition, University of Minnesota.

Title III–English Language Acquisition, Language Enhancement, and Academic Achievement Act, Pub. L. No. 107–110, 20 U.S.C. § 6811/6822 (2000).

Title 34B Education part 303 (Early intervention program for infants and toddlers with disabilities: Service coordination). *Code of Federal Regulations, 34*(2) [Parts 300 to 399]. Washington, DC: U.S. Government Printing Office.

Tizard, J., Schofield, W. N., & Hewison, J. (1982). Collaboration between teachers and parents in assisting children's reading. *British Journal of Educational Psychology, 52*, 1–15.

Tobin, R., & Sprague, J. (2000). Alternative education strategies: Reducing violence in schools and community. *Journal of Emotional and Behavioral Disorders, Fall, 8*(3), 177–186.

Tomlinson, C. A. (2001). *How to differentiate instruction in mixed-ability classrooms* (2nd ed.). Alexandria, VA: Association for Supervision and Curriculum Development.

Tomlinson, C. A., Moon, T. R., & Callahan, C. M. (1998). How well are we addressing academic diversity in the middle school? *Middle School Journal, 29*(3), 3–11.

Traub, A. (1999). *Better by design.* Arlington, VA: The New American Schools Development Corporation.

Tremblay, R. E. (2000). The development of aggressive behavior during childhood: What have we learned in the past century? *International Journal of Behavioral Development, 24*, 129–141.

Trivette, C. M., & Dunst, C. J. (2005). Recommended practices: Family-based practices. In S. Sandall, M. L. Hemmeter, B. J. Smith, & M. E. McLean (Eds.), *DEC recommended practices: A recommended guide for practical application in early intervention/early childhood special education* (pp. 107–126). Arlington, VA: Council for Exceptional Children.

Trusty, J., Watts, R. E., & Erdman, P. (1997). Predictors of parents' involvement in their teens' career development. *Journal of Career Development, 23*(3), 189–201. (EJ 540 414)

Tuckman, B. W., & Jensen, M. A. C. (1977). States in small group development revisited. *Group and Organizational Studies, 2*, 419–442.

Turnbull, A. P., Brotherson, M. J., & Summers, J. A. (1985). The impact of deinstitutionalization of families. In R. Bruininks & K. Lakin (Eds.), *Living and learning in the least restrictive environment* (115–152). Baltimore: Paul H. Brookes.

Turnbull, A. P., & Turnbull, H. R. (1996). Self-determination within a culturally responsive family systems perspective: Balancing the family mobile. In L. E. Powers, G. H. S. Singer, & J. Sowers (Eds.), *Promoting self-competence in children and youth with disabilities: On the road to autonomy* (pp. 195–220). Baltimore: Paul H. Brookes.

Turnbull, A. P., & Turnbull, H. R. (1999). *Self-determination: Focus on the role of families in supporting individuals with significant cognitive disabilities.* Portland: Oregon Health & Science University, Center on Self-Determination.

Turnbull, A. P., & Turnbull, H. R. (2001). *Families, professionals, and exceptionality: A special partnership* (4th ed.). Upper Saddle River, NJ: Merrill/Prentice Hall.

Turnbull, A. P., & Winton, P. J. (1984). Parent involvement policy and practice: Current research and implications for families of young, severely handicapped children. In J. Blacher (Ed.), *Severely handicapped young children and their families* (pp. 377–397). New York: Academic Press.

Turnbull, H. R. III, Turnbull, A. P., Wehmeyer, M. L., & Park, J. (2003). A quality of life framework for special education outcomes. *Remedial and Special Education, 24,* 67–74.

Tyack, D. (1992). Health and social services in public schools: Historical perspectives. *The future of children, 2*(1), 19–31.

Tylor, E. B. (1993). *Primitive culture: Research into the development of mythology, philosophy, religion, art, and customs.* London: John Murray.

Ulrich, M. E., & Bauer, A. M. (2003). Levels of awareness. *Teaching Exceptional Children, 35,* 20–23.

UNI Department of Teaching. (2003). *Rubric for collaboration.* Cedar Falls: University of Northern Iowa, 1998–2002. Retrieved July 21, 2005, from http://www.sdcoe.k12.ca.us/score/actbank/collaborub.html

United Nations. (2005). *Implementing child rights in early childhood, general comment no. 7* (September 12–30, 2005). Convention on the Rights of the Child, Committee on the Rights of the Child, Forty-First Session, Geneva.

University of Central Florida. (2004). *Learning modules series for building teacher preparation capacity through partnerships with families* (p. 7). Orlando: University of Central Florida. Retrieved August 12, 2006, from http://www.teacherfamilies.org

University of Illinois at Chicago National Research & Training Center. (2002). *Self-determination framework for people with psychiatric disabilities.* Chicago, IL: Author. Retrieved August 2, 2006, from http://www.psych.uic.edu/UICNRTC/sdframework.pdf

University of Michigan Health System. (2004). *Developmental delay.* Ann Arbor: University of Michigan.

Urdan, T., & Klein, S. (1998). *Early adolescence: A review of the literature.* Unpublished paper prepared for the U.S. Department of Education, Office of Educational Research and Improvement. Washington, DC.

U.S. Census Bureau. (2000). *Profile of selected social characteristics: 2000. Census 2000.* Retrieved August 10, 2005, from http://factfinder.census.gov/

U.S. Chamber of Commerce. (2004). *Disability employment 101: Learn to tap your 'hire' potential.* Washington, DC: Author.

U.S. Department of Commerce. (1999). *Population profile of the United States, 1999.* Washington, DC: Author.

U.S. Department of Education. (2000a). *Eliminating barriers to improving teaching.* Washington, DC: Government Printing Office.

U.S. Department of Education. (2000b). *Learning without limits: An agenda for the Office of Postsecondary Education.* Washington, DC: Author.

U.S. Department of Education. (2000c). *A new era: Revitalizing special education for children and their families: Report of the President's Commission on Excellence in Special Education.* Jessup, MD: Ed Pubs.

U.S. Department of Education. (2001). Challenges to providing secondary education and transition services for youth with disabilities. In *Twenty-third annual report to Congress on the implementation of the Individuals with Disabilities Education Act* (pp. I-19–I-31). Washington, DC: U.S. Government Printing Office.

U.S. Department of Education. (2002a). *Meeting the highly qualified teachers challenge: The secretary's annual report on teache rquality: 2002.* Jessup, MD: Ed. Pubs.

U.S. Department of Education. (2002b). *No Child Left Behind: A desktop reference.* Washington, DC: Author.

U.S. Department of Education. (2004, March 2). *Letter to chief state school officers regarding inclusion of students with disabilities in state accountability systems.* Washington, DC: Author.

U.S. Department of Education. (2005). *Biennial evaluation report to Congress on the Implementation of the State Formula Grant (2002–2004), English Language Acquisition, Language Enhancement and Academic Achievement Act* (ESEA, Title III, Part A). Washington, DC: Author. Retrieved from http://www.ncela.gwu.edu/oela/biennial05/full_report.pdf

U.S. Department of Education, Family Involvement Partnership for Learning. (1996). *America goes back to school: A place for families and the community.* Washington, DC: Author.

U.S. Department of Education, Institute of Education Sciences. (2003a). *Condition of education.* Washington, DC: National Center for Education Statistics.

U.S. Department of Education, Institute of Education Sciences. (2003b). *What works: Providing evidence in education.* Washington, DC: Author. Retrieved July 28, 2005, from http://wwcinfo@w-w-c.org

U.S. Department of Education, National Center for Education Statistics. (2002). *The condition of education 2002.* Washington, DC: Author. (NCES 2002-025)

U.S. Department of Education, National Center for Education Statistics. (2003). *Prekindergarten in U.S. Public Schools: 2000–2001.* Washington, DC: Author. (NCES 2003-019)

U.S. Department of Education, National Educational Research Policy and Priorities Board. (2000). *National conference on curriculum, instruction and assessment in the middle grades: Linking research and practice, 2000,* Washington, DC: Author.

U.S. Department of Education, Office of Educational Research and Improvement. (1997a). *Family involvement in children's education.* Washington, DC: Author. Retrieved September 2, 2005, from http://www.ed.gov/pubs/faminvolve/execsumm.html

U.S. Department of Education, Office of Educational Research and Improvement. (1997b). *Fitting the pieces together: Education reform that works.* Washington, DC: Author.

U.S. Department of Education, Office of Postsecondary Education. (2004). *Meeting the highly qualified teachers challenge: The secretary's third annual report on teacher quality.* Washington, DC: Author.

U.S. Department of Education, Office of Safe and Drug-Free Schools. (1999a). *Guidelines for submitting safe, disciplined and drug-free schools programs for designation as promising or exemplary.* Washington, DC: Author.

U.S. Department of Education, Office of Safe and Drug-Free Schools. (2003b). *Middle school drug prevention and school safety program coordinators grant recipients.* Washington, DC: Author.

U.S. Department of Education, Office of Special Education. (1999b). *OSEP federal monitoring update.* Washington, DC: Author.

U.S. Department of Education, Office of Special Education. (2001). *Twenty-third annual report to Congress on the implementation of the Individuals with Disabilities Education Act.* Washington, DC: Author.

U.S. Department of Education, Office of Special Education. (2002). *Twenty-fourth annual report to Congress on the implementation of the Individuals with Disabilities Education Act.* Washington, DC: Author.

U.S. Department of Education, Office of Special Education. (2003). *Twenty-fifth annual report to Congress on the Implementation of the Individuals with Disabilities Education Act.* Washington, DC: Author.

U.S. Department of Education, Office of Special Education and Rehabilitative Services. (2002). *A new era: Revitalizing special education for children and their families.* Washington, DC: Author.

U.S. Department of Education, Office of Special Education and Rehabilitative Services, Office of the Assistant Secretary. (2003). *National Symposium on Learning Disabilities in English Language Learners, October 14–15, 2003: Symposium Summary,* Washington, D.C., 2004.

U.S. Department of Education, Office of Special Education Programs. (1999). *Twenty-first annual report to Congress on the implementation of the Individuals with Disabilities Education Act* Washington, DC: Author.

U.S. Department of Education & U.S. Department of Justice (1998). *Safe and smart: Making the after-school hours work for kids.* Washington, DC: Author.

U.S. Department of Health and Human Services. (2001). *Report of the Surgeon General's conference on children's mental health: A national action agenda.* Rockville, MD: Author.

U.S. Department of Health and Human Services. (2003). *President's New Freedom Commission on Mental Health Final Report: Achieving the promise: Transforming mental health care in America.* Washington, DC: Author. (DHHS Pub. No. SMA-03-3832)

U.S. Department of Health and Human Services, Administration for Children and Families, Children's Bureau. (2003). *School-based child maltreatment programs: Synthesis of lessons learned.* Washington, DC: Author.

U.S. Department of Health and Human Services, Administration for Children, Youth and Families. (2001a). *Building their futures: How Early Head Start programs are enhancing the lives of infants and toddlers in low-income families.* Washington, DC: Author.

U.S. Department of Health and Human Services, Administration for Children, Youth and Families. (2001b). *The family and child experiences survey, third report.* Washington, DC: Author.

U.S. Department of Health and Human Services, Substance Abuse and Mental Health Services Administration. (2001a). *Annual report to Congress on the evaluation of the Comprehensive Community Mental Health Services Program for Children and Their Families.* Washington, DC: Author.

U.S. Department of Health and Human Services, Substance Abuse and Mental Health Services Administration. (2001b). *Key principles in providing integrated behavioral health services for young children and their families: The starting early starting smart experience.* Washington, DC: Casey Family Programs and Author.

U.S. Department of Justice. (2003). *America's law enforcement and mental health project (Public Law 106–515).* Washington, DC: Author.

U.S. Department of Labor, Bureau of Labor Statistics. (2004). *Teachers: Preschool, kindergarten, elementary, middle, and secondary.* Retrieved August 27, 2005, from http://stats.bls.gov/oco/ocos069.htm

U.S. Department of Labor, Office of Disability Employment Policy. (2001a). *Accommodating employees with hidden disabilities*. Washington, DC: Author.

U.S. Department of Labor, Office of Disability Employment Policy. (2001b). *On the job: Employees and employers in their own words*. Washington, DC: Author.

U.S. Department of Labor, Office of Disability Employment Policy. (2001c). *Personal assistance services in the workplace*. Washington, DC: Author.

U.S. Department of Labor, Office of Disability Employment Policy. (2001d). *The ticket to work and self-sufficiency program*. Washington, DC: Author. (SSA Publication No. 05-10061)

U.S. Department of Labor, Office of Disability Employment Policy. (2004). *Working while disabled: A guide to plans for achieving self-support*. Washington, DC: Author. (SSA Publication No. 05-11017)

U.S. Department of Labor, Office of Disability Employment Policy. (2005). *Opening doors to job accommodations*. Washington, DC: Author. Retrieved July 22, 2005, from www.dol.gov/odep/pubs/ek98/jan.htm

U.S. Government Accountability Office. (2003a). *Child welfare and juvenile justice: Federal agencies could play a stronger rule in helping states reduce the number of children placed solely to obtain mental health services*. Washington, DC: GPO. (GAO-03-397)

U.S. Government Accountability Office. (2003b). *Federal actions can assist state in improving postsecondary outcomes for youth*. Washington, DC: GPO. (GAO- 03-773)

U.S. Government Accountability Office. (2003c). *No Child Left Behind Act: More information would help states determine which teachers are highly qualified*. Washington, DC: GPO. (GAO-03-631)

U.S. Government Accountability Office. (2003d). *Numbers of formal disputes are generally low and states are using mediation and other strategies to resolve conflicts*. Washington, DC: GPO. (GAO-03-897)

U.S. Government Accountability Office. (2003e). *Study of initiatives for addressing school violence: Examination of 4 promising prevention programs*. Washington, DC: GPO. (GAO/HEHS-95-106)

U.S. Government Accountability Office. (2004a). *No Child Left Behind Act: Additional assistance and research on effective strategies would help small rural districts*. Washington, DC: GPO. (GAO-04-909)

U.S. Government Accountability Office. (2004b). *No Child Left Behind Act: Improvements needed in education's process for tracking states' implementation of key provisions*. Washington, DC: GPO. (GAO-04-734)

U.S. Government Accountability Office. (2004c). *Special education: Additional assistance and better coordination needed among education offices to help states meet the NCLBA teacher requirements*. Washington, DC: GPO. (GAO-04-659)

U.S. Government Accountability Office. (2005a). *Individuals With Disabilities Education Act: Education should provide additional guidance to help states smoothly transition children to preschool*. Washington, DC: GPO. (GAO-06-26)

U.S. Government Accountability Office. (2005b). *No Child Left Behind Act: Most students with disabilities participated in statewide assessment, but inclusion options could be improved*. Washington, DC: GPO. (GAO-05-618)

U.S. General Accounting Office. (1999). *Study of 12 states' coordination of services for children with disabilities*. Washington, DC: GPO. (GAO/HEHS-00-20)

U.S. General Accounting Office. (2000a). *At-risk youth: School-community collaborations focus on improving student outcomes*. Washington, DC: GPO. (GAO-01-66)

U.S. General Accounting Office. (2000b). *Title I preschool education. More children served, but gauging effect on school readiness difficult*. Washington, DC: Author. (GAO/HEHS-00-171)

U.S. General Accounting Office. (2001a). *Student discipline: Individuals With Disabilities Education Act*. Washington, DC: GPO.

U.S. General Accounting Office. (2001b). *Workforce Investment Act: New requirements create need for more guidance*. Washington, DC: GPO. (GAO-02-94T)

U.S. General Accounting Office. (2002). *School dropouts: Education could play a stronger role in identifying and disseminating promising prevention practices*. Washington, DC: GPO. (GAO-02-240)

U.S. Office for Civil Rights. (2002). *Students with disabilities preparing for postsecondary education: Know your rights and responsibilities*. Washington, DC: U.S. Department of Education.

U.S. Office of Juvenile Justice and Delinquency Prevention. (2001, September). Truancy reduction: Keeping students in school. *Juvenile Justice Bulletin*.

U.S. Office of Special Education. (1998). Special education: State program improvement grants program, *Federal Register, 63*(95), 27407. Washington, DC: Author.

U.S. Office of Special Education. (1999a). *Continuous improvement monitoring process: 1999–2000 monitoring manual*. Washington, DC: Author.

U.S. Office of Special Education. (1999b). *Twenty-first annual report to Congress on the implementation of the Individuals With Disabilities Education Act*. Washington, DC: Author.

U.S. Office of Special Education. (2000b). *Twenty-second annual report to Congress on the implementation of the Individuals With Disabilities Education Act*. Washington, DC: Author.

U.S. Office of Special Education. (2001). *Twenty-third annual report to Congress on the implementation of the Individuals With Disabilities Education Act*. Washington, DC: Author.

U.S. Office of Special Education. (2002a). *Number, percentage (based on the total for all settings), and difference from national baseline of infants and toddlers birth through age 2 served in different early intervention settings under Part C, December, 2000*. Data Analysis System, Office of Special Education. Washington, DC: Author.

U.S. Office of Special Education. (2002b). *Strategic plan for 2002–2007*. Washington, DC: Author.

U.S. Office of Special Education. (2002c). *Twenty-fourth annual report to Congress on the implementation of the Individuals With Disabilities Education Act*. Washington, DC: Author.

U.S. Office of Special Education. (2003a). *New Technical Assistance Initiative*, Washington, DC: Author. (OSEP Memo 03-9)

U.S. Office of Special Education. (2003b). *Twenty-fifth annual report to Congress on the implementation of IDEA*. Washington, DC: Author.

U.S. Public Health Service. (2000). *Report of the Surgeon General's conference on children's mental health: A national action agenda, Department of Health and Human Services*. Washington, DC: Author.

U.S. Senate. *Final S 1248 Committee Report Language, Individuals With Disabilities Education Improvement Act*, P. L. 108–185, November 3, 2003.

U.S. Social. Security Administration. (2004). *Working while disabled: A guide to plans for achieving self-support*. Washington, DC: Author. (SSA Publication No. 05-11017)

Utley, C. A., & Obiakor, F. E. (2001a). Learning problems or learning disabilities of multicultural learners: Contemporary perspectives. In C. A. Utley & F. E. Obiakor (Eds.), *Special education, multicultural education, and school reform: Components of quality education for learners with mild disabilities* (pp. 90–117). Springfield, IL: Charles C. Thomas.

Utley, C. A., & Obiakor, F. E. (2001b). Multicultural education and special education: Infusion for better schooling. In C. A. Utley & F. E. Obiakor (Eds.), *Special education, multicultural education, and school reform: Components of quality education for learners with mild disabilities* (pp. 3–29). Springfield, IL: Charles C. Thomas.

Vaishnav, A. (2000, August 29). Program aims to ease move to kindergarten. In *The Boston Globe* (pp. B1–B2).

Valdez-Noel, K. (2004). *Developing community schools as a strategic plan for 'adequate yearly progress.'* Washington, DC: Institute for Education Policy Studies, George Washington University.

Valencia, R. B., & Black, M. S. (2002). Mexican Americans don't value education!—On the basis of the myth, mythmaking, and debunking. *Journal of Latinos and Education, 1*(2), 81–103.

Valentine, J. W., Clark, D. C., Hackman, D. G., & Petzko, V. N. (2002). *A national study of leadership in middle level schools, Volume 1: A national study of middle level leaders and school programs*. Reston, VA: National Association of Secondary School Principals.

Valle, J., & Aponte, E. (2002). IDEA and collaboration: A Bakhtinian perspective on parent and professional discourse. *Journal of Learning Disabilities, 35*(5), 469–479.

Van Reusen, A. K., & Bos, C. S. (1990). I Plan: Helping students communicate in planning conferences. *Teaching Exceptional Children, 22*(4), 30–32.

Van Reusen, L., Bos, C., Schumaker, J., & Deschler, D. (2002). *The self-advocacy strategy for enhancing student motivation and self-determination*. Lawrence, KS: Edge Enterprise.

Vars, G. F. (1998). You've come a long way, baby! In R. David (Ed.), *Moving forward from the past: Early writings and current reflections of middle school founders* (pp. 222–233). Columbus, OH: National Middle School Association.

Vaughn, S., Bos, C., & Schumm, J. S. (1997). *Teaching mainstreamed, diverse, and at-risk students in the general education classroom*. Needham Heights, MA: Allyn & Bacon.

Vaughn, S., Bos, C., & Schumm, J. S. (2003). *Teaching exceptional, diverse and at-risk students in the general education classroom*. Boston: Allyn & Bacon.

Vela Microboard Association. (2004). *What is a Vela Microboard?* Surrey, BC, Canada: Author.

Villa, R., & Thousand, J. (Eds.) (1995). *Creating an inclusive school*. Alexandria, VA: Association for Supervision and Curriculum Development.

Villa, R., & Thousand, J. (1996). Instilling collaboration for inclusive schooling as a way of doing business in public schools. *Remedial & Special Education, 17*(3), 169–182.

Villa, R., & Thousand, J. (1999). *Restructuring for caring and effective education: Piecing the puzzle together.* Baltimore: Paul H. Brookes.

Vinson, N. B., Brannan, A. M., Baughman, L. N., Wilce, M., & Gawron, T. (2001). The system-of-care model: Implementation in twenty-seven communities. *Journal of Emotional and Behavioral Disorders, 9*(1), 30–42.

Virginia Department of Education. (2004, May). *Annual report on discipline, crime and violence: School year 2003–04.* Richmond, VA: Author.

Vocational Rehabilitation Act of 1973, P. L. 93–122, 29 U.S.C. §§ 701 *et seq.* (1973).

Volkmar, F. R., & Greenough, W. T. (1972). Rearing complexity affects branching of dendrites in the visual cortex of the rat. *Science, 176,* 1445–1447.

Volkow, N. (2005). Confronting the rise in abuse of prescription drugs. *National Institute on Drug Abuse Notes, 19*(5), 3.

Volpe, R., Batra, A., Bomio, S., & Costin, D. (1999*). Third generation school-linked services for at-risk children.* Toronto, ON, Canada: Dr. R. G. N. Laidlaw Research Centre, University of Toronto, Institute of Child Study, Department of Human Development and Applied Psychology.

Voltz, D. L., Dooley, E., & Jefferies, P. (1999). Preparing special educators for cultural diversity: How far have we come? *Teacher Education and Special Education, 22*(1), 66–77.

Von Bertalanffy, L. (1968). *General system theory: Foundations, development, applications.* New York: George Braziller.

Voz, W., & Griego Jones, T. (1997). Effects of parental involvement on academic achievement of Latino high school students. *Research & Opinion, 11*(1). Milwaukee: Center for Urban Initiatives & Research, University of Wisconsin.

Vreeberg-Izzo, M., Hertzfeld, J., Simmons-Reed, E., & Aaron, J. (2001). Promising practices: Improving the quality of higher education for students with disabilities. *Disability Studies Quarterly, 21*(1).

Vygotsky, L. S. (1962). *Thought and language.* Cambridge, MA: MIT Press.

Vygotsky, L. S. (1978). *Mind in society; the development of higher psychological processes.* Cambridge, MA: Harvard University Press.

Wagner, C. (2001). *Cultural reciprocity aids collaboration with families.* Arlington, VA: Council for Exceptional Children. Retrieved June 15, 2005, from http://ericec.org/digests/e614.html. ERIC/OSEP Digest #E614

Wagner, C., & Burnette, J. (2000). *Five strategies to reduce overrepresentation of culturally and linguistically diverse students in special education.* Arlington, VA: Council for Exceptional Children. (ERIC/OSEP Digest #E596)

Wagner, M. (1991). Secondary school performance. In M. Wagner, L. Newman, R. D'Amico, E. D. Jay, P. Butler-Nalin, & C. Marder, *Youth with disabilities: How are they doing? The first comprehensive report from the National Longitudinal Transition Study.* Menlo Park, CA: SRI International.

Wagner, M., & Blackorby, J. (1996). Transition from high school-to-work or college: How special education students fare. *The Future of Children: Special Education for Students with Disabilities, 6*(1), 103–120.

Wagner, M., & Blackorby, J. (2004). *Overview of findings from wave I of the Study of the Special Education Elementary Longitudinal Study.* Menlo Park, CA: SRI International.

Wagner, M., Blackorby, J., Cameto, R., & Newman, L. (1993). *What makes a difference? Influences on postschool outcomes of youth with disabilities. The third comprehensive report from the National Longitudinal Transition Study of Special Education Students.* Menlo Park, CA: SRI International.

Wagner, M., Cadwallader, T. W., & Marder, C. (2003). *Life outside the classroom for youth with disabilities. A report from the National Longitudinal Transition Study-2 (NLTS2).* Menlo Park, CA: SRI International.

Wagner, M., Cameto, R., & Guzman, A. (2003). Who are secondary students in special education today? *NLFS2 Data Brief, 2*(1). Menlo Park, CA: SRI International.

Wagner, M., Cameto, R., & Newman, L. (2003). *Youth with disabilities: A changing population. A report from the National Longitudinal Transition Study-2 (NLTS2).* Menlo Park, CA: SRI International.

Wagner, M., Golan, S., & Valdes, K. (2003). *California's Healthy Start Services Initiative: Summary of evaluation findings.* Menlo Park, CA: SRI International, Retrieved August 20, 2003, at http://www.sri.com/policy/cehs/hsevalsm/hsevalsm.html

Wagner, M., & Gomby, D. (2000). Evaluating a statewide school-linked services initiative: California's Healthy Start. In J. M. Marquart & E. Konrad (Eds.). *New directions in program evaluation: Evaluation of human services integration initiatives.* San Francisco: Jossey-Bass.

Wagner, M., Marder, C., & Cardoso, D. (2002). Characteristics of children's households. In M. Wagner, C. Marder, & J. Blackorby, (with D. Cardoso). *The children we serve: The demographic characteristics of elementary and middle school students with disabilities and their households.* Menlo Park, CA: SRI International.

Wagner, M., Newman, L., & Cameto, R. (2003). *Youth with disabilities: A changing population: An earlier comparison of information reported by parents of NLTS and NLTS2 students.* Menlo Park, CA: SRI International.

Wagner, M., Newman, L., & Cameto, R. (2004). *National Longitudinal Transition Study 2: Changes over time in the secondary school experiences of students with disabilities: Findings from the NLTS and NLTS 2.* Menlo Park, CA: SRI International.

Wagner, M., Newman, L., Cameto, R., Garza, N., & Levine, P. (2005). *After high school: A first look at the post-school experiences of youth with disabilities. A report from the National Longitudinal Transition Study-2 (NLTS-2).* Menlo Park, CA: SRI International.

Wagner, T. (1998). Change as collaborative inquiry: A 'constructivist' methodology for reinventing schools. *Phi Delta Kappan, 79*(7), 512–517. Retrieved August 8, 2005, from http://www.schoolredesign.com/srn/server

Wald, P., & Boehm, W. (2002). *The balancing act: Trust and task, presentation for the Instructional Strategies for the Coteaching Classroom workshop,* ASCD 2002 Teaching and Learning Conference, New Orleans, LA.

Wald, P., & Castleberry, M. (2000). *Educators as learners: Creating a professional learning community in your school.* Alexandria, VA: Association for Supervision and Curriculum Development.

Waldron, N. J., & McLeskey, J. (1998). The effects of an inclusive school program on students with mild and severe learning disabilities. *Exceptional Children, 64,* 395–405.

Wallach, C. A., Lambert, M. B., Copland, M., & Lowry, L. K. (2005). *Distributing leadership: Moving from high school hierarchy to shared responsibility.* Seattle: The Small Schools Project, Center on Reinventing Public Education, University of Washington.

Walter, R. (1993). Development of vocational education. In C. S. Anderson & L. C. Ramp (Eds.), *Vocational education in the 1990s, II. Sourcebook for strategies, methods, and materials* (pp. 1–20). Ann Arbor, MI: Prakken Publications, Inc.

Walther-Thomas, C. S. (1997a). *We gain more than we give: Teaming in middle schools* (pp. 487–521). Columbus, OH: National Middle School Association,.

Walther-Thomas, C. S. (1997b). Co-teaching experiences: The benefits and problems that teachers and principals report over time. *Journal of Learning Disabilities, 30*(4), 395–407.

Walther-Thomas, C. S. (2002). Wanted a few good teachers: Developing inclusive programs for students with special needs. In T. S. Dickinson (Ed.), *Cases and commentary: A middle school casebook.* Columbus, OH: National Middle School Association.

Walther-Thomas, C. S., Bryant, M., & Land, S. (1996). Planning for effective co-teaching: The key to successful inclusion. *Remedial and Special Education, 17*(4), 255–264. (EJ 527 660)

Walther-Thomas, C. S., Korinek, L., & McLaughlin, V. (1999). Collaboration to support students' success. *Focus on Exceptional Children, 32*(3), 1–18.

Walther-Thomas, C. S., Korinek, L., McLaughlin, V., & Williams, B. (2000*). Collaboration for inclusive education: Developing successful programs.* Needham Heights, MA: Allyn & Bacon.

Wandry, D., & Pleet, A. (2002). *The role of families in secondary transition: A practitioner's facilitation guide.* Arlington, VA: Council for Exceptional Children.

Wang, M., Haertel, G., & Walberg, H. (1998). *The effectiveness of collaborative school-linked services, Publication Series No. 1 Mid-Atlantic Laboratory for Student Success (LSS).* Philadelphia, PA: Temple University Center for Research in Human Development and Education (CRHDE).

Wang, M., Haertel, G., & Walberg, H. (2002). The effectiveness of collaborative school-linked services. In L. C. Rigsby, M. C. Reynolds, & M. C. Wang (Eds.), *School/community connections: Exploring issues for research and practice.* San Francisco: Jossey-Bass.

Ward, M., & Wehmeyer, W. (1995). The spirit of the IDEA mandate: Student involvement in transition planning [Special Issue]. *Journal of Vocational Special Needs Education, 17,* 108–111.

Ward, M. J. (1996). Coming of age in the age of self-determination: An historical and personal perspective. In D. J. Sands & M. L. Wehmeyer (Eds.), *Self-determination across the life span* (pp. 1–14). Baltimore: Paul H. Brookes.

Warger, C. (2001). *Research on full service schools and students with disabilities.* Arlington, VA: The Council for Exceptional Children. (ERIC/OSEP Digest #E616)

Warger, C., & Burnette, J. (2000). *Five strategies to reduce overrepresentation of culturally and linguistically diverse students in special education.* Washington, DC: ERIC Clearinghouse on Disabilities and Gifted Education. Retrieved November 23, 2005, from http://www.ed.gov/databases/ERIC_Digests/ed447627.html

Warren, J., & Edwards, M. (2001, August). *The impact of high stakes graduation tests on school dropout.* Paper presented at the annual meeting of the American Sociological Association, Anaheim, CA.

Warren-Little, J., Gearhart, M., Curry, M., & Kafka, J. (2003). Looking at student work for teacher learning, teacher community and school reform. *Phi Delta Kappan, 85*(3), 185–192.

Wasow, E. (2000). Families and schools: New lenses, new landscapes. In N. Nager & E. Shapiro (Eds.), *Revisiting a progressive pedagogy. The developmental interaction approach.* Albany: State University of New York Press.

Way, W. L., & Rossmann, M. M. (1996a). *Learning to work: How parents nurture the transition from school to work. Family matters . . . in school to work transition.* Berkeley, CA: National Center for Research in Vocational Education. (Ed 391 885)

Way, W. L., & Rossmann, M. M. (1996b). *Lessons from life's first teacher: The role of the family in adolescent and adult readiness for school-to-work transition.* Berkeley, CA: National Center for Research in Vocational Education. (Ed 396 113)

Wayne, A. J., & Youngs, P. (2003). Teacher characteristics and student achievement gain: A review. *Review of Educational Research, 73*, 89–122.

Weast, J. (2003, June 2). Achievement gains by at-risk students on 2003 CTBS prompt implications for continued local, national improvements. Rockville, MD: *Montgomery County Newsletter, Bulletin.*

Weaver, G. R. (1994). Understanding and coping with cross-cultural adjustment stress. In G. R. Weaver (Ed.). *Culture, Communication and Conflict: Readings in Intercultural Relations*, 169–189. Needham Heights, MA: Ginn Press.

Webb, N., & Farivar, S. (1999). Developing productive group interaction in middle school mathematics. In A. M. O'Donnel & A. King (Eds.), *Cognitive perspectives on peer learning* (pp. 117–149). Hillsdale, NJ: Lawrence Erlbaum Associates.

Webb, N., Farivar, S., & Mastergeorge, A. (2002). Productive helping in cooperative groups. *Theory Into Practice, 41*, 13–20.

Webb, N. M., & Palincsar, A. S. (1996). Group processes in the classroom. In D. C. Berliner & R. C. Cafree (Eds.), *Handbook of educational psychology* (pp. 841–873). New York: Simon & Shuster Macmillan.

Webb, R. B., & Barnash, K. (1997). *Coral Springs Middle School: School climate and school improvement.* Gainesville: Research and Development Center for School Improvement, College of Education, University of Florida.

Webb, R. B., & Kilgore, K. (1995). Restructuring and the dilemmas of school improvement. *Just and Caring Education, 1*(2), 163–179.

Webster-Stratton, C., Reid, M. J., & Hammond, M. (2001). Preventing conduct problems, promoting social competence: A parent and teacher training partnership in Head Start. *Journal of Clinical Child Psychology, 30*(3), 283–302.

Wehman, P. (2001). *Life beyond the classroom: Transition strategies for young people with disabilities* (3rd ed.). Baltimore: Paul H. Brookes.

Wehman, P. (Ed.) (2002). *Individual transition plans: The teacher's curriculum guide for helping youth with special needs* (2nd ed.). Austin, TX: PRO-ED.

Wehmeyer, M. (1996). Self-determination as an educational outcome: Why is it important to children, youth and adults with disabilities? In D. J. Sands & M. L. Wehmeyer (Eds.). *Self-determination across the lifespan: Independence and choice for people with disabilities* (pp. 1–14). Baltimore: Paul H. Brookes.

Wehmeyer, M. (2003). Transition principles and access to the general education curriculum. In C. A. Kochhar-Bryant & D. S. Bassett (Eds*.), Aligning transition and standards-based education: Issues and strategies.* Arlington, VA: Council for Exceptional Children.

Wehmeyer, M., Field, S., Doren, B., Jones, B., & Mason, C. (2004). Self-determination and student involvement in standards-based reform. *Exceptional Children, 70*(4), 413–425. Arlington, VA: Council for Exceptional Children.

Wehmeyer, M., & Sands, D. (Eds.). (1998). *Making it happen: Student involvement in education planning, decision making, and instruction.* Baltimore: Paul H. Brookes.

Wehmeyer, M., & Schwartz, M. A. (1997). Self-determination and positive adult outcomes: A follow-up study of youth with mental retardation and learning disabilities. *Exceptional Children, 63*, 245–255.

Wehmeyer, M. L. (1992). Self-determination and the education of students with mental retardation. *Education and Training in Mental Retardation, 27*, 302–314.

Wehmeyer, M. L. (1999). A functional model of self-determination: Describing development and implementing instruction. *Focus on Autism and Other Developmental Disabilities, 14*(1), 53–61.

Wehmeyer, M. L., Abery, B., Mithaug, D. E., Powers, L. E., & Stancliffe, R. J. (2003). *Theory in self-determination: Foundations for educational practice.* Springfield, IL: Charles C. Thomas.

Wehmeyer, M. L., Agran, M., & Hughes, C. (1998). *Teaching self-determination to students with disabilities: Basic skills for successful transition.* Baltimore: Paul H. Brookes.

Wehmeyer, M. L., & Kelchner, K. (1995). *The ARC's self-determination scale.* Arlington, TX: The ARC.

Wehmeyer, M. L., & Kelchner, K. (1996). Perceptions of classroom environment, locus of control and academic attributions of adolescents with and without cognitive disabilities. *Career Development for Exceptional Individuals, 19*(1), 15–29.

Wehmeyer, M. L., Kelchner, K., & Richards, S. (1996). Essential characteristics of self-determined behavior in individuals with mental retardation. *American Journal on Mental Retardation, 100*(6), 632–642.

Weinberg, G. M. (2001). *An introduction to general systems thinking.* New York: Dorset House Publishing.

Weiss, H. B. (1988). Family support and education programs: Working through ecological theories of human development. In H. B. Weiss & F. H. Jacobs (Eds.), *Evaluating family programs* (pp. 3–36). New York: Aldine De Gruyter.

Weiss, H. B., Woodrum, A., Lopez, M. E., & Kraemer, J. (1993). *Building villages to raise our children: From programs to service systems.* Cambridge, MA: Harvard Family Research Project.

Welch, M., & Brownell, K. (2002). Are professionals ready for educational partnerships? The evaluation of technology-enhanced course to prepare educators for collaboration. *Teacher Education and Special Education, 25*(2), 133–144.

Welch, M., & Sheridan, S. (1995). *Educational partnership: Serving students at risk.* Fort Worth, TX: Harcourt Brace.

Welch, M., & Tulbert, B. (2000). Practitioners' perspectives of collaboration: A social validation and factor analysis. *Journal of Educational and Psychological Consultation, 11*(3&4), 357–378.

Wellman, B., & Lipton, L. (2004). *Data-driven dialogue: A facilitator's guide to collaborative inquiry.* Sherman, CT: MiraVia.

Wenger, E. (1998, June). Communities of practice: Learning as a social system. *Systems Thinker.* Retrieved May 15, 2004, from http://www.co-I-1.com/coil/knowledge-garden/cop/lss/shtml

Wenger, E. (2004). *Learning for a small planet: A research agenda.* Retrieved January 11, 2005, from http://www.ewenger.com/theory/

Wenger, E., McDermott, R., & Snyder, W. M. (2002). *Cultivating communities of practice.* Cambridge, UK: Cambridge University Press.

Wenger, E., & Snyder, W. (2000, January–February). Communities of practice: The organizational frontier. *Harvard Business Review*, 139–145.

Werner, E. E., & Smith, R. S. (1982). *Vulnerable but invincible: A longitudinal study of resilient children and youth.* New York: Adams, Bannister, Cox.

West, J., & Idol, L. (1990). Collaborative consultation in the education of mildly handicapped and at-risk students. *Remedial and Special Education, 11*(1), 22–31.

West, L. (1991). *Effective strategies for dropout prevention.* Rockville, MD: Aspen Publishers.

West, L., Corbey, S., Boyer-Stephens, A., Jones, B., Miller, R. J., & Sarkees-Wircenski, M. (1999). *Integrating transition planning into the IEP process* (2nd ed.). Reston, VA: Council for Exceptional Children.

West, L. L., & Kochhar, C. A. (1995). Transition policy and legislation for the 21st century. *The Journal for Vocational Special Needs Education, 17*, 83–84.

Westat. (2006). *IDEA annual report tables.* Rockville, MD: Author. Retrieved September 3, 2006, from IDEAdata@westat.com

Westberg, J. (1996). *Fostering learning in small groups: A practical guide.* New York: Springer.

Wheatley, M. (1994). *Leadership and the new science: Discovering order in a chaotic world* (2nd ed.). San Francisco: Berrett-Koehler Publishers.

Whelley, T., Hart, D., & Zafft, C. (2002). *Coordination and management of services and supports for individuals with disabilities from secondary to postsecondary education and employment,* Honolulu: National Center for Research on Post-Secondary Education, University of Hawaii.

Wherry, J. (2001). *Selected parent involvement research: A summary of selected research.* Fairfax Station, VA: The Parent Institute.

White, D., & Kochhar-Bryant, C. A. (2004). *Alternative education.* Washington, DC: George Washington University, Hamilton Fish Institute on Schools and Community Violence.

Whitehurst, G. (2003, January). *Institute of Educational Sciences: What's different? What difference does it make?* Research policy notes from the annual conference of the American Education Research Association.

Wigfield, A., Eccles, J., Mac Iver, D., Reuman, D., & Midgley, C. (1991). Transitions during early adolescence: Changes in children's domain-specific self-perceptions and general self-esteem across the transition to junior high school. *Developmental Psychology, 27*(4), 552–565.

Wiggins, G., & McTighe, J. (2005). *Understanding by design* (2nd ed.). Upper Saddle River, NJ: Merrill/Prentice Hall.

Will, M. (1986). *Educating children with learning problems: A shared responsibility. A report to the secretary.* Washington, DC: U.S. Department of Education.

Williams, K. (2003, Winter). A middle school within a K–8 school. *Middle Matters, 3.*

Williams, V. I., & Cartledge, G. (1997). Passing notes to parents. *Teaching Exceptional Children, 30*(1), 30–34.

Williamson, R., & Johnston, J. (1999, March). Challenging orthodoxy: An emerging agenda for middle level reform. *Middle School Journal*, 10–17.

Willis, S. (1995). When parents object to classroom practice. *Education Update, 37*(1), 1, 6, 8.

Wilson, L., & Horch, H. (2004, September). Implications of brain research for teaching young adolescents. *Middle School Journal*, 57–61.

Wilson, M. (2001). The case for sensorimotor coding in working memory. *Psychonomic Bulletin & Review, 8*(1), 57.

Winer, M., & Ray, K. (1994). *Collaboration handbook: Creating, sustaining, and enjoying the journey.* St. Paul, MN: Amherst H. Wilder Foundation.

Winkelman, P. H. (1999). Family involvement in education: The apprehensions of student teachers. In M. S. Ammon (Ed.), *Joining hands: Preparing teachers to make meaningful home–school connections* (pp. 16–36). Sacramento: California Department of Education.

Winnecott, D. W. (1965). *The maturational processes and the facilitating environment: Studies in the theory of emotional development.* London: Hogarth.

Winzer, M. A., & Mazurek, K. (1998). *Special education in multicultural contexts.* Upper Saddle River, NJ: Merrill/Prentice Hall.

Wirt, W. (1923). Ways and means for a closer union between the school and the non-school activities. In *Addresses and proceedings of the sixty-first annual meeting of the National Education Association* (p. 446). Washington, DC: National Education Association.

Wishman, A., Kates, D., & Kaufmann, R. (2001, March). *Funding for early childhood mental health services and supports.* Washington, DC: Center for Mental Health Services and Substance Abuse and Mental Health Services Administration, U.S. Department of Health and Human Services.

Wolanin, T., & Steele, P. (2004). *Higher education opportunities for students with disabilities.* Washington, DC: The Institute for Higher Education Policy.

Wolcott, L. (1998, January–February). Planning with teachers: Practical approaches to collaboration. *Emergency Librarian*, 9–14.

Wolfe, P. (2001). *Brain matters: Translating research into classroom practice.* Alexandria, VA: Association for Supervision and Curriculum Development.

Wolfensberger, W. (1972). *The principle of normalization in human services.* Downsview, ON, Canada: G. Allan Roeher Institute.

Wolfensberger, W. (1983). *Reflections on the status of citizen advocacy.* Downsview, ON, Canada: National Institute on Mental Retardation.

Wood, G. E., & Shors, T. J. (1998). Stress facilitates classical conditioning in males, but impairs classical conditioning in females through activational effects of ovarian hormones. *Proceedings of the National Academy of Sciences, 95*(7), 4066.

Wood, J. W. (1998). *Adapting instruction to accommodate students in inclusive settings.* Upper Saddle River, NJ: Merrill/Prentice Hall.

Wood, M. (1998). Whose job is it anyway? Educational roles in inclusion. *Exceptional Children, 64*, 181–195.

Wood, W. M., Test, D. W., Browder, D., Algozzine, R. F., & Karvonen, M. (1999). *Self-determination curriculum materials.* Charlotte: University of North Carolina, Self-Determination Synthesis Project.

Wood, W. M., Test, D. W., Browder, D. M., Algozzine, B., & Karvonen, M. (2000). *A summary of self-determination curricula and components.* Retrieved July 22, 2005, from http://www.uncc.edu/sdsp/sd_curricula.asp

Woodruff, D., Osher, D., Hoffman, C. C., Gruner, A., King, M. A., Snow, S. T., & McIntire, J. C. (1999). *The role of education in a system of care: Effectively serving children with emotional or behavioral disorders. Systems of care: Promising practices in children's mental health series, Volume III.* Washington, DC: Center for Effective Collaboration and Practice, American Institutes for Research. Retrieved August 15, 2005, from http://cecp.air.org/promisingpractices/1998monographs/vol3.pdf

Woolcock, M., & Narayan, D. (2000). Social capital: Implications for development theory, research and policy. *The World Bank Research Observer, 15*(2), 225–249. Washington, DC: The International Bank for Reconstruction and Development.

Wooton, S., & Horne, T. (2002). *Strategic thinking.* Dover, NH: Kogan Page.

Workforce Investment Act Amendments of 2005, S. 1021, 109th Cong. (2005).

Workforce Investment Act of 1998, P. L. No. 105-220, § 112 Stat. 936 (1998).

Wright, K., Daniel, T., & Himelreich, K. (2000). *Preparation for building partnerships with families: A survey of teachers, teacher educators, and school administrators.* Lexington, KY: Commonwealth Institute for Parent Leadership.

Yamauchi, L. (2003). Making school relevant for at-risk students: The Wai'anae High School Hawaiian Studies Program. *JESPAR, 8*(4), 379–390.

Yates, J. R., & Ortiz, A. (1998). Issues of culture and diversity affecting educators with disabilities: A change in demography is reshaping America. In R. J. Anderson, C. E. Keller, & J. M. Karp (Eds.),

Enhancing diversity: Educators with disabilities in the education enterprise. Washington, DC: Gallaudet University Press.

Yorks, L., & Kasl, E. (Eds.). (2002). *Collaborative inquiry as a strategy for adult learning: Creating space for generative learning.* [New Directions for Adult and Continuing Education, no. 94]. San Francisco: Jossey-Bass.

Yoshikawa, H. (1995). Long-term effects of early childhood programs on social outcomes and delinquency. *The Future of Children, 5*(3), 51–75.

Young, K. T., Davis, K., Schoen, C., & Parker, S. (1998). Listening to parents: A national survey of parents with young children. *Archives of Pediatric Adolescent Medicine, 152,* 25–62.

Young, R. A., Valach, L., Paseluikho, M. A., Dover, C., Matthes, G. E., Paproski, D. L., & Sankey, A. M. (1997). The joint action of parents and adolescents in conversation about career. *Career Development Quarterly, 46*(1), 72–86. (EJ556550)

Ysseldyke, J. E. (1993). *Educational outcomes and indicators for early childhood (Age 3).* Minneapolis: University of Minnesota, College of Education, National Center on Educational Outcomes.

Ysseldyke, J. E. (1994a). *Educational outcomes and indicators for grade 4.* Minneapolis: University of Minnesota, College of Education, National Center on Educational Outcomes.

Ysseldyke, J. E. (1994b). *Educational outcomes and indicators for grade 8.* Minneapolis: University of Minnesota, College of Education, National Center on Educational Outcomes.

Ysseldyke, J. E., Olsen, K., & Thurlow, M. (1997). *NCEO synthesis report 27: Issues and considerations in alternate assessments.* Minneapolis: University of Minnesota, National Center on Educational Outcomes.

Ysseldyke, J. E., & Thurlow, M. (1993). *Developing a model of educational outcomes.* [National Center for Education Outcomes, Report No. 1, October]. Minneapolis: University of Minnesota, College of Education, National Center on Educational Outcomes.

Ysseldyke, J. E., Vanderwood, M. L., & Shriner, J. G. (1997). Changes over the past decade in special education referral to placement probability. *Diagnostique, 23*(1), 193–201.

Zahn-Waxler, C., & Radke-Yarrow, M. (1990). The origins of empathic concern. *Motivation and Emotion, 14*(2), 107–130.

Zehler, A. M., Fleischman, H. L., Hopstock, P. J., Pendzick, M. L., & Stephenson, T. G. (2003). *Descriptive study of services to LEP students and LEP students with disabilities, 4, Special topic report: Findings on special education LEP students.* Arlington, VA: Development Associates, Inc.

Zehr, M. A. (2003). Culture clash. *Education Week, 22*(21), 26–30.

Zellman, G., & Waterman, J. (1998). Understanding the impact of parent school involvement on children's educational outcomes. *Journal of Educational Research, 91*(6), 370–381.

Zemke, R. (1999). Don't fix that company. *Training, 36,* 26, 28.

Zickel, J., & Arnold, E. (2001, November). Putting the I in IEP. *Educational Leadership, 59*(3), 71–73.

Zigmond, N. (2003). Searching for the most effective service delivery model for students with learning disabilities. In H. L. Swanson, K. Harris, & S. Graham, *Handbook of learning disabilities.* New York: Guilford Press.

Zigmond, N., & Rice, D. (1999). Co-teaching in secondary schools: Teacher reports of developments in Australian and American classrooms. *Learning Disabilities Research and Practice, 2000, 15*(4), 190–197. (ERIC Document Reproduction Sservice No. ED432558/SP038679)

Ziguras, S., & Stuart, G. (2000). A meta-analysis of the effectiveness of mental health case management over 20 years. *Psychiatric Services, 51,* 1410–1421.

Zionts, P. (1997). *Inclusion strategies for students with learning and behavior problems: Perspectives, experiences and best practices.* Austin, TX: PRO-ED.

Zipper, I., Hinton, C., Weil, M., & Rounds, K. (1993). *Family-centered service coordination: A manual for parents.* Brookline, MA: Brookline Books.

Zuckerman, A. (2003, March). *The challenge of creating a developmental approach to youth employment.* Paper prepared for the William T. Grant Forum on Reforming Publicly Funded Youth Systems, Aspen Institute, New York.

AUTHOR INDEX

SUBJECT INDEX